Information

CONTENTS

© Copyright by the Publishers, Geographers' A-Z Map Company Ltd.,
Vestry Road, Sevenoaks, Kent. TN14 5EP Telephone: 0732 451152
Showrooms: 44 Gray's Inn Road, London WC1X 8LR Telephone: 01-242 9246

Edition 4   ISBN 0 85039 131 8
An A to Z Publication

MAP REFERENCES IN THIS GUIDE

1. Address and telephone number followed by letter, number and page number (in heavy type) refer to the central London Maps to be found at the back of the Guide e.g. **Athenaeum Hotel,** 116 Piccadilly, W1. 01-499 3464 **2B 48**
2. Those preceded by AZ refer to Geographers' London A–Z Street Atlas from and including Edition 12, and coloured Edition 1. All previous and other format atlases use a reference system not compatible with this guide, e.g. **London Park Hotel,** Elephant and Castle, SE11. 01-735 9191 **AZ 4B 78**
3. Those without map reference numbers are outside the above areas 1 and 2.

TELEPHONE NUMBERS

From a telephone in the London telephone area dial only the 7 figures after the hyphen; do not dial the 01-

ABBREVIATIONS

Arc.	Arcade	Grn.	Green	Pk.	Park
Av.	Avenue	Gro.	Grove	Pas.	Passage
Bri.	Bridge	H.Q.	Headquarters	Pl.	Place
Bldgs.	Buildings	Hrs.	Hours	Rd.	Road
Cent.	Century	Ho.	House	S.	South
Cir.	Circle	Junct.	Junction	Sq.	Square
Comm.	Common	La.	Lane	Sta.	Station
Ct.	Court	Lit.	Little	St.	Street
Cres.	Crescent	Lwr.	Lower	Ter.	Terrace
Dri.	Drive	Mans.	Mansions	Up.	Upper
E.	East.	Mkt.	Market	Wlk.	Walk
Embkmt.	Embankment	M.	Mews	W.	West
Gdns.	Gardens	N.	North	Yd.	Yard
Ga.	Gate	Pal.	Palace		
Gt.	Great	Pde.	Parade		

Within the scope of a guide and directory of this nature, it is inevitable that some details covered in the text will change. While every attempt is made to bring each edition as up-to-date as possible, we still recommend you check variables, like opening hours, before setting out.

Every possible care has been taken to ensure that the information shown in this publication is accurate, and whilst the Publishers would be grateful to learn of any errors, they regret they can accept no responsibility for any loss or expense thereby caused.

ACCOMMODATION

HOTEL BOOKING
London Visitor & Convention Bureau, 26 Grosvenor Gdns., SW1. Mail only.
Hotel Accommodation Service: All price categories. Deposit must be paid, deductible from final hotel bill.
Personal Callers: 1. Victoria Station forecourt. **2C 63**
　　　　　　　　Daily 09.00–20.30, later in summer months.
　　　　　　　　2. Heathrow Central Station, London Airport.
　　　　　　　　Daily 08.00–19.30.
Advanced Booking: Head Office. By mail, four weeks in advance.
Concordia/Hotel (Tourist Bookings Ltd) Platform 9 Victoria Station, 01-828 4646 **2C 63**

...tel Booking Service, 13 Golden Sq., W1. 01-437 5052/5053/5054
...tel Bookings International Hotac,
Heathrow Airport Terminal 1 01-759 2710, Terminal 2 897 0821, Terminal 3 897 0507
Gatwick Airport, Crawley. 30266
Hotelguide, 8 Charing Cross Rd., WC2. 01-836 5561 **3C 35**

HOTELS

**Arranged into three price categories, and those near to London Airports.
"Rooms****" indicates total rooms with bath and/or shower, rooms
without and also single room information is given where available. Tariff
includes English Breakfast unless stated otherwise.
KEY TO SERVICES: T. Telephone. T.V. Television. R. Radio. LV. Laundry
and/or Valet. HM. Hairdressing and/or Manicure. GP. Garage and/or Parking. BP.
Banqueting and/or Party Rooms. CR. Conference Rooms. CC. Some Credit
Cards accepted. NP. Night Porter.**

Higher price range Hotels.
Athenaeum Hotel, 116 Piccadilly, W1. 01-499 3464 **2B 48**
Rooms 112, 33 Apartments. English Breakfast not included. "The Restaurant"
English-French cuisine, Theatre Bookings, Florist. ALL SERVICES.
Belgravia Sheraton, 20 Chesham Pl., SW1 01-235 6040 **1D 61**
Rooms 89. Breakfast not included. Restaurant serving fine wines and cuisine,
Pianist. ALL SERVICES except GP. BP.
Britannia Hotel, Grosvenor Sq., W1. 01-629 9400 **2A 32**
Rooms 435, 234 single. English Breakfast not included. Restaurant "The Terrace
Room", English/French cuisine. Disco except Mon., shopping arcade. ALL SERVICES.
Cadogan Hotel, 75 Sloane St., SW1. 01-235 7141 **1C 61**
Rooms 69, 10 single. Breakfast not included. Restaurant "Lillies", English cuisine,
ALL SERVICES except HM. GP.
Cavendish Hotel, Jermyn St., SW1. 01-930 2111 **3D 33**
Rooms 255, 154 single. English Breakfast not included. Ribblesdale Restaurant.
Theatre agent. ALL SERVICES.
Claridge's, Brook Street, W1 01-629 8860 **2B 32**
Rooms 191, 61 single. Breakfast not included. Two Restaurants—French/Danish
cuisine. Pianist Fri Dinner and Sat Lunch & Dinner. Foyer Quartet. ALL SERVICES.
Churchill, The, Portman Sq., W1. 01-486 5800 **1D 31**
Rooms 489 can be single or twin. Breakfast not included. Restaurant "The No.
10". International cuisine. ALL SERVICES.
Cumberland, Marble Arch, W1. 01-262 1234 **1C 31**
Rooms 905, 436 single. English Breakfast not included. Carvery, also Restaurant
and Coffee Shop. ALL SERVICES except G.P.
Dorchester, Park La., W1. 01-629 8888 **1A 48**
Rooms 280, 77 single. English Breakfast not included. Restaurants "Terrace
Restaurant" and "Grill Room". International cuisine and "Cuisine Naturelle". Dancing
in Terrace Restaurant except Sun. Theatre Desk, Bookstall, Florist, Shopping
corridor. ALL SERVICES.
Dukes Hotel, St. James's Pl., SW1. 01-491 4840 **1D 49**
Rooms 52, 8 single. English Breakfast not included. "Dukes Restaurant",
English/French cuisine. ALL SERVICES except GP.
Goring Hotel, Beeton Pl., Grosvenor Gdns., SW1. 01-834 8211 **1C 63**
Rooms 100, 46 single. English Breakfast not included. Restaurant, French cuisine.
ALL SERVICES except HM. GP.
Grosvenor House, Park La., W1. 01-499 6363 **3D 31**
Rooms 478, 123 single. English Breakfast not included. Restaurants "La Fontaine"
and "La Piazza". Piano in Park Lounge afternoons. Dentist, Doctor,
Gymnasium, Sauna, Shops, Swimming, Theatre ticket agent. ALL SERVICES.
Hilton, Park La., W1. 01-493 8000 **1A 48**

Rooms 455. English Breakfast not included. Restaurants "International" and "Roof Garden". French cuisine. Dancing, closed Sun.

Holiday Inn Chelsea, 17/25 Sloane St., SW1 01-235 4377 **1C 61**
Rooms 206. Breakfast not included, Papillon Restaurant, International cuisine, pianist evenings & Sun. Lunch. Swimming Pool. ALL SERVICES except GP.

Holiday Inn Marble Arch, 134 George St., W1. 01-723 1277 **1B 30**
Rooms 241, English Breakfast not included. Two Restaurants, Sauna; Swimming Whirlpool, Mini Gym. ALL SERVICES except HM.

Hotel Inter Continental, One Hamilton Place, W1 01-409 3131 **2A 48**
Rooms 500. Breakfast not included. 3 Restaurants. International cuisine, ALL SERVICES also sauna, gym, health club, secretarial services. theatre booking, car hire.

Howard Hotel, Temple Pl., WC2. 01-836 3555 **2B 36**
Rooms 141, Breakfast not included. Restaurant. French cuisine. Walled Garden. ALL SERVICES except HM.

Hyde Park Hotel, 66 Knightsbridge, SW1. 01-235 2000 **2C 47**
Rooms 186, 19 suites. English Breakfast not included. Park Restaurant, French cuisine, closed Sat., Oak panelled Grill Room Restaurant.

Inn On The Park, Hamilton Pl., W1. 01-499 0888 **2A 48**
Rooms 228. English Breakfast not included. Restaurants "Four Seasons" and "Lanes". English/Classical French cuisine. ALL SERVICES except HM.

Kensington Palace Hotel, De Vere Gardens, W8. 01-937 8121 **3A 44**
Rooms 298, 65 single. English Breakfast not included. "Pavillion Coffee House". British/Continental cuisine. ALL SERVICES except GP.

Londonderry Hotel, Park La., W1. 01-493 7292 **2A 48**
Rooms 150. Breakfast not included. Isle de France Restaurant. French/English cuisine. Le Prive Night Club. ALL SERVICES except HM. BP. CR.

Lowndes Hotel, Lowndes St., SW1. 01-235 6020 **3D 47**
Rooms 80. Breakfast not included. "The Adam Room", French cuisine. ALL SERVICES except HM. BP. CR.

Marriott, Grosvenor Sq., W1 01-493 1232 **2A 32**
Rooms 228. English Breakfast not included, Restaurants "Regent Lounge" and "Diplomat". ALL SERVICES except HM.

May Fair International, Stratton St., W1 01-629 7777 **3C 33**
Rooms 322. Breakfast not included. Le Chateau Restaurant. French cuisine. Comprehensive selection of studio and suite accommodation, many with jacuzzi bathrooms. ALL SERVICES except HM. GP.

New Piccadilly, Piccadilly W1 01-734 8000 **3A 34**
Rooms 150, 110 single, 30 suites. Breakfast not included. Oak Room and Terrace Garden "Conservatory" Restaurants.

Portman Intercontinental Hotel, 22 Portman Sq., W1. 01-486 5844 **1C 31**
Rooms 278, 87 single. English Breakfast not included. Restaurant "Truffles". French cuisine. ALL SERVICES except HM.

Ritz Hotel, Piccadilly, W1. 01-493 8181 **1C 49**
Rooms 142, 59 single. English Breakfast not included. Ritz Restaurant, French and International cuisine, a la carte. Ritz Casino. SERVICES T. LV. HM. BP. CC. NP.

Royal Garden Hotel, Kensington High St., W8. 01-937 8000 **2D 43**
Rooms 395. English Breakfast not included. Restaurants "Royal Roof" closed Sun. (Band Mon.-Sat. Dinner), "Garden Cafe", traditional French, English and International cuisine. ALL SERVICES.

Royal Westminster, Buckingham Palace Rd., SW1. 01-834 1821 **1C 63**
Rooms 136, 8 single. English Breakfast not included. Restaurants "Brasserie Saint Germain"; "Cape Saint Germain". ALL SERVICES except HM. GP.

St. George's Hotel, Langham Pl., W1. 01-580 0111 **3C 17**
Rooms 83, 3 single. English Breakfast not included. Summit Restaurant. French cuisine. ALL SERVICES except HM.

Savoy, The Strand, WC2. 01-836 4343 **3A 36**
Rooms 152, 48 suites. English Breakfast not included. Restaurants "Savoy Grill",

ne River Restaurant, Grand Hotel style with riverside setting. Dancing
tly except Sun. ALL SERVICES including many special facilities. 24 hr chauffeur
-hire, ticket agency, Savoy shopping arcade.

elfridge Hotel, Orchard St., W1. 01-408 2080 **1D 31**
Rooms 298. English Breakfast not included. Restaurants "Orchard Terrace" and
"Fletchers" International cuisine. ALL SERVICES except HM.

Sheraton Park Tower, 101 Knightsbridge, SW1 01-235 8050 **3C 47**
Rooms 295. Breakfast not included, "The Restaurant", traditional English cuisine.

Westbury Hotel, New Bond St., W1. 01-629 7755 **2C 33**
Rooms 244, 92 single. English Breakfast not included. The Westbury Restaurant
International cuisine. ALL SERVICES except HM.

White's, Lancaster Ga., W2. 01-262 2711 **2B 28**
Rooms 62, 25 single. Charcoal Grill, a la carte. ALL SERVICES except HM. GP.

Middle price range Hotels.

Bloomsbury Crest Hotel, Coram St., WC1. 01-837 1200 **1C 19**
Rooms 239. English Breakfast not included. Scribes Restaurant. SERVICES: T. TV.
R. GP. CR. CC.

Bonnington House, Southampton Row, WC1. 01-242 2828 **2D 19**
Rooms 148, (plus 94 without bath) 148 single. Restaurant, English/French cuisine.
SERVICES: T. TV. R. LV. BP. CR. NP. CC.

Charing Cross Hotel, Strand, WC2 01-839 7282 **3D 35**
Rooms 218, 113 singles. Betjeman Carving Room Restaurant. ALL SERVICES.

Charles Dickens Hotel, Lancaster Gate, W2 01-262 5090 **2B 28**
Rooms 192. Parking nearby. A Ladbroke Hotel.

Clifton Ford Hotel, Welbeck St., W1. 01-486 6600 **3A 16**
Rooms 219, 71 single. English Breakfast not included. Restaurant "Clifton Ford",
International cuisine. ALL SERVICES except HM.

Clive Hotel, Primrose Hill Rd., NW3 01-586 2233 **AZ 7D 44**
Rooms 84. Grove Restaurant. Car Park and Conference facilities. A Ladbroke Hotel.

Curzon Hotel, Stanhope Row, W1 01-493 7222 **1B 48**
Rooms 70. "Charming Park Room" Restaurant. Car Parking. A Ladbroke Hotel.

Flemings Hotel, Half Moon St., W1. 01-499 2964 **1C 49**
Rooms 87, 47 single. Breakfast not included. Langoustine Restaurant. ALL
SERVICES except HM. GP.

Great Northern, King's Cross, N1. 01-837 5454 **2D 11**
Rooms 60 (plus 27 without bath), 18 single (7 without bath). Carvine Restaurant.
ALL SERVICES except HM.

Holiday Inn Swiss Cottage, 128 King Henry's Rd., NW3 01-722 7711 **AZ 7B 44**
Rooms 291, 98 single. King Henry's Restaurant, International cuisine. Pianist
nightly, ALL SERVICES, plus indoor pool, saunas, solarium.

Hospitality Inn, 104 Bayswater Rd., W2 01-262 4461 **3A 28**
Rooms 175, 95 single. English Breakfast not included. Restaurant. English fare.
ALL SERVICES.

Kensington Close Hotel, Wrights La., W8. 01-937 8170 **3C 43**
Rooms 530, 206 single. English Breakfast not included. Restaurants "Kensington
Grill Room" and "Chandelier Restaurant", English fare. Own Leisure Centre. ALL
SERVICES except HM.

Leinster Towers Hotel, Leinster Gdns., W2 01-262 4591 **1A 28**
Rooms 163. Coronet Restaurant. Conference facilities. Parking nearby. A Ladbroke
Hotel.

London Tara Hotel, Wrights La., W8. 01-937 7211 **3C 43**
Rooms 850. Restaurants "Brasserie", "Poachers", International cuisine. ALL
SERVICES except HM.

London West Hotel, Lillie Rd., SW6 01-385 1255 **AZ 1E 75**
Rooms 500. Breakfast not included. Earls Carver Restaurant. Extensive exhibition
and conference facilities. Underground car parking.

Marlborough Crest Hotel, Bloomsbury St,. WC1 01-636 5601 **3C 19**

Rooms 169. All with many private facilities. Restaurant "Brasserie St Martin". AL SERVICES except HM. GP. A Crest Hotel.

Park Lane Hotel, Piccadilly, W1. 01-499 6321 **1B 48**
Rooms 324, 54 suites. English Breakfast not included. 2 Restaurants. English/French cuisine. ALL SERVICES.

Park Plaza Hotel, Lancaster Gate, W2 01-262 5022 **2C 29**
Rooms 403. Royal Carver Restaurant. Car Parking nearby. A Ladbroke Hotel.

Regent Crest Hotel, Carburton St., W1. 01-388 2300 **2C 17**
Rooms 320, 6 suites. Breakfast not included. Restaurant "Boulevard". Cafe and Tiffany Bar. ALL SERVICES except HM. A Crest Hotel.

Regent Palace, Piccadilly Circus, W1. 01-734 7000 **2A 34**
Rooms without bath or shower 1034, 570 single. Carvery, and Coffee Shop. Private Disco except Sun. ALL SERVICES except GP.

Rembrandt Hotel, Thurloe Pl., SW7. 01-589 8100 **2A 60**
Rooms 200. Breakfast not included. Restaurant "Masters" full carvery plus A la Carte. Own Health and Fitness Centre. ALL SERVICES except HM. GP.

Royal Angus, 39 Coventry St., W1. 01-930 4033 **3B 34**
Rooms 92, 25 single. Breakfast not included. Angus Steak House. SERVICES T. TV. R. LV. CC. NP.

Royal Kensington, 380 Kensington High St., W14. 01-603 3333 **AZ 3H 75**
Rooms 400. Breakfast not included. Restaurant "Royal Carver". A Ladbroke Hotel.

Royal Scot Hotel, 100 King's Cross Rd., WC1. 01-278 2434 **AZ 3K 61**
Rooms 349, 28 single. English Breakfast not included. Restaurant "Dumbarton Drums", English and French cuisine. ALL SERVICES.

Royal Trafalgar Thistle Hotel, Whitcomb St., WC2. 01-930 4477 **3B 34**
Rooms 108, 48 single. English Breakfast not included. Hamilton Brasserie and Battle of Trafalgar Pub. SERVICES T. TV. R. LV. CC. NP.

Rubens Hotel, Buckingham Palace Rd., SW1. 01-834 6600 **1C 63**
Rooms 191, 31 singles. English Breakfast not included. "Masters Restaurant" and "Library Lounge". SERVICES, T. R. LV. BP. CR. CC. NP. Barber.

Russell Hotel, Russell Sq., WC2 01-837 6470 **1C 19**
Rooms 319. English Breakfast not included. Carvery Restaurant, Oakroom Grill and Bars. Gift Shop, Ticket agent, Photo-stat. ALL SERVICES except HM. GP.

St Ermin's Hotel, Caxton St., SW1. 01-222 7888 **3A 50**
Rooms 296. English Breakfast not included. Restaurants. A Stakis Hotel.

St. James Court, Hotel & Apartments, Buckingham Ga., SW1. 01-834 6655 **1A 64**
Rooms 391 plus 18 Suites and 92 Apartments. Breakfast not included. Four Restaurants. Own Business Centre. Own Health and Leisure Centre. ALL SERVICES.

Sherlock Holmes Hotel, Baker St., W1 01-486 6161 **1D 15**
Rooms 148. Restaurant "Ristorante Moriarti". Conference facilities. Car Parking nearby. A Ladbroke Hotel.

Strand Palace Hotel, Strand, WC2 01-836 8080 **2A 36**
Rooms 770. Breakfast not included, "Carvery" and Coffee Shop. Theatre Desk, shops and all SERVICES except GP.

Tower Thistle Hotel, St Katharine's Way, E1 01-481 2575 **1D 57**
Rooms 826, 104 singe. Carvery, also Princes Room Restaurant; and Coffee Shop. ALL SERVICES except HM. Executive facilities available.

The Waldorf, Aldwych. WC2 01-836 2400 **2A 26**
Rooms 310, 109 singles, Restaurant, French cuisine. ALL SERVICES except GP.

Wembley International Hotel, Empire Way, 01-902 8839 **AZ 4F 41**
Rooms 322. Car Parking. Wembley Conference Centre adjacent. A Ladbroke Hotel.

Lower price range Hotels.
Bailey's Hotel, 140 Gloucester Rd., SW7. 01-373 6000 **2B 58**
Rooms 154, 53 single. English Breakfast not included. Restaurant English-Indian, a la carte. SERVICES: T. TV. R. LV. BP. CR. CC. NP.

Bedford Hotel, Southampton Row, WC1 01-636 7822 **2D 19**
Accommodation for 250. Sun terrace and gardens. Licenced Coffee Shop. Garage facilities. An Imperial Hotel.

Bedford Corner, Bayley St., WC1. 01-580 7766 **3B 18**
Rooms 54, 34 single. Restaurant "Bayleys". Bedford Arms Bar and Wine Bar. SERVICES: T. TV. LV. BP. CR. CC. NP.

Coburg Hotel, Bayswater Rd., W2. 01-229 3654 **3D 27**
Rooms 125. Restaurant. SERVICES T. TV. R. BP. CR. CC.

County Hotel, Upper Woburn Pl., WC1. 01-387 5544 **3B 10**
Accommodation for 224. Restaurant and Bar. Travel facilities and Car Parking. An Imperial Hotel.

Cranley Gardens Hotel, 8 Cranley Gardens, SW7. 01-373 3232 **3B 58**
Rooms 84. Car Parking nearby. A Ladbroke Hotel.

Ebury Court, 26 Ebury St., SW1. 01-730 8147 **2B 62**
Rooms 12 (plus 27 without bath). Restaurant "Ebury Court", English cuisine. SERVICES: T. TV. R. LV. CC. NP.

Embassy House Hotel, 31 Queen's Ga., SW7. 01-584 7222 **1B 58**
Rooms 69. Restaurant, Bar. SERVICES: T. TV. R. LV. CR. CC. NP.

Georgian House Hotel, 87 Gloucester Pl,. W1. 01-486 2211 **2C 15**
Rooms 20, 2 singles. English Breakfast not included. SERVICES: T. TV. CC.

Hotel Tria, 35/37 St Stephens Gdns., W2 01-221 0450 **AZ 6J 59**
Rooms 43. "Davids Restaurant", Garden Patio. SERVICES: T. TV. R. A Sty-al Hotel.

Imperial Hotel, Russell Sq., WC1. 01-837 3655 **2D 19**
Accommodation for 650. "Day and Night" Grill. Car Hire and shopping facilities. ALL SERVICES. An Imperial Hotel.

Leicester Court Hotel, 41 Queen's Gate Gdns., SW7. 01-584 0512 **2B 58**
Rooms 60 (plus 20 without bath), 10 single (5 without bath). Restaurant. SERVICES: T. R. LV. BP. CR. CC. NP.

London Park Hotel, Elephant and Castle, SE11. 01-735 9191 **AZ 4B 78**
Rooms 300 (plus 94 without bath), 119 single (36 without bath). Restaurant. Telex, copying machines available. ALL SERVICES except HM.

Mount Pleasant Hotel, Calthorp St., WC1. 01-837 9781 **AZ 1B 20**
Rooms 89 (286 without bath), 199 single. Restaurant. Garden. SERVICES: T. R. CR. CC. NP.

New Ambassadors Hotel, Upper Woburn Pl., WC1. 01-387 1456 **3B 10**
Rooms 70 (30 without bath), 10 single. Restaurant and Bars. SERVICES: T. TV. R. LV. GP. BP. CR. CC. NP.

President Hotel, Russell Sq., WC1. 01-837 8844 **1D 19**
Accommodation for 700. "Day and Night" Grill, Restaurant "Saracen Carver". Shopping arcade, car hire, bank, ALL SERVICES except BP. CR. An Imperial Hotel.

Prince of Wales Hotel, De Vere Gdns., W8. 01-937 8080 **3A 44**
Rooms 177 (plus 126 without bath), 83 single (49 without bath). English Breakfast not included. Restaurant "Caernarvon Room". ALL SERVICES.

Royal Adelphi Hotel, 21 Villiers St., WC2. 01-930 8764 **3D 35**
Rooms 55 (34 without bath), English Breakfast not included. SERVICES T. TV. R.

Royal Bayswater, 122 Bayswater Rd., W2. 01-229 8887 **3D 27**
Rooms 38 (plus 15 without bath), 12 single. SERVICES: T. V. LV. CC. NP.

Royal National Hotel, Bedford Way, WC1. 01-637 2488 **1C 19**
Accommodation for over 2,000. Carver and speciality Restaurants. Shopping arcade, ticket booking. SERVICES: T. TV. R. HM. GP. An Imperial Hotel.

Royal Norfolk, 25 London St., W2. 01-402 5221 **1C 29**
Rooms 60. English Breakfast not included. Restaurant. SERVICES: T. TV. R. LV. CC. NP. A Sty-al Hotel.

Somerset House Hotel, 6 Dorset Sq., NW1. 01-723 0741 **1C 15**
Rooms 28, 10 single. Restaurant. SERVICES: T. TV. R. LV. GP. CC. CR.

Tavistock Hotel, Tavistock Sq., WC1. 01-636 8383 **1C 19**

Accommodation for 500. Tavistock Restaurant. An Imperial Hotel with ticket and car hire services.

Waverley House, 130/134 Southampton Row, WC1. 01-833 3691 **2D 19**
Rooms 77 plus 32 single. Restaurants "Deans Brasserie" and "Aquarian".
SERVICES: T. TV. R. LV. BP. CR. CC. NP.

Wilbraham Hotel, Wilbraham Pl., SW1. 01-730 8296 **2D 61**
Rooms 50 (11 without bath), 10 single. Breakfast not included. SERVICES: T. TV. LV. NP.

Y Hotel, 112 Gt. Russell St., WC1. 01-637 1333 **3B 18**
Rooms 168, 48 single. Breakfast not included. ALL SERVICES except BP. HM.

London Airport (Heathrow)

Ariel Hotel, Bath Rd., Hayes, Middlesex. 01-759 2552
Rooms 177, 81 single. English Breakfast not included. Ariel Grill Restaurant. ALL SERVICES.

Arlington Hotel, Shepiston La., Hayes, Middlesex. 01-573 6162
Rooms 80, 17 single. English Breakfast not included. Restaurant, International cuisine. ALL SERVICES except HM. Free telephone and also mini-coach from London Airport.

Berkeley Arms Hotel, Bath Rd., Cranford. 01-897 2121
Rooms 42, 20 single. English Breakfast not included. Restaurant, Carvery, A la Carte. Ornamental Garden. ALL SERVICES except HM.

Excelsior Hotel, Bath Rd., W. Drayton, Middx. 01-759 6611
Rooms 571, 69 single. English Breakfast not included. Three Restaurants"Draitone Manor", "Carvery" and 24 hour Coffee Shop. ALL SERVICES, also hotel shops, baby sitting service, sauna/massage, heated outdoor swimming pool, free coach services.

Grenada Hotel, Lampton Rd., Hounslow, Middx. 01-570 8794
Rooms 50 without bath, 20 single. Bar. TV Lounge. No Credit Cards. SERVICES: GP.

Heathrow Ambassador Hotel, London Rd., Slough, Berks. Slough 684001
Rooms 112. Breakfast not included. ALL SERVICES except HM. Near Airport and Windsor.

Heathrow Penta Hotel, Bath Road, Hounslow. Middx. 01-897 6363
Rooms 670, 89 single. Breakfast not included. Two Restaurants. ALL SERVICES, also swimming pool, health club/sauna, travel agency, shop.

Holiday Inn, Stockley Rd., W. Drayton, Middx. 0895 445555
Rooms 400. English Breakfast not included. A la Carte Restaurant. Coffee Shop. ALL SERVICES except HM. Also has indoor swimming pool, sauna, solarium, tennis, golf.

Master Robert Motel, 366 Great West Rd., Hounslow, Middx. 01-570 6261
Rooms 63, 10 single. English Breakfast not included. Griffin Steak House and Carvery. ALL SERVICES except HM.

Post House, Sipson Rd., W. Drayton, Middx. 01-759 2323
Rooms 594, 52 single. 2 Restaurants, 2 Bars. ALL SERVICES except HM.

Sheraton-Heathrow Hotel, Colnbrook By Pass, Longford, W. Drayton. 01-759 2424
ALL SERVICES.

Sheraton Skyline, Bath Rd., Hayes, Middx. 01-759 2535
Rooms 354. English Breakfast not included. The Colony Room Restaurant. ALL SERVICES, also indoor swimming pool and tropical garden. Sauna/massage, shops.

Skyway Hotel, Bath Rd., Hayes, Middx. 01-759 6311
Rooms 450. Restaurant.

London Airport (Gatwick)

Gatwick Moat House, Longbridge Roundabout, Gatwick. 02934 5599
Rooms 124. The Buttery Restaurant. ALL SERVICES except HM.

Gatwick Hilton International, Gatwick Airport, Horley, Surrey. Crawley 518080

Of International Hilton reputation.
Gatwick Penta Hotel, Povey Cross Rd., Horley. 0293 785533
Rooms 260. English Breakfast not included. Pavilion Restaurant. ALL SERVICES
except HM.
Gatwick Piccadilly, see Gatwick Moat House
Post House, Povey Cross Rd., Horley. 0293 771621
Rooms 220, 34 single. 2 Restaurants. ALL SERVICES.

HOSTELS
Also consult "LONDON—HOTELS, RESTAURANTS AND BUDGET
ACCOMMODATION" from London Visitor & Convention Bureau. "HOSTEL AND
RESIDENTIAL CLUBS IN LONDON FOR WOMEN AND GIRLS" from
Y.W.C.A.
London Hostels Association, 54 Eccleston Sq., SW1. 01-834 1545. Bookings 01-
828 3263 **3C 63.** Accommodation for young office workers.
St Mungo Community Housing Association, 83 Endell St., WC2. 01-240 5431
(24 hours) **1C 35**
YMCA Young Men's Christian Association, National Council, 640 Forest Rd.,
E17. 01-520 5599 **Central London Hostel; London City YMCA,** Luwum Ho.,
8 Errol St., EC1 01-628 8832 **1D 23;** other Hostels throughout London.
YWCA Young Women's Christian Association, 16 Gt. Russell St., WC1. 01-580
4827 **3B 18.** Admin. H.Q., 2 Weymouth St., W1. 01-631 0657 **2A 16**
Accommodation and advisory service 01-430 1524 Central London Hostel; Helen
Graham Ho., Gt Russell St., WC1 01-430 0834 **3B 18;** other Hostels throughout
London
Youth Hostels Association. Dormitory accommodation for members only.
Zebra Trust, 25 Harrington Gdns., SW7. 01-373 7311 **3A 58**
Community houses for students and their families of all nationalities.

CAMP & CARAVAN SITES
Abbey Wood, Co-operative Woods Camping Site, Federation Rd., SE2. 01-310
2233 **AZ 4B 84.** Open all year. Maximum stay two weeks.
Crystal Palace, Crystal Palace Parade, SE19. 01-778 7155 **AZ 6F 111.**
Eastway Camping Site, Temple Mills La., E15. 01-534 6085 **AZ 4D 48**
Hackney Marsh, International Camping, Millfields Rd., E5. 01-985 7656 **AZ 4J 47**
Picketts Lock Centre, Picketts Lock La, N9. 01-803 4756 **AZ 2E 18**
Sewardstone Caravan Park, Sewardstone Rd., E4 01-529 5689 **AZ 7J 9**
Tent City, Old Oak Common La., W3 01-743 5708 **AZ 5A 58**

ADVICE — see also Societies, 24 Hours/Emergencies

Age Concern, Gt. London, 54 Knatchbull Rd., SE5. 01-737 3456 **AZ 2B 94**
Help for the Aged, information on welfare organisations.
Alcoholics Anonymous, 01-834 8202
Help, discussion, group meetings for people who want to stop drinking. Use of
first names preserves anonymity. Office: 11 Redcliffe Gdns., SW10. 01-352
9779
Banking Ombudsman, Citadel Ho., 5/11 Fetter La., EC4. **1C 37** If you have a
difficult dispute with your bank, the Banking Ombudsman can try to settle it,
if the bank concerned is in the scheme. Complaints must be followed up within
six months of your final failure to agree with the bank concerned.
British Red Cross, 9 Grosvenor Cres., SW1. 01-235 5454 **3A 48**
Help for the aged, handicapped and sick. Active in volunteer work in hospitals,
residential and private homes. Organises holidays. Missing persons tracing
dept.
Childminders, 67a Marylebone High St., W1. 01-935 9763. 01-935 2049 **2A 16**

Babysitters supplied to homes and Hotels in central London and most suburban areas. Nanny service also available.

Church Army, Winchester Ho., Independents Rd., SE3 01-318 1226 **AZ 3H 97** Social work for homeless, aged, unmarried mothers, rehabilitation of prisoners, alcoholics and drug addicts. Runs hostels, holiday homes, youth clubs.

Citizens Advice Bureau, National H.Q., Admin. only, 31 Wellington St., WC2. 01-379 6841 See list of Local Branches. Advice on everyday problems relating to Law, Legal Aid, Housing and Rents, any matters of Consumer Protection.

Commission for Racial Equality, Elliot Ho., 10 Allington St., SW1. 01-828 7022 **1C 63** Established to help enforce the 1976 Race Relations Act, to work towards the elimination of discrimination and promote equality of opportunity and good relations between people of different racial groups. The Act makes racial discrimination unlawful in employment, housing, education, provision of goods, facilities and services.

Community Relations Councils. Exist to encourage co-operation and communications between different ethnic groups in neighbourhoods. Most London boroughs have one; address from Citizens Advice Bureaux.

Consumers Association, 14 Buckingham St., WC2. 01-839 1222 **3D 35** Will supply information of local consumer groups. Concerned with standards of consumer goods and services. Monthly reports in the form of "WHICH?" Magazine, also quarterly on Motoring and Money. A number of information publications on specific problems and decisions, e.g. buying a house.

Daily Telegraph Telephone Information Service. 01-353 4242 General information. Office hours.

Disabled, Information Service for: Central Council for the Disabled, 25 Mortimer St., W1. 01-637 5400 **3D 17** Advice and information. Recommends hotels and travel facilities.

Families Anonymous, 88 Caledonian Rd., N1. 01-278 8805 For relatives and friends concerned and/or involved in the abuse of drugs.

Financial Advice Centre, Mary Ward Centre, 42 Queen Sq., WC2. 01-831 7079 **2D 19.** Offers free financial advice by appointment, Mon. and Wed. 18.30 to 20.30.

Gamblers Anon, 17–23 Blantyre St., Cheyne Wlk., SW10. 01-352 3060 **AZ 7B 76** Advice, group meetings, gamblers stay anonymous using first names.

Health Service Commissioner: Ombudsman. Investigates complaints of maladministration within the National Health Service, after the appropriate authorities have investigated. Complaints must normally be made within 12 months of maladministration becoming apparent. You may complain direct to the Health Service Ombudsman, Church House, Smith Sq., London SW1. 01-212 7676

Insurance Ombudsman, 31 Southampton Row, WC1. 01-242 8613 **2D 19** If you have a difficult dispute with your insurance company, the Insurance Ombudsman can try to settle it, if the company concerned is in the scheme. Complaints must be followed up within six months of your final failure to agree with the company concerned.

Legal Aid and Advice. Citizens Advice Bureau can supply information of the nearest Legal Advice Centres, legal advice can be obtained from MARY WARD LEGAL CENTRE, 42 Queen Sq., WC1. 01-831 7009 **2D 19** The Law Society, 113 Chancery La., WC2. 01-242 1222 **1C 37,** administers the Legal Aid Scheme, publishes a booklet "Legal Aid and Advice".

Local Authorities Ombudsman. Investigates complaints against Local Councils (except Parish Councils), Joint Planning Boards, Water and Police Authorities. Information from Local Ombudsman, 21 Queen Anne's Gate, London SW1. 01-222 5622 **1C 65**

London Marriage Guidance Council, 76a New Cavendish St., W1. 01-580 1087. **3B 16** Help with any marriage problem. Marriage counselling. Advice on emotional problems and preparation for marriage.

London Youth Advisory Centre, 26 Prince of Wales Rd., NW5. 01-267
4792 **AZ 6E 44** Advice for young people with legal, medical, sexual problems.
Marie Stopes House, 108 Whitfield St., W1. 01-388 0662/2585/4843 **2A 18**
Advice on abortion, birth control, family planning, pregnancy testing,
sterilization.
National Childbirth Trust, 9 Queensborough Ter., W2. 01-221 3833 **2A 28**
Information relating to childbirth in particular Natural Childbirth, post- and antenatal
care and exercises.
National Council for One Parent Families, 255 Kentish Town Rd., NW5. 01-267
1361. **AZ 7F 45** Advice and practical help.
Parliamentary Commissioner for Administration: Ombudsman.
Investigates complaints of maladministration in Government Departments via
Members of Parliament only. Complaints must normally be made within 12
months of maladministration becoming apparent. Exclusions: Nationalised
Industries, Foreign Affairs, Criminal or Civil proceedings, Government commercial
transactions, personnel matters affecting civil servants or servicemen. General
enquiries, Church House, Smith Sq., London SW1. 01-212 7676. **1C 65**
Patients' Association, 18 Charing Cross Rd., WC2 01-240 0671
Represents, and furthers the interests of patients, provides assistance and advice.
Prisoners' Wives Service, 51 Borough High St., SE1 01-403 4095
Assists wives and families of men in prison.
Release, 1 Elgin Av., W9. 01-289 1123 01-603 8654 24 hrs. **AZ 4J 59**
Information and referral service for personal problems, Legal, Medical, Social.
Open during office hours, access to doctors, solicitors, library on drugs.
Salvation Army Advice Bureau HQ., 101 Queen Victoria St., EC4. 01-236 5222
2B 38 Social work for homeless, aged, unmarried mothers, rehabilitation of prisoners,
alcoholics and drug addicts. Runs hostels and holiday homes.
Samaritans, 39, Walbrook, EC4. 01-283 3400 24 hrs. **2D 39** Help and friendship
for the suicidal or despairing. For local branches see page 205.
St. Martin-in-the-Field's Social Service Unit, St. Martin's Pl., WC2. 01-930 4137
3C 35. Help for any personal problems in time of crisis. 10.00–20.00
"Students Nightline", emergency service see page 205.
Universal Aunts Ltd., 250 Kings Rd., SW3. 01-351 5767 **AZ 9E 144**
A large range of personal services; help for both residents and visitors. Can include
baby sitting, proxy parents, travel/escorting, accommodation, shopping,
sightseeing, general day to day problem solving.

AUCTIONEERS

**See Companies for catalogues, dates of viewing and sales. Most large sales
are advertised in "The Times" on Tuesdays and the "Daily Telegraph" on
Mondays. The main companies for the auction of valuables are:**
Bonham & Sons Ltd., Montpelier St., SW7. 01-584 9161 **3B 46**
Bonhams, New Chelsea Galleries, 65 Lots Rd., SW10. 01-352 0466 **AZ 7A 76**
Antique and modern furniture. Art and valuables. Valuations 01-584 9161
Christies, St. James's, 8 King St., SW1. 01-839 9060 **1D 49**
Fine Art and Wine.
Christies, S. Kensington, 85 Old Brompton Rd., SW7. 01-581 2231 **3C 59**
Antique furniture, art and valuables. Free valuation service.
Gibbons, Stanley, 399 Strand, WC2. 01-836 8444. **2A 36.** Stamps only.
Glendining & Co., 7 Blenheim St., W1. 01-493 2445 **1B 32** Coins and Medals.
Harmer, H. R. Ltd., 41 New Bond St., W1. 01-629 0377 **2C 33.** Stamps only.
Harvey's, 14 Neal St,. WC2. 01-240 1464 **1C 35**
Phillips, 7 Blenheim St., W1. 01-629 6602 **1B 32**
Phillips, West 2, 10 Salem Rd., W2. 01-221 5303 **2D 27**
Phillips, Marylebone, Hayes Pl., NW1. 01-723 2647 **2B 14**

Fine art, furniture and valuables. Valuation Dept. 01-409 2593
Sotheby & Co., 34 New Bond St., W1. 01-493 8080. **2C 33**
Fine art, furniture and valuables.

BANKS (National and International Headquarters)

INSTITUTE OF BANKERS, 10 Lombard St., EC3. 01-623 3531 **2A 40**

National Girobank, *10 Milk St., EC2. 01-600 6020* 1C 39 *The National Girobank provides a broad range of corporate and personal banking facilities; it operates through more than 20,000 UK post offices. See page 111*

Afghan National Bank, 22 Finsbury Sq., EC2. 01-628 4721 **2A 24**
African Continental Bank, 24 Moorgate, EC2. 01-628 7131 **3D 23**
Algemene Bank Nederland, 61 Threadneedle St., EC2. 01-628 4272 **1A 40**
Allied Bank Int., 6 Frederick's Place, EC2. 01-606 9741 **1D 39**
American Express Bank, 30 Monument St., EC3. 01-283 3488 **2A 40**
Arab Bank, 8/14 St. Martin-le Grand, EC1. 01-606 7801 **1B 38**
Associated Japanese Bank (Int)., 29 Cornhill, EC3. 01-623 5661 **1A 40**
Atlantic Int. Bank, 65/66 Queen St., EC4. 01-248 9001 **2C 39**
Australia & New Zealand Banking Group, 55 Gracehurch St., EC3. 01-280 3100 **2A 40**
Banca D'Italia, 39 King St., EC2. 01-606 4201 **1D 39**
Banca Nazionale del Lavoro, 33/35 Cornhill, EC3. 01-623 4222 **1A 40**
Banco de Bilbao, 100 Cannon St., EC4. 01-623 3060 **1B 38**
Banco Nacional de Mexico, 77 London Wall, EC2. 01-638 9171 **3A 24**
Banco Totta & Acores 68 Cannon St., EC4. 01-236 1515 **1B 38**
Bank fur Gemeinwirtschaft, 83 Cannon St., EC4. 01-248 6731 **1B 38**
Bank Hapoalim, 22 Lawrence La., EC2. 01-600 0382 **1C 38**
Bank Indonesia, 10 City Rd., EC1. 01-638 9043 **1A 24**
Bank of America, 25 Cannon St., EC4. 01-634 4000 **2C 39**
Bank of Baroda, 31 King St., EC2. 01-606 8888 **1D 39**
Bank of British Columbia, 27 Old Jewry, EC2. 01-606 8577 **1D 39**
Bank of Ceylon, 1 Aldermanbury Sq., EC2. 01-606 5597 **3C 23**
Bank of China, Mansion House Pl., EC4. 01-626 8301 **2D 39**
Bank of England, Threadneedle St., EC2. 01-601 4444 **1A 40**
Bank of India, Kent Ho., 11 Telegraph St., EC2. 01-628 3165 **1D 39**
Bank of Ireland, 2 Lombard St., EC3. 01-626 2575 **2A 40**
Bank of Japan, 27/32 Old Jewry, EC2. 01-606 2454 **1D 39**
Bank of Montreal, 9 Queen Victoria St., EC4. 01-236 1010 **2A 38**
Bank of New England, 119 Finsbury Pavement, EC2. 01-638 2331 **2A 24**
Bank of New York, 147 Leadenhall St., EC3. 01-626 2555 **1B 40**
Bank of New Zealand, 91 Gresham St., EC2. 01-726 4060 **1C 39**
Bank of Nova Scotia, 33 Finsbury Sq., EC2. 01-638 5644 **2A 24**
Bank of Oman, Coventry Ho., 3 South Pl., EC2. 01-638 2271 **2A 24**
Bank of Scotland, 38 Threadneedle St., EC2. 01-628 8060 **1A 40**
Bank of Tokyo, Northgate Ho., 20 Moorgate, EC2. 01-638 1271 **3C 23**
Bank Saderat Iran, 5 Lothbury, EC2. 01-606 0951 **1D 39**
Banque Belge, 4 Bishopsgate, EC2. 01-283 1080 **1B 40**
Banque Française, Morgan Ho., 1 Angel Ct., EC2. 01-726 4020 **1A 40**
Banque Nationale de Paris, 8 King William St., EC4. 01-626 5678 **2A 40**
Barclays Bank, 54 Lombard St., EC3. 01-626 1567 **1A 40**
Barclays Bank Int., 54 Lombard St., EC3. 01-283 8989 **1A 40**
British Bank of the Middle East, 18c Curzon St., W1. 01-493 8331 **1A 48**
British Linen Bank, 55 Bishopsgate, EC2. 01-588 7911 **1B 40**
Canadian Imperial Bank, 55 Bishopsgate, EC2. 01-628 9858 **1B 40**
Central Bank of India, 42 New Broad St., EC2. 01-588 7841 **3A 24**

Chase Manhattan, Woolgate Ho., Coleman St., EC2. 01-726 5000 **1D 39**
Citibank NA, Citibank Ho., 336 Strand, WC2. 01-240 1222 **3D 35**
Clydesdale Bank, 30 Lombard St., EC3. 01-626 4545 **1A 40**
Commonwealth Trading Bank of Australia, 8 Old Jewry, EC2. 01-600 0822 **1D 39**
Co-operative Bank, 78/80 Cornhill, EC3. 01-626 6543 **1A 40**
County Bank, 10/11 Old Broad St., EC2. 01-638 6000 **1A 40**
Coutts & Co. 440 Strand, WC2. 01-379 6262 **3D 35**
Crédit Lyonnais, 84 Queen Victoria St., EC4. 01-248 9696 **2A 38**
Crédit Suisse, 24 Bishopsgate, EC2. 01-623 3488 1B 40
Credito Italiano, 17 Moorgate, EC2. 01-606 9011 **3D 23**
Deutsche Bank, 6 Bishopsgate, EC2. 01-283 4600 **1B40**
European Banking Co., 10 Devonshire Sq., EC2. 01-621 0101 **3C 25**
First Commercial Bank, 2 South Pl., EC2. 01-628 2612 **2A 24**
First National Bank of Boston, 5 Cheapside, EC2. 01-236 2388 **1C 39**
F. N. Bank of Chicago, Long Acre, WC2. 01-240 7240 **2C 35**
First Wisconsin National Bank, 5 St. Helen's Pl., EC3. 01-588 7633 **1B 40**
Ghana Commercial Bank, 69 Cheapside, EC2. 01-248 2384 **1C 39**
Girard Trust Bank, 15 Trinity Sq., EC3. 01-488 2434 **2C 41**
Grindlays Bank, 23 Fenchurch St., EC3. 01-626 0545 **2B 40**
Gulf Bank, 1 College Hill, EC4. 01-248 2843 **2D 39**
Habib Bank Ltd., 12 Finsbury Cir., EC2. 01-588 7881 **3A 24**
Hambros Bank, 41 Bishopsgate, EC2. 01-588 2851 **1B 40**
Harris Trust & Savings Bank, Bucklersbury Ho., 3 Queen Victoria St., EC4. 01-248 0364 **2A 38**
Hong Kong & Shanghai Banking, 99 Bishopsgate, EC2. 01-638 2366 **1B 40**
Hungarian Int. Bank, 95 Gresham St., EC2. 01-606 5371 **1C 39**
Japan Int. Bank, 107 Cheapside, EC2. 01-600 0931 **1D 39**
Kyowa Bank, Princes Ho., 95 Gresham St., EC2. 01-606 9231 **3C 23**
Lloyds Bank International, 40 Queen Victoria St., EC4. 01-248 9822 **2A 38**
Lloyds Bank, 71 Lombard St., EC3. 01-626 1500 **1A 40**
Lombard N. Central, 31 Lombard St., EC3. 01-623 6744 **1A 40**
London Interstate Bank, 140 London Wall, EC2. 01-606 8899 **3A 24**
Manufacturers Hanover Trust, 7 Princes St., EC2. 01-600 5666 **1D 39**
Mellon Bank N.A., 6 Devonshire Sq., EC2. 01-626 9828 **3C 25**
Middle East Bank, 1 Lombard St., EC3. 01-283 2201 **1A 40**
Midland Bank, 27 Poultry, EC2. 01-606 9911 **1D 39**
Mitsubishi Bank, 1 King William St., EC2. 01-606 6644 **2A 40**
Mitsui Bank, 34 King St., EC2. 01-606 0611 **1D 39**
Moscow Narodny Bank, 24 King William St., EC4. 01-623 2066 **2A 40**
National Australia Bank, 6/8 Tokenhouse Yd., EC2. 01-606 8070 **1A 40**
National Bank of Abu Dhabi, 90 Bishopsgate, EC2. 01-626 8961 **1B0**
National Bank of Canada, Princes Ho., 95 Gresham St., EC2. 01-726 6581 **1C 39**
National Bank of Detroit, 28 Finsbury Circus, EC2. 01-920 0921 **3A4**
National Bank of Egypt, 2 Honey La., EC2. 01-726 4237 **1C 39**
National Bank of Greece, 50 St. Mary Axe, EC3. 01-626 3222 **1B 40**
National Bank of Kuwait, 99 Bishopsgate, EC2. 01-920 0262 **1B 40**
National Bank of New Zealand,100 Pall Mall, SW1. 01-930 7366 **1A 50**
National Bank of Nigeria, 2 Devonshire Sq., EC2. 01-247 5561 **3C 25**
National Bank of Pakistan, 18 Finsbury Circus, EC2. 01-588 1511 **3A 24**
National City Bank – Cleveland, 66 Queen St., EC4. 01-248 1456 **2C 39**
National Westminster Bank, 41 Lothbury, EC2. 01-726 1000 **1D 39**
Nedbank, 20 Abchurch La., EC4. 01-623 1077 **1A 40**
Orion Royal Bank, 1 London Wall, EC2. 01-600 6222 **3C 23**
Overseas Union Bank, 61 Coleman St., EC2. 01-628 0361 **1D 39**
Philippine National Bank 103 Cannon St., EC4. 01-623 0031 **1B 38**
Rothschild N. M. & Sons, St. Swithins La., EC4. 01-280 5000 **2D 39**
Royal Bank of Canada, 6 Lothbury, EC2. 01-920 9212 **1D 39**

Royal Bank of Scotland, 60 Lombard St., EC3. 01-621 1234 **1A 40**
Sanwa Bank, 1 Undershaft, EC3. 01-283 5252 **1B 40**
Saudi International Bank, 99 Bishopsgate, EC2. 01-638 2323 **1B 40**
Scandinavian Bank, 2 Cannon St., EC4. 01-236 6090 **1B 38**
Societe Generale, 60 Gracechurch St,. EC3. 01-626 5400 **2A 40**
Standard & Chartered Banking Group, 10 Clements La., EC4. 01-623 7500 **2A 40**
State Bank of India, 1 Milk St., EC2. 01-600 6444 **1C 39**
Swiss Bank Corporation, 99 Gresham St., EC2. 01-606 4000 **3C 23**
Tokai Bank, P. & O. Building, Leadenhall St., EC3. 01-283 8500 **1B 40**
Toronto Dominion Bank, 62 Cornhill, EC3. 01-283 8700 **1A 40**
Trust Bank of Africa, 20 Cannon St., EC4. 01-236 7424 **1B 38**
Trustee Savings Bank, S.E.H.Q., 237 Union St., SE1. 01-928 3344 **2A 54**
Union Bank of Finland, 46 Cannon St., EC4. 01-248 3333 **1B 38**
Union Bank of Norway, Old Deanery, Dean's Ct., EC4. 01-248 0462 **1B 38**
Union Bank of Switzerland, 117 Old Broad St., EC2. 01-638 2800 **1A 40**
United Bank, 29 Mincing La., EC3. 01-623 5773 **2B 40**
United Bank of Kuwait, 3 Lombard St., EC3. 01-626 3422 **1A 40**
Wells Fargo Bank NA, 9 Long Acre, WC2. 01-836 3434 **2C 35**
Williams & Glyn's Bank, 20 Birchin La., EC3. 01-623 4356 **2A 40**
Yorkshire Bank, 56 Cheapside, EC2. 01-236 9813 **1C 39**
Zivnostenska Banka, 104/106 Leadenhall St., EC3. 01-623 3201 **1B 40**

BRIDGES AND TUNNELS: The River Thames

The River Thames is London's principal natural feature giving fine visual settings for many of the Capital's great buildings, and provides an ideal tree-lined promenade for walks or boating trips. Tower Bridge Walkway has perhaps the most dramatic river views. The Thames Barrier AZ 2A 82 with its enormous rising steel gates has been constructed to prevent the river flooding Central London; there are viewing facilities and exhibition on the south side.

Historically the Thames was London's "main road", used as a means of easy local transportation and at the same time linking the City directly with the world's other ports. The introduction of the 16th-century coach marked the beginning of the end for the Watermen and their wherries, and the size of modern ships and container systems has removed the Port of London Authority's activities to Tilbury.

Albert Bridge. AZ 6C 76 Built 1873. R. M. Ordish. Combination of cantilever and suspension principles, 711 ft long in three spans.

Barnes Bridge. AZ 2A 90 Road (now pedestrian) and Rail Bridge, begun 1846.

Battersea Bridge. AZ 7B 76
Built 1887–90. Sir J. Bazalgette. Iron structure replaces one of wood built 1772.

Blackfriars Bridge. 3A 38
Built 1865–9. J. Cubitt. Replaces an earlier bridge built as a memorial to W. Pitt.

Blackwall Tunnel. AZ 1F 81 Poplar to East Greenwich. Two tunnels, the first built 1892–97; the second added 1967. Length 6,164 ft. with open approaches.

Chelsea Bridge. AZ 6F 77 Built 1937. Suspension bridge 700 ft. long.

Chiswick Bridge. AZ 2J 89
Built 1933. Has the longest concrete arch of all the Thames bridges, 150 ft.

Greenwich Tunnel. AZ 5E 80
Isle of Dogs to Greenwich. Pedestrian tunnel; 1902. Length 1,217 ft.

Hammersmith Bridge. AZ 5D 74
Opened 1887. Sir J. Bazalgette. Suspension bridge, has partly gilt iron pylons.

Hampton Court Bridge. Reinforced concrete bridge of 1933.

Hungerford Footbridge. 1A 52
Runs alongside Charing Cross Railway Bridge. The original Hungerford Bridge was a suspension bridge designed by Brunel, removed 1861 the chains being used for Clifton suspension bridge at Bristol.
Kew Bridge. AZ 6F 73 Opened 1903. Sir John W. Barry and Cuthbert Brereton. Stone, three spans.
Officially the King Edward VII Bridge.
Kingston Bridge. AZ 2D 118 Brick construction, 1828. Widened 1941.
Lambeth Bridge. 2D 65 Built 1929–32. The original bridge opened in 1862 was erected on the site of an ancient horse-ferry.
London Bridge. 3A 40
Present bridge built 1967–73. Harold King and Charles Brown. Pre-stressed concrete. Until mid-18th cent. London Bridge was the only bridge across the Thames. The first bridge was built by the Romans, later followed by other constructions in wood. In 1176 Peter of Colechurch began to erect a stone bridge, completed 1209; 905 ft. long, 19 pointed arches with houses, shops and a chapel. Later heads of traitors were impaled on spikes on the drawbridge gate. The medieval bridge remained until the 19th cent. when a granite bridge designed by J. Rennie was constructed, since transported to Lake Havasu City, Arizona, U.S.A.
Putney Bridge. AZ 3G 91 1884. Sir J. Bazalgette. Stone bridge 189 ft. long.
Richmond Bridge. AZ 5D 88 Built 1774–77. J. Paine and K. Couse. The only 18th-cent. bridge left in London. Classical style, five graduated arches.
Rotherhithe Tunnel. AZ IJ 79
Rotherhithe to Wapping. Earlier and first successful tunnel by Sir M. I. Brunel and Son I. K. Brunel. Started 1825, completed and opened to pedestrians 1843 after many mishaps. Adapted for use by underground trains. The pumping engine house, Rotherhithe St., AZ 2J 79, renovated by the Brunel Society, with restored Rennie pumping engine, is open summer Sundays 11.00–16.00. Later tunnel 1904–8, vehicle tunnel 6,277 ft. long.
Southwark Bridge. 3C 39 Built 1913–21, Sir Ernest George.
Tower Bridge. 1D 57
1886–94. Sir John W. Barry and Sir Horace Jones. Hydraulically operated roadways between twin Victorian Gothic towers to let ships through.
TOWER BRIDGE WALKWAY 01-403 3761: 142 ft. above the river and closed since 1909; re-opened in 1982 with museum of machinery. Open: 10.00–18.30, 16.45 in winter months. Last ticket 45 min prior. Closed Xmas Bank Hols. Admission charge.
Twickenham Bridge. AZ 5C 88 Built 1933, concrete.
Vauxhall Bridge. AZ 5J 77
Opened 1906. Sir M. Fitzmaurice and W. E. Riley. The first to be crossed by tramcars.
Wandsworth Bridge. AZ 3K 91
1873. J. H. Tolme. Lattice girder bridge, reconstructed 1936–40.
Waterloo Bridge. 3A 36
1937–45. Sir Giles Gilbert Scott. Steel and concrete, 5 arches each about 240 ft. wide. Replaced an earlier bridge by John Rennie known as Strand Bridge.
Westminster Bridge. 3D 51
1854–62. Thomas Page. Cast-iron construction replacing the 18th-cent. crossing.
Woolwich Tunnel. AZ 2E 82 1909–12. Pedestrian tunnel, 1655 ft. long.

BUILDING SOCIETIES

BUILDING SOCIETIES ASSOCIATION 3 Saville Row, W1. 01-437 0655 **2C 33**

Abbey National, Abbey Ho., 27 Baker St., NW1. 01-486 5555 **1C 15**

Aid to Thrift, 38 Finsbury Sq., EC2. 01-638 0311 **AZ 5B 142**
Alliance and Leicester, 49 Park La., W1. 01-629 6661 **2D 31**
Anglia, 12 Wigmore St., W1. 01-580 3836 **1A 32**
Argyle, 105 Seven Sisters Rd., N7. 01-272 3935 **AZ 3K 45**
Bolton, 235/237 Baker St., NW1. 01-935 0138 **1C 15**
Bradford & Bingley, 161 Piccadilly, W1. 01-499 0124 **3A 34**
Bristol & West, 95 Regent St., W1. 01-734 0996 **1C 33**
Britannia, 60 Kingsway, WC2. 01-405 1781 **1A 36**
Burnley, 129, Kingsway, WC2. 01-405 9851 **3A 20**
Catholic, 7 Strutton Ground, SW1. 01-222 6736 **1B 64**
Chelsea, 255 Kensington High St., W8. 01-602 0066 **3B 42**
Cheltenham & Gloucester, 68 Baker St., W1. 01-935 0016 **1C 15**
City & Metropolitan, 37 Ludgate Hill, EC4. 01-236 3556 **1A 38**
City of London, 34 London Wall, EC2. 01-920 9100 **3C 23**
Civil Service, 40 Buckingham Gte., SW1. 01-828 5115. **3C 49**
Clapham Permanent, 31 St. Johns Hill, SW11. 01-228 0839 **AZ 4B 92**
County of London Permanent, 375 Lewisham High St., SE13. 01-852 4189
AZ 6D 96
Ealing & Acton, 55 The Mall, Ealing, W5. 01-579 3066 **AZ 7E 56**
Gateway, 227 Regent St., W1. 01-408 2424 **1C 33**
Greenwich, 281 Greenwich High Rd., SE10. 01-858 8212 **AZ 7D 80**
Guardian, 120 High Holborn, WC1. 01-242 0811 **3D 19**
Halifax, Halifax Ho., 51/55 Strand, WC2. 01-930 0793 **3D 35**
Haverstock, 94–96 Commercial St., E1. 01-247 5582 **AZ 5E 142**
Hearts of Oak & Enfield, 8 The Town, Enfield. 01-366 4348 **AZ 3J 7**
Hendon, 9 Central Cir., NW4. 01-202 6384 **AZ 5D 26**
Huddersfield & Bradford, 6 Maddox St., W1. 01-491 3330 **2C 33**
Immigrants, 45 Lisson Grove. NW10. **AZ 3B 138**
Lambeth, 118 Westminster Bri. Rd., SE1. 01-928 1331 **3B 52**
Leeds & Holbeck, 73 Kingsway, WC2. 01-242 7313 **3A 20**
Leeds Permanent, 159 Fenchurch St., EC3. 01-623 9551 **2B 40**
Leicester, 85 Kingsway, WC2. 01-242 5182 **3A 20**
Liverpool Victoria, Victoria Ho., Southampton Rw., WC1. 01-405 4377 **2D 19**
London Commercial, Guildford Ho., 137 Grays Inn Rd., WC1. 01-242 6674 **1B 20**
London Permanent, 14 Tufton St., SW1. 01-222 3581 **1C 65**
London & South of England, 246 Upper St., N1. 01-226 3066 **2B 62**
Mornington, 158 Kentish Town Rd., NW5. 01-267 2971 **AZ 7F 45**
Nationwide, New Oxford Ho., High Holborn, WC1. 01-242 8822 **3D 19**
Newcastle, 77 Baker St., W1. 01-935 6069 **1C 15**
Northern Rock, 17 Conduit St., W1. 01-499 3563 **2C 33**
Paddington, 125 Westbourne Gro., W2. 01-229 7164 **AZ 7H 59**
Peckham Permanent, 14 Hanover Pk., SE15. 01-639 2254 **AZ 1G 95**
Portman, 40 Portman Sq., W1. 01-935 0981 **1D 31**
Property Owners,4 Cavendish Pl., W1. 01-580 5864 **3C 17**
St. Pancras, 200 Finchley Rd., NW3. 01-794 2331 **AZ 1B 60**
St. Stephens, 70 Chepstow Rd., W2. 01-229 8397 **1B 26**
Saffron Walden & Essex, 2 Romford Rd., E15. 01-534 8141 **AZ 6G 49**
Skipton, 81 High Holborn, WC1. 01-242 8147 **3D 19**
Thrift, 3-4 Turnpike Pde., Green Lanes, N15. 01-889 6023 **AZ 3B 30**
Town & Country, 215 Strand, WC2. 01-583 0981 **2A 36**
Victoria Permanent, 99 Aldwych, WC1. **2A 36**
Walthamstow, 869 Forest Rd., E17. 01-531 3231 **AZ 4J 31**
Westminster, 45 Weymouth St , W1 01-486 1913 **2A 16**
Woolwich Equitable, Equitable Ho , Woolwich New Rd., SE18. 01-854 2400
AZ 5E 82

CATHEDRALS AND CHURCHES

Including details of services in Church of England and Roman Catholic places of worshipfor other denominations see section WORSHIP. Church of England enquiry centre 01-222 9011: London Diocesan office 01-821 9351

All Hallows by the Tower, Byward St., EC3. 01-481 2928 **3C 41**
Rebuilt in Gothic style by Lord Mottistone after bad World War II damage; reopened 1957. New spire added to the surviving 17th cent. brick tower. 14th. cent. barrel vault, crypt, and many other historic features. Chapel of Toc H.
SERVICES: Sun. 11.00, 16.00, 17.30, Mon. 12.15, Tues. 08.30, 13.10, Wed. 12.35, Thurs. 18.15, Fri. 13.10.
All Hallows, London Wall, London Wall, EC4. 01-638 0971
3A 24
Rebuilt on an early foundation in 1765–7 by the younger George Dance. Brick with Portland stone tower and cupola; north wall is part of the Roman and Medieval City Wall. H.Q. of Council for Places of Worship.
All Hallows, Staining, Mark La., EC3. **2C 41** 15th cent. perpendicular tower only.
All Saints, Margaret St., W1. 01-636 1788 **3D 17**
Mid-19th cent. church by Butterfield in Gothic style. 230 ft. spire. Interior of mosaics, frescos, marbles and carvings. Well known for its music.
SERVICES: Sun. 08.00, 10.20, 11.00, 17.15, 18.00. Weekdays 07.30, 17.45, 18.30 and Thurs. 13.00.
All Souls, Langham Place, Langham Pl., W1. 01-580 4357
3C 17
Built by John Nash 1822–24 as part of his Regent Street town planning scheme. Circular portico of corinthian columns and slender needle spire.
SERVICES: Sun. 09.30, 11.00, 18.30. Tues. 12.30. Thurs. 13.10.
Brompton Oratory see **Oratory, The.**
Chapel Royal St. James's, Ambassador's Ct., St. James's Palace, SW1. **1D 49**
Built as part of St. James's Palace for Henry VIII. Painted ceiling attributed to Holbein. Has been the scene of many Royal marriages.
SERVICES: Sun. 08.00, 11.15 Oct. to Good Fri.
Chapel Royal of St. John, White Tower, Tower of London, EC3. **3C 41**
The oldest church in London, built about 1080 as part of the White Tower; established by William the Conqueror to protect and control the City. Tunnel vaulted nave, massive circular pillars. Crypt contains instruments of torture, execution axe, block from 17th cent. No regular services.
Chapel Royal of St. Peter-ad-Vincular, Tower of London, EC3. **3C 41**
Chiefly Tudor after restoration during Henry VIII's reign although its origins go back to the 12th cent. Buried in front of the altar are Anne Boleyn, Catherine Howard, Dukes of Northumberland and Somerset; and in the precincts Lady Jane Grey, Lord Guildford Dudley, the Duke of Monmouth and Scottish Lords Kilmarnock, Balmerino and Lovat.
SERVICES: Sun. 11,00, Thurs. 18.15 in July and Aug.
Chelsea Old Church, Cheyne Walk, SW3. 01-352 5627 **AZ 7B 76**
South Chapel 1528, by Sir Thomas More; rest of church much restored after World War II bomb damage. Chained books presented by Sir Hans Sloane. 16th cent. monument to Sir Thomas More.
SERVICES: Sun. 08.00, 10.00, 11.00, 12.00, 18.00, Thurs. 08.00, Fri. 12.00, Saints Days 08.00
Christchurch, Newgate, Newgate St., EC1. **1B 38**
Tower and steeple (1703–4) only. wren church once used by the bluecoat boys of Christ's Hospital, bombed 1940.
Christ Church Spitalfields, Commercial St., E1. 01-247 7202 **2D 25**

Built 1723–29 Baroque design by Nicholas Hawksmoor. 225 ft. tower and steeple rise from massive portico of columns. (Interior closed for renovation except for Church Festivals and two-week Summer Music Festival – May/June. Services held at temporary Church 22a Hanbury St., E1. Sun. 11.00, 18.30.

Grosvenor Chapel, S. Audley St., W1. 01-499 1684 **3A 32**
Built 1730 in colonial style architecture. Small tower with octagonal spire. Used by U.S. Armed Forces during World War II.
SERVICES: Sun. 08.15, 10.30, 11.00, Mon. to Sat. 12.30, Wed. 18.30, Thurs. 08.00.

Guards Chapel, Wellington Barracks, SW1. 01-930 4466 **3A 50**
Rebuilt 1963 incorporating surviving aspse of the earlier chapel devastated during World War II. Many internal features include pulpit given by the Royal Family and seven books of Remembrance, one for each regiment of the household brigade.
SERVICES: Sun. 08.00, 11.00, 12.00, 18.30 last Sun. in month.

Holy Sepulchre, Holborn Viaduct, EC4. 01-248 1660 **3A 22**
Otherwise known as St. Sepulchre without Newgate. Founded 12th cent.; rebuilt 15th cent.; repairs by Wren after the Great Fire and 19th cent. alterations; now the largest Parish Church in the City. Medieval tower and porch. Among many historic features are a handbell of 1605 used to rouse condemned prisoners at Newgate on the eve of execution; Musicians Chapel, and Garden of Remembrance for the Royal Fusiliers.
SERVICES: Sun. 09.15, Thurs. 13.20.

Holy Trinity, Sloane St., SW1. 01-730 7270 **3D 61**
Design by Sedding, 1890 "Arts and Crafts Church" with decoration by Henry Wilson, stained glass by Burne-Jones.
SERVICES: Sun. 08.30, 11.00, 12.10, Thurs. 11.30.

Oratory, The, Brompton Rd., SW3. 01-589 4811 **1A 60**
Roman Catholic Church served by secular priests of the Institute of the Oratory. Completed 1884 to designs by Herbert Gribble; dome added 1896–7. Italian Baroque with marbled interior, mosaics, gildings. Altarpieces and carvings from Italy, Statue Cardinal Newman.
MASSES: Sun. 07.00, 08.00, 09.00, 10.00, 11.00, 12.30, 16.30, 19.00.
Weekdays 07.00, 07.30, 08.00, 10.00, 12.30 ex. Sat., Holidays of Obligations 07.00, 08.00, 10.00, 12.15, 13.15, 16.30, 18.00, 20.00. Evening before Hol. of Obligations 17.30.

Queen's Chapel, St. James's Palace, Marlborough Rd., SW1. **1A 50**
Designed by Inigo Jones 1623–27 as a Catholic Chapel for Charles the First's Queen. Wooden coffered ceiling, Carolean panelling and Royal pews.
SERVICES: Sun. 08.30, 11.15 Easter Day to end of July.

Queen's Chapel of the Savoy see **Savoy Chapel.**

St. Alban, Wood Street, Wood St., EC2. **3C 23**
Wren tower 1697–8 only remains, pinnacles removed 1878.

St. Andrew, Holborn, Holborn Circus, EC1. 01-353 3544 **3D 21**
Wren Church of 1684–92 incorporating 15th cent. vestibule. Burnt out 1941, reopened 1961. 18th cent. organ case, gilded altarpiece, altar rails, pulpit, font all from Foundling Hospital Chapel and tomb of its founder Thomas Coram.
SERVICES: Tues. 13.05, Wed. 08.30, Thurs. 13.05.

St. Andrew by the Wardrobe, Queen Victoria St., EC4. 01-248 7546 **2A 38**
Name originates from the church's close proximity to the King's Storehouse or 'Great Wardrobe'. Of early foundation, rebuilt by Wren 1685–95 and again internally by M. Sisson after bombing 1940. Wren period pulpit, 18th cent. chamber organ.
SERVICES: Tues. and Thurs. 12.35, Wed. and Fri. 13.05.

St. Andrew Undershaft, St. Mary Axe, EC3. 01-283 7382 **1B 40**
Tower 15th cent., body of church rebuilt 1520–32. Name derived from the Maypole erected each year outside the church until 1517. Font 1631 by Nicholas Stone; Monument to John Stow whose quill pen is renewed by Lord Mayor at a special service; 17th cent. pulpit and organ case Services as announced.

St. Anne and St. Agnes, Gresham St., EC2. 01-373 5566 **3C 23**
Small red brick building, rebuilt by Wren 1676–87. Small western tower has
weather vane shaped as letter A. Internal cross plan with central dome
supported by four columns. World War II damage restored 1963–5.
SERVICES: In English Sun. 11.00, Estonian 1st and 3rd Sun. 16.15 Latvian 2nd and
4th Sun. 17.00.
St. Anne Limehouse, Commercial Rd., E14. **AZ 6J 63**
Nicholas Hawksmoor, English Baroque built 1712–30. Complex of arches and
buttresses, internally austere simplicity.
St. Anne's Soho, 57 Dean St., W1. **2B 34**
Steeple 1802–6 by Cockerell only remains. Wren church destroyed by World War
II bombing.
St. Augustine, Watling St., EC4. **1B 38**
Only Wren tower is left of church built 1680–87; new spire to original design,
incorporated into new St. Paul's Cathedral Choir School.
St. Bartholomew the Great, Smithfield, EC1. 01-606 5171 **3B 22**
Church of Augustinian Priory founded 1123 by Rahere, jester to Henry 1, and later
first Prior. Choir and crossing original Norman work; Lady Chapel and Crypt 14th cent.;
17th cent. brick tower—all heavily restored 1897 by Sir A. Webb. Only pre-
reformation font in the City. Monument to Rahere.
SERVICES: Sun. 09.00, 11.00, 18.30.
St. Bartholomew the Less, St. Barthlolomew's Hospital, EC1. 01-600 9000 **3A 22**
Parish church of St. Bartholomew's Hospital. 15th cent. tower, body of church
rebuilt in octagonal shape 1789; design by G. Dance junior. Many monuments, 17th
cent. onwards.
SERVICES: Sun. 08.00, 10.30, 17.00, Tues. 17.30, Wed. 12.20, Thurs. 17.00, Fri.
13.10.
St. Benet Guild Welsh Church, Queen Victoria St., EC4. 01-723 3104 **2B 38**
Rebuilt 1677–85, Wren. Red brickwork with stone fes*oons; tall tower has lead
dome and steeple. Interior of original galleries (pews reconstructed from originals),
pulpit, font, altar table. Inigo Jones buried here 1652.
SERVICES: Sun. 11.00, 17.00.
St. Botolph Aldersgate, Aldersgate St., EC1 **3B 22**
Rebuilt 1788, Nathaniel Wright. Exterior brown brick with wooden turret and gilded
vane. Barrel vaulted roof. Altar table of 1639 and monuments from earlier
church. Churchyard, often called "Postmen's Park" has art nouveau tiles recording
acts of heroism in everyday life.
SERVICES: Thurs. 12.15.
St. Botolph Aldgate, Aldgate High St., EC3. 01-283 1670 **1C 41**
Rebuilt 1741–44 by George Dance senior. Large brick building, late 19th-cent.
interior alterations by Bentley (architect of Westminster Cathedral) including plaster
work, mosaic floor, pews.
SERVICES: Sun. 10.30, Mon. 13.00, Tues. 17.45, Wed. 13.00, Thurs. 12.10, Fri.
13.20.
St. Botolph Bishopsgate, Bishopsgate, EC2. 01-588 1053 **3B 24**
Rebuilt 1725–9, J. Gold. Brick with stone detailing and tower. Glass dome over
nave roof 1820. Victorian screens and decoration.
SERVICES: Sun. 11.00 last Sun. in month, 08.30 remainder. Tues. 13.10. Wed.
12.35, 13.15. Thurs. 08.15, 12.30.
St. Bride, Bride La., Fleet St., EC4. 01-353 1301 **1D 37**
Dedicated to St. Bridget, a 6th cent. Irish Saint. Rebuilt by Wren 1670–84 and again
after 1940 devastation around the surviving steeple. As a result of the bombing
there is now a Crypt Museum with Roman, Saxon and Medieval finds uncovered
by archaeological digs relating to the history of St. Bride. Rehallowed Dec.
1957. Samuel Pepys baptised here 1663. Regarded as the "Journalists' Church".
SERVICES: Sun. 08.30, 11.00, 18.00.
St. Clement Danes, Strand, WC2. 01-242 8282 **1B 36**
Church of the Royal Air Force. Wren church built 1681 on site of a church thought

to date back to a 9th cent. Danish settlement. Spire added 1719, James Gibbs. Although gutted 1941 the church has been restored to original design; pulpit reconstructed from fragments of the original. Crests of the 735 R.A.F. units have been let into the floor. United States Air Force shrine. Bells play the tune "Oranges and Lemons"
SERVICES: Sun. 08.30, 11.00, 12.15, 15.30. Tues. to Fri. 12.30.

St. Clement Eastcheap, King William St., EC4. 01-248 6121 **2A 40**
Small brick Wren church, 1683–87. Plain interior contrasts with 17th cent. carved canopied pulpit, font cover, panelled walls and huge plaster wreath on the ceiling.
SERVICES: Tues. 08.15. Wed. 12.15. Thurs. 13.00.

St. Dunstan-in-the-East, Idol La., EC3. **3B 40**
Only Wren tower 1702 remains after bombing 1941; steeple on flying buttresses.

St. Dunstan-in-the-West, Fleet St., EC4. 01-242 6027 **1C 37**
Octagonal shaped church by John Shaw, 1831. Stone tower and lantern. 17th cent. clock with bell striking statues from the old church. Statues include one of Elizabeth 1 (from Lud Gate demolished 1760).

Romanian Orthodox Church, see page 203.

St. Edmund the King, Lombard St., EC3. 01–623 6970 **2A 40**
Dedicated to Edmund, King of East Anglia killed 870 by Danes. Wren church, 1670–79 on lines of original, octagonal lead spire added 1706. 17th cent. woodwork, font cover, pews, pulpit.
SERVICES: Wed. 12.10, 13.10. Holy Days 12.10, 13.10.

St. Ethelburga, Bishopsgate, EC3. 01-588 3596 **1B 40**
Tiny Medieval church, 15th cent. and later additions. Restored by Comper 1912 including chancel screen. Modern mural and stained glass.
SERVICES: Tues. 12.10, Thurs. 13.10.

St. Etheldreda or Ely Chapel, Ely Pl., EC1. 01-405 1061 **3D 21**
Chapel once belonging to the Palace of the Bishops of Ely, demolished 1772. Renamed St. Etheldreda's Church on restoration to Roman Catholic worship in 1874. Example of decorated style c. 1290, restored by Sir Giles G. Scott 1935. Large west window c. 1300, south-west doorway the original entrance from Ely Palace.
MASSES: Sun. 09.00, 11.00, 18.00. Mon. to Fri. 08.00, 13.00 Holy days of Obligation 08.00, 13.00, 18.00.

St. George, Bloomsbury, Bloomsbury Way, WC1. **3D 19**
Classical style 1720–31 design by Nicholas Hawksmoor. Portico of corinthian columns, stepped spire topped with statue of George I.
SERVICES: Sun. 10.00, 18.30. Wed. 13.10. Fri. 08.00.

St. George-in-the-East, Cannon Street Rd., E1. 01-481 1345 **AZ 8J 143**
Nicholas Hawksmoor baroque, built 1715–23. Only tower; crowned by octagonal lantern, and side walls survived World War II bombing. Interior rebuilt 1964.
SERVICES: Sun. 10.00, 18.30. Weekdays 17.00. Wed. 08.30. Thurs. 20.00. Fri. 07.30. Sat. 08.30.

St. George, Hanover Square, St. George St., W1. 01-629 0874 **2C 33**
Built 1713–24 design John James. Classical portico, Baroque tower, 16th cent. Flemish glass. Fashionable weddings since late 18th cent. include Disraeli, Lady Emma Hamilton, Theodore Roosevelt, Shelley.
SERVICES: Sun. 08.15, 11.00. Wed. 08.00, 13.10. Fri. 12.10. Saint Days 12.10.

St. George's Roman Catholic Cathedral, St. George's Rd. SE1. 01-928 5256 **1D 67**
Design by Pugin 1840–48. Victorian Gothic, renovated after World War II bombing.
MASSES: Sun. (evening before at 18.30) then: 07.00, 08.00, 09.30, 10.30, 12.30, 17.30, 18.30. Weekdays 07.00, 08.00, 12.30, 19.30. Hols. of Obligation 07.00, 0.800, 09.00, 10.00, 12.30, 17.30, 18.30, 19.30.

St. Giles Cripplegate, Fore St., EC2. 01-606 3630 **2C 23**
Medieval church rebuilt 16th cent. Tower added 17th cent including white wooden turret. Interior restored after World War II damage Still has many monuments— J. Speed, Sir Martin Frobisher and J. Milton Oliver Cromwell married here 1620. Roman and Medieval City Wall close by.

SERVICES: Sun. 08.00, 10.00, 18.00. Wed. 12.40, 13.05.

St. Helen Bishopsgate, St. Helen's Pl., EC3. 01-283 2231 **1B 40**
13th cent. church, two parallel naves—northern one used by Benedictine Nunnery.
15th cent. Squint, 17th cent. wooden sword rest, elaborate south doorway and doors
canopied pulpit, wooden bell turret and many monuments including Sir J. Crosby,
Sir T. Gresham.
SERVICES: Sun. 10.45. Tues. 12.25 and 13.05.

St. James Garlickhythe, Garlick Hill, EC4. 01-236 1719 **2C 23**
Wren church 167484. Three tiered steeple on square tower, restored 1714. Interior
of plaster, gilded detailing—very bright owing to many clear glass windows; dark
woodwork, pews, pulpit, case of Father Smith Organ, ironwork.
SERVICES: Tues. 13.15. 1st Sun. 10.30.

St. James's, Spanish Place, George St., W1. 01-935 0943 **3A 16**
Roman Catholic church. Built in Victorian Early English style 1890, design J. Goldie.
MASSES: 08.30, 10.30, 12.00, 16.00, 19.00. Mon. to Fri. 07.15, 12.30, 18.00. Sat.
08.00, 10.00, 18.00. Hols. of Obligation 07.15, 08.30, 12.00, 13.15, 18.00, 20.00.

St. James's Piccadilly, Piccadilly, W1. 01-734 4511 **3A 34**
Wren built 1676–84, rebuilt after destruction 1940. Decorated barrel vault, galleries,
organ built 1685 for Whitehall Palace given by Mary II. Marble font, reredos,
organ case by Grinling Gibbons. New glass-fibre spire to original design added
1968. Fashionable for marriages. Garden of remembrance dedicated to
Londoners' courage in the Second World War. Has the London **Brass Rubbing
Centre** see page 187.
SERVICES: Sun. 08.15, 09.15, 11.00, 18.00.

St. John Bethnal Green, Cambridge Heath Rd., E2. 01-980 1742 **AZ 4H 63**
Built 1825–8. Design by Soane a composition of pronounced horizontal and vertical
pillars and beams, cube tower with small turret. Interior altered after fire 1870.
SERVICES: Sun. 10.00, Tues. 13.10, Thurs. Fri. & Sat. 09.15.

St. John the Evangelist, Smith Sq., SW1. **1C 65**
Baroque church by Thomas Archer 1713–28. Isolated in centre of square it has
four great corner towers linked by columns and pediments, nicknamed
"Queen Anne's Footstool". Restored as concert hall and arts centre after war
damage, see page 39.

St. John's Clerkenwell, St. John's Sq., EC1. **1A 22**
Rebuilt 1721–3 on site of round church of Order of St. John consecrated 1185.
Norman crypt survives. Private Chapel; admission only via St. John's Gate p. 102.

St. Katherine Cree, Leadenhall St., EC3. 01-283 5733 **1C 41**
Tower 1504, rest rebuilt 1628–31 and consecrated by Archbishop Laud. Pre-fire
Renaissance has mixture of styles—classical pillars, arches and gothic
windows. Guild Church for finance, commerce and industry and headquarters of
the Industrial Christian Fellowship.
SERVICES: Thurs. 13.05.

St. Lawrence Jewry, Gresham St., EC3. 01-600 9478 **1C 39**
Corporation of London Church, one of the largest of Wren's designs, 1670–87,
only tower and walls survived bombing 1940. Restored 1954–7 with replicas
of steeple and ceiling. Original weathervane in form of gridiron recalling the
martyrdom of St. Lawrence.
SERVICES: Wed. 08.30, Fri. 12.15, 13.15. 1st Sun. 09.15.

St. Magnus the Martyr, Lwr. Thames St., EC3. 01-626 4481 **3A 40**
Rebuilt, Wren 1671–87. Tower with projecting clock has octagonal lantern, lead
dome and spire added 1705–6. Stood on approach to Old London Bridge.
Interior has much wood and iron work.
SERVICES: Sun. 11.00, Tues. and Thurs. 12.15, Wed. and Fri. 13.15.

St. Margaret Lothbury, Lothbury, EC2. 01-606 8330 **1D 39**
Rebuilt in white Portland stone, 1686–1700 design by Wren. Corner tower with
lead steeple. Interior rich with woodwork, 17th cent. chancel screen and pulpit
sounding board from All Hallows the Great.
SERVICES: Wed. 12.10.

St. Margaret Pattens, Rood La., EC2. 01-623 6630 **2B 40**
Wren 1684–9, tall lead spire with gilded vane. 17th cent. churchwardens' pews
with carved canopies. 1543 Communion Cup, 18th cent. monuments, sword rests,
punishment bench. Now Christian Study Centre.
SERVICES: Thurs. 13.15.

St. Margaret's Westminster, Parliament Sq., SW1. 01-222 6382 **3C 51**
Parish church of House of Commons. Rebuilt 1504–18, perpendicular style. 16th
cent. Flemish glass in east window, memorials to Lady Dudley, Sir Walter Raleigh,
William Caxton. Modern windows by John Piper. Weddings celebrated here
include Samuel Pepys, John Milton, Winston Churchill; and fashionable
weddings nowadays.
SERVICES: Sun. 08.15, 11.00, first Sun. in month. 11.00, 12.15 the remainder.

St. Martin-in-the-Fields, Trafalgar Sq., WC2. 01-930 0089 **3C 35**
Rebuilt, James Gibbs 1721–6. Famous Corinthian portico, steps, tower and spire
with weather vane topped by crown. Venetian east window white and gold
ceiling work of Italian craftsmen, Font 1689, from previous church. Royal box.
Baptised here were Francis Bacon, John Hampden, Charles II. Crypt contains
whipping post from Charing Cross.
SERVICES: Sun. 08.00, 09.45, 11.15, 16.15. 18.30. Daily 08.00, 08.15, 17.30.

St. Martin Ludgate, Ludgate Hill, EC4. 01-248 6054 **1A 38**
Rebuilt, Wren 1677–87. Delicate lead spire to harmonise with nearby St. Paul's;
internal cruciform shape created by moulded ceiling and columns. Screen separates
noisy Ludgate Hill from body of church. 17th cent. altar-piece and table, pulpit,
organ case. West wall is part of the medieval city wall.
SERVICES: Thurs. 13.15.

St. Mary Abchurch, Abchurch La., EC4. 01-626 0306 **2A 40**
Rebuilt, Wren 1681–7. Square building with painted dome over the total interior by
William Snow 1708. Carved woodwork includes canopied pulpit 1685. Grinling
Gibbons altarpiece, panelled pews, west gallery.
SERVICES: Tues. 12.30, Thurs. 13.00, 1st Wed. of month & Saints' Days 12.30.
Service of healing 2nd Mon. of month. Oct. to July 17.45.

St. Mary Aldermary, Queen Victoria St., EC4. **2C 39**
Rebuilt, Wren in late gothic style, fan vaulting. Opened 1682, tower of original
church partly rebuilt 1703.
SERVICES: Tues. 13.15, Wed. 12.15, Thurs. 13.15, Fri. 12.15, 13.15. Saints' Days
12.15, 13.15.

St. Mary at Hill, Lovat La., EC3. 01–626 4184 **2B 40**
Rebuilt varying stages by Wren 1670–6. East end has enormous projecting clock;
entrance at west through tower and glass-wood screen; gallery and massive
organ above. Ceiling with central dome in Adam style, 1843, contrasts with the
masses of original woodwork, boxed pews with sword rests, pulpit and
sounding board.
SERVICES: Wed. 13.15.

St. Mary le Bow, Cheapside, EC2. 01-248 5139 **1C 39**
Tower and steeple by Wren 1670–83, at 221 ft. is second highest in City, famed
for "Bow Bells". Three aisled Norman Crypt, some Roman brick used in
construction; the round arches or bows gave name to the Court of Arches formerly;
and now held here for deciding Ecclesiastical Law cases. Body of church rebuilt 1961–
64 after bombing 1941.
SERVICES: Tues. 13.05 Diaglogue. Wed. 12.30.

St. Mary-le-Strand , Strand, WC2. 01-836 3126 **2A 36**
Small baroque island church, James Gibbs 1714–17. Three stage steeple above
semi-circular porch. Coffered ceiling to the nave. Prince Charles the "Young Pretender"
is supposed to have been secretly received into the C. of E. here, 1750. Thomas
a Becket rector of previous church.
SERVICES: Sun. 11.00, Tues. 12.15, Thurs. 13.05.

St. Mary Somerset, Upper Thames St., EC4. **2B 38**
Tower only of Wren church, 1695 demolished 1872.

St. Mary Woolnoth, King William St.-Lombard St., EC3. 01-626 9701 **2A 40**
Rebuilt Nicholas Hawksmoor 1716–27. Wide tower with horizontal rustications,
twin turrets rising above high level arcade. Internally cubed with triple groups
of columns in corners. Features include baroque altarpiece, pulpit, ironwork, Father
Smith organ.
SERVICES: Thurs. 13.05.
St. Michael Paternoster Royal, College St., EC4. 01-248 5208 **2D 39**
Rebuilt Wren, 1686–94. Red brick and Portland stone. Tower with steeple of
columns rising in four stages to 128 ft. Interior destroyed in World War II but
restored much to original condition. Grinling Gibbons pulpit, 17th cent. candelabra.
Grave of Dick Whittington who rebuilt the earlier church and founded college
nearby. Headquarers of the Missions to Seamen.
St. Michael-upon-Cornhill, Cornhill, EC3. 01-626 8841 **1A 40**
Rebuilt Wren, 1670–7 with Gothic tower added 1715–22. Interior restored Sir G.
Scott 1857–60. Font of 1672. Carved pelican 1775, monuments to Cowper
family. Peal of 12 bells rung on Sundays.
SERVICES: 1st, 3rd & 5th Sun. 11.00. 2nd & 4th 12.15. Wed. 13.00.
St. Nicholas Cole Abbey, Queen Victoria St., EC4. 01-248 5213 **2C 39**
Wren 1671–81, square tower and lead spire with ship weather vane from St.
Michael Queenhithe dem. 1875. Gutted 1941 but since restored, all woodwork being
17th cent. (some from other churches) see pulpit, font cover, panelled walls.
SERVICES: Wed. 12.15.
St. Olave Hart Street, Hart St., EC3. 01-488 4318 **2C 41**
Dedicated to King Olaf of Norway, martyred 1030. Small medieval city church, 15th
cent., 12th cent. vaulted crypt. Restoration after destruction of 1941 added a new and
larger bell turret and south door porch. Samuel Pepys worshipped and was buried
here, bust in south aisle 1884, and of his wife, 1669. 17th cent. pulpit and altar rail.
Original churchyard has archway with skull and crossbones referred to by Dickens
in "Uncommercial Traveller".
SERVICES: Sun. 11.00, Tues. 13.00.
St Olave Old Jewry, Ironmongers La., EC2. **1D 39**
Tower only of Wren church 1670–6, demolished 1888. Ship weather vane from St.
Mildred Poultry dem. 1872.
St. Paul Covent Garden, Inigo Pl., WC2. 01-836 5221 **2D 35**
Inigo Jones 1633. Designed back to front with the impressive overhanging portico
in Covent Garden Square at the east end, the entrance through quiet gardens.
Rebuilt in 1795 after fire. Known as the actors' church: memorial to Charles
Macklin; and ashes of Dame Ellen Terry. Grave of Grinling Gibbons.
SERVICES: Sun. 11.00, Wed. 08.30. Thurs. 13.05.
St. Paul's Cathedral, St. Paul's Churchyard, EC4. 01-248 2705 **1B 38**
Seat of the Bishopric of London and "Parish Church of the British Commonwealth".
The present Cathedral built 1675–1710 was designed by Sir Christopher Wren.
It follows the traditional Cathedral form of Latin Cross; internal length 463 ft., width
across Transepts 227½ ft., height to top of cross 365 ft. This is the third
Cathedral on the site. The first dated possibly from the ordination of Millitus by St.
Augustine *c.* 604. The second was begun by the Norman Bishop Maurice in
1087 and building continued until *c.* 1286, this cathedral was destroyed in the Great
Fire 1666.
FEATURES:
1. The Ball.
   The Ball 6ft. dia. surmounting the Lantern, is 344ft. or 627 steps high,
   above which is the 15ft. Cross. Accessible only by permission.
b. Carving, Grinling Gibbons.
   Choir Stalls and Organ Case. The Organ built 1697 by Father Smith is now
   in two sections on either side of the Choir.
c. Chapels.
   All Souls Chapel in the Apse is dedicated to American Servicemen who
   lost their lives in World War II while based in this country. Jesus Chapel

containing the Kitchener Memorial in the North-West Tower. North-West Chapel dedicated to St. Dunstan is reserved for private prayer. St. Christopher's Chapel is in the Crypt. South-West Chapel is dedicated to the Order of St. Michael and St. George; has 17th cent. oak screen by Jonathan Maine.

d. Clock Tower.

 The Clock or South Tower contains the largest bell in England, "Great Paul" 16–6

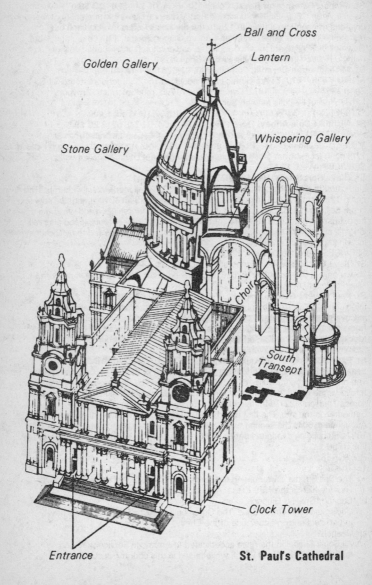

St. Paul's Cathedral

tons, it is rung for five minutes at 13.00. There are also three clock bells the largest of which is "Great Tom" 5–4 tons, it is tolled on the death of a member of the Royal Family, Archbishop of Canterbury, Bishop of London, Dean of St. Paul's or the Lord Mayor of London.

e. The Crypt.
   Extends the entire length of the Cathedral. At the east end is the Chapel of St. Christopher. There are two exhibitions, 1) "Christopher Wren", including his "Great Model" for the Cathedral, 2) "Treasury", gold and silver plate, robes and other ecclesiastical treasures from the diocese of London. Approach by the staircase in the South Transept.

f. Golden Gallery.
   281ft. high, runs around the base of the Lantern and is reached by a series of open metal stairs between the inner and outer Domes. Approach by staircase from Stone Gallery.

g. Ironwork, Jean Tijou.
   Low Choir Screen. Gates to Choir Aisles and Balustrade to the Dean's Staircase, South-West Tower.

h. Library.
   Contains a collection of manuscripts and books begun by Bishop Compton, 1714; retains the original bookcases and panelling. Approach from South Aisle Staircase via South Triforium Gallery.

j. Paintings and Mosaics.
   Inner Dome has eight paintings of the life of St. Paul by Sir J. Thornhill. Quarter Domes mosaics of the Crucifixion, Entombment, Resurrection and the Ascension by Sir W. Richmond. Spandrels a series of mosaics representing St. Matthew and St. John by G. F. Watts; St. Mark and St. Luke by W. E. Britten; and Isaiah, Jeremiah, Ezekiel and Daniel by A. Stephens.

k. Sculpture, Francis Bird.
   Includes the West End Pediment relief of the Conversion of St. Paul and surmounting statues.

ST. PAULS CATHEDRAL

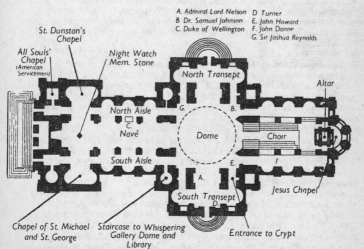

Tombs and Monuments

A. Admiral Lord Nelson
B. Dr. Samuel Johnson
C. Duke of Wellington
D. Turner
E. John Howard
F. John Donne
G. Sir Joshua Reynolds

l. South Triforium Gallery.
   Has a collection of relics, plans and sketches of "Old St. Paul's". Approach from
   the South Aisle Staircase.
m. Stone Gallery.
   182ft. high, runs externally at balustrade level of the Dome giving a 360;dg
   panoramic view of London. Approach by staircase via Whispering Gallery.
n. Tombs, Monuments and Memorials.
   ARCHITECT: Christopher Wren. ARTISTS: William Blake, John Constable,
   Edwin Landseer, Lord Leighton, Sir Joshua Reynolds, P. Wilson Steer, J. W.
   M. Turner, Van Dyck. ENGINEER: John Rennie. LITERARY: John Donne,
   Dr. Johnson, Walter de la Mare. MILITARY: General Abercromby; Admirals
   Beatty, Collingwood, Howe, Jellicoe, Nelson and Rodney; Lord Heathfield,
   Field-Marshal Kitchener, Sir Henry Lawrence, Duke of Wellington.
   MUSICIANS: Sir Hubert Parry, Sir Arthur Sullivan. OTHERS: Sir Max
   Beerbohm, W. Carlile founder of the Church Army, Sir Alexander Fleming of
   penicillin fame, John Howard, Florence Nightingale, Sir George Williams founder
   of Y.M.C.A., Air Transport Auxiliary 1939–45 and a memorial slab to Night
   Watch 1939–45.
o. Whispering Gallery.
   100ft. above the Cathedral floor, runs internally around the circumference
   of the lower Drum. Whispers against the wall on one side can be heard near
   the wall on the opposite side. Approach from staircase off South Aisle.
SERVICES: Sun. 08.00, 10.30, 11.30; evensong 15.15. Weekdays, Mon. to Fri.
07.30, 08.00, 12.30. Sat. 08.00, 10.00, 12.30; plus evensong Mon. to Sat. April
to Oct. 17.00; Oct. to March 16.00. Subject to special events. Admission charge
to Crypt, Galleries
& East End.

St. Paul's Deptford, High St., SE8. 01-692 1419 **AZ 6C 80**
Archer, 1712–30. Semi-circular portico supporting tall tower and spire stand at the
side of square plan church; surrounded by staircases. Interior galleried. Dutch
oak fittings.
SERVICES: Sun. 08.00, 10.00, 19.00. Mon. to Sat. 08.00, 18.00, ex. Thurs. 09.00,
18.00 and Sat. 10.00, 18.00.

St. Peter Cornhill, Cornhill, EC3. 01-626 9483 **1C 40**
Rebuilt Wren, 1677–87. Brick tower, copper dome, spire surmounted by weather
vane in form of St. Peter's key. Carved chancel screen has Lion and Unicorn,
font 1681 with cover from original church. Vestry has keyboard of organ played by
Mendelssohn and his autograph (1840). Organ originally by Father Smith noted for
musical recitals.
SERVICES: Thurs. 12.30.

St. Sepulchre Without Newgate see **Holy Sepulchre.**

St. Stephen Walbrook, Walbrook, EC4. 01-283 3400 **2D 39**
Rebuilt Wren, 1672–77 steeple added 1717. Rectangular interior divided by pillars
supporting eight arches and dome. Original pulpit, altar rails, altar piece, font. Baroque
west screen, organ 1765. Grave of Sir John Vanburgh. Headquarters of Samaritans
since 1953.

St. Vedast, Foster La., EC2. 01-606 3998 **1C 39**
Rebuilt Wren, 1695–1700. Tower surmounted by simple three part steeple,
concave and convex surfaces. Interior rebuilt after destruction 1940, with contemporary
Wren fittings from other churches—organ case, pulpit and font, altar-piece.
SERVICES: Sun. 11.00. Mon. to Fri. 12.15. Mon. 08.00. Sat. 08.30.

Savoy Chapel, Savoy St., WC2. 01-836 7221 **2A 36**
Perpendicular, early 16th cent.; largely rebuilt 1864. Private Chapel of the ruling
monarch as the Duke of Lancaster. Since 1937 also the chapel of the Royal
Victorian Order. At west end are Royal pews and arms of members of the order.
SERVICES: Sun. 11.15. Wed. 12.30.

Southwark Cathedral, Southwark High St., SE1. 01-407 2939 **1D 55**
The Cathedral Collegiate Church of St. Saviour and St. Mary Ovary. Norman church

built by Augustinian Canons was burnt out and reconstructed beginning 13th cent.—Early English Gothic. Nave rebuilt 1890–97. Became a Cathedral 1905.

FEATURES:

a. Harvard Chapel.
    Restored 1907 by Blomfield with money given by Harvard University and in memory of John Harvard baptized in the church 1607. Previously called Chapel of St. John the Evangelist.

b. Choir.
    13th cent. Early English. Five bays, vault rebuilt 19th cent. and choir stalls added.

c. Lady Chapel (or Retro-Choir).
    Early English restored 1832–5. 16th cent. screen on west side.

d. Tower.
    163ft. high. Lower part 13th cent. upper stages 1520. Peal of 12 bells.
    Other features include: Perpendicular altar screen (1520), 16th cent. stubbed doorway, Elizabethan glass. Memorial to Shakespeare and grave of his brother, tomb and effigy of Gower (1408) friend of Chaucer.

SERVICES: Sun. 09.00, 11.00, 15.30. Mon. 17.30. Tues. 08.00, 17.30. Wed. 17.30. Thurs. 08.00, 17.30 (Said Evensong), Fr. 13.10, 17.30. Sat. 12.00. Saints' Days 13.10.

Temple Church, Inner Temple La., EC4. 01-353 1736 **1C 37**

Circular nave 1185, built for Knights Templar; one of few remaining round churches in England. Chancel added 1240, Early English Style. 12th-13th cent. effigies. Reredos 1682, Wren. Restored after World War II damage. See also PLACES OF INTEREST

SERVICES: Sun. 08.30, 11.15. Greater Festivals and 1st. Sun. 12.30. No services Aug. or Sept.

Westminster Abbey, Broad Sanctuary, SW1. 01-222 5152 **3C 51**

Collegiate church of St. Peter in Westminster, under jurisdiction of Dean and Chapter subject only to the Sovereign. All English Sovereigns from William I to Elizabeth II crowned here except Edward V and VIII, and burial place of most English Kings Henry III to George II. Founded by Edward the Confessor on site of earlier building in 1605. Rebuilt in Edward's honour by Henry III in French Gothic style, architect Henry of Rheims and rededicated 1269. Western end of nave completed in 14th cent. by Henry Yevele, architect of Westminster Hall. Henry VII Chapel added in 16th cent., Western towers by Hawksmoor, 18th cent. Interior length 511–4ft., width across transepts 203ft., highest Gothic vault in England 102ft. (Nave); height of Western towers 255ft.

FEATURES

a. Chapels:
    i   Edward the Confessor—contains shrine of Edward, 13th cent, tomb, 15th cent. screen, oak Coronation Chair c. 1297 with Stone of Scone beneath (the Coronation Seat of Kings of Scotland).
    ii Henry VII Chapel—Elaborate Perpendicular Gothic. World famous fan vaulting, flying buttresses; tomb by 16th cent. Florentine sculptor. Banners of the Knights of the Order of the Bath (founded by Richard II) hang over the Stalls.
    iii Islip Chapel—lower storey contains grave of Abbot Islip d. 1532, upper storey: the Nurses' Chapel.
    iv R.A.F. Chapel—dedicated in 1947 to those of the flying forces who lost their lives in the Battle of Britain.
    v   St. George's Chapel—The Old Baptistry, dedicated 1932 to the dead of the First World War.

There are also chapels to St. Andrew, St. Faith, St. Benedict, St. Edmund, St. Nicholas, St. Paul, St. John Baptist, St. John Evangelist, St. Michael, St. Martin and All Saints and Henry V Chantry.

b. Chamber of the Pyx.
    Vaulted chamber 1040–1100, part of Edward Confessor's Church. Later became royal treasury or repository of the "Pyx".

WESTMINSTER ABBEY

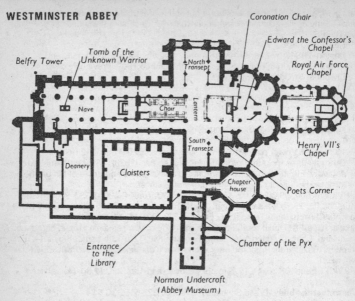

c. Chapterhouse.
   Built for Henry III. Scene of Great Council 1257, and Parliament 1352–1547. 13th cent. tiled pavement, 14th cent. east wall paintings, others of the 15th cent. Roman Sarcophagus.

d. Cloisters.
   13th and 14th cent. Little cloister on site of monks' infirmary.

e. Library.
   Many 16th cent. books, collections on the Abbey and School, see LIBRARIES

f. Norman Undercroft and Museum.
   Part of Edward Confessor's Church now containing the Abbey Collection, see MUSEUMS AND GALLERIES.

g. Sanctuary.
   Setting for the Coronation, mosaic pavement of 1268, medieval tombs.

h. Tombs, Monuments and Memorials.
   The Abbey is a mass of tombs and monuments. Amongst these are many tombs of Royalty; POETS' CORNER with busts of Dryden, Longfellow and Milton, Chaucer's tomb, graves of Browning and Tennyson, ashes of T. S. Eliot and Masefield, monuments to Shakespeare and Dr. Johnson, tablet to Brontë Sisters, medallion to Ben Jonson and many others; including actors, actresses, admirals, architects, schoolmasters, scientists, soldiers and statesmen. Grave of the UNKNOWN WARRIOR buried Nov. 11th 1920 is representative of the British who gave their lives in World War I. Nearby are monuments to Winston Churchill and David Lloyd George.

i. Windows.
   Rose window in South Transept is largest of its kind in England—reglazed 1902 (nearby is Poets' Corner, see above), that in the North 1722, by Sir James Thornhill. East window has glass of 13th, 14th and 15th cent., West window 15th cent. glass; Chapter House has six large windows of "Early Decorated" style.

SERVICES: Sun. 08.00, 10.30, 11.40, 15.00, 18.30. Weekdays 07.30, 08.00, 12.30, 17.00. Sat. 08.00, 09.20, 15.00. Admission charge to Royal Chapels, Poets' Corner, Quire, Statesmen's Aisle, Chapter House, Chapel of the Pyx and Museum. Only the Nave is Open to visitors on Sundays—between services.

Westminster Cathedral, Ashley Pl., SW1. 01-834 7452 **2D 63**
Roman Catholic Cathedral, seat of the Cardinal Archbishop of Westminster, scene of the first mass ever celebrated by a Pope on English soil—Pope John Paul II, in May 1982. Built 1895–1903, J. F. Bentley in Early Christian Byzantine style. Exterior of alternate brick and stone bands, now beautifully offset by modern architecture and piazza. Square Campanile, St. Edward's tower is 284 ft. high, interior 342 ft. long; nave 60 ft. wide has three domed bays. Pillars of nave have Eric Gill reliefs of Stations of the Cross. There are eleven chapels, four relic chambers in the crypt, and tombs of Cardinals Wiseman and Manning. Altar to Canadian Airmen lost in World War II.
MASSES: Sun. 07.00, 08.00, 09.00, 10.30, 12.00, 17.30, 19.00. Weekdays 07.00, 08.00, 08.30, 09.00, 10.30, 12.30, 13.05, 17.30. Christmas Day, Bank Hol. 15.30 instead, 18.00. Holidays of Obligation as weekday services plus 17.30, 19.00. Campanile open usually 10.30 to dusk, admission charge (Viewing Gallery).

CEREMONIES, EVENTS AND FESTIVALS

DAILY:
CEREMONY OF THE KEYS. Tower of London. See also page 105
The Chief Yeoman Warder with an escort of Foot Guards proceed at 21.53 to lock the gates of the Tower. At the Bloody Tower they are challenged. "Queen Elizabeth's Keys" replies the Warden. The Last Post is sounded at 22.00. Application to see this ceremony should be made to the Resident Governor, H.M. Tower of London, EC3.
CHANGING THE GUARD.
1. Buckingham Palace. Changing of the Queen's Guard takes place every morning at 11.30. Alternate days in winter months.
   The ceremony is carried out by one of five regiments of Foot Guards marching to the Band. Duration 30 mins. (In wet weather the Band does not accompany the Guards.)
2. Horse Guards, Whitehall. Changing of the Queen's Life Guard takes place in the small courtyard adjacent to Whitehall daily at 11.00 (Sundays 10.00). The ceremony is held by the two regiments of Household Cavalry, the Royal Horse Guards in Blue and the Life Guards in Red. Duration 20 mins.
3. Windsor Castle, Berkshire. Daily 11.00, Double guard when the Queen is in residence.

ANNUAL:
Venues can change; for current details consult London Visitor and Convention Bureau.
JANUARY:
Ceremony of Charles I. Charing Cross and Banqueting House, Whitehall, SW1.
To commemorate the execution of King Charles I in 1649.
International Boat Show. Earls Court.
Model Engineer Exhibition. Wembley Conference Centre.
Racing and Sporting Motor-Cycle Show, R.H.S. Halls.
Royal Academy of Art—Winter Exhibition. Burlington House, Piccadilly, W1.
FEBRUARY:
Clowns Service. Holy Trinity Church, Dalston, E8.
Crufts Dog Show. Earls Court.
English Folk Dance and Song Society's Festival. Royal Albert Hall, SW7.
National Canoe Exhibition. Crystal Palace, SE19.

FEBRUARY–MARCH:
"Daily Mail" Ideal Home Exhibition. Earls Court.
Stampex National Stamp Exhibition. Royal Horticultural Society Halls.
Trial of the Pyx. Goldsmiths' Hall, Foster La., EC2.
At which the coins of the realm are tested.
MARCH:
Camping and Outdoor Leisure Exhibition. Variable venue.
Chelsea Antiques Fair. Chelsea Old Town Hall, SW3.
London Marathon. Starts at Greenwich.
City of London Art Exhibition. Guildhall, EC2.
London Dinghy Exhibition. Pickets Lock Centre.
National Cross Country Championships. Parliament Hill, NW3.
Oranges and Lemons Service. St. Clement Danes, Strand, WC2. Distribution of
oranges and lemons to school children takes place after a special service.
Spital Service and Procession. Guildhall to St. Lawrence Jewry. The Lord Mayor,
Aldermen and Common Councilmen attend the Spital Sermon, a name derived
from the priory of St. Mary Spittle.
MARCH–APRIL:
Easter Holy Week.
    Bank Holiday Fairs. Sat. and Mon. at Blackheath, Hampstead Heath and
    Wormwood Scrubs.
    Easter Parade. Sun., Battersea Park.
    Easter Procession and Carols. Mon., Westminster Abbey.
    London Horse Harness Parade. Mon., Regent's Park.
    Maundy Money Service. Maundy Thurs. Her Majesty the Queen
    distributes Maundy Money to pensioners at one of the Nation's great churches.
Head of the River Race. Mortlake to Putney.
Oxford v. Cambridge Boat Race. Putney to Mortlake.
Camden Arts Festival. Various venues in Camden.
APRIL:
Greyhound Grand National. White City Stadium.
John Stowe Service. St. Andrew's Undershaft. The quill pen held by the Statue
of John Stowe is replaced. A London school child is presented a prize by the
Lord Mayor for the best essay on London.
National Scout Service. Windsor Castle, Berkshire. The Queen's Scouts and
holders of the Scout Gallantry Awards are reviewed by a member of the Royal
Family prior to a service in St. George's Chapel. Usually Sunday nearest St.
George's Day.
Royal Horticultural Society Spring Flower Show. Royal Horticultural Soc. Halls.
APRIL–MAY:
F.A. Cup Final. Wembley Stadium.
MAY:
Biggin Hill Air Fair. Biggin Hill, Kent.
Chelsea Flower Show. Royal Hospital Chelsea.
Historic Commercial Vehicles Run. London to Brighton.
London Private Fire Brigades Competition. Guildhall Yard, EC2. Competitive
target spraying.
London to Brighton Walk. Westminster Bridge, SW1.
May Day (1st May). Labour Party Procession to Hyde Park.
Oak Apple Day. Chelsea Royal Hospital. Chelsea Pensioners Parade on May 29th,
the anniversary of the restoration of Charles II founder of the hospital.
Pepys Commemoration Service. St. Olave's, Hart St.
Putney and Hammersmith Amateur Regattas. River Thames.
Royal Academy of Art—Summer Exhibition. Burlington Ho., Piccadilly, W1.
Continues till August.
Rugby League Final. Wembley Stadium.
Spring Bank Holiday. Fairs: Blackheath, Hampstead Heath and Wormwood
Scrubs.

JUNE:
Beating Retreat. Horse Guards Parade, SW1.
Election of Sheriffs of the City of London. Guildhall EC2.
Garter Ceremony. Windsor Castle, Berkshire. Procession of the Sovereign and Knights of the Garter from the Royal Apartments to St. George's Chapel.
Greyhound Derby. White City Stadium.
Lords Test Match. Lords Cricket Ground, St. John's Wood Rd.
Quit Rents Ceremony. Mansion House, EC4. Presentation of the Knolly's Rose by a descendant of Sir Robert Knolly (1381), to the Lord Mayor. Midsummer's Day.
Trooping the Colour, Queen's Birthday Parade, Horse Guards Parade, SW1.
JUNE–JULY:
Henley Royal Regatta. Henley-on-Thames, Oxon.
Lawn Tennis Championships. Wimbledon.
Royal National Rose Society Show. St. Albans.
Royal Tournament. Earl's Court.
JULY:
City of London Festival. Enquiries: City of London Information Centre. Concerts held in St. Paul's Cathedral, Guildhall and Mansion House, Mid-July in alternate years.
Promenade Concerts. Royal Albert Hall. Continues till Sept.
Road Sweeping by Vintners Company. Vintners Hall to St. James's Garlickhythe, EC4. A procession to St. James's Garlickhythe after the installation of the New Masters, is lead by the wine porters sweeping the road.
Royal International Horse Show. Wembley Arena.
JULY–AUGUST:
Amateur Athletic Association Championships. Crystal Palace SE19.
Doggett's Coat and Badge Race. London Bridge to Cadogan Pier. A rowing competition for the Thames Watermen, dates from 1716.
Swan Upping. Kingston to Henley-on-Thames. A voyage up the River Thames is undertaken by the Swanmasters of the Queen and the two City Companies of Dyers and Vinters, who share the ownership, for the purpose of counting and marking the Thames Swans.
AUGUST:
Cart Marking. Guildhall Yd., EC2. Annual renewal of licences for City of London street traders.
European Festival of Model Railways, Central Hall.
Oval Test Match. The Oval Cricket Ground, Kennington.
Summer Bank Holiday. Sat. and Sun.
  Fairs: Blackheath, Hampstead Heath and Wormwood Scrubs.
  Greater London Horse Show: Clapham Comm., SW4.
SEPTEMBER:
Battle of Britain Week:
  Commemoration Service. Battle of Britain Sunday. Westminster Abbey. 11.00.
R.A.F. Flypast. Formation flying over Central London. 15th, between 11.00–12.00.
Christ's Hospital Boys' March. Procession of Lord Mayor, Sheriffs, Aldermen and Bluecoats of Hertford School from Holy Sepulchre Holborn to Mansion House for the presentation of gifts by the Lord Mayor.
Promenade Concerts. Royal Albert Hall. Final Night.
Royal Horticultural Society Great Autumn Show. Royal Horticultural Soc. Halls.
Royal National Rose Society Show. Royal Horticultural Society Halls.
SEPTEMBER–OCTOBER:
British Philatelic Exhibition. Variable venue.
Election of the Lord Mayor. The Lord Mayor, Sheriffs and Aldermen proceed from Mansion House to Guildhall to St. Lawrence Jewry for a Service and Sermon. Then returning to Guildhall for the election, after which the Lord Mayor takes the Lord Mayor elect back to the Mansion House in his State Coach.

OCTOBER:

Costermongers' Harvest Festival. St. Martin-in-the-Fields. The street traders' Pearly King and Queen attend a Harvest Festival on first Sunday in October.

Harvest of the Sea Thanksgiving. Service at St. Mary-at-Hill.

Horse of the Year Show. Wembley Arena.

"Improve Your Home" Exhibition, Olympia.

Motorfair. Earl's Court.

Opening of the Law Courts. Takes place at the Royal Courts of Justice on first Mon. in Oct. Prior to this there is an Annual Breakfast at the House of Lords attended by Her Majesty's Judges and Queen's Council and a Special Service at Westminster Abbey.

Quit Rents Ceremony. Royal Courts of Justice, Strand, WC2. Presentation of six horseshoes and nails to the Queen's Remembrancer as payment for property once a Smithy (1235) and of a Billhook and Hatchet in place of rents for a piece of land called The Moors in Shropshire. End of Oct.

Trafalgar Day. Trafalgar Sq. Service and Parade on 21st Oct.

NOVEMBER:

Admission of the Lord Mayor Elect. Procession from Mansion House to Guildhall where the outgoing Lord Mayor hands over the City Insignia. Fri. before the Lord Mayor's Show.

Caravan Camping Holiday Show. Earl's Court.

Guy Fawkes Celebrations. Anniversary of Gun Powder Plot, 5th Nov.

International Furniture Exhibition. National Exhibition Centre, Birmingham.

London Film Festival. Enquiries: National Film Theatre, South Bank, SE1.

Lord Mayor's Show and Procession. The newly elected Mayor is driven from Guildhall to Royal Courts of Justice in his State Coach to be received by the Lord Chief Justice. 2nd Sat. in Nov.

National Chrysanthemum Society Show. Royal Horticultural Society Halls.

R.A.C. International Rally of Gt. Britain. Starting from London Airport, Heathrow.

Remembrance Sunday. Cenotaph, Whitehall, SW1. Annually on the Sunday nearest Nov. 11th, Her Majesty the Queen, the Prime Minister, his ministers and members of the opposition, take up their places by the Cenotaph for two minutes silence at 11.00 in memory of those killed in battle since 1914.

State Opening of Parliament. Her Majesty the Queen is driven from Buckingham Palace to Victoria Tower via Admiralty Arch, in the Irish State Coach.

Veteran Car Run. London to Brighton. Starts from Hyde Park Corner, first Sun. in Nov.

NOVEMBER–DECEMBER:

National Exhibition of Cage Birds. Alexandra Pavilion.

DECEMBER:

Christmas Celebrations. Decorations in Regent St. Carol Singing around Christmas Tree in Trafalgar Sq.

International Show Jumping. Olympia.

Ladies Kennel Association Championship Dog Show. National Exhibition Centre, Birmingham.

Royal Smithfield Show. Earls Court.

DECEMBER–JANUARY:

New Year's Eve Celebrations. "Auld Lang Syne". 31st Dec. 24.00 in Trafalgar Sq.

Winter "Ice Show Spectacular". Wembley Arena.

CINEMAS (Central London)

A.B.C. One & Two, 135 Shaftesbury Av., WC2. 01-836 8861 **1C 35**

A.B.C. Bayswater, 98 Bishop's Bridge Rd., W2. 01-229 4149 **1D 27**

A.B.C. Edgware Rd., Edgware Rd. W2. 01-723 5901 **3D 13**

A.B.C. Fulham Rd., Fulham Rd., SW10. 01-370 2636 **AZ 9B 144**
Barbican 1, Silk St., EC2. 01-628 8795 **2C 23**
Battersea Arts Centre, Lavender Hill, SW11. 01-223 8413 **AZ 3D 92**
Camden Plaza, 211 Camden High St., NW1. 01-485 2443 **AZ 1F 61**
Cannon Baker Street, Marylebone Rd., NW1. 01-935 9772 **2D 15**
Cannon Chelsea, 279 Kings Rd., SW3. 01-352 5096. **AZ 9E 144**
Cannon, Charing Cross Rd., WC2. 01-437 4815 **1B 34**
Cannon Haymarket, Haymarket, SW1. 01-839 1527 **3B 34**
Cannon Oxford St., Oxford St., W1. 01-636 0310 **3B 18**
Cannon, Panton St., SW1. 01-930 0631 **3B 34**
Cannon, Praed St., W2. 01-723 5716 **3D 13**
Cannon Royal, Charing Cross Rd., WC2. 01-930 6915 **2C 35**
Cannon, Tottenham Ct. Rd., W1. 01-636 6148 **3B 18**
Chelsea Cinema, 206 Kings Rd., SW3. 01-351 3742 **AZ 9E 144**
Cinecenta, Piccadilly W1. 01-437 3561 **3A 34**
Curzon, Curzon St., W1. 01-499 3737 **1B 48**
Curzon West End, 93 Shaftesbury Av., W1. 01-439 4805 **2B 34**
Dominion, Tottenham Ct. Rd., W1. 01-580 9562 **3B 18**
Empire 1, Leicester Sq., WC2. 01-437 1234 **2B 34**
Empire 2, Leicester Sq., WC2. 01-437 1234 **2B 34**
Everyman, Holly Bush Vale, NW3. 01-435 1525 **AZ 4A 44**
Gate, Notting Hill Ga., W11. 01-221 0220 **3B 26**
Gate, Bloomsbury, Brunswick Sq., WC1. 01-837 8402 **1D 19**
Gate Mayfair, Mayfair Hotel, Stratton St., W1. 01-493 2031 **3C 33**
Institute of Contemporary Arts, The Mall, SW1. 01-930 3647 **1B 50**
Leicester Square, Leicester Sq., WC2. 01-930 5252 **3B 34**
Lumiere, The; formerly Lane, St. Martins La., WC2. 01-836 0691 **2C 35**
Metro, Rupert St., W1. 01-437 0757 **2B 34**
Minema, 45 Knightsbridge, SW1. 01-235 4225 **2D 47**
Moulin Cinema Complex, 44 Gt. Windmill St., W1. 01-437 1653 **2A 34**
National Film Theatre, South Bank, SE1. 01-928 3232 **1B 52**
Odeon, Haymarket, SW1. 01-930 2738 **3B 34**
Odeon, Kensington High St., W8. 01-602 6644 **AZ 3H 75**
Odeon, Leicester Sq., WC2. 01-930 6111 **3B 34**
Odeon, Marble Arch, 10 Edgware Rd., W2. 01-723 2011 **2C 31**
Odeon, Swiss Cottage, Finchley Rd., NW3. 01-586 3057 **AZ 2H 27**
Odeon, Westbourne Grove, W2. 01-229 3369 **1B 26**
Phoenix, High Rd., E. Finchley, N2. 01-883 2233 **AZ 1B 28**
Plaza 1 2 3 & 4, 25 Regent St., SW1. 01-437 1234 **3A 34**
Premiere, Swiss Centre, Leicester Sq., WC2. 01-439 4470 **2B 34**
Prince Charles, Leicester Pl., WC2. 01-437 8181 **2B 34**
Riverside Studios, Crisp Rd., W6. 01-748 3354 **AZ 5E 74**
Ritzy Brixton, Brixton Oval, Coldharbour La., SW2. 01-737 2121 **AZ 4A 94**
Roxie, 76 Wardour St., W1. 01-439 3657 **2A 34**
Scala, 275 Pentonville Rd., N1. 01-278 8052 **2D 11**
Screen at the Electric, 191 Portobello Rd., W11. 01-229 3694 **AZ 5G 59**
Screen on Baker St., 96 Baker St., NW1. 01-935 2772 **2D 15**
Screen on the Green, Upper St., N1. 01-226 3520 **AZ 2B 62**
Screen on the Hill, 203 Haverstock Hill, NW3. 01-435 3366 **AZ 5C 44**
Warner West End, Cranbourn St., WC2. 01-439 0791 **2B 34**

CITIZENS ADVICE BUREAUX

Addington, la Overbury Cres., New Addington, Croydon, Surrey 01-664 6890
Anerley see **Penge & Anerley.**
Barnes Sheen Lane Centre, 52 Sheen La., SW14. 01-876 1513 **AZ 5J 89**

Battersea, 177 Battersea High St., SW11. 01-228 0272 **AZ 1B 92**
Beckenham, Beckenham Town Hall, Church Av., 01-650 1617 **AZ 1C 126**
Beddington & Wallington, 16 Stanley Pk. Rd., Wallington. 01-669 3435 **AZ 6F 133**
Bethnal Green, St. Margarets Ho., 21 Old Ford Rd., E2. 01-980 2390 **AZ 1L 143**
Bexleyheath, Graham Rd., 01-304 5619
Bow, 86 Bow Rd., E3. 01-980 3728 **AZ 3B 64**
Brentford & Chiswick, Town Hall, Heathfield Ter. W4. 01-994 4846 **AZ 5J 73**
Bromley, The Old Library, 83 Tweedy Rd., 01-460 8161 **AZ 1J 127**
Carshalton, Hill Ho., Bishopsford Rd., Morden. 01-648 1209 **AZ 7A 122**
Catford, 120 Rushey Green, SE6. 01-690 8455 **AZ 7D 96**
Charing Cross, 33 Charing Cross Road, WC2. 01-839 2825 **2C 35**
Chelsea, Old Town Hall, Kings Rd., SW3. 01-351 2114 **AZ 9E 144**
Chessington, Hook Community Centre, Hook Rd., 01-397 6187
Chiswick see **Brentford & Chiswick.**
City 32 Queen St., EC4. 01-236 1156 **2C 39**
Clapham, 361 Clapham Rd., SW9. 01-733 1946 **AZ 3J 93**
Coombe see **Maldon & Coombe.**
Coulsdon & Purley, 105 Brighton Rd., Purley. 01-660 6800
Cricklewood, 87 Cricklewood Broadway, NW2. 01-450 2407 **AZ 3F 43**
Croydon, 78 Thornton Rd., Thornton Heath. 01-684 9661 **AZ 6K 123**
Dagenham, 383 Heathway. 01-592 1084 **AZ 3F 53**
East Barnet, Town Hall, Station Rd., New Barnet. 01-449 9181 **AZ 5E 4**
Edmonton, Methodist Church, Lwr. Fore St., N9. 01-807 4253 **AZ 4B 18**
Enfield, 10 Little Park Gdns., 01-363 0928 **AZ 3J 7**
Erith, 1 Walnut Tree Rd. Erith 40481
Feltham, 77 Bedfont La. 01-890 2213
Finchley, Hertford Lodge Annex, East End Rd., N3. 01-349 0954 **AZ 2J 27**
Finsbury, 106 Old St., EC1. 01-253 2155 **AZ 3L 141**
Friern Barnet, Priory Hall, Friern Barnet La., N11. 01-361 0727 **AZ 3G 15**
Fulham, 50 Greyhound Rd., W6. 01-385 1322 **AZ 6F 75**
Grahame Park, The Concourse, Hendon, NW9. 01-205 4141 **AZ 1B 26**
Hackney, 236 Mare St., E8. 01-986 8446 **AZ 1H 63**
Hampstead, Oriel Hall, Oriel Pl., NW3. 01-435 0048 **AZ 4A 44**
Hanwell, Hanwell Library, Cherington Rd., W7. 01-579 2950 **AZ 1K 71**
Harlesden, 156 Manor Pk. Rd., NW10. 01-965 5821 **AZ 1B 58**
Harrow, Adjacent to Civic Centre, Station Rd., Harrow. 01-427 9443 **AZ 4K 23**
Hayes, 16 Botwell La. 01-573 4507
Hendon, 25 Bell La., NW4. 01-203 5801 **AZ 4E 26**
Highbury Corner, 326 St. Paul's Rd., N1. 01-359 0619 **AZ 1C 62**
Highgate New Town, 60 Chester Rd., N19. 01-272 5519 **AZ 1C 18**
Holloway, 12 St. John's Way, N19. 01-272 5577 **AZ 2G 45**
Hornchurch, 73 North St. Hornchurch 45983
Hounslow, 51 Grove Rd. 01-570 2983 **AZ 4E 86**
Ilford, Fellowship Ho., Green La. 01-514 1314 **AZ 2H 51**
Kensington, 140 Ladbroke Gro., W10. 01-960 3322 **AZ 4F 59**
Kentish Town, 242 Kentish Town Rd., NW5. 01-485 7034 **AZ 7F 45**
Kilburn, 200 Kilburn High Rd., NW6. 01-624 2007 **AZ 7H 43**
Kings Cross, 74 Marchmont St., WC1. 01-837 9341 **1C 19**
Kingston, 31 St. James Rd. 01-549 0818 **AZ 2D 118**
Malden & Coombe, 41 Blagdon Rd., New Malden. 01-949 4179 **AZ 4B 120**
Merton & Morden, 80 Kingston Rd., SW19. 01-542 9061 **AZ 2F 121**
Mitcham, 326 London Rd., 01-648 1910 **AZ 7E 122**
New Cross, 2 Lewisham Way, SE14. 01-692 6654 **AZ 1B 96**
North Cheam & Worcester Pk., Priory Cres., 01-641 0889 **AZ 4F 131**
North Lambeth, 323 Kennington Rd., SE11. 01-735 9551 **AZ 66 147**
Orpington, 1 Church Hill. Orpington 27732
Paddington, 439/441 Harrow Rd., W10. 01-960 4481 **AZ 3D 58**

Penge & Anerley, Anerley Town Hall, Anerley Rd., SE20. 01-778 0921 **AZ 7G 111**
Pimlico, 99 Tachbrook St., SW1. 01-834 5727 **2D 63**
Plaistow, 661 Barking Rd., E13. 01-471 5223 **AZ 5H 65**
Poplar South, Old Council Offices, Poplar High St., E14. 01-987 6040 **AZ 7D 64**
Richmond, Vestry House, Paradise Rd. 01-940 2501 **AZ 5E 88**
Roehampton, 1 Portswood Pl., Danebury Av., SW15. 01-876 6909 **AZ 6A 90**
Romford, 221 South Street, Romford. Romford 7063414
Royal Courts of Justice, Strand, WC2. 01-405 2225 **1B 36**
Ruislip, Manor Farm, approach via Moat. Ruislip 35212
St. Marylebone, Westminster Co. Ho., Marylebone Rd., NW1. 01-486 6425 **2B 14**
Shoreditch, 491 Kingsland Rd., E8. 01-249 8616 **AZ 1D 142**
Sidcup, 7 Hadlow Rd. 01-300 7804 **AZ 4A 116**
Southgate, Town Hall, Green Lanes, N13. 01-886 6555 **AZ 6E 16**
Stepney Green, Dame Colet Ho., Ben Johnson Rd., E1. 01-790 9077 **AZ 5A 64**
Streatham, Ilex Ho., 1 Barrhill Rd., SW2. 01-674 8993 **AZ 2J 109**
Surbiton, Branch Library, Ewell Rd. 01-399 2360 **AZ 7B 118**
Sutton, Central Library, St. Nicholas Way. 01-643 5291 **AZ 4K 131**
Swiss Cottage, Swiss Cottage Centre, Avenue Rd., NW3. 01-586 3882 **AZ 7B 44**
Thamesmead, 97 Binsey Wlk., SE2. 01-310 0108 **AZ 2C 84**
Toynbee Hall, 28 Commercial St., E1. 01-247 4172 **AZ 4E 142**
Twickenham, 25 London Rd. 01-892 5917 **AZ 7A 88**
Uxbridge, Darren Ho, 65 High St. Uxbridge 56511
Waltham Forest, 167 Hoe St., E17. 01-520 0939 **AZ 4C 32**
Walworth Rd., 199 Walworth Rd., SE17. 01-703 4198 AZ 7C 78
Wandsworth, 609/613 York Rd., SW18. 01-870 6552 **AZ 4A 92**
Welling, Rear 99/101 Welling High St. 01-303 5100 **AZ 3B 100**
Wembley, 501 High Rd. 01-902 5177 **AZ 5D 40**
West Drayton see **Yiewsley & West Drayton.**
West Hendon, 133 W. Hendon Broadway, NW9. 01-202 5177 AZ 5B 26
Willesden, 270–272 High Road, NW10. 01-451 4355 **AZ 6B 42**
Wimbledon, 30 Worple Rd., SW19. 01-947 4946 **AZ 1F 121**
Woolwich, Old Town Hall, Polytechnic St., SE18. 01-854 9607 **AZ 4E 82**
Yiewsley & West Drayton, 106 High St., Yiewsley. W. Drayton 0895 442007

CLUBS

NIGHT CLUBS
Some are only open to members and their guests; for other non-membership restaurants with entertainment are listed under "Dine & Dance" page 45.
Burlesque, 14/16 Bruton Pl., W1. 01-493 0630 **3B 32**
Churchill Suite, 52 Piccadilly, W1. 01-408 0226 **3D 33**
Club de Luxe, 50 Dover St., W1. 01-409 0822 **3C 33**
Directors Lodge, 13 Mason's Yard, Duke St,., SW1. 01-839 6109 **1A 50**
Eve, 189 Regent St., W1 01-734 0557 **2D 33**
La Capannina, 21 Bateman St., W1. 01-439 0033 **1B 34**
Le Reims, 24 Gt. Windmill St., W1. 01-734 5128 **2A 34**
The Office, 16/17 Avery Row, W1. 01-499 6728 **2B 32**
Penthouse, 11 Whitehorse St., W1. 01-493 1977 **1B 48**
Pinstripe, 21 Beak St., W1. 01-437 4294 **2D 33**
Shaftesbury's on the Avenue, 24 Shaftesbury Av,. W1. 01-734 2019 **2B 34**

Striptease
Raymond Revue Bar, Walker's Ct., W1. 01-734 1593 **2A 34**
Internationally known for spectacular entertainments.
Sunset Strip, 30a Dean St., W1. 01-437 7229 2B 34
The Carnival, 12 Old Compton St., W1. 01-437 8337 **2B 34**

WEST END BUSINESS AND PROFESSIONAL CLUBS

Alpine, 74 S. Audley St., W1. 01-499 1542 **3A 32**
American, 95 Piccadilly, W1. 01-499 2303 **1C 49**
American Women's, 95 Piccadilly, W1. 01-491 4024 **1C 49**
Army and Navy, 36 Pall Mall, SW1. 01-930 9721 **1A 50**
Arts, 40 Dover St., W1. 01-499 8581 **3C 33**
Athenaeum, 107 Pall Mall, SW1. 01-930 4843 **1B 50**
Beefsteak, 9 Irving St., WC2. 01-930 5722 **3C 35**
Boodle's, 28 St. James's St., SW1. 01-930 7166 **1D 49**
Brook's, 60 St. James's St., SW1. 01-499 0072 **1D 49**
Buck's, 18 Clifford St., W1. 01-734 2337 **2D 33**
Caledonian, 9 Halkin St., SW1. 01-235 5162 **3A 48**
Canning, 42 Half Moon St., W1. 01-499 5163 **1C 49**
Carlton, 69 St. James's St., SW1. 01-493 1164 **1D 49**
Cavalry & Guards, 127 Piccadilly, W1. 01-499 1261 **2B 48**
Challoner, 59/61 Pont St., SW1. 01-589 5343 **1C 61**
Chelsea Arts, 143 Old Church St., SW3. 01-352 0973 **AZ 5B 76**
City Livery, Sion College, Victoria Embkmt., EC4. 01-353 2431 **2D 37**
City of London, 19 Old Broad St., EC2. 01-588 7991 **1A 40**
City University, 50 Cornhill, EC3. 01-626 8571 **1A 40**
Civil Service, 13 & 15 Gt. Scotland Yd., SW1. 01-930 4881 **1C 51**
Danish, 62 Knightsbridge, SW1. 01-235 5121 **2C 47**
East India, Devonshire, Sports & Public Schools, 16 St. James's Sq., SW1.
01-930 1000 **1A 50**
Eccentric, 9 Ryder St., SW1. 01-930 6133 **1D 49**
English Speaking Union, 37 Charles St., W1. 01-629 0104 **3B 32**
Farmers', 3 Whitehall Ct., SW1. 01-930 3160 **1D 51**
Garrick, 15 Garrick St., WC2. 01-379 6478 **2C 35**
Green Room, 8 Adam St., WC2. 01-379 7946 **3D 35**
Gresham, 15 Abchurch La., EC4. 01-626 7231 **2A 40**
Grosvenor, Carmel Hall, Bourne St., SW1. 01-730 2934 **3A 62**
Guild of Freemen of the City of London, 4 Dowgate Hill, EC4. **2D 39**
Hurlingham, Ranelagh Gdns., SW6. 01-736 8411 **AZ 3G 91**
Irish, 82 Eaton Sq., Sw1. 01-235 4164 **2A 62**
Kennel, 1/4 Clarges St., W1. 01-493 6651 **2C 49**
Lansdowne, 9 Fitzmaurice Pl., Berkeley Sq., W1. 01-629 7200 **3C 33**
London Rowing, Embankment, Putney, SW15. 01-788 0666 **AZ 3F 91**
National Liberal, Whitehall Pl., SW1. 01-930 9871 **1D 51**
Naval, 38 Hill St., W1. 01-493 7672 **3B 32**
Naval and Military, 94 Piccadilly, W1. 01-499 5163 **1C 49**
Norwegian, 21 Cockspur St., SW1. 01-930 3632 **1C 51**
Oriental, Stratford House, Stratford Pl., W1. 01-629 5126 **1A 32**
Overseas Bankers, 7 Lothbury, EC2. 01-606 5883 **1A 40**
Oxford and Cambridge University, 71 Pall Mall, SW1. 01-930 6942 **1A 50**
Pratt's, 14 Park Pl., SW1. 01-493 0397 **1D 49**
Press, 76 Shoe La., EC4. 01-353 2644 **1D 37**
Reform, 104 Pall Mall SW1. 01-930 9374 **1B 50**
Rotary Club of London, 6 York Ga., NW1. 01-487 5429 **1A 16**
Royal Air Force, 128 Piccadilly, W1. 01-499 3456 **2B 48**
Royal Automobile, 89 Pall Mall, SW1. 01-930 2345 **1A 50**
Royal Ocean Racing, 20 St. James's Pl., SW1. 01-493 5252 **1D 49**
Royal Thames Yacht, 60 Knightsbridge, SW7. 01-235 2121 **2C 47**
St. Stephen's, 34 Queen Anne's Ga., SW1. 01-222 1382 **3B 50**
Savage, 9 Fitzmaurice Pl., W1. 01-493 1094 **3C 33**
Savile, 69 Brook St., W1. 01-629 5462 **2A 32**
Ski Club, 118 Eaton Sq., Sw1. 01-235 2378 **1B 62**
Spanish, 5 Cavendish Sq., W1. 01-580 2750 **3C 17**

Thames Rowing, Embankment, Putney, SW15. 01-788 0676 **AZ 3F 91**
Travellers', 106 Pall Mall, SW1. 01-930 8688 **1B 50**
Turf, 5 Carlton Ho. Ter., SW1. 01-930 8555 **1B 50**
Union Jack, 91 Waterloo Rd., SE1. 01-928 6401 **2C 53**
United Nursing Services, 40 South St., W1. 01-499 1564 **3A 32**
United Oxford & Cambridge University, 71 Pall Mall, SW1. 01-930 4152 **1A 50**
University Women's, 2 Audley Sq., W1. 01-499 6478 **1A 48**
Victory Ex-services, 63 Seymour St., W2. 01-723 4474 **1B 30**
Wellington, 116 Knightsbridge, SW1. 01-584 4521 **3B 46**
White's, 37 St. James's St., SW1. 01-493 6671 **1D 49**
Wig & Pen, 229 Strand, WC2. 01-583 7255 **1C 37**

COMMONWEALTH REPRESENTATIVES

COMMONWEALTH INSTITUTE Kensington High St., W8. 01-602 3252 **3A 42**
COMMONWEALTH SECRETARIAT, Marlborough Ho., Pall Mall, SW1. 01-839 8411 **1A 50**
ROYAL COMMONWEALTH SOCIETY, 18 Northumberland Av., WC2. 01-930 6733 **IC 51**

Antigua & Barbuda, 15 Thayer St., W1. 01-486 7073 **3A 16**
Australia, Commonwealth of, Australia Ho., Strand, WC2. 01-438 8000 **2B 36**
Bahamas, 39 Pall Mall, SW1. 01-930 6967 **1A 50**
Bangladesh, 28 Queen's Ga., SW7. 01-584 0081 **1B 58**
Barbados, 6 Up. Belgrave St., SW1. 01-235 8686 **1A 62**
Belize, 15 Thayer St., W1. 01-486 8381 **3A 16**
Botswana, 6 Stratford Pl., W1. 01-499 0031 **1B 32**
Brunei, 49 Cromwell Rd., SW7. 01-581 0521 **2C 59**
Canada (Dominion of), MacDonald Ho., 1 Grosvenor Sq., W1. 01-629 9492 **2A 32**
Information, Consular Section, Library, Gallery, Tourist Bureau, etc. are at Canada Ho., Trafalgar Sq., SW1. 01-629 9492 **3C 35**
Cyprus, 93 Park St., W1. 01-499 8272 **2D 31**
Dominica, 1 Collingham Gdns., SW5. 01-370 5194 **3A 58**
Fiji, 34 Hyde Park Ga., SW7. 01-584 3661 **3B 44**
Gambia, 57 Kensington Court, W8. 01-937 6316 **3D 43**
Ghana, 13 Belgrave Sq., SW1. 01-235 4142 **1D 61**
Grenada, 1 Collingham Gdns., SW5. 01-373 7809 **3A 58**
Guyana, 3 Palace Ct., Bayswater Rd., W2. 01-229 7684 **3C 27**
India (Republic of), India Ho., Aldwych, WC2. 01-836 8484 **2A 36**
Jamaica, 50 St. James's St., SW1. 01-499 8600 **1D 49**
Kenya (Republic of), 45 Portland Pl., W1. 01-636 2371 **2B 16**
Lesotho, 10 Collingham Gdns., SW5. 01-373 8581 **3A 58**
Malawi, 33 Grosvenor St., W1. 01-491 4172 **2B 32**
Malaysia, 45 Belgrave Sq., SW1. 01-235 8033 **3A 48**
Malta, 16 Kensington Sq., W8. 01-938 1712 **3D 43**
Mauritius, 32/33 Elvaton Pl., SW7. 01-581 0294 **1B 44**
New South Wales, 66 Strand, WC2. 01-839 6651 **3D 35**
New Zealand, New Zealand Ho., 80 Haymarket, SW1. 01-930 8422 **3B 34**
Nigeria (Fed Rep of), Nigeria Ho., 9 Northumberland Av., WC2. 01-839 1244 **1D 51**
Papua New Guinea, 3rd floor, 14 Waterloo Pl., SW1. 01-930 0922 **1A 50**
Saint Lucia, 10 Kensington Court, W8. 01-937 9522 **3D 43**
Saint Vincent & the Grenadines; as St Lucia.
Seychelles, 50 Conduit St., W1. 01-439 0405 **2C 33**
Sierra Leone, 33 Portland Pl., W1. 01-636 6483 **2B 16**
Singapore (Republic of), 2 Wilton Cres., SW1. 01-235 8315 **3D 47**

Sri Lanka, 13 Hyde Park Gdns., W2. 01-262 1841 **2D 29**
Swaziland, 58 Pont St., SW1. 01-581 4976 **1C 61**
Tanzania, 43 Hertford St., W1. 01-499 8951 **1B 48**
Tonga, New Zealand Ho., 80 Haymarket, SW1. 01-839 3287 **3B 34**
Trinidad & Tobago, 42 Belgrave Sq., SW1. 01-245 9351 **3A 48**
Uganda, 58/59 Trafalgar Sq., WC2. 01-839 5783 **3C 35**
Victoria, Victoria Ho., Melbourne Pl., WC2. 01-836 2656 **2B 36**
Western Australia, 115 Strand, WC2. 01-240 2881 **2A 36**
Zambia (Republic of), 2 Palace Ga., W8. 01-589 6655 **3A 44**
Zimbabwe, 429 Strand, WC2. 01-836 7755 **3D 35**

CONCERT HALLS: Opera, Ballet, Music Hall, Folk, Jazz, Rock venues

Ballet Rambert, 94 Chiswick High Rd., W4. 01-995 4246
Performances at Sadlers Wells Theatre and Jeannetta Cochrane Theatre.
Barbican Arts Centre Concert Hall, Silk St., EC2.
Box Off: Reservations & Enquiries 01-628 8795; Credit Card bookings 638 8891
Central Hall, Storeys Ga., SW1. Admin. 01-222 8010. Box Office 01-222 6289
3B 50
Coliseum, St. Martin's La., WC2. 01-836 3161. **3C 35**
English National Opera. Also visiting Opera and Ballet Companies.
Conway Hall, Red Lion Sq., WC1. 01-242 8032 **2A 20**
Court Theatre, Holland Park. **3A 42**
Performances include ballet, dance, plays, concerts—Summer season only, open air.
Crystal Palace Concert Bowl. AZ 6H 111
Open Air Concerts—Summer season only.
Fairfield Halls, Park La., Croydon. 01-688 9291 **AZ 3D 134**
Guildhall School of Music and Drama, Barbican, EC2. 01-628 2571 **2D 23**
Kenwood Lakeside Concert Bowl, Hampstead La., NW3. **AZ 1C 44.** Open Air
Concerts—Summer season only.
Logan Hall, Inst. of Education, 20 Bedford Way, WC1. 01-636 1500 ext. 264 **1C 19**
London Festival Ballet.
Performances at Royal Festival Hall, Coliseum and Sadlers Wells Theatre.
London School of Contemporary Dance, The Place, 17 Dukes Rd., WC1. 01-387 0161 **3B 10**
National Poetry Centre, Poetry Society, 21 Earls Court Sq., SW5. 01-373 7861
AZ 3J 75. Evening poetry readings etc. Information section.
Purcell Room, South Bank, SE1. **1B 52** see Queen Elizabeth Hall.
Queen Elizabeth Hall, South Bank, SE1. **1B 52**
Box Off.: Ticket Reservations 01-928 3191. General Information 01-928 3002.
Postal Booking Enquiries 01-928 2972.
Riverside Studios, Crisp Rd., W6. 01-748 3354 **AZ 5E 74**
Round House, Chalk Farm Rd., NW1. 01-267 2564 **AZ 7E 44**
Royal Albert Hall, Kensington Gore, SW7. 01-589 8212 **3C 45**
Royal Ballet, see Royal Opera House.
Royal Ballet School, (Upper School) performances at Royal Opera House and
Sadlers Wells Theatre; (Lower School) at Sadlers Wells Theatre. End of
Summer term.
Royal College of Music, Prince Consort Rd., SW7. 01-589 3643 **3C 45**
Royal Festival Hall, South Bank, SE1. **1B 52**
Box Off.: Ticket Reservations 01-928 3191. General Information 01-928 3002.
Postal Booking Enquiries 01-928 2972.
Royal Military School of Music, Kneller Hall, Kneller Rd., Twickenham 01-
898 5533 **AZ 6H 87**

Royal Opera House, Covent Garden, WC2. **2D 35**
Administration 01-240 1200. Box Office 01-240 1066. Royal Opera & Ballet.
Sadlers Wells Theatre, Rosebery Av., EC1. 01-837 1672 **AZ 1H 141**
New Sadlers Wells Opera & Ballet and Opera by Visiting Companies.
St. John's Smith Square, Smith Sq., SW1. 01-799 2168. Box Off. 222 1061 **1C 65**
St. Pancras Town Hall, Euston Rd., NW1. 01-278 4444 **2C 11**
Wembley Arena, Empire Way. 01-902 1234 **AZ 1F 41**
Wigmore Hall, 36 Wigmore St., W1. 01-935 2141 **3B 16**

FOLK, JAZZ, ROCK VENUES

Bulls Head, Barnes Bridge, SW13. 01-876 5241 **AZ 2A 90**
Bunjies Folk Cellar, 27 Litchfield St., WC2. 01-240 1796 **2C 35**
Cellar Folk Club, Cecil Sharp House, 2 Regents Pk. Rd., NW1. **AZ 1D 60**
Chat's Place, 44 Brooksby's Walk, E9. 01-986 6714 **AZ 5K 47**
Dingwalls, Commercial Pl., Chalk Farm Rd., NW1. 01-267 4967 **AZ 7E 44**
Golden Lion, 490 Fulham Rd., SW6. 01-385 3942 **AZ 9B 144**
•**Greyhound,** 175 Fulham Palace Rd., W6. 01-385 0526 **AZ 5E 74**
Hammersmith Palais, 242 Shepherds Bush Rd., W6. 01-748 2812 **AZ 4E 74**
Hampstead Folk Club, The Enterprise, Chalk Farm Rd., NW1. **AZ 7E 44**
Hogs Grunt, 100 Cricklewood La., NW2. 01-450 8969. **AZ 4F 43**
Hope & Anchor, 207 Upper St., N1. 01-359 4510 **AZ 2B 62**
Jazz Centre Society, 35 Gt. Russell St., WC1. 01-580 8532 **3C 19** (at the 100
Club)
Marquee, 90 Wardour St., W1. 01-437 6603 **1A 34**
Moonlight Club, 100 West End La., NW6. 01-624 7611 **AZ 5J 43**
Nashville Room, 171 North End Rd., W14. 01-603 6071 **AZ 4G 75**
National Jazz Centre, 9/10 Floral St., WC2. 01-240 3235 **2D 35**
Due to open 1986.
New Merlin's Cave, Margery St., WC1. 01-837 2097 **AZ 2G 141**
Pindar of Wakefield, 328 Gray's Inn Rd., WC1. C1-837 1753 **AZ 2E 140**
Pizza Express, 10 Dean St., W1. 01-439 8722 **1A 34**
Prospect of Whitby, 57 Wapping Wall, E1. 01-481 1095 **AZ 2L 149**
Riverside Studios, Crisp Rd., W6. 01-748 3354 **AZ 5E 74**
Rock Garden, The Piazza, Covent Garden, WC2. 01-240 3961 **2D 35**
Ronnie Scott's, 47 Frith St., W1. 01-439 0747 **1B 34**
Round House, Chalk Farm Rd., NW1. 01-267 2564 **AZ 7E 44**
Starlight, Railway Hotel, 100 West End La., NW6. 01-624 7611 **AZ 5J 43**
White Lion, 14 Putney High St., SW15. 01 788 1540 **AZ 4G 91**
100 Club, 100 Oxford St., W1. 01-636 0933 **1A 34**
101 Club, 101 St Johns Hill, SW11. 01-223 8309 **AZ 4B 92**

LUNCHTIME CONCERTS

For current details in the City: City Information Centre, 01-606 3030
All Hallows by the Tower, Byward St., EC3. 01-709 2928 **3C 41**
Bishopsgate Institute, 230 Bishopsgate, EC2. 01-247 6844 **2C 25**
Guildhall School of Music & Drama, Barbican EC2. 01-628 2571 **2D 23**
Holy Sepulchre, Holborn Viaduct, EC4. 01-248 1660 **3A 22**
St. Botolph Aldgate, Aldgate High St., EC3. 01-283 1670 **1C 41**
St. Bride, St. Bride La., Fleet St., EC4. 01-353 1301 **1D 37**
St. James's Piccadilly, Piccadilly, W1. 01-734 4511 **3A 34**
St. John's Smith Square, Smith Sq., SW1. 01-799 2168 **1C 65**
St. Lawrence Jewry, Gresham St., EC3. 01-600 9478 **1C 39**
St. Margaret's Lothbury, Lothbury, EC2. 01-606 8330 **1D 39**
St. Martin-in-the-Fields, Trafalgar Sq., WC2. 01-930 0089 **3C 35**
St. Mary-at-Hill, Lovat La., EC3. 01-626 4184 **2B 40**
St. Mary le Bow, Cheapside, EC2. 01-248 5139 **1C 39**
St. Mary Woolnoth, King William St., EC4. 01-626 9701 **2A 40**
St. Michael-upon-Cornhill, Cornhill, EC3. 01-626 8841 **1A 40**
St. Olave Hart Street, Hart St., EC3. 01-488 4318 **2C 41**

St. Paul's Cathedral, EC4. 01-248 2705 **1B 38**
St. Peter, Cornhill, Cornhill, EC3. 01-626 9483 **1B 40**
St. Stephen, Walbrook, Walbrook, EC4. 01-283 3400 **2D 39**
Southwark Cathedral, Borough High St., SE1. 01-407 2939 **1D 55**

MUSIC HALL

Aba Daba Music Hall, 328 Grays Inn Rd., WC2. 01-722 5395 **AZ 2E 140**
(Pindar of Wakefield P.H.) Lively entertainments in small restaurant-pub setting.
Cockney Cabaret & Music Hall, 18 Charing Cross Rd., WC2. 01-408 1001 **2C 35**
A Cabaret, Dancing, Restaurant night-spot. Wed. to Sat.
Hoxton Hall Theatre, 128 Hoxton St., N1. 01-739 5431 **AZ 1D 142**
Built in 1863. One of London's oldest Music Halls, small, intimate saloon style with
balconies. Victorian style entertainments at times throughout the year.
Players Theatre Club, Hungerford Arches, Villiers St., WC2. 01-839 1134 **3D 35**
An original Victorian Music Hall entertainment with theatre bar and snack bar plus
restaurant. Performances known as the "Late Joys" (dating from the 1820's
management) begin at 20.00 nightly; closed Sunday. Temporary membership
available.
Wiltons Music Hall, Graces Alley, Wellclose Sq., E1. **AZ 9H 143**
An original Victorian hall founded 1851; undergoing restoration under the auspices
of the London Music Hall Trust and London Music Hall Protection Society.

CONFERENCE & TRADE EXHIBITION CENTRES

London Visitor & Convention Bureau, 26 Grosvenor Gdns., SW1. 01-730 3450
1B 62
*Impartial advice and assistance on every aspect of the conference and exhibition
business. Help is available free to those planning events in London.*
Confravision. *British Telecom public videoconferencing service, linking London to
eight major cities in the UK, USA, Canada and West Germany. Further
information and bookings 01-239 1517. International bookings 01-936 3009.*

Alexandra Palace/Pavilion, Wood Green, N22. 01-883 6477 **AZ 2H 29**
Barbican Centre for Arts & Conferences, Silk St., EC2. 01-638 4141 **2C 23**
Bloomsbury Conference Agency, (University of London), Room 106, Senate
House, Malet St., WC1. 01-636 8000 **2C 19**
C.B.I. Conference Centre, Centre Point, New Oxford St., WC1. 01-379 7400 **1B 34**
Central Hall, Storey's Ga., SW1. 01-222 8010 **3B 50**
C.F.S. Conference Centre, 22 Portman Close, W1. 01-486 2881 **1D 31**
City Conference Centre, 76 Mark La., EC3. 01-481 8493 **2C 41**
City University, Northampton Sq., EC1. 01-253 4399 **AZ 4B 46**
Commonwealth Institute, Kensington High St., W8. 01-603 4535 **3A 42**
Conference Forum, Sedgwick Centre, E1. 01-481 5204 **1D 41**
Earls Court, Warwick Rd., SW5. 01-385 1200 **AZ 5J 75**
Kensington Town Hall, Hornton St., W8. 01-937 5464 **3C 43**
Limehouse Studios, Canary Wharf, W. India Docks, E14. 01-987 2090 **AZ 1C 80**
London Press Centre, 76 Shoe La., EC4. 01-353 6211 **1D 37**
Olympia, Hammersmith Rd., W14. 01-385 1200 **AZ 3G 75**
The Podium, Market Towers, 1 Nine Elms La., New Covent Garden, SW8. 01-720
9200 **AZ 7G 77**
Queen Elizabeth II Conference Centre, Broad Sanctuary, SW1. 01-928 3666 **3C
51**
Rainbow Suite & Kensington Exhibition Centre, 99 Kensington High St., W8.
01-603 4535 **3C 43**
Regent's College, Regent's Park, NW1. 01-486 2558 **3D 7**
Royal Albert Hall, Kensington Gore, SW7. 01-589 3203 **3C 45**

Royal Festival Hall, South Bank, SE1, 01-928 3641 **1B 52**
Wembley Arena & Conference Centre, Empire Way. 01-902 8833 **AZ 1F 41**
World Trade Centre, St. Katharine-by-the-Tower, E1. 01-488 2400 **3D 41**

CONSULATES, EMBASSIES AND LEGATIONS

Afghanistan, *Embassy,* 31 Prince's Ga., SW7. 01-589 8891 **3D 45**
Algeria, *Embassy,* 54 Holland Pk., W11. 01-221 7800 **AZ 1G 75**
America United States of, *Consulate & Embassy,* 24 Grosvenor Sq., W1. 01-499 9000 **2A 32**
Argentina, *Argentine interests are dealt with through the Brazilian Embassy.*
Austria, *Consulate & Embassy,* 18 Belgrave M. W., SW1. 01-235 3731 **1D 61**
Bahrain, *Embassy,* 98 Gloucester Rd., SW7. 01-370 5132 **2A 58**
Belgium, *Consulate General & Embassy,* 103 Eaton Sq., SW1. 01-235 5422 **1A 62**
Bolivia, 106 Eaton Sq., SW1. 01-235 2257 **1A 62**
Brazil, *Consulate General,* 6 Deanery St., W1. 01-499 7441 **1A 48**
  Embassy, 32 Green St., W1. 01-499 0877 **2D 31**
Bulgaria, *Embassy,* 186/8 Queen's Ga., SW7. 01-584 9400 **3B 44**
Burma, *Embassy,* 19a Charles St., W1. 01-499 8841 **1B 48**
Cameroon, *Embassy,* 84 Holland Pk, W11. 01-727 0771 **AZ 1G 75**
Chile, *Consulate,* 12 Devonshire St., W1. 01-580 1023 **2B 16**
  Embassy, 12 Devonshire St., W1. 01-580 6392
China, *Embassy,* 31 Portland Pl., W1. 01-636 5726 **2C 17**
  Consular Section, 31 Portland Pl., W1. 01-636 5637
Colombia, *Embassy,* 3 Hans Cres., SW1. 01-589 9177 **1C 61**
Costa Rica, 93 Star St., W2. 01-723 1772 **3A 14**
Cuba, *Embassy,* 167 High Holborn, WC1. 01-240 2488 **3D 19**
Czechoslovakia, *Embassy,* 25 Kensington Pal. Gdns., W8. 01-229 1255 **3C 27**
  Consular Dept, 30 Kensington Pal. Gdns., W8. 01-727 9431
Denmark, *Embassy,* 55 Sloane St., SW1. 01-235 1255 **1C 61**
Dominican Republic, *Honorary Consulate,* 6 Queen's Mansions, Brook Green, W6. 01-602 1885 **AZ 3F 75**
Ecuador, *Consulate,* Flat 3b, 3 Hans Cres., SW1. 01-584 2648 **1C 61**
  Embassy, Flat 3b, 3 Hans Cres., SW1. 01-584 1367
Egypt, *Consulate,* 19 Kensington Pal. Gdns., W8. 01-229 8818 **1C 43**
  Embassy, 26 South St., W1. 01-499 2401 **3A 32**
El Salvador, *Embassy,* 9 Welbeck Ho., 62 Welbeck St., W1. 01-486 8182 **1B 32**
Ethiopia, *Embassy,* 17 Prince's Ga., SW7. 01-589 7212 **3D 45**
Finland, *Embassy,* 38 Chesham Pl., SW1. 01-235 9531 **1A 62**
France, *Consulate General,* 24 Rutland Ga., SW7. 01-581 5292 **3A 46**
  Embassy, 58 Knightsbridge, SW1. 01-235 8080 **2C 47**
Gabon, *Embassy,* 48 Kensington Ct., W8. 01-937 5285 **3D 43**
German Democratic Rep., *Embassy,* 34 Belgrave Sq., SW1. 01-235 9941 **AZ 1A 62**
German Federal Republic, *Embassy,* 23 Belgrave Sq., SW1. 01-235 5033 **1A 62**
  Visa Matters 01-235 0165. Passports for German Nationals 01-235 0282
Greece, *Embassy,* 1a Holland Pk. 01-727 8040 **AZ 1G 75**
Haiti, *Embassy,* 33 Abbots Ho., St. Mary Abbots Terrace, W14. **AZ 3E 59**
Holy See, 54 Parkside, SW19 01-946 1410 **AZ 4F 107**
Honduras, *Consulate & Embassy,* 47 Manchester St., W1. 01-486 3380 **3D 15**
Hungary, *Embassy,* 35 Eaton Pl., SW1. 01-235 4048 **1A 62**
  Consulate, 01-235 2664
Iceland, *Embassy,* 1 Eaton Ter., SW1. 01-730 5131 **2D 61**
Indonesia, *Embassy,* 38 Grosvenor Sq., W1. 01-499 7661 **3A 32**
Iran, *Embassy,* 27 Princes Ga., SW7. **3D 45**

Iraq, *Embassy,* 21 Queen's Ga., SW7. 01-584 7141 **1B 58**
Ireland, Republic of, *Embassy,* 17 Grosvenor Pl., SW1. 01-235 2171 **3B 48**
Israel, *Consulate & Embassy,* 2 Palace Grn., W8. 01-937 8050 **2D 43**
Italy, *Embassy,* 14 Three Kings Yd., W1. 01-629 8200 **1A 62**
  Consulate-General, 38 Eaton Pl., SW1. 01-235 9371 **1A 62**
Ivory Coast, *Embassy,* 2 Up. Belgrave St., SW1. 01-235 6991 **3A 48**
Japan, *Embassy,* 46 Grosvenor St., W1. 01-493 6030 **2B 32**
Jordan, *Embassy,* 6 Up. Phillimore Gdns., W8. 01-937 3685 **3B 42**
Korea, *Embassy,* 4 Palace Ga., W8. 01-581 0247 **3A 44**
Kuwait, *Embassy,* 45/6 Queen's Ga., SW7. 01-589 4533 **1B 58**
Laos, *Embassy,* 7 Heath Drive, NW3. 01-794 0011 **AZ 4K 43**
Lebanon, *Embassy,* 21 Kensington Pal. Gdns., W8. 01-229 7265 **1C 43**
  Consular Section, 15 Palace Gdns. M., W8. 01-727 6696 **1C 43**
Liberia, *Embassy,* 21 Prince's Ga., SW7. 01-589 9405 **3D 45**
Libya, *Libyan interests are dealt with through the Saudi Arabian Embassy.*
Luxembourg, *Embassy,* 27 Wilton Cres., SW1. 01-235 6961 **3D 47**
Mexico, *Embassy,* 8 Halkin St., SW1. 01-235 6393 **3A 48**
Monaco, *Consulate-General,* 4 Audley Sq., W1. 01-629 0734 **1A 48**
Mongolia, *Embassy,* 7 Kensington Ct., W8. 01-937 0150 **3D 43**
Morocco, *Embassy,* 49 Queen's Ga. Gdns., SW7. 01-581 5001 **2B 58**
Nepal, *Embassy,* 12a Kensington Pal. Gdns., W8. 01-229 1594 **1C 43**
Netherlands, *Consulate & Embassy,* 38 Hyde Pk. Ga., SW7. 01-584 5040 **3B 44**
Nicaragua, *Consulate & Embassy,* 8 Gloucester Rd., SW7. 01-584 4365 **1A 44**
Norway, *Embassy,* 25 Belgrave Sq., SW1. 01-235 7151 **1A 62**
Oman, *Embassy,* 44a/b Montpelier Sq., SW7. 01-584 6782 **3B 46**
Pakistan, 35 Lowndes Sq., SW1. 01-235 2044 **3C 47**
Panama, *Consulate General,* 24 Tudor St., EC4. 01-353 4792 **2D 37**
  Embassy, 109 Jermyn St., SW1. 01-930 1591 **3A 35**
Paraguay, *Consulate,* Braemar Lodge, Cornwall Gdns., SW7. 01-937 6629
  AZ 3K 75
  Embassy, Braemar Lodge, Cornwall Gdns., SW7. 01-937 1253
Peru, *Consulate General,* 52 Sloane St., SW1. 01-235 6867 **1C 61**
  Embassy, 52 Sloane St., SW1. 01-235 1917
Philippine, *Embassy,* 9a Palace Grn., W8. 01-937 1600 **2D 43**
Poland, *Embassy,* 47 Portland Pl., W1. 01-580 4324 **2B 16**
Portugal, *Consular Section,* 62 Brompton Rd., SW3. 01-581 8722 **3B 46**
  Embassy, 11 Belgrave Sq., SW1. 01-235 5331 **3D 47**
Qatar, *Embassy,* 27 Chesham Pl., SW1. 01-235 0851 **1D 61**
Romania, *Embassy,* 4 Palace Grn., W8. 01-937 9666 **2D 43**
San Marino, *Consulate-General,* 86 Park La., W1. 01-499 6363 **3D 31**
Saudi Arabia, *Embassy,* 30 Belgrave Sq., SW1. 01-235 0831 **1A 62**
  Consular Section, 30 Belgrave Sq., SW1. 01-235 0303
Senegal, *Embassy,* 11 Phillimore Gdns., W8. 01-937 0925 **3B 42**
Somali, Democratic Republic, *Embassy,* 60 Portland Pl., W1. 01-580 7148 **2C 17**
South Africa, *Embassy,* S. Africa Ho., Trafalgar Sq., WC2. 01-930 4488 **3C 35**
Soviet Socialist Republics, Union of,
  Consular Section, 5 Kensington Pal. Gdns. W8. 01-229 3215 **1C 43**
  Embassy, 13 Kensington Pal. Gdns., W8. 01-229 3628 **1C 43**
Spain, *Consular Section,* 20 Draycott Pl., SW3. 01-581 5921 **3C 61**
  Embassy, 24 Belgrave Sq., SW1. 01-235 5555 **1A 62**
Sudan, *Embassy,* 3 Cleveland Row, SW1. 01-839 8080 **1D 49**
Sweden, *Consulate & Embassy,* 11 Montagu Pl., W1. 01-724 2101 **3C 15**
Switzerland, *Embassy,* 16 Montagu Pl., W1. 01-723 0701 **3C 15**
Syria, *Embassy,* 8 Belgrave Sq., SW1. 01-245 9012 **3D 47**
Thailand, *Embassy,* 30 Queen's Ga., SW7. 01-589 0173 **1B 58**
Togo, 30 Sloane St., SW1. 01-235 0147 **3C 47**
Tunisia, *Embassy,* 29 Prince's Ga., SW7. 01-584 8117 **3D 45**
Turkey, *Embassy,* 43 Belgrave Sq., SW1. 01-235 5252 **3A 48**

United Arab Emirates, 30 Prince's Ga., SW7. 01-581 1281 **3D 45**
United States, see America, United States of
Uruguay, *Consulate & Embassy,* 48 Lennox Gdns., SW1. 01-589 8835 **2B 60**
Venezuela, *Embassy,* 1 Cromwell Rd., SW7. 01-584 4206 **2D 59**
Viet-nam, *Embassy,* 12 Victoria Rd., W8. 01-937 1912 **3A 44**
Yemen Arab Republic, *Embassy,* 41 South St., W1. 01-629 9905 **3A 32**
Yemen, People's Democratic Republic of, *Embassy,* 57 Cromwell Rd., SW7. 01-584 6607 **2B 58**
Yugoslavia, *Embassy,* 5 Lexham Gdns., W8. 01-370 6105 **AZ 4J 75**
Zaire, *Embassy,* 26 Chesham Pl., SW1. 01-235 6137 **1D 61**

COURTS

Central Criminal Court, Old Bailey, EC4. 01-248 3277 **1A 38**
Royal Courts of Justice, Strand, WC2. 01-405 7641 **1B 36**

COUNTY COURTS
Barnet, Kingmaker Ho., Station Rd., New Barnet. 01-440 5948 **AZ 5E 4**
Bloomsbury & Marylebone, 7 Marylebone Rd., NW1. 01-637 8703 **2B 14**
Bow, 96 Romford Rd., E15. 01-555 3421 **AZ 6G 49**
Brentford, Alexandra Rd., High St., Brentford, Middx. 01-560 3424 **AZ 6D 72**
Bromley, Court Ho., College Rd., Bromley, Kent. 01-464 9727 **AZ 1J 127**
Clerkenwell, 33 Duncan Ter., N1. 01-359 7347 **AZ 1J 146**
Croydon, Law Courts, Barclay Rd., Croydon. 01-681 2533 **AZ 3D 134**
Edmonton, Court Ho., 59 Upper Fore St., Upper Edmonton, N18. 01-807 1666 **AZ 6B 18**
Ilford, Buckingham Rd., Ilford, Essex. 01-478 1132 **AZ 2H 51**
Kingston-upon-Thames, St. James's Rd., Kingston. 01-546 8843 **AZ 2D 118**
Lambeth, Cleaver St., Kennington Rd., SE11. 01-735 4425 **AZ 5A 78**
The Mayors & City of London Court, Guildhall, Basinghall St., EC2. 01-606 3030 **3D 23**
Shoreditch, 19 Leonard St., EC2. 01-253 5184 **AZ 3B 142**
Uxbridge, 114 High St., Uxbridge, Middx. Uxbridge 30441
Wandsworth, 76/78 Up. Richmond Rd., Putney, SW15. 01-870 2212 **AZ 4B 90**
West London, 43 North End Rd., W14. 01-602 8444 **AZ 4H 75**
Westminster, 82 St. Martin's La., WC2. 01-240 1405 **2C 35**
Willesden, 9 Acton La., NW10. 01-965 0261 **AZ 3J 57**
Woolwich, Powis, St., SE18. 01-854 2127 **AZ 3E 82**

CROWN COURTS
Croydon, Law Courts, Barclay Rd., Croydon. 01-681 2533 **AZ 3D 134**
and Foresters·Hall, Westow St., SE19. 01-771 9991 **AZ 6E 110**
Inner London Sessions Ho., Newington Causeway, SE1. 01-407 7111 **3C 55**
Kingston upon Thames, Canbury Park Rd., 01-549 5241 **AZ 1E 118**
Knightsbridge, 1 Hans Crescent, SW1. 01-589 4500 **3B 46**
Middlesex Guildhall, Broad Sanctuary, SW1. 01-222 8161 **3C 51**
and—41 Craven Park, NW10. 01-965 5963 **AZ 1K 57**
Snaresbrook, Court Ho., Holybush Hill, E11. 01-989 6666 **AZ 6H 33**
and—177 High Rd., S. Woodford, E18. 01-504 7148 **AZ 1J 33.** Court Ho., The Ridgeway, Chingford, E4. 01-529 6362 **AZ 1K 19**
Surbiton, 17 Ewell Road, 01-399 6691 **AZ 7B 118**

JUVENILE COURTS
Inner London Area
Enquiries to Senior Chief Clerk, P.O. Box 5, 185 Marylebone Rd., NW1. 01-262 3211 **2B 14**
Camden, 163a Seymour Pl., W1. 01-725 4345 **2B 14**

Greenwich, 7 Blackheath Rd., SE10. 01-853 8345 **AZ 1D 96**
Hackney, 51 Holloway Rd., N7. 01-607 6757 **AZ 2H 45**
Hammersmith, 163a Seymour Pl., W1. 01-725 4345 **2B 14**
Islington, 51 Holloway Rd., N7. 01-607 6757 **AZ 2H 45**
Kensington & Chelsea, 163a Seymour Pl., W1. 01-725 4345 **2B 14**
Lambeth, 217 Balham High Rd., SW17. 01-672 6547 **AZ 2E 108**
Lewisham (North), 4 Kimpton Rd., SE5. 01-703 0909 **AZ 1D 94**
Lewisham (South), 7 Blackheath Rd., SE10. 01-853 8345 **AZ 1D 96**
Southwark, 4 Kimpton Rd., SE5. 01-703 0909 **AZ 1D 94**
Tower Hamlets, 58b Bow Rd., E3. 01-488 5345 **AZ 3B 64**
Wandsworth, 217 Balham High Rd., SW17. 01-672 6547 **AZ 3E 108**
Westminster, 163a Seymour Pl., W1. 01-725 4345 **2B 14**

MAGISTRATES' COURTS
Inner London Area
Bow Street, Bow St., WC2. 01-434 5345 **1D 35**
Camberwell Green, D'Eynsford Rd., SE5. 01-703 0909 **AZ 1D 94**
Clerkenwell, 78 King's Cross Rd., WC1. 01-278 6541 **AZ 1E 104**
Greenwich, 9 Blackheath Rd., SE10. 01-853 8345 **AZ 1D 96**
Guildhall Justice Room, 65–70 Basinghall St., EC2. 01-606 3030 **3D 23**
Hampstead, 55 Downshire Hill, NW3. 01-725 4345 **AZ 4B 44**
Highbury Corner, 51 Holloway Rd., N7. 01-607 6757 **AZ 2H 45**
Horseferry Rd., 70 Horseferry Rd., SW1. 01-434 5345 **2B 64**
Mansion House Justice Room, Mansion Ho., EC4. 01-626 2500 **1D 39**
Marlborough St., 21 Gt. Marlborough St., W1. 01-434 5345 **1D 33**
Marylebone, 181 Marylebone Rd., NW1. 01-725 4345 **2B 14**
Old Street, 335 Old St., EC1. 01-488 5345 **AZ 3L 141**
South Western, 175a Lavender Hill, SW11. 01-228 9201 **AZ 3D 92**
Thames, Aylward St., E1. 01-488 5345 **AZ 7M 143**
Tower Bridge, 211 Tooley St., SE1. 01-407 4232 **2C 57**
Wells Street, 59 Wells St., W1. 01-725 4345 **3D 17**
West London, Southcombe St., W14. 01-741 6345 **AZ 4G 75**
Woolwich, Market St., SE18. 01-853 8345 **AZ 4E 82**

Outer London Area
Acton, Winchester St., W3. 01-992 9014 **AZ 2J 73**
Barking, East St., Barking, Essex. 01-594 5311 **AZ 1G 67**
Barnet, 7c High St., Barnet, Herts. 01-449 9541 **AZ 3B 4**
Bexley, Pincott Rd., Bexleyheath. 01-304 5211 **AZ 5G 101**
Brentford, Market Pl., Brentford. 01-568 9811 **AZ 7C 72**
Bromley, Court Ho., South St., Bromley, Kent. 01-466 6621 **AZ 2J 127**
Croydon, Law Courts, Barclay Rd., Croydon. 01-686 8680 **AZ 3D 134**
Ealing, Green Man La., W13. 01-579 9311 **AZ 1A 72**
Feltham, Hanworth Rd., Feltham, Middx. 01-890 4811 **AZ 1A 102**
Harrow, Court Ho., Rosslyn Cres., Wealdstone. 01-427 5146 **AZ 4K 23**
Havering, Court Ho., Main Rd., Romford. Romford 42341
Hendon, Court Ho., The Hyde, NW9. 01-200 1141 **AZ 4A 26**
Highgate, Bishops Rd., N6. 01-340 3472 **AZ 6E 28**
Ilford, 850 Cranbrook Rd., Barkingside, Ilford. 01-551 4461 **AZ 7E 34**
Kingston upon Thames, 34 Mkt. Pl., Kingston. 01-546 5603 **AZ 2D 118**
Richmond upon Thames, Parkshot, Richmond. 01-948 2101 **AZ 4D 88**
Stratford, Gt. Eastern Rd., E15. 01-534 8523 **AZ 7F 49**
Sutton, Court Ho., Throwley Way, Sutton, Surrey. 01-642 4231 **AZ 5K 131**
Tottenham, Court Ho., Lordship La., N17. 01-808 5411 **AZ 2A 30**
Uxbridge, Harefield Rd., Uxbridge, Middx. Uxbridge 30771
Wallington, Shotfield, Wallington, Surrey. 01-669 1281
Waltham Forest, 1 Farnan Av., Walthamstow, E17. 01-531 3121 **AZ 2C 32**

West Ham, Court Ho., West Ham La., E15. 01-534 8443 **AZ 7G 49**
Willesden, St. Mary's Rd., NW10. 01-965 3113 **AZ 1A 58**
Wimbledon, 80a The Broadway, SW19. 01-543 4145 **AZ 6H 107**

CORONERS COURTS
City of London, Milton Ct., EC2. 01-606 3030 **2D 23**
Battersea, Sheepcote La., SW11. 01-228 6044 **AZ 2D 92**
Croydon, The Law Courts, Barclay Rd. 01-681 5019 **AZ 3D 134**
Hackney, Mare St., E8. 01-985 1454 **AZ 1H 63**
Hammersmith, 77 Fulham Palace Rd., W6. 01-748 1813 **AZ 5E 74**
Hornsey, Myddelton Rd., N8. 01-348 4411 **AZ 4J 29**
Lewisham, Ladywell Rd., SE13. 01-690 2327 **AZ 5C 96**
Poplar, 127 Poplar High St., E14. 01-987 3614 **AZ 7D 64**
Southwark, Tennis St., SE1. 01-407 5611 **2D 55**
St. Pancras, Camley St., NW1. 01-387 4882 **AZ 7H 45**
Walthamstow, Queen's Rd., E17. 01-520 7246 **AZ 6B 32**
Westminster, 65 Horseferry Rd., SW1. 01-834 6515 **2B 64**

DANCING

BALLROOMS
Cafe de Paris, 3 Coventry St., W1. 01-437 2036 **2B 34**
Tea Dance 15.00, 17.45 Evenings from 19.30.
Empire Ballroom, Leicester Sq., WC2. 01-437 1446 **2B 34**
Evenings from 20.00.
Hammersmith Palais, Shepherds Bush Rd., W6. 01-748 2812 **AZ 4E 74**
Nightly at varying times. Ballroom & Disco Dancing.
Ritz, High Rd., Tottenham, N17. 01-808 4179 **AZ 4F 31**
Mon., Thurs., Fri. and Sat. 21.00 'til 02.00.
The Studio, 158 Streatham Hill, SW2. 01-674 5868 **AZ 2J 109**
Tiffanys, 111 The Broadway, SW19. 01-542 3869 **AZ 7J 107**

DANCE CLASSES
English Folk Dance and Song Society, Cecil Sharp House, 2 Regent's Park Rd.,
NW1. 01-485 2206 **AZ 1D 60**
Folk singing and dancing. The society exists to preserve and popularise English
Folk Music. Library of books and records. Shop stocking every kind of folk music,
dance, song and lore books/records/music/instruments/gifts. Open to public
09.30–17.30 Mon. to Sat., plus 18.00–21.00 Sat.
Pineapple Dance Studios, 7 Langley St., WC2. 01-836 4004 **2C 35**
Classes held in all types of dancing from Classical Ballet to Go-Go. Also Hire of
Studios, Retail Shop 09.00–21.00 Mon. to Sat.
Also at 60 Paddington St., W1. 01-487 3444 **2D 15** and 38 Harrington Rd., SW7.
01-581 0466 **2C 59**

DINE AND DANCE AT HOTELS AND RESTAURANTS
For Music Hall see page 40.
Apollonia, 17a Percy St., W1. 01-636 4140 **3A 18**
Traditional taverna with Greek dancing, also entertainments. Thurs, Fri & Sat.
Barbarella, 428 Fulham Rd., SW6. 01-385 9977 **AZ 2G 91** and **Barbarella 2,** 43
Thurloe St., SW7. 01-584 2000
Italian restaurants, disco dance-floors. Closed Sun.
Beefeater, Ivory Ho., St. Katharines Dock, E1. 01-408 1001 **3D 41**
Pageantry/entertainments, dancing to 24.00. Daily from 20.00.
Caledonian Suite, 6 Hanover St., W1. 01-408 1001 **1C 33**
Cabaret, Dancing, RestaurantScottish style.
Dorchester Hotel, Park La., W1. 01-629 8888 **1A 48**

Music and Dancing nightly except Sun. in the Terrace Room.
Gallipoli, 7-8 Bishopsgate Churchyard, EC2. 01-588 1922 **3B 24**
Dancing, Cabaret, Belly dancers. Closed Sun.
Hippodrome, Charing Cross Rd., WC2. 01-437 4311 **2C 35**
(Formerly Talk of the Town). Full Restaurant and fast food Restaurant. Six bars.
Bands, live performances, video. Discotheque setting with elaborate technical
features. 21.00–04.00 Mon. to Sat.
L'Hirondelle, Swallow St., W1. 01-734 6666 **3D 33**
Dinner and Dancing from 20.30 to two bands, sophisticated cabaret at 23.00 and
01.30 daily. Closed Sun.
London Hilton Hotel, Park La., W1. 01-493 8000 **1A 48**
In the Roof Restaurant every day except Sun.
Martinez, 25 Swallow St., W1. 01-734 5066 **3D 33**
Spanish restaurant, dancing by candlelight nightly.
Mimmo & Pasquale's le Palme, 62/65 Wilton Rd., SW1. 01-834 0716 **2C 63**
Italian restaurant, guitar music and dancing. Mon. to Sat.
Royal Garden Hotel, Kensington High St., W8. 01-937 8000 **2D 43**
In the Royal Roof Restaurant nightly except Sun.
Savoy Hotel, Strand, WC2. 01-836 4343 **3A 36**
Dancing nightly except Sun. in the Savoy Restaurant.
Shakespeare's Tavern & Playhouse, Blackfriars La., EC4. 01-408 1001 **2A 38**
Entertainment includes play excerpts. Dancing 'til Midnight.
Stork Club, 99 Regent St., W1. 01-734 3686 **3D 33**
Floor show twice nightly and dancing to resident orchestra. Daily. Dinner and
Dancing from 20.30.
Vecchiomondo, 118 Cromwell Rd., SW7. 01-373 7756 **2A 58**
Italian restaurant, disco dancing nightly.

DISCOTHEQUES

*There are many Disco's which enjoy changing popularity. Pubs often have Disco
Rooms. * Indicates membership necessary.*
Busby's, 157 Charing Cross Rd., WC2. 01-734 6963 **1B 34**
21.00–02.00 Wed. 21.00–03.00 Sat. Laser Show, multi-screen video. Food bar,
wine cocktail bar, disco bar.
Hippodrome, for "the greatest disco in the world" see above.
Park Discotheque, 38 Kensington High St., W8. 01-937 7744 **3B 42**
21.00–03.00 Mon.–Sat. Video, Cocktail Bar, Restaurant. Private functions Sun.
Purple Pussycat Dicso, 307 Finchley Rd., NW3. 01-794 2801
Illuminated floor. Restaurant and bars. 21.00–0300 nightly **AZ 4H 27**
Ritzi Park, 201–203 Wardour St., W1. 01-437 5979
Open 21.00–03.30 Mon.–Sat. **1A 34**
Samantha's, 3 New Burlington St., W1. 01-734 6249 **2D 33**
21.00–03.00, Sat. 04.00, Sun. 20.00–01.30.
St. Moritz, 159 Wardour St., W1. 01-437 0525 **1A 34**
*20.00–03.00. Closed Sundays.
Stringfellows, 16/19 Upper St. Martins La., WC2. 01-240 5534 **2C 35**
20.00–03.00. Closed Sun. Restaurant. Membership optional.
Studio Valbonne, 62 Kingly St., W1. 01-439 7242 **1D 33**
21.00–03.30. Closed Sun. Restaurant, three bars. Disco and live entertainment and
video.
Xenon, 196 Piccadilly, W1. 01-734 9344 **3A 34**
21.00–03.30. Discotheque with live entertainment.

EMPLOYMENT & UNEMPLOYMENT OFFICES

EMPLOYMENT OFFICES AND JOB CENTRES
Acton, Job Centre, 164 High St., W3. 01-993 0831 **AZ 1H 73**
Balham, Job Centre, 122 Balham High St., SW12. 01-673 2193 **AZ 3E 108**
Barking, Job Centre, 60 East St., 01-591 0666 **AZ 1G 67**
Barnet, Job Centre, 74 High St., 01-441 3456 **AZ 3B 4**
Beckenham & Penge, 2 Beckenham Rd., Beckenham. 01-650 5055 **AZ 1K 125**
Becontree, Job Centre, 714 Green La., Dagenham. 01-597 2121 **AZ 2H 51**
Bermondsey, Brunel Rd., SE16. 01-237 2864 **AZ 5L 149**
Bexley, Job Centre, 196 Broadway, Bexleyheath. 01-304 5121 **AZ 4E 100**
Borough, Job Centre, 92 Borough High St., SE1. 01-403 2055 **2D 55**
Brixton, Job Centre, 442 Brixton Rd., SW9. 01-733 5522 **AZ 3A 94**
Bromley, Job Centre, Westmoreland Rd. 01-460 9911 **AZ 5G 127**
Burnt Oak, Job Centre, Burnt Oak Broadway, 01-951 0411 **AZ 7C 12**
Camberwell, Collyer Pl., SE15. 01-639 4377 **AZ 1F 95**
Camden Town, Jobshop, 104 St. Pancras Wy., NW1. 01-485 4181 **AZ 7G 45**
Capital Radio Jobshop, Euston Road, NW1. 01-388 1288 **1D 17**
Catford, Job Centre, 62 Rushey Green, SE6. 01-690 9811 **AZ 7D 96**
Cathedral Place, Job Centre, 43 Cathedral Pl., EC4. 01-248 2141 **1B 38**
Central London, Job Centre, 213 Oxford St., W1. 01-439 7131 **1D 33**
Chiswick, Job Centre, 319 Chiswick High Rd., W4. 01-995 4071 **AZ 5G 73**
Clapham Junction, Job Centre, 155 Falcon Rd., SW11. 01-223 5283 **AZ 2C 92**
Croydon, 17 Dingwall Rd. 01-688 3881 **AZ 2D 134**
Dagenham, Chequers La. 01-592 4533 **AZ 4F 69**
Deptford, Job Centre, 122 Deptford High St., SE8. 01-691 8723 **AZ 6C 80**
Downham, Job Centre, 415 Bromley Rd., Bromley. 01-698 1114 **AZ 2D 126**
Ealing, Job Centre, 39 High St., W5. 01-579 9342, **AZ 7D 56**
East Finchley, Job Centre, 99 High Rd., N2. 01-444 5131 **AZ 1B 28**
East Ham, Job Centre, 2 Heigham Rd., E6. 01-552 5631 **AZ 7C 50**
Edgware Road, Job Centre, 182 Edgware Rd., W2. 01-724 1351 **3A 14**
Edmonton, Job Centre, 135 Lower Fore St., N18. 01-803 0066 **AZ 4B 18**
Eltham, Job Centre, 4 Pound Pl., SE9. 01-859 5711 **AZ 6E 98**
Enfield & Ponders End, 318 High St., Ponders End. 01-805 0516 **AZ 5D 8**
Enfield Town, Job Centre, 36 The Town, 01-367 5251 **AZ 3J 7**
Erith, 7 Queen's Rd. Dartford 348111
Feltham, Job Centre, 76 The Centre, High St. 01-890 6665
Finchley, Job Centre, 60 Ballard's La., N3. 01-349 2033 **AZ 1J 27**
Fulham, Job Centre, 376 North End Rd., SW6. 01-381 1900 **AZ 4G 75**
Golders Green, Job Centre, 11 Golders Green Rd., NW11. 01-458 8366 **AZ 6G 27**
Hackney, Job Centre, 394 Mare St., E8. 01-533 1121 **AZ 1H 63**
Hainault, 19 New North Rd. 01-500 0095
Hammersmith, Job Centre, 73 King St., W6. 01-741 1525 **AZ 4C 74**
Harrow, Job Centre, 7 Manor Pde., Sheepcote Rd. 01-863 8566 **AZ 6K 23**
Hayes, Job Centre, 50 Station Rd., Hayes. 01-848 3761
Heathrow, Job Centre, Building 865, Heathrow Airport North Side, Norwood Crescent, Hounslow. 01-759 9718
Holborn, Job Centre, 275 High Holborn, WC1. 01-242 9256 **3B 20**
Holloway, Medina Rd., N7. 01-607 4431 **AZ 3A 46**
Hornchurch, North St. Hornchurch 74922
Hotel & Catering Trades, Job Centre, 3 Denmark St., WC2. 01-836 6622 **1B 34**
Hounslow, Job Centre, 216 High St., 01-572 2561 **AZ 3F 87**
Ilford, Job Centre, 88 High Rd., 01-514 2727 **AZ 2G 51**
Kensington, Job Centre, 198 Kensington High St., W8. 01-937 6976 **3B 42**

Kentish Town, Job Centre, 178 Kentish Town Rd., NW5. 01-267 9551 **AZ 7F 85**
Kilburn, Job Centre, 292 Kilburn High Rd., NW6. 01-328 6543 **AZ 7H 43**
King's Cross, Barnsbury Rd., N1. 01-837 8811 **AZ 1A 62**
Kingston upon Thames, Job Centre, 19 Fife Rd. 01-549 5921 **AZ 2E 118**
Lewisham, Holbeach Rd., SE6. 01-318 7174 **AZ 7C 96**
Leytonstone, Job Centre, 616 High Rd., E11. 01-558 0941 **AZ 4G 49**
Loughton, Job Centre, 284 High Rd., Loughton. 01-508 6181 **AZ 2E 20**
Mitcham, Job Centre, 246 London Rd., Mitcham. 01-640 7221 **AZ 7E 122**
Morden, Job Centre, 41 London Rd., Morden. 01-640 2953 **AZ 1J 121**
Orpington, Job Centre, The Walnuts, High St. Orpington 73121
Palmers Green, Job Centre, 348 Green Lanes, N13. 01-882 4666 **AZ 6E 16**
Plaistow, Job Centre, Balaam St., E13. 01-476 2000 **AZ 4J 65**
Poplar, Burdett Rd., E14. 01-987 4101 **AZ 4A 64**
Richmond, Job Centre, 19 Kew Rd. 01-948 5351 **AZ 3E 88**
Romford, Job Centre, 16 North St. Romford 44201
Ruislip, Job Centre, 126 High St. Ruislip 76455
St. Marylebone, 46 Lisson Gro., NW1. 01-262 3477 **2B 14**
Shoreditch, 57 Kingsland Rd., E2. 01-729 1666 **AZ 1D 142**
Sidcup, Job Centre, 15 Market Pde., Sidcup High St. 01-300 7711 **AZ 4A 116**
Southall,68 The Broadway. 01-843 2222 **AZ 1C 70**
Stepney, Settles St., E1. 01-247 3242 **AZ 6H 143**
Stockwell, Job Centre, 219 Clapham Rd., SW9. 01-733 6261 **AZ 3J 93**
Stratford, Job Centre, 66 Broadway, E15. 01-519 7900 **AZ 7F 49**
Streatham, Job Centre, 103 Streatham High Rd., SW16. 01-677 1221 **AZ 4J 109**
Sutton, Job Centre, 240 High St. 01-643 0731 **AZ 4K 131**
Swiss Cottage, Job Centre, 120 Finchley Rd., NW3. 01-794 0941 **AZ 4H 27**
Tooting Broadway, Job Centre, 24 Mitcham Rd., SW17. 01-767 3414 **AZ 5D 108**
Tottenham, Job Centre, 624 High Rd., N17. 01-808 4581 **AZ 4F 31**
Twickenham, Job Centre, 20 York St. 01-892 9025 **AZ 1A 104**
Uxbridge, Job Centre, 208 High St., Uxbridge. Uxb. 56556
Victoria, Job Centre, 119 Victoria St., SW1. 01-828 9321 **1C 63**
Walthamstow, Job Centre, 263 Hoe St., E17. 01-520 8900 **AZ 4C 32**
Watney Market, Job Centre, 25 Watney Mkt., E1. 01-790 9033 **AZ 8K 143**
Wealdstone, Job Centre, 31 High St. 01-863 9966 **AZ 2J 23**
Wembley, Job Centre, 528 High Rd., Wembley. 01-903 9491 **AZ 5D 40**
West Drayton, Job Centre, High St., Yiewsley. West Drayton 440661
West Ealing, Job Centre, 156 Broadway, W13. 01-567 3010 **AZ 1K 71**
West End, Job Centre, 195 Wardour St., W1. 01-439 4541 **1A 34**
Westminster, Chadwick St., SW1. 01-222 8060 **1B 64**
West Norwood, Job Centre, 19 Knight's Hill, SE27. 01-761 1461 **AZ 5B 110**
Westway Jobshop, 140 Ladbroke Grove, W10. 01-969 0914 **AZ 4F 59**
Willesden, Job Centre, 161 High St., NW10. 01-965 6506 **AZ 2B 58**
Wimbledon, Job Centre, 56 Wimbledon Hill Rd., SW19. 01-947 6694 **AZ 6G 107**
Wood Green, Job Centre, 2a Lymington Av., N22. 01-889 0991 **AZ 2A 30**
   Job Centre, 54 High Rd., N22. 01-889 0991 **AZ 1K 29**
Woolwich, 115 Powis St., SE18. 01-854 5333 **AZ 3E 82**

UNEMPLOYMENT BENEFIT OFFICES
Barking, 510 Ripple Rd., 01-594 4084 **AZ 1H 67**
Barnet, Raydean Ho., 17 Western Pde, Gt. North Rd., 01-449 5522 **AZ 5D 4**
Battersea, Beechmore Rd., SW11. 01-720 8911 **AZ 1D 92**
Beckenham, 2 Beckenham Rd. 01-650 5055 **AZ 1K 125**
Bermondsey, Brunel Rd., SE16. 01-237 1943 **AZ 5L 149**
Bexley, 74 Trinity Place, Bexley Heath. 01-304 8415 **AZ 4F 101**
Borough, Keyworth Ho., Keyworth St., SE1. 01-928 8077 **AZ 6K 147**
Brixton, 372 Coldharbour La., SW9. 01-274 3241 **AZ 4A 94**
Brentford, Power Rd., W4. 01-994 6480 **AZ 4G 73**
Bromley, 2 Ethelbert Rd., 01-460 9911 **AZ 3J 127**

Camberwell, Collyer Pl., SE15. 01-639 4377 **AZ 1F 95**
Camden Town, 106 St. Pancras Way, NW1. 01-485 4181 **AZ 7G 45**
Canning Town, Freemasons Rd., E16. 01-476 2761 **AZ 5K 65**
Croydon, 17 Dingwall Rd., 01-688 3881 **AZ 2D 134**
Dagenham, Chequers La. 01-592 4533 **AZ 4F 69**
Deptford, Meridian Ho., Royal Hill, SE10. 01-853 5544 **AZ 7E 80**
Ealing, 140/152 Uxbridge Rd., W13. 01-567 3090 **AZ 1B 72**
East Ham, 473 Barking Rd., E6. 01-472 3316 **AZ 1D 66**
Enfield, 318 High St., Ponders End. 01-805 6060 **AZ 5D 8**
Erith, 7 Queen's Rd. Erith 349221
Eltham, 1 Passey Pl., SE9. 01-859 7611 **AZ 6D 98**
Feltham, 76 The Centre, High St., 01-751 0916
Finchley, 40 Ballards La., N3. 01-349 9241 **AZ 1J 27**
Forest Hill, Heron Ho., 32 Dartmouth Rd., SE23. 01-699 9288 **AZ 3H 111**
Fulham, Wyfold Rd., SW6. 01-385 2241 **AZ 7G 75**
Hackney, Spurstowe Ter., Dalston La., E8. 01-254 6171 **AZ 6F 47**
Hammersmith, 200 Shepherds Bush Rd., W6. 01-603 3456 **AZ 4E 74**
Harrow, Station Rd., Wealdstone, 01-863 9424 **AZ 4K 23**
Hayes, 235 Viveash Close, Nestles Av. 01-573 5626
Hainault, 19 New North Rd. 01-500 0095
Hendon, 2a Rundell Cres., NW4. 01-202 0826 **AZ 5D 26**
Holloway, Medina Rd., N7. 01-607 4431 **AZ 3A 46**
Hornchurch, 40 North St. Hornchurch 76611
Hornsey, 431/433 Hornsey Rd., N19. 01-263 3191 **AZ 2J 45**
Hounslow, 565 London Rd., Isleworth. 01-560 2177 **AZ 3G 87**
Ilford, 564/570 High Rd., Seven Kings. 01-590 5601 **AZ 2G 51**
Kings Cross, 1 Barnsbury Rd., N1. 01-837 8811 **AZ 1A 62**
Kingston, Water La. 01-546 2204 **AZ 1D 118**
Lewisham, Holbeach Rd., SE6. 01-690 1183 **AZ 7C 96**
Leyton, Grosvenor Park Rd., E17. 01-520 5500 **AZ 5D 32**
Mill Hill, 120 Bunns La., NW7. 01-959 3686 **AZ 6F 13**
Orpington, The Walnuts, High St. Orpington 26721
Poplar, Burdett Rd., E14. 01-987 4101 **AZ 4A 64**
Richmond, 1 Parkshot Ho., 19 Kew Rd. 01-940 6011 **AZ 3E 88**
Romford, 30 Main Rd. Romford 22111
Ruislip, 41/45 Windmill La., Ruislip 59271
St. Marylebone, 46 Lisson Grove, NW1. 01-262 3477 **2B 14**
Shoreditch, 57 Kingsland Rd., E2. 01-729 1666 **AZ 1D 142**
Sidcup, 15 Sidcup Hill. 01-300 7711 **AZ 4B 116**
Southall, 68 The Broadway. 01-843 2222 **AZ 1C 70**
Stepney, Settles St., E1. 01-247 3242 **AZ 6H 143**
Stratford, Station St., E15. 01-534 5151 **AZ 7F 49**
Streatham, Crown Ho., Station Approach, Streatham High Rd., SW16. 01-677 8122 **AZ 4J 109**
Sutton, Lodge Pl. 01-642 7621 **AZ 5K 131**
Tooting, 67/95 Upper Tooting Rd., SW17. 01-642 1248 **AZ 4D 108**
Tottenham, 625 High Rd., N17. 01-808 4581 **AZ 4F 31**
Uxbridge, Mill Ho., Riverside Way, Uxbridge 72366
Waltham Cross, 235 High St. Waltham Cross 23307
Wembley, Chantry Ho., Olympic Way. 01-902 8854 **AZ 3G 41**
Westminster, Chadwick St., SW1. 01-222 8060 **1B 64**
Willesden, Chancel Ho., Neasden La., NW10. 01-459 8844 **AZ 1A 42**
Wimbledon, 12 Southey Rd., SW19. 01-542 5681 **AZ 7J 107**
Wood Green, 38/46 Station Rd., N22. 01-889 2621 **AZ 2K 29**
Woolwich, Spray St., SE18. 01-854 2441 **AZ 4F 83**

EXHIBITION HALLS   see also MUSEUMS AND GALLERIES

National Exhibition Centre, Birmingham. 021-780 4141
Seven Halls staging important exhibitions plus Conference Centre, Hotels,
Restaurants, Car Park, etc. Direct access from M6/M42 Motorway,
Birmingham Airport and B.R. Birmingham International Station.

Alexander Palace & Pavilion, Muswell Hill, N10. 01-883 6477 **AZ 2H 29**
Multi-purpose venue for exhibitions, events, entertainments and meetings; the
restored Palace is due to re-open 1988 to complement the modern Pavilion.
Barbican Centre for Arts & Conferences, Silk St., EC2. 01-588 8211 **2C 23**
Extensive trade exhibition facilities linked to the Arts and Conference Centre.
Building Centre, 26 Store St., WC1. 01-637 1102. Enquiry Service: Winkfield Row
884999 **2B 18**
Permanent exhibition display stands and information on all aspects of building and
maintaining the home. Open: 09.30–17.30 Mon. to Fri.
Business Design Centre, 52 Upper St., N1. 01-226 9355 **AZ 1A 62**
Trade exhibitions within the restored Royal Agricultural Hall (The Aggie) built 1861,
now a showcase for the contract design trade.
Commonwealth Institute, 230 Kensington High St., W8. 01-603 4545 **3A 42**
Information centre and exhibition galleries of and about the Commonwealth. Open
10.00–17.30 Mon.–Sat., 14.30–18.00 Sun. Recorded Information 01-602 3257
Crafts Centre, Fed. of Brit. Crafts Soc. 43 Earlham St., WC2. 01-836 6993 **1C 35**
Exhibitions of furniture, jewellery, pottery etc., work may be commissioned. Open
10–17.30 Mon. to Fri.11.00–17.00 Sat.
Crafts Gallery, Crafts Council, 12 Waterloo Pl., SW1. 01-930 4811 **3B 34**
Show case for artist/craftsmen, open 10.00–17.00 Tues. to Sat; 14.00–17.00 Sun.
Craftsman Index, slide library, research facilities.
Design Centre, Council of Industrial Design, 28 Haymarket, SW1. 01-839 8000
3B 34
1. Permanent Exhibition of best in British industrial design and periodic exhibitions
on specific subjects. 2. Design Index—visual reference library with stockists,
prices etc., free access to public. 3. Designer selection service—will recommend
individual designers. Open Mon.–Tues. 10.00–18.00. Wed.–Sat. 10.00–20.00. Sun.
13.00–18.00
Earls Court Exhibition Halls, Lillie Rd., SW5. 01-385 1200 **AZ 5J 75**
Annual events can include the Int. Boat Show, Crufts Dog Show, Caravan Camping
Holiday Show, London Furniture Show, Royal Tournament and Royal
Smithfield Show, "Daily Mail" Ideal Home Exhib., Int. Motor Cycle Show.
Olympia Exhibition Halls, Hammersmith Rd., W14. 01-603 3344 **AZ 3G 75**
Annual events can include Camping and Outdoor Holiday Exhibition, London
Fashion Exhibition, International Showjumping Championships.
Royal Horticultural Society Halls, Vincent Sq., SW1. 01-834 4333 **2A 64**
Annual exhibitions can include the Horticultural Society Flower Shows, Spring,
Summer and Autumn, National Rose and Chrysanthemum Society Shows.
Wembley Arena, Conference and Exhibition Centre, Empire Way. 01-902 8833
AZ 4F 41 Multi-purpose centre holding important events, exhibitions, conferences,
concerts.

FURTHER EDUCATION   (Colleges, Polytechnics and Universities)

STUDENTS NIGHTLINE emergency service p. 205.
Asterisk * denotes Schools and Colleges of the University of London.

Acton Technical College, Mill Hill Rd., W3. 01-993 2344 **AZ 2H 73**
Architectural Association School of Architecture, 34 Bedford Sq., WC1. 01-636 0974 **3B 18**
Avery Hill College, See Thames Polytechnic
Barking College of Tech., Dagenham Rd., Romford. Romford 66841
Barnet College, Wood St. 01-440 6321 **AZ 4A 4**
***Bedford College,** Se Ryl Holloway & Bedford New College
Beth Jacob Teachers Seminary, 10a Woodberry Down, N4. 01-800 4719 **AZ 7C 30**
***Birkbeck College,** Malet St., WC1. 01-580 6622 **2B 18**
British College of Naturopathy & Osteopathy, 6 Netherhall Gdns., NW3. 01-435 7830 **AZ 6A 44**
Brit. Inst. of International & Comparative Law, 17 Russell Sq., WC1. 01-636 5802 **1C 19**
***British Inst. in Paris,** 15 Woburn Sq., WC1. 01-636 8000 **2C 19**
***British Postgraduate Medical Fed.,** 33 Millman St., WC1. 01-831 6222 **1A 20**
British School of Osteopathy, 1 Suffolk St., SW1. 01-930 9254 **3B 34**
Brixton College, 56 Brixton Hill, SW2. 01-737 1166 **AZ 7J 93**
Bromley College of Tech., Rookery La., Bromley Comn. 01-462 6331 **AZ 6B 128**
Brunel University, Kingston La., Hillingdon. Uxbridge 37188
Camberwell School of Art & Crafts, Peckham Rd., SE5. 01-703 0987 **AZ 1E 94**
Carshalton College of Fur. Ed., Nightingale Rd. 01-647 0021 **AZ 3D 132**
***Cardiothoracic Inst., Fulham Rd., SW3. 01-352 8121 3D 59**
Central School of Art & Design, Southampton Row, WC1. 01-405 1825 **3A 20**
Central School of Speech & Drama, 64 Eton Av, NW3. 01-722 8183 **AZ 7B 44**
***Charing Cross & Westminster Medical School,** The Reynolds Building, St. Dunstan's Rd., W6. 01-748 2040 **AZ 5F 75**
***Chelsea College,** See Kings College
Chelsea School of Art, Manresa Rd., SW3. 01-351 3844 **AZ 5C 76**
City & East London College, Pitfield St., N1. 01-253 6883 **AZ 3E 62**
City & Guilds of Lon. Art Sch., 124 Kennington Pk. Rd., SE11. 01-735 2306 **AZ 6A 78**
City & Guilds College, see Imperial College of Science.
City Lit., Stukeley St., WC2. 01-242 9872 **1D 35**
City of London Polytechnic, 117 Houndsditch, EC3. 01-283 1030 **1C 41**
City University, Northampton Sq., EC1. 01-253 4399 **AZ 3B 62**
College for the Distributive Trades, 30 Leicester Sq., WC2. 01-839 1547 **3B 34**
College of Law, The, 27 Chancery La., WC2. 01-242 3757 **1C 37**
College of Physical Education, 16/18 Paddington St., W1. 01-486 4804 **2D 15**
Cordwainers Technical College, 182 Mare St., E8. 01-985 0273 **AZ 1H 63**
***Courtauld Inst. of Art,** 20 Portman Sq., W1. 01-935 9292 **1D 31**
Croydon Coll. of Design & Tech., Fairfield, Croydon. 01-688 9271 **AZ 2D 134**
Digby-Stuart College, Roehampton La., SW15. 01-876 2967 **AZ 4C 90**
Ealing College of Higher Education, St. Mary's Rd., W5. 01-579 4111 **AZ 2D 72**
East Ham College of Tech., High St. S., E6. 01-472 1480 **AZ 2D 66**
Edmonton College of Fur. Ed., Montagu Rd., N18. 01-803 7311 **AZ 5C 18**
Enfield College, Montague Rd., N18. 01-803 7311 **AZ 5C 18**
Erith College of Tech., Tower Rd., Belvedere. Erith 42331
E.S.S.R.A. School of Economic Studies, 177 Vauxhall Bridge Rd., SW1. 01-834 4979 **3D 63**
Garnett College, Downshire Ho., Roehampton La., SW15. 01-789 6533 **AZ 4C 90**
Goldsmiths' College, Lewisham Way, SE14. 01-692 7171 **AZ 1B 96**
Guildhall School of Music & Drama, Barbican, EC2. 01-628 2571 **2D 23**
***Guy's Hospital Medical & Dental Sch.,** St. Thomas St., SE1. 01-407 7600 **1A 56**
Hackney College, 89–115 Mare St., E8. 01-985 8484 **AZ 1H 63**
Hammersmith & W. London Coll., Gliddon Rd., W14. 01-741 1688 **AZ 7G 75**
Haringey College, Park Rd., N11. 01-888 7123 **AZ 7C 16**

Harrow College of Further Education, Uxbridge Rd., Hatch End, Pinner. 01-428 0121

Harrow College of Higher Education, Watford Rd., Harrow. 01-864 5422 **AZ 7A 24**

Hendon College of Fur. Ed., The Burroughs, NW4. 01-202 3811 **AZ 4D 26**

*Heythrop College, 11 Cavendish Sq., W1. 01-580 6941 **3C 17**

Hounslow Borough College, London Rd., Isleworth. 01-568 0244 **AZ 3G 87**

*Imperial College of Science & Tech., Exhibition Rd., SW7. 01-589 5111 **1C 59**

Inchbald School of Design, 7 Eaton Gt., SW1. 01-730 5508 **2D 61**

*Institute of Advanced Legal Studies, 17 Russell Sq., WC1. 01-637 1731 **2C 19**

*Institute of Archaeology, 31 Gordon Sq., WC1. 01-387 6052 **2B 18**

*Institute of Cancer Research, Royal Cancer Hosp., 17a Onslow Gdns., SW7. 01-352 8133 **3C 59**

*Institute of Child Health, 30 Guildford St., WC1. 01-242 9789 **1A 20**

*Institute of Classical Studies, 31 Gordon Sq., WC1. 01-387 7696 **1B 18**

*Institute of Commonwealth Studies, 27 Russell Sq., WC1. 01-580 5876 **2C 19**

*Institute of Education, 20 Bedford Way, WC1. 01-636 1500 **1C 19**

*Institute of Germanic Studies, 29 Russell Sq., WC1. 01-580 2711 **2C 19**

*Institute of Historical Research, Senate Ho., Malet St., WC1. 01-636 0272 **2B 18**

*Institute of Laryngology & Otology, 330 Grays Inn Rd., WC1. 01-837 8855 **AZ 3K 61**

*Institute of Latin-American Studies, 31 Tavistock Sq., WC1. 01-387 5671 **1B 18**

*Institute of Obstetrics & Gynaecology Queen Charlotte's Maternity Hosp., Goldhawk Rd., W6. 01-741 8351 **AZ 4B 74**

*Institute of United States Studies, 31 Tavistock Sq., WC1. 01-387 5534 **3B 10**

Jews' College, London, 44a Albert Rd., NW4. 01-203 6427 **AZ 4F 27**

Kensit Memorial College, 104 Hendon La., N3. 01-349 9408 **AZ 3G 27**

Kilburn Polytechnic, Priory Pk. Rd., NW6. 01-328 8241 **AZ 1H 59**

*King's College London, Strand, WC2. 01-836 5454 **2B 36**

Chelsea Campus; 552 King's Rd., SW10. 01-351 2488 **AZ 7A 76**

Kensington Campus; Campden Hill Rd., W8. 01-937 5411 **2B 42**

*Kings College School of Medicine & Dentistry, Denmark Hill, SE5. 01-274 6222 **AZ 4D 94**

Kingston College of Fur. Ed., Kingston Hall Rd. 01-546 2151 **AZ 3D 118**

Kingston Polytechnic, Penrhyn Rd. 01-549 1366 **AZ 4E 118**

Kingsway—Princeton College, Sidmouth St., WC1. 01-278 0541 **3D 11**

London Academy of Music & Dramatic Art, 226 Cromwell Rd., SW5. 01-373 9883 **AZ 4K 75**

London Business School, Sussex Pl., NW1. 01-262 5050 **3C 7**

London College of Business Studies, 60 South Molton St., W1. 01-493 3401 **1B 32**

London College of Fashion, 20 John Prince's St., W1. 01-629 9401 **1C 33**

London College of Furniture, 41 Commercial Rd., E1. 01-247 1953 **AZ 6G 63**

London College of Music, 47 Gt. Marlborough St., W1. 01-437 6120 **1D 33**

London College of Osteopathy, 8 Boston Pl., NW1. 01-262 5250 **1B 14**

London College of Printing, Elephant and Castle, SE1. 01-735 8484 **AZ 4B 78**

London College of Secretaries, 24 Queensbury Pl., SW7. 01-589 9211 **2C 59**

*London Hospital Medical College, Turner St., E1. 01-377 8800 **AZ 6J 143**

London Institute, c/o London Coll. of Fashion, see above.

London International Film School, 24 Shelton St., WC2. 01-240 0168 **1C 35**

London Opera Centre, 490 Commercial Rd., E1. 01-790 4468 **AZ 6G 63**

London School of Accountancy, 17 Longford St., NW1. 01-388 7232 **AZ 4F 61**

*London School of Economics & Political Science, Houghton St., WC2. 01-405 7686 **1A 36**

*London School of Hygiene & Tropical Medicine, Keppel St., WC1. 01-636 8636 **2B 18**

London School of Nautical Cookery, 202 Lambeth Rd., SE1. 01-261 9535 **1C 67**

Maison de L'Institute de France a Londres, 8 Queen's Gate Terr., SW7. 01-584 7392 **1B 58**

Maria Assumpta College of Ed., 23 Kensington Sq., W8. 01-937 6434 **3C 43**

Merchant Navy College, Greenhithe, Kent. Greenhithe 845050

Merton Tech. College, Morden Pk., London Rd., Morden. 01-640 3001 **AZ 5J 121**

*Middlesex Hospital Medical School, Mortimer St., W1. 01-636 8333 **3D 17**

Middlesex Polytechnic, Admission Off., 114 Chase Side, N14. 01-886 6599 **AZ 6K 5**

Missionary School of Medicine, 2 Powis Pl., WC1. 01-837 5832 **2D 19**

Montessori Maria Training Organisation, 26 Lyndurst Gdns., NW3. 01-435 3646 **AZ 5B 44**

Montessori St. Nicholas' Training Centre, 23 Prince's Ga., SW7. 01-584 9232 **3D 45**

Morley College, 61 Westminster Bridge Rd., SE1. 01-928 8501 **1C 67**

North East London Polytechnic, Longbridge Rd., Dagenham. 01-590 7722 **AZ 4A 52**

North East Surrey Coll. of Tech., Reigate Rd., Ewell, Surrey. 01-394 1731.

North London College, Camden Rd., Holloway, N7. 01-609 9981 **AZ 7G 45**

Norwood Hall Institute of Horticultural Education, Norwood Green, Southall, Middx. 01-574 2261 **AZ 4E 70**

Nuffield College of Surgical Sciences, 35 Lincoln's Inn Fields, WC2. 01-405 3474 **1B 36**

Open University, London Region, 527 Finchley Rd., NW3. 01-794 0575 **AZ 4H 27**

Orpington College, The Walnuts, High St. Orpington 39336

Paddington College, 25 Paddington Grn., W2. 01-402 6221 **2C 13**

Pitmans Central College, 154 Southampton Row, WC1. 01-837 4481 **2D 19**

Polytechnic of Central London, 309 Regent St., W1 01-580 2020 **3C 17**

Polytechnic of North London, Holloway Rd., N7. 01-607 2789 **AZ 2H 45**

Polytechnic of the South Bank, Borough Rd. SE1. 01-928 8989 **3A 54**

*Queen Elizabeth College, See King's College

*Queen Mary College, Mile End Rd., E1. 01-980 4811 **AZ 5L 143**

Queen's College, 43 Harley St., W1. 01-580 1533 **3B 16**

Ravensbourne College of Art & Design, Walden Rd., Chislehurst. 01-468 7071 **AZ 6D 114**

Redbridge Technical College, Little Heath, Romford. 01-599 5231

Richmond Adult College, Clifden Rd., Twickenham. 01-891 5907 **AZ 1E 103**

Richmond upon Thames College, Egerton Rd., Twickenham. 01-892 6656 **AZ 7J 87**

Roehampton Inst. of Higher Education, Grove Ho., Roehampton La., SW15. 01-878 5751 **AZ 4C 90**

Rose Bruford Coll. of Speech & Drama, Lamorbey Park, Burnt Oak La., Sidcup. 01-300 3024 **AZ 6A 100**

Royal Academy of Dancing, 48 Vicarage Cres., SW11. 01-223 0091 **AZ 1B 92**

Royal Academy of Dramatic Art, 62 Gower St., WC1. 01-636 7076 **1B 18**

Royal Academy of Music, Marylebone Rd., NW1. 01-935 5461 **1A 16**

Royal Academy Schools, Royal Academy of Arts, Piccadilly, W1. 01-734 9052 **3D 33**

Royal Ballet School, 155 Talgarth Rd., W14. (Upper School.) 01-748 6335 **AZ 4F 75**

Royal College of Art, Kensington Gore, SW7. 01-584 5020 **3B 44**

Royal College of Defence Studies, 37 Belgrave Sq., SW1. 01-235 1091 **3A 48**

Royal College of General Practitioners, 14 Princess Ga., SW7. 01-581 3232 **3D 45**

Royal College of Midwives, 15 Mansfield St., W1. 01-580 6523 **3B 16**

Royal College of Music, Prince Consort Rd., SW7. 01-589 3643 **3C 45**

Royal College of Nursing, 20 Cavendish Sq., W1. 01-409 3333 **1B 32**

Royal College of Obstetricians & Gynaecologists, 27 Sussex Pl., NW1. 01-262 5425 **3B 6**

Royal College of Organists, Kensington Gore, SW7. 01-589 1765 **3B 44**

Royal College of Pathologists, 2 Carlton Ho. Ter., SW1. 01-930 5861 **1B 50**

Royal College of Physicians, 11 St. Andrews Pl., NW1. 01-935 1174 **3B 8**

Royal College of Psychiatrists, 17 Belgrave Sq., SW1. 01-235 2351 **1D 61**

Royal College of Surgeons, 35 Lincoln's Inn Fields, WC2. 01-405 3474 **1B 36**

Royal College of Veterinary Surgeons, 32 Belgrave Sq., SW1. 01-235 4971 **1A 62**

Royal Dental Hosp. School, 32 Leicester Sq., WC2. 01-930 8831 **3B 34**

*Royal Free Hospital School of Medicine, Rowland Hill St., NW3. 01-794 0500 **AZ 5C 44**

*Royal Holloway & Bedford New College, Egham Hill, Egham, Surrey. Egham 34455

*Royal Postgraduate Medical School, Hammersmith Hospital, Du Cane Rd., W12. 01-743 2030 **AZ 6B 58**

Royal School of Needlework, 25 Prince's Ga., SW7. 01-589 0077 **3D 45**

*Royal Veterinary College, Royal College St., NW1. 01-387 2898 **AZ 7G 45**

*St. Barts' Hosp. Medical College, West Smithfield, EC1. 01-606 7404 **3B 22**

*St. George's Hosp. Medical School, Cranmer Ter., SW17. 01-672 1255 **AZ 5B 108**

St. Martin's School of Art, 109 Charing Cross Rd., WC2. 01-437 0611 **1B 34**

St. Mary's College, Strawberry Hill, Twickenham. 01-892 0051 **AZ 3K 103**

*St. Mary's Hospital Medical School. Norfolk Pl., W2. 01-723 1252 **3D 13**

*St. Thomas's Hospital Medical School, Lambeth Palace Rd., SE1. 01-928 9292 **3A 52**

Schiller International University, 5–55 Waterloo Rd., SE1. 01-928 1372 **1B 52**

School of Computer Technology, 104/108 Oxford St., W1. 01-636 6441 **1A 34**

*School of Environmental Studies, Gower St., WC1. 01-387 7050 **1A 18**

*School of Oriental & African Studies, Malet St., WC1. 01-637 2388 **2B 18**

*School of Pharmacy, 29 Brunswick Sq., WC1. 01-837 7651 **3D 11**

*School of Slavonic & E. European Studies, Malet St., 01-637 4934 **2B 18**

*Slade School of Fine Art (University Coll.), Gower St., WC1. 01-387 7050 **1A 18**

Southgate Technical College, High St., N14. 01-886 6521 **AZ 1C 16**

Southall College of Tech., Beaconsfield Rd., Southall. 01-574 3448 **AZ 1B 70**

South East London College, Lewisham Way, SE4. 01-692 0353 **AZ 1B 96**

Southlands College, 65 Wimbledon Park Side, SW19. 01-946 2234 **AZ 2F 107**

South London College, Knight's Hill, SE27. 01-670 4488 **AZ 5B 110**

South Thames College, Wandsworth High St., SW18. 01-870 2241 **AZ 5J 91**

Southwark College, The Cut, SE1. 01-928 9561 **2A 54**

South West London College, Tooting Broadway, SW17. 01-672 2441 **AZ 5D 108**

Spurgeon's College, 189 South Norwood Hill, SE25. 01-653 0850 **AZ 1E 124**

Sutton College of Liberal Arts, St. Nicholas Way, Sutton. 01-661 5060 **AZ 4K 131**

Thames Polytechnic, Wellington St., SE18. 01-854 2030 **AZ 4E 82**

Tottenham College of Technology, High Rd., N15. 01-802 3111 **AZ 4F 31**

Trinity College of Music, 11 Mandeville Pl., W1. 01-935 5773 **1A 32**

*University Coll. Hosp. Medical School, University St., WC1. 01-387 9300 **1A 16**

*University College London, Gower St., WC1. 01-387 7050 **1A 18**

University of London, Senate House, Malet St., WC1. 01-636 8000 **2B 18**

Uxbridge Technical College, Park Rd. Uxbridge. 30411

Vauxhall Coll. of Building & Fur. Ed., Belmore St., SW8. 01-928 4611 **AZ 1H 93**

Waltham Forest College, Forest Rd., E17. 01-527 2311 **AZ 4J 31**

*Warburg Institute, Woburn Sq., WC1. 01-580 9663 **1B 18**

*Westfield College, Kidderpore Av., NW3. 01-435 7141 **AZ 4J 43**

West Ham College, Welfare Rd., E15. 01-555 1422 **AZ 7G 49**

West London Institute of Higher Education, 300 St. Margaret's Rd., Twickenham. 01-891 0121 **AZ 4B 88**
Westminster College, Battersea Park Rd., SW11. 01-720 2121 **AZ 2C 92**
*Westminster Medical School, See Charing Cross & Westminster
Whitelands College, West Hill, SW15. 01-788 8268 **AZ 7F 91**
Willesden College of Tech., Denzil Rd., NW10. 01-451 3411 **AZ 5B 42**
Wimbledon School of Art, Merton Hall Rd., SW19. 01-540 0231 **AZ 1G 121**
Woolwich College for Further Ed., Villas Rd., SE18. 01-855 1216 **AZ 4G 83**
Working Men's College, Crowndale Rd., NW1. 01-387 2037 **AZ 2G 61**

GOVERNMENT DEPARTMENTS

Departments of State, Nationalised Industries and other Public Offices.

Advisory, Conciliation & Arbitration Service, 11–12 St. James's Sq., SW1. 01-214 6000 **1A 50**
Agricultural & Food Research Council, 160 Gt. Portland St., W1. 01-580 6655 **1C 17**
Agriculture, Fisheries & Food, Min. of, Whitehall Pl., SW1. 01-233 3000 **1C 51**
Arts Council, 105 Piccadilly, W1. 01-629 9495 **3D 33**
Associated British Ports, 150 Holborn, EC1. 01-430 1177 **3C 21**
Bank of England, Threadneedle St., EC2. 01-601 4444 **1A 40**
Boundaries Commission, St. Catherines Ho., Kingsway, WC2. 01-242 0262 **1A 36**
British Aerospace, Brooklands Rd,. Weybridge 0932 53444
British Airports Authority, Gatwick Airport, West Sussex. 0293 517755
British Airways, H.Q., Speedbird Ho., Heathrow Airport, Middx. 01-759 5511
British Broadcasting Corp., Portland Pl., W1. 01-580 4468 **3C 17**
British Coal, Hobart Ho., Grosvenor Pl., SW1. 01-235 2020 **1B 62**
British Council, 10 Spring Gdns., SW1. 01-930 8466 **1C 51**
British Gas Corporation, Rivermill Ho., 152 Grosvenor Rd., SW1. 01-821 1444 **AZ 6F 77**
British Railways Board, Euston Sq., PO Box 100, NW1. 01-262 3232 **3A 10**
British Shipbuilders, 136 Sandyford Rd., Newcastle upon Tyne. 326772
British Standards Institution, 2 Park St., W1. 01-629 9000 **2D 31**
British Steel Corporation, 9 Albert Embankment, SE1. 01-735 7654 **3D 65**
British Technology Group, 101, Newington Causeway, SE1. 01-403 6666 **AZ 7L 147**
British Telecom, 81 Newgate St., EC1. 01-356 5000 **1B 38**
British Tourist Authority, Thames Tower, Blacks Rd., W6. 01-846 9000 **AZ 4E 74**
British Waterways Board, Melbury Ho., Melbury Ter., NW1. 01-262 6711 **1B 14**
Britoil, 150 Vincent St., Glasgow. 041 204 2525
Cabinet Office, 70 Whitehall, SW1. 01-233 3000 **2C 51**
Cable Authority, 38/44 Gillingham St., SW1. 01-821 6161 **2C 63**
Central Electricity Generating Board, Sudbury Ho., 15 Newgate St., EC1. 01-634 5111 **1B 38**
Central Office of Information, Hercules Rd., SE1. 01-928 2345 **1C 67**
Central Public Health Laboratory, 61 Colindale Av., NW9. 01-200 4400 **AZ 3K 25**
Charity Commission, 14 Ryder St., SW1. 01-214 6000 **1D 49**
Church Commissioners, 1 Millbank, SW1. 01-222 7010 **1D 65**
Civil Aviation Authority, CAA Ho., 45 Kingsway, WC2. 01-379 7311 **1A 36**
Civil Service Commission, Alencon Link, Basingstoke. 0256 29222
College of Arms, Queen Victoria St., EC4. 01-248 2762 **2B 38**
Commissioner for Local Administration, Ombudsman (In England), 21 Queen Anne's Gate, SW1. 01-222 5622 **3B 50**

Commission for Racial Equality, Elliot Ho., 10/12 Allington St., SW1. 01-828 7022 **1C 63**

Commonwealth Secretariat, Marlborough House, Pall Mall. 01-839 8411 **1A 50**

Countryside Commission, Crescent Pl., Cheltenham, Glos. 0242 521381

Criminal Injuries Compensation Board, 19 Alfred Pl., WC1. 01-631 4467 **2A 18**

Crown Estate Commisioners, 13 Carlton Ho. Ter., SW1. 01-214 6000 **1B 50**

Customs & Excise, H.M., Kings Beam Ho., Mark La., EC3. 01-626 1515 **2B 40**

Data Protection Registrar, Springfield Ho., Water La., Wilmslow, Cheshire. 0625 535777

Defence, Ministry of, Whitehall, SW1. 01-218 9000 **2D 51**

Design Council, 28 Haymarket, SW1. 01-839 8000 **3B 34**

Development Commission, 11 Cowley St., SW1. 01-222 9134 **1C 65**

Duchy of Cornwall, 10 Buckingham Ga., SW1. 01-834 7346 **3C 49**

Duchy of Lancaster, Lancaster Pl., Strand, WC2. 01-836 8277 **3D 35**

Education & Science, Dept. of, Elizabeth Ho., York Rd., SE1. 01-934 9000 **2B 52**

Electricity Council, 30 Millbank, SW1. 01-834 2333 **3D 65**

Employment, Dept. of, Caxton Ho., Tothill St., SW1. 01-213 3000 **3B 50**

Energy, Dept. of, Thames Ho. S., Millbank, SW1. 01-211 3000 **2D 65**

English Heritage. See Historic Buildings & Monuments Comm.

Environment, Dept. of, 2 Marsham St., SW1. 01-212 3434 **1B 64**

Equal Opportunities Commission, 1 Bedford St., WC2. 01-379 6323 **2D 35**

European Parliament Information Office, 2 Queen Anne's Ga., SW1. 01-222 0411 **3B 50**

Export Credits Guarantee Dept., Aldermanbury Ho., Aldermanbury, EC2. 01-382 7000 **1C 39**

Foreign & Commonwealth Office, Downing St., SW1. 01-233 3000 **2C 51**

Forestry Commission,231 Corstorphine Rd., Edinburgh. 031-334 0303

Friendly Societies, Registry of, 15–17 Gt. Marlborough St., W1. 01-437 9992 **1D 33**

Gaming Board, 163–173 High Holborn, WC1. 01-240 0821 **3A 20**

General Register Office, see Population Censuses and Surveys

Government Actuary's Dept., 22 Kingsway WC2. 01-242 6868 **1A 36**

Government Chemist, Laboratory of the (*Dept. of Trade & Industry*), Cornwall Ho., Stamford St., SE1. 01-928 7900 **1C 53**

Health Service Commissioner, Ombudsman, Church Ho., Gt. Smith St., SW1. 01-212 7676 **1C 65**

Health & Social Security Dept., Alexander Fleming Ho., Elephant & Castle, SE1. 01-407 5522 **AZ 8K 147**

Historic Buildings & Monuments Commission for England (English Heritage), 23 Saville Row, W1. 01-734 6010 **2D 33**

Home Office, 50 Queen Anne's Gate, SW1. 01-213 3000 **3A 50**

Houses of Parliament, SW1 **3D 51.** General Information 01-219 3000. Parliamentary Information; *Commons* 01-219 4272, *Lords* 01-219 3107

Housing Corporation, 149 Tottenham Court Rd., W1. 01-387 9466 **1D 17**

Industry, Dept. of, See Trade & Industry

Inland Revenue, Somerset Ho., Strand, WC2. 01-438 6622 **2A 36**

Inner London Education Authority, County Hall, SE1 01-633 5000 **2A 33**

Land Registry, H.M., Lincoln's Inn Fields, WC2. 01-405 3488 **1B 36**

Law Commission, 37/38 John St., WC1. 01-242 0861 **1B 20**

Law Officers' Dept., Attorney-General's Chambers, Ryl. Courts of Justice, WC2. 01-405 7641

London Docklands Development Corp., West India Ho., Millwall Dock, E4. 01-515 3000 **AZ 3C 80**

London Fire and Civil Defence Authority, Albert Embankment, SE1. 01-582 3811 **2A 66**

London Residuary Body, St. Vincents Ho., 30 Orange St., WC2. 01-930 0613 **3B 34**

Lord Chancellor's Department, House of Lords, Houses of Parliament, SW1. 01-219 3000 **3D 51**

Management & Personnel Office, Whitehall, SW1. 01-273 3000 **2C 51**

Manpower Services Commission, Selkirk Ho., 166 High Holborn, WC1. 01-836 1213 **3C 19**

Medical Research Council, 20 Park Cres., W1. 01-636 5422 **1B 16**

Monopolies Commission, New Ct., 48 Carey St., WC2. 01-831 6111 **1B 36**

Museums and Galleries Commission, 2 Carlton Gardens, SW1. 01-930 0995 **1A 50**

National Audit Office, Audit House, Victoria Embankment, EC4. 01-353 8901 **2D 37**

National Bus Company, 172 Buckingham Pal. Rd., SW1. 01-730 3453 **3B 62**

National Consumer Council, 18 Queen Anne's Ga., SW1. 01-222 9501 **3B 50**

National Economic Development Office, Millbank Tower, 21 Millbank, SW1. 01-211 6998 **3D 65**

National Freight Co., Ltd. 45 St. Peters St., Bedford. 67444

National Savings, Dept. for,375 Kensington High St., W14. 01-603 2000 **AZ 3H 75**

National Trust, 36 Queen Anne's Ga., SW1. 01-222 9251 **3A 50**

National Water Council, 1 Queen Anne's Gate, SW1. 01-222 8111 **3B 50**

Natural Environment Research Council. Polaris Ho., North Star Av., Swindon. 40101

Nature Conservancy, Northminster Ho., Peterborough 0733 40345

Northern Ireland Office, Whitehall, SW1. 01-233 3000 **3C 51**

Office of Arts & Libraries, St. George St., SW1. 01-233 3073 **3C 51**

Office of Fair Trading, Field Ho., Breams Bldgs., EC4. 01-242 2858 **1C 37**

Office of Telecommunications, 50 Holborn Viaduct, EC1. 01-353 4020 **3A 22**

Ordnance Survey, Romsey Rd., Maybush, Southampton. 775555

Overseas Development Admin., Eland Ho., Stag Pl., SW1. 01-213 3000 **1C 63**

Parliamentary Commissioner for Administration, Ombudsman, Church Ho., Gt. Smith St., SW1. 01-212 7676 **1C 65**

Passport Office, Clive Ho., Petty France, SW1. 01-213 3434 **3A 50**

Patent Office, 25 Southampton Bldgs., Chancery Lane, WC2. 01-405 8721 **3C 21**

Paymaster General, Southerland Ho., Russell Way, Crawley. 27833

Pensions Appeal Tribunals, St. Dunstan's Ho., Fetter La., EC4. 01-404 4954 **1C 37**

Police Complaints Dept., 10 Gt. George St., SW1. 01-213 5392 **3C 51**

Population Censuses and Surveys, St. Catherine's Ho., 10 Kingsway, WC2. 01-242 0262 **1A 36**

Port of London Authority, Leslie Ford Ho., Tilbury Docks, Essex. 03752 3444

Post Office, 33 Grosvenor Pl., SW1. 01-235 8000 **3A 48**

Privy Council Office, 68 Whitehall, SW1. 01-233 3000 **2C 51**

Public Prosecutions, Director of, 4–12 Queen Anne's Ga., SW1. 01-213 3000 **3B 50**

Public Record Office, Chancery Lane, WC2. 01-405 0741 **1C 37.** Ruskin Ave., Kew. 01-876 3444 **AZ 1D 73**

Public Trustee Office, 24 Kingsway WC2. 01-405 4300 **1A 36**

Royal Mint, Llantrisant, Pontyclun, Mid Glamorgan. Llantrisant. 222111

Science Research Council, as for Natural Environment Research Co.,

Scottish Office, Dover Ho., Whitehall, SW1. 01-233 3000 **2C 51**

Stationery Office, H.M. *Head Office,* St. Crispins, Duke St., Norwich 0603 622211. *Shop,* 49 High Holborn, WC1. 01-211 5656 **3B 20**

Trade and Industry, Dept. of, 1 Victoria St., SW1. 01-215 7877 **3B 50**

Transport, Dept of, 2 Marsham St., SW1. 01-212 3434 **2B 64**

Treasury, Her Majesty's, Parliament St., SW1. 01-233 3000 **3C 51**

Trinity House, Corporation of, Trinity Ho., Tower Hill, EC3. 01-480 6601 **2C 41**

United Kingdom Atomic Energy Authority, 11 Charles II St., SW1. 01-930 5454 **3B 34**
United Nations Information Centre, Ship Ho., 20 Buckingham Ga., SW1. 01-630 1981 **3C 49**
Welsh Office, Gwydyr Ho., Whitehall, SW1. 01-233 3000 **2C 51**

HEALTH AND BEAUTY

MEDICHECK. *A 45 minute private examination of your physical condition by experienced doctor: Marie Stopes House, 108 Whitfield St., W1. 01-388 2585* **2A 18**

CENTRAL BATHING, SAUNA, HOT BATHS AND TURKISH BATHS
Note: Pools usually close earlier during winter months
Chelsea Sports Centre, Chelsea Manor St., SW3. 01-352 6985 **AZ 5C 76**
Swimming Classes for mothers and infants, beginners five to sixteen years, adults and also competitive training. Pool open from 08.30 Daily. Also Hot Baths and Sauna.
Dolphin Square Sports Centre, Grosvenor Rd., SW1. 01-828 1681 **AZ 5G 77**
Swimming Pool, 12.00–21.00. Sat. and Sun. 09.00–18.00.
Kensington Sports Centre, Walmer Rd., SW11. 01-727 9923 **AZ 7G 59**
Main pool and learner pool open daily; Sun. am only. Also Multi-gym; Solarium, Hot Baths.
Marshall St. Leisure Complex, Marshall St., W1. 01-439 4678 **1D 33**
Swimming from 08.30, Sat. from 09.00. Closed Sun. Also swimming classes, keep fit.
Oasis Sports Centre, 32 Endell St., WC2. 01-836 9555 **1C 35**
Indoor and heated outdoor pool open daily. Sun. am only. (Outdoor summer only). Also swimming classes; sauna.
Porchester Centre, Queensway, W2. 01-798 3689 **1D 27**
Swimming pool open daily, closed Sun. Baths and showers, also Turkish and Russian baths at various times.
Queen Mother Sports Centre, Vauxhall Bri. Rd., SW1. 01-798 2125 **2D 63**
Swimming and diving pools open daily.
Seymour Leisure Centre, Bryanston Pl., W1. 01-798 1421 **3B 14**
Swimming; sauna and jacuzzi; also steam baths. Closed Sun.
Swiss Cottage Sports Centre, Avenue Rd., NW3. 01-278 4444 **AZ 7B 44**
Main pool and learner pool open daily.

BEAUTY SALONS AND SPECIALISTS
Aromatherapy Clinic, 4a William St., SW1. 01-235 4106 **3C 47**
Health and Beauty treatments for face and body based on Neuromuscular therapy, using natural oils and herbs. By appointment 09.30–17.30 Mon. to Fri. Products on sale.
Beauchamp Beauty Clinic, 42 Beauchamp Pl., SW3. 01-589 1853 **1B 60**
The health and beauty specialists of Knightsbridge. Open 09.00–18.00 Tues., Wed., Fri. to 20.00 Mon. & Thurs.
Body Shop, Unit 13, The Market, Covent Garden, WC2. 01-836 2183 **2D 35**
Large and distinctive range of own make natural cosmetics, perfumes, skin and beauty products; includes men's own range and vegan recommended products. Mail order available. Also at 32/34 Gt. Marlborough St., W1.; 203 Kensington High St., W8. and many other branches.
Crabtree & Evelyn, 6 Kensington Church St., W8. 01-937 9335 **2C 43**
Good range of naturally based toiletries alongside traditional food products. Mail order and gift wrapping services. 09.30–18.00 Mon. to Sat.
Culpeper, 21 Bruton St., W1. 01-629 4559 **3C 33**
Herbalists—Herbal Remedies, Medicinal Herbs, Culinary Herbs, Herbal

Cosmetics, Pot Pourri. Mail order service. Open 09.30–17.30 Mon. to Sat. Also at 9 Flask Walk, NW3. **AZ 4A 44** & The Market, Covent Garden WC2. **2D 35**
Floris, 89 Jermyn St., SW1. 01-930 2885 **3A 34**
Perfumers to the Court of St. James since George IV, specializes in exclusive products for men.
Joan Price's Face Place, 33 Cadogan St., SW3. 01-589 9062 **3B 60**
All facial and body beauty treatments, specialists in facial make-up. Free use and advice about different leading brands, no appointment Mon. to Fri. Private make-up sessions by appointment 10.00–18.00 Mon. to Fri. Connaught St. branch 10.00–18.00 Mon. to Fri. 10.00–17.00 Sat. **1B 30**
Katherine Corbett, Second Floor, 21 South Molton St., W1. 01-629 2210 **1B 32**
Skin specialist. Free advice on the care of problem skin. Own range of skin care cosmetics.
Penhaligons, 41 Wellington St., WC2. 01-836 4973 **2A 36**
For traditional handmade fragrances and toilet waters. Also at 28a Brook St., W1. **2B 32** and Burlington Arcade, W1. **3D 33**
Taylor of London, 179 Sloane St., SW1. 01-235 4653 **3C 47**
Exclusive range of own perfumes for both sexes, also toiletries, pot pourri etc. Perfumers since 1887.

HAIRDRESSERS

Most large Department Stores have hairdressing salons. Kensington High St., Knightsbridge, Brompton and Kings Roads all have many salons. For reduced rates or a free service most salons have a students evening. Here are a few of the more well known.

Andre Bernard, 41 Knightsbridge, SW1. 01-235 6851 **3C 47**
Hairdressing, beautician, pedicure, manicure. Mon. to Fri. 09.00–17.30, 12.30 Sat.
Crimpers, 80a Baker St., W1. 01-486 4522 **2D 15**
Unisex, by appointment. Mon. to Fri. 09.30–17.30; to 20.00 Thurs.; 09.00–17.00 Sat. Also at 63/67 Heath St., NW6. 01-794 0262 appts as above. 231 Brompton Rd., SW3. 01-584 3671 appts as above except to 20.00 Wed. not Thurs.
Leonard, 6 Upper Grosvenor St., W1. 01-629 5757 **2D 31**
Female hairdressing. Mon. to Sat. 09.00–17.00.
Michaeljohn, 23a Albemarle St., W1. **3C 33**. 01-629 6969 (M), 01-499 7529 (F). Hairdressing, manicure and pedicure. Mon. to Sat. 09.00–18.00.
Ricci Burns, 94 George St., W1. 01-935 3657 **1B 30**
Unisex, by appointment. 09.00–17.00, 11.50 Sat.
Sweeny's, 48 Beauchamp Pl., SW3. 01-589 3066 7 **1B 60**
Male and female, by appointment. 10.00–18.00, Sat. 16.00.
Trumper, 9 Curzon St., W1. 01-499 1850 **1B 48**
Male, by appointment 09.00–17.00, 12.00 Sat.
Vidal Sassoon, 130 Sloane St., SW1. 01-730 7288 **3C 47**
Hairdressing for women. Hair treatments, manicure. 09.00–16.30 Mon., Tues., Wed., Sat. 17.00 Thurs. and Fri. Also at 60 S. Moulton St., W1. 01-491 8848 **1B 32**, 44 Sloane St., SW1 01-235 7791 **3C 47** and 11 Floral St., WC2 **2C 35**
Hairdressing for men 44 Sloane St., SW1. 01-235 1957, 56 Brook St., W1. 01-493 5428 **2A 32** and 11 Floral St., WC2. 01-240 9635 **2C 35**

HEALTH AND PHYSICAL CULTURE CLUBS AND CENTRES

City Gymnasium, New Union St. (Tenter St.), EC2. 01-628 0786 **2D 23**
Fitness and rehabilitation. Gymnasium open Men, 09.30–17.45 Mon., Wed., Fri., 08.00–12.00 Tues., Thurs. Women, 12.30–17.45 Tues., Thurs. Postal address Britannic Ho., Moor Lane, EC2.
Dave Prowse's Fitness Centre, 12 Marshalsea Rd., SE1. 01-407 5650 **2C 55**
Two fully equipped weight training gyms, providing keep fit, bodybuilding, weight reduction and gaining, sports training, pre-ski routines, sunbeds. Open 09.30–21.00 Mon. to Fri. Free trials before joining.

Edward Sturges Gymnasium, 106 Pavilion Rd., SW1. 01-235 4234 **1C 61**
Gymnasium open daily for men, women and children.
Lucas-Tooth Gymnasium, Heathcote St., WC1. 01-837 9851 **AZ 4K 61**
General fitness classes 18.00 Mon. to Thurs. Games Players classes including
circuit training 18.00 Tues. & Wed. Specialists in training P.E. Instructors.
Ravelle's Health Club, Portsea Pl., W2. 01-402 7684 **1B 30**
Fitness, toning, sauna, slimming, weight training. Separate facilities for men and
women. Open 10.30–21.00 Mon. to Fri., 18.00 Sat. Also at 52 Brunswick
Centre, WC1. 01-278 2754 **1D 19**
Sanctuary, The, 11 Floral St., WC2. 01-240 9635 **2D 35**
Health Club for Women with tropical indoor setting. Swimming pool, sauna, steam
room, solarium etc., beauty treatments. Open 10.00–22.00 Mon. to Fri; to 18.00 Sat;
12.00–20.00 Sun.
Town and Country Health and Beauty Salon, 2 Yeoman's Row, SW3. 01-584
7702 **1A 60** Every aspect of health and beauty treatment for Ladies. Figure,
facial, manicure, pedicure. Also yoga, keep fit, steam cabinets, sauna, showers.
Membership and single treatments. Open 10.00–21.00 Mon. to Fri.
Westside Health Centre, 201 Kensington High St., W8. 01-937 5386 **3B 42**
Individual and group keep fit, dance classes for men and women. All beauty
treatments, facial and body. Gymnasium, sauna, suntanning, rest rooms,
restaurant. Open 08.00–21.00 Mon. to Sat. 10.30–16.30 Sun.
Yoga Centre, 13 Hampstead Hill Gdns., NW3. 01-794 4119 **AZ 4B 44**
Basic all-round training in Yoga under the direction of Sri Nandi, established 1948.
Personal appointments 10.00–17.00 Mon. to Fri. Evening classes 19.00–20.00
Tues., Wed.

HOSPITALS

For Emergency Casualties see page 204.

BLOOD TRANSFUSION SERVICES (National), ring for details
City Centre: Moor Ho., London Wall, EC2. 01-628 4590
N.E London Area: Crescent Dri., Brentwood, Essex. Brentwood 223545
N.W. London Area: N. London Blood Transfusion Centre, Deansbrook Rd.,
Edgware,   Middx. 01-952 5511
S.E. & S.W. London Areas: S. London Blood Transfusion Centre, 75 Cranmer Terr.,
   SW17. 01-672 8501
West End Centre: 26 Margaret St., W1. 01-580 8772

CHEST RADIOGRAPHY (chest X-ray) SERVICES, ring for details
N.E. London Area: 118 Hermon Hill, E18. 01-530 4510
N.W. London Area: by referral through GP only
S.E. London Area: New Cross Hosp. Avonley Rd., SE14. 01-639 4380
S.W. London Area: by referral through GP only

Acton, Gunnersbury La., W3. 01-992 2277 **AZ 2G 73**
Albert Dock Seamen's, Alnwick Rd., E16. 01-476 2234 **AZ 6A 66**
Aldersbrook Unit, Aldersbrook Rd., Wanstead, E11. 01-989 7776 **AZ 2K 49**
All Saints, Austral St., Southwark, SE11. 01-828 9811 **2D 67**
Angas Home, Cudham, Sevenoaks, Kent. Biggin Hill 72003
Arrazi, 29–31 Devonshire St., W1. 01-486 7131 **2A 16**
Athlone House (Caenwood), Hampstead La., N6. 01-348 5231 **AZ 1B 44**
Atkinson Morley's, Copse Hill, Wimbledon, SW20. 01-946 7711 **AZ 1C 120**
Avenue Clinic, 12 Avenue Rd., NW8. 01-722 7131 **AZ 7B 44**
Barking, Upney La., Barking, Essex. 01-594 3898 **AZ 6J 51**
Barnes, South Worple Way, SW14. 01-878 4981 **AZ 3K 89**
Barnet General, Wellhouse La., Barnet, Herts. 01-440 5111 **AZ 4A 4**

Bearsted Memorial, Lordship Rd., N16. 01-802 1189 **AZ 1D 46**
Beckenham, 379 Croydon Rd., Beckenham, Kent. 01-650 0125 **AZ 4K 125**
Beckenham Maternity, Stone Park Av., Beckenham, Kent. 01-650 2213 **AZ 4C 126**
Belgrave Hosp. for Children, Clapham Rd., SW9. 01-274 6222 **AZ 3J 93**
Bethlem Royal, The, Monks Orchard Rd., Eden Park, Beckenham, Kent. 01-777 6611 **AZ 1C 136**
Bethnal Green, Cambridge Heath Rd., E2. 01-980 3413 **AZ 4K 143**
Bexley, Old Bexley La., Bexley, Kent. Crayford 526282
Bolingbroke, Wandsworth Common, SW11. 01-223 7411 **AZ 5A 92**
Bowden House Clinic, London Rd., Harrow-on-the-Hill, Middx. 01-864 0221 **AZ 2J 39**
Bowley Private Clinic, Ladbroke Terr., W11. 01-221 1040 **3A 26**
Brentford, Boston Manor Rd., Brentford Middx. 01-560 3930 **AZ 4B 72**
British Home & Hosp. for Incurables, Crown La., Streatham, SW16. 01-670 8261 **AZ 5A 110**
British Hospital for Mothers & Babies, Samuel St. Woolwich, SE18. 01-854 8016 **AZ 4D 82**
Bromley, Cromwell Av., Bromley, Kent. 01-460 9933 **AZ 4K 127**
Brompton Hospital, Fulham Rd., SW3. 01-352 8121 **3D 59**
Brook General, Shooter's Hill Rd., Woolwich, SE18. 01-856 5555 **AZ 1F 97**
Brookside Young Peoples, Barley La., Ilford, Essex. 01-559 5188 **AZ 7A 36**
Broomhills, Old Bexley Lane, Bexley, Kent. Crayford 526282
Cane Hill, Coulsdon, Surrey. Downland 52221
Carshalton, Beddington & Wallington District (*War Memorial*), The Park, Carshalton, Surrey. 01-647 5534 **AZ 6D 132**
Cassel Hosp. for Functional Nervous Disorders, Ham Common, Richmond, Surrey. 01-940 8181/4 **AZ 4D 104**
Castlewood Day, 25 Shooter's Hill, SE18. 01-856 4970 **AZ 1E 98**
Central Middlesex, Acton La., NW10. 01-965 5733 **AZ 3J 57**
Chadwell Heath, Grove Rd., Romford, Essex. 01-599 3007 **AZ 5B 36**
Charing Cross see **New Charing Cross.**
Charter Clinic, 1/5 Radnor Walk, SW3. 01-351 1272 **AZ 5C 76**
Chase Farm (Enfield District), The Ridgeway, Enfield, Middx. 01-366 6600 **AZ 2G 7**
Cheam, London Rd., North Cheam, Sutton, Surrey. 01-337 4488 **AZ 2E 130**
Chelsea Hosp. for Women, Dovehouse St., SW3. 01-352 6446 **AZ 9B 144**
Chepstow Lodge, 6 Chepstow Pl., W2. 01-727 3531 **2C 27**
Cheyne, Woodland Way, West Wickham, Kent. 01-777 1955 **AZ 4D 136**
Cheyne Spastics Centre, 61 Cheyne Wlk., SW3. 01-352 8434 **AZ 7B 76**
Child Guidance Training Centre, 120 Belsize La., NW3. 01-435 7111 **AZ 6B 44**
Children's, 321 Sydenham Rd., SE26. 01-778 7031 **AZ 4J 111**
Chingford, Larkshall Rd., Chingford, E4. 01-529 7141/2/3 **AZ 5K 19**
Chiswick, Netheravon Rd., W4. 01-994 1124 **AZ 4B 74**
Churchill Clinic, 80 Lambeth Rd., SE1. 01-928 5633 **2A 66**
City of London Maternity, Hanley Rd., N4. 01-272 5441 **AZ 1J 45**
Claybury, Woodford Bridge, Woodford Green, Essex. 01-504 7171
Clayponds, Occupation La., W5. 01-560 4011 **AZ 4D 72**
Clementine Churchill, Sudbury Hill, Harrow, Middx. 01-422 3464 **AZ 3J 39**
Colindale, Colindale Av., NW9. 01-200 1555 **AZ 3K 25**
Coppetts Wood, Coppetts Rd., Muswell Hill, N10. 01-883 9792 **AZ 7J 15**
Cromwell, Cromwell Rd., SW5. 01-370 4233 **AZ 8A 144**
Croydon General, London Rd., Croydon, Surrey. 01-688 7755 **AZ 1K 123**
Cumberland, Whitford Gdns., Mitcham, Surrey. 01-648 1144 **AZ 3D 122**
Dagenham, Rainham Road South, Dagenham, Essex. 01-592 0034
Devonshire, 29 Devonshire St., W1. 01-486 7131 **2A 16**
Dispensaire Francais, 2 Osnaburgh St., NW1. 01-387 5132 **1C 17**
Dulwich, E. Dulwich Gro , SE22. 01-693 3377 **AZ 5E 94**

Dunoran Home, 4 Park Farm Rd., Bromley, Kent. 01-467 3701 **AZ 1B 128**
Ealing, Uxbridge Rd., Southall, Middx. 01-574 2444 **AZ 2G 71**
Eastern, Homerton Gro., Homerton, E9. 01-985 1193 **AZ 5K 47**
East Ham Memorial, Shrewsbury Rd., Forest Gate, E7. 01-472 3322 **AZ 5B 50**
Eastman Dental, Gray's Inn Rd., WC1. 01-837 7251 **AZ 2E 140**
East Roding District, see Barking, Chadwell Heath or King George
Edenhall, 11 Lyndhurst Gdns., Hampstead, NW3. 01-794 0066 **AZ 5B 44**
Edgware General, Burnt Oak, Edgware, Middx. 01-952 2381 **AZ 7C 12**
Elizabeth Garrett Anderson, 144 Euston Rd., NW1. 01-387 2501 **2B 10**
Elstree Private, Green St., Shenley, Herts. 01-953 6941
Eltham & Mottingham, Passey Pl., Eltham, SE9. 01-850 2611 **AZ 6D 98**
Enfield District (Chase Farm), The Ridgeway, Enfield. 01-366 6000 **AZ 2G 7**
Erith & District, Park Cres., Erith, Kent. Erith 30161
Evelina Children's, Southwark Bri. Rd., SE1. 01-407 4747 **2B 54**
Farnborough, Farnborough Common, Orpington, Kent. Farnborough 53333
Finchley Memorial, Granville Rd., Finchley, N12. 01-349 3121 **AZ 7F 15**
Fitzroy Nuffield, 10/12 Bryanston Sq., W1. 01-723 1288 **3C 15**
Forest, Roebuck La., Buckhurst Hill, Essex. 01-504 2285 **AZ 1F 21**
Forest Gate, Forest La., Forest Gate, E7. 01-534 5064 **AZ 5G 49**
Friern, Friern Barnet Rd., New Southgate, N11. 01-368 1288 **AZ 5J 15**
Fulham see **New Charing Cross.**
Galsworthy House, Kingston Hill, Kingston-upon-Thames, Surrey. 01-549 9861
AZ 1G 119
Garden Clinic, The, 46 Sunny Gardens Rd., NW4. 01-203 0111 **AZ 2D 26**
Gardiner Hill Unit, Burnwood La., SW17. 01-767 4626 **AZ 3A 108**
German, Ritson Rd., Dalston, E8. 01-254 5202 **AZ 6G 47**
Goldie Leigh, Lodge Hill, Welling, SE2. 01-311 9161 **AZ 6B 84**
Goodmayes, Barley La., Ilford, Essex. 01-590 6060 **AZ 5A 36**
Gordon, 126 Vauxhall Bri. Rd., SW1. 01-828 9811 **3A 64**
Greentrees, Tottenhall Rd., N13. 01-889 1041 **AZ 6F 17**
Greenwich District, Vanbrugh Hill, Greenwich, SE10. 01-858 8141 **AZ 6H 81**
Grove Park, Marvels La., Lee, SE12. 01-857 1191 **AZ 2K 113**
Guy's, Saint Thomas St., SE1. 01-407 7600 **1A 56 & 2D 55**
Guy's Dental, Hospital & School; as above
Hackney, Homerton High St., E9. 01-985 5555 **AZ 5K 47**
Halliwick House see **Friern Hospital.**
Hammersmith, Du Cane Rd., Shepherd's Bush, W12. 01-743 2030 **AZ 6B 58**
Harefield, Harefield, Middx. Harefield 3737
Harestone, Harestone Drive, Caterham, Surrey. Caterham 42226
Harley Street Clinic, 35 Weymouth St., W1. 01-935 7700 **2B 16**
Harold Wood, Gubbins La., Harold Wood, Essex. Ingrebourne 45533
Harrow, Roxeth Hill, Harrow, Middx. 01-864 5432 **AZ 2H 39**
Harts, Woodford Green, Essex. 01-504 7244/5 **AZ 5D 20**
Hayes Cottage, Grange Rd., Hayes, Middx. 01-573 2052
Henderson, 2 Homeland Drive, Sutton, Surrey. 01-661 1611
Hendon District, 357 Hendon Way, NW4. 01-202 4511 **AZ 6D 26**
Hereford Lodge, Hereford Rd., W2. 01-727 3531 **1C 27**
Highbury Home, 1 Highbury Ter., Highbury, N5. 01-226 2938 **AZ 5B 46**
Hillingdon, Hillingdon, Uxbridge, Middx. Uxbridge 38282
Hither Green, Hither Green Lane, SE13. 01-698 4611 **AZ 5E 96**
Holly House Private, High Rd., Buckhurst Hill, Essex. 01-505 6425 **AZ 2E 20**
Homeopathic, see Royal London Homeopathic
Hornsey Central, Park Rd., Crouch End, N8. 01-340 6244 **AZ 4G 29**
Hosp. for Sick Children, The, Gt. Ormond St., WC1. 01-405 9200 **1A 20**
Hosp. for Tropical Diseases, 4 St. Pancras Way, NW1. 01-387 4411 **AZ 7G 45**
Hosp. for Women, The, Soho Sq., W1. 01-580 7928 **1B 34**
Hostel for Deaf Children, 6 Castlebar Hill, Ealing, W5. 01-997 8480 **AZ 5C 56**
Hosp. of St. John & St. Elizabeth, 60 Grove End Rd., NW8. 01-286 5126 **1C 5**

Hostel for Deaf Children & Mothers, 8 Castlebar Hill, Ealing, W5. 01-997 0134 **AZ 5C 56**
Hostel of God, 29–32 North Side, Clapham Comm., SW4. 01-622 5343 **AZ 4E 92**
Hounslow (Nurses Home), Bath Rd., Hounslow, Middx. 01-570 2486 **AZ 1A 86**
Humana Hospital, Wellington Pl., NW8. 01-586 5959 **2D 5**
Ilford Maternity, Eastern Av., Ilford, Essex. 01-554 8811 **AZ 6H 35**
Invalid & Crippled Children's, Balaam St., Plaistow, E13. 01-472 1131 **AZ 4J 65**
Inverforth House, North End Way, Hampstead, NW3. 01-455 6601/4 **AZ 2A 44**
Italian, Queen Sq., WC1. 01-831 6961 **2D 19**
Jewish Home & Hosp. at Tottenham, The, 295 High Rd., South Tottenham, N15. 01-800 5138 **AZ 4F 31**
Jubilee, Woodford Green, Essex. 01-504 8891 **AZ 5D 20**
King Edward VII's Hosp. for Officers, Beaumont Ho., Beaumont St., W1. 01-486 4411 **2A 16**
King George, Eastern Av., Ilford, Essex. 01-554 8811 **AZ 6H 35**
Kingsbury, Honeypot La., NW9. 01-204 2292 **AZ 7J 11**
King's College, Denmark Hill, SE5. 01-274 6222 **AZ 4D 94**
King's College Dental, Hospital & School as above
Kingston, Galsworthy Rd., Kingston-upon-Thames, Surrey. 01-546 7111 **AZ 1H 119**
Lambeth, Brook Dri., Kennington Rd., SE11. 01-735 8141 **2D 67**
Langthorne, Leytonstone, E11. 01-539 5511 **AZ 4F 49**
Leamington Park, Wales Farm Rd., Acton, W3. 01-992 8632 **AZ 5K 57**
Leigham Clinic, The Lodge, 76 Leigham Ct. Rd., SW16. 01-677 1241 **AZ 2J 109**
Lennard, Lennard Rd., Bromley Common, Bromley, Kent. 01-460 9933
Lewisham, High St., Lewisham, SE13. 01-690 4311 **AZ 6D 96**
Leytonstone House, High Rd., Leytonstone, E11. 01-989 7701/4 **AZ 6G 49**
London, The (*Whitechapel*), Whitechapel Rd., E1. 01-247 5454 **AZ 6G 143**
See also **Mile End Hosp.** and **St. Clements Hosp.**
London Bridge Hospital, Tooley St., SE1. 01-407 3100 **1A 56**
London Chest, Bonner Rd., E2. 01-980 4433 **AZ 2J 63**
London Clinic, The, 20 Devonshire Pl., W1. 01-935 4444 **1A 16**
London Clinic of Psycho-Analysis, 63 New Cavendish St., W1. 01-580 4952/3/4 **2B 16**
London Foot, 33 Fitzroy Sq., W1. 01-636 0602 **1D 17**
London Hosp. Dental Institute, Stepney Way, E1. 01-247 5454 **AZ 6J 143**
London Jewish, Stepney Grn., E1. 01-790 1222 **AZ 5M 143**
Lugano, 3 Powell Rd., Buckhurst Hill, Essex, 01-504 7611 **AZ 1F 21**
Maida Vale Hosp. for Nervous Diseases, 4 Maida Vale, W9. 01-286 5172 **3B 4**
Manor, Christchurch Rd., Epsom, Surrey. Epsom 26291
Manor House, North End Rd., Golders Green, NW11. 01-455 6601/4 **AZ 1J 43**
Marlborough, 38 Marlborough Pl., NW8. 01-624 8605 **AZ 2A 60**
Maudsley, The, Denmark Hill, SE5. 01-703 6333 **AZ 4D 94**
Mayday, Mayday Rd., Thornton Heath, Surrey. 01-684 6999 **AZ 6B 124**
Medical Rehabilitation Centre, 152 Camden Rd., NW1. 01-485 1124 **AZ 7G 45**
Memorial, Shooter's Hill, Woolwich, SE18. 01-856 5511 **AZ 1F 97**
Metropolitan, Kingsland Rd., E8. 01-254 6862 **AZ 3E 62**
Metropolitan Ear, Nose & Throat, Saint Mary Abbots Hosp., Marloes Rd., W8. 01-937 8181 **AZ 3K 75**
Middlesex, The, Mortimer St., W1. 01-636 8333 **3D 17**
Mildmay Mission, Hackney Rd., E2. 01-739 2331 **AZ 3F 63**
Mile End (London Hospital), Bancroft Rd., E1. 01-980 4855 **AZ 3K 63**
Molesey, High St., East Molesey, Surrey. 01-979 5060
Moorfields Eye, City Rd., EC1. 01-253 3411 **AZ 2B 62**
Moorfields Eye, High Holborn Branch, WC1. 01-836 6611 **1D 35**
Morris Markowe Unit, Kingston Rd., New Maldon, Surrey. 01-942 0779 **AZ 3H 119**
Mothers' (*Salvation Army*), Lower Clapton Rd., E5. 01-985 6661 **AZ 3H 47**

Mottingham, see **Eltham**
Mount Pleasant, North Rd., Southall, Middx. 01-574 1394 **AZ 7E 54**
Mount Vernon & The Radium Institute, Northwood, Middx. Northwood 26111
National, The, Queen Sq., Bloomsbury, WC1. 01-837 3611 **2D 19**
National, The (*Branch Hosp.*), Gr. North Rd., N2. 01-883 8235 **AZ 5C 28**
National Heart, The, Westmoreland St., W1. 01-486 0824 **2A 16**
National Temperance, Hampstead Rd., NW1. 01-387 9300 **2D 9**
Neasden, Brentfield Rd., NW10. 01-459 2251/4 **AZ 6K 41**
Nelson, Kingston Rd., Merton, SW20. 01-540 7261 **AZ 2F 121**
Neurosurgical Unit (Guys, King's College & Maudsley Hospitals), De Crespigny Park, SE5. 01-703 6333 **AZ 2D 94**
New Charing Cross, Fulham Palace Rd., W6. 01-748 2040 **AZ 5E 74**
New Cross, Avonley Rd., New Cross, SE14. 01-639 4380 **AZ 7J 79**
New End, New End, Hampstead, NW3. 01-435 7131 **AZ 3A 44**
Newham Maternity, Forest La., E7. 01-555 3262 **AZ 5G 49**
New Royal Free, The, See Royal Free, Pond St., NW3
New Victoria, The, "Coombe Manor", Coombe La. W., Kingston-upon-Thames, Surrey. 01-949 1661 **AZ 1H 119**
Normansfield, Kingston Rd., Teddington, Middx. 01-977 7583 **AZ 5B 104**
North London Nuffield, Cavell Dri., Enfield. 01-366 2122 **AZ 2F 7**
North Middlesex, Silver St., N18. 01-807 3071 **AZ 4J 17**
Northwick Park, Watford Rd., Harrow, Middx. 01-864 5311 **AZ 7A 24**
Northwood, Pinner & District, Pinner Rd., Northwood, Middx. Northwood 24182
Norwood & District, Hermitage Rd., SE19. 01-653 1171 **AZ 7C 110**
Nuffield House, Guy's Hosp., St. Thomas St., SE1. 01-407 7600 **1A 56**
Obstetric, Huntley St., WC1. 01-387 9300 **1A 18**
Oldchurch, Oldchurch Rd., Romford, Essex. Romford 46090 **AZ 6K 37**
Old Court Clinic, 19 Montpelier Rd., W5. 01-998 2848 **AZ 5D 56**
Orme Lodge, Gordon Av., Stanmore, Middx. 01-954 3305 **AZ 7E 10**
Orpington, Sevenoaks Rd., Orpington, Kent. Orpington 27050/8
Paddington Clinic & Day, 217–221 Harrow Rd., W2. 01-286 4800 **AZ 3D 58**
Paddington Green Children's, Paddington Grn., W2. 01-723 1081 **2C 13**
Park Clinic, The, 14 Seagry Rd., E11. 01-989 0113 **AZ 6J 33**
Perivale Maternity, Greenford, Middx. 01-997 5661 **AZ 3K 55**
Plaistow, Samson St., Plaistow, E13. 01-472 7001 **AZ 2A 66**
Plaistow Maternity, see **Newham**
Portman Clinic, 8 Fitzjohns Av., NW3. 01-794 8262 **AZ 4A 44**
Prince of Wales's General, The, Tottenham, N15. 01-808 1081 **AZ 4F 31**
Princess Grace 42/52 Nottingham Pl., W1. 01-486 1234 **1D 15**
Princess Louise Hosp., Saint Quintin Av., W10. 01-969 0133 **AZ 5E 58**
Priory, The, Priory La., Roehampton, SW15. 01-876 8261 **AZ 6A 90**
Purley & District War Memorial, Brighton Rd., Purley, Surrey. 01-660 0177
Putney, Lower Common, SW15. 01-789 6633 **AZ 3D 90**
Queen Charlotte's Maternity, Goldhawk Rd., W6. 01-748 4666 **AZ 4B 74**
Queen Elizabeth Hosp. for Children, Hackney Rd., E2. 01-739 8422 **AZ 3F 63**
Queen Elizabeth Military, Stadium Rd., SE18. 01-856 5533 **AZ 7D 82**
Queen Mary's, Roehampton, SW15. 01-789 6611 **AZ 6C 90**
Queen Mary's, Frognal Av., Sidcup, Kent. 01-302 2678 **AZ 6A 116**
Queen Mary's Hosp. for Children, Carshalton, Surrey. 01-643 3300
Queen Mary's Hosp. for the East End, West Ham La., E15. 01-534 2616 **AZ 7G 49**
Queen's, Queen's Rd., Croydon, Surrey. 01-689 2211 **AZ 6B 124**
Rame House, Church La., SW17. 01-672 9543 **AZ 5D 108**
Rosslyn, 15/17 Rosslyn Rd., Twickenham. 01-891 3173 **AZ 6C 88**
Roxbourne, Rayners La., South Harrow, Middx. 01-422 1450 **AZ 5D 22**
Royal, Kew Foot Rd., Richmond, Surrey. 01-940 3331 **AZ 4E 88**
Royal Ear, Huntley St., WC1. 01-387 9300 **1A 18**
Royal Free, The, Pond St., Hampstead, NW3. 01-794 0500 **AZ 5C 44**

Royal Hosp. & Home for Incurables, West Hill, Putney, SW15. 01-788 4511/3 **AZ 7F 91**

Royal London Homoeopathic, Gt. Ormond St., WC1. 01-837 8833 **1A 20**

Royal Marsden Hosp., Fulham Rd., SW3. 01-352 8171 **3D 59**

Royal Marsden, The, Surrey Branch, Downs Rd., Sutton, Surrey. 01-642 6011

Royal Masonic, Ravenscourt Pk., W6. 01-748 4611 **AZ 4C 74**

Royal National Orthopaedic, Outpatients Dept. only; 45/51 Bolsover St., W1. 01-387 5070 **1C 17**

Royal National Orthopaedic, Country Hosp. & Convalescent Branch, Brockley Hill, Stanmore, Middx. 01-954 2300 **AZ 1H 11**

Royal National Throat, Nose & Ear, Golden Sq., W1. 01-437 4058 **2D 33**

Royal National Throat, Nose & Ear, Grays Inn Rd., WC1. 01-837 8855 **AZ 3K 61**

Royal Northern Hosp., Holloway Rd., N7. 01-272 7777 **AZ 2H 45**

Royal Star & Garter Home for the Disabled Sailors, Soldiers & Airmen, Richmond Hill, Surrey. 01-940 3314 **AZ 6E 88**

Rush Green, Dagenham Rd., Romford, Essex. Romford 46066 **AZ 4J 53**

Saint Andrew's, Devons Rd., E3. 01-987 2030 **AZ 5C 64**

Saint Andrews House, Dollis Hill La., NW2. 01-452 5451 **AZ 4B 42**

Saint Ann's General, St. Ann's Rd., Tottenham, N15. 01-800 0121 **AZ 5C 30**

Saint Anthony's, North Cheam, Sutton, Surrey. 01-330 3351 **AZ 2E 130**

Saint Bartholomew's, West Smithfield, EC1. 01-600 9000 **3B 22**

Saint Bernard's, see Ealing

Saint Charles', St. Charles Sq., Exmoor St., W10. 01-969 2488 **AZ 5G 59**

Saint Clements, (London Hospital), Bow Rd., E3. 01-980 4899 **AZ 3B 64**

Saint Christopher's Hospice, 51/53 Lawrie Park Rd., SE26. 01-778 9252 **AZ 6H 111**

Saint David's Home, Castlebar Hill, Ealing, W5. 01-997 5121 **AZ 5C 56**

Saint Francis', St. Francis' Rd., E. Dulwich, SE22. 01-693 3377 **AZ 4E 94**

Saint George's, Blackshaw Rd., SW17. 01-672 1255 **AZ 4A 108**

Saint George's, Suttons La., Hornchurch, Essex. Hornchurch 43531

Saint Giles, St. Giles Rd., Camberwell, SE5. 01-703 0898 **AZ 7E 78**

Saint Helier, Wrythe La., Carshalton, Surrey. 01-644 4343 **AZ 1A 132**

Saint James', Sarsfield Rd., Balham, SW12. 01-672 1222 **AZ 1D 108**

Saint John & Saint Elizabeth, see Hosp. of

Saint John's, Kingston La., Uxbridge, Middx. Uxbridge 38282

Saint John's, Morden Hill, Lewisham, SE13. 01-852 4467 **AZ 2E 96**

Saint John's, Saint John's Hill, SW11. 01-874 1022 **AZ 4B 92**

Saint John's, Amyand Pk. Rd., Twickenham, Middx. 01-891 3101 **AZ 7A 88**

Saint John's Hosp. for Diseases of the Skin, Lisle St., WC2. 01-437 8383 **2B 34**

Saint John's Hosp. for Diseases of the Skin In-Patient Department, Homerton Gro., E9. 01-985 7061 **AZ 5K 47**

Saint Joseph's Nursing Home, 15 Church St., Lwr. Edmonton, N9. 01-807 8383 **AZ 7J 7**

Saint Joseph's Home for Handicapped Women & Girls, Burlington La., Chiswick, W4. 01-994 4641 **AZ 7K 73**

Saint Joseph's Hospice, Mare St., Hackney, E8. 01-935 0861/2/3 **AZ 1H 63**

Saint Leonard's, Nuttall St., N1. 01-739 8484 **AZ 2E 62**

Saint Luke's, Hereford Rd., Bayswater, W2. 01-727 3531 **2C 27**

Saint Luke's Hosp. for the Clergy, 14 Fitzroy Sq., W1. 01-388 4954 **1D 17**

Saint Luke's—Woodside, Woodside Av., Muswell Hill, N10. 01-883 8311. **AZ 5D 28**

Saint Mark's Hosp. for Diseases of the Rectum and Colon, City Rd., EC1. 01-253 1050 **AZ 2B 62**

Saint Mary Abbot's, Marloes Rd., Kensington, W8. 01-937 8201 **AZ 3K 75**

Saint Mary's Harrow Road, Harrow Rd., W9. 01-286 4884 **AZ 3D 58**

Saint Mary's, Upper Rd., Plaistow, E13. 01-472 6621 **AZ 3J 65**

Saint Mary's, Praed St., Paddington, W2. 01-262 1280 **3D 13**

Saint Mary's Cottage, Upper Sunbury Rd., Hampton, Middx. 01-979 4451

Saint Mary's Maternity, St. James's Rd., W. Croydon, Surrey. 01-684 6999 **AZ 7C 124**

Saint Matthew's, Shepherdess Wlk., N1. 01-253 4218 **AZ 2C 62**

Saint Michael's, 19 Chase Side Cres., Enfield, Middx. 01-363 8234 **AZ 1H 7**

Saint Michael's, Cleveland Gdns., Worcester Park, Surrey. 01-337 1301

Saint Nicholas', 79 Tewson Rd., Plumstead, SE18. 01-854 2455 **AZ 5J 83**

Saint Olave's, Lower Rd., Rotherhithe, SE16. 01-237 6622 **AZ 3J 79**

Saint Pancras, 4 St. Pancras Way, NW1. 01-387 4411 **AZ 7G 45**

Saint Paul's, Endell St., WC2. 01-836 9611 **1D 35**

Saint Peter's, Henrietta St., WC2. 01-836 9347 **2D 35**

Saint Philip's, Sheffield St., WC2. 01-242 9831 **1A 36**

Saint Raphael's, Coopers La. Rd., Barvin Pk., Potters Bar, Herts. Potters Bar 52282

Saint Stephen's, Fulham Road., SW10. 01-352 8161 **AZ 2G 91**

Saint Stephen's, Mays La., Barnet, Herts. 01-440 5111 **AZ 6A 4**

Saint Teresa's Maternity, The Downs, SW20. 01-947 3142/5 **AZ 7F 107**

Saint Thomas', Lambeth Pal. Rd., SE1. 01-928 9292 **3A 52**

Saint Vincent's Orthopaedic, Eastcote, Pinner, Middx. 01-866 0151

Samaritan Hosp. for Women, Marylebone Rd., NW1. 01-402 4211 **2B 14**

Scio House, Portsmouth Rd., Putney, SW15. 01-788 3462 & 8705 **AZ 7D 90**

Shaftesbury, 172 Shaftesbury Ave., WC2. 01-836 2711 **1C 35**

Southall-Norwood, The Green, Southall, Middx. 01-574 2616 **AZ 2D 70**

Southgate, see Wood Green.

South London Hosp. for Women & Children, Clapham Comm., SW4. 01-673 7788 **AZ 4E 92**

South Middlesex, Mogden La., Isleworth, Middx. 01-892 2841 **AZ 5K 87**

South Side Home, 4 Streatham Comm, SW16. 01-764 8777 **AZ 6J 109**

South Western, Landor Rd., Stockwell, SW9. 01-928 9292 **AZ 3J 93**

Southwood, Southwood La., Highgate, N6. 01-340 8778 **AZ 7E 28**

Springfield, Glenburnie Rd., SW17. 01-672 9911 **AZ 3D 108**

Stanmore Cottage, Old Church La., Stanmore, Middx. 01-954 0257 **AZ 5G 11**

Surbiton General, Ewell Rd., Surbiton, Surrey. 01-399 7111 **AZ 7B 118**

Sutton General, Cotswold Rd., Sutton, Surry. 01-642 6090

Tavistock Clinic, 120 Belsize La., NW3. 01-435 7111 **AZ 6B 44**

Teddington Memorial, Hampton Rd., Teddington, Middx. 01-977 2212 **AZ 5H 103**

Thames Ditton, Weston Green Rd., Thames Ditton, Surrey. 01-398 1130

Thorpe Coombe, 714 Forest Rd., Walthamstow, E17. 01-521 8881 **AZ 4J 31**

Tolworth, Red Lion Rd., Tolworth, Surbiton, Surrey. 01-390 0102

Tooting Bec, Tooting Bec Rd., SW17. 01-672 9933 **AZ 3E 108**

Trinity Hospice, 29/32 Clapham Common N. Side, SW4. 01-622 9481 **AZ 4E 92**

Turret, The, 16 Streatham Comn. S., SW16. 01-764 8778 **AZ 6J 109**

Twyford Abbey Nursing Home, Twyford Abbey Rd., NW10. 01-965 6312 **AZ 3F 57**

University College, Gower St., WC1. 01-387 9300 **1A 18**

University College Dental, Mortimer Mkt., WC1. 01-387 0351 **1A 18**

Unit for Deaf Children & Parents, see Hostel for.

University College Hosp. Private Patients' Wing, Grafton Way, WC1. 01-387 9300 **1A 18**

Uxbridge & District Cottage, Harefield Rd., Uxbridge, Middx. Uxbridge 33085

Victoria, Pettits La., Romford, Essex. Romford 42461

Victoria Maternity, Wood St., Barnet, Herts. 01-440 5111 **AZ 4A 4**

Waddon, Purley Way, Croydon, Surrey. 01-684 6999 **AZ 7K 123**

Wandle Valley, Mitcham Junction, Mitcham, Surrey. 01-648 9441 **AZ 7D 122**

Wanstead, Hermon Hill, Wanstead, E11. 01-989 6699 **AZ 5J 33**

Warlingham Park, off Chelsham Rd., Warlingham, Surrey. 01-820 2101

Weir Maternity, Weir Rd., SW12. 01-673 7799 **AZ 7G 93**

Welbeck Street Nursing Home, 27 Welbeck St., W1. 01-486 7631 **3A 16**

Wellington Private, Wellington Pl., NW8. 01-586 5959 **AZ 3B 60**
Wembley, Fairview Av., Wembley, Middx. 01-903 6633 **AZ 3D 40**
Western Opthalmic, Marylebone Rd., NW1. 01-402 4211 **2B 14**
West Hendon, The, Goldsmith Av., The Hyde, NW9. 01-205 2367 **AZ 5A 26**
West London, Hammersmith Rd., W6. 01-748 3441 **AZ 4F 75**
West Middlesex, Twickenham Rd., Isleworth, Middx. 01-560 2121 **AZ 5A 88**
Westminster, Dean Ryle St., Horseferry Rd., SW1. 01-828 9811 **2C 65**
Westminster Children's, Vincent Sq., SW1. 01-828 9811 **2A 64**
Westmoor House, 244 Roehampton La., SW15. 01-788 2122 **AZ 4C 90**
Whipps Cross, Whipps Cross Rd., E11. 01-539 5522 **AZ 5F 33**
Whitechapel, (London Hosp.) Whitechapel Rd., E1. 01-247 5454 **AZ 5G 63**
Whittington, Highgate Hill, N19. 01-272 3070 **AZ 1F 45**
Whittington Home, 20 Broadlands Rd., N6. 01-340 3410 **AZ 7D 28**
Willesden General, Harlesden Rd., NW10. 01-459 1292 **AZ 1C 58**
Wilson, Cranmer Rd., Mitcham, Surrey. 01-648 3021 **AZ 4D 122**
Wimbledon, Thurstan Rd., Copse Hill, SW20. 01-946 1103 **AZ 7D 106**
Winifred House Convalescent Hosp. for Children, Barnet Gate, Arkley, Barnet,
Herts. 01-449 3343
Wood Green & Southgate, Bounds Green Rd., N11. 01-889 1981 **AZ 6B 16**
York Clinic, Guy's Hosp., Borough High St., SE1. 01-407 7600 **2D 55**

INSURANCE COMPANIES (National and International Headquarters)

BRITISH INSURANCE ASSOCIATION, Aldermary Ho., Queen St. EC4. 01-248 4477
1D 39

Abbey Life Ass., 8 East Harding St., EC4. 01-248 9111 **1D 37**
Canada Life Ass., 2 High St., Potters Bar. Potters Bar 51122
City of Westminster, 3 London Wall Buildings, EC2. 01-638 5737 **3C 23**
Commercial Union Ass., St. Helens, 1 Undershaft, EC3. 01-283 7500 **1B 40**
Co-operative Ins. Society, Branches throughout London.
Eagle Star Ins., 1 Threadneedle St., EC2. 01-588 1212 **1A 40**
Equitable Life Ass. Society, 4 Coleman St., EC2. 01-606 6611 **1D 39**
General Accident, Fire & Life Ass., 74 Cheapside, EC2. 01-606 1030. **1C 39**
Guardian Royal Exchange Ass. Group, Royal Exchange, EC3. 01-283 7101 **1A 40**
Hambro Life Ass., 9 Sackville St., W1. 01-434 3211 **3D 33**
Hearts of Oak Benefit Society, Aviation Ho., Kingsway, WC2. 01 404 0393 **1A 36**
Legal and General Ass. Society, Finland Ho., 56 Haymarket, SW1. 01-839 6595
3B 34
London and Manchester Ass., Imperial Ho., Dominion St., EC2. 01-628 8000 **2A 24**
London Life Association, 215 Bishopsgate, EC2. 01-377 0660 **3B 24**
National Mutual Life Ass., 5 Bow Churchyard, EC4. 01-236 1566 **1C 39**
National Provident, 48 Gracechurch St., EC3. 01-623 4200 **2A 40**
Norwich Union Ins. Group, 51 Fenchurch St., EC3. 01-623 2575 **2B 40**
Pearl Ass., High Holborn, WC1. 01-405 8441 **1C 35**
Phoenix Ass., Phoenix Ho., King William St., EC4. 01-626 9876 **2A 40**
Provident Mutual Life Ass., 25 Moorgate, EC2. 01-626 3232 **1D 39**
Provincial Ins., 222 Bishopsgate, EC2. 01-247 6533 **1B 40**
Prudential Ass., 142 Holborn Bars, EC1. 01-405 9222 **3C 21**
Refuge Ass., 241 Upper St., N1. 01-226 0603 **AZ 2B 62**
Royal Exchange Ass., see **Guardian Royal Exchange Ass. Group.**
Royal Ins. Co., 1 Cornhill EC3. 01-283 4300 **1A 40**
Royal Ins. UK., 34 Lime St., EC3. 01-283 4135 **1B 40**
Royal Life Ins., John Adam Ho., John Adam St., WC2. 01–930 7800 **3D 35**
Scottish Life Ass., 36 Poultry, EC2. 01-606 0935 **1D 39**

Scottish Union & National Insurance Co., 51 Fenchurch St., EC3. 01-623 2575 **2B 40**
Sun Alliance & London Ins. Group, 1 Bartholomew La., EC2. 01-588 2345 **1A 40**
Sun Life Ass. of Canada, 2 Cockspur St., SW1. 01-930 5400 **3B 34**
Sun Life Ass. Society, 107 Cheapside, EC2. 01-606 7788 **1C 39**
United Friendly Ins., 42 Southwark Bridge Rd., SE1. 01-928 5644 **3B 54**

LIBRARIES

Besides books, Libraries usually stock newspapers, periodicals and records. They are also a source of neighbourhood information, ie events and clubs. For local Libraries consult the appropriate Borough Council.

Barbican Library, Barbican, EC2. 01-638 0569. **2C 23**
Renewals 01-638 0568. The largest of the City's Lending Libraries with a computerised issue system housed within the Barbican Centre for Arts and Conferences. Open 09.30–17.30 Mon., Wed., Thurs. & Fri.; to 19.30 Tues; to 12.30 Sat. Large general book collection with special sections on fine and performing arts, music and children's books. Also records, cassettes, scores and basic reference collection; more specialised reference information available at Guildhall Library, City Business Library, St. Bride Printing Library, see below.
Charing Cross Library, 4 Charing Cross Rd., WC2. 01-930 3274 **3C 35**
(After 17.00 and Sat. 01-240 1170). Renewals 01-240 2989. Book and music lending library open Mon. to Fri. 09.30–19.00, Sat. 09.30–13.00. The music library has a large collection of some 13,000 records of music and speech. Scores can be borrowed with most records, musicassettes are now included in the record library.
Guildhall Library, Aldermanbury, EC2. 01-606 3030 **1C 39**
Reference Library. Open Mon. to Sat. 09.30–17.00. Library of the Corporation of London founded *c.*1425 and especially rich in material on London. For Lending Library see Barbican. For other specialist City Reference Libraries see City Business Library and St. Bride Printing Library.
  Principal contents: Deposited archives of the City of London Parishes, Wards and Guilds; of the Diocese of London and of many business houses. Print room with 30,000 prints & drawings, 30,000 maps, 23,000 minor illustrations. Special collections include English History, Genealogy, Heraldry, Commerce and Statistics. Law reports. Election literature and tracts.
CORPORATION OF LONDON RECORD OFFICE: 01-606 3030
  The official depository of records of the Corporation, regarded as the most complete collection of ancient municipal records in existence. Includes Charters
  granted by William the Conqueror, Henry II and later Kings and Queens up to 1957. Continuous series of judicial rolls and books from 1252 and Council meetings from 1275; financial records from the 16th cent. and records of London Bridge from the 12th cent. Readers' room open 09.30–17.00 Mon. to Fri.
Marylebone Library, Marylebone Rd., NW1. 01-828 8070 **2C 15**
Renewals 01-935 2629. Book and music lending library: Open Mon. to Fri. 09.30–20.00. Sat. 09.30–17.00. Special collections include: History, Ashbridge Collection, Sherlock Holmes Collection and Medical Library with its comprehensive general medical collection including nursing and dentistry—most British and American text books, medical periodicals and world health organisation publications.
Mayfair Library, S. Audley St., W1. 01-499 2351 **3A 32**
Renewals 01-493 7485. Book lending library open Mon. to Fri. 09.30–19.00, Sat. 09.30–13.00. Foreign Languages collection has material in over 100 different languages. Aims to provide grammars, dictionaries, literary histories and where possible literary texts both in the original and translation.

Victoria Library, 160 Buckingham Palace Rd., SW1. 01-730 7371 **3B 62**
Renewals 01-730 6601. Book and Music Lending Library open Mon. to Fri. 09.30–
19.00, Sat. 09.30–17.00. For records see Charing Cross Library.
(1) CENTRAL MUSIC LIBRARY The Library's scope is virtually unlimited (with
    exception of scores of jazz and modern popular music and gramophone
    records) and consists of about 78,000 items headed as follows:
Books about music arranged in classified order. Music subdivided into a principal
section of scores arranged alphabetically by groups and a lesser section of
sheet music of short pieces under instruments groupings. There are also miniature
scores, song collections, instrumental collections and tutors and orchestral parts.
(2) ENGLISH LITERARY TEXTS AND CRITICISM.
Westminster Central Reference Library, St. Martin's St., WC2. 01-798 2036.
3B 34
Open Mon. to Fri. 10.00–19.00. Sat. 10.00–17.00. Fine Art Library. 01-798 2038
(1) GROUND FLOOR. Specialises in commerce and technology providing ready
    access to thousands of volumes ranging from standard legal works to
    studies of the latest developments in automation. Dictionaries in many
    languages and of many industries. Directories on an international basis of
    companies, products and professions as well as the normal telephone, telex
    directories, etc., of most countries of the world. Government publications
    include industrial, social and regional statistics, statutes and statutory
    regulations and reports on every aspect of the national economy. All
    command papers and House of Commons papers are available as well as
    publications of separate Departments. Documents of international Bodies
    including UN, EEC, GATT and OECD, and comparative data on world powers
    and developing countries. Atlases and Gazetteers of Gt. Britain, the World
    and over 18,000 maps including Ordnance Survey sheets, geological maps,
    road maps, town plans and charts of British Coastal Waters. Time tables of sea, air,
    road and rail services in Gt. Britain and rail services for most of Europe. Local
    authority guides and town directories. Publications of the British Standards
    Institution. The complete Times on microfilm, all British Standards, and over
    500 periodicals.
(2) FIRST FLOOR. Information on a wealth of general subjects and also the Pavola
    Memorial collection.
(3) SECOND FLOOR. Contains the Fine Art library. Painting, Drawing and
    Sculpture are the principal topics; but also included are ceramics,
    glassware, coins, tapestry, carpets, furniture, jewellery, interior design,
    costume, goldsmith's work and silverware, arms and armour and numorous other
    subjects. The Preston Blake Library contains over 700 volumes by and about
    the great English poet, painter, engraver and mystic William Blake.

SPECIALIST REFERENCE LIBRARIES:
Local Reference Libraries should have one or all the following volumes that
catalogue the 1000s of specialist subject libraries available for study and
research. (1) "British Archives", a guide to archive resources in UK. (2) "Aslib
Directory" in 2 vols.—the Association of Specialist Libraries and Information
Bureaux. (3) "Libraries, Museums and Galleries Year Book", published by the
Library Association. Ridgmount St., WC1. 01–636 7543.

*Most government departments and ministries, have libraries concerned with their
specific interests usually available to the public, sometimes prior application
is necessary.*
Arts Council Poetry Library, 105 Piccadilly, W1. 01-629 9495 **3D 33**
Poetry since 1930, reference and lending. 10.00–17.30 Mon. and Tues. to 18.00
Wed.–Fri.
Australia House, Strand, WC2. 01-438 8170 **2B 36**
Literature, history, law, social sciences, government publications relating to
Australia. Open 09.00–17.15 weekdays, 09.00–12.00 Sat.
BBC Hulton Picture Library: See Radio Times Hulton Picture Library.

Bishopsgate Institute, 230 Bishopsgate, EC2.**2C 25**
Collections on early Co-op movement and London history, also prints and
watercolours. Open 09.30–17.30 Mon. to Fri.
Reference 01-247 6844. Lending 01-247 8895
Blind, Libraries for—see National Library for the Blind and Talking Book Service.
British Library, Reference Division, Gt. Russell St., WC1. 01-636 1544 **2C 19**
Intended for research and reference which cannot be carried out elsewhere and is
limited to ticket holders. Comprises the Departments of Printed Books
(including maps, music and stamps), of Manuscripts, of Oriental Manuscripts and
Printed Books. Each department has a reading room, for tickets apply to British Library
(Readers' Tickets); hours of opening vary. Interested visitors can usually see inside
the main Reading Room with its vast domed roof. Selected items of great
historical interest are exhibited in the Library Galleries page 75 (British Museum)—
open as for British Museum.
Publishers are required by law to deposit a copy of every book published in the
United Kingdom. See below for Newspaper Library, Science Reference Library and
National Sound Archive.
British Library of Political & Economic Science, Houghton St., WC2. 01-405
7686 **1A 36** Social Sciences, special collections include Fry Library of Internat. Law and
Webb Trade Union and Local Government collections. Research by special permit.
Open 10.00–21.30 Mon. to Fri. (17.00 in Aug.), 10.00–17.00 Sat. (closed July
and Aug.).
British Music Information Centre, 10 Stratford Pl., W1. 01-499 8567 **1B 32**
Reference Library of Contemporary British music, scores, tapes and records. Open
11.00–17.00 Mon. to Fri.
Canada House, Trafalgar Sq., SW1. 01-629 9492 **3C 35**
Reference Library of books, periodicals, government publications relating to
Canada. Open 10.00–17.00 Mon. to Fri.
Central Music Library see Victoria Library, preceding.
Central Reference Library see Westminster Central Ref. Library, preceding.
Chemical Society, Burlington Ho., Piccadilly, W1. 01-734 9971 **3D 33**
All aspects of chemistry open for research only.
City Business Library, Gillett Ho. Basinghall St., EC2. 01-638 8215 **3D 23**
British and Foreign directories, trade publications, national and overseas
newpapers, official publications and statistical information. Open 09.30–17.30
Mon. to Fri.
Commonwealth Institute of Entomology, 56 Queen's Ga., SW7. 01-584 0067
1B 58 Applied entomology and related subjects; reference work. Open 09.00–17.00
Mon. to Fri.
Commonwealth Institute Library, Kensington High St., W8. 01-603 4535 **3A 42**
All aspects of the commonwealth today and its members. Open for reference
10.00–18.00 Mon. to Sat.
Courtauld Institute of Art, 20 Portman Sq., W1. 01-935 9292 **1D 31**
History of Art, photographic section open to public; book section to members of
Academic Institutions only. Open 10.00–18.00 Mon. to Fri.
Fawcett Library, City of London Polytechnic. Old Castle St., E1. 01-283 1030
3D 25
Women in society, social, legal and economic, etc., photographs, press cuttings
especially of suffragette movement. Open Mon. to Fri.
Geological Museum Library, Inst. of Geological Sciences, Exhibition Rd., SW7.
01-589 3444 **1D 59.** Geology and allied sciences, maps of world, photographs
of Brit. Geology. Open for reference 10.00–16.00 Mon. to Fri.
Geological Society, Burlington Ho., Piccadilly, W1. 01-734 5673 **3D 33**
Geology including maps. Non-fellows admission charge. Open 10.00–17.00 Mon.
to Fri., 20.00 Wed.
Goethe Institute, 50 Princes Gate, SW7. 01-581 3344 **3D 45**
German books and English books about Germany; newspapers, periodicals,

records. Information service. Open for reference and lending 10.00–20.00 Mon. to Thurs. 10.00–13.00 Sat. Closed Fridays.

Gray's Inn Library, South Sq., WC1. 01-405 4177 **2C 20**
Established c. 1555, about 38,000 books. The Holker Library. Legal subjects, available for historical research 09.00–20.00 weekdays.

Greater London Record Office, 40 Northampton Rd., E1. 01-633 5000, Map room 7193 **1C 21**
History, topography, Greater London local government. Photographs, prints, drawings, maps. Open for reference 10.00–16.45 Tues to Fri. to 19.30 Tues.

Guy's Hospital Medical Library, St. Thomas St., SE1. 01-407 7600 **1A 56**
The Wills Library, medicine, dentistry and allied subjects. Special permission required. Open 09.00–22.00.

Horniman Museum Library, 100 London Rd., SE23. 01-699 2339 **AZ 1H 111**
Ethnology, prehistoric man, natural history, musical instruments and topics dealt with in museum. Open for reference 10.30–18.00 Tues. to Sat., 14.00–18.00 Sun.

House of Lords Library, Palace of Westminster, SW1. 01-219 3000 (Admin.) **3D 51**
Main collection—parliamentary history, peerage, law. Also English and French literature, genealogy, heraldry, etc. Written application for research to Librarian. Open Sitting Days 10.30–13.30, otherwise 10.30–16.30.

Imperial War Museum Library, Lambeth Rd., SE1. 01-735 8922 **1D 67**
1st and 2nd World Wars, other operations since 1914 of British and Commonwealth Forces. Also Photographs and Film Collections. Prints can be purchased. Reading room open 10.00–17.00 Tues. to Fri.

India House Library, Aldwych, WC2. 01-836 8484 **2A 36**
Orientalist books and manuscripts. Founded 1801 by Honourable East India Co. Open for reference 09.00–17.15 Mon. to Fri.

Inner Temple Library, Inner Temple, EC4. 01-353 2959 **2C 37**
Legal and legal historical materials, topography, genealogy. Available to accredited scholars only—written application. Open 10.00–18.00, Law vacations 10.00–16.00.

Institute of Advanced Legal Studies, 17 Russell Sq., WC1. **2C 19**
Legal subjects, available for special research only on written application to Librarian.

Institute of Bankers, 10 Lombard St., EC3. 01-623 3531 **2A 40**
Banking and finance, economics, law, management, social sciences. By special written request. Open 09.00–17.00 Mon. to Fri.

Institute of Historical Research, University of London, Senate Ho., Malet St., WC1. 01-636 7950 **2C 19.** History, bibliographies, guides to archives and printed sources. Open on permission from the office.

Jews' College, Kinloss Gdns., N3. 01-346 7467 **AZ 3H 27**
All aspects of Judaica and Hebraica, bible, language, art. Open for research, term time 09.00–17.00 Mon. to Thurs., 10.00–13.00 Fri. and Sun. Vacations 09.00–17.00 Mon., Tues., Thurs. 09.00–1900 Wed. Closed Aug., Jewish and Public Hols.

King's College Library, 160 Strand, WC2. 01-836 5454 **2B 36**
All subjects studied in the college, a centre for Military Archives. Open on letter of recommendation, term time 09.30–20.45 Mon. to Thurs., 19.15 Fri., 12.45 Sat. Vacation 09.30–16.30 Mon. to Fri., 12.00 Sat.

Lambeth Palace Library, Lambeth Palace Rd., SE1. 01-928 6222 **2A 66**
Theology, inter-church relations, canon law, liturgy, church history. Open by arrangement with Librarian, 10.00–17.00 Mon. to Sat.

Law Notes Lending Library, 25 Chancery La., WC2. 01-405 0780 **1C 37**
Legal works of reference and English legal textbooks. Available to public by annual subscription. Open 09.30–17.00 Mon. to Fri.

London Library, 14 St. James's Sq., SW1. 01-930 7705 **1A 50**
General subjects but excluding legal, medical and scientific works. By subscription.

Marx Memorial Library, 37a Clerkenwell Grn., EC1. 01-253 1485 **1D 21**

100,000 books, pamphlets, etc., special collections on Spanish Civil War, Chartism, Third World. Open pm Mon. to Fri., am Sat. Closed Thurs.

Middle Temple Library, Garden Ct., EC4. 01-353 4303 **2C 37**
Legal, medicine, English literature, county histories, also special collections. Bona fide enquiries, written application to Librarian. Open 09.30–19.00 Mon. to Fri.

Museum of London Library, London Wall, EC2. 01-600 3699 **3C 23**
Library and print room specialising on all London topics, including a suffragette collection. Open for research by appointment only, Tues. to Fri. 10.00–17.00.

National Art Library, Victoria & Albert Mus., Exhibition Rd., SW7. 01-589 6371 **1D 59**
Reference library of fine and applied art of all periods and countries and special collections. Open 10.00–17.00 weekdays, regular reader needs ticket.

National Film Archive, 81 Dean St., W1. 01-437 4355 **1A 34**
Cinema films, television recordings, film stills and posters. (British Film Institute.) Open by appointment only, 10.00–18.00 daily.

National Library for the Blind, Cromwell Rd., Bredbury, Stockport. 061-494 0217
For the blind and partially sighted. Postal service of books in Braille and Moom.

National Listening Library, see Talking Books.

National Maritime Library, Nat. Maritime Museum, Romney Rd., SE10. 01-858 4422 **AZ 6F 81.** Maritime affairs, special collection of atlases also Gosse collection of piracy. Ticket holders only. 10.00–13.00, 14.00–17.00 Mon. to Fri., 10.00–17.00 Sat.

National Monuments Record, Fortress Ho., 23 Savile Row, W1. 01-734 6010 **2D 23** Historic buildings and archaeology of England, photographs and drawings. Open 10.00–17.30 Mon. to Fri. (Ryl. Comm. on Historical Monuments).

National Sound Archive, 29 Exhibition Rd., SW7. 01-589 6603 **3C 45**
National archive of sound recordings. Music, many languages, every production of National and Royal Shakespeare Theatres. Open for listening 10.00–17.30 Mon. to Fri., to 21.00 Thurs.

Natural History Library, Nat. History Mus., Cromwell Rd., SW7. 01-589 6323 **2C 59**
All aspects of natural history especially taxonomic studies. Drawings and Paintings. Open for reference purposes 10.00–17.00 Mon. to Sat.

New Zealand House, 80 Haymarket, SW1. 01-930 8422 **3B 34**
Reference library of Government publications and statistics, books etc., on New Zealand, South Pacific and Antarctic. Open 10.00–16.30 Mon. to Fri.

Newspaper Library, Colindale Av., NW9. 01-200 5515 **AZ 4C 26**
Daily newspapers except those published in London pre-1801. Most weekly periodicals. Duplicate "Times" from 1801 are kept in British Library. Open 10.00–17.00 Mon. to Sat.

Patent Office Library see Science Reference Library.

Pharmaceutical Society, 1 Lambeth High St., SE1. 01-735 9141 **2A 66**
Pharmacy and pharmaceutical research. Open for reference 09.00–17.00 Mon. to Fri.

Polish Library, Polish Social & Cultural Ass., 238 King St., W6. 01-741 0474 **A2 7C 74** Books, Maps etc. relating to Poland. Open daily. Closed Sun.

Public Record Office see p. 101.

Radio Times Hulton Picture Library, BBC Publications, 35 Marylebone High St., W1. 01-580 5577 **2A 16** Photographs, drawings, colour transparencies; over 8,000,000 pictures available. Open 09.30–17.30 Mon. to Fri. for reproduction enquiries only.

Royal Academy of Arts Library, Burlington Ho., Piccadilly, W1. 01-734 9052 **3D 33.** Fine arts and allied subjects. Open by arrangement 14.00–17.00 Mon. to Fri.

Royal Aeronautical Society, 4 Hamilton Pl., W1. 01-499 3515 **2A 48**
Aeronautical science and history including photographs, prints and slides. Open by arrangement 09.30–17.00 weekdays.

Royal Artillery Institution Library, Old Royal Military Academy, Academy Rd.,

SE18. 01-856 5533 ext. 2524 **AZ 7E 82.** Open for Research on artillery and related subjects.

Royal Astronomical Society, Burlington Ho., Piccadilly, W1. 01-734 4582 **3D 33**
Open for Astronomy and Geology research on sponsorship by a Fellow.

Royal Botanical Gardens Library, Kew, Surrey. 01-940 1171 **AZ 7F 73**
Plant taxonomy, anatomy, physiology, horticulture, enonomic botany and cyto-genetics. Paintings, engravings, photographs. Open for research on application to Director 09.00–17.30 Mon. to Thurs., 17.00 Fri., 16.15 Sat.

Royal College of Physicians Library, St. Andrews Pl., NW1. 01-935 1174 **3B 8**
History and biography of medicine, medical education. Open for research on application to Harveian Librarian. 10.00–17.00 Mon. to Fri.

Royal College of Surgeons of England Library, Lincoln's Inn Fields, WC2. 01-405 3474 **1C 36**
Surgery with its specialities. Medical or scientific workers and students on introduction of Fellows or members. Open 10.00–18.00 Mon. to Fri., 10.00–12.30 Sat.

Royal Entomological Society, 41 Queen's Ga., SW7. 01-584 8361 **1B 58**
Entomology, diaries, photographs. Open on introduction by Fellow 09.30–17.00 Mon. to Fri.

Royal Geographical Society, 1 Kensington Gore, SW7. 01-589 5466 **3C 45**
All aspects of geography, cartography. Map and Atlas room open to public, Library for research on payment of fee and at Director's approval. 09.30–17.30 weekdays, 09.30–13.00 Sat.

Royal Horticultural Society, Vincent Sq., SW1. 01-834 4333 **2A 64**
All branches of horticulture, reference works on botany. Open on application to secretary, 09.30–17.30 Mon. to Fri.

Royal Institute of British Architects, 66 Portland Pl., W1. 01-580 5533 **2B 16**
Architecture, its related arts and sciences, Sir Bannister Fletcher Library. Open for reference 10.00–19.00 Mon., Wed., Thurs. and Fri., 20.30 Tues., 17.00 Sat.

Royal Institution of Gt. Britain, 21 Albermarle St., W1. 01-409 2992 **3C 33**
Physical sciences, especially physics, history of sciences, portraits. Open on application to Librarian 09.30–17.30.

St. Bride Institute Printing Library, Bride La., Fleet St., EC4. 01-353 4660 **1D 37**
Reference collection relating to technology, design and history of printing and allied trades. Open 10.00–17.30 Mon. to Fri.

St. Paul's Library, St. Paul's Cathedral, EC4. 01-248 2705 **1C 38**
Theology, Fathers Canon Law, Classics, Liturgiology. Open for research 11.30–15.00 Tues. to Sat.

Science Library, Science Museum, Exhibition Rd., SW7. 01-589 3456 **1C 59**
Literature and history of science and technology 17th cent. onwards. All important scientific publications. Open 10.00–17.30, weekdays.

Science Reference Library 25 Southampton Buildings, Chancery La., WC2. 01-405 8721 ext. 3344 & 3345. **3C 21**
(British Library Reference Division) The National Library of modern science, technology and commerce; for patents, trade marks and designs. All information readily available. Open weekdays and main building Sat. am. Business Information Service 01-404 0406.

Soanes Museum Library, Sir John, 13 Lincoln's Inn Fields, WC2. 01-405 2107 **3A 20.** Part of the Soane collection, nothing added since 1837; art and architecture. Open for research 10.00–17.00 Tues. to Sat. Closed August.

Society of Antiquaries of London, Burlington Ho., Piccadilly, W1. 01-437 9954 **3D 33.** British and Foreign archaeology, history, heraldry, early printed books, brass rubbings. Open on introduction by a Fellow and for specific enquiries, 10.00–17.00 weekdays.

South Africa House, Trafalgar Sq., WC2. 01-930 4488 **3C 35**
Reference library of directories, Government statistics etc. and some general works relating to South Africa. Open 09.30–12.30, 14.00–16.00 weekdays.

Talking Book Libraries. Postal Service only. British Talking Book Service for the

Blind, Mt. Pleasant, Wembley. 01-906 6666. National Listening Library for the Handicapped, 12 Lant St., SE1. 01-407 9417

Vaughan Williams Memorial Library, 2 Regents Park Rd., NW1. 01-485 2206 **AZ 3H 27.** English Folk Dance and Song Society, Books, Records on Folk Music and related subjects. Open 09.30–17.30 Mon. to Sat.

Wellcome Institute of the History of Medicine, 183 Euston Rd., NW1. 01-387 4477 **3A 10** History of medicine and allied sciences, Reading Room, Photographic Dept. Open 10.00–17.00 Mon. to Fri., 09.30–16.30 Sat.

Westminster Abbey Library, The Cloisters, SW1. 01-222 5152 **3C 51** Classics, theology, law, history, science and maths. Many 16th cent. books, works relating to the Abbey and School. Open by appointment for research 10.00–13.00, 14.00–16.00 Mon. to Fri. Closed Aug.

LONDON BOROUGHS

CITY OF LONDON, Corporation of London, Guildhall, EC2. 01-606 3030 **3D 23**

Barking, Civic Centre, Wood Lane, Dagenham, Essex., 01-592 4500 **AZ 4D 52**

Barnet, Town Hall, The Burroughs, Hendon, NW4. 01-202 8282 **AZ 4D 26**

Bexley, Council Offices, Broadway, Bexleyheath. 01-303 7777 **AZ 4G 101**

Brent, Brent Town Hall, Forty La., Wembley, Middx. 01-903 1400 **AZ 2H 41**

Bromley, Civic Centre, Rochester Av., Bromley, Kent. 01-464 3333 **AZ 2K 127**

Camden, Town Hall, Euston Rd., NW1. 01-278 4444 **2C 11**

Croydon, Tabener Ho., Park La., Croydon. 01-686 4433 **AZ 3B 134**

Ealing, Town Hall, New Broadway, Ealing, W5. 01-567 2424 **AZ 7D 56**

Enfield, Civic Centre, Silver St., Enfield, Middx. 01-366 6565 **AZ 3J 7**

Greenwich, Town Hall, Wellington St., SE18. 01-854 8888 **AZ 4E 82**

Hackney, Town Hall, Mare St., Hackney, E8. 01-986 3123 **AZ 1H 63**

Hammersmith & Fulham, Town Hall, King St., W6. 01-748 3020 **AZ 4C 74**

Haringey, Civic Centre, High Rd., N22. 01-881 3000 **AZ 1K 29**

Harrow, Civic Centre, Station Rd., Harrow, 01-863 5611 **AZ 4K 23**

Havering, Town Hall, Main Rd., Romford. Romford 46040

Hillingdon, Civic Centre, High St., Uxbridge. Uxb. 50111

Hounslow, Civic Centre, Lampton Rd., Hounslow. 01-570 7728 **AZ 2F 87**

Islington, Town Hall, Upper St., N1. 01-226 1234 **AZ 2B 62**

Kensington & Chelsea (Royal Borough of), Town Hall, Hornton St., W8. 01-937 5464 **3C 43**

Kingston-upon-Thames (Royal Borough of), Guildhall, Kingston-upon-Thames. 01-546 2121 **AZ 2D 118**

Lambeth, Town Hall, Brixton Hill, SW2. 01-274 7722 **AZ 7J 93**

Lewisham, Lewisham Town Hall, Catford, SE6. 01-690 4343 **AZ 7D 96**

Merton, Town Hall, Broadway, Wimbledon, SW19. 01-946 8070 **AZ 7J 107**

Newham, Town Hall, Barking Rd., E16. 01-472 1430 **AZ 5H 65**

Redbridge, Town Hall, High Rd., Ilford, Essex. 01-478 3020 **AZ 2G 57**

Richmond-upon-Thames, Municipal Offices, York Ho., Twickenham, Middx. 01-891 1411. Information Centre 01-940 9125 **AZ 1B 104**

Southwark, Town Hall, Peckham Rd., SE5. 01-703 6311 **AZ 1E 94**

Sutton, Civic Offices, St. Nicholas Way, Sutton, Surrey. 01-661 5000 **AZ 4K 131**

Tower Hamlets, Town Hall, Patriot Sq., E2. 01-980 4831 **AZ 1L 143**

Waltham Forest, Town Hall, Forest Rd., E17. 01-527 5544 **AZ 4C 31**

Wandsworth, Municipal Bldgs., Wandsworth High St., SW18. 01-871 6000. **AZ 5J 91**

Westminster, City of, Westminster City Hall, Victoria St., SW1. 01-828 8070 **1A 64**

MUSEUMS AND PICTURE GALLERIES

Listings of commercial Art Galleries and current exhibitions are given in "Arts Review", "Art Monthly" and the National Press.

Baden Powell House, Queen's Gate, SW7. 01-584 7030 **2B 58**
Mementoes of Baden Powell founder of the Scout Movement. The house, a memorial to Powell, is a centre and a hostel for scouting. Open: 09.00–18.00 Daily.

Barnet Museum, Wood St., Barnet. 01-449 0321 **AZ 4A 4**
Local history collection. Open: Library hours.

Battle of Britain Museum, see Royal Air Force Museum.

Bear Gardens Museum & Arts Centre, 1 Bear Gdns., Bankside, SE1. 01-928 6342 **3C 39.** Collection of Elizabethan Theatre and Bankside history (plus performances and entertainments), in late 18th cent. warehouse, site of 16th cent. Hope playhouse. Open Sat. & Sun. 10.30–17.30. Weekdays by appt. Admission charge.

Bethnal Green Museum of Childhood, Cambridge Heath Rd., E2. 01-980 2415 **AZ 4H 63.** Being developed as a Museum of Childhood. Notable toy collection; also Spitalfields silks and 19th cent. manufactures. Opened in 1872, housed in an iron and glass building—design by Sir W. Cubitt. Branch of the Victoria and Albert Museum. Open: Mon. to Sat. 10.00–18.00, Sun. 14.30–18.00. Closed Fridays.

Bomber Command Museum, see Royal Air Force Museum.

British Piano and Musical Museum, 368 High St., Brentford. 01-560 8108 **AZ 7C 72**
A collection of piano and mechanical musical instruments to be heard as well as seen. Open: Sat. and Sun. for six summer months, 14.00–17.00. Adm. charge.

British Dental Association Museum, 64 Wimpole St., W1. 01-935 0875 **3B 16**
History of dental surgery. By appointment.

British Library Galleries, see Libraries page 70 and British Museum below.

British Museum, Gt. Russell St., WC1. 01-636 1555 **2C 19**
HISTORY: The museum was founded in 1753 when the trustees were given charge of the treasures bequeathed to the nation by Sir Robert Cotton and Sir Hans Sloane. Building designed by Sir Robert Smirke and built 1823–52. Reading Room designed by Sidney Smirke was added in 1857, Karl Marx being among the many to have worked there; see **British Library** page 68. For the Ethnography department see **Museum of Mankind;** and for the Natural History Section see the **Natural History Museum.**
PRINCIPAL CONTENTS:
1. King Edward VII Gallery—A selection of works taken from the whole museum.
2. Upper Floor—Prehistory and Roman Britain including the Mildenhall Treasure.
3. Ground Floor and the Duveen Basement Galleries—Greek, Roman, Egyptian and Assyrian sculpture including the Elgin Marbles and Rosetta Stone.
4. Ground Floor—British Library Galleries: Printed books and manuscripts including Lindisfarne Gospels and Magna Carta.
5. Print Room—one of the great collections of European prints and drawings. Students Room for study; adm. by ticket, apply to Director's Office.
SERVICES: Lectures, Films, Snack Bar, Car Park, Publications & Replicas.
Open: Mon. to Sat. 10.00–17.00, Sun. 14.30–18.00. Closed Christmas Eve and Day, Boxing Day, Good Friday, New Year's Day.

Bromley Museum, Orpington Library, The Priory, Church Hill, Orpington. Not confined to local history. Open Library Hours.

Broomfield Museum, Broomfield Park, N13. 01-882 1354 **AZ 5D 16**
Local History Collection. Open daily (except Mondays Oct. to Easter).

Bruce Castle Museum, Lordship La., N17. 01-808 8772.**AZ 1E 30**
Local History Collection and Middlesex Regiment Museum. Open: 10.00–17.00.
Sat. 10.00–12.30, 13.30–17.00. Closed Wed., Sun.
Chartered Insurance Institute's Museum, The Hall, 20 Aldermanbury, EC2. 01-
606 3835 **3C 23.** Institute's Collection. Open: 10.00–17.30 Mon. to Fri.
Church Farm House Museum, Greyhound Hill, NW4. 01-203 0130 **AZ 3D 26**
Local History Collection and temporary exhibition of local interest. Open: 10.00–
13.00, 14.00–17.30; Tues. 10.00–13.00. Sun. 14.00–17.30.
Clockmaker's Company Museum, Guildhall Library, EC2. 01-606 3030 **1D 39**
Historical collection of clocks and watches. Open: 09.30–16.45 Mon. to Fri.
Courtauld Institute Galleries, Woburn Sq., WC1. 01-636 2095 **1B 18**
Collection of paintings bequeathed by Samuel Courtauld and Lord Lee of Fareham.
Works by Botticelli, Bellini, Tintoretto; English and Dutch portraits;
impressionist and post impressionist paintings. Furniture, sculpture and other
objets d'art. Lee, Gambier-Parry and Fry collections and Witt collection of Old
Master drawings. Open: 10.00–17.00 Mon. to Sat., 14.00–17.00 Sun. Closed Bank
Holidays.
Court Dress Collection, see Kensington Palace p. 97.
Cuming Museum, Walworth Rd., SE17. 01-703 3324 **AZ 9L 147**
History and archaeology of Southwark and Lambeth. Open: 10.00–17.30. Sat.
17.00. Closed Sun.
Dulwich College Picture Gallery, College Rd., SE21. 01-693 5254 **AZ 7E 94**
Opened in 1814, London's first public art gallery, designed by Sir John Soane.
Includes works by Rembrandt, Hogarth, Gainsborough, Reynolds, Raphael,
Veronese, Canaletto, Tiepolo, Rubens, Van Dyck, Murillo, Poussin and Watteau.
See also **Soane's Museum** page 81. Open: 10.00–13.00. 1400–17.00 Tues. to Sat.,
14.00–17.00 Sun. Closed Mondays.
Epping Forest Museum, Queen Elizabeth's Hunting Lodge, Rangers Rd., E4.
Local History collection including history of mammals and birds in the area.
16th cent. shooting lodge. Open: 14.00–18.00 Wed. to Sun. Admission charge.
Faraday Museum, Royal Institution, 20 Albermarle St., W1. 01-409 2992 **3C 33**
Material on Faraday's work and life including his own laboratory and equipment.
Open: 13.00–16.00 Tues. and Thurs. Admission charge.
Forty Hall Museum, Forty Hill, Enfield. 01–363 8196
Local history museum. House built 1629–1700, plaster ceilings. Open: Excepting
closed Mondays; open daily.
Foundling Hospital Art Treasures, Thomas Coram Foundation, 40 Brunswick
Sq., WC1. 01–278 2424 **3D 11.** Sometimes closed for functions.
Includes pictures by Hogarth, Gainsborough and Knellar given to raise money for
the Foundling Hospital; a charity founded in 1739 for the care of destitute children.
Score of Handel's Messiah. Open: 10.00–16.00 Mon. to Fri. Admission charge.
Geffrye Museum, Kingsland Rd., E2. 01-739 8368 **AZ 1D 142**
Period rooms showing the development of furniture, crafts and domestic
equipment from 1600; space devoted to children's work and interests.
Almshouses, 1715 for the widows of Ironmongers Company members. Open:
10.00–17.00 Tues. to Sat., 14.00–17.00 Sun.
Geological Museum, Exhibition Rd., SW7. 01-589 3444 **1C 59**
HISTORY: Opened in 1841 as the Museum of Economic Geology and moved to
present building in 1935. Museum of the Institute of Geological Sciences, an
important research centre.
CONTENT: Huge collection of rocks, minerals and fossils, including moon rock.
Also models and dioramas. Regional Geology and scenery of Great Britain. Economic
geology and mineralogy of the world. Special exhibitions include, Gemstones,
Treasures of the Earth, Britain before Man, The story of the Earth, British
Fossils.
SERVICES: Films and Lectures. Library, Literature, Maps, Photos, Souvenir shop.
Open: 10.00–18.00 Mon. to Sat., 14.30–18.00 Sun. Closed Christmas Eve and
Day, Boxing Day, Good Fri.

Greenwich Museum, see Plumstead Museum.

Guildhall Art Gallery, Guildhall, EC2. 01-606 3030 **1D 39**
Pictures from the Corporation of London collection; also special loan exhibitions
and exhibitions by art societies. Open: 10.00–17.00 Mon. to Sat. Closed
Christmas Day, Boxing Day, Good Fri., Spring and Summer Hol. Mons.

Gunnersbury Park Museum, Gunnersbury Park, W3. 01-992 1612 **AZ 3G 73**
Local history and archaeology. Also Rothschild relics including maps, prints and
coaches in early 19th cent. mansion formally belonging to the Rothschilds.
Open: pm Daily. Closed Christmas Eve, Day, Boxing Day, Good Fri.

Hayes and Harlington Museum, Hayes Library, Golden Crescent, Hayes. Small
local collection. Open: Library hours.

Hayward Gallery, Belvedere Rd., SE1. 01-928 3144 **1B 52**
Arts Council special and loan exhibitions, open air sculpture courts. Opened in
1968 as part of the South Bank Arts Centre. Open: 10.00–20.00 Mon.-Wed.
10.00–18.00 Thurs., Fri. & Sat., 12.00–18.00 Sun. Closed Christmas Eve and Day,
Good Fri. Admission charge.

Heinz Gallery, Ryl. Inst. of British Architects, Portman Sq., W1 **1D 31**
Architectural drawings from the Institute's collections exhibited in rotation. Open:
11.00–17.00 Mon. to Fri. (also 10.00–01.00 Sat. and Sun. during exhibitions).

Herald's Museum, see Tower of London.

Heritage Motor Museum, Syon Park, Brentford. 01-560 1378 **AZ 1D 88**
A collection of over 100 cars showing the development of the motor vehicle from
1895. Open 10.00–17.00 daily (16.00 winter). See also Syon House.

Historic Ship Collection, see St. Katharine's Dock page 102.

Horniman Museum, London Rd., SE23. 01–699 1872 **AZ 1H 111**
Deals with man and his environment, ethnographical and natural history
collections, musical instruments. Library. Art Nouveau building design by C.
Harrison Townsend, 1901. Open: 10.30–18.00 Mon. to Sat., 14.00–18.00 Sun.

Imperial War Museum, Lambeth Rd., SE1. 01-735 8922 **1D 67**
HISTORY: Occupies buildings designed 1812 by Lewis as Bethlehem Hospital, a
hospital for the insane and origin of the word Bedlam. Museum founded 1917.
CONTENT: All aspects of warfare since 1914 in which British and Commonwealth
forces have been involved. Equipment and exhibits used by and relating to
Royal Air Force, Royal Navy, Army and other services. Captured enemy equipment
includes a German one-man submarine. A selection of the museum's works
of art, paintings, drawings, prints by War artists including Paul Nash, John Piper,
Anthony Gross; sculpture by Epstein and others. Voluntary admission charges.
LIBRARY: Collection of books, periodicals, papers, maps, films and photographs.
SERVICES: Lectures, films, cafe.
Open: 10.00–17.50 Mon. to Sat., 14.00–17.50 Sun. Closed Christmas Eve and
Day, Boxing Day, Good Fri., New Year's Day. Reference depts., by appt., Mon. to Fri.

Independent Broadcasting Authority Television Gallery, 70 Brompton Rd.
SW3. **3B 46.** Illustrates the history of television. Open by appointment.

Institute of Contemporary Arts, Nash Ho., The Mall, SW1. 01–930 3647 **1B 50**
Centre for the Arts of today, 3 galleries, 2 cinemas, video library and theatre.
Restaurant, Bar. Open: 12.00–23.00 all week. Varying charges for different
events. Entrance by membership, day membership available for visitors.

Iveagh Bequest, Kenwood House, Hampstead La., NW3. 01–348 1286 **AZ 1C 44**
Collection of Paintings including works by Boucher, Gainsborough, Guardi, Hals,
Rembrandt, Reynolds, Romney, Turner, Van Dyck, Vermeer bequeathed to
the nation by Lord Iveagh in 1927 along with Kenwood and other contents. See
also Kenwood House and Grounds—PLACES OF INTEREST. Open: 10.00–
19.00. April to September, otherwise 10.00–17.00 or dusk Closed Christmas Eve
and Day, Good Fri. Admission charge.

Jewish Museum, Woburn Ho , Upper Woburn Pl , WC1. 01-388 4525 **3B 10**
Jewish antiquities and relics illustrating Jewish life and worship Open: 10.00–
16.00 Tues. to Fri. (except winter Fri. to 12.45) Sun 10 30–12.45. Closed
Mon., Sat., Bank & Jewish Hols.

London Hospital Medical College Museum, Turner St., E1. **AZ 6J 143**
Museum of pathology. Open: College hours during the day. 01-377 8800.
London Toy & Model Museum, October House, 23 Craven Hill, W2. 01-262 9450
2B 28. Shows history of commercially made toys and models, features period
shop displays. Open: 10.00–17.30, Tues. to Sat. 11.00–17.00 Sun. Closed Mon.
Admission charge.
London Transport Museum, Wellington St., WC2. 01-379 6344 **2D 35**
Historic vehicles and exhibits: early steam and electric locomotives, horse buses,
motor buses (including the famous 'B' type), tram cars, trolley buses. Also
posters, tickets, signs, etc. In the historic Covent Garden Flower Mkt. Hall. Open:
Daily 10.00–18.00, closed Christmas Day and Boxing Day. Admission charge.
Martinware Pottery Collection, District Library, Osterley Park Rd., Southall.
AZ 3D 70. Open Library hours.
M.C.C. Cricket Museum, Lords Cricket Ground, St. John's Wood Rd., NW8. **2D
5**
History of cricket and of Lords. Open: During match days or by appointment.
Admission charge.
Middlesex Regiment Museum see **Bruce Castle Museum.**
Museum of Blindiana, Royal National Institute for the Blind, 224 Gt. Portland St.
W1. **1C 17.** Open: by appointment. 01-388 1266
Museums of Economic Botany, Royal Botanical Gardens, Kew. **AZ 7F 73**
Collections of plant products within General, Wood, and Reference Museums
(latter not open to the public). Open: 10.00–16.50 Daily (17.50 Sun.) or dusk if earlier.
Closed Christmas Eve and Day, Boxing Day, Good Fri. 01-940 1171.
Museum of Garden History, see Lambeth Palace, p. 98.
Museum of London, London Wall, EC2. 01-600 3699 **3C 23**
HISTORY: Opened 1976, formed from the former Guildhall and London Museums.
CONTENTS: Arranged in chronological order to present a visual history of London
from prehistoric times to the present day. Exhibits include the Lord Mayor's Coach,
Great Fire of London Room, 18th-cent. prison cell, 19th-cent. shops.
LIBRARY AND PRINT ROOM: Specializing in all London topics.
SERVICES: Lectures, Education Department, Shop, Refreshments.
Open: 10.00–18.00 Tues. to Sat. 14.00–18.00 Sun. Closed Mon., Christmas Day
and Boxing Day.
Museum of Mankind, 6 Burlington Gardens, W1. 01-437 2224 **3D 33**
Ethnography Department of the British Museum. Exhibitions portraying the lives
and culture of peoples throughout the world. Films, students' room. Open:
10.00–17.00 Mon. to Sat., 14.30–18.00 Sun. Closed Christmas Eve and Day,
Boxing Day, Good Fri., New Year's Day.
Museum of the Order of St. John, St. John's Gate, EC1. 01-253 6644 **1A 22**
The most comprehensive collection of relics to the Medieval Order outside Malta;
together with the history of the St. John Ambulance Brigade. Open: 10.00–
18.00 Tues. and Fri.; to 16.00 Sat. See also St. John's Gate p.102.
Museum of the Pharmaceutical Society of Great Britain, 1 Lambeth High St.,
SE1. 01-735 9141 **2A 66.** Society's collection on pharmacy. Open: By appointment.
Musical Museum, see British Piano and Musical Museum.
National Army Museum, Royal Hospital Rd.; SW3. 01-730 0717 **AZ 6D 76**
HISTORY: Originally at the Royal Military Academy, Sandhurst it is now housed in
a specially designed new building next to Chelsea Royal Hospital.
CONTENT: Covers the history of the Army from Henry VII up to the present day,
including the Falklands War. Also the history of Commonwealth armies until their
independence, including the Indian Army up to partition in 1947. The displays
illustrate important campaigns, the evolution of uniforms and weaponry, also notable
orders, decorations, insignia and honours. Art Gallery has portraits by Reynolds,
Gainsborough etc.
READING ROOM: Book and army lists, prints, drawings, photographs.
Open: 10.00–17.30 Mon. to Sat., 14.00–17.30 Sun. Closed Christmas Eve and
Day, Boxing Day, Good Fri., New Year's Day.

National Gallery, Trafalgar Sq., WC2. 01-839 3321 **3C 35**
HISTORY: Founded 1824. The gallery built 1834–7 was designed by William Wilkins, columns from Carlton House were adopted for the portico.
CONTENT: Covers all major European artists and movements from 13th to 19th cent. Arranged under schools: British, Early Netherland, Early German, Dutch, Flemish, French, Italian and Spanish. Reserve collections in the basement. See Tate Gallery for Modern Painting, sculpture and the National Gallery of English Art (16th cent. onwards).
SERVICES: Lectures, large collection of reproductions, mounting and framing service. Restaurant.
Open: 10.00–18.00 Mon. to Sat., 14.00–18.00 Sun. Closed Christmas Eve and Day, Boxing Day, Good Fri.

National Maritime Museum, Romney Rd., SE10. 01-858 4422 **AZ 6F 81**
Shows the maritime history of Great Britain from Tudor times to the Second World War. Special exhibitions include relics, portraits of Admiral Nelson and Battle of Trafalgar exhibits; new Boat Archaeology Gallery; figureheads, ships models, State Barge of 1689, paddle steamer, Shackleton's boat, navigation room, print room and a large collection of seascapes, naval scenes and portraits by Hogarth, Reynolds, Gainsborough, Turner, Van de Velde and others. Print room and library available for study and reference. An annexe of the museum, at the Old Royal Observatory, Flamsteed House, exhibits astronomical and navigational equipment. See also Greenwich, page 93. Open: 10.00–18.00 Mon. to Sat., 14.00–17.30 Sun. (Closes 17.00 winter). Closed most Bank Holidays. Admission charge.

National Museum of Artillery, The Rotunda, Green Hill, SE18. 01-856 5533 ext. 385. **AZ 5D 82.** Firearms collections exhibited in a metal tent designed by Nash, originally erected in St. James's Park, 1814. See also Royal Artillery Regimental Museum. Open. Mon. to Fri. 12.00–17.00. Sat & Sun. 13.00–17.00. Closes 16.00 April to Oct.

National Museum of Labour History, Limehouse Town Hall, Commercial Road, E14. 01-515 3229 **AZ 6G 63.** Depicts the rise of the Labour movement. Open: 09.30–17.00. Mon. to Friday.

National Portrait Gallery, 2 St. Martin's Pl., WC2. 01-930 1552 **3C 35**
Portraits of Royalty and well-known British men and women from the Middle Ages to the present day, works by Gainsborough, Holbein and Reynolds. The purpose of the gallery is to illustrate British History by focussing on significant historical and literary characters. Shop selling prints, cards, books and records. Open: 10.00–17.00 Mon. to Fri., 10.00–18.00 Sat., 14.00–18.00 Sun. Closed Christmas Eve and Day, Boxing Day, Good Fri.

National Postal Museum, King Edward St., EC1. 01-432 3851 **3B 22**
Philatelic collections from Great Britain and the World. Drawings, documents, library. Open: 10.00–16.30 Mon. to Thurs. to 16.00 Fri.

Natural History Museum, (British Museum, Dept. of), Cromwell Rd., SW7. 01-589 6323 **2C 59**
HISTORY: The nucleus of the collection is that of Sir Hans Sloane (d. 1753). Present building designed by Alfred Waterhouse was opened in 1880 and is an important research centre. CONTENT: There are departments of zoology including the whale and mammal galleries, entomology, palaeontology including reconstructed Dinosaur and Pterodactyl, mineralogy, botany. Special Exhibitions— Introducing Ecology, Human Biology, Dinosaurs & Their Living Relatives, Man's Place in Evolution, Origin of Species, British Natural History. Children's centre. Library for reference and study.
SERVICES: Tours, lectures, films, cards, books, souvenirs, cafeteria.
Open: 10.00–18.00 Mon. to Sat., 14.30–18.00 Sun. Closed Christmas Eve and Day, Boxing Day, Good Fri., New Year's Day.

Passmore Edwards Museum, 115 Romford Rd., E15. 01–519 4296 **AZ 6G 49**
Local History, Essex archaeology etc. Open 10.00–18.00 Mon., Tues., Wed., Fri.; 10.00–20.00 Thurs.; 10.00–13.00, 14.00–17.00 Sat. Closed Bank Hols.

Percival David Foundation of Chinese Art, 53 Gordon Sq., WC1. 01-387 3909
1B 18. Collection of Chinese ceramics and library of Chinese art. Open: 10.35–
17.00 Tues. to Fri., 14.00–16.00 Mon., 10.30–13.00 Sat. Closed Bank Hols.
Plumstead Museum, 232 Plumstead High St., SE18. 01-855 3240 **AZ 4H 83**
Local History, stuffed mammals etc. Open: 10.00–13.00, 14.00–17.00 Tues. to
Sat. except Mon. 14.00–20.00. Closed Wed. and Sun.
Pollocks Toy Museum, 1 Scala St., W1. 01-636 3452 **2A 18**
Collection of toys and dolls of many periods, toy theatres, optical effect toys. Sells
replicas, toy cut-out theatres, gingerbread men and sweets. Open: 10.00–
17.00 Mon. to Sat. Admission charge.
Public Record Office Museum, Chancery La., WC2. 01-405 0741 **1C 37**
Public archives, documents and state papers. Historical items include Domesday
Book and Magna Carta; Signatures and Documents connected with Byron,
Chaucer, Cardinal Wolsey, Florence Nightingale, Guy Fawkes, Napoleon, Nelson,
Shakespeare, Wellington, Wesley and Sovereigns of England from Richard II to
Elizabeth II. Open: 13.00–16.00 Mon. to Fri. Closed Christmas Eve and Day, Boxing
Day, Good Fri., Bank Hol. Mons. See also page 98.
Queen's Gallery, Buckingham Palace Rd., SW1. **3C 49**
Changing exhibitions selected from the Royal collection of paintings and art
treasures. Open: 11.00–17.00 Tues. to Sat., 14.00–17.00 Sun. Admission
charge.
Royal Academy of Arts, Burlington House, Piccadilly, W1. 01-734 9052 **3D 33**
Founded in 1768 and Sir Joshua Reynolds appointed the first president. Best
known for its annual summer exhibition of works by living artists (May to Aug.)
its opening being the start of the London season. Open: 10.00–18.00 daily.
Admission charge for exhibitions. Publications Dept., shop, picture framing.
Restaurant.
Royal Air Force Museum, Hendon, NW9. 01-205 2266 **AZ 2C 26**
Opened in 1972, it portrays the history of aviation: aircraft from World War I
onwards; 100 years of aviation history from the military balloonists of the
1870's onwards; including technical equipment, uniforms, photographs. Research
centre with books, photos, records etc. SERVICES: Lectures, films,
Restaurant, Car Park. Open: 10.00–18.00 Mon. to Sat., 14.00–18.00 Sun. Closed
Christmas Day, Boxing Day, Good Fri., New Year's Day. **Battle of Britain Museum,**
opened 1978. A collection of British, German and Italian aircraft engaged in the
Battle include: Spitfire, Hurricane, Messerschmitt, Heinkel, Junkers, etc., also
equipment, uniforms, etc. Admission charge. **Bomber Command Museum**
includes an extensive range of famous bomber aircraft. Admission charge.
Royal Artillery Regimental Museum, Old Royal Military Academy, Academy Rd.,
SE18. 01-856 5533 ext. 2523 **AZ 7E 82.** Uniforms, pictures, dioramas etc. See
also **National Museum of Artillery.** Open: 10.00–12.30, 14.00–16.00 Mon. to Fri.
Royal College of Music, Prince Consort Rd., SW7. 01-589 3643 **3C 45**
A museum of instruments from all over the world, includes the Donaldson
Collection. Open by appointment.
Royal College of Surgeons' Museum, Lincoln's Inn Fields, WC2. 01-405 3474
1B 36 Medical museum, including the Hunter Collection. Open: Members of
the Medical Profession and others on application to the Secretary.
Royal Fusiliers Regimental Museum see **Tower of London.**
St. Bartholomew's Hospital Pathological Museum, West Smithfield, EC1. 01-
600 9000 **3B 22.** Open: primarily for medical students and research. By appt.
St. Bride's Crypt Museum, St. Bride's Church, Bride La., EC4. 01-353 1301 **1D
37**
Illustrates the history of St. Bride's; includes archaeological finds. Also the history
of print etc. Open: 09.00–17.00 daily.
St. Thomas's Hospital Operating Theatre Museum, St Thomas St., SE1. **1A 56**
Early 19th cent. operating theatre, operating equipment, and stories of some
famous characters involved. Open: 12.30–16.00 Mon., Wed., Fri. Admission
charge.

Science Museum, Exhibition Rd., SW7. 01-589 3456 **1C 59**
HISTORY: Originally part of the South Kensington Museum proposed by the Prince
Consort after the Great Exhibition of 1851. Became known as the Science
Museum in 1909.
CONTENT: Science and technology collections with working models and
dioramas. Sections on motive power; weights and measures; electric power;
road and rail transport including Puffing Billy; gas manufacture and distribution;
meteorology; time measurement; astronomy; map making and surveying;
chemistry and nuclear power; air and sea navigation; physics and allied subjects;
space exploration and rockets. Children's gallery. Library of pure and applied science.
Includes the galleries of the Wellcome Historical Medical Museum; exhibits
include complete 1905 Pharmacy and 1980 Operating Theatre.
SERVICES: Lectures, films, Tea Bar.
Open: 10.00–18.00 Mon. to Sat., 14.30–18.00 Sun. Closed Christmas Eve and
Day, Boxing Day, Good Fri., New Year's Day.
Serpentine Gallery, Kensington Gardens, W2. 01-402 6075 **2C 45** Arts Council
exhibitions of contemporary art. Open daily during exhibitions.
Sir John Soane's Museum, Lincoln's Inn Fields, WC2. 01-405 2107 **2B 20**
Founded by Soane, consists of the house to his own design, his personal collection
of works of art including Hogarth's "Rakes Progress"; furniture antiquities,
books and drawings as arranged by him before his death in 1837. Open: 10.00–
17.00 Tues. to Sat. Closed all August and Bank Hols.
Tate Gallery, Millbank, SW1. 01-821 1313 **3C 65**
HISTORY: The National Collection of British Art made possible by the bequest
from Sir Francis Chantrey 1841. Other bequests followed, including the
collection of Henry Tate who also financed the building of the gallery. Designed by·
Sidney R. J. Smith it was opened in 1897. Additional galleries have since been
added to house collections of Modern Foreign Painting and Modern Sculpture and
the Turner Collection.
CONTENT: British Painting from the 16th cent. to the present day, including the
collection of Turner paintings, and Blake paintings, water-colours, drawings and prints.
Lower ground floor covers the Modern Foreign art movements and their principal
artists. The sculpture collection includes works by Henry Moore. There are
also special exhibitions and retrospectives.
SERVICES: Lectures, large collection of postcards, books, reproductions.
Restaurant. Open: 10.00–17.50 Mon. to Sat., 14.00–17.50 Sun. Closed
Christmas Eve and Day, Boxing Day, Good Fri., New Year's Day.
Telecom Technology Showcase, Baynard Ho., Queen Victoria St., EC4. 01-248
7444 **2B 38.** The story of Telecommunications; includes many working models
and video presentations. Open 09.00–17.00 Mon. to Fri.
Theatre Museum. Due to open in Covent Garden Flower Market **2D 35,** during
1987. A branch of the Victoria and Albert Museum it will include its theatre
collections; and the contents of the British Theatre Museum from Leighton House.
Will include material on the history of Ballet and Diaghilev.
University College Collections, Gower St., WC1. **1A 18**
Flaxman Gallery: Models and Drawings by Flaxman beneath the Central dome,
can be seen during college hours. Egyptology department museum: Open: 10.00–
12.00, 13.30–17.00 Mon. to Fri. Zoology and Comparative Anatomy: By
appointment.
University of London: Dept. of Geology Museum, Queen Mary College, Mile
End Rd., E1. **AZ 5J 63.** Open: 10.00–16.00 Mon. to Fri. By appointment.
Valence House Museum, Becontree Av., E17. 01-592 2211 **AZ 1F 33**
Local history including Fanshawe Portraits in 17th-cent. Manor House still partly
moated. Open by appointment.
Vestry House Museum, see **Walthamstow Museum.**
Victoria and Albert Museum, Cromwell Rd., SW7. 01-589 6371 **1D 59**
HISTORY: Grew out of the Museum of Manufactures opened in 1852 and later

became the South Kensington Museum. Present buildings designed by Aston Webb were begun in 1899.
COLLECTION: Fine and applied art from all countries, styles and periods arranged in two groups. (1) Primary Collections: all arts brought together by style, period or nationality. (2) Departmental Collections: exhibits grouped on the basis of departments, e.g. sculpture, textiles, woodwork etc. Dept. of Prints, Drawings, Paintings and Photographs holds the National Collection of Art Photographs; photographic galleries opened for the first time in 1982.
LIBRARY: The National Art Library, containing books, pamphlets, periodicals and a photographic collection.
SERVICES: Lectures, restaurant. Crafts Shop, Books, Postcards etc.
Open: 10.00–17.50 Mon. to Thurs. and Sat. 14.30–17.50 Sun. Closed Fridays, Christmas Eve and Day, Boxing Day. Voluntary admission charges.
Wallace Collection, Hertford House, Manchester Sq., W1. 01-935 0687 **3A 16**
Bequeathed to the nation by Lady Wallace (d. 1897). The house formerly Manchester House was built 1776–78 for the 4th Duke of Manchester. Amongst its paintings, furniture and other works of art, the French 17th, 18th cents. are well represented. Paintings by Rembrandt, Rubens, Holbein, Gainsborough, Pieter de Hooch, Hals, Van Dyck, Watteau. Large collection of arms and armour. Open: 10.00–17.00 Mon. to Sat., 14.00–17.00 Sun. Closed Christmas Eve and Day, Boxing Day, Good Fri., New Year's Day, May Day.
Walthamstow Museum, Old Vestry House, Vestry Rd., E17. 01-527 5544 **AZ 4D 32**
Local History collection in early 18th cent. workhouse. Open: 10.00–13.00, 14.00–17.30 Mon. to Fri. to 17.00 Sat. Closed Sun. & Bank Hols.
Wellcome Historical Medical Museum, see **Science Museum.**
Wellington Museum, Apsley House, 149 Piccadilly, W1. 01-499 5676 **2A 48**
Paintings, works of art and personal relics of the Duke of Wellington. See also Apsley House—PLACES OF INTEREST. Open: 10.00–18.00 Tues., Wed., Thurs. and Sat., 14.30–18.00 Sun. Closed Mon., Fri. & Bank Hols. Admission charge.
Westminster Abbey Collection, Westminster Abbey, Broad Sanctuary, SW1. 01-222 5152 **3C 51.** The museum of Abbey Treasures is housed in the Norman Undercroft, it contains wax effigies carried at funerals of persons buried in the Abbey including Elizabeth I, Charles II, Mary II, William III, Queen Anne, wooden effigies of Edward III, Henry VII, Mary I; old seals and charters, 14th, 15th cent. chests. Coronation Chair made for Mary II. Open: Daily 10.30–16.00. Closed Christmas Day, Good Fri. Admission charge.
Whitechapel Art Gallery, Whitechapel High St., E1. 01-377 0107 **AZ 7F 142**
Stages loan exhibitions, features modern art movements. Building designed by C. H. Townsend 1899. Open: 11.00–17.50 Tues to Sun.
William Morris Gallery, Water House, Lloyd Park, Forest Rd., E17. 01-527 5544 **AZ 4J 3**
Memorial to Morris including a collection of his designs, personal relics, examples of craftsmanship (carpets, woodwork etc.). Also Brangwyn's work. Open: 10.00–13.00, 14.00–17.00 Tues. to Sat., 10.00–12.00, 14.00–17.00 every first Sun. Closed Bank Hols.
Wimbledon Lawn Tennis Museum, Church Rd., SW19. 01-946 6131 **AZ 5G 107.**
Shows history and development of tennis. Open: 11.00–17.00 Tues. to Sat. 14.00–17.00 Sun. (Except during Championships—ring for details). Admission charge.
Wimbledon Society's Museum, Village Club, Ridgeway, SW19. **AZ 7E 106.** Local and natural history. 14.30–17.00 Sat. only.
Wimbledon Windmill and Museum, SW19. 01-788 7655 **AZ 3D 106,** Sat. and Sun. 14.00–17.00 (Summer). History of windmills and milling.

NEWSPAPERS, NEWS AGENCIES AND PRESS CUTTING AGENCIES

Foreign Press Ass., 11 Carlton House Terr., SW1. 01-930 0445 **1B 50**
London International Press Centre, 76 Shoe La. 01-353 4757 **1D 37**
Press Ass., 85 Fleet St., EC4. 24 hrs. 01-353 7440 **1D 37**

NEWSPAPER OFFICES
Daily Express, Fleet St., EC4. 01-353 8000 **1D 37**
Daily Mail, Northcliffe Ho., Tudor St., EC4. 01-353 6000 **2D 37**
Daily Mirror, Holborn Circus, EC1. 01-353 0246 **3D 21**
Daily Star, The, Fleet St., EC4. 01-353 8000 **1D 37**
Daily Telegraph, 135 Fleet St., EC4. 01-353 4242 **1D 37**
Economist, 25 St. James's St., SW1. 01-839 7000 **1D 49**
Financial Times, Bracken Ho., Cannon St., EC4. 01-248 8000 **2C 39**
Guardian, 119 Farringdon Rd., EC1. 01-278 2332 **1D 21**
Irish Times, 85 Fleet St., EC4. 01-353 8981 **1D 37**
Jewish Chronicle, 25 Furnival St., EC4. 01-405 9252 **3C 21**
News of the World, 1 Pennington St., EC1. 01-481 4100 **AZ 7H 63**
New Statesman, 14 Farrington La., EC1. 01-253 2001 **AZ 4A 62**
Observer, 8 St. Andrews Hill, EC4. 01-236 0202 **2A 38**
Scotsman, The, Pemberton Ho., East Harding St., EC4. 01-353 9051 **1D 57**
Standard, The, 118 Fleet St., EC4. 01-353 8000 **1D 37**
Sun, 1 Pennington St., E1. 01-481 4100 **AZ 7H 63**
Sunday Express, Fleet St., EC4. 01-353 8000 **1D 37**
Sunday Mirror, Holborn Cir., EC1. 01-353 0246 **3D 21**
Sunday People, 9 New Fetter La., EC4. 01-353 0246 **3D 21**
Sunday Telegraph, 135 Fleet St., EC4. 01-353 4242 **1D 37**
Sunday Times, 1 Pennington St., E1. 01-481 4100 **AZ 7H 63**
The Times, 1 Pennington St., E1. 01-481 4100 **AZ 7H 63**
Today, News (UK) Ltd. Allen Ho., 70 Vauxhall Bri. Rd., SW1. 01-630 1333 **2D 63**

NEWS AGENCIES
Parliamentary Press Gallery, House of Commons. 01-219 4700

A.D.N., 47 Fleet St., EC4. 01-353 5428 **1C 37**
Associated Press, 12 Norwich St., EC4. 01-353 1515 **3C 21**
Central News Service, Southwark Crown Ct., Battlebridge La., SE1. 01-378 6081 **AZ 1E 78**
D.M. News Service, 226 Strand, WC2. 01-353 6434 **2A 36**
Economic News Agency, 12 Petersham Pl., SW7. 01-589 6891 **1A 58**
Exchange Telegraph, 1 E. Harding St., EC4. 01-353 1080 **1D 37**
Fowlers Press Agency, 226 Strand, WC2. 01-353 6612 **2A 36**
Fleet Street News Agency, 68 Exmouth Mkt., EC1. 01-278 5661 **AZ 4A 62**
Gemini News Service, 21 John St., WC1. 01-353 2567 **1B 20**
Internews, Dulwich Rd., SE4. 01-737 1012 **AZ 5A 94**
London News & Photographic Service, 68 Exmouth Mkt., EC1. 01-278 5661 **AZ 4A 62**
Press Association, 85 Fleet St., EC4. 01-353 7440 **1C 37**
Reuters, 85 Fleet St., EC4. 01-250 1122 **1C 37**
Southam News Services, 43 Fleet St., EC4. 01-583 7322 **1C 37**
Tass News Agency, Communications Ho., Gough Sq., EC4. 01-353 9831 **1D 37**
United Press International, 8 Bouverie St., EC4. 01-353 2282 **1D 37**
United Press Int. Photo Library, 24 Bride St., EC4. 01-353 9665 **1B 48**

PRESS CUTTING AGENCIES
Associated Press Cuttings, 52 Fetter La., EC4. 01-353 7191 **1C 37**
Durrants Press Cuttings Ltd., 103 Whitecross St., EC1. 01-588 3671 **1C 23**
Foreign Press Clipping Service, see Press Clipping Bureau.

International Press Cutting Bureau, 70 Newington Causeway, SE1. 01-403 0608 **AZ 3C 78**
Newsclip (U.K.) Ltd., 52 Fetter La., EC4. 01-353 7191 **1C 37**
Press Clipping Bureau, Hale Ho., Green Lanes, N13. 01-882 0155 **AZ 6E 16**

OPEN AIR ENTERTAINMENT

ANIMALS
Enclosures, aviaries and sanctuaries can be seen in the following parks:
   Brockwell Pk., Dulwich Rd., SE24. **AZ 5A 94**
   Clissold Pk., Green Lanes, N4. **AZ 3C 46**
   Dulwich Pk., College Rd., SE21. **AZ 7E 94**
   Golders' Hill Pk., Sandy Rd., NW3. **AZ 2K 43**
   Holland Pk., W8. **3A 42**
   Maryon Wilson Pk., Charlton Pk. Rd., SE7. **AZ 6B 82**
   Regent's Pk., NW1. **2A 8 and 1D 7**
   St James's Pk., SW1. **2A 50**
   Sydenham Wells Pk., Wells Pk. Rd., SE26. **AZ 3G 111**
   Victoria Pk., Victoria Pk. Rd., E9. **AZ 1J 63**
   Waterlow Pk., Highgate High St., N6. **AZ 1E 44**
Crystal Palace Children's Zoo, Crystal Palace Park, SE20. 01-778 4487 **AZ 6H 111**
Open Easter to Sept., Weekdays 13.30–17.30, weekends, Bank and School Hols. 11.00–18.00. Elsewhere in Park are rowing boats, adventure playground etc.
Chessington Zoo, Leatherhead Rd., Chessington, Surrey. Epsom 27227. Set in the grounds of the 17th cent. Mansion "Burnt Stub", contains most animals. Feeding times are every hour on the hour starting at 11.00 with the great apes. Other attractions include a new two-acre Bird Garden, Pets' Corner with Pony and Donkey rides and many animals from home and abroad, Model Railway, Miniature Railway, Playfield, Model Village, Dinosaur Park, and Circus (summer). Restaurant, Cafe, Car Park.
Open: 10.00–17.00 Weekdays, 10.00–18.00 Weekends. Closes 16.00 winter months. Admission charge.
London Zoo, Regent's Park, NW1. 01-722 3333 **1A 8**
London Zoo opened in 1828. Now contains over 6,000 animals. Special attractions include Aquarium, Snowdon Aviary (an outdoor home for birds), Elephant and Rhinoceros Pavilion, Children's Zoo and Farm and Nocturnal Hall where day and night are reversed. Feeding times: Sea Lions 12.00, 15.30 (winter 14.30) not Fri. Penguins 14.30, Pelicans 14.45, Eagles 15.15 not Thurs, Reptiles 14.30 Fri. only. Other attractions include animal rides and elephant bathing. Restaurant, Cafe, Car Park. Open 09.00 summer, 10.00 winter to 18.00 or dusk whichever is earlier. Closed Christmas Day. Admission charges.
Windsor Safari Park, Royal Windsor, Berks. Windsor 69847.
Drive-round game reserve and many animal enclosures including performing whales and dolphins, exotic birds, reptile house, kiddies' corner. Restaurant, Cafe, Car Park. Open from April to end Sept. daily 10.00–17.00 or dusk if earlier.

ART EXHIBITIONS
Green Park. 2C 49. Railings on Piccadilly side. Weekends.
Hampstead, Heath St., NW3. **AZ 3A 44**
Hampstead Arts Council. Weekends June to Aug.
Hyde Park. 3B 30 Railings on Bayswater Rd. side. Sundays.
Terrace Gardens, The, Richmond. AZ 6E 88
Richmond Art Group. Weekends in May and June.
Victoria Embankment Gardens, WC2. **3D 35** During May.

LONDON ZOO

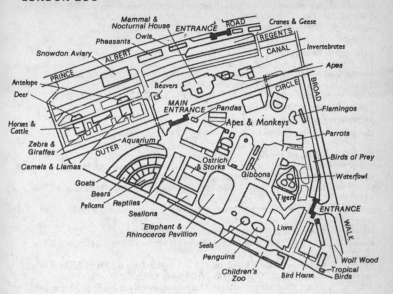

BRASS BANDS
Times of concerts in parks vary; see adjacent notice boards for details of events and performing bands.
Changing the Guard. Buckingham Palace, SW1. **3C 49**
Daily at 11.30, alternate days in winter months, see also page 29.
Hyde Park, W1. **1D 47**
June and July, Sunday afternoon and evening performances.
Lincoln's Inn Fields, WC2. **3B 20**
Lunchtime concerts during May, June, July and Aug., see notices.
Regent's Park, NW1. **1A8**
Sunday afternoon and evening performances during summer months, see notices.
Royal Military School of Music, Kneller Hall, Twick. 01-894 1245 **AZ 6H 87**
Concerts Wed. evenings May to Sept., 20.00. Admission charge.
St. James's Park, SW1. **2B 50**
Daily performances June, July and August, see notices.
St. Paul's Cathedral Steps, St. Paul's Churchyard, EC4.
12.00 Thursdays, alternating weekly with concerts in Paternoster Sq. from May or June then July, Aug. and Sept.
Victoria Embankment Gardens, SW1. **3D 35.**
May, June, July. Afternoon and evening performances, daily, see notices.

BUSKERS
Traditionally perform to waiting queues at leading cinemas and theatres and in recent years in subway corners.
The Market, Covent Garden, **2D 35.** This pedestrian shopping precinct is the daily venue for licensed buskers performing jazz, classical music, Punch and Judy
c, (10.00–20.00 except in bad weather), see also page 91.

CONCERTS

Symphony concerts are organized at: **Crystal Palace Concert Bowl. AZ 6H 111, Holland Park Court Theatre. 3A 42.** and **Kenwood Lakeside. AZ 1C 44,** during the summer months, see press notices for details.

FAIRS

Blackheath Bank Holiday Fair, Blackheath, SE3. **AZ 1F 97**
Easter, Spring and Summer Bank Holidays.
Hampstead Heath Bank Holiday Fair, Nr. North End Way, NW3. **AZ 2A 44**
Easter, Spring and Summer Bank Holidays.
Wormwood Scrubs Bank Holiday Fair, Wormwood Scrubs, W12. **AZ 5B 58**
Easter, Spring and Summer Bank Holidays.

NATURE TRAILS & TOWN TRAILS

Canal Walks: It is possible to walk some 40 miles along London's canal network. The Grand Union Canal and Regents Canal towing path extends from Limehouse **AZ 6B 64,** via Regents Park **1A 6,** and Little Venice **2A 12** to Uxbridge; and is usually open 09.00 to sunset. For guided walks see page 189. Further details from London Visitor & Convention Bureau.
Coach House and Dutch Barn Trails, Horniman Gdns., London Rd., SE23. **AZ 1H 111**
In the grounds of the Horniman Museum, teaching packs available from Museum or kiosk. Gardens open dawn to dusk.
Natural History Museum Trail, Cromwell Rd., SW7. **2C 59**
Indoor trail around various galleries. Trail sheets from the Children's Centre. 10.00–16.30 Sat. and during school holidays.
Railway Trail, from London Rd. **AZ 1H 111** to Langton Rise **AZ 7H 95** SE23. Along the line of disused railway. Open 09.00–16.00 Mon. to Fri., 09.00–18.00 Sat. and Sun. Teaching Pack from Horniman Museum, London Rd. No unaccompanied children or dogs.
Silver Jubilee Walkway. An eleven-mile circular route marked by a silver crown emblem set at intervals in the pavement. Route and information from London Visitor & Convention Bureau. Passes Westminster Abbey, Houses of Parliament, Tower of London, St Paul's Cathedral etc.
Walk around Historic Southwark. Route and information from London Visitor & Convention Bureau.
Blind Persons Nature Trail, Church Wood, Trent Park. **AZ 1A 6**
Braille information posts at intervals beside log-edged woodland path.

THEATRE

Court Theatre, Holland Park, W8. **3A 42**
Traditional theatre, contemporary Dance and Ballet productions during June and July. No advance booking. See press notices.
Regent's Park Open Air Theatre, Inner Circle, Regent's Park, NW1. 01-486 2431/2
3D 7. Shakespeare presented by the New Shakespeare Company during June, July and Aug. Wine tent, refreshments. Seats bookable.

PLACES OF INTEREST

See also Bridges, Cathedrals and Churches, Museums and Galleries Squares and Streets, Statues and Monuments.

Abbey Mills Pumping Station, Abbey La., E15. **AZ 2E 64**
A fine example of Victorian Civil Engineering, these pumping engines enclosed in an iron Cathedral of domes and cupola crowned towers, are still in working order. Built in 1868 to the design of J. Bazalgette, chief engineer to the Metropolitan

Board of Works who superintended the construction of the London drainage system and the Thames Embankments. Applications to visit: see TOURS AND SIGHTSEEING EXCURSIONS.

Admiralty, Whitehall, SW1. **1C 51**
Consisting of two parts, the earlier built 1722–6 to the design of T. Ripley surrounds a small courtyard off Whitehall, approached through an Adam screen of 1760. Behind this is a later building in the Italian Palladian style (1895) which connects the Admiralty Arch on the North side. Once the administrative and operational centre of the Royal Navy and later the Headquarters of the Civil Service Department.

Admiralty Arch, The Mall, SW1. **1C 51**
This triple archway separating the Mall from Trafalgar Square was built in 1910 as part of the national memorial to Queen Victoria. The centre arch is opened only for State and Royal processions.

Albany, Piccadilly, W1. **3D 33**
A Georgian mansion built to the design of Sir W. Chambers in 1770, later converted into "residential chambers for bachelor gentlemen". Famous residents have included Canning, Byron, Macaulay and Gladstone.

Alexandra Palace, Muswell Hill, N22. **AZ 2H 29**
This the second hall on the site to be destroyed by fire, is expected to reopen in 1988, completely restored and modernised as a venue for exhibitions, events, sports and meetings. Known affectionately as "Ally Pally" and famed for its enormous concert organ, it commands panoramic views of London, the extensive grounds being open to the public.

Apsley House (Wellington Museum), 149 Piccadilly, W1. 01-499 5676 **2A 48**
The home of the Duke of Wellington from 1817–52. The original building was an Adam design although little survived the modifications by B. Wyatt 1828–30, which included the refacing of the exterior, addition of a portico and redecoration of the interior. It is now the Wellington Museum and contains trophies of the Napoleonic Wars. See also **Wellington Museum.**
Open 10.00–18.00 Tues., Wed., Thurs., Sat. 14.30–18.00 Sun. Admission charge.

Auction Rooms see also Auctioneers page 11.
    CHRISTIES, 8 King St., 01-839 9060 SW1. founded 1766. **1D 49**
    SOTHEBY'S, 34 New Bond St., W1. 01-493 8080 founded 1744. **2C 33**
Are both known internationally as specialists in auctioning fine art, rare books, furniture, silver, jewellery etc. Auctions are advertised in *The Times* on Tuesdays and *Daily Telegraph* on Mondays.

Bank of England, Threadneedle St., EC2. **1D 39**
Incorporated by Royal Charter in 1694 to finance the French wars. Nationalized in 1946 the Bank of England is now the Government's bank. Its vaults contain the nation's gold reserve, it manages the National Debt, the Note issue and administers the Exchange Control Regulations. The Bank occupying this site since 1734 was rebuilt between 1788–1833 to the design of Sir J. Soane. His striking, original interiors are preserved only in drawings to be seen at Soane's Museum, the perimeter wall being the sole survivor of rebuilding between 1925–39 by Sir H. Baker. Over the portico in Threadneedle Street are sculptures by Sir C. Wheeler. Liveried messengers and gate-keepers can be seen in the entrance hall which leads to Garden Court, once the churchyard of St. Christopher-le-Stocks (a Wren church demolished 1781) and a restored Roman mosaic. Until the 1970's a military guard protected the bank at night, a measure instigated, during the Gordon Riots, 1780.

Bankside, Southwark, SE1. **3C 39**
Bankside during the Elizabethan period was similar in character to Soho today. Outside the strict rule of the City, popular taste found vent in the agglomeration of pubs, "stewes" (brothels), animal-baiting pits and theatres, including Shakespeare's Globe. The Bear Gardens Museum & Arts Centre on the site of Hope Playhouse and Bear Baiting Ring has an exhibition of Bankside history and scale models of specific playhouses.

Banqueting House, Whitehall, SW1. **1C 51**
The Banqueting House completed in 1622 is the only surviving building of Whitehall
Palace destroyed by fire in 1698. Commissioned by James I it represents along
with the Queen's House, Greenwich, the introduction of the Italian Palladian Style
into England by the architect Inigo Jones. It has a ceiling painted by Rubens in
1630 for Charles I who nineteen years later was to walk from a window to his
execution. Open Tues. to Sat. 10.00–17.00 Sun. 14.00–17.00. Admission
charge.

Barbican, EC2. 01-628 8795 **2C 23**
A post-war redevelopment designed to reintroduce a balanced residential and
cultural life back to the business City. Pedestrians are segregated from traffic on
elevated levels, accommodation is grouped around squares. The historic Church
of St. Giles and a length of the Roman and Medieval City Wall are incorporated. The
precinct includes: Barbican Centre for Arts and Conferences. Museum of London,
Guildhall School of Music and Drama, City of London School for Girls. Opened
in 1982 the Barbican Arts Centre is the London equivalent of the Lincoln Centre,
New York or the Pompidou Centre, Paris; facilities include: Barbican Hall,
Barbican Theatre, The Pit (studio theatre), Barbican Library, Art Gallery, Cinemas,
roof-top Conservatory, restaurants and car park.

Battersea Park, Battersea, SW11. **AZ 7D 76**
Formerly Battersea Fields the scene of a duel between the Duke of Wellington
and Lord Winchelsea in 1829. It was laid out as a park in the 1850's. The
Festival Gardens were added in 1951 for the Festival of Britain on the lines of the
Tivoli Gardens in Copenhagen. Includes sub-tropical garden, botanical wild
flower gardens, boating and fishing lakes, open air theatre and concert pavilion,
110 ft Japanese Peace Pagoda.

Belfast H.M.S., Symon's Wharf, Vine La., SE1. 01-407 6434 **1C 57**
The largest, most powerful cruiser built for the Royal Navy. Moored opposite the
Tower of London it now houses a R.N. museum. Open 11.00–18.00 summer,
11.00–16.00 except Tues. winter. Closed Christmas, N. Year, Good Friday, May
Day. Admission charge. Part of Imperial War Museum. Ferry runs from Tower
Pier.

Billingsgate, EC3. **3B 40**
The name of London's oldest market and since the 17th cent. the capital's principal
fish market. Trading moved to new premises at the West India Docks E14. in
1982, and the historic area of cobbled streets and alleys are scheduled for
redevelopment, although the façade of the 1874 market building will be retained.

Blackfriars, EC4. **2A 38**
An area deriving its name from the Dominican Priory founded in 1221 just outside
the City Wall. This was important enough by 1283 for Edward I to order the
rebuilding of the wall so as to encompass the Priory. The dissolution of the
monasteries saw its surrender to the Crown and what remained by 1666 was
destroyed in the Great Fire.

Blackheath, SE3. **AZ 1F 97**
The common is an open area of 267 acres. The Danes camped here in 1011; Wat
Tyler and his followers in 1381; Jack Cade in 1450; Henry VI with his Lancastrians in
1452; Lord Audley and the Cornish rebels in 1497. Here also James I introduced
golf to England. Blackheath is connected to Greenwich Park forming a mile
long stretch of parkland. To the south east is The Paragon, 1792, consisting of a
crescent of seven villas with connecting colonnades and Morden College a home for
City Merchants founded 1695.
    RANGERS HOUSE, Chesterfield Walk, SE10. 01-853 0035. 18th cent. home of 4th
      Earl of Chesterfield, his bow-fronted Gallery added 1749 now houses a
      Gallery of 16th to 18th cent. English Portraits. Open 10.00–17.00 (to 16.00 Nov.
      to Jan.).

Boston Manor, Boston Manor Rd., Brentford. **AZ 4B 72**
Tudor and Jacobean mansion with fine plaster ceilings, set in parkland. Open
14.00–17.00 Sat. only, May to Sept. Admission charge.

Buckingham Palace and the Queen Victoria Memorial

British Museum see MUSEUMS AND GALLERIES.

Brixton Windmill, Blenheim Gardens, Brixton Hill, SW2. **AZ 7J 93**
Tower windmill 1816, last used 1934, restored by Greater London Council. Open
Daily 09.00–16.00, 18.00 May to Sept. Closed Christmas.

Buckingham Palace, The Mall, SW1. **3C 49**
London home of the Sovereign. Changing the Guard is at 11.30 alternate days in
winter months; the Royal standard flies from the centre flagpole when the
Royal Family are in residence. Originally built 1703 for the Duke of Buckingham,
remodelled 1825 by Nash for George IV and again in 1913 by Sir A. Webb as
part of the National Memorial to Queen Victoria.
See also **Royal Mews** and **Queen's Gallery,** MUSEUMS AND GALLERIES.

Bunhill Fields, City Road, EC1. **1D 23**
Until 1852 the chief non-conformist burial ground, J. Bunyan, D. Defoe, W. Blake,
I. Watts and many of the Wesley family are buried here. John Wesley is buried in the
Wesley Chapel graveyard and George Fox is buried in the Quaker burial ground off
Roscoe St. **1C 23**

Burlington House, Piccadilly, W1. 01-734 9052 **3D 33**
Old Burlington House 1715 built for the Third Earl of Burlington is faced by a two
winged Victorian extension, forming a central quadrangle. In the centre is a
statue of Sir J. Reynolds first President of the Royal Academy of Arts founded in
1768 which has held an annual summer exhibition of works by living artists
since 1769, (although not moving to Piccadilly until 1869). Also the home of the
Royal Academy Schools, famous pupils have included Constable and Turner.
The extension contains several Royal Societies.

Cabinet War Rooms, Clive Steps, King Charles St., SW1. 01-930 6961 **2C 51**
One of the Second World War bunkers used by Winston Churchill and his staffs.
All rooms are restored to their war time appearance. Open 10.00–17.15 Tues.
to Sun. Admission charge.

Canonbury Tower, Canonbury Pl., N1. **AZ 6B 46**
Tudor brick tower containing oak panelled rooms and staircase. Famous residents
have included Sir Francis Bacon and Oliver Goldsmith. Viewing by appointment—
Tavistock Repertory Co. 01-226 5111

Carlyle's House, 24 Cheyne Row, SW3. 01-352 7087 **AZ 7B 76**
18th cent. home of Thomas Carlyle from 1834 until his death 1881. Museum. N.T.
Open April to end Oct, every day except Mon, Tues and Good Fri. 11.00–17.00,
or sunset if earlier. Admission charge.

Cenotaph see STATUES AND MONUMENTS.

Central Criminal Court, Old Bailey, EC4. 01-248 3277 **1A 38**
Known as the Old Bailey. Occupies the site of Newgate Prison demolished 1907.
Public are admitted to the Public Galleries when courts are in session. Court No. 1 is
the scene of important trials.

Central Hall, Storey's Ga., SW1. 01-222 7472 **3B 50**
London headquarters of the Methodist movement. Also frequently used for
Concerts, Conferences and Exhibitions; and venue in 1946 of the first session of the
General Assembly of the United Nations. The **Imperial Collection** is housed here;
an authentic replica collection of Crown Jewels from over 15 countries. Open
Mon. to Sat. Closed Sun. Admission charge.

Charlton House, Charlton Rd., SE7. **AZ 7J 81**
Jacobean house of 1607 with three storied porch, long gallery, stable block and
summer house. Used partly as a Public Library.

Charterhouse, Charterhouse Sq., EC1. **1A 22**
The site of a Carthusian Priory founded 14th cent. Original buildings extant are
mainly 16th cent. notably the Elizabethan Great Hall and Gatehouse, the
Chapel, 17th cent. Library and remains of the monastic buildings in Masters and
Washhouse Courts. A hospital for eighty poor brethren and school for forty poor boys
was established in 1611 (removed to Godalming 1872). The brethren must be
bachelors or widowers over sixty and be members of the Church of England.

Chelsea Physic Garden, 66 Royal Hospital Rd., SW3. **AZ 6D 76**

Botanic garden est. 1673 for the propogation and study of new species; several staple industries in former British Colonies were derived therefrom. 14.00–17.00 Sun. and Wed. Easter to Oct. and Bank Hols. Admission charge. Entrance in Swan Walk.

Chelsea, Royal Hospital, Royal Hospital Rd., SW3. 01-730 0161 **AZ 5E 76**
Home for 500 old or invalid soldiers—the Chelsea Pensioners, who may be seen wearing a scarlet frock-coat in the summer and a blue tunic in winter. Founded in 1682 by Charles II by popular belief at the instigation of Nell Gwyn. The principal buildings are designs by Wren with additions by R. Adam and Soane. The Royal Hospital Museum has plans, maps, medals etc, also Wellington exhibits. Statue of Charles II by Grinling Gibbons stands in the central courtyard. The annual Chelsea Flower Show takes place in the grounds. Open 10.00–12.00, 14.00–16.00, 14.00–16.00 Sun. Closed Christmas.

Cheshire Cheese, Ye Olde, Wine Office Ct., EC4. 01-353 6170 **1D 37**
Famous for its pudding served from Oct. to April and low oak beams, rebuilt 1667 after the Great Fire. Traditionally the haunt of Dr. Johnson, Boswell and Goldsmith.

Chiswick House, Burlington La., W4. 01-994 3299 **AZ 7K 73**
Palladian villa by Lord Burlington and W. Kent 1720–30. Symmetrical design built up of simple geometrical forms contrasted with intricate detailing. The main front is composed of two double approach stairways flanking a dominant portico at first floor level. The interior is a series of connected rooms with sensitive decoration by Kent which takes into account the relationships of linking spaces. The central room has a clerestory pierced by semi-circular windows which from the outside visually echo the surmounting dome. The garden also by Kent was a forerunner of the English Landscape Park, creating a natural setting as foil to classical architecture. Open 09.30–18.30 Daily in Summer. 09.30–16.00 Wed. to Sun. only in Winter. Closed Christmas.

Clarence House, Stable Yard, SW1. **2D 49**
Home of H.R.H. the Queen Mother. Designed by Nash 1825 for the Duke of Clarence later William IV.

Cleopatra's Needle, Victoria Embankment, WC2. **3A 36**
From Heliopolis approximately 3,500 years old, set up on the embankment in 1878. The hieroglyphics record praises of Thothmes III and victories of Rameses the Great.

College of Arms, Queen Victoria St., EC4. 01-248 2762 **2B 38**
Sometimes called the Herald's Office, it is the official authority in all matters relating to armorial bearings and pedigrees and received its present charter from Elizabeth I in 1555. The college has been on this site since 1554; its present building is a design by Wren completed 1682. The Corporation comprises three Kings of Arms, six Heralds and four Pursuivants who assist the Earl Marshal to arrange State Ceremonies. The panelled Earl Marshall's Court is open 10.00–16.00 Mon. to Fri. only. Bookshop and souvenirs. See also the Herald's Museum housed in the Tower of London.

Commonwealth Institute, 230 Kensington High St., W8. 01-603 4535 **3A 42**
Information centre, reference library, cinema, art gallery and exhibition galleries of and about the Commonwealth. The modern building was a result of money and gifts of materials contributed by Commonwealth Countries. Open Mon. to Fri. 10.00–17.30, 14.30–18.00 Sun. Closed Christmas Eve and Day, Good Fri., Boxing Day.

County Hall, Westminster Bri., SE1. **2A 52**
Opened by George V in 1922 as the headquarters of the London County Council; later HQ of the Greater London Council, disbanded 1986.

Covent Garden, WC2. **2D 35**
Originally "Covent Garden", this area was laid out as residential Piazza by Inigo Jones for the Earl of Bedford 1631–5. A small market given Royal Charter in 1671 grew into London's wholesale fruit and veg market, since removed to Nine Elms. The restored Market Buildings opened in 1980 as a lively environment of shops, boutiques, cafes, offices/studios, promenades and landscaped areas. This is also

the daily venue (10.00–20.00 except in bad weather) for a great variety of buskers performing jazz, classical music, Punch and Judy etc, etc. A plaque near St. Pauls Church (see page 23) records that here, the first of Punch's Puppet Shows in England took place, a fact noted in Samuel Pepy's diary for 1662. The former Flower Market Hall houses the London Transport Museum and will contain the Theatre Museum when completed. Nearby is the Royal Opera House.

Cromwell House, Highgate High St., N6. **AZ 1E 44**
Large red brick 17th cent. house, contains an elaborate oak staircase. Open by appointment, Church Missionary Society, 157 Waterloo Rd., SE1. 01-928 8681

Crosby Hall, Cheyne Wlk., SW3. 01-352 9663 **AZ 7B 76**
15th cent. Hall originally part of Crosby Place, a mansion on Bishopsgate, moved to this site in 1910. Oak Hammerbeam roof with oriel window. Open 10.00–12.00, 14.00–17.00, 14.00–17.00 Sun. when not in use for functions—check.

Crystal Palace, Sydenham, SE19. **AZ 5G 111**
Site of Paxton's cast iron and glass palace originally constructed in Hyde Park for the Great Exhibition 1851, re-erected here but destroyed by fire in 1936. Two relics of the exhibition are plaster prehistoric animals on islands in the boating lake and the clock of King's Cross Station. Within the park is the National Sports Centre opened 1964.

Customs House, Lwr. Thames St., EC3. **3B 40**
The present building is 19th cent. although there has been a customs house on the site since the 14th cent. Imposing Thames frontage 490 ft. long.

Cutty Sark see **Greenwich.**

Dickens House, 48 Doughty St., WC1. 01-405 2127 **1B 20**
Home of Charles Dickens from 1837–39 during which period he wrote parts of Pickwick Papers, Oliver Twist, Nicholas Nickleby and Barnaby Rudge. Now a Dickens Museum and Library. Open 10.00–17.00. Closed Sun. and Bank Hols. Admission charge.

Downing Street see STREETS AND SQUARES.

Dulwich, SE21. **AZ 7E 94**
One of London's villages which like Highgate manages to retain a rural atmosphere despite being surrounded by suburbia. Dulwich College was founded in 1619 by Edward Alleyn. There are the Old College Buildings the 17th cent. home of Alleyn's college including almshouses and chapel. Dulwich Park, a toll house, the 19th cent. College by C. Barry and the Dulwich College Picture Gallery. Opened in 1814 the gallery was London's first public art gallery, designed by Soane, see MUSEUMS AND GALLERIES.

Eastbury Manor House, Eastbury Sq., Barking. **AZ 1K 67**
Red brick Elizabethan Manor House, 1572; property of the National Trust. Let to the Borough of Barking, viewing only by written appointment with the Borough Engineer, Town Hall, Barking.

Eltham Palace, Court Yard, SE9. **AZ 6D 98**
Medieval Royal Palace, although only the 15th cent. Great Hall with its oak hammerbeam roof, and the moat bridge survive. An ancient monument open Thurs. & Sun. 10.00–12.15, 14.15–18.00 (Winter to 16.00). Nearby are Avery Hill Winter Gardens, (Avery Hill Park **AZ 6H 99**) an iron and glass structure with central dome built 1890. Cool House, Temperate House and Tropical House are stocked with tropical and exotic plants. Open as for park.

Epping Forest, Essex.
Covers an area about 10 miles along by about 2 miles at its widest point from Wanstead to Epping. Comprises mainly oak, beech, birch and hornbeam; and supports much wildlife including a herd of black fallow deer. There is a Forest Museum housed in the Queen Elizabeth's Hunting Lodge, Rangers Rd., Chingford.

Eros see STATUES AND MONUMENTS.

Fenton House see **Hampstead.**

Fulham Palace, Fulham Palace Rd., SW6. **AZ 2G 91**
Official residence of the Bishop of London. The buildings range from 16th-19th cent.; amongst the oldest are the gateway and quadrangle.

George Inn, Borough High St., SE1. 01-407 2052 **1D 55**
One side of a galleried Inn, 1677. Famous as a coaching terminus in 18th and 19th
centuries when it surrounded three sides of a courtyard, and access to the rooms was
along covered balconies. Now property of National Trust.

Goldsmiths' Hall see **Livery Hall.**

Gray's Inn, Holborn, WC1. 01-405 8164 **2B 20**
One of the four great Inns of Court. Entered through an archway next to 22 on the
North side of High Holborn, its name originates from the de Gray family. The buildings
were badly damaged by bombing in World War II but have been restored—including
the Elizabethan Hall containing a late 16th cent. carved screen; the Library, Chapel
and Gatehouse in Gray's Inn Sq. Gardens laid out by Francis Bacon. For access
to buildings apply to the Under Treasurer. See also **Inns of Court and Chancery.**

Green Park, SW1. **2C 49**
Originally an extension to St. James's Park on land bought by Charles II, 1667. On
the Piccadilly side are gates from Old Devonshire House. On the east side is
Queen's walk overlooked by former mansions and the Ritz Hotel.

Greenwich, SE10. **AZ 6G 81**

CUTTY SARK, King William Wlk., SE10. 01-858 3445. The last and fastest of the
    tea clippers built in competition with steam ships. Launched 1869 her best
    day's run was 363 miles. Contains a maritime museum. Open 10.30–17.00.
    Sun., Good Fri. and Boxing Day 14.30–17.00. Open later in summer. Closed
    Christmas Eve and Day. New Year's Day. Admission charge.

GREENWICH PARK. Royal Park laid out for Charles II by Le N;xcotre landscape
    gardener to Louis XIV. See view over London from Flamsteed House, 1694 (home
    of General Wolfe), also Rangers House page 88 and Vanbrugh Castle, 1717–26.

GIPSY MOTH IV. Sir Francis Chichester's round the world yacht.

NATIONAL MARITIME MUSEUM, Romney Rd., SE10. 01-858 4422. Incorporates
    the Queen's House and two wings and the Old Royal Observatory. Shows the
    maritime history of Great Britain, see **National Maritime Museum,** MUSEUMS
    & GALLERIES.

OLD ROYAL OBSERVATORY, 01-858 1167. Founded 1675 by Charles II, the
    Observatory moved to Herstmonceux, Sussex in 1950. The buildings
    include Flamsteed House, the Meridian Building and Greenwich Planetarium
    (summer shows in school hols.), and are now an annex of the National
    Maritime Museum exhibiting astronomical and navigational equipment. A mast
    on the east turret carries the time ball which falls at 13.00 daily, "Greenwich
    Mean Time" is British Standard Time; the zero meridian of longitude is marked
    by a brass strip. Open 10.00–17.30, Sun. 14.30–17.30. Closed most Bank
    Holidays. Admission charge.

QUEEN'S HOUSE, Romney Rd., SE10. Commissioned by James I as a home for
    Queen Anne of Denmark this design, by Inigo Jones between 1619–37 is
    with the Banqueting House, Whitehall, the forerunner of classical architecture
    in England. Outstanding internal features include the hall, a perfect 40 ft.
    cube with gallery around the upper floor and the cantilevered Tulip Staircase.
    Now houses the National Maritime Museum.

ROYAL NAVAL COLLEGE, King William Wlk, SE10. 01-858 2154. On the site of
    Greenwich Palace or the Royal Palace of Placentia which was built in 1423
    for the Duke of Gloucester later becoming a favourite residence of the Tudor
    monarchs. The Palace was rebuilt by a succession of architects as
    Greenwich Hospital, a Navy hospital which itself became a college for training
    Naval Officers in 1873. West block 1664–9 by J. Webb. East block and twin
    towers forming a symmetrical group with an axis on the Queen's House by
    Wren, 1699–1703, other additions by Vanburgh, 1728. Open to the public are the
    "Painted Hall' with Baroque decoration by Thornhill, 1707–26, and the Chapel,
    decoration by James Stuart, 1789. Open 14.30–17.00. Closed Thurs.
    Admission charge.

ST. ALPHEGE'S CHURCH, Greenwich High Rd., SE10. Traditionally the site of the
    martyrdom of Alphege, Archbishop of Canterbury by the Danes 1011. Henry VIII was

baptized in the medieval Church, rebuilt 1712–30 by N. Hawksmoor and J. James. Tombs of Thomas Tallis and General Wolfe.

Guildhall, Corporation of London, Gresham St., EC2. 01-606 3030 **3D 23**
Centre of the City of London's civic government for 1,000 years during the development from the ancient Court of Husting to the modern Common Council. Here the 84 Livery Companies annually elect the Lord Mayor (the first Lord Mayor was elected 1192) and Sheriffs, banners of the twelve principal companies hang from the walls. Also used for municipal meetings, presentation of the freedom of the City and State Banquets. Foundations date from 1411—see The Medieval Crypt half of which survived both Great Fire 1666 and 1940 bombs. See also Guildhall Library, Museum, Art Gallery and Clockmakers Company Museum. For the Corporation of London Record Office, see **Guildhall Library.** Open 10.00–17.00. Mon. to Sat. Sundays 1st May to end of Sept. 14.00–17.00 only. Closed Christmas Day, Boxing Day, Good Fri. and special events.

Gunnersbury Park, Popes La., Acton, W5. 01-992 1612 **AZ 3G 73**
Regency Mansion and park once a home of the English Rothschilds. Now a museum of local interest. Open pm daily. Closed Good Fri., Christmas Day and Boxing Day.

Gipsy Moth IV see **Greenwich.**

Ham House, Petersham, Surrey. 01-940 1950 **AZ 1C 104**
Jacobean mansion, 1610; lavish Baroque interior much as left by the Duke of Lauderdale a favourite of Charles II. An annexe of the Victoria and Albert museum containing a collection of Stuart furniture, largely original. Grounds are a centre for Polo playing on summer Sundays. A National Trust property. Open Apr. to Sept., 14.00–18.00. Oct. to Mar. 12.00–16.00. Closed Mon. (excluding Bank Hols.), Good Fri., Christmas Day and Eve, Boxing Day, N. Years Day. Admission charge.

Hampstead, NW3. **AZ 4A 44**
Still retains in parts something of a village character. At the highest point a complex maze of small streets and alleys harbours many surprise views and architectural settings. Church Row, Holly Walk, Holly Mount and environs. Famous pubs include Holly Bush on Holly Mount; Old Bull and Bush, North End Way; Jack Straws Castle, North End Rd., and The Spaniards, Spaniards Rd. Hampstead Heath reaches the height of 440 ft. at Whitestone Pond. Nearby are held the Summer Bank Holiday Fairs. Parliament Hill 319 ft. commands an extensive view of London, a popular place for kite flying. There are facilities for many sports, including the lido. Natural ponds on other parts of the Heath are also used for swimming. See also **Kenwood.**

FENTON HOUSE, Hampstead Grove, NW3. 01-435 3471. Built 1693 exhibits furniture, porcelain, and the Benton Fletcher collection of early keyboard instruments. Walled garden. Open 11.00–17.00, Sat to Wed. April to end of Oct. 14.00–17.00.Sat. & Sun. in March. Admission charge. National Trust Property.

KEATS HOUSE, Wentworth Pl'., Keats Grove, NW3. 01-435 2062. Keats' Regency home (1815) between 1818–20. Museum of personal relics. Open 10.00–13.00, 14.00–18.00. daily. 14.00–17.00 Sundays and Easter, Spring & Summer Bank Hols. Closed other Bank Hols.

Hampton Court Palace, Hampton Ct., Middlesex. 01-977 8441 **AZ 4A 118**
Royal Palace built in three stages around three courtyards. Begun by Cardinal Wolsey 1515–20 around Base Court, Clock Court. Additions by Henry VIII include the Great Hall. Wren additions for William and Mary include S.E. wing with Fountain Court, Banqueting House, State Rooms, Orangery. Decoration by Vanbrugh, Verrio, Thornhill, Grinling Gibbons and Jean Tijou. Other features include the Great Vine, 1769, the Maze, formal gardens, Henry VIII's tennis courts, Astronomical clock and landscape park. To the North is Bushey Park with a mile long Chestnut Avenue planted 1699 to plans of Wren. Within the park roams a herd of deer. Open Summer months 09.00–18.00 weekdays. 11.00–18.00 Sundays. Winter months closes earlier. Closed Good Fri., Christmas Eve and Day, Boxing Day, Jan. 1st. Park and Gardens until 21.00 or dusk. Admission charge.

Henry VIII's Wine Cellar, Min. of Defence, Horseguards Av., SW1. **1D 51**
Originally built for Cardinal Wolsey as part of Whitehall Palace, see Banqueting
House. This Tudor Cellar 56 ft. long was moved en bloc when the Ministry of
Defence building was constructed. Open Sat. 14.30–17.30 Summer only.

Highgate, N6. **AZ 1E 44**
Stands on the same range of hills as Hampstead and has a similar mellow quality
although here the village is concentrated around the centre, Pond Square. See The
Grove; 17th and 18th cent. houses, No. 3 being once the home of Coleridge,
Highgate School founded 1565, The Flask 17th cent. Inn on West Hill,
Waterlow Park, Dick Whittington Stone and Cat at the bottom of Highgate Hill,
Highgate Cemetery, Swains La., Lower section has tombs of Karl Marx and George
Eliot; Upper section is wild and overgrown—eerie Egyptian catacombs.

Hogarth's House, Hogarth La., W4. 01-994 6757 **AZ 6A 74**
Queen Anne country home of Hogarth 1749–64. Now a museum of his drawings,
engravings and personal relics. Open Apr. to Sept. 11.00–18.00, Sun. 14.00–18.00.
Oct. .o Mar. 11.00–16.00 Sun. 14.00–16.00. Closed Tuesdays; 1st two weeks
Sept., last three weeks Dec., and Jan 1st. Admission charge.

Holland House and Park, Holland Wlk., W8. **3A 42**
Jacobean mansion of the Earl of Holland, largely destroyed by bombs in 1941.
Restored east wing dating from about 1640 is now part of the King George VI
memorial youth hostel. Of the centre section only the lower storey survives and
is used as a backcloth for summer performances of the open air Court Theatre. The
park includes Dutch and Rose gardens, Orangery, Woodland and an area for open
air concerts.

Honourable Artillery Company H.Q., City Rd., E1. **1A 24**
The oldest regiment in the British Army has had headquarters here since 1642;
the centre block, Armoury House, dating from 1735. Supplies the guard of honour for
Lord Mayor's Shows and for Royalty visiting the City; and fires all salutes from the
Tower of London. Museum open by appointment. 01-606 4644.

Horse Guards, Whitehall, SW1. **1C 51**
Design by W. Kent 1750–60, occupies the site of the Guard house of Old Whitehall
Palace. Mounted Guards of the Household Cavalry stand at the Whitehall
entrance during the day, the guard is changed at 11.00 (10.00 Sun.) when a new
guard arrives from Hyde Park Barracks; the ceremony lasts –4 hour. The
Household Cavalry comprises two regiments: The Life Guards (scarlet tunics) and
the Royal Horse Guards (blue tunics). Besides alternating on duty at Horse Guards they
provide the personal bodyguard for the Sovereign on state occasions. Horse
Guards' Parade on the St. James's Park side is the site of the tilt-yard of
Whitehall Palace; and here in June on the occasion of H.M. the Queen's official
birthday the Trooping the Colour takes place.

House of St. Barnabas-in-Soho, 1 Greek St., W1. 01-437 1894 **1B 34**
18th cent. mansion; interior has carved woodwork, rococco plasterwork and
wrought-iron staircase balustrade. Small paved garden. Occupied by a charity founded
1846 to help destitute and homeless. Open Wed. 14,00–16.15, Thurs. 11.00–
12.30. Closed Bank Hol. Mon.

Houses of Parliament, Palace of Westminster, SW1. 01-219 3000 **3D 51**
Stands throughout the world as symbol of democratic government. The Victorian
Gothic building 1840–68, design by Barry and Pugin is on the site of the Old Palace of
Westminster, a royal residence from Edward the Confessor to the time of Henry
VIII. Being the permanent home of Parliament from 1547 the Old Palace having escaped
the intended destruction by Guy Fawkes, 1605, was destroyed by fire in 1834
except for Westminster Hall and the Jewel Tower; other surviving sections
were incorporated into the new building, the Cloister 1526–9 and the Crypt 1292–
7. Within the Houses of Parliament the House of Lords lies to the south and the
Commons to the north (rebuilt after destruction by bombing 1941) and access to
both is from the Central Lobby. On the South-East corner is the Victoria Tower:
the Sovereign's entrance for the State opening of Parliament. On the North side is
the Clock Tower with Big Ben. The House when in session usually meets

Big Ben and Westminster Bridge

Mon. to Thurs. 14.30 onwards, Fri. 11.00. This is indicated by the Union Jack flying from Victoria Tower or a light in the Clock Tower at night. For admission to the public gallery either queue at St. Stephen's entrance or write to your M.P. otherwise open only by arrangement with your Member of Parliament.

Hyde Park, W2. **3B 30** and **1C 47**

A Royal Park since 1536. Used by Henry VIII and Elizabeth I as a deer hunting ground. It was first opened to the public by James I. The Serpentine formed in 1730 is a centre for leisure activities including boating, fishing and swimming. The park adjoins Kensington Gardens at the Serpentine Bridge, design by G. Rennie 1826. Riding takes place in Rotten Row; "Tub-Thumping" at Speakers' Corner is most active on Sundays; nearby is Marble Arch and the site of Tyburn gallows where public executions took place until 1783. At Hyde Park Corner are Apsley House and an entrance screen of three arches by D. Burton 1828; a statue of Lord Byron; and of Achilles in honour of Wellington. Near the Police Station in centre of the park is a bird sanctuary with an Epstein memorial to the naturalist W. H. Hudson. The Great Exhibition 1851, housed in Paxton's Crystal Palace stood on the south side just to the east of the Albert Memorial. There is a bandstand on Serpentine Road. Restaurants are at either end of the Serpentine, refreshment kiosks are situated at Speaker's Corner and the northern end of Broad Walk in Kensington Gardens.

Inner Temple see **Temple.**

Inns of Court and Chancery.

The four Great Inns of Court, Inner and Middle Temple, Gray's Inn and Lincoln's Inn, form the function of university to the Legal Profession. Their history began with the establishment of the Temple as the headquarters in England of the Knights Templars (an Order of military crusaders founded 1119 at Jerusalem with the object of recovering Palestine from the Saracens). Temple Church was consecrated in 1185. The crusading orders were suppressed in 1312 and the Temple was granted to the Knights Hospitallers of St. John. They leased it to professors of the common law and their students. At the abolition of orders of chivalry by Henry VIII the lawyers took over the precincts. By the 15th cent. there were nine Inns of Chancery; and it was customary for students of law to enter one of these before passing on to an Inn of Court (see Staple Inn).

Jewel Tower, Old Palace Yd., SW1. **3C 51**

14th cent. corner tower of the Old Palace of Westminster, contains a museum of relics. Open 10.30–16.00 Mon. to Sat. Closed Christmas Eve and Day, Boxing Day.

Johnson's House, 17 Gough Sq., EC4. 01-353 3745 **1D 37**

Home of Dr. Johnson 1748–59, during the compilation of his Dictionary, it contains a Museum of relics. Open 11.00–17.30 weekdays. October to April 11.00–17.00. Closed Sundays and Bank Holidays. Admission charge.

Keats House see **Hampstead.**

Kensington Gardens, W2. **3B 28** and **2B 44**

Once the private park of Kensington Palace with its Orangery and Sunken Garden. Many formal avenues of trees include The Broad Walk and Flower Walk. The Round Pond is a centre for sailing model boats; Long Water has a fountain layout at its northern end. Statuary includes Peter Pan; a statue of William III; Queen Victoria by her daughter Princess Louise; Physical Energy an equestrian work by Watts; a memorial to J. H. Speke. See adjoining Hyde Park.

Kensington Palace, Kensington Gdns., W2. 01-937 9561 **1D 43**

Originally Nottingham House, converted into a Royal Palace for William III in 1689 to designs by Wren. Interior alterations by W. Kent 1722–4. Home of Queen Victoria 1819–37 and is still a Royal Residence. Open to the public are the "State Rooms" and "Court Dress Collection"—historical costumes 1750–1930's. Open Daily 09.00–17.00. Sun. 13.00–17.00. Closed Christmas Eve & Day, Boxing Day, N. Years Day, Good Fri. Admission charge.

Kenwood, Hampstead, NW3. 01-348 1286 **AZ 1B 44**

Mansion of the first Earl of Mansfield, rebuilt 1767–9 and designed by R. Adam

with 1795 additions by Saunders. Bequeathed to the nation by Lord Iveagh in 1927
complete with his collection of paintings and furniture. Works by Boucher,
Gainsborough, Guardi, Hals, Rembrandt, Reynolds, Romney, Turner, Van Dyck,
Vermeer. Set in parkland adjoining Hampstead Heath, open air concerts are
held beside the lake in summer months. Open 10.00–19.00. Closes 17.00 Oct.,
Feb., and March; 16.00 Nov. to Jan. Closed Christmas Eve and Day, Good Fri.
Admission charge. Park open 08.00 to dusk.

Kew Bridge Steam Engines, Green Dragon La., Brentford. 01-568 4757 (not Mon.
& Tues) **AZ 5F 73**
Five huge beam engines, two restored and working under steam, earliest built
1820 pumped London's water supply for 100 years. Also rotative engines,
forge and Water Supply Museum. Open Sat., Sun. and Bank Holiday Mons. 11.00–
17.00. Admission charge.

Kew Gardens, Richmond. 01-940 1171 **AZ 7F 73**
Founded in 1759 by Princess Augusta. Officially the Royal Botanical Gardens. Its
main function is identification and research. Within the 300 acres are a vast
variety of garden and landscape park; hothouses; lake and water garden; Kew
Palace (or Dutch House) 1631; three Museums of Economic Botany; Orangery and
Pagoda by Sir W. Chambers. Palm House 1844–8 by R. Turner is one of the earliest
buildings in iron and glass, with originality the result of functional design. Open:
Gardens 10.00–20.00 or dusk, closed Christmas Day. Museums 10.00–16.50
(17.50 Sun.) or dusk, closed Good Fri., Christmas Eve and Day, Boxing Day.
Palace Apr. to Sept. Daily 11.00–17.30. Herbarium and Library for research.

Lambeth Palace, Lambeth Rd., SE1. 01-928 8282 **2A 66**
London residence of the Archbishops of Canterbury. 13th cent. crypt, Lollards
Tower c. 1450, entrance gate 1490, Great Hall rebuilt 1663 now houses the library of
manuscripts and books. Open by appointment. The **Tradescant Trust** 01-373
4030, is developing the adjacent St. Mary at Lambeth Church as a Museum
of Garden History, and centre for gardeners and their societies in honour of the
Tradescants, gardeners to Charles I, and responsible for the introduction of
many exotic plants and trees.

Lancaster House, Stable Yd., SW1. **2D 49**
Victorian Mansion built 1825 for the Duke of York. Completed 1840 by Sir R. Smirke
with florid decoration by Sir C. Barry. Grand staircase and State rooms. Used
mainly for Government Conferences. Open Easter to Mid-Dec., 14.00–18.00. Sat,
Sun. & Bank Hols. except during functions. Admission charge.

Leadenhall Market, Gracechurch St., EC3. **1B 40**
A market site for over 600 years, Victoria glass and iron hall, 1881.

Leighton House, 12 Holland Park Rd., W14. 01-602 3316 **AZ 3H 75**
Home of Lord Leighton 1866–96, who himself decorated much of the interior
which includes ancient Persian tiling and carving, an exceptional Arabian Hall with
fountain. Permanent exhibition of High Victorian Art (Burne-Jones, Millais, Pynter
etc.), period decoration, furniture plus temporary exhibitions. Open 11.00–
17.00 Mon. to Sat., Garden open April to September. Closed Bank Holidays.

Lincoln's Inn, Chancery La., WC2. 01-405 1393 **3B 20**
One of the four great Inns of Court. Its name originates from the Earl of Lincoln
who established a school of law in the 15th cent. Amongst the 18th cent. squares and
gardens are the Old Hall 1492 and 1624, Gateway facing Chancery La., 1518,
Chapel with open undercroft 1623, New Hall and Library 1845. Open: Halls,
Library and Chapel, 10.00–16.30 Mon. to Fri. on application at the Porter's Lodge,
Chancery Lane. 01-405 6360. See also **Inns of Court and Chancery.**

Lincoln's Inn Fields, WC2. **3A 20**
Laid out 1618 by Inigo Jones. Once a famous duelling ground now an oasis of
plane trees, tennis and netball courts, refreshment hut. On the north side is Sir J.
Soanes House (Museum) 1792; on the west side, Lindsey House 1640 attributed
to Inigo Jones; on the south side Royal College of Surgeons 1835, by Sir C. Barry.

Linley Sambourne House, 18 Stafford Ter. W8. 01-994 1019 **3B 42**

The Victorian Society. Home of "Punch" cartoonist L. Sambourne 1870–1910.
Victorian decor + cartoons. Open March to Oct. 10.00–16.00 Wed. 14.00–17.00 Sun.
Little Venice, Warwick Ave., W2. **2A 12**
Where Regent's Canal and Paddington Basin meet at Browning Pool. A colony of
artists live in converted barges. The Zoo waterbus runs to London Zoo. A mural
to Robert Browning in Warwick Crescent. See also Canal Walks p. 84.
Livery Halls.
Livery Companies are the successors of the religious and social fraternities of the
11th cent., but later became connected with particular trades and crafts. There
are over 80 Livery Companies, many with their own halls in the City. Of the 36
before the war only two were left undamaged and twenty were totally
destroyed. Perhaps the most famous Company is the Goldsmiths', responsible
since 1281 for the Trial of the Pyx (the testing of newly minted coins), which
has been held annually at Goldsmiths' Hall since 1870. A number of Halls are
accessible between May and Oct.; details from the City of London Information
Centre.
Lloyds, Lime St., EC3. 01-623 7100 **1B 40**
The international insurance market, and world centre of shipping intelligence.
Lloyds started life in Edward Lloyds coffee house, Tower Street in 1689. Given
official status in 1871 by act of Parliament. The exciting modern building has
external observation lifts giving access for the public to the Underwriting Room
Viewing Gallery and exhibition of Lloyds history. The famous Lutine Bell is rung
once for bad news and twice for good news.
London Bridge see BRIDGES AND TUNNELS.
London Bridge City, Tooley St., SE1 **1A 56–1C 57**
A new traffic free environment of offices. shops and leisure facilities is being
developed on the south bank of the Thames incorporating the Victoria Hays
Dock buildings now called "Hays Galleria". A riverside walk will eventually link
London Bridge and Tower Bridge,
London City Wall. From **3D 41** to **2A 38**
Built originally by the Romans 2nd cent. A.D. incorporating an earlier fort at the
N.W. corner. About 2 miles long. Rebuilt in Medieval times and extended on
the west to encompass Blackfriars. There were six gates in the Roman Wall,
Aldersgate, Aldgate, Bishopsgate, Cripplegate, Newgate and Ludgate;
Moorgate being added in 1415. The Wall can still be seen:
(1) Tower of London. **3D 41;** (2) Behind Tower Hill Tube Station. **2D 41;** (3) All
Hallows, London Wall. **3B 24;** (4) St. Alphage's Churchyard, London Wall. **3D
23;** (5) Barbican near St. Giles' Church. **3C 23;** (6) Car Park south of St. Giles (West
Gateway open Mon to Fri. 12.30–14.30). **3C 23;** (7) Noble Street. **3C 23;** (8)
Post Office, King Edward St. **3B 22.**
London Dungeon, Tooley St., SE1. 01-403 0606 **1A 56**
Waxwork tableaux portraying gruesome and macabre events. Not recommended
to the nervous or unaccompanied children. Open 10.00–17.45 (16.30 Oct. to
March). Admission charge.
London Planetarium, Marylebone Rd., NW1. 01-486 1121 **1D 15**
Shows the relative position of stars and planets in either hemisphere or at different
periods of time; also illustrates journeys into space. Presentations regularly
11.00–17.00 Daily. Closed Christmas Day. Admission charge. LASERIUM: An
abstract audio-visual entertainment using a Krypton gas laser; evenings only, ring 01-
486 2242 for programme.
London Stone, Cannon St., EC4. **2D 39**
Believed to have been the millarium from which the Romans measured distances
out of the City, let into the wall opposite Cannon Street Station.
Madame Tussauds, Marylebone Rd., NW1. 01-935 6861 **1D 15**
Waxwork exhibition of famous and notorious characters both historical and
contemporary. Tussaud's first opened in London 1802 with an exhibition of death
masks from the French Revolution. Daily 10.00–17.30, to 18.00 July & August.
Admission charge. See also Royalty & Empire exhibition, Windsor.

Manresa House, Putney Heath, SW15. **AZ 6D 90**
Country Villa *c.* 1760. Ionic portico and curved staircase overlooking Richmond Pk.
Mansion House, Bank, EC4. **1D 39**
Official residence of the Lord Mayor of London. Built 1739–53 to designs by G.
Dance. Lord Mayor's Banquets and State Receptions are held in the Egyptian
Hall. The Justice Room is one of the two Magistrates Courts in the City—the other
is The Guildhall. Open on some Sats., by application to the Private Secretary.
Marble Arch, W1. **2C 31**
Designed by Nash as gateway to Buckingham Palace, it was too narrow for the
State Coach, and was re-erected as a gate to Hyde Park 1851.
Marble Hill House, Richmond Rd., Twickenham. 01-892 5115 **AZ 7B 88**
Built 1728 for Henrietta Howard later Countess of Suffolk. A small Palladian style
villa with park abutting the River Thames. Open 10.00–17.00. Nov. to Jan.
10.00–16.00. Closed Fri., Christmas Eve and Day. Admission charge. Upstream
stood Orleans House although only Gibbs' baroque Octagon of 1720 survives; adjacent
is Orleans House Gallery **AZ 1C 104**
Marlborough House, Pall Mall, SW1. 01-930 9249 **1A 50**
Commissioned by the first Duke of Marlborough, original design by Wren 1709–
10 with later additions. In 1850 it became the official residence of the Prince
of Wales. Now a Commonwealth Conference Centre. Adjoining the House is
Queen's Chapel 1627, design by Inigo Jones. Open by arrangement with
Administration Officer; excepting services in Queen's Chapel—Sundays 08.30,
11.15 between Easter Day and end July.
Middlesex Guildhall, Broad Sanctuary, SW1. **3C 51**
The former County Hall built 1905–13, now accommodates the Middlesex Quarter
Sessions.
Monument, The see STATUES AND MONUMENTS.
National Gallery see MUSEUMS AND GALLERIES.
Nelson's Column see STATUES AND MONUMENTS.
New Scotland Yard, Broadway, SW1. **1B 64**
Headquarters of the Metropolitan Police since 1967, formerly sited on Victoria
Embankment. Houses the Flying Squad, Murder Squad, Criminal Record
Office and Traffic Control Dept.
Old Bailey see **Central Criminal Court.**
Old Curiosity Shop, Portsmouth St., WC2. **1A 36**
Tudor house which claims to be the original of Dickens' "Old Curiosity Shop". Now
an antique and tourist souvenir shop.
Old Royal Observatory see **Greenwich.**
Osterley Park House, Osterley. 01-560 3918 **AZ 6G 71**
An Elizabethan house built for Sir T. Gresham. Remodelled by R. Adam 1761–
78 including architectural work, interior decoration, furniture and carpets, with
his original drawings displayed. Elizabethan stables. Parkland with woodland,
lakes and the M4 Motorway. A National Trust property. Open, House: Apr. to
Sept. 14.00–18.00, Oct. to Mar. 12.00–16.00. Closed Mon. (except some Bank
Hols.), Good Fri., Christmas Day, Boxing Day, New Years Day. Admission
charge. Park: 10.00 to dusk.
Palace of Westminster see **Houses of Parliament**
Parliament Square see SQUARES AND STREETS
Petticoat Lane see SQUARES AND STREETS, & MARKETS.
Piccadilly Circus see SQUARES AND STREETS.
Pitshanger Manor, Walpole Pk., Ealing, W5. **AZ 1C 72**
Country House of Sir J. Soane from 1801. Rebuilt to try out ideas used later in his
town house, Lincoln's Inn Fields. Now Ealing Public Library.
Portobello Road see SQUARES AND STREETS AND MARKETS.
Post Office Tower see **Telecom Tower.**
Prince Henry's Room, 17 Fleet St., EC4. 01-353 7323 **1C 37**
Half-timbered building of 1610 incorporating the gateway to Inner Temple Lane.

large first floor room with Jacobean plaster ceiling and oak panelling. Open 13.45–17.00 Mon. to Fri., 13.45–16.00 Sat. Closed Bank Holidays.

Public Record Office, Chancery La., WC2. 01-405 0741 **1C 37** and Ruskin Av., Kew. 01-876 3444 **AZ 7G 73**

Repositories for National records, public archives and state papers, with public search rooms for research and study. Modern records dept. is at Kew. Open: 0930–17.00 Mon. to Fri.; last call for documents at 15.30. Readers' tickets on application to the Secretary. For Public Record Office Museum see p. 80.

Queen Anne's Gate, SW1. **3B 50**

Secluded street of Georgian houses built 1704, some with elaborate canopies. Statue of Queen Anne. Palmerston born at No. 20. Nos. 40–44 H.Q. of National Trust.

Queen's House see **Greenwich.**

Regent's Park, NW1. **1D7 and 2A 8**

Royal Park planned in 1811 by Nash for the Prince Regent. Part of a massive town planning scheme involving the building of Regent Street and terraces surrounding the Park. Large boating lake has six islands with many species of birds. Queen Mary's Gardens within the Inner Circle. Open Air Theatre. Playing fields for cricket, football, hockey, netball, rugby, athletics track and tennis courts. Bandstand, central refreshment pavilion. The Zoo and Regent's Canal are to the Northern side. The classical façades of Nash are now well contrasted by two good modern buildings, the Royal College of Physicians and the London Mosque.

Richmond-upon-Thames. AZ 5D 88

Market town atmosphere retained in narrow winding shopping streets and alleyways. Large square green includes Maids of Honour Row 1724 and other Georgian Houses, Tudor Gateway of Richmond Palace. Riverside walks, Richmond Bridge 1774, Richmond Park, a Royal Park first enclosed 1637 by Charles I, survives as a natural English landscape of oaks and undergrowth; herds of deer and other wild life, Pen Ponds for angling, Adam's Pond for model boats, Isabella Plantation a wooded garden with miniature brook, White Lodge built for George II is now home of Royal Ballet School (Lower) 01-876 5547; Pembroke Lodge is now a Restaurant.

Roman Bath, 5 Strand La., WC2. **2B 36**

Brick bath of uncertain origin, 15 ft. 6 in. long fed by spring. National Trust property. Not open, but the interior is visible from pathway.

Royal Academy of Arts see MUSEUMS AND GALLERIES

Royal Albert Hall, Kensington Gore, SW7. 01-589 3203 **3C 45**

Completed 1871 to the design of Captain Fowke and General Scott. The oval amphitheatre can seat 8,000. Promenade Concerts July to Sept., and other concerts throughout the year. Also Boxing, Tennis, Wrestling, Meetings and Conferences.

Royal Botanic Gardens see **Kew.**

Royal Courts of Justice, Strand, WC2. 01-930 6000 **1B 36**

Built 1874–82 to house the Supreme Court of Judicature. Courts generally sit between 10.30–16.30 weekdays. Small exhibition of Costumes, Maces and Scrolls. Access to public galleries on both sides of the main entrance.

Royal Exchange, Cornhill, EC3. **1A 40**

Founded 1564 by Sir T. Gresham (the weather vane incorporates the Grasshopper family crest). The original building was destroyed in the Great Fire 1666; the second in 1838. The present building by Sir W. Tate opened 1844 has a glass roofed quadrangle now houses the London International Financial Futures Exchange 01-623 0444; viewing gallery open 11.30–14.00 Mon. to Fri.

Royal Festival Hall, South Bank, SE1. 01-928 3002 **1B 52**

Built 1951 for the Festival of Britain, its enlarged river frontage was added 1962–5. Main Hall seats 3,000, acoustics highly praised. See also **South Bank Arts Centre.**

Royal Geographical Society, 1 Kensington Gore, SW7. 01-589 5466 **3C 45**

Founded 1830. Lowther Lodge, designed by Norman Shaw 1874 houses a Map room available to the public for viewing. Open 10.00–17.00 Mon. to Fri. Closed Good Fri. & Christmas. Library by appointment.

Royal Hospital, Chelsea see **Chelsea, Royal Hospital.**

Royal Mews, Buckingham Palace Rd., SW1. **1C 63**
Houses the Queen's Coaches and Horses. State Coach designed by Sir W. Chambers 1762 for George III, Irish State Coach bought 1852 by Queen Victoria, Glass State Coach bought 1910 by George V. Open 14.00–16.00 Wed. and Thurs. only. Closed Royal Ascot Week.

Royal Mint, Tower Hill, EC3. **3D 41**
Home of the Royal Mint between 1811 and the early 1970's; now transferred to Llantrisant near Cardiff. Prior to 1811 the mint occupied part of the Tower of London. Trial of the Pyx, the testing of newly minted coins is performed by the Goldsmiths' Company annually in March, see **Livery Halls.**

Royal Opera House, Covent Garden, WC2. 01-240 1200 **2D 35**
The Royal Opera Company with famous international artists and the Royal Ballet Company perform here throughout the year (for opera in English translation see English National Opera at the Coliseum page 38). Built 1856–8 this is the third theatre on the site, its great portico has sculpture panels by Flaxman and Rossi from the previous building. The interior is of white, gold and deep crimson, there are displays of memorabilia connected with historic performers and performances.

Royal Naval College see **Greenwich.**

St. Bartholomew's Hospital, West Smithfield, EC1. 01-600 9000 **3B 22**
Founded in 1123 as part of an Augustinian Priory (see St. Bartholomew the Great Church) by Rahere, Henry II's jester. After the suppression of the priory, the Hospital was refounded in 1546 by Henry VIII; and has since been rebuilt and often enlarged. The Gatehouse with London's only statue of Henry VIII dates from 1702; in the Great Hall 1730–34 are paintings by Hogarth, Reynolds and Lawrence. St. Bart's is a parish in its own right, and the original hospital church St. Bartholomew the Less *c.* 1150 is the Parish Church.

St. James's Palace, SW1. Pall Mall, SW1. **2A 50**
Built 1532 by Henry VIII on the site of a Norman leper hospital dedicated to St. James the Less. The home of sovereigns before Buckingham Palace, now the official residence of the Prince of Wales. Foreign ambassadors are still accredited to the "Courts of St. James". The Chapel Royal, Ambassadors' Court has been the scene of many Royal Marriages; its painted ceiling 1540 is attributed to Holbein. The Presence Chamber of Tapestry Room bears the initials of Henry VIII and Anne Boleyn. Decorations by William Morris 1881. Tudor Gatehouse facing St. James's Street. H.Q. of the Gentlemen at Arms formed 1509 and Yeomen of the Guard (Beefeaters) formed 1485—together the Sovereign's dismounted bodyguard at state ceremonies. The Queen's Chapel in Marlborough Rd., designed 1623–7 by Inigo Jones was built as a Catholic Chapel for Charles I's Queen; has Royal Pews, wooden coffered ceiling and carolean panelling.

St. James's Park, SW1. **2A 50**
The oldest Royal Park, formerly laid out for Charles II by Le Nôtre, the French landscape gardener; redesigned by Nash in 1827 for George IV. Parkland, walks, meandering lake; duck island bird sanctuary has many species of duck, geese and also pelicans. Bandstand. Refreshment pavilion.

St. John's Gate, St. John's La., EC1. 01-253 6644 **1A 22**
Built in 1504 as a gateway to the Priory of the Knights Hospitallers of St. John. The order was revived in 1831 and is well known for its hospital and ambulance work. Also to be seen are the historical museum (p. 78) and nearby Priory Church with its Norman Crypt (p. 21).

St. Katharine's Dock, St. Katharine's Way, E1. **3D 41**
Built in 1827 to designs by Thomas Telford, since 1968 redeveloped into a mix of leisure and international trade facilities. New buildings include London World Trade Centre and Tower Hotel. Historic structures incorporated are the Italianate

Ivory House of 1854, timber warehouse *c.* 1800 now "Dickens Inn", the Dockmaster's Ho. and two bridges. With shopping arcades and cobbled promenades the complex centres round the 240 mooring Yacht Haven and Maritime Trust **Historic Ship Collection.** 01-481 0043; includes herring drifter, steam coaster, steam tug, Thames sailing barge, and light ship.

St. Martin-in-the-Fields see CATHEDRALS AND CHURCHES.

St. Paul's Cathedral see CATHEDRALS AND CHURCHES.

Science Museum see MUSEUMS AND GALLERIES.

Smithfield, Charterhouse St., EC1. **2A 22**

The Central Meat Market buildings dating from the 1860's occupies an area historically called "Smoothfield". This was the site of St. Bartholomew's Fair from 9th to 19th cent. Tournaments and executions took place here and Catholic and Protestant Martyrs were burnt at the stake.

Somerset House, Strand, WC2. **2A 36**

The south wing built 1776–86 to designs by Sir William Chambers houses the Probate and Divorce Registry, the east wing added 1829–34 by Sir R. Smirke is now King's College, and the west wing 1851–6 by Sir J. Pennethorne occupied by the Board of Inland Revenue. On the site of a 16th cent. Palace begun by the Duke of Somerset, Lord Protector of Edward VI but still unfinished at his execution in 1552. Later occupants included Elizabeth I and the Queens of James I, Charles I and II.

South Bank Arts Centre, SE1. **1B 52**

The variety of public buildings on this, the site of the 1951 Festival of Britain, illustrates the development of British architectural design between the construction of the Royal Festival Hall and National Film Theatre 1951, the Queen Elizabeth Hall, Purcell Room and Hayward Gallery 1967 and finally the National Theatre 1976. Jubilee Gdns. date from the Queen's Silver Jubilee 1977. Refreshments are open to the public in the Royal Festival Hall and National Theatre.

Southwark Cathedral see CATHEDRALS AND CHURCHES.

Spanish and Portuguese Synagogue, Bevis Marks, EC3. 01-626 1274 **1C 41**

The oldest Synagogue in England, founded in Creechurch Lane in 1657 rebuilt on this site in 1701. Brass chandeliers from Amsterdam. Services: Daily 07.30 Sat. and Sun. 08.00.

Speakers' Corner, Hyde Park, W2. **2C 31**

Hyde Park became a popular centre for orators during the Victorian era; some meetings organised by the Reform League in 1855 and 1859 ending in mass riot. In 1872 a specific area at the north-east of Hyde Park was assigned for public assembly known since as "Orators' Corner".

Staple Inn, Holborn, WC2. **3C 21**

16th cent. Hall and Courtyard. Once an Inn of Chancery, and home of Dr. Johnson 1759–60. Restored after destruction by a flying bomb 1944. Holborn is straddled at this point by twin silver griffins (the site of Holborn Bars) marking the City boundary. See also **Inns of Court and Chancery.**

Stock Exchange, Old Broad Street, EC2. 01-588 2355 **1A 40**

Founded in 1801. The market place for stocks and shares where members are divided into jobbers (or dealers) and brokers, until recently exclusive to men, women are now able to deal and take positions on the exchange. Housed in a new tower block the trading floor has a public gallery and small cinema. Open 09.45–15.15, last guided tour 14.30, working days only; advisable to book.

Strawberry Hill, St. Mary's College of Education, Waldegrave Rd., Twickenham. **AZ 4K 103.** Home of Horace Walpole 1750–87. Converted into a neo-gothic castle by various architects to Walpole's ideas. Open by appointment with the Principal.

Syon House, London Rd., Brentford. 01-560 0881 **AZ 1C 88**

HOUSE: originally a 15th cent. convent. Interior, redesigned by R. Adam 1762–69 for the Duke of Northumberland, is a sequence of five rooms. Entrance Hall in white, Ante Room with columns set against pale green walls, Dining Room in gold, white and red with a screened apse at either end, Drawing Room in deep red

and Library once the Tudor Long Gallery, has elaborate plaster work. Open: Easter to Sept. 12.00–17.00 Sun. to Thurs.; Sun. only in Oct. Closed Fri. and Sat.
GARDENS: Landscaped by Capability Brown with the Great Conservatory (1827) by Dr Fowler now containing an Aviary and Aquarium in addition to many interesting plants and cacti, Open: daily 10.00–18.00 or dusk in winter months, closed Christmas Day & Boxing Day (conservatory closed winter months).
SYON PARK GARDEN CENTRE: 01-568 0134. Set within the landscape park it combines information centre, botanical garden, pleasure garden and nursery. Open: daily 09.30–17.15, 10.00–17.45 Sun.; or dusk in winter months. Closed Christmas and Boxing Day. Other attractions include London Butterfly House 01-560 7272 and Heritage Motor Museum—see Museums. Admission charges.

Telecom Tower, Howland St., W1. **2D 17**
The renamed "Post Office Tower" is 620 ft. high; built to facilitate telecommunications without interference from other tall buildings.

Temple, The, EC4. **2C 37** Inner—01-353 8462; Middle—01-353 4355.
Comprises two Inns of Court: the Inner and Middle Temples, Inner Temple Lane is entered through the 17th cent. archway supporting Prince Henry's Room; Middle Temple Lane through a gateway by Wren 1685. Badly damaged by bombing in 1941 the alleys, courtyards, halls and gardens have been rebuilt and today represent one of the most relaxing areas of London. Middle Temple Hall was opened by Elizabeth I 1576 and has an elaborate double hammerbeam roof. Inner Temple Hall crypt, survives from the 14th cent. Temple Church consists of a Norman round church 1185 with an oblong chancel added *c.* 1240; reredos by Wren 1682, 12–13th cent. effigies of crusaders. Open, Middle Temple Hall 10.00–12.00, 15.00–16.30 Mon. to Fri.; also Sat. when staff are available, closed Public Holidays. Inner Temple Hall 11.00–12.00 weekdays only, closed Public Holidays. Temple Church 14.00–16.30 daily except for Public Holidays and Christmas Day (except for Services) see page 27. See also Inns of Court and Chancery.

Temple Bar, Fleet St., EC4. **1C 37**
Historically the Western entrance of the City of London. The Wren gate erected after the Great Fire 1666 was removed in 1878 and re-erected in Theobalds Park, Waltham Cross. The Bar is now marked by a memorial capped with the unofficial badge of the City, a griffin. When the sovereign visits the City she is met, and accompanied from, here by the Lord Mayor.

Temple of Mithras, Queen Victoria St., EC4. **2D 39**
Place of worship from *c.* A.D. 90 to 350. devoted to the Roman God of Mithras. Unearthed in 1954 the remains are in the basilican form of apse, nave and side aisles. Roman finds are now in the Museum of London.

Thames Barrier see River Thames p. 14.

Tower Bridge see BRIDGES AND TUNNELS.

Tower of London, Tower Hill, EC3. 01-709 0765 **3C 41**
First built by William the Conqueror to both protect and control the City, it has been continually added to over the centuries. During its history the Tower has served as Fortress, Palace, Prison, and has housed the Royal Mint, Public Records, Royal Observatory and, Predecessor of the London Zoo, the Royal Menagerie. The Inner Ward is defended by a wall with thirteen towers, an inner moat; then an outer wall and outer moat. In the centre is the Great Tower or Keep called "The White Tower". Occupied as a Palace until the reign of James I, it was the custom for the monarch to lodge in the Tower before the coronation and ride in procession through the City to Westminster Abbey. For opening hours, etc., see below after YEOMEN WARDERS.

BELL TOWER. 13th cent. Sir Thomas More, Princess Elizabeth and James Duke of Monmouth were imprisoned here. Curfew is still rung just before 21.00 or dusk.

BEAUCHAMP TOWER 13th to 16th cent Semi-circular tower of three stories. The middle chamber has inscriptions of former prisoners.

BLOODY TOWER. 13th to 14th cent Believed to be the scene of the notorious

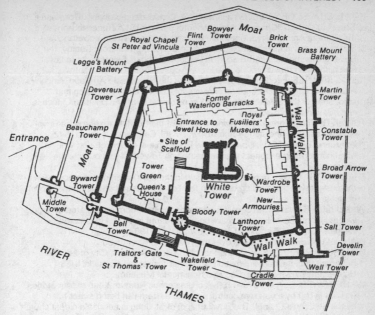

Plan of the TOWER OF LONDON

murder of "The Princes in the Tower": Edward V and his brother the Duke of York.
   Other prisoners were Jeffreys, Laud, Percy and Raleigh.
CEREMONY OF THE KEYS. Enacted nightly at 22.00 when the main gates are
   locked. On the return of the keys the sentry challenges "Halt, who comes
   there?" The Chief Warder replies: "The Keys". "Whose Keys?"—"Queen
   Elizabeth's Keys". The ceremony can be seen, written application to the
   Resident Governor.
CROWN JEWELS. Most of the regalia of the English Monarchy was sold or melted
   down during the Commonwealth. At the restoration in 1660 some were
   recovered and new pieces made to resemble the original. The oldest Sovereign's
   Crown extant is the King Edward the Confessor's Crown made for the
   Coronation of Charles II in 1661. The Crown of Queen Elizabeth II made 1911 is
   set with the "Koh-i-Noor" diamond. The Royal Sceptre includes the larger
   of the "Stars of Africa"—the largest cut diamond in the world.
HERALDS' MUSEUM. Opened in 1980 by the College of Arms Trust, see also
   page 89. Shows the history and development of heraldry through the ages.
KEEP see WHITE TOWER.
NEW ARMOURIES. Mainly 18th and 19th cent. collections. Firearms, oriental
   weapons and armour including a suit of elephant armour.
QUEEN'S HOUSE. Residence of the Governor. Timber-framed house c. 1530 once
   the prison of Anne Boleyn and Lord Nithsdale. Adjoining is Yeoman Gaolers'
   House where Lady Jane Grey was held.
RAVENS. There are six ravens cared for by a Yeoman Warder, their cage being
   beside Lanthorn Tower. There is a legend that the Tower will fall if it loses its ravens.
REGIMENTAL MUSEUM. The Royal Fusiliers Museum (see also Waterloo
   Barracks).
ROMAN WALL. 2nd cent. City Wall runs either side of a Bastion, later incorporated
   in the 12th cent. Wardrobe Tower.

ROYAL CHAPEL OF ST. PETER ad VINCULA. Consecrated probably in the early 12th cent., rebuilt 13th cent. and again after a fire in 1512. Buried in front of the altar are Anne Boleyn, Catherine Howard, Dukes of Northumberland and Somerset; and in the precincts: Lady Jane Grey, Lord Guildford Dudley, the Duke of Monmouth and the Scottish Lords Kilmarnock, Balmerino and Lovat. See below for admission.

ROYAL SALUTES. Fired from Tower Wharf by the Honourable Artillery Company. A Salute of 62 guns are fired on anniversaries of the birth, accession and coronation of the Sovereign and of 41 guns on the birth of a prince or princess and other important occasions.

TOWER GREEN. A brass plate marks the site of the Scaffold reserved for Royal or noble persons; including Anne Boleyn (1536), Catherine Howard (1542), Lady Jane Grey (1554), all buried in the Royal Chapel of St. Peter ad Vincula. Most condemned prisoners were executed on Tower Hill just outside the Tower.

TRAITORS' GATE. The river entrance. Used in the days when river transport was the easiest way of travelling between the Tower, Westminster and other Royal Palaces.

WAKEFIELD TOWER. 13th cent. round tower. Vaulted room on the ground floor where Henry VI is believed to have been murdered in 1471. Housed the Public Records 1360–1856 and the Crown Jewels 1870–1967.

WALL WALK, gives good views over the Tower and Riverscape.

WATERLOO BARRACKS. Headquarters of the Royal Fusiliers, City of London Regiment until their amalgamation with other fusilier regiments in 1968. Houses the Crown Jewels. See also Regimental Museum.

WHITE TOWER. Built *c.* 1078–1100. A characteristic Norman Keep of four stories. Divided in half by a massive central wall, the eastern half being sub-divided by the St. John's Chapel. The Royal Chapel of St. John is London's oldest church and shows Norman ecclesiastical architecture in perfect condition. The Armouries have displays under the following principal headings: Swords from the Middle Ages to the 19th cent., the development of armour, items of armour and weapons of famous Tudor and Stuart personages, the development of fire-arms, relics of famous soldiers, collections of ordnance and instruments of torture.

YEOMEN WARDERS. (Popularly called Beefeaters.) Formed by Henry VIII and now consist of about 40 ex-service men. They normally wear a blue costume, changed on ceremonial occasions for one of red and gold, both of which are of Tudor origin, similar to that of the Yeoman of the Guard, see St. James's Palace.

Open: Mar. to Oct. 09.30–17.00, Mon. to Sat.; 14.00–17.00 Sun. Nov. to Feb. 09.30–16.00, Mon. to Sat. only. Conducted tours by Yeoman Warders start from Byward Tower covering the external areas of the Tower and admission to the Royal Chapel of St. Peter ad Vincula. Closed Christmas Eve and Day, Boxing Day, Easter and Bank Hol. Mon. Admission charge, extra charges to Crown Jewels and Regimental Museum. Jewel House closed in Feb. for cleaning.

Trafalgar Square see SQUARES AND STREETS.

Tyburn, Marble Arch, W1. **2C 31**

On a spot now marked by a stone slab stood Tyburn Tree, a triangular gallows where the execution of common criminals took place; the last being in 1783.

University College, London, Gower St., WC1. 01-387 7050 **1A 18**

Founded in 1826 the college provides courses in the faculties of arts, Law, science, engineering and economics and in medical sciences. Incorporated in the college is the Slade School of Fine Art founded 1871, the Galton Laboratory, the Bartlett School of Architecture and the School of Librarianship and Archives. To be seen by visitors are the Flaxman Gallery and an Egyptology Collection. University College was incorporated in the University of London in 1907—its largest college.

University of London, Senate Ho., Gower St., WC1. 01-636 8000 **2C 19**

Founded in 1836 as an examination organization. It became a teaching university in 1900 being the first to admit women to degrees in 1878. The headquarters house the Senate House and Library. For individual colleges see FURTHER EDUCATION.

Victoria and Albert Museum see MUSEUMS AND GALLERIES.

Wallace Collection see MUSEUMS AND GALLERIES

Wesley's House and Chapel, 47 City Rd., EC1. 01-253 2262 **1A 24**
Home of John Wesley 1779–91. Stands beside Wesley's Chapel the crypt of which contains The Museum of Methodism. In the churchyard is John Wesley's tomb. Open 10.00–16.00 Mon. to Sat. and by arrangement. Closed Bank Holidays. Admission charge. See also Worship p. 203.

Westminster Abbey see CATHEDRALS AND CHURCHES.

Westminster Cathedral see CATHEDRALS AND CHURCHES.

Westminster Hall, Parliament Sq., SW1. **3D 51**
The main surviving fragment of the Old Palace of Westminster founded by Edward the Confessor and used as a Royal residence until the 16th cent. The Hall was built for William II and completed 1099. Richard II added the massive hammerbeam roof and the full sized statues of Kings of which eleven survive, from the 12th to 19th cent. it was principally used as the meeting place for the Courts of Justice. Sir Thomas More, Guy Fawkes, Charles I were sentenced here. See also Jewel Tower and Houses of Parliament. Not open except by arranagement with Member of Parliament.

Whitefriars Crypt, 30 Bouverie St. EC4. **1D 37**
Crypt of the 15th cent. Carmelite Priory. Restored by "News of the World" under whose old offices it is situated.

Whitehall see SQUARES AND STREETS.

Windsor, Berkshire.
The traditional home of English Monarchs. Dominating the town the massive castle was established by William the Conqueror, rebuilt in stone by Henry II since when many additions have been made by consecutive sovereigns, making it now the largest castle in England. The Middle Ward contains the Round Tower established by Henry II, the Lower Ward encompasses St. George's Chapel begun 1475. The Upper Ward is made up of State Apartments, these being mainly of Charles II and 19th cent. origin containing carving by Gibbons, ceiling paintings by Verrio; collections of armour, furniture and fine art, in particular Leonardo da Vinci sketches and drawings by Holbein also the Queen's dolls house designed by Sir E. Lutyens. St. George's Chapel the Chapel of the Dean and Canons of Windsor and the Order of the Garter features fan vaulting of perpendicular architecture, elaborately carved stalls (at the back of which are affixed plates recording Knights of the Garter, the earliest being 1390) and tombs including those of Prince Imperial, Princess Charlotte of Wales and Duke of Clarence an art nouveau design by Sir A. Gilbert. Windsor Great Park is a vast area of parkland 6 miles long by 5 miles at its widest point; some 4,800 acres encompassing Home Park with Frogmore House and the Royal mausoleum of Victoria and Albert; Savill Gardens, Virginia Water, the polo centre at Smith's Lawn and the Windsor Safari Park (for details see page 84). Combermere Barracks has the Household Cavalry Museum. The Guildhall built 1689 is attributed to Wren and has a Local History Museum.

Open: CASTLE: The Precincts 10.00 to Sunset daily; State Apartments and Queen Mary's Dolls' House daily except when the Queen is in residence, usually for two spring months. Subject to closure at short notice, Tel. Windsor 68286. St. George's Chapel enquiries Tel. Windsor 65538. Admission charges. CAVALRY MUSEUM: 10.00–13.00, 14.00–17.00 Mon. to Fri., Sundays 10.00–12.00, 13.00–17.00 Easter to Sept. only. Closed Bank Hols. Tel. Windsor 68222. GUILDHALL April to Sept. 13.30–16.30 daily. Admission charge. Madame Tussaud's exhibition ROYALTY & EMPIRE is open 09.30–17.30 Daily. Adm. Charge.

York House, York St., Twickenham. **AZ 1A 104**
18th cent. childhood home of Queen Anne, interior has the original panelling and

staircase. Now municipal offices. Open by arrangement, London Borough of Richmond-upon-Thames.

York Watergate, Embankment Gdns., WC2. **3D 35**
Built 1626 as the river entrance to York House, home of the Duke of Buckingham.

POLICE STATIONS

CITY POLICE
Headquarters, 26 Old Jewry, EC2. 01-606 8866 **1D 39**
'A' Division (Traffic), 37 Wood Street, EC2. 01-606 8866 **1C 39**
'B' Division, Snow Hill, 5 Snow Hill, EC1. 01-606 8866 **3A 22**
'C' Division, Bishopsgate, 182 Bishopsgate, EC2. 01-606 8866 **1B 40**
'D' Division, Wood Street, EC2. 01-606 8866 **1C 39**

METROPOLITAN POLICE
Headquarters, New Scotland Yard, 10 The Broadway, SW1. 01-230 1212 **1B 64**
Acton, 250 High St., W3. 01-900 7212 **AZ 1H 73**
Addington, Addington Village St., Croydon. 01-680 6212 **AZ 5D 136**
Albany Street, 60 Albany St., NW1. 01-725 4212 **3C 9**
Arbour Square, East Arbour St., E1. 01-488 5212 **AZ 6K 63**
Banstead, 168 High Steet, Banstead. 01-680 6212
Barking, 6 Ripple Rd. 01-593 8232 **AZ 1H 67**
Barkingside, 1 High St. 01-551 4211 **AZ 3G 35**
Barnes, 92 Station Rd., SW3. 01-577 1212 **AZ 2B 90**
Barnet, 26 High St. 01-200 2212 **AZ 3B 4**
Battersea, 112 Battersea Bridge Rd., SW11. 01-350 1122 **AZ 7C 76**
Beckenham, 45 High St. 01-697 9231 **AZ 2C 126**
Belvedere, 2 Nuxley Rd. 01-853 8212 **AZ 6F 85**
Bethnal Green, 458 Bethnal Green Rd., E2. 01-488 5212 **AZ 4F 63**
Bexleyheath, 39 Broadway, 01-853 8212 **AZ 4E 100**
Biggin Hill, 195 Main Road, Biggin Hill, Kent. 0959 74030
Boreham Wood, Elstree Way, Boreham Wood. 01-200 2212
Bow, 111 Bow Rd., E3. 01-488 5212. **AZ 3B 64**
Bow Street, 28 Bow St., WC2. 01-434 5212 **1D 35**
Brentford, The Half Acre. 01-577 1212 **AZ 6D 72**
Brick Lane, 66 Brick La., E1. 01-733 5678 **AZ 4F 63**
Brixton, 367 Brixton Rd., SW9. 01-326 1212 **AZ 3A 94**
Brockley, 4 Howson Rd., SE4. 01-853 8212 **AZ 4A 96**
Bromley, Widmore Rd., 01-697 9212 **AZ 2J 127**
Bushey, 43 Clay Hill, Bushey 01-200 2212
Caledonian Road, 470 Caledonian Rd., N7. 01-609 4111 **AZ 2J 61**
Camberwell, 22a Camberwell Church St., SE5. 01-703 0866 **1D 94**
Cannon Row, Victoria Embankment. 01-434 5212 **3D 51**
Carter Street, 292 Walworth Rd., SE17. 01-703 0844 **AZ 4C 78**
Catford, 333 Bromley Rd., SE6. 01-697 9212 **AZ 1D 112**
Cavendish Road,47 Cavendish Rd., SW12. 01-326 1212 **AZ 6G 93**
Chadwell Heath, 14 Wangey Rd. 01-326 1212 **AZ 7D 36**
Chelsea, 2 Lucan Pl., SW3. 01-741 6212 **7D 36**
Cheshunt, 101 Turner's Hill, Cheshunt, Herts. 01-367 2222
Chigwell, 24 Brook Prde., High Rd. 01-501 2231 **AZ 5K 21**
Chingford, Kings Head Hill, E4. 01-529 8666 **AZ 7J 9**
Chislehurst, 47 High St. 01-697 9212 **AZ 6F 115**
Chiswick,205 Chiswick High Rd., W4. 01-577 1212 **AZ 5G 73**
City Road, 4 Shepherdess Walk, N1. 01-488 5212 **AZ 2C 62**
Clapham, 51 Union Gro., SW8. 01-326 1212 **AZ 2H 93**
Cobham, 91–93 Portsmouth Rd., Cobham. 0932 2041

Collier Row, 22 Collier Row La., Romford. 0708 29212 **AZ 1H 37**
Croydon, 71 Park Lane. 01-680 6212 **AZ 3D 134**
Dagenham, 561 Rainham Road S. 01-593 8232 **AZ 4H 53**
Dalston, 39 Dalston La., E8. 01-488 5212 **AZ 6F 47**
Deptford, 116 Amersham Vale, SE14. 01-697 9212 **AZ 7B 80**
Ealing, 67 Uxbridge Rd., W5. 01-900 7212 **AZ 7E 56**
Earlsfield, 522 Garratt La., SW17. 01-947 6121 **AZ 6K 91**
East Dulwich, 173–183 Lordship La., SE22. 01-299 0111 **AZ 5F 95**
East Ham, 4 High Street S., E6. 01-593 8232 **AZ 2D 66**
East Molesey, 1 Walton Rd., East Molesey. 01-979 0977
Edgware, Whitchurch La. 01-900 7212 **AZ 7J 11**
Edmonton, 320 Fore St., N9. 01-803 3311 **AZ 4B 18**
Eltham, 20 Well Hall Rd., SE9. 01-853 8212 **AZ 3C 98**
Enfield, 41 Baker St. 01-367 2222 **AZ 2J 7**
Epsom, Church St. 037-274 0411 **AZ 7C 130**
Erith, 22 Erith High St., 01-853 8212
Esher, 113 High Street, Esher, Surrey. 0372 67261
Farnborough, Farnborough Common, Farnborough, Orpington. 01-697 9212.
Feltham, 34 Hanworth Rd., Feltham 01-577 1212 **AZ 1A 102**
Finchley, 193 Ballard's La., N3. 01-200 2212 **AZ 1J 27**
Forest Gate, 370 Romford Rd., E7. 01-593 8232 **AZ 6G 49**
Fulham, Heckfield Pl., SW6. 01-741 6212 **AZ 7J 75**
Gerald Road, 5 Gerald Rd., SW1. 01-434 5212 **2A 62**
Gipsy Hill, 66 Central Hill, SE19. 01-326 1212 **AZ 6E 110**
Golders Green, 1069 Finchley Rd., NW11. 01-200 2212 **AZ 6H 27**
Greenford,21 Oldfield La. 01-900 7212 **AZ 4G 55**
Greenwich, 31 Royal Hill, SE10. 01-853 8212 **AZ 7E 80**
Hackney, 2 Lower Clapton Rd., E5. 01-488 5212 **AZ 3H 47**
Ham, 18 Ashburnham Rd. 01-948 3661 **AZ 3B 104**
Hammersmith, 226 Shepherds Bush Rd., W6. 01-741 6212 **AZ 4E 74**
Hampstead, 26–4 Rosslyn Hill, NW3. 01-725 4212 **AZ 4B 44**
Hampton, 68 Station Rd. 01-577 1212 **AZ 7E 102**
Harlesden, 75 Craven Park, NW10. 01-900 7212 **AZ 1K 57**
Harold Hill, Gooshays Drive. 0708 29212
Harrow, 74 Northolt Rd. 01-900 7212 **AZ 4F 39**
Harrow Road, 325 Harrow Rd., W9. 01-725 4212 **AZ 3D 58**
Hayes, 755 Uxbridge Rd., 01-900 7212
Heathrow Airport, Hounslow. 01-897 7373
Hendon, 133 Brent St., NW4. 01-200 2212 **AZ 4E 26**
Highbury Vale, 211 Blackstock Rd., N5. 01-226 1113 **AZ 2B 46**
Highgate, 407 Archway Rd., N6. 01-340 6275 **AZ 6E 28**
Holborn, 70 Theobald's Rd., WC1. 01-725 4212 **2A 20**
Holloway, 284 Hornsey Rd., N7. 01-263 9090 **AZ 2J 45**
Hornchurch, 74 Station La. 0708 29212
Hornsey, 98 Tottenham La., N8. 01-348 5201 **AZ 5J 29**
Hounslow, 5 Montague Rd. 01-577 1212 **AZ 3F 87**
Hyde Park, North of Serpentine, W2. 01-434 5212 **3B 30**
Ilford, 40 High Rd. 01-553 3400 **AZ 2G 51**
Isle of Dogs, 160 Manchester Rd., E14. 01-488 5212 **AZ 5E 80**
Islington, 277 Upper St., N1. 01-226 3291 **AZ 2B 62**
Kenley, 94 Godstone Rd. 01-680 6212
Kennington Road, 49 Kennington Rd., SE1. 01-326 1212 **1C 67**
Kensington, 72 Earl's Court Rd., W8. 01-741 6212 **AZ 2J 75**
Kentish Town, 12a Holmes Rd., NW5. 01-725 4212 **AZ 5F 45**
Kilburn, 38 Salusbury Rd., NW6. 01-900 7212 **AZ 1G 59**
Kingsbury, 5 The Mall, Kenton, Harrow. 01-900 7212 **AZ 6F 25**
Kingston-upon-Thames, 5 High St. 01-546 7777 **AZ 3D 118**
King's Cross Road, 76 King's Cross Rd., WC1. 01-837 4233 **AZ 5K 61**

Lavender Hill, 176 Lavender Hill, SW11. 01-228 8565 **AZ 3D 92**
Lee Road, 418 Lee High Rd., SE12. 01-697 9212 **AZ 3E 96**
Leman St., 74 Leman St., E1. 01-488 5212 **AZ 6F 63**
Lewisham, 2 Ladywell Rd., SE13. 01-697 9212 **AZ 5C 96**
Leyton, 215 Francis Rd., E10. 01-556 8855 **AZ 1E 48**
Leytonstone, 470 High Rd., E11. 01-556 8855 **AZ 4G 49**
Limehouse, 29 West India Dock Rd., E14. 01-488 5212 **AZ 7C 64**
Loughton, 158 High Street, Loughton. 01-508 2136
Marylebone Lane, 1–9 Seymour St., W1. 01-725 4212 **1C 31**
Mill Hill, 11 Dean's Drive. 01-200 2212 **AZ 5E 12**
Mitcham, 58 Cricket Green. 01-640 5533 **AZ 4D 122**
Muswell Hill, Fortis Green, N2. 01-444 7171 **AZ 4C 28**
New Malden, 184 High St. 01-942 1113 **AZ 4A 120**
Norbury, 15-16 London Rd., SW16. 01-680 6212 **AZ 1K 123**
Northwood, 2 Murray Rd. 01-900 7212
North Woolwich, Pier Rd., E16. 01-593 8232 **AZ 2E 82**
Norwood Green, 190 Norwood Rd., Southall. 01-900 7212 **AZ 3C 70**
Notting Hill, 101 Ladbroke Rd., W11. 01-741 6212 **AZ 1H 75**
Orpington, 17 Homefield Rise. 01-697 9212
Paddington Green, 4 Harrow Rd., W2. 01-725 4212 **2D 13**
Peckham, 177 Peckham High St., SE15. 01-639 4333 **AZ 1G 95**
Penge, 175 High St., SE20. 01-697 9212 **AZ 6J 111**
Pinner, Bridge St. 01-900 7212 **AZ 3C 22**
Plaistow, 444 Barking Rd., E13. 01-474 1113 **AZ 5H 65**
Plumstead, 216 Plumstead High St., SE18. 01-853 8212 **AZ 4H 83**
Ponders End, 204 High St. 01-367 2222 **AZ 5D 8**
Poplar, 2 Market Way, E14. 01-515 3228 **AZ 6D 64**
Potters Bar, The Causeway, Potters Bar. 01-200 2212
Putney, 215 Upper Richmond Rd., SW15. 01-788 1113 **AZ 4B 80**
Rainham, 3 New Rd. 0708 29212
Richmond, 8 Red Lion St. 01-577 1212 **AZ 5D 88**
Rochester Row, 63 Rochester Row, SW1. 01-434 5212 **2A 64**
Roehampton, 117 Danebury Av., SW15. 01-788 1103 **AZ 6A 90**
Romford, 19 Main Rd. 0708 29212
Rotherhithe, 99 Lower Rd., SE16. 01-237 0582 **AZ 2J 79**
Ruislip, The Oaks. 01-900 7212
Shepherd's Bush, 252 Uxbridge Rd., W12. 01-741 6212 **AZ 1C 74**
Shooter's Hill, SE18. 01-853 8212 **AZ 1E 98**
Sidcup, 87 Main Rd. 01-853 8212 **AZ 3H 115**
Southall, 67 High St. 01-900 7212 **AZ 1D 70**
Southgate, 25 Chase Side, N14. 01-803 3311 **AZ 6K 5**
Southwark, 323 Borough High St., SE1. 01-407 8044 **3C 55**
South Norwood, 83 High St., SE25. 01-680 6212 **AZ 4F 125**
St. Ann's Road, 289 St. Ann's Rd., N15. 01-801 2443 **AZ 5C 30**
St. John's Wood, 20–4 Newcourt St., NW8. 01-725 4212 **1A 6**
St. Mary Cray, 79 High St. 0689 73211
Staines, 2 London Road, Staines. 0784 50261
Stoke Newington, 33 Stoke Newington High St., N16. 01-488 5212 **AZ 3F 47**
Stoneleigh, 358 Kingston Rd., Ewell. 01-393 9874.
Streatham, 101 Streatham High Rd., SW16. 01-326 1212 **AZ 4J 109**
Sunbury, 67-71 Staines Rd. East, Sunbury. 01-897 7373
Surbiton, 299 Ewell Rd. 01-399 1113
Sutton, 6 Carshalton Road W. 01-680 6212 **AZ 5A 132**
Sydenham, 179 Dartmouth Rd., SE26. 01-697 9212 **AZ 3H 111**
Teddington, 18 Park Rd. 01-577 1212 **AZ 6K 103**
Thamesmead, 1 Tavy Bridge, SE2. 01-310 0580 **AZ 2C 84**
Titmuss Av., Thamesmead Estate, SE28. 01-311 2055 **AZ 7B 68**
Tooting, Mitcham Rd., SW17. 01-672 9922 **AZ 5D 108**

Tottenham, 398 High Rd., N17. 01-801 3443 **AZ 4F 31**
Tottenham Court Road, 56 Tottenham Court Rd., W1. 01-725 4212 **2A 18**
Tower Bridge, 209 Tooley St., SE1. 01-407 6213 **2C 57**
Trinity Rd., 76 Trinity Rd,. SW17. 01-672 9922 **AZ 4A 92**
Twickenham, 41 London Rd. 01-577 1212 **AZ 7A 88**
Upminster, 223 St. Mary's La., Upminster. 0708 29212
Uxbridge, 49 Windsor St. 01-900 7212
Vine Street, 10 Vine St., W1. (formerly Piccadilly Pl.) 01-434 5212 **3A 34**
Wallington, 84 Stafford Rd. 01-680 6212 **AZ 6G 133**
Waltham Abbey, 35 Sun Street, Waltham Abbey. 0992 716222
Walthamstow, 360 Forest Rd., E17. 01-520 0911 **AZ 4J 31**
Wandsworth, 146 High St., SW18. 01-870 9011 **AZ 5J 91**
Wanstead, Spratt Hall Rd., E11. 01-989 1113 **AZ 6J 33**
Wapping, 98 Wapping High St., E1. 01-488 5212 **AZ 1G 79**
Waterloo Pier, Victoria Embankment, WC2. 01-434 5212 **2B 36**
Wealdstone, 78 High St. 01-900 7212 **AZ 2J 23**
Welling, 60 High St. 01-304 3161 **AZ 3B 100**
Wellington Arch, Hyde Park Corner, SW1. 01-434 5212 **2A 48**
Wembley, 603 Harrow Rd. 01-900 7212 **AZ 4K 39**
Westcombe Park, 11 Combedale Rd., SE10. 01-853 8212 **AZ 5J 81**
West End Central, 27 Savile Row, W1. 01-434 5212 **2D 33**
West Drayton, Station Rd. 01-900 7212
West Ham, 18 West Ham La., E15. 01-593 8232 **AZ 7G 49**
West Hampstead, 21 Fortune Green Rd., NW6. 01-725 4212 **AZ 4J 43**
West Hendon, West Hendon Broadway, Edgware Rd., NW9. 01-200 2212.
AZ 5B 26
West Wickham, 9 High Street, West Wickham, Kent. 01-777 0383 **AZ 1D 136**
Whetstone, 1170 High Rd., N20. 01-200 2212 **AZ 7F 5**
Willesden Green, 96 High Rd., NW10. 01-900 7212 **AZ 6B 42**
Wimbledon, 15 Queen's Rd., SW19. 01-947 4141 **AZ 6J 107**
Winchmore Hill, 687 Green Lanes, N21. 01-803 3311 **AZ 6E 16**
Woodford, 509 High Rd., Woodford Green. 01-505 6131 **AZ 6C 20**
Woolwich, 29 Market St., SE18. 01-853 8212 **AZ 4E 82**
Wood Green, 347 High Rd., N22. 01-888 1113 **AZ 1K 29**
Worcester Park, 154 Central Rd., 01-330 2831 **AZ 1C 130**

POST OFFICES

Customer Service Information, 01-250 2888
Enquiries Office, 01-606 9876
Emergency Service, Trafalgar Square, see p. 205. **National Girobank,** see p. 12.

Abbey Wood, 90 Abbey Wood Rd., SE2. 01-311 2798 **AZ 4B 84**
Acton, 23 King St., W3. 01-992 0128 **AZ 1J 73**
Addiscombe, 275 Lwr. Addiscombe Rd. 01-654 2596 **AZ 2E 134**
43 Albermarle St., W1. 01-493 5620 **3D 33**
111 Baker St., W1. 01-935 3701 **2D 15**
Balham, 92a Balham High Rd., SW12. 01-673 4602 **AZ 3E 108**
Barking, 9 Ripple Rd. 01-594 2164 **AZ 1H 67**
Barnet, 63 High St. 01-449 9137 **AZ 3B 4**
Battersea, *District Off.,* 202 Lavender Hill, SW11. 01-228 4145 **AZ 3D 92**
    52 Lavender Hill, SW11. 01-228 4222 **AZ 3D 92**
    19 Northcote Rd., Battersea Rise, SW11. 01-223 5986 **AZ 5C 92**
    14 York Rd., SW11. 01-228 2171 **AZ 4A 92**
Beckenham, 22 Rectory Rd., 01-650 4736 **AZ 1C 126**
Bellingham, 12 Randlesdown Rd., SE6. 01-698 3985 **AZ 4C 112**

Belsize Park, 210 Haverstock Hill, NW3. 01-794 4841 **AZ 5C 44**
Bermondsey, 59 Old Kent Rd., SE1. 01-237 3455 **AZ 4E 78**
Bethnal Green, 223 Bethnal Green Rd., E2. 01-739 3540 **AZ 4F 63**
   286 Cambridge Heath Rd., E2. 01-980 5715 **AZ 4H 63**
   138 Roman Rd., E2. 01-980 2260 **AZ 3J 63**
Bexley Heath, 157 The Broadway. 01-303 5722 **AZ 4E 100**
302 Bishopsgate, EC2. 01-247 6903 **2C 25**
Blackfriars, 52 Blackfriars Rd., SE1. 01--928 4816 **3A 54**
Blackheath Village, Blackheath Gro., SE3. 01-852 1809 **AZ 2H 97**
Bloomsbury, 33 Marchmont St., WC1. 01-837 3978 **3C 11**
   71 Southampton Row, WC1. 01-636 3593 **2D 19**
   30 Store St., WC1. 01-636 1880 **2B 18**
Borough, 19a Borough High St., SE1. 01-407 1001 **1D 55**
Bow, 130 Bow Rd., E3. 01-980 3624 **AZ 3B 64**
Brentford, 207 High St. 01-560 8661 **AZ 7C 72**
Brixton, 250 Ferndale Rd., SW9. 01-274 1503 **AZ 4J 93**
Broadway, SW1. 01-222 7528 **1A 64**
15 Broadwick St., W1. 01-437 6842 **1A 34**
Bromley, 3 East St. 01-460 8911 **AZ 2J 127**
Brondesbury, 295 Kilburn High Rd., NW6. 01-624 5231 **AZ 7H 43**
Camberwell Green, 25 Denmark Hill, SE5. 01-703 9022 **AZ 4D 94**
Camden Town, 10 Parkway, NW1. 01-485 3550 **AZ 1F 61**
Canning Town, 22 Barking Rd., E16. 01-476 2326 **AZ 5H 65**
33 Cannon St., EC4. 01-248 1576 **2C 39**
Carshalton, 27 High St. 01-647 9472 **AZ 4E 132**
Catford, 187 Rushey Grn., SE6. 01-698 1812 **AZ 7D 96**
Chancery La., 2 Bishops Ct., WC2. 01-242 8600 **3C 21**
Charlton, 10 Charlton Church La., SE7. 01-858 0937 **AZ 5A 82**
Chelsea, 232 King's Rd., SW3. 01-352 1565 **AZ 7K 75**
   World's End, 351 King's Rd., SW3. 01-351 1187 **AZ 7K 75**
Chessington, Elm Rd. 01-397 1808
Chingford, 104 Station Rd., E4. 01-529 2721 **AZ 1A 20**
   24 Old Church Rd., Chingford Mount, E4. 01-529 3592 **AZ 4H 19**
Chislehurst, 9 High St. 01-467 3932 **AZ 6F 115**
Chiswick, 1 Heathfield Ter., W4. 01-994 4568 **AZ 5J 73**
Clapham Common, 161 Clapham High St., SW4. 01-622 1892 **AZ 4H 93**
Clerkenwell, Mount Pleasant, Rosebery Av., EC1. 01-837 4272 **1C 21**
Colliers Wood, 6 Christchurch Rd., SW19. 01-542 3667 **AZ 1B 122**
Cricklewood, 193 Cricklewood Broadway, NW2. 01-452 1241 **AZ 3F 43**
Croydon, 1 Addiscombe Rd. 01-688 3651 **AZ 3E 134**
   10 High St. 01-688 4980 **AZ 3C 134**
Dagenham, 499 Gale St. 01-592 5147 **AZ 5C 52**
   214 Heathway. 01-592 0568 **AZ 3F 53**
Ealing, 11 High St., W5. 01-567 4615 **AZ 7D 56**
Earls Court, 185 Earls Court Rd., SW5. 01-370 2841 **AZ 3J 75**
East Acton, 71 Old Oak Common La., W3. 01-743 1021 **AZ 5A 58**
East Dulwich, 76 Lordship La., SE22. 01-693 2924 **AZ 5F 95**
East Finchley, 11 Viceroy Pde., High St., N2. 01-883 7535 **AZ 3C 28**
   6 Lyttelton Rd., N2. 01-458 5651 **AZ 5A 28**
East Ham, Wakefield St., E6. 01-472 0581 **AZ 1B 66**
East Sheen, 367 Upper Richmond Rd. W., SW14. 01-876 4087 **AZ 4G 89**
4 Eccleston St., SW1. 01-730 1162 **2B 62**
Edgware Rd., 1 Star St., W2. 01--723 7522 **3D 13**
   291 Edgware Rd., W2. 01-262 7056 **1C 13**
Elephant & Castle, 91 Newington Butts, SE1. 01-703 9223 **AZ 4B 78**
Eltham, 33 Court Yd., SE9. 01-850 1504 **AZ 6D 98**
Enfield, 27 Church St. 01-363 9191 **AZ 3H 7**
Erith, 89 Erith High St. Erith 33139

165 Euston Rd., NW1. 01-387 3121 **3B 10**
328 Euston Rd., NW1. 01-387 3201 **1C 17**
81 Farringdon Rd., EC1. 01-242 7008 **2D 21**
Feltham, 88 High St. 01-890 2676
60 Fenchurch St., EC3. 01-488 3937 **2C 41**
Finchley Church End, 59 Ballards La., N3. 01-346 4714 **AZ 1J 27**
Finsbury Park, 290 Seven Sisters Rd., N4. 01-800 3705 **AZ 3K 45**
Finsbury Sq., 20 City Rd., EC1. 01-606 6502 **1A 24**
40 Fleet St., EC4. 01-353 7101 **1C 37**
Forest Gate, 16 Woodgrange Rd., E7. 01-534 3147 **AZ 5K 49**
Forest Hill, 24 Dartmouth Rd., SE23. 01-699 5458 **AZ 3H 111**
Fore St., EC2. 01-628 9345 **3D 23**
Friern Barnet, 1 Halliwick Court Pde., N12. 01-368 6897 **AZ 5J 15**
Fulham, 14 Farm La., SW6. 01-385 7401 **AZ 7J 75**
  256 Fulham Rd., SW10. 01-352 7388 **AZ 2G 91**
Golders Green, 881 Finchley Rd., NW11. 01-455 7672 **AZ 1J 43**
  1197 Finchley Rd., NW11. 01-455 9327 **AZ 5H 27**
7 Gt. Portland St., W1. 01-636 2205 **1D 33**
202 Gt. Portland St., W1. 01-636 9935 **2C 17**
Greenford, 225 Oldfield La. 01-578 2540 **AZ 1H 55**
Greenwich, 261 Greenwich High Rd., SE10. 01-858 0977 **AZ 7D 80**
Hackney, Paragon Rd., E9. 01-985 4090 **AZ 6J 47**
Hammersmith, 5 Queen Caroline St., W6. 01-748 5011 **AZ 5E 74**
Hampstead, 79 Hampstead High St., NW3. 01-435 0924 **AZ 4A 44**
Hanwell, 139 Uxbridge Rd., W7. 01-567 3217 **AZ 1K 71**
Harlesden, 2 Wendover Rd., NW10. 01-965 5593 **AZ 2B 58**
Harringay, 509 Green Lanes, N4. 01-340 2860 **AZ 4B 30**
Harrow, 51 College Rd. 01-863 0366 **AZ 6J 23**
Hayes, 52 Station Rd. 01-573 2799
Hendon, 131 Brent St., NW4. 01-202 8522 **AZ 4E 26**
Hendon Central, 14 Vivian Av., NW4. 01-202 6661 **AZ 5D 26**
Herne Hill, 134 Herne Hill, SE24. 01-274 1288 **AZ 5C 94**
Highbury, 5 Highbury Corner, N5. 01-607 4668 **AZ 6C 46**
Holborn, 52 High Holborn, WC1. 01-242 8676 **3B 20**
Holloway, 482 Holloway Rd., N7. 01-272 0450 **AZ 2H 45**
Hornsey, 28 Topsfield Pde., Crouch End, N8. 01-340 7263 **AZ 5J 29**
138 Houndsditch, EC3. 01-283 3501 **1C 41**
Hounslow, 9 Holloway St. 01-570 3433 **AZ 3F 87**
Hoxton, 205 Old St., EC1. 01-253 4038 **AZ 3E 62**
Hyde, The, 213 Edgware Rd., NW9. 01-205 6128 **AZ 2J 25**
Ilford, 9 Clements Rd. 01-478 6969 **AZ 3F 51**
Isleworth, 466 London Rd. 01-560 3366 **AZ 3G 87**
Islington, 238 Essex Rd., N1. 01-226 4160 **AZ 1B 62**
  32 High St., N1. 01-837 2329 **AZ 2A 62**
Kennington Park, 410 Kennington Rd., SE11. 01-735 3150 **AZ 3A 78**
Kensal Rise, 85 Chamberlayne Rd., NW10. 01-969 2916 **AZ 1E 58**
Kensington, 257 Kensington High St., W8. 01-602 6651 **AZ 3H 75**
  15 Young St., W8. 01-937 3626 **3D 43**
Kentish Town, 212 Kentish Town Rd., NW5. 01-485 4718 **AZ 7F 45**
Kilburn, 79 Kilburn High Rd., NW6. 01-624 3678 **AZ 7H 43**
Kilburn Park, 9 Chippenham Gdns., NW6. 01-328 1138 **AZ 5H 41**
King Edward St., EC1. 01-601 9103 **3B 22**
Kingsbury, 439 Kingsbury Rd., NW9. 01-204 8265 **AZ 5G 25**
Kings Cross, 13 Euston Rd., NW1. 01-278 5076 **2D 11**
Kingsland, 118 High St., E8. 01-254 0158 **AZ 6F 47**
Kingston-upon-Thames, 42 Eden St. 01-546 3191 **AZ 2D 118**
18 Kingsway, WC2. 01-405 9389 **1A 36**
55 Knightsbridge, SW1. 01-235 2385 **2D 47**

Lambeth, 125 Westminster Bri. Rd., SE1. 01-928 5504 **3B 52**
10 Lancelot Pl., SW7. 01-589 0633 **3B 46**
Leadenhall St., 5 Whittington Ave., EC3. 01-626 1623 **1B 40**
Lee Green, 151 Lee Rd., SE3. 01-852 2425 **AZ 3H 97**
Lewisham, 107 High St., SE13. 01-852 2810 **AZ 6D 96**
Leyton, 553 Lea Bridge Rd., E10. 01-539 4181 **AZ 3J 47**
Leytonstone, 30 Cathall Rd., Harrow Grn., E11. 01-539 6197 **AZ 2F 49**
   783 High Rd., E11. 01-539 3002 **AZ 4G 49**
Lombard St., 86 King William St., EC4. 01-626 1820 **2A 40**
Lower Edmonton, 1 South Mall, N9. 01-807 3380 **AZ 3B 18**
Ludgate Circus, 16 New Bridge St., EC4. 01-353 4159 **AZ 6B 62**
121 Lupus St., SW1. 01-834 3604 **AZ 5F 77**
Maida Hill, 377 Harrow Rd., W9. 01-969 0634 **AZ 3D 58**
Maida Vale, 20 Clifton Rd., W9. 01-286 5493 **1B 12**
Marble Arch, 43 Seymour St., W1. 01-723 0867 **1C 31**
Marylebone, 28 Marylebone High St., W1. 01-935 7838 **2A 16**
Mayfair, 22 Queen St., W1. 01-499 3522 **1B 48**
Merton, High St., SW19. 01-542 4465 **AZ 7K 107**
Mill Hill, 27 The Broadway, NW7. 01-959 1510 **AZ 5F 13**
Mitcham, 7 Langdale Pde., Upper Green E. 01-648 5439 **AZ 3D 122**
Moorgate, South Pl., EC2. 01-606 7641 **2A 24**
Morden, 25 Abbotsbury Rd. 01-648 2737 **AZ 5K 121**
15 Mount St., W1. 01-499 1849 **3A 32**
Muswell Hill, 420 Muswell Hill Broadway, N10. 01-883 3785 **AZ 4F 29**
New Cross, 480 New Cross Rd., SE14. 01-692 3765 **AZ 7K 79**
New Cross Gate, 199 New Cross Rd., SE14. 01-639 6658 **AZ 7K 79**
New Fetter La., EC4. 01-353 1345 **3D 21**
50 Newman St., W1. 01-636 9995 **3A 18**
Norbury, 1346 London Rd., SW16. 01-764 2218 **AZ 1K 123**
North Finchley, 751 High Rd., N12. 01-445 9778 **AZ 4F 15**
Northwood, Green La. Northwood 21043
Norwood, 35 Westow St., SE19. 01-653 3882 **AZ 6E 110**
Notting Hill, 224 Westbourne Gro., W11. 01-229 0082 **1A 26**
Notting Hill Gate, 190 Kensington Church St., W8. 01-229 2009 **3B 26**
Old St., 59 Old St., EC1. 01-253 7747 **1B 22**
Orpington, 214 High St., Orpington 20259
Paddington, 291 Edgware Rd., W2. 01-262 7056 **2D 13**
   41 Spring St., W2. 01-723 0279 **1C 29**
   1 Star St., W2. 01-723 7522 **3A 14**
Palmers Green, 364 Green Lanes, N13. 01-886 5350 **AZ 6E 16**
44 Parliament St., SW1. 01-930 8947 **2C 51**
Peckham, 121 Peckham High St., SE15. 01-639 4294 **AZ 1G 95**
Peckham Rye, 199 Rye La., SE15. 01-639 7068 **AZ 2G 95**
Penge, 100 High St., SE20. 01-778 2455 **AZ 6J 111**
Pinner, Bridge St. 01-866 1295 **AZ 3C 22**
Plaistow, 371 Barking Rd., E13. 01-476 5165 **AZ 5H 65**
Poplar, 22 Market Sq., E14. 01-987 3469 **AZ 6D 64**
Portman Square, 132 Wigmore St., W1. 01-935 6357 **1D 31**
Purley, 6 Purley Pde., High St., 01-660 0471
Putney, 214 Upper Richmond Rd., SW15. 01-788 4104 **AZ 4B 90**
118 Queensway, W2. 01-229 5257 **2D 27**
Rainham, 32 Wennington Rd. Rainham 54230
Raynes Park, 1a Amity Gro., SW20. 01-946 1208 **AZ 1E 120**
Regent Street, 3 Heddon St., W1. 01-734 5556 **2D 33**
   11 Regent St., SW1. 01-930 9538 **3A 34**
Richmond, 83/84 George St. 01-940 2361 **AZ 5D 88**
Romford, 64 South St. Romford 64021, ext. 59
Ruislip, 48 High St. Ruislip 32297

87 St. James's St., SW1. 01-930 4124 **1D 41**
St. John's Wood, 28 Circus Rd., NW8. 01-722 0996 **1D 5**
St. Lukes, 59 Old St., EC1. 01-253 7747 **1B 22**
Seething La., EC3. 01-623 6602 **2C 41**
Shepherds Bush, 65 The Green, W12. 01-743 2860 **AZ 2E 74**
Shoreditch, 176 High St., E1. 01-739 7717 **AZ 4E 62**
Sidcup, 89 Sidcup High St., 01-300 4421 **AZ 4A 116**
Sloane Sq., 9 King's Rd., SW1. 01-730 1832 **3D 61**
13 Soho St., W1. 01-437 3235 **1B 34**
Southall, 38 The Broadway. 01-574 4361 **AZ 1C 70**
3 Southampton St., Strand, WC2. 01-836 5344 **2D 35**
South Ealing, 89 South Ealing Rd., W5. 01-567 4686 **AZ 2D 72**
Southfields, 265 Wimbledon Park Rd., SW19. 01-788 2970 **AZ 2G 107**
Southgate, 100 Crown La., N14. 01-886 3086 **AZ 1B 16**
   Hampden Sq., 1 Onslow Pde., N14. 01-368 5641 **AZ 1A 16**
South Kensington, 25 Exhibition Rd., SW7. 01-589 2018 **1D 59**
   41 Old Brompton Rd., SW7. 01-589 7984 **3C 59**
   152 Gloucester Rd., SW7. 01-370 2071 **3B 58**
South Lambeth, 186 Wandsworth Rd., SW8. 01-622 9858 **AZ 3F 93**
   591 Wandsworth Rd., SW8. 01-622 6566 **AZ 3F 93**
65 South Moulton St., W1. 01-629 2480 **2B 32**
South Norwood, 243 Selhurst Rd., SE25. 01-653 2542 **AZ 6E 124**
South Tottenham, 316 High Rd., N15. 01-808 0355 **AZ 4F 31**
Southwark, 52 Blackfriars Rd., SE1. 01-928 4816 **1A 54**
South Woodford, 139 George La., E18. 01-989 2138 **AZ 2J 33**
Spitalfields Market, 107 Commercial St., E1. 01-247 5225 **2D 25**
Stamford Hill, 250 Stamford Hill, N16. 01-800 4967 **AZ 2F 47**
Stanmore, 35 Church Rd. 01-954 4107 **AZ 5G 11**
Stepney, 597 Commercial Rd., E1. 01-790 2157 **AZ 6G 63**
Stockwell, 2 Stockwell Rd., SW9. 01-274 6493 **AZ 2K 93**
Stoke Newington, 138 High St., N16. 01-254 6688 **AZ 3F 47**
Stratford, 413 High St., E15. 01-534 1484 **AZ 2E 64**
Streatham, 136 High Rd., SW16. 01-769 6251 **AZ 4J 109**
   225 High Rd., SW16. 01-769 0984 **AZ 4J 109**
Streatham Hill, 45c Streatham Hill, SW2. 01-674 3138 **AZ 2J 109**
Sutton, 19 Grove Rd. 01-643 8911 **AZ 6J 131**
Swiss Cottage, 18 Harben Pde., NW3. 01-722 6719 **AZ 7A 44**
Sydenham, 44 Sydenham Rd., SE26. 01-778 7495 **AZ 4J 111**
Teddington, 19 High St. 01-977 4225 **AZ 5K 103**
Temple Fortune, 1197 Finchley Rd., NW11. 01-455 9327 **AZ 4H 27**
The Hyde, 213 Edgware Rd., NW9. 01-205 6128 **AZ 2J 25**
Theobalds Rd., WC1. 01-405 5810 **2A 20**
Thornton Heath, 1 The Drive. 01-653 3766 **AZ 4D 124**
24 Throgmorton St., EC2. 01-588 3314 **1B 40**
Tooting,2 Gatton Rd., SW17. 01-672 4089. **AZ 4C 108**
Tottenham, 555 High Rd., N17. 01-808 7314 **AZ 4F 31**
   824 High Rd., N17. 01-808 5345 **AZ 4F 31**
Trafalgar Square, 24 William IV St., WC2. 01-930 9580 **3C 35**
69 Tufton St., SW1. 01-222 5109 **2C 65**
Twickenham, 109 London Rd., 01-892 6616 **AZ 7A 88**
Upper Clapton, 41 Mount Pleasant La., E5. 01-806 2574 **AZ 2H 47**
Upper Edmonton, 18 Sterling Way. N18. 01-807 4902 **AZ 5J 17**
Upper Holloway, 14 Junction Rd., N19. 01-272 1955 **AZ 3G 45**
Upper Tooting, 1 Trinity Rd., SW17. 01-672 6306 **AZ 4A 92**
Uxbridge, Crown Wlk. Uxbridge 35911
167 Vauxhall Bridge Rd., SW1. 01-834 1611 **3A 64**
110 Victoria St., SW1. 01-834 0509 **1D 63**
Wallington, 1 Ross Pde. 01-647 4519 **AZ 6F 133**

Walthamstow, 267 High St., E17. 01-520 4551 **AZ 5A 32**
  58 St. James St., E17. 01-520 5331 **AZ 5A 32**
  87 Wood St., E17. 01-520 2591 **AZ 3E 32**
Walworth, 234 Walworth Rd., SE17. 01-703 5733 **AZ 4C 78**
Wandsworth, 1 Arndale Wlk., SW18. 01-874 5534 **AZ 5K 91**
Wanstead, 75 High St., E11. 01-989 4208 **AZ 5J 33**
Waterloo, 57 Waterloo Rd., SE1. 01-928 6785 **1C 53**
Welling, 2a Hook La. 01-303 2734 **AZ 4K 99**
Wembley, 397a High Rd., 01-902 2236 **AZ 5D 40**
West Brompton, 256, Fulham Rd., SW10. 01-352 7388 **AZ 2G 91**
West Drayton, 52 Station Rd. W. Drayton 42307
West Ealing, 189 Uxbridge Rd., W13. 01-567 3142 **AZ 1B 72**
West Hampstead, 128 West End La., NW6. 01-624 7874 **AZ 5J 43**
West Kensington, Blythe Rd., W14. 01-603 3663 **AZ 3F 75**
  88 North End Rd., W14. 01-385 9148 **AZ 4G 75**
125 Westminster Bridge Rd., 01-928 5504 **3A 52**
West Norwood, 12 Knights Hill, SE27. 01-670 1809 **AZ 5B 110**
West Wickham, 92 Station Rd. 01-777 6387
Whetstone, 1327 High Rd., N20. 01-445 8473 **AZ 7F 5**
Whitechapel, 29 Cable St., E1. 01-709 4784 **AZ 7G 63**
  2 White Church La., E1. 01-247 6375 **AZ 6G 63**
Willesden, 114 Church Rd., NW10. 01-459 0731 **AZ 7A 42**
  78 High Rd., NW10. 01-459 4005 **AZ 6B 42**
Wimbledon, 1 Compton Rd., SW19. 01-946 4191 **AZ 6H 107**
Wood Green, 12 The Broadway, High Rd., N22. 01-888 1017 **AZ 1K 29**
Woolwich, Thomas St., SE18. 01-854 2349 **AZ 4F 83**
Worcester Park, 4 Green La., 01-337 3467 **AZ 1C 130**
14 York Rd., SW11. 01-228 2171 **AZ 4A 92**

PUBLIC HOUSES

A selection of Pubs of every period, mood and inclination. Restaurant hours are subject to alteration, check by telephone.

Anchor, The, 1 Bankside, SE1. 01-407 1577 **3C 39**
Courage. Food. Historic riverside Inn close to site of Shakespeare's Globe Theatre. Rebuilt *c.* 1750. Displays of Elizabethan objects found during renovation. Restaurant open 12.00–14.15, 19.00–22.15 Mon. to Sat., closing 13.00 and 21.00 Sun. Riverside yard with views of St. Pauls and City.
Angel, 101 Bermondsey Wall E., SE16. 01-237 3608 **AZ 2H 79**
Historic riverside pub, 16th cent. origin. Period prints. Balcony with views over the Pool of London. Restaurant open for lunch and dinner.
Blackfriar, The, 174 Queen Victoria St., EC4. 01-236 5650 **2A 38**
Free House. Food. On site of Dominican Priory, rebuilt 1903 with "Art Nouveau" interior.
Bulls Head Tavern, Strand-on-the-Green, W4. 01-994 1204 **AZ 6G 73**
Full range of beers. Cromwellian House, beside the river. Lunch served daily.
Bull and Bush, North End Way, NW3. 01-455 3685 **AZ 2A 44**
Taylor Walker, of music hall song fame. Interior restored Victorian, collection relating to Florrie Forde and music hall, set on Hampstead Heath.
Bunch of Grapes, 207 Brompton Rd., SW3. 01-589 4944 **1A 60**
Free House. Food. Victorian pub, glass work includes snob screens between bars.
City Barge, Strand-on-the-Green, W4. 01-994 2148 **AZ 6G 73**
Courage. Russian Stout. Food. Inn dates from 1484, Parliament clock 1792. Restaurant open 12.30–14.30 Mon. to Fri. Conservatory for adults with children.

Cutty Sark Tavern, Ballast Quay, SE10. 01-858 3146 **AZ 5F 81**
Free House. Georgian Riverside Tavern, timber interior. Restaurant open 12.00–
14.15, 19.00–22.15. Closed Sat. lunch, Sun. Terrace by river.

Dickens Inn, St. Katharine's Way, E1. 01-488 2208 **3D 41**
Converted 19th cent. warehouse; part of St. Katharine's Dock redevelopment,
with Yacht Haven and Historic Ship Collection adjacent. Restaurants up stairs.

Dirty Dick's, 202 Bishopsgate, EC2. 01-283 5888 **3C 25**
Free House. Food. Pub founded by the 18th cent. miser Nathaniel Bentley, original
wine vaults complete with cobwebs.

Finch's, "King's Arms", 190 Fulham Rd., SW10. **AZ 2G 91**
Free House. Victorian interior and atmosphere. Writers and artists local.

Flask, 77 Highgate West Hill, N6. 01-340 7260 **AZ 2E 44**
Taylor Walker. Food. Historic 17th cent. Inn. Outside benches very popular on
summer evenings.

George Inn, 77 Borough High St., SE1. 01-407 2056 **1D 55** (National Trust).
Whitbread. Food. Only surviving galleried pub in London. Restaurant. Open 12.30–
14.00, 19.00–21.00. Closed Sun. Courtyard, occasional plays.

Grapes, 76 Narrow St., E14. 01-987 4396 **AZ 7A 64**
Ind Coope. Dickens room and fish restaurant. Pub balcony overlooking the river.

Grenadier, 18 Wilton Row, SW1. 01-235 3074 **3D 47**
Watney. Food. Collections of Wellingtonia, Wine labels, history of the Grenadiers.
Restaurant serving lunch and dinner.

Greyhound, 175 Fulham Palace, Rd., W6. 01-385 0526 **AZ 5E 74**
Watney. Victorian original with modern extensions, Rock music/entertainment
20.30–23.00 daily.

Holly Bush, Holly Mount, Heath St., NW3. 01-435 2892 **AZ 4A 44**
Ind Coope. Food. Historic pub, literary connections, interior Victorian with mirrors
and advertisements.

Hoop and Grapes, 47 Aldgate High St., EC3. 01-480 5739 **1D 41**
Bass Charrington. Food. Dating back to 13th cent., thought to be London's oldest
pub, part scheduled as an ancient monument. Micawber Room Restaurant
open for lunch weekdays and Sun., closed Sat.

Jack Straw's Castle, North End Way, NW3. 01-435 8374 **AZ 2A 44**
Bass Charrington. The original Inn was associated with Dick Turpin and Dickens.

King's Arms, see Finch's "King's Arms".

King's Head and Eight Bells, 50 Cheyne Wlk., SW3. 01-352 1820 **AZ 7B 76**
Whitbread. Hot and cold food served daily.

Lamb, 94 Lamb's Conduit St., WC1. 01-405 0713 **1A 20**
Young's. Food. Victorian interior, music hall photos and Hogarth prints. Garden.

Lamb and Flag, 33 Rose St., WC2. 01-836 4108 **2C 35**
Courage. Director's Bitter and Best Bitter. Historic pub (1623) with literary
associations. Old Prints. Once known as the "Bucket of Blood".

London Apprentice, 62 Church St., Old Isleworth, Middx. 01-560 3538 **AZ 3B 88**
Watney. Food. Historic Riverside Pub, 15th cent. and Georgian architecture. Name
derives from the City Livery Co. apprentices who used to row up to Isleworth.
Restaurant serves lunch and dinner.

Mayflower, The, 117 Rotherhithe St., SE16. 01-237 4088 **AZ 2J 79**
Bass Charrington. Food. 17th cent. Inn beside jetty of "The Mayflower". Original
decor, carvings, model ships and farm implements. Restaurant open 12.00–
13.45., 18.30–21.30. Closed Sat. lunch, Sun.

Nag's Head, 10 James St., WC2. 01-836 4678 **2D 35**
McMullen's of Hertford. Food. Prints etc. relating to Drury Lane and Covent Garden
Theatres. Lunch. Bar food daily.

Old Mitre Tavern, 1 Ely Ct., off Ely Pl., EC1. 01-405 4751 **3D 21**
Ind Coope. Food. Built 1546 as part of the Bishop of Ely's Palace. Associations
with Elizabeth I and Dr. Johnson.

Pindar of Wakefield, 328 Gray's Inn Rd., WC1. 01-837 1753 **AZ 3K 61**

Courage. Food. Rebuilt on historic pub site. Old Time Music Hall with restaurant in pub setting.

Printer's Devil, 98 Fetter La., EC4. 01-242 2239 **3C 21**
Whitbread. Food. Printers and journalists Pub, historically the "devil" was the apprentice. Collection of early prints.

Prospect of Whitby, 57 Wapping Wall, E1. 01-481 1095 **AZ 1J 79**
Chef & Brewer London Hosts. Food mid-day. Riverside Inn with long history. Live music daily except Mon. evening. Restaurant open lunch and dinner daily. Traditional English Roast Suns. 12.00–14.00. Terrace overlooking river.

Punch Tavern, 99 Fleet St., EC4. 01-353 8338 **1D 37**
Bass Charrington. Food. Victorian interior, glass, mirrors. Drawings and Photographs of and relating to Punch magazine.

Red Lion, 2 Duke of York St., SW1. 01-930 2030 **3A 34**
Ind Coope. Hot and cold bar meals, except Sun. Victorian, noted for engraved mirrors and glass.

St. Stephen's Tavern, 10 Bridge St., SW1. 01-930 2541 **3D 51**
Whitbread. Historic pub close to Houses of Parliament, the M.P.'s local; "division" bell in Tavern Bar—open 11.00–15.00, 17.30–23.00, closed Sun. evening.

Salisbury, 90 St. Martin's La., WC2. 01-836 5863 **2C 35**
Ind Coope. Food. The actors' local. Large, dark, cool Victorian interior; engraved glass, mirrors, brasswork.

Sherlock Holmes, 10 Northumberland St., WC2. 01-930 2644 **3D 35**
Whitbread. Bar snacks. Souvenirs, pictures and reconstruction of Holmes's flat in Baker Street. Restaurant 12.00–14.00, 19.00–21.30. Closed Sun.

Samuel Pepys, 48 Upper Thames St., EC4. 01-248 3048 **2C 39**
Bass Charrington. Food lunch time. Decor depicting the life of Samuel Pepys. Restaurant, open 12.00–14.15, 18.15–22.15. Closed Sat. lunch. Terrace over river.

Sir Christopher Wren, 17 Paternoster Sq., EC4. 01-248 1708 **1B 38**
Watney. Food. Wren period decor, blacksmiths equipment, Longmans first editions. Restaurant open 12.00–15.00 Mon. to Fri.

Spaniard's Inn, Spaniard's Rd., NW3. 01-455 3276 **AZ 2A 44**
Charrington (Vintage Inn). Food. 400 year old pub. Dick Turpin associations. Beer Garden.

Square Rigger, King William St., EC4. 01-623 1963 **2A 40**
Bass Charrington. Snacks. Decor in form of Square Rigged Ship. Restaurant open 12.00–15.00. Closed Sat., Sun.

Tattershall Castle, Victoria Embankment, SW1. 01-839 6548 **1D 51**
Free House; and Nightclub. Former Humber Ferry Paddle Steamer, built 1934.

Watermans Arms, Glenaffric Av., E14. 01-515 9302 **AZ 4F 81**
Ind Coope. Food. Victorian riverside pub. Early 1900's entertainment, groups, singer, drag, 20.30–23.00 Tues. to Sat.

Williamson's Tavern, Bow La., EC4. 01-248 6280 **1C 39**
Free House. Post 1666, alleged the oldest Hostelry in the City. Restaurant, traditional English Fare.

Ye Grapes, Shepherd Market, W1. 01-499 1563 **1B 48**
Free House. Food. Small Victorian Pub. Restaurant, open 12.00–14.45. Closed evenings and Sun.

Ye Olde Cheshire Cheese, Wine Office Ct., EC4. 01-353 6170 **1D 37**
Free House. Food. Very famous pub with history going back to 1538, rebuilt after the Great Fire. The journalists' local, and traditionally also of Dr. Johnson. Lunch can include the famous pudding served between Oct. and April.

Ye Olde Cock Tavern, 22 Fleet St., EC4. 01-353 9706 **1C 37**
Truman. Export draught bitter. Food. Dickensian decor, journalists' pub, literary associations. Restaurant, lunch only. Closed Sun.

Ye Olde Watling, 29 Watling St., EC4. 01-248 6235 **1C 39**
Charrington (Vintage Inn). Only draught beer. National Headquarters of the Society for Preservation of Beer from the Wood. Food. Built 1668. Used as Wren's

office and hostel for builders during construction of St. Paul's Cathedral. Collection of measuring jugs. Restaurant, open 11.30–15.00, closed Sat., Sun.

WINE BARS
Serving wines, sherry, port, cocktails etc. A selection of bars retaining traditional atmospheres.
Crusting Pipe, The Market, Covent Garden, WC2. 01-836 1415 **2D 35**
In ex-market vaults; brick arches, candlelight, sawdust. Excellent cold buffet; also restaurant for lunch and dinner.
El Vinos, 47 Fleet St., EC4. 01-353 6786 **1C 37**
Very popular, journalists, women not served at the bar. Food.
Fino's, 123 Mount St., W1. 01-492 1640 **3D 31** and branches.
Gordon's Wine Cellars, 47 Villiers St., WC2. 01-930 1408 **3D 35**
Bar overlooking the embankment. Good food and ambience.
Cork & Bottle, 44/46 Cranbourn St., WC2. 01-734 7807 **2C 35**
"Award Winner"; extensive wine lists; good food; Spanish guitar music nightly.

RADIO AND TELEVISION

BRITISH BROADCASTING CORPORATION Broadcasting House, Portland Place, W1. 01-580 4468 **3C 17**
For tickets to Public Performances write well in advance including S.A.E. to B.B.C. Radio and Television Ticket Unit, address as above.
Radio London, 35a Marylebone High St., W1. 01-486 7611 **2A 16.** "Call In" 486 7744 1457 kHz/*206 m.* VHF 94.9 MHz. London news, weather and traffic reports, music, community affairs.
B.B.C. Radio 1. Medium wave 1485 kHz/*202 m.* 1089 kHz/*275 m.* 1053 kHz/*285 m.* VHF 88–91 Mhz at certain times. Disc.-Jocky pop music ;pl news, weather every half hour.
B.B.C. Radio 2. Medium wave 693 kHz/*433 m.* 909 kHz/*330 m.* VHF 88–91 MHz. 24 hrs broadcasting light music, sport, quizzes ;pl news, weather on the hour.
B.B.C. Radio 3. Medium wave 1215 kHz/*247 m.* VHF 90–92 MHz. Classical music, drama, lectures, arts critics. Open University VHF only, at certain times.
B.B.C. Radio 4. U.K. Med. wave (London) 720 kHz/*417 m.* Long wave 200 kHz/*1500 m.* VHF 92–95 MHz. News, drama, discussions, current affairs, quizzes. Open University VHF only, at certain times.
B.B.C. Television. Television Centre, Wood La., W12 **AZ 6E 58.** Lime Grove Studios, W12 **AZ 2E 74.** Television Theatre. Shepherds Bush Grn., W12 **AZ 2E 74.** 01-743 8000.
B.B.C. World Service. World news, current affairs, music, drama etc., broadcast throughout the world, wavelengths and programmes from external services.
External Services, Bush House, Strand, WC2. 01-240 3456 **2A 36**
B.B.C. Publications, 35 Marylebone High St., W1. 01-580 5577 **2A 16**
Paris Theatre Studios, Regent St., SW1. **2A 34**

INDEPENDENT BROADCASTING AUTHORITY, 70 Brompton Rd., SW3. 01-584 7011 **3B 46**
Capital Radio, Euston Tower, NW1. 01-388 1288 **1D 17.** "Phone-in" 01-484 5255. 1548 kHz/*194 m.* VHF 95.8 MHz. 24 hrs. broadcasting music, pop, light, progressive, commercials; London programmes, news, weather, discussions, phone-ins.
London Broadcasting, P.O. Box 261, Communications Ho., Gough Sq., EC4. 01-353 1010 **1D 37** "Phone-in" 01-353 8111.
1151 kHz/*260 m.* VHF 97.3 MHz. 24 hrs. broadcasting, news, National and International, commercials, London programmes, weather, traffic reports, talks, discussions, what's-on and reviews.
Breakfast-Time T.V., Hawley Cres. NW1. 01-267 4300 **AZ 7F 45**

Channel 4, 60 Charlotte St., W1. 01-631 4444 **4A 18**
Independent T.V. News, ITN House, 48 Wells St., W1. 01-637 2424 **3D 17**
London Weekend Television, Kent Ho., South Bank T.V. Centre, SE1. **3C 37.** 01-261 3434.
Thames Television, 306 Euston Rd., NW1. **1D 17.** 01-387 9494
London weekday programmes.
ITV Publications, 247 Tottenham Court Rd., W1. 01-323 3222 **3B 18**
Limehouse TV Studios, Canary Wharf, West India Dock, E14. 01-987 2090
AZ 1D 80

REGISTRARS

POPULATION CENSUSES AND SURVEYS AND GENERAL REGISTER OFFICE,
St. Catherines Ho., 10 Kingsway WC2. 01-242 0262 1A 36
Births, Deaths and Marriages, General Enquiries, Search Rooms. Open 08.30–16.30 Mon. to Fri. For Probate Registry see Somerset Ho., Strand WC2. 01-405 7641 open 09.30–16.30 Mon. to Fri.

Registration must be made in the appropriate registration district, if in doubt check by telephone. Abbreviations: M=Marriages. B=Births. D=Deaths.

Acton, Town Hall, Winchester St., W3. *M* 01-992 5566 **AZ 2J 73**
Barking, 198 Longbridge Rd. *M* 01-594 4239 *B & D* 594 1700 **AZ 6H 51**
Barnet, 29 Wood St., Barnet. *M* 01-449 2098 *B & D* 449 0900 **AZ 4A 4**
Beckenham, see Bromley North
Beddington & Carshalton, Town Hall, Woodcote Rd., Wallington. *B & D*
  01-669 5066 **AZ 6F 133**
Bethnal Green, Town Hall, Cambridge Heath Rd., E2. *B & D* 01-980 4831
AZ 4H 63
Bexley Heath, Broadway, Bexleyheath, *B & D* 01-304 1665 **AZ 4E 100**
Brent, 249 Willesden La., NW2. 01-459 6188 **AZ 6E 42**
Brentford & Chiswick, see Hounslow
Bromley North, 4 Beckenham La. *B, D & M* 01-460 2201 **AZ 2G 127**
Bromley South, Farnborough Hosp. Farnborough Comn. *B & D.* Farn. (Kent) 52138
Camberwell, 34 Peckham Rd., SE5 *B, D & M* 01-703 6311 **AZ 1E 94**
Camden, Town Hall, Euston Rd., NW1 *B, D & M* 01-278 4366 **2C 11**
Chelsea, see Kensington & Chelsea
City, Town Hall, Rosebery Av., EC1. *B, D & M* 01-837 2121 *M* 4941 **1C 21**
  St. Barts Hosp. W. Smithfield, EC1. *B & D* 01-600 9000 **3B 22**
Croydon, Mint Walk. *B, D & M* 01-686 4433 **AZ 3C 134**
Dagenham, Rush Green Lodge, Dagenham Rd., Romford. *B & D* Rom. 49895
Ealing, Town Hall, Uxbridge Rd., W5. *B & D* 01-579 2424 **AZ 1B 72**
Edmonton, see Enfield
Enfield, Gentleman's Row, Enfield. *B, D & M* 01-367 5757 **AZ 3H 7**
Finchley, see Hendon
Fulham, Town Hll, 553 Fulham Rd., SW6 *M* 01-385 6423 *B & D* 385 1146 **AZ 2G 91**
Greenwich, Town Hall, Wellington St., SE18. *B, D & M* 01-854 8888 **AZ 4E 82**
Hackney, Town Hall, Mare St., E8. *B, D & M* 01-986 3123 **AZ 1H 63**
Hammersmith, Nigel Playfair Av., W6 *B, D & M* 01-748 3020 **AZ 5D 74**
  Woodmans Mews, Scrub La., W12. *B & D* 01-743 1842 **AZ 5D 58**
Harringey, Civic Centre, High Rd., N22. *B, D & M* 01-888 7228 **AZ 1K 29**
Harrow, Civic Centre, Station Rd. *B, D & M* 01-863 5611 **AZ 4K 23**
Havering, Langtons, Billet La., Hornchurch. *B, D & M* Hornchurch 52555
Hayes, see Hillingdon
Hendon, 182 Burnt Oak Broadway, Edgware 01-952 0876 **AZ 7C 12**

Hillingdon, 150 Royal La., *B. & D* Uxbridge 36490
Hounslow, 88 Lampton Rd., 01-570 7728 **AZ 2F 78**
Ilford, see Redbridge
Isleworth, Town Hall, Treaty Rd., Hounslow *B & D* 01-570 7728 **AZ 3F 87**
Islington, N: Archway Central Hall, Arch., Clo., N14 *B & D* 01-272 3121 **AZ 6D 28**
   S: Town Hall, Rosebury Av., EC1 *B, D & M* 01-837 2121 **1C 21**
Kensington & Chelsea, Old Town Hall, Kings Rd., SW3 *B, D & M* 01-351 3941
AZ 7K 75
Kingston upon Thames, 35 Coombe Rd. *B, D & M* 01-546 0920 **AZ 1G 119**
Lambeth, 357/361 Brixton Rd., SW9 *M* 01-737 0011 **AZ 3A 94**
Lewisham, 368 Lewisham High St., SE13. *B, D & M* 01-690 2128 **AZ 6D 96**
Merton, Morden Cott., Morden Hall Rd. *M* 01-540 5011 *B & D* 5012 **AZ 3K 121**
Newham, 82 West Ham La., E15. *B, D & M* 01-534 4545 **AZ 7G 49**
Orpington, see Bromley South
Park Royal, Barretts Green Rd., NW10. *B & D* 01-965 3735 **4E 41**
Poplar, Town Hall, Bow Rd., E3 *B, D & M* 01-980 4414 *M* 1222 **AZ 3B 64**
Redbridge, 794 Cranbrook Rd., Barkingside *B, D & M* 01-551 4379 **AZ 7E 34**
Redhill, see Hendon
Richmond & Barnes, 1 Spring Ter., Rich. *M* 01-940 2853 *B & D* 2651 **AZ 5E 88**
Ruislip, see Uxbridge
Sidcup, 71 Sidcup Hill. *B, D & M* 01-300 4537 **AZ 4B 116**
Southall, Town Hall, High St. *B & D* 01-574 2311 **AZ 1D 70**
Southwark, Municipal Off., Walworth Rd., SE17. *B, D & M* 01-703 5464 **AZ 4C 78**
Stepney, 1 Philpot St., Commercial Rd., E1. *B, D & M* 01-790 6098 **AZ 6G 63**
Stoke Newington, see Hackney
Sutton & Cheam, 25 Worcester Rd., Sutton. *M* 01-661 5086 *B & D* 5087
AZ 7J 131
Syon Park, see Hounslow
Twickenham, 91 Queens Rd., Twickenham. *B & D* 01-892 3865 **AZ 1A 104**
Uxbridge, Hillingdon Civic Centre, Uxbridge. *B & D* Uxb. 50111 *M* 38508
Waltham Forest, 106 Grove Rd., E17. *B, D & M* 01-520 8617 **AZ 6D 32**
Wandsworth, Town Hall, Wandsworth High St., SW18. *B, D & M* 01-874 6464
  AZ 5J 91
Wembley, Library, Ealing Rd. *B & D* 01-902 7167 **AZ 6E 40**
Westminster, Council Ho., Marylebone Rd., NW1. *B, D & M* 01-828 8070 **2C 15**
Willesden, 269 Willesden La., NW2. *B & D* 01-459 5263 *M* (No. 249) 6188
AZ 6E 42
Wimbledon, Q. Hall, Queens Rd., SW19. *B & D* 01-946 1875 **AZ 6J 107**

RESTAURANTS

**A selection of restaurants in Central London. Opening hours are always liable
to variation, check by telephone. CC. indicates some credit cards are
accepted. For meals in hotels see page 2.**
For Cabaret/Theatre Restaurants, see Dine & Dance p. 45.

A L'ecu de France, 111 Jermyn St., SW1. 01-930 2837 **3A 34**
French cuisine, classic food and ambience. Pianist evenings. Open 12.00–15.00
Mon. to Fri. 18.00–23.00 Mon. to Thurs. (18.30–23.20 Fri. and Sat).
American Hamburger Restaurant, 455 Oxford St., W1. 01-629 1602 **2D 31**
American and International menu. Open 11.00–24.00 daily.
Anchor, The, 1 Bankside, SE1. 01-407 1577 **3C 39**
Historic riverside Inn near site of Shakespeare's Globe Theatre. Open 12.00–14.15,
19.00–22.15; Sun. 12.00–13.00, 19.00–21.00 C.C.
Anemos Taverna, 34 Charlotte St., W1. 01-636 2289 **3A 18**
Greek cuisine. Open: 12.00–15.00, 18.00–24.00.

Au Jardin des Gourmets, 5 Greek St., W1. 01-437 1816 **3C 34**
French cuisine. Open: 12.30–14.30, 18.30–23.15, Sun. 18.30–23.15. Private rooms available. CC.
Baron of Beef, Gutter La., EC2. 01-606 6961 **1C 39**
Traditional English Fare. Open: 12.00–15.00, 17.30–21.00 (last orders), closed Sat., Sun., Bank Hols. Available for private functions Sat. and Sun. CC.
Bentley's, 11/15 Swallow St., W1. 01-734 4756 **3D 33**
Famous Seafood and Oyster Bar. Open: 12.00–15.00, 18.00–23.00 Mon. to Sat.
Bizzarro, 20 Craven Rd., W2. 01-723 6029 **1C 29**
Italian cuisine. Four-piece live band (evenings). Open: 12.00–15.00, 18.00–02.30; Closed Sun. CC.
Borgo Santa Croce, 112 Cheyne Walk, SW10. 01-352 7534 **AZ 1A 76**
Italian cuisine; national specialities and vegetarian available. Open 12.30–14.30, 19.00–23.15. Closed Sun. Private rooms available.
Café Royal, 68 Regent St., W1. 01-437 9090 **3A 34**
Grill Room: Famous meeting place for celebrities. French cuisine. Open: 12.00–15.00, 18.00–23.00. Closed Sun.
Also Nichols Restaurant: French cuisine. Open: 12.00–15.00, 17.30–23.00, 12.00–14.00 Sun. Private Banqueting suites available. CC.
Calabash, Africa Centre, 38 King St., WC2. 01-836 1976 **2D 35**
Authentic African cuisine in atmospheric setting. Open for lunch Mon. to Fri., dinner Mon. to Sat.
Chambeli, The, 12 Gt. Castle St., W1. 01-636 0662 **1C 33**
North Indian cuisine. Open: 12.00–15.00, 18.30–23.30. Mon. to Sat. Also at 146 Southampton Row, WC1. 01--837 3925.
Chicago Pizza Pie Factory, 17 Hanover Sq., W1. 01-629 2669 **1C 33**
American menu, decor and music to match, video tapes. Open: 11.45–23.30 Mon. to Sat. 12.00–22.30 Sun.
Dickens Inn by the Tower, St. Katharines Way, E1. 01-488 2208 **3D 41**
English and Continental dishes. Converted 19th cent. warehouse; Pickwick Room 01-488 2208. Dickens Room 01-488 9932
Dumpling Inn, 15a Gerrard St., W1. 01-437 2567 **2B 34**
Peking cuisine. Open: 12.00–24.00. CC.
Elysee Restaurant, 13 Percy St., W1. 01-636 4804 **3A 18**
French, Greek cuisine, Greek cabaret twice nightly, music 21.00–03.00. Open: 12.00–15.00, 18.00–03.00. Closed Christmas Day only. Private rooms available. Roof garden. CC. No lunch Sat.
L'Epicure, 28 Frith St., W1. 01-437 2829 **2B 34**
French cuisine. Open: 12.00–14.30, 18.00–23.15, Sat. 18.00–23.15. Closed Sun. Small Party Room. CC.
Fair Lady, from 250 Camden High St., NW1. 01-485 4433 **AZ 1F 61**
Canal boat restaurant. Three hour cruise, Regent's Park to Little Venice return. English cuisine. Dinner cruise Tues.–Sat. 19.30. Lunch Sun. only 12.30.
Farringdons, 41 Farringdon St., EC4. 01-236 3663 **3D 21**
English food served in atmospheric railway vaults setting, complete with candles and stone floors. Open Lunch Mon. to Fri. and dinner Mon. to Sat.
Fook Lam Moon, 10 Gerrard St., W1. 01-437 5712 **2B 34**
Cantonese and Peking menu, esp. seafoods; also vegetarian. Open 12.00–23.30 Mon. to Sat. 12.00–22.30 Sun.
Gallery Rendezvous, 53 Beak St., W1. 01-734 0445 **2A 34**
Peking cuisine, Open: 12.00–23.15. Private facilities available CC.
Gallipoli, 7–8 Bishopsgate Churchyard, EC2. 01-588 1922 **3B 34**
Turkish cuisine. Dancing 18.00–03.00. Cabaret. Belly-dancers twice nightly. Open: 11.00–15.00, 18.00–03.00. Closed Sun.
Gay Hussar, 2 Greek St., W1. 01-437 0973 **1B 34**
Hungarian cuisine. Open: 12.30–14.30, 17.30–24.00. Private room available. Closed Sun.
Gaylord, 16 Albemarle St., W1. 01-493 7756 **3C 33**

Authentic Tandoori, Mughlai and Kashmiri cuisine. Open: 12.00–15.00, 18.00–24.00 daily.

George Inn, The, 77 Borough High St., SE1. 01-407 2056 **1D 55**
English cuisine. Only surviving galleried pub in London. Occasional Dickensian and Shakespearian plays in the courtyard (summer). Open: 12.30–14.00, 19.00–21.30. Whitbread P.H.

George and Vulture, 3 Castle Court, EC3. 01-626 9710 **1A 40**
Free House. Old Dickens House. Chops, steaks cooked on open grills. Open: 12.00–15.00. Closed Sat., Sun.

Kerzenstuberl, 9 St. Christopher's Pl., W1. 01-486 3196 **1A 32**
Austrian food, decor and music. Open: 12.00–15.00, 18.00–24.00, not lunch on Sat. Closed Sun.

L'Opera, 32 Great Queen St., WC2. 01-405 9020 **1D 35**
French cuisine, opulent decor, close to the Royal Opera House. Open 12.30–14.30, 18.00–24.00. Sat. 18.00–24.00. Closed Sun. CC.

La Coree, 56 St. Giles High St., WC2. 01-836 7235 **1C 35**
Authentic Korean cuisine with decor to match. Open 12.00–15.00, 18.00–23.00 Mon. to Sat. Closed Sun.

La Cucaracha, 12 Greek St., W1. 01-734 2253 **1B 34**
Mexican cuisine, white-washed underground rooms. Mexican music nightly. Open 12.30–14.30, 18.30–23.30 daily. CC.

Last Days of the Raj, 22 Drury La., WC2. 01-836 1628 **1D 35**
Many Indian specialities, also vegetarian menu. Open 12.00–14.30, 18.00–23.30 Mon. to Sat. 18.30–23.30 Sun.

Le Gavroche, 43 Upper Brook St., W1. 01 499 1826 **2D 31**
French, first restaurant in Britain to be awarded the Michelin 3 star rating. Open 12.00–14.00, 19.00–23.00 Mon. to Fri. Closed Sat. and Sun. CC.

Leiths Restaurant, 92 Kensington Pk. Rd., W11. 01-229 4481 **2A 26**
Of "Leiths Good Food" parentage. French cuisine also vegetarian menu. Open 19.00–24.00

Les Halles, 57 Theobalds Rd., WC1. 01-242 6761 **2A 20**
French cuisine; 12.00–1430, 19.00–10.30. Closed Sat. and Sun.

Ley Ons, 56/58 Wardour St., W1. 01-437 6465 **1A 34**
Famous for Hong Kong, Cantonese cuisine. Open 12.00–23.30 Mon. to Sat. 12.00–23.00 Sun.

Lowiczanka, 1st floor, 238/246 King St., W6. 01-741 3225 **AZ 4C 74**
Polish cuisine served in the atmosphere of the Polish Social and Cultural Centre; dancing and music Fri. and Sat. evenings. Open for lunch and dinner except no dinner Tues.

Man Fu Kung, 29/30 Leicester Sq., WC2. 01-839 2939 **2B 34**
Huge Chinese restaurant with late night entertainment/music. Open 10.30–01.00; from 12.00 Sundays.

Martinez, 25 Swallow St., W1. 01-734 5066 **3D 33**
Spanish, continental cuisine. Dancing. Guitarist evenings. Open: 12.00–15.00, 18.30–002.00. Sat. 18.00–03.00. Sun. till 24.00. Private party rooms available. CC.

Maxim's de Paris, Panton St., SW1. 01-839 4809 **3B 34**
French cuisine in distinctive "Paris art nouveau" setting. Open 12.00–15.00 Mon. to Fri. 18.30–23.45 Mon. to Sat.

Mayflower, The, 117 Rotherhithe St., SE16. 01-237 1898 (4088 reservations) **AZ 2J 79**
First floor restaurant overlooking the river. Menu includes complete 17th cent. meal. 17th cent. Inn besides the jetty of "The Mayflower". Open: 12.00–13.45, 18.30–21.30, closed Sat. lunch. Closed Sun. Bass Charrington.

Mignon Hungarian Restaurant, 2 Queensway, W2. 01-229 0093 **1D 27**
Hungarian food, decor and live music. Open: 12.00–15.00, 18.00–01.00 Tues. to Sun. Closed Mon.

Mr Bumble, 23 Islington Green, N1. 01-354 1952 **AZ 1B 62**

Traditional English food, roasts, pies, pudding a speciality. Open 12.30–14.30 Tues. to Sat. 19.30–23.00 Mon. to Sat. 12.30–15.00 Sun.

Mr Kong, 21 Lisle St., WC2. 01-437 7341 **2B 34**
Cantonese cuisine, also some Peking and Szechuan. Seafood a speciality. Open 12.00–01.45.

Old Vienna, 94 New Bond St., W1. 01-629 8716 **1B 32**
Austrian cuisine. Traditional Singing and Dancing. Open: 12.00–15.00, 18.00–01.00. 18.00–01.00 Sat. Closed Sun. CC.

Prospect of Whitby, 57 Wapping Wall, E1. 01-481 1095 **AZ 1J 79**
International cuisine. Riverside Inn with long history, Pepys, Judge Jeffreys, Dickens, connections. Live music in pub. Open: 12.00–14.15, 19.00–22.15. Closed Sat. Lunch. Traditional English Roast Sun. Lunch. Closed Sun. evening.

Relais de Amis, 17b Curzon St., W1. 01-499 7595 **1B 48**
French Mediterranean cuisine. Open 12.00–15.30, 18.00–24.30. Private rooms available. CC.

Richoux, 172 Piccadilly, W1. 01-493 2204 **3D 33**
English traditional dishes, afternoon teas and late dinners. No booking. Also at 86 Brompton Rd., **3B 46.** 41a South Audley St., **3A 32**

Rugantino, 26 Romilly St., W1. 01-734 3854 **2B 34**
Italian cuisine. Open 12.00–15.00, 18.00–24.00; Closed Sun., Bank Hols. CC.

Rules, 35 Maiden Lane, WC2. 01-836 5314 **2D 35**
Traditional English fare. Pre-Theatre suppers. Open 12.15–14.30, 18.00–23.15. Mon. to Sat. Closed Sun.

St. Paul's Tavern, 56 Chiswell St., EC1. 01-606 3828 **2D 23**
English cuisine. Display of prints of St. Paul's Cathedral and old London. Open: 11.00–15.00, 17.30–23.00. Closed Sat. and Sun. Whitbread P.H.

Sakura, 9 Hanover St., W1. 01-629 2961. **1C 33**
Authentic Japanese cuisine and matching decor. Open 12.00–14.30, 17.30–21.30 Tues. to Sat. Closed Mon.

Samuel Pepys, 48 Upper Thames St., EC4. 01-248 3048 **2C 39**
English cuisine. Decor depicts life of Pepys. Open: 12.00–14.00, 18.00–21.30. Sat. 18.00–22.00. Closed Sun. Terrace overlooking river.

Scott's, 20 Mount St. W1. 01-629 5248 **3A 32**
Sea food menu. Cocktail Bar. Open: 12.30–15.00, 18.00–23.00. Private rooms available. CC. Closed Sun.

Serpentine Restaurant, Hyde Park, W2. 01-723 8784 **1D 45**
Overlooking Serpentine. English/Continental cuisine. Speciality Charcoal Grilled Steaks. Open: 12.00–15.00, 18.00–23.00, Sun. 12.00–16.00, 19.00–23.00. CC.

Sheekey's, 29 St. Martin's Ct., WC2. 01-240 2565 **2C 35**
Est. 1896. Sea Food cuisine. Open: 12.15–20.30, Sat. 12.15–14.30. Closed Sun. CC.

Sherlock Holmes, 10 Nothumberland St., WC2. 01-930 2644 **3D 35**
English/French cuisine. Re-construction of Sherlock Holmes's Baker St. flat, exhibits. Open: 12.00–14.00, 19.00–21.30. Closed Sun. Whitbread P.H.

Simpson's in the Strand, 100 Strand, WC2. 01-836 9112 **2A 36**
Renowned English cuisine, beef and lamb carved at the table. Closed Sun. Open 12.00–15.00, 10.00–22.00. CC.

Simpson's Restaurant, 38–4 Cornhill, EC3. 01-626 9985 **1A 40**
English cuisine. Open: 12.00–15.00. Closed Sat., Sun.

Surprise, 12 Gt. Marlborough St., W1. 01-434 2666 **1D 33**
American specialities. 12.00–15.00; 18.00–23.45 Mon. to Sat. 11.45–15.00 Sun. CC.

Sweetings, 39 Queen Victoria St., EC4. 01-248 3062 **2C 39**
Sea food specialties. Open: 12.00–14.30. Closed Sat., Sun., Bank Hols.

Swiss Centre, Leicester Sq., WC2. 01-734 1291 **3B 34**
Four restaurants, Chesa, Taverne, Locanda, Rendezvous; variety of cooking, also cafe, Imbiss—for light meals.

Terrazza Restaurant, 19 Romilly St., W1. 01-437 8991 **2B 34**

Italian cuisine. Open: 12.00–15.00, 18.00–24.00 Daily. CC.
Tiberio, 22 Queen St., W1. 01-629 3561 **1B 48**
Italian cuisine. Dancing nightly. Open: 12.00–14.30, 20.00–24.00. Closed Sat.
lunch and Sun., Bank Hols. CC.
Tiddy Dolls Eating House, 55 Shepherd Mkt., W1. 01-499 2537 **1B 48**
English cuisine. Live entertainment, grand piano, Elizabethan players etc. Open:
18.00–00.30 daily. Private party rooms available. CC.
1520 AD Tudor Rooms, 17 Swallow St., W1. 01-240 3978 **3D 33**
Medieval style theatre restaurant; continuous entertainment throughout the
banquet from Henry VIII and his Court. Open from 19.30 daily, closed Sunday.
Disco dancing.
Tui, 19 Exhibition Rd., SW7. 01-584 8359 **2D 59**
Authentic Thai food. Open 12.00–14.30, 18.30–23.00; Sun. 12.30–14.30, 19.00–
22.30.
Villa Dei Cesari, 135 Grosvenor Rd., SW1. 01-828 7453 **AZ 6F 77**
Italian cuisine. Live music and dancing. Open: 20.00–02.30. Closed Mon. "Ancient
Rome" decor in riverside setting.
Williamson's Tavern, Bow La., EC4. 01-248 6280 **1C 39**
Traditional English cuisine. Built after Great Fire 1666, alleged the oldest Hostelry
in the City. Free House.
Wiltons, 55 Jermyn St., W1. 01-629 9955 **3A 34**
Famous fish restaurant. Open: 12.30–14.30, 18.30–22.15 Mon. to Fri. Sat dinner
only.
Ye Olde Watling, 29 Watling St., EC4. 01-248 6235 **1C 39**
Old English cuisine. Built 1668. Served as office for Wren during building of St.
Paul's. Open: 11.30–15.00. Closed Sat., Sun. Vintage Inns Bass Charrington.

INEXPENSIVE RESTAURANTS, BISTROS, VEGETARIAN & HEALTH FOODS

**The Vegetarian Society, 53 Marloes Rd., W8. have lists of vegetarian
restaurants and health food shops.**
American, The, 335 Fulham Rd., SW10. **AZ 1A 76**
American specialities. Open: 11.00–24.00 daily, also Fri. and Sat. to 24.30.
Baalbek, 18 Hogarth Pl., off Hogarth Rd., SW5. **AZ 4K 75**
Family restaurant, Lebanese and some Vegetarian dishes. Open: 12.00–23.00
Mon. to Sat. Closed Sun.
Continental Bar, 30 Charing Cross Rd., WC2. 01-836 4233 **1B 34**
Middle Eastern specialities. Open 09.00–24.00. Sun. from 10.00.
Cranks Health Foods, 8 Marshall St., W1. **2D 33**
Health food and vegetarian. Classical music on tape. Open 10.00–23.00 Mon. to
Sat. Closed Sun., Public Hols. Also at 9/11 Tottenham St., W1 and The Market,
Covent Garden, WC2. **2A 18**
Flanagans, 11 Kensington High St., W8. **3D 43**
English cuisine—fish speciality, steak and kidney puddings, game pies etc. Honky-
Tonk Pianist evenings. Open 12.00–14.30, 18.00–23.45. Private facilities
available. CC. Also at 100 Baker St., W1. **2D 15**
Food for Thought, 31 Neal St., WC2. **1C 35**
Health and vegetarian foods. Open: 12.00–20.00 Mon. to Fri.
Golden Horn, 134 Wardour St., W1. **1A 34**
Turkish cuisine. Open: 12.00–23.30. Closed Sun. Party rooms available. CC.
Godinda's Vegetarian Restaurant, 9 Soho St., W1. **1B 34**
Vegetarian, natural whole food. Open 11.30–20.00.
Habitat, 206 King's Rd., SW3. Self-service, store hours. **AZ 7K 75**
Hard Rock Cafe, 150 Old Park Lane, W1. **2B 48**
American dishes; bar. Open seven days a week.
Institute of Contemporary Arts, Nash Ho., The Mall, SW1. **1B 50**
Self-service. Centre for contemporary art and those attracted to it. Open 12.00–
20.00 all week.

Lyons Corner House, 450 Strand, WC2. **3C 35**
Good basic English food with children's menu. Open daily.
Manna, 4 Erskine Rd., NW3. **AZ 7D 44**
Vegetarian whole food. Open 06.30–24.00 daily.
Nuthouse, 26 Kingly St., W1. **2D 33**
Vegetarian health food on two floors. Open 10.30–19.00 Mon. to Fri., to 17.00 Sat.
Pied Piper Video Cafe, 8 Argyll St., W1. **1D 33**
Eat surrounded by TV monitors and overhead video screens—resident "Video-Jockey".
Pizza Express, 29 Wardour St., W1. and branches see p. 124.
American style piazza chain. Open: 11.30–24.00 daily.
Raw Deal, 65 York St., W1. **2B 14**
Vegetarian. Guitarist Thurs., Sat. evenings. Open: 10.00–22.00, 23.00 Sat. Closed Sun.
Wren, The, St. James's Church, Piccadilly, W1. **3A 34**
Home-made fare. Open 10.00–20.00 Mon. to Fri., to 17.00 Sat. Sun. lunch following Sung Eucharist 12.30 Sundays.

AFTERNOON TEA
Bendicks, 195 Sloane St., SW1. **3C 47**
Purveyors of handmade chocolates—other branches at 55 Wigmore St., W1. **1A 32** and 20 Ryl. Exchange, EC3. **1A 40** (Chocolates only)
Brown's Hotel, Dover St., W1. **3C 33**
Ceylon Tea Centre, 22 Regent St., SW1. **3A 34**
Charing Cross Hotel, Strand, WC2. **3D 35**
Claridges Hotel, Brook St., W1. **2B 32**
Dickins & Jones, 224 Regent St., W1. **1D 33**
Dorchester Hotel, Park La., W1. **1A 48**
D. H. Evans, 318 Oxford St., W.1. **1B 32**
Fortnum and Mason, 181 Piccadilly, W1. **3D 33**
Fourth floor restaurant 15.30–17.00 Soda Fountain 14.45–18.00 (open until 23.30 Jermyn St. entrance).
Harrods, Knightsbridge, SW1. **3B 46**
Hyde Park Hotel, 66 Knightsbridge SW1. **2C 47**
Kardomah, 14 Brompton Rd., SW1. **3C 47**
Myur, 343 Oxford St., W1. **1B 32**
New Piccadilly Hotel, Piccadilly, W1. **3A 34.**
Park Lane Hotel, Piccadilly, W1. **1B 48**
Richoux Ltd., 86 Brompton Rd., SW3. **3B 46.**41a South Audley St., W1. **3A 32** 172 Piccadilly **3D 33.**
Ritz Hotel, Piccadilly, W1. **1C 49**
Savoy Hotel, Savoy Court, WC2. **3A 36**
Search Tansley & Co., 136 Brompton Rd., SW3. **1B 60** and 30 Pavilion Rd., SW1. **3C 47**
Selfridge Hotel, Orchard St., W1. **1D 31**
Tatlers Cafe, 95 Old Brompton Rd., SW7. **3C 59**
Westbury Hotel, New Bond St., W1. **2C 33**
Twinings, 216 Strand, WC2. **1C 37**
Waldorf Hotel, Aldwych, WC2. 2A 36

CHAIN GROUP RESTAURANTS
Aberdeen Steak Houses: 124 Brompton Rd., SW3. **2A 60.** 147 Charing Cross Rd., WC2. **1B 34.** 175 Earl's Court Rd., SW5. **AZ 3J 75.** 171 Edgware Rd., W2. **1B 30.** 53 Shaftesbury Av., W1. **2B 34.** 82/166 Victoria St., SW1. **1C 63.** 108 Wigmore St., W1. **1A 32.**
Angus Steak Houses: 39 Coventry St., W1. **3B 34.** 4 Glasshouse St., W1. **3A 34.** 42 Kensington High St., W8. **3C 43.** 28/31 Leicester Sq., WC2. **3B 34.** 74 Regent St., W1. **3A 34.** 396 Strand, WC2. **3D 35**

Garners Steak Houses: 28 Berkeley St., W1. **3C 33.** 179 Brompton Rd., SW3.
2A 60. 3 Charing Cross Rd., WC2. **1B 34.** 29 Cockspur St., SW1. **3B 34.** 40
Haymarket, SW1. **3B 34.** 16 Jermyn St., SW1. **3A 34.** 399a Oxford St., W1. **1A 32.**
11a Lwr. Regent St., SW1. **3A 34.** 56 Whitcombe St., WC2. **3B 34.**
Kardomahs: 8 Byward St., EC3. **3C 41.** 81 Gloucester Rd., SW7. **1A 58.** 307 High
Holborn, WC1. **3B 20.** 2 Kingsway, WC2. **1A 36.** 11 Poultry, EC2. **1D 39.**
London Steak Houses: 96 Dulwich Village, SE21. **AZ 6E 94.** 18 High St.,
Wimbledon, SW19. **AZ 5F 107.**
Kentucky Fried Chicken: 14 Argyll St , W1 **1D 33.** 158/180 Bishopsgate, EC2.
3C 25. 194 Earl's Court Rd., SW5. **AZ 3J 75.** 1 Euston Rd., NW1. **1C 17.** 53
Haymarket, SW1. **3B 34.** 56 Kings Rd., SW3. **3C 6129/289** Oxford St., W.1. **1C 33.**
8 Pembridge Rd., W11. **1B 26** 265 Regent St., W.1. **3A 34.** 6 Sherwood St.,
W.1. **2A 34.** 407 Strand, WC2. **2D 35.** 71 Tottenham Court Rd., W1. **1A 18.** 64/122
Victoria St., SW1. **1A 64.**
McDonald's Hamburgers: 122 Baker St., W1. **1C 35.** 208 Earls Ct. Rd., SW5.
AZ 3J 75. 178/180 Edgware Rd., W2. **1B 30.** 57 Haymarket, SW1. **3B 34.** 108
Kensington High St., W8. **3C 43.** 53 King William St., EC4. **2A 40.** 1/4 Marble Arch,
W1. **2C 31.** 8/10 Oxford St., W1. **1A 34.** 310 Regent St., SW1. **1A 64.** 65
Shaftesbury Av., W1. **2B 34.** 35 Strand, WC2. **3D 35.** 155 Victoria St., SW1. **1A 64.**
134 Tottenham Ct. Rd., W1. **2A 18.**
Pizza Express: 30 Coptic St., WC1. **3C 19.** 10 Dean St., W1. **1B 34.** 363 Fulham
Rd., SW10. **AZ 2G 91.** 15 Gloucester Rd., SW7. **1A 58.** 64 Heath St., NW3.
AZ 3A 44. 84 High St., Wimbledon, SW19. **AZ 5F 107.** 137 Notting Hill Ga., W11.
3B 26. 26 Porchester Sq., W2. **AZ 6K 59.** 14 High Parade, Streatham High
Rd., SW16. **AZ 4J 109.** 29 Wardour St., W1. **1A 34.**
Pizza Hut: 67 Duke St., W1. **1A 32.** 149 Earl's Court Rd., SW5. **AZ 3J 75** 183 High
Rd., N22. **AZ 1K 29.** 238 Kilburn High Rd., NW6. **AZ 7H 43** 39 New Broadway,
W5. **AZ 7D 56.** 103 Queensway, W2. **1D 27**114 Streatham Hill, SW2. **AZ 2J 109.**
169 Upper St., N1. **AZ 2B 61.**
Pizzaland: 25 Argyll St., W1. **1D 33.** 187 Baker St., NW1. **1C 15.** 58 Berwick St.,
W1. **1A 34.** 20 Brompton Rd., SW1. **3B 46.** 44 Cranbourn St., WC2. **2B 34.** 75
Gloucester Rd., SW7. **1A 58.**46 Hampstead High St., NW3. **AZ 4A 44.** 80 King's
Rd., SW3. **3C 61.** 14 Leicester Sq., WC2. **3B 34.** 15 New Burlington St., W1.
2D 33. 10 Pembridge Rd., W11. **3B 26.** 101 Putney High St., SW15. **AZ 4G 91.** 76
Queensway W2. **2D 27.** 61 Shaftesbury Av., W1. **2B 34.** 51 St. Martin's La.,
WC2. **2C 35.**
Quality Inns: 128 Baker St., W1. **1C 15.** 1 Coventry St., W1. **3B 34.** 22 Leicester
Sq., WC2. **3B 34.** 192 Oxford St., W1. **1D 33** 191 Victoria St., SW1. **1C 63.**
Spaghetti Houses: 39 Charlotte St., W1. **2A 18.** 24 Cranbourn St., WC2. **2B 34.**
74 Duke St., W1. **1A 32.** 15 Goodge St., W1. **2A 18.** 4 Hans Rd., SW3. **1B 60.**
77 Knightsbridge, SW1. **3D 47.** 20 Sicilian Av., WC1. **3D 19.**
Strikes: 120 Bayswater Rd., W2. **3A 28.** 126 Baker St., W1. **1C 15.** 24 Charing
Cross Rd., WC2. **1B 34.** 157 Earls Court Rd., W2 **AZ 3J 75.** 43 Haymarket,
SW1. **3B 34.** 17 Irving St., SW1. **3B 34.** 124 Southampton Row, WC1. **3A 20.** 166
Tottenham Court Rd., W1. **1A 18.** 124 Victoria St., SW1. **1C 63.** 1 Warwick
Way, SW1. **3C 63.**
Tennessee Pancake Houses: 1 Argyll St., W1. **1D 33** 39/103 Charing Cross Rd.,
WC2. **1B 34.** 36 Glasshouse St. **3A 34.** 25 London St., W2. **1C 29**
Wimpy Bars: 161 Bishopsgate, EC2. **3C 25.** 342 Edgware Rd., WC2. **3A 14.**
Piccadilly Circus, W1. **3A 34.** 85 Gloucester Rd., SW7. **1A 58.** 113 Baker St., W1.
1C 15. 100 Notting Hill Ga., W11. **3B 26.** 70 Queensway, W2. **1D 27.** 27 Euston
Rd., NW1. **1C 17** 333 Vauxhall Bridge Rd., SW1. **2D 63.**

SHOPPING

REFERENCE TO SHOPPING ROUTE MAPS

☆ Banks
✳ Books
Clothing
● Female   ♣ Children
○ Male   □ Shoes
◐ Uni-sex
■ Department Store
▥ Hi-Fi, Radio, TV, Video

❖ Jewellery
⊠ Photographic, Optical, Scientific
➡ Public House
❀ Records
▦ Restaurant ,Cafe
✳ Souvenirs, Gifts
⊖ Underground Stations

BEAUCHAMP PLACE, BURLINGTON ARCADE, JERMYN AND SLOANE STREETS: Four select, high-class shopping areas made up of small specialist shops, people who make and sell shirts, shoes, pipes, chocolates or perfume, many up-to-date fashion boutiques, jewellery, gift and furniture shops, antiques are everywhere.

BOND STREETS: New and Old Bond Streets are essentially concerned with quality, where goods often go unmarked and prices left to the imagination. Fashion, jewellery, antiques, fine art abound; other specialists include beauty salons, watches, optical equipment.

CARNABY STREET: Made a big noise in fashion during the late 1960's, now a Union Jack tourist attraction, pedestrianized with coloured pavement.

CHARING CROSS ROAD, TOTTENHAM COURT ROAD: None of the glitter and show of other popular shopping streets, these provide a basic service. Charing Cross Rd. is a centre for book shops, also newsagents stocking foreign newspapers; music, musical instruments and record shops. Tottenham Court Rd. features modern furniture and accessories, electrical, Hi-Fi and optical goods.

COVENT GARDEN: Since the departure of the wholesale fruit and vegetable market to Nine Elms, Covent Garden has been transformed. The restored central market hall and piazza are now a pedestrian shopping centre, here and in the surrounding small streets are a wide variety of shops: food, crafts, books, fashion, gifts, perfumiers, herbalists and art galleries; also many restaurants and pubs. See also page 89.

KENSINGTON HIGH STREET: Multiple use High Street of stores and small shops, a lively fashion centre extending into Kensington Church Street, a centre for antique shops.

KINGS ROAD: As much of a parade as a place to buy trendy clothes with the pubs providing a grandstand for the elite. Towards the south antique shops take over from clothes including the Chelsea Antique Market.

KNIGHTSBRIDGE, BROMPTON RD. AND FULHAM RD.: The fashionable Knightsbridge and northern Brompton Rd. focus on two exclusive department stores, surrounded by quality fashion and shoe shops, hairdressers and specialists in oriental carpets. Brompton Rd. begins with fashion boutiques, Fulham Rd. ends with antiques and restaurants, in between is a fast-growing shopping centre where local food shops, hairdressers, florists etc. still rub shoulders with the 20th-cent. affluent image.

OXFORD STREET: Perhaps the most popular and well-known shopping area. Vast range of clothing shops from the trendy boutiques through the established chain stores to the renowned department stores. Many shoe shops, jewellers, record shops and places for refreshment.

PICCADILLY: a diverse mixture of quality fashion and food stores, small specialist shops, i.e. leather and travel goods, tobacconists, hotels, airline and tourist offices and showrooms. Open-air art market beside Green Park weekends.

BEAUCHAMP PL

BROMPTON RD.
HENRYS Handbags: Travel Goods
CANNIBAL ●
CROCHETTA ●
Shirts, Blouses, VALBRIDGE ◐
Confectioners FOUQUET
REJECT CHINA SHOP
BEAUCHAMP PLACE SHOP ◐
Antique Maps MAP HOUSE
MONSOON ●
JONES ✧
POMODORO PIZZA ▩
FOOTLIGHTS ●
KEN LANE ✧
Pharmacy HEAVEN SCENT
PANTON ●
LACOSTE ○
BORSHTCH 'N TEARS ▩
FOLLI FOLLIES ✧

GROVE TAVERN →

ASHLEY BLAKE ◐
DELISS □
Hairdressers EDMONDS
SONNYS GAURMET ▩
MAROUCH II ▩
BEACHAMP PLACE SHOP ●

Tapestry LUXURY NEEDLEPOINT

REJECT CHINA SHOP
SPAGHETTI ●
BILL BENTLEY ▩
WALTON ST.

BROMPTON RD.
REJECT CHINA SHOP
▩ PASTA
CHINACRAFT Fine China. Crystal
● JANET REGER
CHINACRAFT Fine China. Crystal
● ADELE DAVIS
● LAVA
● RASCALS
□ SHUZANA
● KANGO
▩ DUMPLING HOUSE
* BREAK OF DAY Porcelain, Objets d'art
● CAROLINE CHARLES
● TAN GIUDICELLI
▩ RESTORANTE ITALIANO
⊠ OPTICIAN
● WHISTLES
STANLEY LESLIE Antique Silver.
        Sheffield Plate
● BIANCA FURS
● PADDY CAMPBELL
● OLD ENGLAND
JULIE LOUGHNAN Model Horses. Toys
● SARAH SPENCER
NEEDLE NEEDS Tapestry equipment
▩ SAN LORENZO
SELECTA VIDEO
● MAISON PANACHE
* SYLVIA'S
● SCRUPLES
● BRUCE OLDFIELD
HALLIDAYS Handcarved Mantlepieces
DANS UN JARDIN Perfumer
▩ VERBANMLLA
WALTON ST.

JERMYN STREET

HAYMARKET
PICCADILLY CIRCUS TUBE ⊖
COCKNEY PRIDE →
REGENT STREET
SMILES ▩
SNOOKER ○
ALFRED ○
Hairdressers IVAN'S
HERBIE FROGG ○
Hats Shirts BATES ○
HAWES & CURTIS ○
EAGLE PL.
NATIONAL WESTMINSTER ☆
SIMPSON ■
CHURCH PL.

ST. JAMES'S CHURCH
HILDITCH & KEY ○
PRINCES ARCADE
Antiques MAYORCAS
Fine Gifts. Porcelain VON POSH *
Bathroom requisites CZECH & SPEAKE
Fountain Restaurant FORTNUM & MASON ■ ▩
DUKE ST.
Tobacconists Gift Shop DUNHILL *

PICCADILLY ARCADE

Shirts NEW & LINGWOOD ○
UNO MENSWEAR ○
WILTONS RESTAURANT ▩

Carpets Tapestry's VICTOR FRANCIS
Fine Art HEIM GALLERY
VINCCI ○
MOKARIS ▩
FRANCO'S ▩
ST. JAMES'S STREET

HAYMARKET
REGENT STREET
▩ ROWLEYS ON JERMYN ST.
○ PICCADILLY MAN'S SHOP
□ A. JONES & SON
BABMAES ST.
▩ A LECU de FRANCE
○ TIE RACK
● RACSON Woollens
GOLD-PFEIL Handbags. Travel Goods
○ T. M. LEWIN
□ CEASAR
○ FRANCESCA SMALTO
○ BRUNO
* UGGETTI Fine Gifts. Glass. Porcelain
DUKE OF YORK ST.
○ HARVIE & HUDSON Shirts
□ RUSSELL & BROMLEY
PAXTON & WHITFIELD Provisions
E.R. COOPER Chemist
M. EKSTEIN Antiques
FLORIS Perfumers
○ HILDITCH & KEY
○ TREVELYAN
○ JULES BAR
□ FOSTER & SON Shoes. Leather Goods
○ S. CONWAY Shirts
✧ ANDREW GRIMA
DUKE ST.
ARTHUR DAVIDSON Antiques
○ HARVIE & HUDSON Shirts
JOAN PALMER Florist
○ ULTIMO
○ FRANCHESCO
○ HILDITCH & KEY
BURY ST.
○ TURNBULL & ASSER
○ JAMES DREW
○ VINCCI
□ TRICKER
◀ VINCCI
ST. JAMES'S STREET

OXFORD

Left side:

TOTTENHAM COURT ROAD
TOTTENHAM COURT RD. TUBE ⊖
HORNE BROS O
THE TOTTENHAM ➤
McDONALD'S HAMBURGERS ▦
VIRGIN RECORD MEGASTORE ▦
CANNON CINEMA 1 2 3 & 4
H.WOLFE ❖
VIRGIN RECORD MEGASTORE ▦
+ Tapes, Video, Etc.
SOUVENIR SHOP ✳
LLOYDS BANK ☆
BARRATT ☐
JEANS WEST ◑
NATIONAL WESTMINSTER ☆
OPENED ●
MIMIKA ●
ANGUS STEAK HOUSE ▦
WANT SHE WANTS ●
HANWAY ST.

RATHBONE PL.
DUNN O
JEAN MACHINE ◑
SALISBURY HANDBAGS
PERRY'S PL.
McDONALD Hi-Fi ▥
ARISTOS ●
IBIZA ●
FREEMAN HARDY WILLIS ☐
DIXONS ⊠
NEWMAN ST.
JEAN MACHINE ◑
Chemist Dept Store UNDERWOODS
VIRGIN GAMES CENTRE
SMITH O
NAT. WESTMINSTER BANK ☆
BERNERS ST.

PLAZA ON OXFORD STREET ●O
Shopping Centre ▦

WELLS ST.
Sports Wear SUPERSPORTS ◑
NICKLEBYS O
MISTER BYRITE ◑
ADAM & EVE CT.
WIMPY ▦
DOLCIS ☐
HMV RECORD MEGASTORE ▦
JOHN KENT O
Unisex Hairdressers SUPERCUTS
MR HOWARD O
TAKE 6 O
WINSLEY ST.

NOW ●
MOTHERCARE ✚
PETER LORD ☐
GT. TITCHFIELD ST.
RAVEL ☐
FAITH ☐
QUALITY INN ▦
MARKET CT.
MIDLAND BANK ☆
C & A ■

GT. PORTLAND ST.
BURGER KING ▦
P. BROWN O
BURTON O
TOP SHOP ●
TOP MAN O
OXFORD CIRCUS TUBE ⊖

REGENT STREET
OXFORD CIRCUS TUBE ⊖

Right side:

CENTRE POINT
CHARING CROSS ROAD
O COLES
⊖ TOTTENHAM COURT RD. TUBE
☐ K SHOES
✳ CLAUDE GILL Books
O PETER BROWN
⊠▥ TANDY
▦ PIZZA HUT
☐ ANELLO & DAVIDE
RYMAN STATIONERS
● JOHN KENT
● JEAN CENTRE
☐ THE BOOTSTORE
● LEATHER MATE
O BRICKS
SOHO ST.
❖ RATNERS
⊠ HILTON CAMERAS
◑ J. MART
▦ 79 BAR/RESTAURANT
● TORO
◑ MARMALADE
▦ WENDY HAMBURGERS
DEAN ST.
O TIE RACK
CARD SHOP
O WOODHOUSE
✳ SOUVENIR SHOP
GT. CHAPEL ST.
SILVERDALE Travel Goods
☐ COBRA Soprts Shoes
❖ THE JEWELLERS GUILD
PHARMACY
✳ ATHENA Books/Posters/Cards
● BENETTON
● STRAVAGANZA
WARDOUR ST.
✳ SOUVENIRS
● INSTYLE
● DETROIT CLOTHING CO.
● CASCADE
● HARVEST

BERWICK ST.
● RISA
☐ DERBER
O COLES
BOOTS. Chemist
● JANE NORMAN
◑ THE SALES Leisurewear. Camping
☐ SHELLEY'S SHOES
POLAND ST.
❖ ERNEST JONES
■ MARKS & SPENCER
☐ SAXONE
☐ DOLCIS
▦ STRIKES
◑ THE SCOTCHOUSE
● PAIGE
RAMILLIES ST.
❖ ZALES
▦ RECORDS
■ LITTLEWOOD'S
☐● WALLIS
❖ RATNERS
HILLS PL.
● BENETTON
✳ SOUVENIRS
● LISA
⊖ OXFORD CIRCUS TUBE
ARGYLL ST.
▦ TAKAWAY FOOD
⊖ OXFORD CIRCUS TUBE
✳ WEDGWOOD GIFT CENTRE
REGENT STREET
⊖ OXFORD CIRCUS TUBE

OXFORD
CIRCUS

Left side (north) — REGENT STREET / OXFORD CIRCUS TUBE ⊖ to MARBLE ARCH TUBE ⊖

- REGENT STREET
- OXFORD CIRCUS TUBE ⊖
- HENNES ●
- **JOHN PRINCES ST.**
- MISTER BYRITE ○
- BALLY □
- RAVEL □
- H. SAMUEL ❖
- BRITISH HOME STORES ■
- LORD PETER □
- JANE NORMAN ●
- NICKLEBY'S ○
- ZALES ❖
- PHARMACY
- WALLIS ●
- **HOLLES ST.**
- JOHN LEWIS ■
- **OLD CAVENDISH ST.** ■
- D. H. EVANS ■
- **CHAPEL PL.**
- K. SHOES □
- DERBER □
- BENETTON ●
- GREEN & SYMONDS ❖
- BANK OF SCOTLAND ☆
- **VERE ST.**
- DEBENHAMS ■
- **MARLEYBONE LA.**
- STRATFORD COURT HOTEL
- DOLCIS □
- **MARYLEBONE LA.**
- SOUVENIR SHOP ✳
- DETROIT CLOTHING CO. ◑
- NATIONAL WESTMINSTER ☆
- BOND STREET TUBE ⊖
- **STRATFORD PL.**
- LILLY & SKINNER □
- TAKE SIX ○
- BARRIE ○
- **GEES CT.**
- BALLY □
- RICHARDS ●
- **JAMES ST.**
- C & A. ■
- **BIRD ST.**
- GILDA ●
- JANE NORMAN ●
- BARRATT □
- **DUKE ST.**
- SELFRIDGES ■
- **ORCHARD ST.**
- MARKS & SPENCER ■
- NATIONAL WESTMINSTER ☆
- ETAM ●
- MICHAEL BARRIE ○
- BALLY □
- RUSSELL & BROMLEY □
- RAVEL □
- ERNEST JONES ❖
- SAXONE □
- **PORTMAN ST.**
- LITTLEWOODS ■
- BENETTON ●
- DOROTHY PERKINS ●
- PAIGE ●
- SALISBURY HANDBAGS
- DOLCIS □
- GREEN & SYMONDS ❖
- EVANS OUTSIZE ●
- **OLD QUEBEC ST.**
- JULIES PANTRY ▨
- MARBLE ARCH TUBE ⊖

Center: OXFORD CIRCUS — STREET — MARBLE ARCH

Right side (south) — REGENT STREET / OXFORD CIRCUS TUBE ⊖ to MARBLE ARCH TUBE ⊖

- REGENT STREET
- OXFORD CIRCUS TUBE ⊖
- **SWALLOW PASSAGE**
- BENETTON ●
- RICHARDS ●
- DOROTHY PERKINS ●
- GREEN & SYMONDS ❖
- SCOTTISH WOOLLENS
- ERNEST JONES ❖
- CHELSEA GIRL/MAN ◑
- JEAN JEANIE ◑
- DEEP PAN PIZZA CO. ▨
- MR. HOWARD ○
- TUCCINI ●
- GUGGENHEIM'S ▨
- **HAREWOOD PL.**
- SAXONE □
- BABERS □
- OLYMPUS. Sportswear. equipment ◑
- RATNERS ❖
- GEE 2 ○
- JOHN KENT ○
- **DERING ST.**
- STEFANEL ●
- CHEMIST
- **NEW BOND ST.**
- DOLCIS □
- SOUVENIR SHOP ✳
- CHAMPAGNE ●
- **WOODSTOCK ST.**
- SACHA □
- THORNTONS Confectioners
- **SEDLEY PL.**
- JOHN KENT ○
- H. M. V. RECORD SHOP ▨
- RATNERS ❖
- **S. MOLTON ST.**
- **DAVIES ST.**
- TOP SHOP & TOP MAN ◑
- BOND STREET TUBE ⊖
- WEST ONE SHOPPING ARCADE ◑
- FAITHS □
- BOOTS Chemist ■
- COLES ○
- EVERON ●
- **GILBERT ST.**
- GARNERS STEAK HOUSE ▨
- **BINNEY ST.**
- BERTIE □
- WOODHOUSE ○
- NATIONAL WESTMINSTER BANK ☆
- **DUKE ST.**
- HORNE BROS. ○
- BURTON & TOP SHOP ◑
- **LUMLEY ST.**
- JEAN JEANIE ◑
- WIMPY ▨
- **BALDERTON ST.**
- MIDLAND BANK ☆
- LISA ●
- BENETTON ●
- LONDON HOUSE Cashmere Woollens
- JEAN MACHINE ◑
- BARCLAYS ☆
- **N. AUDLEY ST.**
- AMERICAN HAMBURGER
- MOTHERCARE ❖ ●
- NOW ●
- ABERDEEN STEAK HOUSE ▨
- HENNES ●
- JOHN KENT ○
- CARD SHOP
- REVONE ●
- **PARK ST.**
- CHINACRAFT
- C & A. ■
- MARBLE ARCH TUBE ⊖
- PARK LANE

HYDE PARK CORNER TUBE ⊖   ⊖ HYDE PARK CORNER TUBE

KNIGHTSBRIDGE

HYDE PARK

☆ BARCLAYS BANK
OLD BARRACK YD.
SAMAD'S ORIENTAL CARPETS
PANACHE Chocolates
HEAD GARDENER Hairdressers
WELLINGTON PHARMACY
ANDRE BERNARD Hairdressers
EDWARD GOODYEAR Florist
MINEMA Cinema

MADELENE ●
FABIAN FURS ●
HELLUA ●
Corsetiere LEWIS ●
GERMAN FOOD CENTRE
SEAFOOD RESTARUANT ▦
Antiques YOUNGROSE

WILTON PL.
GORGISSIMA
PIAFF
61 KNIGHTSBRIDGE
DOMINIC Wine Merchants
● WAKEFORDS
● YVETTE
□ ALAN Mc AFEE
▦ TAVOLA CALOLA
▦ SPAGHETTI HO.
● RUSSELL & BROMLEY
● BRADLEYS
● LUCIENNE PHILIPS
MAYFAIR CARPET GALLERY
KINGS CUTLERY

ALAN INTERNATIONAL SCHOOL
OF HAIRDRESSING
GERTRUDE CAROL ●
ALBERT GATE
NATIONAL WESTMINSTER ☆
HYDE PARK HOTEL
KNIGHTSBRIDGE TUBE ⊖

●●

WILLIAM ST.
SHERATON PARK TOWER HOTEL

SCOTCH HO. ◑

SEVILLE ST.
■ HARVEY NICHOLS
SLOANE ST.
⊖ **KNIGHTSBRIDGE TUBE**
☆ BARCLAYS

PARK MANSIONS ARCADE
BARCLAYS INTERNATIONAL ☆

CRECY ●
SIGNOR SASSI ▦
GRANT □
TATTERSALLS TAVERN ➜

● LUCY'S
● WALLIS
● STEFANEL
● MIDAS
BROMPTON ARCADE
● BENETTON
● ROBINA
● FIOR Fashion Accessories
□ SAXONE
HOOPER CT.
● NEXT
● SAINT LAURENT
● CHARLES JOURDAN
▦ CUL DE SAC
● RUSSELL & BROMLEY
● LOWE
GINGER GROUP Hairdressers

KNIGHTSBRIDGE GREEN
RAPHAEL STREET
ROYAL BANK OF SCOTLAND ☆
FIORUCCI ◑
CHINACRAFT
JULIES PANTRY ▦
Stationery RYMAN
Sports Wear THE SKIRACQUET ◑
Footwear / Footcare SCHOLL □

● FOGAL
○ NEXT

BROMPTON

BANQUE NATIONAL de PARIS ☆
TIE RACK ○
BOOTS ■
Department Store / Chemist
WAREHOUSE ●
LANCELOT PL.
LEBANON JEWELLERY ❖
FRETTE ●
Chocolates RICHOUX
LANVIN ○
REGINE ●
VERSACE ●
THE HIGHLAND SHOP ◑
JAEGER ◑
Porcelain, Glass GALLERY ROSENTHAL ✲

❖ GRAFF
□ RAYNE
● JANE NORMAN
● BERK Woollens, Cashmere
❖ CIRO PEARLS
❖ MAPPIN & WEBB Silversmiths
□ IVORY
□ BALLY
❖ KUTCHINSKY
● MISS SELFRIDGE
□ RUSSELL & BROMLEY
☆ LLOYDS
○ CECIL GEE
KNIGHTSBRIDGE TUBE
HANS CRES.
■ HARRODS
HANS RD.
☆ BARCLAYS
□ JONES
● FELLINI
☆ NATIONAL WESTMINSTER
BROMPTON PL.

ROAD

Kitchen & Bathroom Interiors DOMA
ABERDEEN STEAK HOUSE ▦
Hairdresser R. FIELDING
FORCES HELP SOCIETY
& LORD ROBERTS FURNITURE

Pastrycooks GLORIETTE ▦
MONTPELIER ST.

BROMPTON ROAD FULHAM ROAD

Left side:

MONTPELIER ST.
CROWN & SEPTRE ✦
CHIARI □
Food & Wine STEARCY
Antiques VANDEKAR
Foodhall HOUSE OF LEBANON

Antiques JOHN KEIL
Antiques JELLINEK & SAMPSON
Kitchens & Bathrooms HUMPERSONS
Antiques MICHAEL HOGG
Hairdressers OLOFSON
CRANE KALMAN GALLERY
NATIONAL WESTMINSTER ☆
CHEVAL PL.

BROMPTON SQ.
COTTAGE PL.
THE ORATORY
CROMWELL RD.
FLORIST
NEWSAGENT
WINE GALLERY ▦
SKYE CERAMIC TILES

NORTH TER.

ALEXANDER SQ.

SOUTH TER.
Patisserie ST. QUENTON
MARIO ▦
PLANTATION ●
Italian Tiles DOMUS

LA BRASSERIE ▦
Carpets WALDORF

PELHAM ST.

SYDNEY PL.
MIDLAND BANK ☆
GREAT EXPECTATIONS ●♣
Custom built furniture ANTARTICA
SYDNEY MEWS
Antiques KAPLAN
THE CRANLEY ✦
MONSOON ●
China & Gifts PARROTS ✳
ALI BEN ACCOLTO ▦
Gifts, Objet d'Art OCCASIONS ✳
SAN FREDIANO ▦
PIERO DE MONZI ◐
TATTERS ●
SYDNEY CL.
Nightware NIGHTOWLS ●
SUMNER PL.

Right side:

BROMPTON PL.
O AUSTIN REED
BEAUFORT GDNS.
O HIGH & MIGHTY
▦ GARNERS STEAK HO.
REJECT CHINA SHOP
BEAUCHAMP PL.
HENRYS. Handbags. Travel Goods
❖ LAKHA'S
■ WARING & GILLOW Traditional & Modern
Furniture. Fabrics, Household Gds
OVINGTON GDNS.
□ BALLY
⊠ DOLLAND & AITCHISON Optician
GEE BEE Antiques
UNDERWOODS Chemist Dept Store
✦ BUNCH OF GRAPES
YEOMANS ROW
INTERNATIONAL Supermarket
● CAROLYN BRUNN
▦ AL BUSTAN
GOUGH BROS Wine Merchants
MIDNIGHT SHOP Delicatessen
▦ SHAHEEN
EGERTON TER.
CHATSWORTH CARPETS
◑ SUN & SNOW Sports & Ski Shop
CRIMPERS Unisex Hairdresser
▦ GOOD EARTH
❖ HARDY Silver & Goldsmith
☆ MIDLAND BANK
SHURA Handbags. Travel Goods
● CALMAN LINKS Furriers
▦ ST. QUENTIN
THE REJECT SHOP Furniture Housewares
EGERTON GDNS.
EGERTON CRES.
✦ HOUR GLASS
● CAROLYN BRUNN
DAVID JAMES GALLERY
LALANS Foodshop
▦ VINO BISTRO
KRIOS GALLERY
MR LIGHT Lighting Specialist
HAMILTONS GALLERY
FLORIST
DRAYCOTT AV.
■ CONRAN Modern Furnishings
SLOANE AV.
▦ HAN'S CHINESE RESTAURANT
LUCIAN PL.
ELYSTAN ST.
CHELSEA GLASSWORKS Glass. Tiles
WHITTARD Tea & Coffee
KIMBOLTON ROW
SLEEPING COMPANY Bed Linen
▥ CHELSEA VIDEO CENTRE
❖ The WATCH GALLERY
✳ OGGETTI Fine Gifts. Glass. Porcelain
LONDON LIGHTING Co.
DIVERTIMENTI Tableware. Cooking Utensils
SLEEPING COMPANY Bed Linen
J.K. HILL Handmade Pottery
ETOILE HAIRDRESSER
▦ TANDOORI
● RITVA WESTENIRS Wedding Gowns
WINDSOR Food & Wine
● LAURA ASHLEY
PELHAM GALLERIES Antiques
PAPERCHASE Papers. Posters. Cards
POND PL.
▦ MERIDANA
BURY WLK.
SOLEIADO Quilt Bags. Fabrics
L'ODEON Antiques
❖ THEO FANNELL
SYDNEY ST.
ASHOKA TRANDOORI
● TOUCH

NEW BOND STREET · **OLD BOND ST**

Left (West side)	Right (East side)
OXFORD STREET	**OXFORD STREET**
DOLCIS □	● BERKERTEX BRIDES Bridalwear
ROLAND CARTIER ○	○ FRANCISCO M.
Woollens W. BILL ◐	ANDREWS Chemist
OLD VIENNA ▦	✚ BAMBINO
GRANT □	● HENRY'S
BLENHEIM ST.	**DERING ST.**
K. GEIGER □	● MINA
ROYAL BANK OF SCOTLAND ☆	PRATESI Linen
Linen Shop FRETTE	□ MIDAS
Woollens BRAININ OF BOND ST. ◐	⊠ PEARLE Opticians
ALAN Mc AFEE □	▦ BRASSIERIE, Cafe / Bar
NEWBAR ❖	● PLEASE MUM
CACHAREL ○	□ CARVELA
IVORY □	○ RIVOLI
DANIEL HECHTER ○	□ RAYNE
LUCY'S ●	❖ BENTLEY
LANVIN ○	⊠ DIXONS
Stationer RYMAN	**BROOK ST.**
RUSSELL & BROMLEY □	● FENWICKS
BROOK ST.	✳ SMYTHSON
BARCLAYS ☆	JASONS Fabrics
SAINT LAURENT ●	WHITE HOUSE Linen
MAGLI □	CHAPPELL Music. instruments, records
BALLY □	□ KURT GEIGER
CROMBIE ❖	□ PINET
OPPORTUNITIES ●	**MADDOX ST.**
CECIL GEE ○	❖ MASSADA
LANCASHIRE CT.	◐ REGINE
HERBIE FROGG ○	SIMMONDS Fabrics
Cameras, Hi-Fi WALLACE HEATON ⊠	○ HERBIE
MIDLAND BANK ☆	● AUSTIN
GROSVENOR ST.	● FOGAL
CHINACRAFT	SOTHEBY & Co. Auctioneers
BEALE & INMAN ○	● BENETTON
GORGISSIMA ●	○ HUBERT
SAINT LAURENT ○	□ CESAR
ROBINA ●	◐ CELINE Leatherware
BLOOMFIELD PL.	❖ TESSIERS Antique Jewellers & Plate
MARIE CLARE ●	□ RUSSELL & BROMLEY
ZELLI ○	**CONDUIT ST.**
RALPH LAURFN ◐	○ PHILIP LANDA
Travel Goods LOUIS VUITTON	❖ MOIRA
IRELAND HO. ◐	❖ FIOR
BRUTON ST.	○ BASILE
HERMES ○	**CLIFFORD ST.**
EMANUEL UNGARO ●	❖ WATCHES OF SWITZERLAND
VALENTINO ●	❖ PATEK PHILIPPE
CHURCH'S SHOES □	❖ GEORG JENSEN Silversmiths
SAVOY TAILORS GUILD ○	❖ PIAGET
GRAFTON ST.	❖ ADLER
Gifts, Porcelain, Antiques ASPREY & Co. ✳❖	❖ HENNELL
CHRISTENSEN ●	❖ PHILIP ANTROBUS
COLLINGWOOD ❖	● ADELE DAVIS
PORTS ●	❖ ANNE BLOOM
KARL LARGERFIELD ●	❖ BOOTY
LALAOUNIS ❖	● PLATINUM SHOP
CARTIER ❖	○ TROUSER HO.
ROSSETTI □	● ELIENNE AIGNER
CHAUMET ❖	❖ ROLEX Watches
KUTCHINSKY ❖	☆ NATIONAL WESTMINSTER
BOUCHERON ❖	**BURLINGTON GDNS.**
Leather Goods LOEWE	● FERRAGAMO
CHANNELL ●	○ PIERRE CARDIN
Leather Goods GUCCI □	○ SULKA
Woollens W. BILL ◐	❖ CLOUGH Pawnbrokers
ROYAL ARCADE	● ALAN Mc AFEE
Chocolates CHARBONNEL ET WALKER	❖ DELMAN
BALLY □	● RAYNE
STAFFORD ST.	BENSON & HEDGES Tobacconist
MIDLAND BANK ☆	● BRAININ CASHMERES
Handbags. Travel Goods ANDREW SOO'S	● JINDO FUR SALON
FEREDAY ❖	✳ SILVER CRYSTAL SUITE Glassware.
LLOYDS ☆	❖ BIJOUX
PIED a TERRE ROUGE □	○ FENZI
Amber SAC FRERES ❖	⊠ MEYROWITZ Optical Goods
CIRO PEARLS ❖	❖ TYME Watches
PICCADILLY	**PICCADILLY**

SLOANE ST.
MIDLAND BANK ☆
PETER JONES ■
CODOGAN GDNS.
SAXONE □
RECORDS 🏛
SIDNEY SMITH ●
CECIL GEE ○
BLUSHES 🏛
Perfumers BODY SHOP
JEAN MACHINE ◑
PIZZA HUT 🏛
Chemist UNDERWOODS
RUSSELL & BROMLEY □
CAROL ●
BLACKLANDS TER.
PASHU ◑
LINCOLN ST.
ARROWS 🏛
NEXT ●
PIZZALAND 🏛
SOLO ●
HOBBS □
SACHA □
STEFANEL ●
SISLEY ●
BALLY □
BENETTON ●
WALLIS ●
CHELSEA KITCHEN 🏛
TRANSPORT □
ANDERSON ST.
REISS ○
TRYON ST.
JUST MEN ○
BERTIE □
CUE ○
Boots, Sainsbury PRECINCT SHOPPING ■
L'AGGREESSE ○
MAGLIA ○
FIKIPSI ●
FERRARI □
FIORUCCI ●
RAVEL □
012 BENETTON ✚
BYWATER ST.
Bakers BEATON
FASHION STORE ●
MARKHAM ➡
MARKHAM PHARMACY
MARKHAM SQ.
BARCLAYS ☆
SHELLYS □
MARKHAM ST.
BENETTON ●
Stationers RYMAN
Bookshop HATCHARDS ※
JUBILEE PL.
LLOYDS ☆
CHELSEA LEATHER ◑
Card Shop SCRIBBLER
CHOYS 🏛
JANE ●
BURNSALL ST.
TIPO ○
PHOTO ●
CAPRIKORN ◑
Hi-Fi Radio ASHBY ⪣
SOLDIER BLUE ●
CURIO LEATHER ◑
CADEY ●
ANGUS STEAK HOUSE 🏛
LEATHERS ●
STUDIO 194 ●
Supermarket WAITROSE ■
Modern Furniture, Furnishings, HABITAT ■
CHELSEA MANOR ST.
POST OFFICE ☆
THE REJECT SHOP ■
Modern Furniture & Furnishings

SLOANE SQUARE

⊖ **SLOANE SQUARE TUBE**
SLOANE GDNS.
※ SMITHS Bookshop
☆ NATIONAL WESTMINSTER
LOWER SLOANE ST.
CHEMIST
☆ LLOYDS
☆ BARCLAYS
□ LACES
● WHISTLES
□ MIDAS
☆ POST OFFICE
BROOMFIELDS
INTERNATIONAL Supermarket
NEWSAGENTS
WINE MARKET
○ GLIDER
BOOTS Chemist
○ ACROBA
DUKE OF YORK'S HEADQUARTERS
CHELTENHAM TER.
☆ NATIONAL WESTMINSTER
◑ FAMILY
○ GEE 2
🏛 WHEELERS
● MONSOON
⪣ MARTINS Hi. T. V., Radio
□ PIED a TERRE
🏛 RECORD STORE
WALPOLE ST.
SAFEWAY Supermarket
ROYAL AV.
🏛 DRUMMONDS Cafe/Bar
● CHINESE LAUNDRY
● ARTE
● SLOT MACHINE
◑ LEATHERWEAR
WELLINGTON SQ.
◑ GEE 2
R. FIELDING Hairdressers
THE BODY SHOP Herbalists Perfumers
○ WHITES
● STRINGS
○ TAKE SIX
SMITH ST.
◑ WORKSHOP
● JONES
● CHOPRA
● SUGAR CANE
□ OFFICE
◑ REVIEW
● SCRUFFS
◑ GREAT GEAR MARKET
● SERGE
○ CHARCOAL
🏛 GOOD EARTH
○ GITENE
○ SPRINT
○ STIRLING COOPER
○ CARVIL
● TRIP
● CHAMPAGNE
○ LOGO
● RIVAAZ
● HUGO
RADNOR WLK.
➡ CHELSEA POTTER
WINE SHOP
◑ AWARDS
SHAWFIELD ST.
● PINTO SPORTSWEAR
🏛 PICASSO
○ JONES
○ QUINCY
ANTIQUARIUS ANTIQUE MARKET
FLOOD ST.
◑ JAEGAR
○ QUARZO
○ BOY

KINGS ROAD

OXFORD STREET
TOTTENHAM COURT RD. TUBE ⊖
FASHION STORE ●
W.I. BURGERS ▩
FALCONBERG CT.
ANNE SUMMERS
Theatre ASTORIA
SUTTON ROW
MEXICANA PIZZA HOUSE ▩
ABERDEEN STEAK HOUSE ▩

Chemist UNDERWOODS
BATTISTAS ▩
GOSLETT YD.
RECORD SHOP ▩
COLLETTS INTERNATIONAL ✳
Bookshop and Records ▩
BRITISH FILM INSTITUTE
Books WATERSTONES ✳
MANETTE ST.
Books & Records FOYLES ✳
ST. MARTINS SCHOOL OF ART
COLLEGE FOR THE DISTRIBUTIVE TRADES
Cinema CANNON
DEEP PAN PIZZA ▩
SNACK BAR ▩
COACH & HORSES ➡
OLD COMPTON STREET
Books, Tapes, Video LOVEJOYS ✳

CAMBRIDGE ➡
SHAFTESBURY AV.
MIDLAND BANK ☆
WELSH PRESBYTERIAN CHURCH
LE RENOIR ▩
HOLLYWOOD FOODHALL
Chemist UNDERWOODS

PLAYTHINGS SOUVENIRS ✳

NEWPORT CT.
HAPPY GARDEN CHINESE RESTAURANT ▩
LEICESTER SQ. TUBE ⊖
LITTLE NEWPORT ST.
GARFUNKELS ▩
Night Club/Restaurant HIPPODROME
CRANBOURN ST.
Tobacconist ARJAY
ALPINE ▩
PARIS TEXAS PANCAKE HOUSE ▩
BEAR ST.
BEAR & STAFF ➡
Cinema CANNON
HUNTS COURT
CITIZENS ADVICE BUREAU
BARCLAYS ☆
TRATTORIA IMPERIA ▩
NEWSAGENT
BRITISH SCHOOL OF MOTORING
Art & Crafts Materials CASS ARTS
GREEK TAVERNA ▩
IRVING ST.
GARNERS STEAK HO ▩
ORANGE ST.

NATIONAL PORTRAIT GALLERY

CHARING CROSS ROAD

NEW OXFORD STREET
CENTRE POINT TOWER BLOCK
ANDREW BORDE ST.
⊖TOTTENHAM COURT RD. TUBE
✳ BOOKSMITH Books & Magazines
▩ DEEP PAN PIZZA
▩ KENTUCKY FRIED CHICKEN
F.D. & H. Music & Musical Instruments
DENMARK PL.
◑ LEISURE WEAR, CAMPING
MUCCI BAG STORE
▩ SNACK BAR
ROCK STOP Musical Instruments
PRONTAPRINT Copy Service
DENMARK ST.
✳ HELLENIC BOOK SERVICE
MACARIS Musical Instruments
▩ BOOKS ETC. Books/Stationery/
Maps/Cards, Etc.
FLITCROFT STREET
PHOENIX Theatre

PHOENIX STREET
▩ FRENCH FRANKS Patisserie/Cafe
▩ PAYTON PLAICE
NEW COMPTON ST.
☐ ANELLO & DAVIDE Theatrical Costume.
Fabrics, Dancing Shoes.
PHARMACY
▩ COVENT GARDEN RECORDS
Compact Disc. Centre
SHAFTESBURY AV.
▩ WENDY HAMBURGERS
LITCHFIELD ST.
✳ ZWEMMER Fine Art Books
✳ AL HODA Bookshop
SMITH Tobacconist, Snuff
✳ ZWEMMER Oxford Univ., Press Bookshop
✳ SHIPLEY Secondhand Books
✳ SILVER MOON Secondhand Books
✳ COLLETS London Bookshop
✳ ANY AMOUNT OF BOOKS
Antiquarian & Secondhand Books
✳ HENRY PORDES Books
Antiquarian & Secondhand Books
○ MENSFAIR CENTRE
◑ SCOT CENTRE
✳ SOLOSY Books Newsagent
✳ READS Antiquarian & Secondhand Books
GT. NEWPORT ST.
➡ PORCUPINE
⊖LEICESTER SQ. TUBE

▩ ANGUS STEAK HO.
CRANBOURN ST.
⊖LEICESTER SQ. TUBE
ST. MARTINS CT.
WYNDHAMS Theatre
ST.MARTINS CT.
▩ CONTINENTAL BAR
▩ STRIKES
CECIL CT.
○ LIPMAN
STAMPS & COINS
✳ HOLBORN BOOKSHOP Books, Newsagent
▩ 'THE DYNASTY'
▩ OVAL PLATTER
PUBLIC LIBRARY
GARRICK Theatre
ST.MARTINS LANE
DUNCAN ST.
☆ POST OFFICE
ST MARTIN IN THE FIELDS

TRAFALGAR SQUARE

EUSTON ROAD
WARREN STREET TUBE 🚇
McDONALD'S HAMBURGERS 🍴
EASTERN BAZZAR ●
MANNY HARRIS ●
CHEMIST
Stationers QUADRANT
Chemist UNDERWOODS
GRAFTON WAY
NORTHUMBERLAND ARMS ➡
LAL QILA 🍴
PIRRONI'S 🍴
Leather Goods PARAMOUNT
MIDFORD PLACE
Adaptable Seating Specialists ADEPTUS
CANNONS CAFE/BAR 🍴
MAPLE ST.
NATIONAL WESTMINSTER ☆
Tools BUCK & RYAN
DEEP PAN PIZZA 🍴
NATIONAL WESTMINSTER ☆
HOWLAND ST.
Creative Lighting LIGHTSTYLE
KINGSLEY ⊠
Radio Hi-Fi TELESONIC ⅲ
LLOYDS ☆
Furniture Makers WESLEY BARRELL
ELITE ELECTRONICS ⅲ
WHITEFIELD MEMORIAL CHURCH
Pharmacy PONDEROSE
TOTTENHAM ST.
MESSRS C. 🍴
TRAVEL SHOP
GOODGE STREET TUBE
KENTUCKY FRIED CHICKEN 🍴
BERNIGRA 🍴
SCIENTOLOGY LONDON
Stationery RYMAN
Furniture & Furnishings DELCOR
GUGGENHEIMS 🍴
GOODGE ST.
LENNARDS ☐
SARDAR PUNJAB 🍴
POLICE STATION
KIRKMAN PL.
CLASSIQUE FOOD STORE
PROOPS ⅲ
AU MONTMARTRE 🍴
CRAIG Hi-Fi ⅲ
RISING SUN ➡
WINDMILL ST.
Hi-Fi Radio LASKYS ⅲ
MIDLAND BANK ☆
PERCY ST.
LAWRENCE & LAURENCE ❖
CANNON CINEMA
Audio Visual SPATIAL ⅲ
P N R AUDIOVISION ⅲ
STEPHEN ST.
WELBECK VIDEO ⅲ
AUDIO 1 ⅲ
ADIDAS SPORTSWEAR ◑
LAND OF VIDEO
BRIANS VIDEO ⅲ
THE VIDEO SHOP ⅲ
TUDOR PL.
Fashion Shoes CREATION ☐
GULTRONICS HI FI ⅲ
RECORD SHOP ⊛
VIDEO SHOP ⅲ
Hi-Fi CARE ⅲ
BLUE POSTS ➡
HANWAY ST.
VIDEO HI FI CENTRE ⅲ
WIMPY 🍴
HORNES O.
TOTTENHAM COURT RD. TUBE 🚇
OXFORD STREET

EUSTON ROAD
☆ MIDLAND BANK
BEAUMONT PLACE
■ MAPLES Trad. / Mod. Furniture.
Fabrics. Household Gds.
GRAFTON WAY
⊠ FOX TALBOT PHOTOGRAPHERS
⊠ FOTO INN Photographic Equipment
WORLD OF LEATHER Furnishers
🍴 GARFUNKEL'S
UNIVERITY ST.
🍴 STRIKES RESTAURANT
● CHIXY COCOS
SHURA Handbags / Travel Goods
● HOUSE OF SAREES
MORTIMER MKT.
☆ ROYAL BANK OF SCOTLAND
➡ MORTIMER ARMS
CAPPER ST.
IRAQ CULTURAL CENTRE
⊠ MORGAN CAMERA CO.
QUEENS YD.
ELNA SEWING MACHINES
➡ NEW INN
LONDON SOFA-BED CENTRE
⊠ SCIENTIFIC & TECHNICAL Optical & Electric
Graphic Supplies
☆ BARCLAYS
TORRINGTON PL.
■ HABITAT Modern Furniture & Furnishings
■ HEALS Modern Furniture. Fabrics.
Household Gds. & Childrens Toys

ALFRED MEWS
ⅲ GULTRONICS
☆ NATIONAL BANK OF GREECE
CHENIES ST.
■ REJECT SHOP Modern Household Goods
● LUCYS
PAPERCHASE Paper. Cards. Posters
APOLLO FOODSTORE
⊠ DOLLONDS Photographic & Optical
Equipment
SOFAS & SOFA BEDS
ⅲ SARAYS Hi-Fi
⊠ EUROCALC Calculators
UNDERWOOD Chemist
STORE ST.
ⅲ HI FI EXPERIENCE
ⅲ GALAXY AUDIO VISUAL
JAEGGI Kitchen Equipment
ⅲ Q TRONICS
ⅲ VIDEO CITY
☆ BARCLAYS
BAYLEY ST.
ⅲ HARP ELECTRONICS
🍴 PIZZALAND
ⅲ BUDGET SOUND SYSTEMS
ⅲ A to Z ELECTRONICS
ⅲ AUDIO ACCESSORIES.
ⅲ ASK ELECTRONICS
UNDERWOODS Chemist
ⅲ SONIC. PHOTO CENTRE
ⅲ LASKYS Hi-Fi Radio
BEDFORD AV.
ⅲ VIDEO WORLD
YMCA (LONDON CENTRAL) Y HOTEL
🍴 CLOUDS RESTAURANT
GT. RUSSELL ST.
☆ LLOYDS BANK
UNDERWOODS Chemist
DOMINION Cinema
◖ TOP SHOP
O BURTON
TOTTENHAM COURT RD. TUBE
NEW OXFORD STREET

TOTTENHAM COURT ROAD

KENSINGTON

KENSINGTON GARDENS & PALACE
ROYAL GARDEN HOTEL

KENSINGTON PALACE GDNS.
PALACE GRN.
Fashion Arcade HYPER HYPER ◑
Hairdressers R. FIELDING
RAVEL ☐
OLD COURT PL.
JEAN ARCADE ◑
TOWER RECORDS ▦
Silver & Goldsmiths H. SAMUEL ❖
NEWSAGENT
BARCLAYS ☆
KENSINGTON CHURCH ST.
ST MARY ABBOTS CHURCH
DERBER ☐
ABERDEEN STEAK HOUSE ▦
JEAN MACHINE ◑
MIDLAND BANK ☆
NATIONAL WESTMINSTER ☆
BENETTON ●
Stationers RYMAN
LAURA ASHLEY ●
ALFRED SNOOKER ○

KENSINGTON CHURCH WALK
PETER LORD ☐
DISCOUNT RECORDS ▦
TOP MAN ○
Travel Shop THOMAS COOK

McDONALD'S HAMBURGERS ▦
LLOYDS ☆
HORNTON ST.
ARAB BANK ☆
TOBACCONISTS
MOTHERCARE ●✚
CHELSEA MAN/CHELSEA GIRL ●◑
OLYMPUS SPORTSWEAR ◑
Newsagents Bookshop SMITHS

COUTTS & CO ☆
CAMPDEN HILL RD.

KENTUCKY FRIED CHICKEN ▦
RICHARDS ●
Food SAFEWAY
ARGYL RD.
C. & A. ■

FRIENDS ●
GOCCIA ○

Chemist Dept. Store UNDERWOODS ■
Hairdressers JACKIE AT RAMON
CROCODILE ●
Artists Materials REEVES
HALIFAX
JAEGER ●
FRANK JOSEPH ❖
Sports Outfitters SNOW & ROCK ◑
BURTON ○
Discount Electrical TEMPO ▥
HARTS FOODHALL
OXFAM
EVANS OUTSIZES ●
PHILLIMORE GDNS.
BARCLAYS ☆
Antiques KENSINGTON FURNITURE BAZAAR
LINEA RIVA
Interior Design & Furnishing
ALBASHA PALACE ▦
HOLLAND WALK
HOLLAND PARK
COMMONWEALTH INSTITUTE

HIGH

➜ THE GOAT
▦ DINOS
▦ GARFUNKELS
▦ FLANAGANS
☒ OPTICIAN
▦ WHEELER'S ALCOVE
❖ CHRICHTON Silversmiths
○ TRANQUILLE
○ VATRES
▦ FU TONG
▦ STICK & BOWL
○ PAPPION
KENSINGTON CT.
▦ PARIS PERSIAN RESTAURANT
◑ PERSEPOLIS
◑ SLICK WILLIES
◖ SHARCO FASHIONS
▦ BISTINGO ITALIANO
◑ RODEO DRIVE
KENSINGTON MARKET
☆ NATIONAL WESTMINSTER BANK

YOUNG ST.
■ BARKERS
DERRY ST.
■ BRITISH HOME STORES
■ MARKS & SPENCER
◑ JEAN JEANIE
●✚ HENNES
⊖ **KENSINGTON HIGH ST. TUBE**
○ DETROIT
● BOOTS Chemist
☐ BALLY
WRIGHTS LA.
● BENETTON
☐ BARRATT
● NEXT
SALISBURY Handbags, Fancy Gds.
○ WOODHOUSE
THORNTONS Confectioners
☐ SAXONE
❖ RATNERS
● NEXT
◑ DOROTHY PERKINS
☐ SAXONE
● MANNAN'S
☒▥ DIXON'S Hi-Fi. PHOTOGRAPHIC
☐ RAVEL
ADAM & EVE MWS.
☐ DOLCIS
PAPIER STUDIO Cards & Papers
CHEMIST
▦ PIZZA INN
☐ K SHOES
▥ TASHA Hi Fi, TV
✳ WATERSTONE'S BOOKSHOP
ALLEN ST.
●✚ MEENYS
✳ ST. PAUL Bookshop
SUPERDRUG Chemist
BODYSHOP Perfumiers
◑ INTERSPORT Sportswear & equipment

✳● MITSUKIKU, Japanese Gifts etc.
● KAY FASHIONS
CHEMIST
◑ ALPINE SPORTS
R. DYAS Ironmongers
GOUGH BROS. Wine Merchants
ABINGDON RD.
EARLY LEANING CENTRE Toys, Games
RYMAN Stationers
YOUNG WORLD Toy and Childrens
Book Centre
✳ THE TREE HOUSE Gifts

STREET

CARNABY ST.

GT. MARLBOROUGH ST.	**GT. MARLBOROUGH ST.**
PEPE ●	○ MERC
THE SHAKESPEARE ➜	**FOUBERTS PL.**
FOUBERTS PL.	● SUPREME
ST. TROPEZ ●	◐ PIONEER
LADY LISA ◐	◐ RAJ ENTERPRISES
	LOWNDES CT.
	◐ CHANDIS
GEAR ✱	● RUBY FASHIONS
ANITAS ●	**MARLBOROUGH CT.**
CEREX ✱	◐ SOCCER SCENE
JEAN MASTERS ◐	◐ DONIS
MELANDDI ○	● KAY BOUTIQUE
GANTON ST.	**GANTON ST.**
RUBY FASHIONS ●	✱ CARNABY CENTRE
FASHION SHOP ●	○ SNOOPING AROUND
Tobacconist INDERWICKS	● CATCH
GIFT SHOP ✱	○ TURBO GEAR
CAPRICORN □	◐ RAWHIDE LEATHER WEAR
ANITAS AGAIN ●	✱ GIFT SHOP
IN GEAR ✱	○ MELANDDI
HEAVEN ◐	**BROADWICK ST.**
LISA ●	◐ RAJ ENTERPRISES
ANCHORAGE ◐	✱ CASCADE
BEAK ST.	◐ LISA SUPERSTORE

PICCADILLY

PICCADILLY CIRCUS ⊖	**REGENT STREET**
REGENT STREET	✦ MODANI
TOWER RECORDS ▩	CANNON CINEMA
Shopping Precinct CENTRE AT THE CIRCUS ▩	BRITISH CALEDONIAN AIRWAYS
BANK OF SCOTLAND ☆	SHARATON PATISSERIE
AIR ST.	✱ CLAUDE GILL. Books
Rainwear CORDING ○	□ SAXONE
Fil a Fil ○	○ BARON OF PICCADILLY
NEW PICCADILLY HOTEL	**EAGLE PLACE**
Airline LUFTHANSA	☆ NATIONAL WESTMINSTER
ALITALIA	■ SIMPSON Fashion Dept Store
EGYPTAIR	UNDERWOOD CHEMIST
PICCADILLY PL.	TRANS WORLD AIRLINE
WALES TOURIST OFFICE	☆ BANK OF CREDIT & COMMERCE
SWALLOW ST.	**CHURCH PLACE**
Belgian World Airlines SABENA	ST. JAMES'S CHURCH
LLOYDS ☆	☆ MIDLAND BANK
SACKVILLE ST.	BRITISH ACADEMY OF FILM
ITALIAN TRADE CENTRE	& TELEVISION ARTS
AIREY & WHEELER ○	PAN AMERICAN
PAKISTAN INTERNATIONAL AIRLINE	✱ COLERIDGE Porcelain. Glass. Gifts
ALBANY COURTYARD	**PRINCESS ARCADE**
CYRUS CARPETS	▩ CAFE TORINO
	✱ HATCHARDS Bookshop
Royal Academy BURLINGTON HOUSE	◐ SWAINE ADENEY BRIGG & SONS
	Outfitters & Leather Goods
BURLINGTON ARCADE	■ FORTNUM & MASON Food & Fashion
WEATHERALL ○	Dept Store
ZIMBABWE AIRLINES	**DUKE STREET ST. JAMES'S**
TYME. Watches ✦	FRENCH RAIL
OLD BOND STREET	FRENCH TOURIST OFFICE
	UTA FRENCH AIRLINE
ALBEMARLE ST.	MAITLANDS Chemist
NATIONAL WESTMINSTER ☆	**PICCADILLY ARCADE**
	✱ GERED WEDGWOOD CHINA
BANK OF CREDIT & COMMERCE ☆	▩ RICHOUX
DOVER ST.	✱ ONE SEVEN ONE Gifts
AEROFLOT	REVELATION Travelgoods
IRAN AIRWAYS	⠿ WESTMINSTER AUDIO Hi-Fi. Radio. T.V.
GULF AIRWAYS	✱ THE CONNOISEUR Gifts
BERKELEY ST.	✱ LEATHER & SNOOK China & Glass
TALBOT. MOTORS	◐ PICCADILLY CASHMERE
SAAB MOTORS	○ KENT & CURWEN
GREEN PARK TUBE ⊖	**St. JAMES'S STREET**
MERCADES MOTORS	☆ BARCLAYS
STRATTON ST.	**ARLINGTON ST.**
MIDLAND BANK ☆	○ ANGELLO
SALLY VIKING LINE	✦ GOLDEN GARDEN
BOLTON ST.	● GRIFFIN FURS
JVC INFORMATION CENTRE	◐ THE LONDON STORE Designer Knitwear
THE XEROX STORE	RITZ HOTEL
CLARGES ST.	**GREEN PARK**
	⊖ **GREEN PARK TUBE**

BURLINGTON GDNS.
Household Linen IRISH LINEN Co.
Tobacconist SULLIVAN POWEL
Shirts, Woollens, S. FISHER ◑
DEMAS ❖
KEN LANE ❖
RICHARD OGDEN ❖
THE PEN SHOP
Antique Silver CHRISTIE
Antiques GERALD SATTIN
HOLMES ❖
Shirts, Knitwear S. FISHER ◑
Outfitters BERK ◑
SIMEON ●
THE PEWTER SHOP
Toys. Miniatures HUMMEL
Fine Art MacCONNAL-MASON
Woollens, Childrens wear. Hosier JONES ◑♣
China Glass CHINACRAFT
Cashmere, Woollens PYM
Cutlery CLEMENTS
JAMES DREW ●
WETHERALL ◑
PICCADILLY

BURLINGTON ARC

BURLINGTON GDNS.
● N. PEAL Shirts, Knitwear
D. L. LORD Leather Goods
O DONALDSON, WILLIAMS, WARD Tailors

❖ ARMOUR WINSTON
❖ GOLDSMITHS & SILVERSMITHS ASSN.
● BERK Knitwear

C. BARRETT Antiques
❖ S. T. ROOD
N. PEAL Shirts Knitwear
PENHALIGONS Perfumers
◑ SCOTT Knitwear
□ A. JONES Bootmakers
H. SIMMONS Tobacconist

ZELLI Porcelain Gifts
CLEMENTS Cutlery
❖ JOHNSON, WALKER & TOLHURST
O LORDS Shirts, Woollens
❖ B. BARNETT Jewellers
PICCADILLY

KNIGHTSBRIDGE
KNIGHTSBRIDGE TUBE ⊖
BARCLAYS ☆
BANCO DE BILBAO ☆
ATKINSON ❖
Butcher COBB
BASIL ST.
JOSEPH ●
LA CICOGNA ♣
BROWNS ●
NEW MAN O
BERTIE □
WOODHOUSE O
BALLY □
ANDRE BOGAERT ❖
GARNERS ▦
PIEDATERRE ●
ERREUNO □
IB JORGENSEN ●
HOLIDAY INN CHELSEA
ELLE ITALIAN SHOP ●
ISSEY MIYAKE ●
PLEASE MUM ♣
LONDON BEDDING CENTRE
Car Sales ASTON MARTIN
HANS CRES.
Antiques GEORGE SPENCER
FENDI ●
MARIO SABA ❖
UNGARO ●
BLEYLE ●
Gallery NEW ART CENTRE
Furs KONRAD ●
HARABEL'S ●
Unisex Hairdressing VIDAL SASSOON
ST. MARCO'S BATHROOMS
Antiques DE HAVILLARD
SLOANE PEARLS ❖
IVOR GORDON ❖
HANS ST.

PONT ST.

CADOGAN GTE.
CADOGAN GDNS.
Gifts PRESENTS ✱
VIDAL SASSOON
COLES O
Foodhall PARTRIDGE
Interior Design, Decoration J. CHURCHILL
Hairdressers R. FIELDING
Household Gds. GENERAL TRADING Co. ■
MIDLAND BANK ☆
SLOANE SQUARE

SLOANE STREET

KNIGHTSBRIDGE
■ HARVEY NICHOLS
□ MAGLI
● COUNTRY CASUALS
※ TRUSLOVE & HANSON Books
☆ MIDLAND BANK
O FRANCO SMOLTO
● ELEGANCE MATERNELLE
TOUCH OF CLASS Porcelain, Glassware
DESCAMPS LINEN
□ PIPIN
BENDICKS Chocolates
● MONSOON
● FRIENDS
O CELCIL GEE
HARRIET ST.

❖ DIBDIN
◑ COURTENAY
♣ THE GLOUCESTER
☆ NATIONAL WESTMINSTER
LAURA ASHLEY Fabrics. Wallpapers
CADOGAN HEALTH CLUB
PULBROOK & GOULD Florist
TAYLOR OF LONDON Perfumers
◑ GORDON LOWES
NEVILLE DANIEL Beauty Salon
◑ VALENTINO
SLOANE STREET FOOD SUPERSTORE
● MURRY ARBEID
MOORE of SLOANE ST. Chemist
● JOSEPH
CHARLES HAMMOND Furnishings
O NICHOLAS OF LONDON
● JAEGER
▦ RIB ROOM
☆ COUTTS & CO. BANK
CADOGAN PL.

PONT ST.

CADOGAN PL.
♣ CHILDRENS BAZAAR
ELLIS ST.
EUROPA 80 Supermarket
JACUZZI Bath Centre
WILBRAHAM PL.
BARGET Kitchens & Interiors
SLOANE TER.
CHEMIST
CHURCH OF HOLY TRINITY
☆ NATIONAL WESTMINSTER
SLOANE SQUARE

REGENT STREET (left / west side)

- Musical Centre. BOOSEY & HAWKES ※
- DON GENNORO
- **MARGARET ST.**
- NEWSAGENT
- China & Cutlery 285 REGENT ST.
- CHEMIST
- PEN SHOP
- TIE RACK O
- WATCHES OF SWITZERLAND ✤
- **GT. CASTLE ST.**
- FURS & SHEEPSKINS ●
- GARFUNKEL'S
- Underwear THERMAWEAR O✤
- HENNES O
- **OXFORD CIRCUS TUBE** ⊖
- **OXFORD STREET**
- **OXFORD CIRCUS TUBE** ⊖
- BENETTON O
- **PRINCES ST.**
- DALAH O
- CARD SHOPS
- TAKE SIX O
- LINDY
- **HANOVER ST.**
- AER LINGUS
- **MADDOX ST.**
- PRAVINS ✤
- Tailoring. Fabrics. Woollens TOPS
- Hairdressers R. FIELDING
- FURS ●
- K SHOES □
- **CONDUIT ST.**
- GREEK TOURIST OFFICE
- Cashmere, Woollens SCOTCH HOUSE ◐
- PETER TREVOR ✤
- WONDERLAND ✤
- **NEW BURLINGTON PL.**
- NOBLE FURS ●
- REGENT TEXTILES
- ROYAL JORDANIAN AIRLINE
- ALL WOOLLENS
- SAUDI AIRLINE
- QANTAS AIRLINE
- **NEW BURLINGTON ST.**
- BURBERRYS ●O
- Wine HEDGES & BUTLER
- **NEW BURLINGTON MWS.**
- Wool Merchants WOOLLEN CENTRE
- **HEDDON ST.**
- SCOTTISH WOOLLENS
- China. Glass WILSON GILL
- MIDLAND BANK ☆
- **HEDDON ST.**
- JOHN KENT O
- AIREY & WHEELER O
- TEXTILE SHOP
- PENCRAFT
- TRUSTEES SAVINGS BANK ☆
- **VIGO ST.**
- AUSTIN REED ●O
- PETER LORD □
- Woollens TAX FREE SHOP
- **SWALLOW ST.**
- THE CLOTH HOUSE
- Tie Shop WEATHERALL O
- Glassware LINE OF SCANDINAVIA
- ACUMAN O●
- SALISBURYS ✤
- **MAN IN THE MOON PAS.**
- BRITISH AIRWAYS
- CHINACRAFT
- Travel Goods SILVERDALE
- BRITISH AIRWAYS
- **AIR ST.**
- Shopping Precinct CENTRE AT THE CIRCUS
- TOWER RECORDS ▧
- **PICCADILLY CIRCUS TUBE** ⊖
- **PICCADILLY**

Centre: **REGENT** — OXFORD CIRCUS — **STREET** — THE QUADRANT — PICCADILLY CIRCUS

REGENT STREET (right / east side)

- **LITTLE PORTLAND ST.**
- McDONALD'S HAMBURGERS
- UNDERWOOD. Chemist
- **MARGARET ST.**
- WENDY HAMBURGERS
- SCOTTISH OMNIBUS
- INTOURIST/MOSCOW INFORMATION SERVICE
- TORINO PATISSERIE
- **GREAT CASTLE ST.**
- TOP SHOP ●
- TOP MAN O
- **OXFORD CIRCUS TUBE** ⊖
- **OXFORD STREET**
- **OXFORD CIRCUS TUBE** ⊖
- WEDGWOOD GIFT CENTRE
- RATNERS ✤
- BALLY □
- LAURA ASHLEY ●
- THORNTONS CONFECTIONERS
- TIE RACK O
- NATIONAL WESTMINSTER ☆
- **LITTLE ARGYLE ST.**
- DICKINS & JONES ■
- **GT. MARLBOROUGH ST.**
- LIBERTY & Co. ●
- LAURA ASHLEY Fashions & Fabrics ●
- **FOUBERT'S PL.**
- JAEGER ●
- CHINACRAFT
- HAMLEYS. Toys. Games. Sport
- LONDON HOUSE Woollens O●
- BOOTS Chemist Dept Store ■
- DIXONS ☒
- CIRO PEARL ✤
- BERK SCOTTISH SHOP O●
- BOOKENDS Bookshop ※
- **TENSION CT.**
- MAPPIN & WEBB Goldsmiths ✤
- NEXT ◐
- GERED China
- LISA ●
- **BEAK ST.**
- LAWLEYS China & Glass
- BALLY □
- JAEGAR MAN O
- COUNTRY CASUALS ◐
- DELTA & AIR CANADA
- DALAH FABRICS
- REJECT CHINA SHOPS Porcelain
- LLOYDS ☆
- **REGENT PL.**
- IBERIA AIRLINE
- YUGOTOURS
- T & J PERRY ✤
- BURTON O
- GARRARD GOLDSMITHS ✤
- **GLASSHOUSE ST.**
- AQUASCUTUM O
- MITSUKIKU. Japanese Shop ＊●
- WATERSTONE'S Bookshop ※
- SCOTCH HOUSE Woollens O●
- QUADRANT ARCADE
- SAXONE □
- ALEXANDRA. Business Wear
- ANGUS STEAK HO. ▧
- **AIR ST.**
- NICHOLS ▧
- CAFE ROYAL ▧
- ESTRIDGE Knitwear ●●O
- DUNNS Hats O
- BARCLAYS ☆
- SUN ALLIANCE INSURANCE BUILDING
- **PICCADILLY CIRCUS TUBE** ⊖

REGENT STREET: Planned and built in the 19th cent. by John Nash as a processional way for the Prince Regent. Regent Street has a quality of grace and refinement reflected in its many fashion, china, jewellery and gift shops.

ANTIQUES Explore areas like Islington, Marylebone, Kensington and Chelsea. Bond Streets and Mayfair are a class on their own.

Antique Markets and Supermarkets: Open normal shopping hours except when referred to MARKETS.

Antiquarius Arcade, 135 Kings Rd., SW3. 01-351 5353 **AZ 7K 75**
Antique Bazaar, 6 Church St., NW8. **2D 13**
Antique Supermarket, 3 Barrett St., SW1. **1A 32**
Bayswater Antique Market, 122 Bayswater Rd., W2. **3D 27**
Bond Street Antique Centre, 124 New Bond St., W1. 01-351 5353 **1B 32**
Bond Street Silver Galleries, 111 New Bond St., W1. 01-493 6180 **1B 32**
Camden Passage see MARKETS.
Chelsea Antique Market, 245a Kings Rd., SW3. 01-352 9695 **AZ 7K 75**
Farringdon Road Market see MARKETS.
Grays Mews Antique Mkt., 1 Davis Mws., W1. 01-629 7034 **2D 15**
London Silver Vaults, Chancery Ho., Chancery La., WC2. 01-242 3844 **3B 20**
New Caledonian Mkt., see Markets
Portobello Antique Market, see Markets
Portobello Road Market, see Markets.

BOOKS A Selection of good general bookshops and some specialists. See also Department Stores and the Charing Cross Rd.–Gt. Russell St. area.

Books Etc Ltd., 118 Charing Cross Rd., WC2. 01-379 6838 **2C 35** and branches.
Claude Gill, 23 Oxford St., W1. **1A 34**
Collets Bookshops, 129 & 66 Charing Cross Rd., WC2. 01-734 0782 **2C 35**
Compendium, 240 Camden High St., NW1. 01-267 1525 **AZ 1F 61**
Foyles, 119 Charing Cross Rd., WC2. 01-437 5660 **2C 35**
Hatchards, 187 Piccadilly, W1. 01-437 3924 **3D 33**
Mowbrays, 28 Margaret St., W1. 01-580 2812 **3C 17**
Penguin Bookshop, Unit 10, The Market, Covent Garden, WC2. 01-379 7650 **2D 35**
Selfridges, 400 Oxford St., W1. 01-629 1234 **1A 32**
Smith W. H., Kingsway. 01-836 5951 **1A 36** and other branches throughout London.
Truslove and Hanson, 205 Sloane St., SW1. 01-235 2128 **3C 47**
Waterstone & Co., 121 Charing Cross Rd., WC2. 01-434 4291 **2C 35** and branches.

Specialists (for sheet music see also Chappell's, page 149).
Books for Cooks, 15 Blenheim Cres., W11. 01-221 1992 **AZ 7G 59**
Catholic Bookshop, 4 Brownhill Rd., SE6. 01-461 0896 **AZ 7D 96**
Children's Book Centre, 229 Kensington High St., W8. 01-937 0362 **3B 42**
Christian Literature Crusade, Cathedral Pl., EC4. 01-248 6274 **1B 38**
Cinema Bookshop, 13 Gt. Russell St., WC1. 01-637 0206 **3C 19**
Collets Chinese Bookshop, 40 Gt. Russell St., WC1. 01-580 7538 **3C 19**
Dance Books, 9 Cecil Ct., WC2. 01-836 2314 **2C 35**
Dillon's University Bookshop, 82 Gower St., WC1. 01-636 1577 **1B 18**
Science and academic subjects, computer section, language learning dept.
Economists Bookshop, Clare Mkt., Portugal St., WC2. 01-405 5531 **1A 36**
French's Theatre Bookshop, 52 Fitzroy St., W1. 01-387 9373 **1D 17**
Plays, theatre and opera books, sound effects on cassette and record.
Foyles Educational, 37 Up. Berkeley St., W1. 01-723 9257 **2D 31** Textbooks.
Grant & Cutler, 11 Buckingham St., WC2. 01-839 3136 **3D 35**
Foreign Literature, French, German, Italian, Portuguese, Spanish. Periodicals.
Hachette, 4 Regent Pl. W1. 01-734 5633 **2D 33.** In French and about France.
H.M. Stationery Office, 49 High Holborn, WC1. 01-211 5656 **3B 20**

Official books and publications, O.S. maps, guides.
Kimptons Medical Bookshop, 205 Gt. Portland St., W1. 01-580 6381 **1C 17**
Lewis, H. K., 136 Gower St., WC1. 01-387 4282 **1A 18.** Medical books and
literature.
London Art Bookshop, 7 Holland St., W8. 01-937 6996 **2B 42.** Art, architecture,
crafts.
Motor Books, 33 St. Martin's Court, WC2. 01-836 5376 **2C 35.**
Transportation and military.
Museum Bookshop, 36 Gt Russell St., WC1. 01-580 4086 **3C 19**
Archaeology.
Oyez Stationery, 191 Fleet St., EC4. 01-405 2847 **1C 37.** Law and related
subjects.
Peter's Music Shop, 119 Wardour St., W1. 01-437 1456 **1A 34** Sheet Music and
books on music.
St. George's Gallery, 8 Duke St., SW1. 01-930 0935 **3D 33** Fine Art; exhibition
catalogues.
Travel Bookshop, 13 Blenheim Cres,. W11. 01-229 5260 **AZ 7G 59**
Turret Bookshop, 42 Lambs Conduit St., WC1. 01-405 6058 **1A 20** Poetry.
Watkins Bookshop, 19 Cecil Ct., WC2. 01-836 2182 **2C 35** Alternative religion
and medicine.
Zwemmer, 24 Litchfield St., WC2. 01-836 4710 **2C 35** Arts and architecture.

CLOTHING **See the preceding shopping route maps for the larger shopping
areas where male, female and children's shops and boutiques are pin-
pointed with a special key.**
See also DEPARTMENT STORES, especially Barkers, British Home Stores,
C & A, Debenhams, Dickins & Jones, D. H. Evans, Harrods, Harvey Nichols, John
Lewis, Liberty, Lillywhites, Littlewoods, Marks & Spencer, Peter Jones, Selfridges,
Simpson, Top Shop.

Bridal Wear
Berkertex Brides, 81 New Bond St., W1. 01-629 9301 **1B 32**
Pronuptia de Paris, 19 Hanover St., W1. 01-493 9152 **1C 33**

Cashmere and Woollens
Berk, 46 Burlington Arc., W1. 01-493 0028 **3D 33**
Bill, W., 93 New Bond St. and 28 Old Bond St., W1. 01-629 2554 **2C 33**
Brainin Cashmeres, 11 Old Bond St., W1. 01-493 2607 **3D 33**
Scotch House, 2 Brompton Rd., SW1. 01-581 2151 **3B 46**

Fur
Calman Links,241 Brompton Rd., SW3. 01-581 1927 **1A 60**
Furs for All, 205 Regent St., W1. 01-734 7770 **1C 33**
Noble Furs, 183 Regent St., W1. 01-734 6394 **1C 33**

Hats
Bates, 21a Jermyn St., SW1. 01-734 2722 **3D 33** Hatter
Dunn, 228 Piccadilly, W1. 01-930 3744 **3D 33** and branches. Men's hats
Herbert Johnson, 13 Old Burlington St., W1. 01-439 7397 **2D 33** All hats, civil and
military, men and women.
Lock, James, 6 St. James's St., SW1. 01-930 8874 **1D 49** Famous for bowler hats.
Simone Mirman, 11a West Halkin St., SW1. 01-235 2656 **1D 61** Fashion hats.

Leather and Suede
Celine of Paris, 28 New Bond St., W1. 01-493 9000 **2C 33**
Loewe, 25 Old Bond St., W1. 01-493 3914 **3D 33**

Maternity
Elegance Maternelle, 199 Sloane St., SW1. 01-235 6140 **3C 47**
Mothercare, 461 Oxford St., W1. 01-629 6621 **2C 31** and branches
Young Motherhood, 22 Baker St., W1. 01-935 4549 **1C 15**

Shirts
Beale & Inman, 131 New Bond St., W1. 01-493 1048 **2C 33**
Budd Ltd., 3 Piccadilly Arc., W1. 01-493 0139 **3D 33**
Harvie & Hudson, 77 Jermyn St., SW1. 01-930 3949 **3D 33**
Turnbull & Asser, 71 Jermyn St., SW1. 01-930 0502 **3D 33**

Shoes Oxford Street has many many branches of the main shoe retailers.
Anello & Davide, 94 Charing Cross Rd., WC2. 01-836 5019 **2C 35** Dance and
theatrical shoe makers. 33/35 Oxford St., W1. **1A 34** for fashion shoes.
Church & Co., 58 Burlington Arcade, W1. 01-493 8307 **3D 33** Men's shoes.
Ferragamo, 24 Old Bond St., W1. 01-629 5007 **3D 33** Women's shoes.
Geiger, K., 95 New Bond St., W1. 01-499 2707 **2C 33** Women's shoes.
Gucci, 27 Old Bond St., W1. 01-629 2716 **3D 33** Women's shoes.
Lobb J., 9 St. James's St., SW1. 01-930 3664 **1D 49** Handmade men's and
women's shoes.
Pinet, F., 95 Jermyn St., SW1. 01-930 5307 **3D 33** Men's shoes.
Rayne, 57 Brompton Rd., SW3. 01-589 5560 **3B 46.** 15 Old Bond St., W1. **3D 33,**
152 Regent St., W1. 01-734 5952 **1C 33** Women's shoes.
Trickers, 67 Jermyn St., SW1. 01-930 6395 **3D 33** Men's handmade shoes.

DECOR/CRAFTS Explore Covent Garden and environs **2D 35** an area dotted
with small retail outlets for creative and unusual products, Museums and
Galleries, gift shops are also worth exploring.
Africa Centre, 38 King St., WC2. 01-836 1973 **1D 35**
Authentic crafts, goods and souvenirs.
Asprey, 165 New Bond St., W1. 01-493 6767 **2C 33**
Gold and silverware, jewellery, leather, antiques.
Briglin Pottery, 23 Crawford St., W1. 01-935 0605 **3B 14**
A working pottery with craft products for sale.
Casa Pupo, 60 Pimlico Rd., SW1. 01-730 7111 **3A 62**
Spanish household furnishings, especially tiles.
Collectors Corner, Cardington St., NW1. 01-387 9400 **2D 9**
British Rail Memorabilia—name plates, timetables, railway equipment.
Covent Garden General Store, 111 Long Acre, WC2. 01-240 0331 **1C 35**
Gifts, basketware, toys, stationery.
Crafts Centre, 43 Earlham St., WC2. 01-836 6993 **1C 35**
Handmade ceramics.
Craftsman Potter's Shop, Marshall St., W1. 01-437 7605 **1D 33**
Handmade ceramics.
Fortnum & Mason, Piccadilly, W1. 01-734 8040 **3D 33**
Quality gifts and ornaments.
General Trading Co., 144 Sloane St., SW1. 01-730 0411 **3D 61**
Modern and antique objet d'Art, gifts and accessories.
Glasshouse, 65 Long Acre, WC2. 01-836 9785 **2C 35**
All handmade glassware; you can watch it being made.
Modern household furnishings.
Halcyon Days, 14 Brook St., W1. 01-629 8811 **2C 33**
Objets d'Art and antiques.
Heals, 196 Tottenham Ct. Rd., W1. 01-636 1666 **2A 18**
Twentieth cent. furnishings.
Inca, 45 Elizabeth St., SW1. 01-730 7941 **2A 62**
Crafts and hand-knits from Peru.
Irish Shop, 11 Duke St., W1. 01-935 1366 **1A 32**
Handmade crafts, fabrics and knitwear, Waterford Crystal.
Kiwi Fruits, 25 Bedfordbury, WC2. 01-240 1423 **2C 35**
The New Zealand shop, authentic craft and art works.
Lawleys, 154 Regent St., W1. 01-734 2621 **1C 33**
Porcelain ornaments, limited editions.
Mitsukiku, 15 Old Brompton Rd., SW7. 01-589 1725 **2C 59** and branches.

Japanese crafts, goods, ornaments, origami.
Naturally British, 13 New Row, WC2. 01-240 0551 **2C 35**
Unusual household goods, ornaments, toys, gifts, jewellery.
Neal Street Shop, 29 Neal St., WC2. 01-240 0136 **1C 35**
Decorative and household goods.
Oggetti, 133 Fulham Rd., SW3. 01-581 8088 **3A 60** and Jermyn St., SW1. **3A 34**
Fine modern gifts, glassware, porcelain.
Presents, 129 Sloane St., SW1. 01-730 5457 **3C 47**
Modern gifts, games, puzzles, objets d'art.
Royal Copenhagen Porcelain, 15 New Bond St., W1. 01-629 3622 **3C 33**
Porcelain figures, ornaments. With Georg Jensen silverware/jewellery.
Russian Shop, 278 High Holborn, WC1. 01-405 3538 **3B 20**
Crafts, toys and other goods.
Schell, Christine, 15 Cale St., SW3. 01-352 5563 **3A 60**
Tortoiseshell and silverware, jewellery.
V & A Crafts Shop, Victoria and Albert Museum, Cromwell Rd., SW7. **1D 59**
Modern, high quality handmade crafts.
Warehouse, 39 Neal St., WC2. 01-240 0931 **1C 35**
Chinese, Indian imports.
Xanadu, 32 Carlyle Sq., SW3. 01-352 0536 **AZ 5B 76**
Gifts and ornaments.
Zelli, 62 Burlington Arcade, W1. 01-493 0203 **3D 33**
Porcelain and miniature bronzes.

DEPARTMENT STORES Most of the Restaurants serve lunch and afternoon tea. On late nights, shops are usually open to 19.00.

Army & Navy, Victoria St., SW1. 01-834 1234 **1A 64**
One of London's oldest established stores now re-housed in a modern building complete with own car park. Extensive range of British and Continental goods for all personal and household requirements. Many services available. Restaurant. Toilets 2nd floor. Late night Fri.
Barkers, Kensington High St., W8. 01-937 5432 **3C 43**
All general requirements supplied including food. Hosiery dept., has all brand names. "Bargain shopping" in the Pontings basement. Restaurant and Snack Bar. Hairdressers Female. Toilets M, LG. F, 2nd. Late night Thurs.
Boots, Regent St., W1. 01-734 4934 **2D 23**, and smaller stores throughout London. Although basically chemists the Boots Stores provide a large variety of merchandise which can include beer and wine kits, books, cards, child care, cosmetics, health foods, photographic, reproductions, stationery, travel goods, toys and small household goods.
British Home Stores, 252 Oxford St., W1. 01-629 2011 **1C 33** and branches. Household goods and clothing of mass market appeal. Food section has large choice of prepacked sandwiches, salads etc. Also fresh cheeses. Late night Thurs.
Burberrys, 18 Haymarket, SW1. 01-930 3343 **3B 34**
Famous for raincoats but there are three floors of classic, quality clothes including suit, overcoats, shoes and authentic tartans. Delivery, repairs and weather-proofing. Toilets M. 2nd floor, F. 1st floor. Late night Thurs.
C. & A., 200, 376 and 505, Oxford St., W1. 01-629 7272 **1D 33, 1A 32** and **2D 31** Large selection of clothing for men, women and children, inexpensive to medium price range. Late night Thurs. Also 160 Kensington High St., W8. **3B 42**
Debenhams, 334 Oxford St., W1. 01-580 3000 **1B 32**
Departments for all clothing and personal goods plus many household requirements. Stocks many leading brand names besides well-known "Debenhams" label. Restaurant and Coffee shops. Toilets 3rd floor. Late night Thurs.
Dickins & Jones, 224 Regent St., W1. 01-734 7070 **1D 33**

Fashion store, medium price range. Also haberdashery, dress fabrics, jewellery etc. Restaurant and Coffee Bar. Toilets 4th floor, also F, 3rd. Late night Thurs.

D. H. Evans, 318 Oxford St., W1. 01-629 8800 **1B 32**

Large stocks of medium price clothing, men, women and children's depts., especially underwear. Also dress materials, wools, cosmetics. Late night Thurs.

Fenwick, 63 New Bond St., W1. 01-629 9161 **1B 32**

Fashion store essentially for young women, also children's dept. (no menswear). Good accessories dept. Also hairdressing, gifts, food hall, restaurant. Toilets F. ground floor. Late night Thurs.

Fortnum & Mason, Piccadilly, W1. 01-734 8040 **1D 33**

Renowned for gourmet foods and wines. Also handmade chocolates, gift and jewellery depts., clothing for male and female. Restaurants, Soda Fountain open 09.00–23.30 (ent. Jermyn St.), Hairdressers Female. Toilets F, 1st. M, 3rd.

Habitat, 206 Kings Rd., SW3. 01-351 1211 **AZ 5C 76** and 196 Tottenham Court Rd., W1. 01-631 3880 **2A 18** Catalogue and Mail Order available.

Modern household furniture, furnishings, fabrics. Large kitchenware and electrical goods depts with emphasis on the "young", and "budget" prices. Also toys and games. Self-service Restaurant at Kings Rd. branch. Late night Wed.

Harrods, Knightsbridge, SW1. 01-730 1234 **3B 46**

A vast storehouse of furnishings, furniture, fashion, food, gifts—all of the highest quality. The huge range of departments and "in house" services undertake to supply all their customers' needs. Restaurants, Cafes, Hairdressers Male and Female. Toilets F, 1st, 2nd & 4th floors, M, LG, 2nd, 3rd, 4th floors. Late night Wed.

Harvey Nichols, Knightsbridge, W1. 01-235 5000 **3C 47**

Exclusive fashion departments and household furniture and furnishings. Large carpet dept., carpets dyed to any colour at no extra cost. Restaurants. Ladies Hairdressers. Toilets F. M. 3rd floor. Late night Wed.

Heals, 196 Tottenham Court Rd., W1. 01-636 1666 **2A 18**

Large stocks of high quality, contemporary and traditional furniture designs, both British and Foreign. Departments on every aspect of furniture and furnishing; also modern children's toys. Heals Restaurant. Toilets 2nd floor.

John Lewis, 278 Oxford St., W1. 01-629 7711 **1C 33**

Large store with departments covering most needs. In their own brand name "Jonelle" a vast range of quality goods are available at lower prices than other similar brands. Renowned for dress and furnishing fabrics. Restaurants. Toilets F, Basement, 1,2,3,4th. M. 2nd, 4th. Late night Thurs.

Liberty, 210 Regent St., W1. 01-734 1234 **1D 33**

Top quality store. Fashion, household furniture and furnishings both modern and antique. Famous Liberty prints, oriental carpets, scarves, glass and china, jewellery depts. Restaurant. Toilets F. 3rd floor, M. 4th floor, Tudor Bldg. Late night Thurs.

Lillywhites, 24 Regent St., SW1. 01-930 3181 **3A 34**

Large sports outfitters. Departments for most sports clothing and equipment. Toilets F. 5th floor, M. 2nd floor. Late night Thurs.

Littlewoods, 506, 207 Oxford St., W1. 01-437 1718 **1D 31** and **1D 33**

Large stocks of medium-priced clothes, male, female and children. Self-service restaurant. Late night Thurs.

Maples, 141 Tottenham Court Rd., W1. 01-387 7000 **1D 17**

Traditional reproduction and modern furniture and furnishings of high quality. Many sample room settings, bedrooms, dining and seating areas.

Marks & Spencer, 173, 458 Oxford St., W1. 01-935 7954 **1D 31** and **1D 33**

Clothes, household furnishings and food. Well known for good quality knitwear. Unsatisfactory fittings can be changed at any branch. Late night Thurs.

Moss Bros. Bedford St., WC2. 01-240 4567 **2D 35**

Famous for its clothes hire service for both sexes, although their main business is selling high quality menswear. Famous also for its sports depts., clothes and equipment; anything for sale may be hired. Catalogue and mail order services. Valet and repairs. Toilets F. 4th floor. M. 2nd floor. Late night Thurs.

Mothercare, 461 & 164 Oxford St., W1. 01-629 6621, 580 1688 **2D 31, 1D 33** 196 Tottenham Court Rd W1 01-636 0192 **2A 18.** 120 Kensington High St, W8 01-937 9781 **3C 43.** By post 0923 31616.
The children's department store. Clothes, nappies, bottles, prams, pushchairs, cots, all the ancillary equipment for the baby and young child. Also toys and maternity ware. Catalogue and mail order. Unsatisfactory fittings can be changed at any store nationally.

Peter Jones, Sloane Sq., SW1. 01-730 3434 **3D 61**
Member of the J. Lewis partnership, carries a larger range of the more expensive fashion, household furniture and furnishings found in other branches. Restaurants. Ladies Hairdressers. Toilets F. 2nd, 4th floors. M. 1st and 4th floors. Late night Wed.

Selfridges, 400 Oxford St., W1. 01-629 1234 **1A 32**
London's second largest store. Departments of almost every household and personal requirement. Extensive kitchen ware, bookshop. Well-known food section includes delicatessen and kosher. Restaurants, Cafes. Toilets F. Basement, 3rd, 4th floors. M. Basement, 1st, 4th floors. Late night Thurs.

Simpsons, 203 Piccadilly, W1. 01-734 2002 **3A 34**
Male and female fashion store, own brand name of suits, trousers and jackets. Large sports dept. High price range. Restaurant. Bar. Toilets F. Ground and 4th floor, M. 1st floor. Late night Thurs.

Top Shop/Top Man, Oxford Circus, W1. 01-636 7700 **1C 33**
Two shops in one building (formerly Peter Robinson), with huge ranges of fashion, clothes, and accessories; but you must first cut your way through the "background music".

Waring & Gillow, 187 Brompton Rd., SW3. 01-589 8201 **1A 60**
Luxury furniture and household furnishings, traditional and modern designs. Late night Thurs.

FOOD AND DRINK See Department Stores: Army & Navy, Fortnum & Mason, Harrods, Marks & Spencer, Selfridges.

Foreign Food and Speciality Shops

Baily & Son, 116 Mount St., W1. 01-499 1883 **3A 32**
Poulterers and Game Dealers.

Beaton, 134 Kings Rd., SW3. 01-589 6263 **3C 61**
Bakers and Confectioners.

Bendicks, 55 Wigmore St., W1. 01-935 7272 **1A32.** 195 Sloane St., SW1. 01-235 4749 **3C 47**
Handmade chocolates.

Berry Bros. & Rudd, 3 St. James's St., SW1. 01-930 1888 **1D 49**
Wine merchants.

Camisa & Sons, 61 Old Compton St., W1. 01-437 4686 **2B 34**
Italian food.

Ceylon Tea Centre, 22 Regent St., SW1. 01-930 8632 **3A 34**

Charbonnel et Walker, 28 Old Bond St., W1. 01-629 4396 **3D 33**
Handmade chocolates.

Cheong-Leen, 4 Tower St., WC2. 01-836 5378 **1C 35**
Chinese food.

Cranks, Marshall St., W1. 01-437 2915 **1D 33**
Health foods.

Drury Tea & Coffee Co., 37 Drury La., WC2. 01-836 2607 **1D 35**
Many blends of tea and coffee.

Dugdale & Adams, 3 Gerrard St., W1. 01-437 3864 **2B 34**
English and Continental Bakers.

Fern, L., 27 Rathbone Pl., W1. 01-636 2237 **3A 18**

Blenders of tea and coffee; bulk mail order accepted.
Floris, 12a Bourchier St., W1. 01-437 5421 **2B 34**
Bakers, confectioners, handmade chocolates.
German Food Centre, 44 Knightsbridge, SW1 01-235 5760 **2D 47**
Grodzinski, 13 Brewer St., W1. 01-437 3302 **2A 34** and branches.
Kosher bakers, confectioners, patisserie.
Hamburger Products, 15 Charlotte Pl., W1. 01-636 0993 **3A 18**
Home-cured and smoked fish.
Hobbs & Co., 29 S. Audley St., W1. 01-409 1058 **3A 32**
Fine English and Foreign delicacies, hand-made chocolates, own prepared patés,
pies, etc.
Justin de Blank, 42 Elizabeth St., SW1. 01-730 0605 **2A 62**. 54 Duke St., W1. 01-
629 3174 **1A 32**
French and English provisions and bakers.
La Vie Clare, 31 Monmouth St., WC2. 01-836 4842 **1C 35**
Organically grown health foods; patisserie.
Lindys Pastrycooks, 36 Berners St., W1. 01-580 4338 **3A 18** and branches.
Patisserie.
Loon Fung Supermarket, 31 Gerrard St., W1. 01–437 1922 **2B 34**
Chinese provisions and utensils.
Maison Bouquillon, 41 Moscow Rd., W2. 01-727 4897 **2C 27**
French patisserie.
Maison Verlon, 12 Bute St., SW7. 01-584 0485 **2C 57**
Austrian and French patisserie.
Osaka, 17 Goldhurst Ter., NW6. 01-624 4983 **AZ 7K 43**
Chinese, Japanese, Middle Eastern and W. Indian foods. Mail order.
Paxton & Whitfield, 93 Jermyn St., SW1. 01-930 9892 **3A 34**
Cheeses and cold meats.
Randall & Aubin, 16 Brewer St., W1. 01-437 3507 **2A 34**
French food.
Richards, 11 Brewer St., W1. 01-437 1358 **2B 34**
Fishmongers, live and boiled crab, lobster, shellfish in season.
Slater & Cooke, Bisney & Jones, 67 Brewer St., W1. 01-437 2026 **2A 34**
Butchers and prepared meats.
Swiss Centre, The, Leicester Sq., W1. 01-734 1291 **2B 34**
Continental provisions, handmade chocolates,etc.
Tea House, 15a Neal St., WC2. 01-240 7539 **1C 35**
Traditional teas and exotic teas, also accessories.
Twinings, 216 Strand, WC2. 01-353 3511 **1C 37**
Tea and coffee merchants.
Whittard & Co., 111 Fulham Rd., SW3. 01-589 4261 **3D 59**
Coffee and tea specialists, herbal teas, mail order in bulk.

HANDICRAFTS, HOBBIES AND LEISURE PURSUITS see also Sports Goods.

Baines Orr (London) Ltd., Dept P222, 1 Garlands Rd., Redhill, Surrey. Redhill
67363
Supplier of semi-precious gemstones, jewellery findings, castings, kits. Catalogue.
Beatties, 112 High Holborn, WC1. 01–405 6285 **3A 20**
Model railways and kits of all kinds.
Buck & Ryan, 101 Tottenham Court Rd., W1. 01-636 7475 **1D 17**
Metal, wood and stone working tools.
Candle Makers Supplies, 28 Blythe Rd., W14. 01-602 4031 **AZ 3F 75**
Candlemaking moulds and materials.
Candle Shop, 30 The Market, Covent Garden, WC2. 01-836 9815 **AZ 2D 35**
Candles, holders and kits. Catalogue.
Cass Arts, 13 Charing Cross Rd., WC2. 01-930 9940 **2C 35** 18 George St.,
Richmond. 01-940 7642 **AZ 5D 88**

Wide range of arts and crafts supplies and equipment.

Cornelissen, 22 Gt. Queen St., WC2. 01-242 3642 **1D 35**
Artists' colourmen, paints, brushes, papers, canvases, easils, etc.

Cowling & Wilcox, 28 Broadwick St., W1. 01-734 9556 **1A 34**
Fine and graphic art materials and equipment.

Craft O'Hans (London), 21 Macklin St., WC2. 01-242 7053 **1D 35**
Enamels, blanks, kilns, cold enamelling.

Dickins & Jones, 224 Regent St., W1. 01-734 7070 **1D 33**
Buttons, fabrics, patterns, wools, trimmings.

Eaton Bag Co., 16 Manette St., W1. 01-437 9391 **1B 34**
Cane, raffia, wooden beads, shells and rocks, minerals and fossils.

Felt & Hessian Shop, 34 Greville St., EC1. 01-405 6215 **2C 21** Manufacturers and dealers of.

Fulham Pottery, 184 New King's Rd., SW6. 01-731 2167 **AZ 2H 91**
Materials and equipment, catalogue.

Gibbons, Stanley, 399 Strand, WC2. 01-836 8444 **2A 36** Postage stamp dealers.

Glassner, S., (Dept PC), 480 Kingston Rd,. SW20. 01-543 1666
Leathercraft supplies, Illustrated catalogue, Callers by appt. only.

Goddard & Gibbs, 41 Kingsland Rd., E2. 01-739 6563 **AZ 3E 62**
Stained Glass supplies.

Green and Stone, 259 King's Rd., SW3. 01-352 0837 **AZ 7K 75**
Specialists in artists materials, drawing supplies etc. Picture framers, restorers, carvers and gilders.

Hamleys, 200 Regent St., W1. 01-734 3161 **1C 33**
Toy superstore, vast range of hobbies kits and models. Soft toys, mechanical toys, etc. Sports equipment.

Handweavers Studios, 29 Haroldstone Rd., E17. 01-521 2281 **AZ 5A 32**
Looms, spinning wheels, yarns, fleeces. Catalogue.

Hobby Centre, 187 Hoxton St., N1. 01-789 8393 **AZ 1E 62**
Models and modelling supplies, kits, military figures.

Hobby Horse, 15 Langton St., SW10. 01-351 1913 **AZ 6A 76**
Beads specialists.

John Lewis, 278 Oxford St., W1. 01-629 7711 **1C 33**
Dressmaking, knitting and related crafts.

Laura Ashley, 183 Sloane St., SW1. 01-235 9728, **3c 47,** 35 Bow St., WC2. **1D 35**
and branches. Dress and furniture fabrics, wallpaper, studio designs.

Liberty, Regent St., W1. 01-734 1234 **1D 33**
Dress fabrics and patterns.

London Graphic Centre, 107 Long Acre, WC2. 01–240 0095 **2C 35**
Letraset and graphics equipment.

Luxury Needlepoint, 36 Beauchamp Pl., SW3. 01-581 5555 **1B 60**
Tapestry materials and equipment.

Paperchase, 216 Tottenham Ct. Rd., W1. 01-580 8496 **1A 18,**167 Fulham Rd., SW3. **3A 60** Coloured, handmade, Japanese papers etc., greetings cards.

Philatelic Sales Counters, Post Office, King Edward St., EC1. **3B 22** and Trafalgar Sq., WC1. **3C 35**

Reeves & Driad, 178 Kensington High St., W8. 01-937 5370 **3B 42**
Paper, dyes, enamelling, embroidery and crochet, weaving, pottery, plaster, wood-carving, jewellery and glass-fibre requirements, fine art, graphics.

Rowney, 11 Percy St., W1. 01-636 8241 **3A 18**
Fine art and graphics materials, Letraset.

Russell & Chapple, 23 Monmouth St., WC2. 01-836 7521 **1C 35**
Canvas, hessian, upholstery.

Seaby, 8 Cavendish Sq., W1. 01-631 3707 **1B 32**
Coins and medals, catalogue.

Spink & Son, 5 King St., SW1. 01-930 7888 **1D 49**
Coins and medals. Catalogue.

Thorp Modelmakers, 98 Gray's Inn Rd., WC1. 01-405 7545 **2B 20**

Balsa wood and model materials.
Tiranti, 21 Goodge Pl., W1. 01-636 8565 **2A 18**
Modelling, moulding, sculpture equipment.
Transatlantic Plastics, 672 Fulham Rd., SW6. 01-736 2231 **AZ 2G 91**
Polythene P.V.C., polyether foam.
Weil & Sons, 63/65 Riding Ho. St., W1. 01-580 3763 **3C 17**
Silk screen supplies, silk, silk paints, dyes, batik equipment.
W.H.I. Tapestry Shop, 85 Pimlico Rd., SW1. 01-730 5366 **3D 62**
Hand-painted designs, threads.
Winsor & Newton, 51 Rathbone Pl., W1. 01-636 4231 **3A 18**
Fine art and graphics equipment.

HOUSEHOLD FURNISHINGS See Department Stores: Army & Navy, Barkers, British Home Stores, Debenhams, Habitat, Harrods, Harvey Nichols, Heals, John Lewis, Liberty, Maples, Peter Jones, Selfridges, Waring & Gillow.

The Design Centre holds exhibitions of the best in British Industrial Design, have a Design Index—a visual reference library of recommended goods giving manufacturer, stockists and prices. Free access for public.

Specialists:
Adeptus, 110 Tottenham Court Rd., W1. 01-387 8722 **1A 18** and branches
Versatile, modern unit seating, catalogue.
Albrizzi, 1 Sloane Sq., SW1. 01-730 6119 **3D 61**
Chrome, brass, glass, perspex furnishings.
Chinacraft, 499 Oxford St., W1. 01-499 9881 **1A 32** and 198 Regent St., W1.
1C 39 50 Brompton Rd., SW3. **1B 60**
China, porcelain, crystal, silverware.
Conran, 77 Fulham Rd., SW7. 01-589 7401 **3A 60**
Top quality modern furniture and furnishings.
Crafts Centre, 43 Earlham St., WC1. 01-836 6993 **1C 35**
Handmade ceramics, pottery.
Craftsman Potter's Shop, Marshall St., W1. 01-437 7605 **2D 33**
Handmade pottery.
Designers Guild, 277 Kings Rd., SW3. 01-351 5775 **3C 61**
Co-ordinated fabrics, wall coverings and accessories.
Divertimenti, 68 Marylebone La., W1. 01-935 0689 **1A 32** 139 Fulham Rd., SW3.
3D 59
Kitchen utensils, china, tableware.
Domus, 260 Brompton Rd., SW3. 01-589 9457 **1A 60**
Italian tiles.
Elizabeth David, 46 Bourne St., SW1. 01-730 3123 **3D 61**
Modern kitchen equipment, utensils.
Felt & Hessian Shop, 34 Greville St., EC1. 01-405 6215 **2C 21**
Manufacturers and dealers of.
Georg Jensen, 15 New Bond St., W1. 01-499 6541 **2C 33**
Silver, stainless steelware, modern tableware, jewellery. Royal Copenhagen Porcelain.
Gered China, 173 Piccadilly, W1. 01-629 2614 **3D 33** and 158 Regent St., W1.
3A 34
Wedgwood, Spode, Coalport and glassware.
Goode, 19 S. Audley St., W1. 01-499 2823 **3A 32**
China, glass and silverware, handpainted porcelain plaques.
Graham & Green, 7 Elgin Cres., W11. 01-727 4594 **AZ 7G 59**
Kitchenware, bamboo furniture, basketware.
Irish Shop, 11 Duke St., W1. 01-935 1366 **1A 32**
Traditional fabrics and knitwear.
Lasky's, 42 Tottenham Court Rd., W1. 01-636 0845 **3B 18** and branches.
Hi-Fi, Radio, TV.

Laura Ashley, 183 Sloane St., SW1. 01-235 9728 **3C 47,** 35 Bow St., WC2. **1D 35**
208 Regent St., W1. **2D 33** and branches.
Furnishing fabrics, wallpaper, studio designs. Dress fabrics and boutique.
Lawley's, 154 Regent St., W1. 01-734 2621 **3A 34**
China, glass, limited editions, ornaments.
Leather & Snook, 167 Piccadilly, W1. 01-493 9121 **3D 33**
China and glass.
Left Handed Shop, 65 Beak St., W1. 01-437 3910 **2D 33**
All gadgets designed for those left-handed.
London Bedding Centre, 26 Sloane St., SW1. 01-235 /542 **3C 47**
Includes shaped, orthopaedic, space-saving designs.
London Lighting Co., 135 Fulham Rd., SW3. 01-589 3612 **3A 60**
Ultra modern lights and lighting ideas.
Mellor, 4 Sloane Sq., SW1. 01-730 4259 **3D 61**
Ironmonger, modern household, kitchenware goods.
Mr. Stone's, 175 Muswell Hill Bdwy., N10. 01-883 8879 **AZ 3F 29**
Floor and wall tiles specialists, also wallpaper and paints.
Osborne & Little, 304 Kings Rd., SW3. 01-352 1456 **AZ 5C 76**
Fabrics and wallcoverings—hand printed, metallics, hessian etc.
Paperchase, 216 Tottenham Court Rd., W1. 01-580 8496 **1A 18**
Modern wallpapers, curtain materials, bedding, towels.
Reject China Shop, 34 Beauchamp Pl., SW3. 01-584 9409 **1B 60** and 134 Regent
St., W1. **3A 34**
China and glassware.
Reject Shop, 209 Tottenham Court Rd., W1. 01-580 2895 **3B 18** 234 Kings Rd.,
SW3 01-352 2750 **AZ 5C 76**
Modern furniture and furnishings.
Rosenthal China Shop, 137 Regent St., W1. 01-734 3076 **3A 34**
Studio designed china, crystal, cutlery, Danish jewellery.
Russell & Chapple, 23 Monmouth St., WC2. 01-836 7521 **1C 35**
Canvas, hessian, upholstery, packing papers, ropes, tarpaulins.
Sandersons, 56 Berners St., W1. 01-636 7800 **3A 18**
Wallpapers and fabrics, selection areas, lay-outs.
Sekers, 15 Cavendish Pl., W1. 01-636 2612 **3C 17**
Furnishing and upholstery fabrics.
Tamesa Fabrics, 343 Kings Rd., SW3. 01-351 1126 **AZ 5C 76**
Modern furnishing and upholstery fabrics, original designs.
Watts & Co., 7 Tufton St., SW1. 01-222 7169 **1C 65**
Handprinted wallpapers and fabrics; original Victorian designs.
Warehouse, 39 Neal St., WC2. 01-240 0931 **1C 35**
Imported household goods, pottery, basketware, kitchenware etc.
Wedgwood, 32/34 Wigmore St., W1. 01-486 5181 **1A 32**
Spacious showrooms of porcelain and tableware.
White House, 51 New Bond St., W1. 01-629 3521 **1B 32**
Linen specialists.
Wray's Lighting Emporium, 600 Kings Rd., SW6. 01-736 8434 **AZ 7K 75**
Large range of old and reproduction light fittings.
Zarach, 48 South Audley St., W1. 01-491 2706 **3A 32**
Modern furniture and furnishings.
Zelli, 62 Burlington Arc., W1. 01-493 0203 **3D 33**
Crown Staffordshire, Coalport, Meissen, miniatures.

**JEWELLERY Old and New Bond Streets, Burlington Arcade are centres for
exclusive handmade jewellery. The specialist area for Gems and
Jewellers is Hatton Garden, EC1. 2C 21. Most shopping areas have a choice
of jewellers. These are among the most popular:**
Andrew Grima, 80 Jermyn St., W1. 01-839 7561 **1D 49**
Bravingtons, 24 Orchard St., W1. 01-935 7870 **1D 31**
Crafts Centre, 43 Earlham St., WC2. 01-836 6993 **1C 35**

Garrards, 112 Regent St., W1. 01-734 7020 **3A 34**
Jones, E., 161, 277, 500 Oxford St., W1. 01-437 2763 **1D 33, 1A 32**
Mappin & Webb, 170 Regent St., W1. 01-734 0906 **3A 34**
Ratners, 61, 219, 313, 373, Oxford St., W1. 01-734 3632 **1D 33, 1A 32**
Samuel, H., 250 Oxford St., W1. 01-493 1682 **1D 33**
Wolf, Herbert, 18 Oxford St., W1. 01-636 7266 **2C 31**

MAPS & GUIDES See also Bookshops, Bookstalls and Department Stores, in particular W. H. Smith at Kingsway and branches throughout London.
Geographers' A-Z Map Co., 44 Gray's Inn Rd., WC1. 01-242 9246 **2C 21**
The complete range of A to Z maps, atlases and guides of London and Britain. Comprehensive collection of other maps and atlases covering Britain and the world.
Cook, Hammond & Kell, 22 Caxton St., SW1. 01-222 2466 **1A 64**
Distributors for the Ordnance Survey Maps, other maps of Britain and Continent.
Sifton Praed, Map Ho., 54 Beauchamp Pl., SW3. 01-589 4325 **1B 60**
Antique and historic maps.
Stanfords, 12 Long Acre, WC2. 01-836 1321 **2C 35**
Large world map and guide collection.

MARKETS The historic wholesale markets of Billingsgate, Covent Garden, Leadenhall and Smithfield are dealt with under PLACES OF INTEREST.
For covered antique "supermarkets" see ANTIQUES.
Berwick Street, W1. **2A 34**
Mon. to Sat. 09.00–18.00. Food, mainly fruit and veg and lots of atmosphere.
Brick Lane, including Sclater St., Club Row, E1. **1D 25**.
Sun. am. Extensive ramble of street stalls, all kinds of merchandise.
Camden Passage, N1. **AZ 1B 62**
A centre for antiques shops and market stalls; market day is Wed. and Sat.
Chapel Market, N1. **AZ 2A 62**
Tues. to Sat. 09.00–18.00. Sun. 09.00–13.00. General goods.
Church Street, NW8. **2D 13**
Mon. to Sat. 09.00–17.30. Thurs. half-day. Antiques, food, junk.
Cut, The, SE1. **2D 53**
Mon. to Sat. 09.00–16.00. Household goods, food.
Farringdon Road, EC1. **1D 21**
Mon. to Sat. 10.00–16.00. Secondhand books.
Leather Lane, EC1. **2C 21**
Lunch-hour market, weekdays. Household and food.
New Caledonian Market, Bermondsey St., SE1. **AZ 3E 78**
Fri. morning antique trade "centre"; before 7 am—alive with dealers and the best chance of a bargain.
Petticoat Lane, Middlesex St., E1. **3C 25**
Perhaps the most famous market "name"; for a Sunday morning like no other, try to squeeze in—just try!
Portobello Road, W11. **2A 26**
Mon. to Sat. 09.00–17.00. "The" market, and Sat. is "the" day. Boutique clothes, antiques, Victoriana, junk, fruit & veg., tourists, trendys, way-outs and even locals.

RECORDS Record dealers can be found in most shopping areas, in most boutique arcades, bookshops and Department Stores. For sheet music and musical instruments see Charing Cross Road (and Chappell's below). Records can be borrowed, see Charing Cross Lending Library under LIBRARIES.
Chappell's, 50 New Bond St., W1. 01-491 2777 **2C 33**
Music Supermarket. Records, tapes, instruments, sheet music publishers.
Coliseum Shop, 31 St Martin's La., WC2. 01-240 0270 **3C 35**
Opera recordings; also books, libretti, scores and videos.

Dobell's Jazz and Folk Record Shop, 21 Tower St., WC2. 01-240 1354 **2C 35**
English Folk Dance & Song Society, 2 Regent's Park Rd., NW1. 01-485 2206 **AZ 1D 60**. Folk records, sheet music, books, instruments.
Harold Moores Records, 2 Gt. Marlborough St., W1. 01-437 1576 **1D 33**
Classical music and historical records specialists.
HMV Music Stores, 363 Oxford St., W1. 01-629 1240 **2C 31**. Trocadero Centre, Piccadilly Circus, 01-439 0447 **2B 34** and 150 Oxford St., W1 **1A 34**
From Classical to Jazz and Country n' Western to Pop and Rock.
Music Discount Centre, 29 Rathbone Pl., W1. 01-637 4700 **3A 18**
Classical music specialists, records and tapes; including transferred historic performances.
Tower Records, Piccadilly Circus, W1. **3A 34**
Record Superstore, open daily till late; also Kensington High St., branch 01-938 3511 **3A 34**.
Virgin Megastore, 30 Oxford St., W1. 01-631 1614 **1A 34**
All classes of recorded music and videos, magazines etc. Cafe.

REPRODUCTIONS AND POSTERS
Most museums and galleries have a good selection of prints.
Arts Council Shop, 8/9 Long Arcre, WC1. 01-836 1359 **2C 35**
Athena Publications, 1 Leicester Sq., WC2. 01-437 6780 **2B 34** and branches.
Do Do, 185 Westbourne Gro., W11. 01-229 3132 **1C 27**
Posters, old signs, tins, mirrors etc. Open Fri. & Sat. only, or by Appt.
London Transport Museum, Covent Garden, WC2. 01-379 6344 **2D 35**
National Gallery, Trafalgar Sq., WC2. 01-839 1912 (publications dept.) **3C 35**
National Portrait Gallery, St. Martin's Pl., WC2. 01-930 1552 **3C 35**
Pallas Gallery, 53 Hoxton Sq., N1. 01-729 4343 **AZ 3E 62**
Paperchase, 167 Fulham Rd., SW3. 01-589 7873 **3A 60**
Print Centre, 29 Earlham St., WC2. 01-836 1904 **1C 35**
Tate Gallery, Millbank, SW1. 01-821 5001 (publications dept.) **3C 65**

SPORTS GOODS see Department Stores especially Harrods, Moss Bros, Lillywhites and Simpsons for popular sports equipment and clothing.
Beale, 194 Shaftesbury Av., WC2. 01-836 9034 **1C 35**
Ships Chandler.
Blacks of Greenock, 53 Rathbone Pl., W1. 01-636 6645 **3A 18**
Camping, climbing, ski-ing.
Blands, 21 New Row, St. Martin's La., WC2. 01-836 9122 **2C 35**
Gunsmiths.
Brook, Alec, 49/53 Harrow Rd., W2. 01-402 5671.
Sports trophy manufacturers.
Cordings, 19 Piccadilly, W1. 01-734 0830 **3A 34**
Weatherproof clothing and footwear.
Farlow, 5b Pall Mall, SW1. 01-839 2423 **1B 50**
Fishing tackle.
Girl Guide Association, 17 Buckingham Pal. Rd., SW1. 01-834 6242 **1C 63**
Camping and outdoor activities.
Hardy Bros., 61 Pall Mall, SW1. 01-839 5515 **1A 50**
Fishing tackle.
Hobbs, 11a Islington High St., N1. 01-837 8611 **AZ 2A 62**
Cricket, football in season.
Lonsdale Sports Equipment, 21 Beak St, W1. 01-437 1526 **2D 33**
Boxing.
Moss Bros., Bedford St., WC2. 01-240 4567 **2D 35**
Many Sports, especially riding and saddlery. Also for Hire.
Olympus Sportswear, 301 Oxford St., W1. 01-409 2619 **2C 31**
Sportswear Superstore; also at 130 Kensington High St., W8.
Pindisports, 14 Holborn, EC1. 01-242 3278 **3C 21**
Camping, climbing and ski-ing.

Purdey, 57 S. Audley St., W1. 01-499 5292 **3A 32**
Gunsmiths.
Queens Ice Skate Shop, Queensway, W2. 01-229 4859 **3D 27**
Scout Shop, 25 Buckingham Pal. Rd., SW1. 01-834 6007 **1C 63**
Camping and outdoor activities.
Snow and Rock Sports, 199 Kensington High St., W8. 01-937 0872 **3B 42**
Skiing and Mountaineering suppliers.
Watts, Capt. O.M. 49 Albemarle St., W1. 01-493 4633 **3C 33**
Yachting.
YHA Adventure Centre, 14 Southampton St., WC2. 01-836 8542 **2D 35**
Outdoor pursuits including camping, climbing and ski-ing.

**TOYS, GAMES AND MODELS see Department Stores especially Habitat
and Heals for modern and constructive toys.**
Beatties, 202 High Holborn, WC1. 01-405 6285 **3A 20**
Model railways, planes, ships, kits.
Dolls House Shop, The Market, Covent Garden. WC2. 01-379 7243 **2D 35**
Top quality hand-built houses and exquisite miniature furniture, furnishings and
figures.
Hambling, 29 Cecil Ct., WC2. 01-836 4704 **2C 35**
"OO" Railway specialists, large selection of accessories, kits.
Hamleys, 200 Regent St., W1. 01-734 3161 **1C 33**. Toy Superstore, floors of every
kind of toy from soft toys to mechanical toys. Kits, models, sports goods.
Hummel, 16 Burlington Arc., W1. 01-493 7164 **3D 33**
Specialists in toy miniatures.
Just Games, 62 Brewer St., W1. 01-437 0761 **2A 34**
All games, traditional and modern.
Oscar's Den, 15 Buckingham Palace Rd., SW1. 01-828 9300 **3B 62**
Handpainted wooden toys, unusual presents; party paraphenalia a speciality.
Pollock's Toy Museum, 1 Scala St., W1. 01-636 3452 **2A 18**
Shop also at The Market, Covent Garden. **2D 35**.
Famous for toy theatres, many other traditional toys.
Tridias Toy Shop, 6 Lichfield Ter, Sheen Rd., Richmond. 01-948 3459 **AZ 5E 88.**
Large range of modern creative and traditional toys, games and things to do.
Annual catalogue just prior to Christmas season; Mail order dept, 124 Walcot St.
Bath.
Tradition, 5a Shepherd St., W1. 01-493 7452 **1B 48**
Military model makers.
Virgin Games Centre, 100 Oxford St., W1. 01-637 7911 **1A 34**
Huge selection with emphasis towards computer games.
W & H Models, 14 New Cavendish St., W1. 01-486 3561 **3A 16**
Kits for scale railways, also cars, boats etc.

SOCIAL SECURITY OFFICES

Headquarters Offices, Alexander Fleming Ho., Elephant & Castle, SE1. General
Enquiries 01-407 5522 **AZ 4B 78**
Emergency Office, Keyworth St., SE1. 01-407 2135 **3A 54** .
Supplementary Benefits and General Enquiries only. Emergency applications by
persons stranded without money and accommodation considered outside
normal office hours. Mon. to Fri. 18.00–22.00, Sat. 09.00–22.00. Sun and Public
Hols. 14.00–22.00.

Acton, Government Bldgs., Bromyard Av., W3. 01-743 5566 **AZ 7A 58**
Balham, 218 Balham High Rd., SW12. 01-673 7722 **AZ 3E 108**
Barking, 14 Cambridge Rd. 01-591 1311 **AZ 7G 51**
Barnet, Raydean Ho., 15 Western Pde., Gt. North Rd. 01-449 5522 **AZ 5D 4**

Battersea, 40 Parkgate Rd., SW11. 01-228 6454 **AZ 7C 76**
Bexley, Westminster Ho., 186 Broadway, Bexleyheath. 01-303 7799 **AZ 4E 100**
Bloomsbury, 1 Tavistock Sq., WC1. 01-388 4151 **1C 19**
  Supplementary Benefits only.
Brixton, 246 Stockwell Rd., SW9. 01-274 7777 **AZ 2K 93**
Bromley, 1 Westmoreland Rd. 01-460 9911 **AZ 5G 127**
Camberwell, 3 Blenheim Gro., SE15. 01-732 1091 **AZ 2G 95**
  Supplementary Benefits and General Enquiries only.
Canning Town, 199 Freemasons Rd., E16. 01-476 3667 **AZ 5K 65**
Chelsea, Waterford Ho., Waterford Rd,. SW6. 01-736 3399 **AZ 7K 75**
City, Adelaide Ho., London Bri., EC4. 01-629 3499 **3A 40**
  Excluding Supplementary Benefits.
Cricklewood, 249 Cricklewood Broadway, NW2. 01-450 8090 **AZ 3F 43**
Croydon, Concord Ho., 454 London Rd., 01-689 8122 **AZ 1B 134**
Crystal Palace, 9 Cargreen Rd., SE25. 01-653 8822 **AZ 4F 125**
Dagenham, 270 Heathway. 01-592 2131 **AZ 3F 53**
  Exluding Supplementary Benefits.
Ealing, Woodgrange Ho., Uxbridge Rd., W5. 01-992 3461 **AZ 7E 56**
Edgware, Middlesex Ho., 29 High St. 01-952 2323 **AZ 6B 12**
Edmonton, St. George's Chambers, 23 S. Mall, N9. 01-803 1313 **AZ 3B 18**
Eltham, 40 Welling High St., Welling 01-301 3822 **AZ 3B 100**
  Supplementary Benefits only.
Eltham, 62 Well Hall Rd., SE9. 01-850 2102 **AZ 3C 98**
  Excluding Supplementary Benefits.
Euston, 1 Melton St., NW1. 01-387 4366 **AZ 3H 61**
Finsbury Park, Archway Tower, 2 Junction Rd., N19. 01-272 7788 **AZ 3C 45**
Greenwich Park, 110 Norman Rd., SE10. 01-858 8070 **AZ 7D 80**
Greenwich W., 110 Norman Rd., SE10. 01-858 8070 **AZ 7D 80**
  Supplementary Benefits and General Enquiries only.
Hackney, 17 Sylvester Rd., E8. 01-986 3200 **AZ 6H 47**
Harlesden, 161 High St., NW10. 01-965 6506 **AZ 2B 58**
Harrow, Bradstowe Ho., Junction Rd. 01-863 5500 **AZ 6J 23**
Hendon, 10 Finchley La., NW4. 01-203 0091 **AZ 4E 26**
Highgate, Archway Tower, 2 Junction Rd., N19. 01-272 3050 **AZ 3G 45**
Hornchurch, Crown Ho., 40 North St. Hornchurch 52533
  Excluding Supplementary Benefits.
Hounslow, 10 Montague Rd. 01-572 7355
Hoxton, 30 Drysdale St., N1. 01-739 8400 **4D 47**
Kennington, 6 Camberwell New Rd., SE5. 01 582 4511 **AZ 7A 78**
  Supplementary Benefits and General Enquiries only.
Kennington Park, 206–210 Kennington Park Rd., SE11. 01-735 8747 **AZ 6A 78**
Kensington, 375 Kensington High St., W14. 01-605 9600 **AZ 3H 75**
Kingston-upon-Thames, 3 Brook St. 01-549 1400 **AZ 2E 18**
Lewisham, 9 Rushey Grn., SE6. 01-698 6144 **AZ 7D 96**
Leytonstone, 1 Lemna Rd., E11. 01-556 8877 **AZ 7G 33**
Neasden, Chancel Ho., Neasden La., NW10. 01-459 8844 **AZ 4A 42**
Notting Hill, 1 Chepstow Pl., W2. 01-229 3456 **1B 26**
Orpington, The Walnuts, High St. Orpington 26721
Paddington, Tresco Ho., 65 Lisson Gro., NW1. 01-402 4155 **AZ 4B 60**
Peckham, 1 Bournemouth Rd., SE15. 01-639 2040 **AZ 2G 95**
Plaistow, 760 Barking Rd., E13. 01-552 5421 **AZ 5H 65**
Poplar, 13 Dod St., E14. 01-987 1231 **AZ 6C 64**
Richmond, Parkshot Ho., Parkshot. 01-940 6011 **AZ 6D 88**
  Excluding Supplementary Benefits.
Romford, 30 Main Rd. Romford 66911
Shoreditch, 3 Bonhill St., EC2. 01-588 5955 **2A 24**

Southwark, Wedge Ho., 32 Blackfriars Rd., SE1. 01-928 4949 **1A 54**
Stepney, 16 Prescot St., E1. 01-480 6721 **AZ 7F 63**
   Excluding Supplementary Benefits.
   58 Nelson St., E1. 01-790 3382 **AZ 6H 63**
   Supplementary Benefits only.
Stoke Newington, 52 Arcola St., E8. 01-254 1244 **AZ 5F 47**
Streatham, Crown Ho., Station App., SW16. 01-677 8122 **AZ 5H 109**
Surbiton, Government Bldgs., Hook Rise, S. Tolworth. 01-337 6611
   Supplementary Benefits only.
Sutton, Sentinel Ho., 6 Sutton Ct. Rd. 01-643 3377 **AZ 6A 132**
   Excluding Supplementary Benefits.
   348 High St. 01-642 4477 **AZ 4K 131**
   Supplementary Benefits only.
Thames N., 31 Scarborough St., E1. 01-709 0611 **AZ 6F 63**
   Supplementary Benefits and General Enquiries only.
Thames S., Keyworth St., SE1. 01-928 8077 **3A 54**
   Supplementary Benefits and General Enquiries only.
Tottenham, 640 High Rd., N17. 01-808 4599 **AZ 4F 31**
Twickenham, 121 Heath Rd. 01-892 5671 **AZ 1K 103**
Uxbridge, Colham Ho., Baker Rd. Uxbridge 38601
Walthamstow, 656a Forest Rd., E17. 01-520 5533 **AZ 4J 31**
Wandsworth, Arndale Ho., Arndale Wlk., SW18. 01-870 1451 **AZ 5K 91**
   Supplementary Benefits only
West End, Colquhoun Ho., Broadwick St., W1. 01-734 7010 **2A 34**
   Excluding Supplementary Benefits.
Westminster, 4 Regency St., SW1. 01-834 8433 **2B 64**
Wimbledon, 3 Palmerston Rd., SW19. 01-543 6211 **AZ 7J 107**
   Excluding Supplementary Benefits.
   30 St. Georges Rd., SW19. 01-947 6531 **AZ 6H 107**
   Supplementary Benefits only.
Woodgrange Park, 544 Romford Rd., E7. 01-472 1411 **AZ 6G 49**
Wood Green, 1 Western Rd., N22. 01-888 8351 **AZ 2K 29**
Woolwich, Woolwich Crown Bldg., 48 Woolwich N. Rd., SE18. 01-854 2275
AZ 5E 82

SOCIETIES AND ASSOCIATIONS

ARTS, BUSINESS, INDUSTRIAL AND PROFESSIONAL
Aeronautical Soc., Royal, 4 Hamilton Pl., W1. 01-499 3515 **2A 48**
Agricultural Soc. of England, Royal, 35 Belgrave Sq., SW1. 01-235 5323 **3D 47**
Architects, Royal Inst. of British, 66 Portland Pl., W1. 01-580 5533 **1B 16**
Architectural Ass., 34 Bedford Sq., WC1. 01-636 0974 **2B 18**
Artists, Royal Soc. of British, 17 Carlton Ho. Ter., SW1. 01-930 6844 **1B 50**
Arts Council of Great Britain, 105 Piccadilly, W1. 01-629 9495 **2B 48**
Arts, Royal Acad. of Burlington Ho., Piccadilly, W1. 01-734 9052 **2B 48**
Arts, Royal Soc. of, 8 John Adam St., WC2. 01-930 5115 **3D 35**
Astronomical Ass., British, Burlington Ho., Piccadilly, W1. 01-734 4145 **2B 48**
Astronomical Soc., Royal, Burlington Ho., Piccadilly, W1. 01-734 4582 **2B 48**
Authors, Playwrights & Composers, Soc of, 84 Drayton Gdns., SW10. 01-373 6642 **AZ 5A 76**
Automobile Ass., Fanum Ho., 5 New Coventry St., WC2. 01-954 7373 **3B 34**
Bankers, Inst. of, 10 Lombard St., EC3. 01-623 3531 **1A 50**
British Council, 10 Spring Gdns., SW1. 01-930 8466 **1C 51**
Civil Engineers, Inst. of, Great George St., SW1. 01-222 7722 **3C 51**

Chartered Accountants in England & Wales, Inst. of, Moorgate Pl., EC2. 01-628 7060 **3D 23**

Chartered Surveyors, Royal Inst. of, 12 Gt. George St., SW1. 01-222 7000 **3C 51**

Chemical Industry, Soc. of, 14 Belgrave Sq., SW1. 01-235 3681 **3D 47**

Chemical Society, 9 Savile Row, W1. 01-437 4231 **2D 33**

Chemistry, Royal Soc. of, Burlington Ho., Piccadilly, W1. 01-734 9971 **3D 33**

Chiropodists, Soc. of, 53 Welbeck St., W1. 01-486 3381 **3A 16**

Civic Trust, 17 Carlton Ho. Ter., SW1. 01-930 0914 **1B 50**

Commerce, Ass. of British Chambers of, 212 Shaftesbury Av., WC2. 01-240 5831 **2B 34**

Commonwealth Soc., Royal, 18 Northumberland Av., WC2. 01-930 6733 **1C 51**

Computer Society, Brit., 13 Mansfield St., W1. 01-637 0471 **3B 16**

Confederation of Brit. Industry, Centre Point, New Oxford St., WC1. 01-379 7400 **3B 18**

Construction Industry Research Ass., 6 Storey's Ga., SW1. 01-222 8891 **3C 51**

Contemporary Arts, Inst. of, Nash Ho., Carlton Ho. Ter., SW1. 01-930 0493 **1B 50**

Directors, Inst. of, 116 Pall Mall, SW1. 01-839 1233 **1B 50**

Economic & Social Research, National Inst. of, 2 Dean Trench St., SW1. 01-222 7665 **1C 65**

Electrical Engineers, Inst. of, Savoy Pl., WC1. 01-240 1871 **3D 35**

English Ass., 1 Priory Gdns., W4. 01-995 4236 **AZ 4A 74**

English Speaking Union, 37 Charles St., W1. 01–629 8995 **3B 32**

Esperanto Ass., 140 Holland Park Av., W11. 01-727 7821 **AZ 1G 75**

Film Inst., British, 127 Charing Cross Rd., WC2. 01-437 4355 **1B 34**

Flower Arrangement Soc. of Gt. Britain, Nat. Ass. of, 21 Denbigh St., SW1. 01-828 5145 **3D 63**

Folk Dance & Song Soc., English, 2 Regent's Pk. Rd., NW1. 01-485 2206 **AZ 1D 60**

Folk Lore Soc., c/o The Library, University College, Gower St., WC1. 01-387 5894 **1A 18**

Gas Engineers, Inst. of, 17 Grosvenor Cres., SW1. 01-245 9811 **3A 48**

Genealogists, Soc. of, 37 Harrington Gdns., SW7. 01-373 7054 **3A 58**

Geographical Soc., Royal, 1 Kensington Gore, SW7. 01-589 5466 **3B 44**

Geological Soc., Burlington Ho., Piccadilly, W1. 01-734 2356 **2B 48**

Graphic Artists, Soc of, 17 Carlton Ho. Ter., SW1. 01-930 6844 **1B 50**

Heraldry Soc., 28 Museum St., WC1. 01-580 5110 **3C 19**

Historical Ass., 59a Kennington Pk. Rd., SE11. 01-735 3901 **AZ 6A 78**

Historical Soc., Royal, University College, Gower St., WC1. 01-387 7532 **1A 18**

Historic & Artistic Works, Int. Inst. for the Conservation of, 6 Buckingham St., WC2. 01-839 5975 **3D 35**

Horticultural Soc., Royal, Horticultural Hall, Vincent Sq., SW1. 01-834 4333 **3A 64**

House-Building Council, National, 58 Portland Pl., W1. 01-637 1248 **1B 16**

Industrial Artists & Designers, Society of, 12 Carlton Ho. Ter., SW1. 01-839 4453 **1B 50**

International Affairs, Royal Inst. of, 10 St. James's Sq., SW1. 01-930 2233 **3A 34**

Landscape Architects, Inst. of, Nash Ho., 12 Carlton Ho. Ter., SW1. 01-839 4044 **1B 50**

Law Society, 113 Chancery La., WC2. 01-242 1222 **3B 20**

Library Ass., 7 Ridgmount St., WC1. 01-636 7543 **2B 18**

Literature, Royal Soc of, 1 Hyde Pk. Gdns., W2. 01-723 5104 **2D 29**

London Motor Cab Proprietors' Ass., Haverstock Hill, NW3. 01-794 2200 **AZ 5C 44**

Mechanical Engineers, Inst. of, 1 Birdcage Walk, SW1. 01-222 7899 **3D 49**

Medical Ass., British, B.M.A. Ho., Tavistock Sq., WC1. 01-387 4499 **3B 10**

Medical Council, General, 44 Hallam St., W1. 01-580 7642 **2C 17**
Medicine, Royal Soc. of, 1 Wimpole St., W1. 01-580 2070 **1B 32**
Metals Society, 1 Carlton House Ter., SW1. 01-839 4071 **1B 50**
Mining & Metallurgy, Inst. of, 44 Portland Pl., W1. 01-580 3802 **1B 16**
Museums Ass., 34 Bloomsbury Way, WC1. 01-404 4767 **3D 19**
National Soc., 17 Carlton Ho. Ter., SW1. 01-930 6844 **1B 50**
Newcomen Soc., Science Museum, Exhibition Rd., SW7. 01-589 1793 **3C 45**
Oil Painters, Royal Inst. of, 17 Carlton Ho. Ter., SW1. 01-930 6844 **1B 50**
Painters in Watercolours, Royal Inst. of, 17 Carlton Ho. Ter., SW1. 01-930 6844 **1B 50**
Pastel Soc., 17 Carlton Ho. Ter., SW1. 01-930 6844 **1B 50**
Philatelic Soc., Royal, 41 Devonshire Pl., W1. 01-486 1044 **1A 16**
Philosophy, Royal Inst. of, 14 Gordon Sq., WC1. 01-387 4130 **1B 18**
Photographic Soc. of Gt. Britain, Royal, The Octagon, Milsom St., Bath. 62841
Physics, The Inst. of, 47 Belgrave Sq., SW1. 01-235 6111 **1A 62**
Poetry Soc, 21 Earls Ct. Sq., SW5. 01-373 7861 **AZ 5K 75**
Psychical Research, Soc. for, 1 Adam & Eve M., W8. 01-937 8984 **3C 43**
Psycho-Analytical Society, British, 63 New Cavendish St., W1. 01-580 4952 **3A 16**
Public Health & Hygiene, Royal Inst. of, 28 Portland Pl., W1. 01-580 2731 **1B 16**
Records Ass., British, The Charterhouse, Charterhouse Sq., EC1. 01-253 0436 **2B 22**
Royal Automobile Club, 89/91 Pall Mall, SW1. 01-930 2345 **1A 50**
Royal Institution of Gt. Britain, 21 Albemarle St., W1. 01-409 2992 **3C 33**
Royal Soc., 6 Carlton Ho. Ter., SW1. 01-839 5561 **1B 50**
Science Technology, Inst. of, Staple Inn, High Holborn. 01-837 2207 **3A 20**
Sculptors, Royal Soc. of British, 108a Old Brompton Rd., SW7. 01-373 5554 **3B 58**
Sociological Ass., British, 10 Portugal St., WC2. 01-242 3388 **1A 36**
Standards Inst., British, 2 Park St., W1. 01-629 9000 **2D 31**
Statistical Soc., Royal, 25 Enford St., W1. 01-725 5882 **2B 14**
Structural Engineers, Inst. of, 11 Up. Belgrave St., SW1. 01-235 4535 **1A 62**
Theosophical Soc. in England, 50 Gloucester Pl., W1. 01-935 9261 **2C 15**
Town & Country Planning Ass., 17 Carlton Ho. Ter., SW1. 01-930 8903 **1B 50**
Trade, National Chamber of, Enterprise Ho., Pack Prime La., Henley. Henley 6161
Trades Union Congress, Gt. Russell St., WC1. 01-636 4030 **3B 18**
Women's Inst., Nat. Fed. of, 39 Eccleston St., SW1. 01-730 7212 **2B 62**

ENVIRONMENT

Ancient Buildings, Soc. for the Protection of, 37 Spital Sq., E1. 01-377 1644 **2C 25**
Ancient Monuments Soc., St. Andrew by the Wardrobe, Q. Victoria St., EC4. 01-236 3934 **2A 38**
Archaeology, Council for British, 112 Kennington Rd., SE11. 01-582 0491 **1C 67**
Birds, Royal Soc. for the Protection of, The Lodge, Sandy, Beds. Sandy 80551
British Trust for Ornithology, Beech Grove, Tring, Herts. Tring 3461
British Trust for Conservation Volunteers, London Ecology Centre, 80 York Way, N1. 01-278 4293 **1D 11**
Civic Trust, 7 Carlton Ho. Ter., SW1. 01-930 0914 **1B 50**
Conservation Society, 12a Guildford St., Chertsey, Surrey. Chertsey 60975
Council for Places of Worship, 83 London Wall, EC2. 01-638 0971 **2C 23**
Countryside Commission, J. Dower House, Crescent Pl., Cheltenham, Gloucestershire. Cheltenham 21381
County Nature Conservation Trusts, c/o Society for Promotion of N.C. The Green, Nettleham, Lincoln. Lincoln 52326
Environmental Trust, 31 Clerkenwell Clo., EC1. 01-251 4818 **1D 21**
Friends of the Earth, 377 City Rd., EC1. 01-837 0731 **1A 24**

Georgian Group, 37 Spital Sq., E1. 01-377 1722 **2C 25**
Greenpeace, 6 Endsleigh St., WC1. 01-387 5370 **3B 10**
Inland Waterways Ass., 114 Regents Pk. Rd., NW1. 01-586 2556 **AZ 1D 60**
Interplanetary Soc., British, 27 S. Lambeth Rd., SW8. 01-735 3160 **AZ 2J 77**
Keep Britain Tidy Group, 11 St. Chads St., WC1. 01-278 9954 **2D 11**
Maritime Trust, 16 Ebury St., SW1. 01-730 0096 **2B 62**
Metropolitan Public Gardens Ass., 4 Carlos Pl., W1. 01-493 6617 **2A 32**
National Gardens Scheme, 57 Lwr. Belgrave St., SW1. 01-730 0359 **1C 62**
National Trust, 42 Queen Anne's Ga., SW1. 01-222 9251 **3A 50**
Nature Conservancy, 19 Belgrave Sq., SW1. 01-235 3241 **3D 47**
Nature, Council for, Zoological Gdns., Regent Pk., NW1. 01-722 7111 **1A 8**
Pilgrim Trust, Fielden Ho., Little College St., SW1. 01-222 4723 **1C 65**
Ramblers' Ass. 1/5 Wandsworth Rd., SW8. 01-582 6826 **AZ 3F 93**
Royal Commission on Historical Monuments, 23 Savile Row, W1. 01-734 6010 **2D 33**
R.S.P.B. see **Birds.**
Rural England, Council for the Protection of, 4 Hobart Pl., SW1. 01-235 4771 **1B 62**
Town & Country Planning Ass., 17 Carlton Ho. Ter., SW1. 01-930 8903 **1B 50**
Victorian Soc., 1 Priory Gdns., W4. 01-994 1019 **AZ 4A 74**
World Wildlife Fund, Godalming. Godalming 20551
Zoological Soc., Outer Circle, Regents Park, NW1. 01-722 3333 **1B 8**

HUMANE
Abortion Law Reform Ass., 88b Islington High St., N1. 01-359 5209 **AZ 2A 62**
Accidents, Royal Soc. for the Prevention of, 1 Grosvenor Cres., SW1. 01-235 6889 **2A 48**
Age Concern, England, 60 Pitcairn Rd., Mitchum. 01-640 5431 **AZ 7D 108**
Aid to Refugees, British Council for, Bondway Ho., Bond Way, SW8. 01-582 6922 **AZ 6J 77**
Amnesty International, 5 Roberts Pl., EC1. 01-251 8371 **1D 21**
Animals, Royal Soc. for the Prevention of Cruelty to, Manor Ho., Horsham, Sussex. Horsham 64181. See also page 199
Anti-Apartheid Movement, 13 Mandela St., NW1. 01-387 7966 **AZ 1G 61**
Barnardo's Dr., Tanners La., Barkingside, Ilford. 01-550 8822 **AZ 3G 35**
Blind, Royal Nat. Inst. for, 224 Gt. Portland St., W1. 01-388 1266 **1C 17**
Blue Cross, Admin., 1 Hugh St, SW1. 01-834 5556 **3B 62**
British Legion, Royal, 8 Pall Mall, SW1. 01-930 8131 **1A 50**
Campaign for the Homeless and Rootless (CHAR), 5 Cromer St., WC1. 01-833 2071 **3D 11**
Cancer Research Campaign, 2 Carlton Ho. Ter., SW1. 01-930 8972 **1B 50**
Care & Resettlement of Offenders, Nat. Ass. for, 169 Clapham Rd., SW9. 01-582 6500 **AZ 3J 93**
Cheshire Foundation Homes for the Sick, 26 Maunsel St., SW1. 01-828 1822 **2B 64**
Chest & Heart Ass., Tavistock Ho. N., Tavistock Sq., WC1. 01-387 3012 **3B 10**
Child Birth Trust, The National, 9 Queensborough Ter., W2. 01-221 3833 **2A 28**
Child Poverty Action Group, 1 Macklin St., WC2. 01-242 3225 **1D 35**
Children, Nat. Soc. for the Prevention of Cruelty to, 1 Riding Ho. St., W1. 01-580 8812 **3C 17**
Children's Bureau, Nat., 8 Wakley St., EC1. 01-278 9441 **AZ 3B 62**
Christian Aid, H.Q., Ferndale Rd., SW9. 01-733 5500 **AZ 4J 93**
Church of England Children's Soc., Old Town Hall, Kennington Rd., SE11. 01-735 2441 **1C 67**
Civil Liberties, Nat. Council for, 21 Tabard St., SE1. 01-403 3888 **3D 55**
Community Service Volunteers, 237 Pentonville Rd., N1. 01-278 6601 **AZ 2K 61**
Cruel Sports, League Against, 83 Union St., SE1. 01-407 0979 **2A 54**
Deaf, Royal Nat. Inst. for, 105 Gower St., WC1. 01-387 8033 **1A 18**

Deep Sea Fishermen, Royal Nat. Mission to, 43 Nottingham Pl., W1. 01-487 5101 **2A 16**

Disabled, Central Council for, 25 Mortimer St., W1. 01-637 5400 **3D 17**

Disabled, John Grooms Ass. for, 10 Gloucester Dr., N4. 01-802 7272 **AZ 2B 46**

Drug Dependence, Inst. for the study of, Kingsbury Ho., 3 Blackburn Rd. NW6. 01-328 5541 **AZ 6K 43**

Epilepsy Ass., British, New Wokingham Rd., Wokingham. Crowthorne 3122

Ex-Services League, British Commonwealth, 48 Pall Mall, SW1. 01-930 8131 **1A 50**

Family Housing Ass., 189a Old Brompton Rd., SW5. 01-373 3176 **3A 58**

Family Planning Ass., 27 Mortimer St., W1. 01-636 7866 **3C 17**

Fauna Preservation Soc., Zoological Gdns., Regents Pk., NW1. 01-586 0872 **1A 8**

Fawcett Society, 46 Harleyford Rd., SE11. 01-587 1287 **6K 77**

Help the Aged, 1 Sekforde St., EC1. 01-253 0253 **1D 21**

Horses, Int., League for the Protection of, 67a Camden High St., NW1. 01-388 1449 **1F 61**

Institute of Cancer Research, 34 Sumner Pl., SW7. 01-352 8133 **3C 59**

Lifeboat Institution, Royal Nat., 202 Lambeth Rd., SE1. 01-928 5742 **1C 67**

Marie Curie Mem. Foundation, 28 Belgrave Sq., SW1. 01-235 3325 **3A 48**

Marie Stopes Clinic, 108 Whitfield St., W1. 01-388 0662 **1D 17**

Marriage Guidance Council, 76a New Cavendish St., W1. 01-580 1087 **3A 16**

Mental Health, Nat. Ass. for, (MIND), 22 Harley St., W1. 01-637 0741 **1B 46**

Mentally Handicapped Children, Royal Soc. for, MENCAP—123 Golden La., EC1. 01-253 9433 **1C 23**

Multiple Sclerosis Soc., 286 Munster Rd., SW6. 01-381 4022 **AZ 7G 75**

Muscular Dystrophy Group, Macaulay Rd., SW4. 01-720 8055 **AZ 3F 93**

N.S.P.C.C. see **Children.**

Nuclear Disarmament, Campaign for, 11 Goodwin St., N4. 01-263 0977 **AZ 2A 46**

One Parent Families, Nat. Council for, 255 Kentish Town Rd., NW5. 01-267 1361 **AZ 7F 45**

Oxfam, London Office, 333 Upper Richmond Rd. West, SW14. 01-876 3599 **AZ 4G 89**

Peace Council, Nat., 29 Gt. James St., WC1. 01-242 3228 **2A 20**

Penal Reform, Howard League for, 320 Kennington Pk. Rd., SE11. 01-735 3317 **AZ 6A 78**

Planned Parenthood, Int., 18 Regent St., SW1. 01-839 2911 **1C 33**

Race Relations, Inst. of, 247 Pentonville Rd., N1. 01-837 0041 **AZ 2K 61**

Red Cross Soc., British, 9 Grosvenor Cres., SW1. 01-235 5454 **3A 48**

Release, 1 Elgin Av., W9. 01-289 1123 **AZ 4J 59**

R.S.P.C.A. see **Animals.**

Sailors Soc. (At Home & Abroad), British, 406 Eastern Av., Gants Hill. 01-554 6285 **AZ 6E 34**

St. John Ambulance Brigade, 1 Grosvenor Cres., SW1. 01-235 5231 **3A 48**

St. Mungo Community Trust, 21 Abercrombie St., SW11. 01-240 5431 **AZ 2C 92**

Salvation Army, Int. Headquarters, 101 Queen Victoria St., EC4. 01-236 5222 **2B 38**

Samaritans, The, 39 Walbrook, EC4. (Crypt of St. Stephen). 01-626 9000 **2D 39**

Save the Children Fund, Mary Datchelor Ho., 17 Grove La., SE5. 01-703 5400 **AZ 1D 95**

Shaftesbury Society, Fairlight Hall, Fairlight Rd., SW17. 01-672 1783 **AZ 4B 108**

Shelter, Nat. Campaign for the Homeless, 157 Waterloo Rd., SE1. 01-633 9377 **2C 53**

Social Service, London Council of, 68 Charlton St., NW1. 01-388 0241 **1A 10**

Soldiers', Sailors' & Airmens' Families Ass., 27 Queen Anne's Ga., SW1. 01-222 9221 **3A 50**

Spastics Society, 12 Park Crescent, W1. 01-636 5020 **1B 16**

Spina Bifida & Hydrocephalus, Ass. for, Tavistock Ho. North, Tavistock Sq., WC1. 01-388 1382 **1B 18**

Temperance Alliance, United Kingdom, 12 Caxton St., SW1. 01-222 5880 **1A 64**

Toc H., 38 Newark St., E1. 01-247 5110 **AZ 5H 63**

Unborn Children, Soc. for the Protection of, 7 Tufton St., SW1. 01-222 5845 **1C 65**

United Nations Children's Fund, 55 Lincoln's Inn Fields, WC2. 01-405 5592 **3A 20**

Vegetarian Soc. of the United Kingdom, 53 Marloes Rd., W8. 01-937 7739 **AZ 3K 75**

Vivisection, British Union for the Abolition of, 16a Crane Gro., N7. 01-607 1545 **AZ 6A 46**

Voluntary Euthanasia Society, 13 Prince of Wales Ter., W8. 01-937 7770 **3A 44**

Voluntary Service, Int., 53 Regent Rd., Leicester. Leic. 541862

Voluntary Service Overseas, 9 Belgrave Sq., SW1. 01-235 5191 **3A 48**

War on Want, 1 London Bridge St., E1. 01-403 2266 **1A 56**

Women's Int. League for Peace and Freedom, 17 Victoria Park Sq., E2. 01-928 1030 **AZ 3J 63**

Women's Royal Voluntary Service, 17 Old Park La., W1. 01-499 6040 **1A 48**

POLITICAL

Bow Group, 240 High Holborn, WC1. 01-405 0878 **3A 20**

Commonwealth Parliamentary Ass., Houses of Parliament, SW1. 01-219 4666 **3D 51**

Communist Party of Gt. Britain, 16 St. John St., EC2. 01-251 4406 **1A 22**

Conservative & Unionist Central Office, 32 Smith Sq., SW1. 01-222 9000 **1C 65**

Co-operative Party, 158 Buckingham Pal. Rd., SW1. 01-730 8187 **3B 62**

European Movement, 1a Whitehall Pl., SW1. 01-839 6622 **1C 51**

Fabian Society, 11 Dartmouth St., SW1. 01-222 8877 **3B 50**

Green Alliance, 60 Chandos Pl., WC2. 01-836 0341 **3C 35**

Labour Party, 150 Walworth Rd., SE17. 01-703 0833 **AZ 4C 78**

Liberal Party Organization, 1 Whitehall Pl., SW1. 01-839 4092 **1C 51**

Social Democratic Party, 4 Cowley St., SW1. 01-222 4141 **1C 65**

Socialist Party of Gt. Britain, 52 Clapham High St., SW4. 01-622 3811 **AZ 4H 93**

Young Conservative Org., 32 Gt. Smith St., SW1. 01-222 9000 **1C 65**

Young Liberals, National League of, 1 Whitehall Pl., SW1. 01-839 2727 **1C 51**

RELIGIOUS

Baptist Ass., London, 4 Southampton Row, WC1. 01-242 7815 **2D 19**

Baptist Union, 4 Southampton Row, WC1. 01-405 9803 **2D 19**

Bible & Medical Missionary Fellowship, 352 Kennington Rd., SE11. 01-735 8227 **1C 67**

Bible Reading Fellowship, 2 Elizabeth St., SW1. 01-730 9181 **3B 62**

Bible Society, 146 Queen Victoria St., EC4. 01-248 4751 **2A 38**

Bible Students Ass., Int., Watch Tower Ho., The Ridgeway, NW7. 01-906 2211 **AZ 4J 13**

Billy Graham Evangelistic Ass., 27 Camden Rd., NW1. 01-267 0065 **AZ 7G 45**

British Council of Churches, 2 Eaton Gate, SW1. 01-730 9611 **2D 61**

British & Foreign Bible Society, see **Bible Society**

Buddhist Society, 58 Eccleston Sq., SW1. 01-834 5858 **3C 63**

Congregational Union, London, City Temple, Holborn Viaduct, EC1. 01-353 5660 **3D 21**

Christian Action, 308 Kennington La., SE11. 01-735 2372 **AZ 5K 77**

Christian Aid, HQ., 240 Ferndale Rd., SW19. 01-733 5500 **AZ 4J 93**

Christian Alliance of Women & Girls, Exton St., SE1. 01-633 0533 **2C 53**

Christian Community in Gt. Britain, 34 Glenilla Rd., NW3. 01-722 3587 **AZ 6C 44**

Christian Economic & Social Research Foundation, 12 Caxton St., W1. 01-222 4001 **1A 64**
Christian Study Centre, St. Margaret Pattens Church, Eastcheap, EC3. 01-623 6630 **2B 40**
Church Army, CSC House, N. Circular Rd., NW10. 01-903 3763 **AZ 3F 57**
Church House, Dean's Yard, SW1. 01-222 9011 **1C 65**
Church Lads Brigade, 15 Etchingham Park Rd., N3. 01-349 2616 **AZ 7E 14**
Church Missionary Society, 157 Waterloo Rd., SE1. 01-928 8681 **2C 53**
Church of England's Children's Soc., Old Town Hall, Kennington Rd., SE11. 01-735 2441 **1C 67**
Church of England Enquiry Centre, Church Ho., Dean's yd., SW1. 01-222 9011 **1C 65**
Church Union, 7 Tufton St., SW1. 01-222 6952 **1C 65**
Friends, Religious Soc. of, Euston Rd., NW1. 01-387 3601 **1C 17**
Hindu Centre, 39 Grafton Ter., NW5. 01-485 8200 **AZ 5D 44**
Int. Soc. Temple for Krishna Consciousness, 9 Soho St., W1. 01-437 3662 **1B 34**
Latin Mass Soc., 3 Cork St., W1. 01-434 2685 **3C 33**
London City Mission, 175 Tower Bridge Rd., SE1. 01-407 7585 **3C 57**
Lord's Day Observance Soc., 47 Parish La., SE20. 01-659 1117 **AZ 6K 111**
Methodist Missionary Soc., 25 Marylebone Rd., NW1. 01-935 2541 **2B 14**
Naval, Military & Air Force Bible Soc., Radstock Ho., Eccleston St., SW1. 01-730 2155 **2B 62**
Open Air Mission, 19 John St., WC1. 01-405 6135 **1B 20**
Order of the Cross, 10 DeVere Gdns., W8. 01-937 7012 **3A 44**
Order of St. John, 6 Grosvenor Cres., SW1. 01-235 7131 **3A 48**
Protestant Truth Soc., 184 Fleet St., EC4. 01-405 4960 **1C 37**
St. Francis, Soc. of, 42 Balaam St., E13. 01-476 5189 **AZ 4J 65**
St. John the Evangelist, Soc. of, 22 Gt. College St., SW1. 01-222 9234 **1C 65**
Salvation Army, 101 Queen Victoria St., EC4. 01-236 5222 **2A 38**
Scientology, Church of, 68 Tottenham Ct. Rd., W1. 01-580 3601 **1D 17**
Spiritualist Ass. of Gt. Britain, 33 Belgrave Sq., SW1. 01-235 3351 **3D 47**
Student Christian Movement, 1 Lambeth Rd., SE1. 01-587 0474 **2A 66**
Society for Promoting Christian Knowledge, Holy Trinity Church, Marylebone Rd., NW1. 01-388 2162 **2B 14**
United Soc. for the Propagation of the Gospel, 15 Tufton St., SW1. 01-222 4222 **1C 65**
World Ass. for Christian Communication, 122 Kings Rd., SW3. 01-589 1484 **3C 61**
World Revival Crusade, 17 Sumburgh Rd., SW12. 01-228 7363 **1C 92**
Young Christian Workers, 21 Tooting Beck Rd., SW17. 01-765 8208 **AZ 3E 108**
Young Men's Christian Ass., National Council, 640 Forest Rd., E17. 01-520 5599 **AZ 4J 31**
Young Women's Christian Ass., 2 Weymouth St., W1. 01-636 9722 **2A 16**

SPORT AND RECREATION

Athletic Ass., Amateur, Francis Ho., Francis St., SW1. 01-828 9326 **1A 64**
Auto-Cycle Union. Millbuck Ho., Corporation St., Rugby. Rugby 70332
Badminton Ass. of England, Nat. Badminton Centre, Bradwell Rd., Loughton Lodge, Milton Keynes. M. Keynes 568822
Bicycle Polo Ass. of Gt. Britain, 5 Puffin Gdns., Peel Common, Gosport, Hants. Fareham 285967
Billiards & Snooker Control Council, Coronet Ho., Queen St., Leeds. 0532 440586
Boxing Ass., Amateur, Francis Ho., Francis St., SW1. 01-828 8568 **1A 64**
Boxing Board of Control, British, Ramillies Bldgs., Hills Pl., W1. 01-437 1475 **1D 33**

British Amateur Baseball Fed., 197 Newbridge Rd., Hull, N. Humberside. Hull 76169

British Amateur Dancers' Ass., 14 Oxford St., W1. 01-636 0851 **1A 34**

British Amateur Gymnastic Ass., 2 Buckingham Avenue E., Slough, Berks. Slough 32763

British Amateur Weight Lifters' Ass., 3 Iffley Turn, Oxford. Oxford 778319

British Amateur Wrestling Ass., 38 Rodney St., Mitcham. 01-640 0316

British Balloon & Airship Club, Kimberley Ho., 47 Vaughan Way, Leicester. Leics. 531051

British Bobsleigh Ass., Nat. Bobsleigh Centre, Thorpe Park, Staines Lane Chertsey, Surrey: Chertsey 60157

British Canoe Union, Flexel Ho., 45 High St., Addlestone, Weybridge, Surrey. Weybridge 41341

British Crown Green Bowling Association, 14 Leighton Av., Maghull, Liverpool. 051-526 8367

British Cycling Federation, 16 Upper Woburn Pl., WC1. 01-387 9320 **3B 10**

British Darts Organisation, 47 Creighton Av., NW10. 01-883 5055

British Handball Ass., 90 Penryn Av., Fishermead, Milton Keynes, Buckinghamshire. Milton Keynes 678389

British Horse Society, National Equestrian Centre, Stoneleigh, Kenilworth, Warwickshire. Coventry 52241

British Ice Hockey Ass., 48 Barmouth Rd., Shirley, Croydon.

British Korfball Ass., 2 Torrington Clo., Mereworth, Maidstone, Kent. 0622 813115

British Mountaineering Council, Crawford Ho., Precinct Centre, Booth Street East, Manchester. 061 273 5835

British Orienteering Fed., Riversdale, Dale Rd., N. Darley Dale, Matlock, Derbys. 0629 734042

British Petanque Ass., 126 Rosebank Rd., Countesthorpe, Leics. 0533 772796

British Racquetball Ass., 50 Tredegar Rd., Wilmington, Dartford, Kent. 0322 72200

British Racing Toboggan Ass., 89 Tenison Rd., Cambridge.

British Show Jumping Ass., National Equestrian Centre, Stoneleigh, Kenilworth, Warwickshire. Coventry 20783/4

British Softball Fed., 22 Osborne Drive, Chandlers Ford, Hants.

British Sub-Aqua Club, 16 Upper Woburn Pl., WC1. 01-387 9302

British Surfing Ass., Room 65, Burrows Chambers, East Burrow Rd., Swansea, West Glamorgan. Swansea 461476

British Tchouk-ball Ass., 65 Shaw Green La., Prestbury, Cheltenham. Gloucestershire. Cheltenham 31154

British Trampoline Fed. Ltd., 152a College Rd., Harrow, Middx. 01-863 7278

British Water Ski Fed. 390 City Rd., EC1. 01-833 2855 **1A 24**

British Wheel of Yoga, Grafton Grange, Grafton, York. 090-12 3386

Camping Club of Gt. Britain, 11 Lower Grosvenor Pl., SW1. 01-828 1012 **1B 62**

Caravan Club, East Grinstead, W. Sussex. E. Grinstead 26944

Central Council of Physical Recreation, Francis House, Francis St., SW1. 01-828 3163 **1A 64**

Clay Pigeon Shooting Ass., 107 Epping New Rd., Buckhurst Hill, Essex. 01-505 6221

County of London Archery Ass., 61 Carey St., WC2. 01-353 9758 **1B 36**

Cricket Council, The, Lord's Cricket Ground, NW8. 01-289 1611/5 **2D 5**

Croquet Ass., Hurlingham Club, Ranelagh Gdns., SW6. 01-736 3148 **AZ 3G 91**

Cruising Ass., Ivory Ho., St Katharines Dock, World Trade Centre, E1. 01-481 0881 **3D 41**

Cycle Speedway Council, 9 Meadow Close, Hethersett, Norwich. Norwich 811304

Cyclists' Touring Club, Cotterell Ho., 69 Meadrow, Godalming. 7217

Eaton Fives Ass., Saintbury Clo., Saintbury, Nr. Broadway, Worcs. 038 685 3465

English Basket Ball Ass., Calomax Ho., Lupton Av., Leeds. 496044
English Bowling Ass., 2a Iddesliegh Rd., Bournemouth, Dorset. B'mouth 22233
English Bowling Fed., 62 Frampton Pl., Boston, Lincs. Boston 66201
English Bowls Council, 15 Datchworth Ct., Village Rd., Enfield, Middx. 01-387 1269
English Curling Ass. 66 Preston Old Rd., Freckleton, Preston, Lancs. 0772 634154
English Folk Dance & Song Society, Cecil Sharp House, 2 Regent's Park Rd., NW1. 01-485 2206 **AZ 1D 60**
English Golf Union, 12a Denmark St., Wokingham, Berks. Wokingham 781952
English Indoor Bowling Ass., 730 Romford Rd., E12. 01-553 5539
English Lacrosse Union, Room 1, Bellfield Ho., Bellfield Av., Cheadle Hulme, Cheshire. 061-486 9784
English Ladies' Golf Ass., P.O. Box 14, 52 Boroughgate, Otley, West Yorkshire. Otley 464010
English Skateboard Ass., Maryland, Mareham-on-the-Hill, Horncastle, Lincs. 065-82 6012
English Table Tennis Ass., 21 Claremont, Hastings, E. Sussex. Hastings 433121
English Volleyball Ass., 13 Rectory Rd., W. Bridgeford, Notts. Nottingham 816324
English Women's Bowling Ass., 2 Inghalls Cottages, Box, Corsham, Wilts. Box 742852
English Women's Bowling Federation, "Devonia", 305 Dugsthorpe Rd., Peterborough, Cambridgeshire. Peterborough 52638
English Womens' Indoor Bowling Ass., 8 Oakfield Rd., Carterton, Oxford. 0993 841344
Fencing Ass., Amateur, 83 Perham Rd., W14. 01-385 7442
Field Sports Soc., British, 26 Caxton St., SW1. 01-222 5407 **1A 64**
Football Alliance, Amateur, Room 33, 6 Langley St., WC2. 01-240 3837 **1C 35**
Football Ass., 16 Lancaster Ga., W2. 01-262 4542 **2B 28**
Football League, Lytham St. Annes, Lancashire. St. Anne's 729421
Gliding Assoc., British, Kimberley Ho., 47 Vaughan Way, Leicester. Leics. 531051
Grand National Archery Soc., National Agricultural Centre, Stoneleigh, Kenilworth, Warwickshire. Coventry 23907
Greyhound Racing Club, Nat., Shipton Ho., Oval Rd., NW1. 01-267 9256 **AZ 1F 61**
Hang Gliding Ass., British, Cranfield Airfield, Cranfield, Beds. 0234 751688
Hockey Ass., 16 Upper Woburn Pl., WC1. 01-387 9315 **3B 10**
Hockey Ass., All England Women's, Argyle Ho., 29 Euston Rd., NW1. 01-278 2340 **AZ 1C 17**
Hover Club of Gt. Brit., 10 Long Acre, Bingham, Notts. 0949 37294
Judo Ass., British, 16 Upper Woburn Pl., WC1. 01-387 9340 **3B 10**
Keep Fit Ass., 16 Upper Woburn Pl., WC1. 01-387 4349 **3B 10**
Lacrosse Ass., All England Women's, 16 Upper Woburn Pl., WC1. 01-387 4430 **3B 10**
Ladies' Golf Union, 12 The Links, St. Andrews, Fife. St. Andrews 75811
Land Yacht Clubs, Brit. Fed. of, New Covert Ho., 23 Loughborough Rd., Holton, Nr Loughborough, Leicestershire. Lough. 880119
Lawn Tennis Ass., Palliser Rd., Barons Ct., W14. 01-385 2366 **AZ 5G 75**
Lawn Tennis Foundation of Gt. Britain, The Queens Club, Palliser Rd., W14. 01-385 4233/4 **AZ 5G 75**
London Football Ass., 4 Aldworth Grove, Lewisham, SE13. 01-690 9626
Long Distance Walking Ass., 11 Thorn Park, Guildford, Surrey.
Martial Arts Commission, 15/16 Deptford Broadway, SE8. 01-691 3433
Modern Pentathlon Ass., la Godstone Rd., Purley, Surrey. 01-668 7855
National Air Rifle and Pistol Ass., 44 High St., Bridgnorth, Shropshire. Bridgnorth 4855
National Anglers' Council, 11 Cowgate, Peterborough, Cambs. Peterborough 54084

National Caving Ass. c/o Dept. of Geography, University of Birmingham. P.O. Box 363, Birmingham.

National Cricket Ass., Lord's Cricket Ground, NW8. 01-289 1611/5 **2D 5**

National Fed. of Anglers, Halliday Ho., 2 Wilson St., Derby. Derby 362000

National Fed. of Sea Anglers, 26 Downsview Cres., Uckfield, E. Sussex. Uckfield 3589

National Rifle Ass., Bisley Camp, Brookwood, Woking, Surrey. Brookwood 2213

National Roller Hockey Ass. of Gt. Britain, 528 Loose Rd., Maidstone, Kent. Maidstone 43155

National Rounders Ass., 3 Danehurst Av., Nottingham. 0602 785514

National Skating Ass., 15–27 Gee St., EC1. 01-253 3824 **1B 22**

Netball Ass., All England, Francis Ho., Francis St., SW1. 01-828 2176 **1A 64**

Olympic Ass., British, 1 John Princes St., W1. 01-408 2029 **1C 33**

Outward Bound Trust, 360 Oxford St., W1. 01-491 1355 **1A 34**

Parachute Ass., British, Kimberley Ho., 47 Vaughan Way, Leicester 59635

Parascending Clubs, Ass. of, Room 6, Exchange Buildings, 34/50 Rutland St., Leicester. Leics. 530318

Physical Recreation, Central Council of, Francis House, Francis St., SW1. 01-828 3163 **1A 64**

Polo Ass., Hurlingham, Abersham Farm, Abersham, Midhurst, West Sussex, Lodsworth 277

RAC Motor Sports Ass. 31 Belgrave Sq., SW1. 01-235 8601

Race Walking Ass., 112 Lennard Rd., Beckenham, Kent. 01-659 4280

Ramblers' Ass. 1/5 Wandsworth Rd., SW8. 01-582 6878 **AZ 3F 93**

Rowing Ass., Amateur, 6 Lower Mall, W6. 01-748 3632 **AZ 5D 74**

Royal Aero Club, Kimberley Ho., 47 Vaughan Way, Leicester. 531051

Royal Pigeon Racing Ass. Redding Ho., The Reddings, Cheltenham, Glos.

Royal Yachting Ass., Victoria Way, Woking, Surrey. Woking 5022

Rugby Fives Ass., 127 Newlands Pk., SE26. 01-659 4159

Rugby Football League, 180 Chapeltown Rd., Leeds. Leeds 624637

Rugby Football Union, Whitton Rd., Twickenham, Middx. **AZ 6J 87**

Salmon & Trout Ass., Fishmongers Hall, London Bri., EC4. 01-626 3531 **3A 40**

Ski-Bob Ass. of Gt. Britain, 26 Broadmeads, Ware, Herts. 0920 61504

Ski Fed. of Gt. Britain, National, 118 Eaton Sq., SW1. 01-235 8227 **2A 62**

Small-Bore Rifle Ass., National, Lord Roberts House, Bisley Camp, Brookwood, Surrey. Brookwood 6969

Speedway Control Board, 31 Belgrave Sq., SW1. 01-235 8601 **3D 47**

Sports Council, 16 Upper Woburn Pl., WC1. 01-388 1277 **3B 10**

Sport & Physical Recreation, Int. Council of, c/o Sports Council.

Squash Rackets Ass., Francis Ho., Francis St., SW1. 01-828 3064 **1A 64**

Swimming Ass., Amateur, Harold Fern Ho., Derby Sq., Loughborough, Leics. Loughborough 30431

Tennis & Rackets Ass., c/o The Queen's Club, Palliser Rd., W14. 01-381 4746

Ten Pin Bowling Ass., British, 19 Canterbury Av., Ilford, Essex. 01-554 9137

Tug-of-War Ass., 57 Lynton Rd., Chesham, Bucks. 0494 783057

Wildfowlers' Ass. of Gt. Britain & Ireland, Marford Mill, Rossett, Wrexham, Clwyd. Rosset 570881

Women's Amateur Athletic Ass., c/o Amateur Athletic Ass.

Women's Cricket Ass., 16 Upper Woburn Pl., WC1. 01-387 3423 **3B 10**

Women's Football Ass., 11 Portsea Mews, W2. 01-402 9388

Women's Squash Rackets Ass., 345 Upper Richmond Rd W., Sheen, SW14. 01-876 6219 **AZ 3D 73**

World Leisure & Recreation Ass., 345 East 46th St., New York, NJ 10017, U.S.A.

Youth Hostels Ass., H.Q. Trevelyan Ho., 8 St. Stephens Hill, St. Albans, Hertfordshire. St. Albans 55215

SPORT AND RECREATION see also SOCIETIES AND ASSOCIATIONS

An annual "Sports Directory" is available from Sports Council (Gt. London & S.E. Region), Jubilee Stand, National Sports Centre, Crystal Palace; 01-778 8600. Lists main sports facilities and governing bodies, indoor sports centres, swimming pools, golf courses, sport for the Disabled.

Sportsline 01-246 8020. Recorded details of sports news.
Sportsline 01-222 8000. Public information service on London's sports facilities.

Brixton Recreation Centre, 27 Brixton Rd., SW9. 01-274 7774 **AZ 3A 94**
Multi-sports centre and swimming pools.
Central Council of Physical Recreation, Francis Ho., Francis St., SW1. 01-828 3163 **1A 64**
Represents the governing bodies of individual sports.
Chelsea Sports Centre, Chelsea Manor St., SW3. 01-352 6985 **AZ 5C 76**
Multi-sports centre and swimming pool.
Dolphin Square Sports Centre, Grosvenor Rd., SW1. 01-828 1681 **AZ 5G 77**
Swimming pool, fitness room, badminton, squash, sauna, solar.
Ealing Northern Sports Centre, Greenford Rd., Greenford. 01-422 5115 **AZ 7G 55**
Multi-sports centre, heated open-air pool (summer only).
Elephant and Castle Recreation Centre, 22 Elephant & Castle, SE1. 01-528 5505 **AZ 4B 78**
Multi-sports centre, free form leisure pool with waves and slides.
Harrow Leisure Centre, Christchurch Av., Harrow. 01-863 5611 **AZ 4K 23**
Multi-sports centre, two indoor and one outdoor pools.
Herne Hill Stadium, Burbage Rd., SE24. **AZ 6C 94**
Centre for cycling meetings.
Hurlingham Club, Ranelagh Gdns., SW6. 01-736 8411 **AZ 3G 91**
Croquet, Lawn Tennis (London Hard Court Championships).
Lee Valley Park: Offices, Myddelton Ho., Bulls Cross, Enfield. Lea Valley 717711
The Lee Valley Regional Park is the only development of its kind in the U.K. stretching some 23 miles from the Bow Road to Ware, Hertfordshire. Besides the various sports centres, facilities include two Country Parks, camping & caravan sites open working farms, boat centre & trips at Broxbourne, country walks and nature reserve. Plans and information available.
Principal developments to date are:
BANBURY SAILING CENTRE, Banbury Reservoir, Walthamstow Av., E4. 01-531 1129 **AZ 6F 19.**
   Sailing instruction centre, facilities available for schools, groups and individuals.
BROXBOURNE LIDO, Broxborne, Herts, Hoddesdon 42841
   Features wave-makers, simulated beach and tropical plants.
EASTWAY SPORTS CENTRE, Quarter Mile La., E10. 01-519 0017 **AZ 4D 48**
   Provides an extensive range of indoor & outdoor facilities. Special feature—
   Eastway Cycle Circuit, a purpose built enclosed 1.6 kilometre road circuit
   available to all users; coaching staff, bike hire.
LEA BRIDGE RIDING CENTRE, Lea Bridge Rd., E10. 01-556 2629 **AZ 3J 47**
   Offers indoor and outdoor facilities for Gymkhanas and jumping events, casual
   riding and hacking. Later a bridleway to other parts of the park and Epping
   Forest.
LEE VALLEY ICE CENTRE, Lea Bridge Rd., E10. 01-533 3151 **AZ 3J 47**
   Skating and coaching. Ice hockey during the season.
PICKETTS LOCK CENTRE, Picketts Lock La., N9. 01-803 4756 **AZ 2E 18**
   The biggest sports, leisure and social complex in Gt. Britain; provides dozens of

different recreational facilities for all age groups and every member of the family.
SPRINGFIELD MARINA, Spring Hill, E5. 01-806 1717 **AZ 7G 31**
About five miles from R. Thames, at present 100 moorings, 120 boats on the hard, marsh to be dredged to form a lake. Clubhouse, Boathouses and Restaurant.

London Bridge Sports Centre, London Bridge, EC4. 01-623 6895 **3A 40**
Squash courts, gym, sauna, massage room, solarium, rest and refreshment rooms. Membership of limited numbers to avoid congestion of facilities.

Motspur Park, North Malden, Motspur Pk.**AZ 6B 120**
Athletics. (Southern Counties Championships).

National Sports Centre, Crystal Palace, SE19. 01-778 0131 **AZ 6G 111**
Membership. Reduced rates for children and families. Venue for National and International Athletics, Basketball, Gymnastics and Swimming. Facilities for authorised users include Athletics, Gymnastics, Judo, Ski Training, Squash, Swimming, Table Tennis, Tennis indoor and outdoor, Weight Training.

Queen Mother Sports Centre, Vauxhall Bridge Rd., SW1. 01-798 2125 **2D 63**
Multi-sports complex, swimming and diving pools.

Queen's Club, Palliser Rd., W14. 01-385 3421.**AZ 5G 75**
Lawn Tennis (London Grass Court Championships). Real Tennis and Rackets.

Royal Albert Hall, Kensington Gore, SW7. 01-589 3203 **3C 45**
Boxing and Wrestling, Gymnastics, Tennis and Table Tennis Tournaments.

Rugby Union International Ground, Whitton Rd., Twickenham, ex Directory. **AZ 6J 87.**
Internationals and most important matches.

Seymour Leisure Centre, Bryanston Pl., W1. 01-798 1421 **3B 14**
Multi-purpose sports centre; swimming pool.

Sobel Sports Centre, Hornsey Rd., N7. 01-607 1632 **AZ 2J 45**
Multi-sports centre.

Sports Council, 16 Upper Woburn Pl., WC1. 01-388 1277 **3B 10**
Administers grants to Sport, runs nine regional sports councils and National Sports Centres. London and SE Regional Office, Jubilee Stand, National Sports Centre, SE19. 01-778 8600.

Swiss Cottage Sports Centre, Winchester Rd., NW3. 01-586 5989 **AZ 7B 44**
Multi-sports centre and swimming pool.

Walnuts Sports Centre, Lych Gate Rd., Orpington. 70533
Multi-sports centre and swimming pool.

Wembley Empire Stadium and Arena, Empire Way. 01-902 8833 **AZ 4F 41**
Stadium: F.A. and League Cup Finals, International Football, Rugby League Cup Final, Women's Hockey International and World Speedway Championships. *Sports Arena:* Badminton (All England Championships), Basketball, Boxing, Cycling, Ice Hockey, Show Jumping, Tennis (Covered Court Championships), Table Tennis. *Squash Centre:* 15 Courts. 01-902 9230

Wimbledon, All England Club, Church Rd., SW19. 01-946 2244 **AZ 5G 107**
Badminton, Lawn Tennis (Wimbledon Fortnight, Amateur Lawn Tennis Championships).

Y.M.C.A. Sports Centre, Tottenham Court Rd., WC1. 01-637 8131 **3B 18**
Multi-sports centre

Parks details—listed in sections below
Alexandra Park, Muswell Hill, N10. **AZ 3F 29.** Archbishop's Park, Carlisle La., SE1. **1A 66.** Avery Hill Park, Avery Hill Rd., SE9. **AZ 6H 99.** Battersea Park, SW11. **AZ 7D 76.** Blackheath, Prince of Wales Rd., SE3. **AZ 1H 97.** Bostall Heath and Woods, Bostall Hill Rd., SE2. **AZ 6C 84.** Castlewood, Stoney Alley, Shooters Hill, SE18. **AZ 2E 98.** Crystal Palace, Crystal Palace Parade, SE19. **AZ 6G 111.** Dulwich Park, College Rd., SE21. **AZ 7E 94.** Eltham Park, Glenesk Rd., SE9. **AZ 3E 98.** Finsbury Park, Seven Sisters Rd., N4. **AZ 3K 45.** Geffreye's Garden, Kingsland Rd., E2. **AZ 3E 62.** Golders Hill Park, West Heath Av., NW11. **AZ 1J**

43. Gunnersbury Park, Lionel Rd., Brentford. **AZ 3E 72.** Hackney Marsh, Homerton Rd., E9. **AZ 5B 48.** Hainault Forest, Romford Rd., Chigwell. **AZ 1F 37.** Hampstead Heath Extension, Hampstead Way, NW11. **AZ 5H 27.** Holland Park, Holland Walk, W8. **3A 42.** Horniman Gardens, London Rd., SE23. **AZ 1H 111.** Jackwood, Stoney Alley, Shooters Hill, SE18. **AZ 6C 84.** Kenwood, Hampstead La., NW3. **AZ 1B 44.** King George's Field (East London Stadium), Burdett Rd., E3. **AZ 4A 64.** Marble Hill, Richmond Rd., Twickenham. **AZ 7B 88.** N. Camberwell Open Space, Addington Sq., SE5. **AZ 6D 78.** Parliament Hill, NW3. **AZ 3D 44.** Parsloes Park, Gale St., Dagenham. **AZ 5C 52.** Ruislip Lido, Reservoir Rd., Ruislip. Shaftesbury Park, Valeswood Rd., Bromley. **AZ 5H 113.** Thames Mead, Lensbury Way, SE2. **AZ 3C 84.** Trent Park, Cockfosters Rd., Barnet. **AZ 3J 5.** Valentine's Park, Cranbrook Rd., Ilford. **AZ 7E 34.** Victoria Park, Victoria Park Rd., E9. **AZ 1J 63.** Wormwood Scrubs, (West London Stadium), Scrubs La., NW10. **AZ 3C 58.**

Royal Parks. Department of the Environment. Parks General Enquiries
GREENWICH PARK, Greenwich, SE10. 01-858 2608 **AZ 7F 81**   [01-212 3434.
HAMPTON COURT and BUSHEY PARK, Middlesex. 01-977 1328 **AZ 3A 118**
HYDE PARK, W2. 01-262 5484, except boating. 01-262 3751 **3B 30** and **1C 47**
OSTERLEY PARK off Jersey Rd., Hounslow 560 2964 **AZ 7H 71**
PRIMROSE HILL, Albert Rd., NW1. **AZ 1D 60**
REGENTS PARK, NW1. 01-486 7905, except Tennis 01-935 8556 **1D 7** and 2A 8
RICHMOND PARK, Richmond Hill, Richmond 01-948 3209 **AZ 7F 89**
ST. JAMES'S PARK, SW1. 01-930 1793 **2A 50**

ATHLETICS
Amateur Athletics Association, Francis Ho., Francis St., SW1. 01-828 9326 **1A 64**
Universities Athletics Union, 28 Woburn Sq., WC1. 01-637 4828 **1B 18**
Track facilities—at Borough Parks including:
Battersea, Finsbury, King George's Field, Parliament Hill, Victoria Park and Wormwood Scrubs. Also at Herne Hill Stadium

BOATING
Amateur Rowing Association, 6 Lower Mall, W6. 01-748 3632 **AZ 5D 74**
British Canoe Union, 45 High St., Addlestone, Weybridge, Surrey. Weybridge 41341
Royal Yachting Association, Victoria Way, Woking, Surrey. Woking 5022.
Boating: 1. at Borough Parks including—Alexandra, Battersea, Crystal Palace, Dulwich, Finsbury, Gunnersbury, Ruislip Lido, Thamesmead, Valentine's and Victoria Parks. 2. Royal Parks—Hyde Park and Regent's Park. 3. Broxbourne Boat Centre, see Lee Valley Park above.
Canoeing: see Canoe Union.
Sailing: Hyde Park, Regent's Park and River Thames, see Yachting Association. See also Springfield Marina and Banbury Sailing Centre above.
Events:
Regattas: Chiswick, Hammersmith, Henley, Kingston, Putney, Richmond, Twickenham and Walton.
Boat Race: Oxford v Cambridge—Putney to Mortlake.

BOWLS
Public Bowling Greens—at Borough Parks including: Battersea, Blackheath, Bostall Heath, Dulwich, Finsbury, Parliament Hill, Parsloes and Victoria Parks. Also in Hyde Park.

CRICKET
The Cricket Council, Lord's Cricket Ground, St. John's Wood Rd., NW8. 01-289 1611. **2D 5**
Governing body for British Cricket, supplies information and runs the Cricket Mus. *Test and County Match Grounds:*

Essex C.C. Club, Army Sports Ground, Leyton High Rd., E10. **AZ 6D 32**
Middlesex C.C. Club, Lord's. **2D 5**
Prospects of play (May–Sept.) 01-286 8011. Ticket enquiries only 01-289 1615.
Surrey C.C. Club, The Oval, Kennington, SE11. 01-735 4911 **AZ 6K 77**
Cricket Pitches—at Borough Parks including:
Avery Hill, Battersea, Blackheath, Bostall Heath, Crystal Palace, Dulwich, Eltham,
Finsbury, Hackney Marsh, Hainault Forest, Hampstead Heath, Holland Park,
Marble Hill, Parliament Hill, Parsloes, Shaftesbury, Victoria, Wormwood Scrubs.
Royal Parks: Bushey, Greenwich, Hyde Park, Regent's and Richmond Park

CROQUET
Croquet Ass. Hurlingham Club. Ranelagh Gdns., SW6. 01-736 3148 **AZ 3G 91**
Fulham Palace/Bishops Park Croquet Lawn (public), Bishops Pk., Rd., SW6.
AZ 2F 91
Summer Wed. and Sundays.

FISHING
National Federation of Anglers, Halliday Hos., 2 Wilson St., Derby. Derby 362000
At Borough Parks including: Alexandra, Battersea, Crystal Palace, Finsbury,
Hainault Forest, Parliament Hill, Trent, Victoria. Permit from Park
Superintendent.
Royal Parks: Hampton Court Ponds, Hyde Park, Serpentine, Osterley and
Richmond Pen Ponds. Permit from The Storeyard, Hyde Park, W2. S.a.e. 50p.
River Thames: Kew to Staines, no licence needed. Grand Union Canal: Rights are
mostly let to the London Angler's Association, 183 Hoe St., E17. 01-520 7477.

FLYING
Royal Aero Club; also **British Gliding Association,** Kimberley Ho., 47 Vaughan
Way, Leicester. Leic. 531051
Nearest facilities for flying:
Essex Gliding Club, North Weald Aerodrome, Essex. N. Weald 2222.
London Gliding Club, Dunstable Downs, Bed., Dunstable 63419.
London School of Flying, Elstree Aerodrome, Herts. 01-953 4753.

FOOTBALL
Amateur Football Alliance, Room 33, 6 Langley St., WC2. 01-240 3837 **1C 35**
Football Association, 16 Lancaster Ga., W2. 01-262 4542 **2B 28**
League Clubs:
Arsenal F.C., Arsenal Stadium, Avenell Rd., N5. 01-359 0131 **AZ 3B 46**
Brentford F.C., Griffin Park, Ealing Rd., Brentford. 01-560 2021 **AZ 5D 72**
Charlton Athletic F.C., The Valley, Floyd Rd., SE7. 01 858 3711 **AZ 5A 82**
Chelsea F.C., Stamford Bridge, Fulham Rd., SW6. 01-385 5545 **AZ 2D 91**
Crystal Palace F.C., Selhurst Park, Whitehorse La., SE25. 01-653 2223 **AZ 4D 124**
Fulham F.C., Craven Cottage, Stevenage Rd., SW6. 01-736 5621 **AZ 1F 91**
Millwall F.C., The Den, Coldblow La., SE14. 01-639 3143 **AZ 7K 79**
Orient F.C. Brisbane Rd., E10. 01-539 2223 **AZ 2D 48**
Queen's Park Rangers F.C., Ellerslie Rd., W12. 01-743 2618 **AZ 1D 74**
Tottenham Hotspur F.C., White Hart Lane, High Rd., N17. 01-808 2618 **AZ 4F 31**
West Ham United F.C., Boleyn Ground, Green St., E13. 01-472 0704 **AZ 6K 49**
Football Pitches: 1. at Borough Parks including—Avery Hill, Battersea, Blackheath,
Bostall Heath, Castlewood, Crystal Palace, Dulwich, Eltham, Finsbury,
Hackney Marsh, Hainault Forest, Hampstead Heath Ext., Holland, Jackwood, King
George's Field, North Camberwell, Parliament Hill, Parsloes, Shaftesbury,
Thamesmead, Victoria, Wormwood Scrubs. 2. Royal Parks—Hyde Park, Regent's
Park and Richmond Park.

GOLF
For details of clubs, Championships, Tournaments etc., consult "Golfer's
Handbook", 256 West George St., Glasgow.
Public Golf Courses:

Addington Court, Featherbed La., Addington, S. Croydon. 01-657 0281
Beckenham Place Park, Beckenham. 01-650 2292 **AZ 6D 112**
Brent Valley Municipal Golf Course, 138 Church Rd., W7. 01-567 4230 **AZ 7H 55**
Bromley Municipal Golf Course, High Elms Rd., Downe. 01-462 7014
Chingford Golf Course, Station Rd., E4. 01-529 2107 **AZ 1A 20**
Coulsdon Court Municipal Golf Course, Coulsdon Rd., Coulsdon. 01-660 0468
Hainault Forest Public Golf Course, Chigwell Rd., Hainault. 01-500 2097
Haste Hill Golf Course, The Drive, Northwood. Northwd. 26485
Horsenden Hill Golf Course, Woodland Rise, Greenford. 01-902 4555 **AZ 6A 40**
Perivale Park Golf Course, Ruislip Rd., Greenford. 01-578 1693 **AZ 4H 55**
Picketts Lock, Picketts Lock La., N9. 01-803 3611 **AZ 2E 18**
Richmond Park Golf Course, Norstead Pl., Putney, SW15. 01-876 3205
AZ 2C 106
Royal Epping Forest Golf Course, Bury Rd., Chingford, E4. 01-529 2758
AZ 1B 20
Ruislip Municipal Golf Course, Ickenham Rd., Ruislip. Ruislip 32004
Ruxley, Sandy La., St. Paul's Cray, Kent. Orpington 71490 **AZ 7D 116**
Trent Park, Bramley Rd., N14. 01-366 7432 **AZ 5A 6**
Twickenham, Staines Rd., Middx. 01-941 2206 **AZ 3F 103**
Wimbledon Common G. C., Camp Rd., Wimbledon, SW19. 01-946 0294
AZ 5E 106

GREYHOUND RACING
National Greyhound Racing Club, Shipton Ho., Oval Rd., NW1. 01-267 9256
AZ 1F 61
Stadiums:
Catford. Adenmore Rd., Catford Bri. SE6. 01-690 2261 **AZ 7C 96**
Hackney Wick. Waterden Rd., E15. 01-986 3511 **AZ 5C 48**
Harringay, Green Lanes, N4. 01-800 3474 **AZ 4B 30**
Romford, London Rd., Romford. Romford 62345
Walthamstow. Chingford Rd., E4. 01-527 7277 **AZ 6H 19**
Wembley. Empire Way, Wembley. 01-902 8833 **AZ 4F 41**
Wimbledon. Plough La., SW17. 01-946 5361 **AZ 5K 107**

HOCKEY
All England Women's Hockey Ass., Argyle Ho., 29 Euston Rd., NW1. 01-278
6340 **AZ 1C 17**
Hockey Association, 16 Upper Woburn Pl., WC1. 01-387 9315 **3B 10**
Hockey Pitches: 1. at Borough Parks including—Avery Hill, Hackney Marsh, Marble
Hill, Parliament Hill, Victoria, Wormwood Scrubs. 2. Royal Parks—Bushey,
Greenwich, Hyde Park, Regent's Park.

HORSE RACING
Jockey Club (Flat), National Hunt Committee (Steeplechasing),
42 Portman Sq., W1. 01-486 4921 **1D 31**
Nearest Courses to London:
Epsom, Epsom Downs, Surrey. Epsom 26311
Kempton Park, Sunbury, Middlesex. Sunbury-on-Thames 82292
Sandown Park, Sandown Park, Esher, Surrey. Esher 63072
Windsor, Royal Windsor Racecourse, Windsor 65235

HORSE RIDING
British Horse Society, National Equestrian Centre, Stoneleigh, Kenilworth.
Coventry 52241
Dulwich Common:
Dulwich Riding School, Dulwich Comm., SE22. 01-693 2944 **AZ 1E 110**
Epping Forest:
Barnfield Riding Stables, Sewardstone Rd., E4. 01-529 5200 **AZ 7J 9**
Queen Elizabeth Riding School, 97 Forest Side, E4. 01-529 1223 **AZ 1C 20**
Hampstead Heath:

Community Stables, City Farm, 232 Grafton Rd., NW5. 01-482 2861 **AZ 5E 44**
Hyde Park:
Bathurst Riding Stables, 63 Bathurst M., W2. 01-723 2813 **2C 29**
Civil Service Riding Club, Royal Mews, SW1. 01-930 7232 **1C 63**
Lilo Blum's Riding Establishment, 32a Grosvenor Cres. M., SW1. 01-235 6846
2D 47
Ross Nye Riding Stables, 8 Bathurst Mews, W2. 01-262 3791 **2C 29**
Moat Mount/Scratchwood/Totteridge Open Spaces:
Belmont Riding School, Belmont Farm, The Ridgeway, NW7. 01-906 1255
AZ 4J 13
London Equestrian Centre, Frith Manor Farm, Lullington Garth, N12. 01-349 1345
AZ 5C 14
Richmond Park and Wimbledon Common:
Kingston Riding Centre, Crescent Rd., Kingston-upon-Thames. 01-546 6361
AZ 7G 105
Roehampton Riding School, Priory La., SW15. 01-876 7089 **AZ 6A 90**
Wimbledon Village Stables, 24a/b High St., SW19. 01-946 8579 **AZ 5F 107**

JUDO
British Judo Association, 16 Upper Woburn Pl., WC1. 01-387 9340 **3B 10**
Budokwai Judo Club, 4 Gilston Rd., SW10. 01-370 1000 **AZ 5A 76**
Judokan Club, Latymer Ct., Hammersmith Rd., W6. 01-748 6787 **AZ 4F 75**
London Judo Society, 89 Lansdowne Way, SW8. 01-622 0529 **AZ 1H 93**
Renshuden Judo Academy, Albany St., NW1. 01-387 8611.**1B 8**

KARATE
Karate Beginners Courses:
Judokan Club, Latymer Ct., Hammersmith Rd., W6. 01-748 6787 **AZ 4F 75**
London Karate Kai, 89 Lansdowne Way, SE18. 01-622 0529 **AZ 1H 93**

LAWN TENNIS
Lawn Tennis Association, Palliser Rd., Baron's Court, W14. 01-385 2366
AZ 5G 75
All England Club, Wimbledon, Church Road, SW19. 01-946 2244 **AZ 5G 107**
Home of "The Championships" and the Lawn Tennis Museum.
Tennis Courts: 1. in most Borough Parks including—Archbishops, Avery Hill,
Battersea, Blackheath, Crystal Palace, Dulwich, Eltham, Finsbury, Golders Hill,
King George's Field, Marble Hill, North Camberwell, Parliament Hill, Parsloes,
Shaftesbury, Victoria, Wormwood Scrubs. 2. Royal Parks—Greenwich,
Hampton, Regent's Park. Also Lincoln's Inn Fields.

MODEL BOATING AND FLYING
There are *Boating Ponds* at Blackheath, Kensington Gardens—Round Pond (Sailing
Boats only), Parliament Hill, Victoria Park & Richmond Park—Adams Pond.*Powered
Flying* is allowed in a regulated zone in Regent's Park (North of Lake).
Kite Flying takes place at Parliament Hill, Primrose Hill and Kensington Gardens
(near the Round Pond).

MOTOR AND MOTOR CYCLE RACING
Auto-Cycle Union, Millbuck Ho., Corporation St., Rugby. 70332
Royal Automobile Club, Motor Sport Division, 31 Belgrave Sq., SW1. 01-235
8601 **1A 62**
Racing takes place at:
Brands Hatch Circuit, Fawkham, Kent. Ash Green 872331
Crayford, London Rd., Crayford. Crayford 522262
Hackney Wick Stadium, Waterden Rd., E15. 01-986 3511 **AZ 5C 48**
Wimbledon Stadium, Plough La., SW17. 01-946 5361 **AZ 5K 107**

NETBALL
All England Netball Association, Francis Ho., Francis St., SW1. 01-828 2176
1A 64
Netball Courts: 1. in Borough Parks including—Archbishops, Battersea, Finsbury,

Geffrye's Garden, Hampstead Heath ext., Parliament Hill, Victoria and Wormwood Scrubs. 2. Royal Parks—Greenwich, Hyde Park, Regent's and Richmond Parks. Also in Lincoln's Inn Fields.

POLO
Hurlingham Polo Association, Abersham Farm, Abersham, Midhurst, West Sussex. Lodsworth 277
Polo takes place at Ham House, Richmond Park and Windsor Great Park.

PUTTING
Putting Greens: at most Borough Parks including—Alexandra, Archbishops, Avery Hill, Castlewood, Dulwich, Eltham, Golders Hill, Hackney Marsh, Hainault Forest, Hornimans Garden, Marble Hill, Parsloes and Victoria Parks. Also Greenwich and Hampton Court.

RUGBY UNION
Rugby Football League, 180 Chapeltown Rd., Leeds. Leeds 624637
Rugby Football Union, Whitton Rd., Twickenham, Middx. **AZ 6J 87**
Rugby Pitches: in Borough Parks including—Avery Hill, Hackney Marsh, Marble Hill, Wormwood Scrubs.
Main London Clubs:
Blackheath. Rectory Field, Charlton Rd., SE3. 01-858 9303 **AZ 7J 81**
Harlequins, R.F.U. Ground, Twickenham. 01-892 3080 **AZ 6J 87**
London Irish. The Avenue, Sunbury-on-Thames. Sunbury-on-T. 83034
London Scottish. Athletic Grd., Twickenham Rd., Richmond. 01-940 0397 **AZ 4C 88**
London Welsh. Old Deer Park, Kew Rd., Richmond. 01-940 2520 **AZ 3E 88**
Richmond. Athletic Ground, Twickenham Rd., Richmond. 01-940 0397 **AZ 4C 88**
Rosslyn Park. Priory La., Upper Richmond Rd., SW15. 01-876 1879 **AZ 4B 90**
Saracens, Green Rd., Southgate, N14. 01-449 3770 **AZ 6A 6**
Wasps, Repton Av., Wembley. 01-902 4220 **AZ 4C 40**

SHOW JUMPING
British Show Jumping Association, National Equestrian Centre, Stoneleigh, Kenilworth. Coventry 20783
Wembley Arena is the main venue for events.

SKATING
National Skating Association, 15/27 Gee St., EC1. 01-253 3824 **1B 22**
Ice Skating Rinks:
Queen's Ice Skating Club, Queensway, W6. 01-229 0172 **3D 27**
Lee Valley Ice Centre, see Lee Valley Park above.
Richmond Ice Rink, Clevedon Rd., E. Twickenham. 01-892 3646 **AZ 6D 88**
Streatham Ice Rink, 386 Streatham High Rd., SW16. 01-769 7861 **AZ 4J 109**
Roller Skating Rink: (Hyde Park and Battersea Park have special areas).
Picketts Lock Sports Centre, see Lee Valley Park above.

SKI-ING
National Ski Federation of Gt. Britain, 118 Eaton Sq., SW1. 01-235 8227 **1A 62**
Instruction Runs:
National Sports Centre, Crystal Palace, SE19. 01-778 0131 **AZ 6G 111**

SQUASH
Squash Rackets Association, Francis Ho., Francis St., SW1. 01-828 3064 **1A 64**
Squash Courts:
Dolphin Square, Chichester St., SW1. 01-828 1681 **2A 72**
Holland Park, Holland Walk, W8. 01-602 2226 **3A 42**
South Bank Squash Centre, 124 Wandsworth Rd., SW8. 01-622 6866 **AZ 3F 93**

Wembley Squash Centre, Empire Way. 01-902 9230 **AZ 4F 41**
Also at Sports Centres, see especially Eastway Centre and Picketts Lock Centre, Lee Valley Park.

STOCK CAR RACING
Speedway Control Board, R.A.C., 31 Belgrave Sq., SW1. 01-235 8601 **1A 62**
Stadiums at:
Harringay, Green Lanes, N4. 01-806 3474 **AZ 4B 30**
Walthamstow, Chingford Row, E4. 01-527 8725 **AZ 6H 19**
Wimbledon, Plough La., SW17. 01-946 5361 **AZ 5K 107**

SWIMMING
Amateur Swimming Association, Harold Fern Ho., Derby Sq., Loughborough, Leics. Loughborough 30431

Water Scene, Mapleton Rd., SW18. 01-870 4955 **AZ 6K 91**
A water "theme park" with four heated open air pools, water slides, diving tubes, children's facilities. Restaurant. Open daily, summer months only.
Broxbourne Lido features wave-makers and simulated beach, see Lee Valley Park;
Elephant & Castle Recreation Centre has free form pool with waves and slides, see above.

Indoor Pools in Central London; for details see HEALTH AND BEAUTY.
Chelsea Sports Centre, SW3. 01-352 6985 **AZ 5C 56**
Dolphin Square, Chichester St., SW1. 01-828 3800 **AZ 5G 77**
Kensington Sports Centre, Walmer Rd., SW11. 01-727 9923 **AZ 7G 59**
Marshall St. Leisure Complex, W1. 01-439 4678 **1D 33**
Oasis Sports Centre, Endell St., WC2. 01-836 3771 **1C 35**
Porchester Centre, Queensway. W2. 01-229 3226 **1D 27**
Queen Mother Sports Centre, Vauxhall Bridge Rd., SW1. 01-798 2125 **2D 63**
Seymour Leisure Centre, Seymour Pl., W1. 01-723 8618 **3B 14**
Swiss Cottage Sports Centre, Avenue Rd., NW3. 01-278 4444 **AZ 7B 44**
Outdoor Pools:
Barking Park, Park Av. 01-594 3527 **AZ 6G 51**
Brockwell Park, Dulwich Rd., SE24. 01-274 7991 **AZ 5A 94**
Chiswick Open Air Baths, Edensor Rd., W4. 01-994 2315 **AZ 7A 74**
Ealing Northern Sports Centre, Greenford Rd., Greenford. 01-422 5115 **AZ 7G 55**
Eltham Park, Glenesk Rd., SE9. 01-850 9890 **AZ 7E 94**
Highbury Fields, Highbury Pl., N5. 01-226 2165 **AZ 6B 46**
Highgate Ponds, Millfield La., N6. (Men only) 01-340 4044 **AZ 2D 44**
Kenwood Pond, Millfield La., N6. (Women only) 01-348 1033 **AZ 2D 44**
Oasis Sports Centre, Endell St., WC2. 01-836 3771 **1C 35**
Parliament Hill, Lissenden Gdns., NW5. 01-485 3873 **AZ 4E 44**
Ruislip Lido, Reservoir Rd., Ruislip 34081
Tottenham Lido, Lordship La., N17. 01-808 2867 **AZ 2A 30**
Victoria Park, Grove Rd., E3. 01-985 6774 **AZ 1K 63**
Outdoor swimming is also possible in three natural ponds on Hampstead Heath and in Hyde Park's Serpentine.

TEN PIN BOWLING
British Ten Pin Bowling Ass., 19 Canterbury Av., Ilford, Essex. 01-554 9173
ABC Princess Bowl, New Rd., Dagenham. 01-592 0347 **AZ 2G 69**
ABC N. Harrow Bowl, Pinner Rd., N. Harrow. 01-863 3491 **AZ 4D 22**
ABC Cine Bowl, Broadway, Bexleyheath. 01-303 3325 **AZ 4E 100**
Airport Bowl, Bath Rd., Harlington. 01-759 1396
Excel Bowl, Kingston Rd., Tolworth. 01-337 0974
Mecca Streatham Bowl, 142 Streatham Hill, SW2. 01-674 5251 **AZ 2J 109**

WRESTLING
Venues include Royal Albert Hall.

SQUARES AND STREETS

A selection of interesting, historic and important places.

Adelphi, WC2. 3D 35
A development planned by three of the Adam Brothers between 1768–74 on land
reclaimed from the Thames. Only two portions survive in the restored Royal
Society of Arts building No. 8 John Adam St. and in No. 7 Adam St.

Baker Street, W1. 1C 15
Laid out late 18th cent. and named after Sir Edward Baker. Ex-residents have
included Mrs. Siddons, Cardinal Wiseman, William Pitt the Younger and
fictitious Sherlock Holmes at equally fictitious No. 221b.

Belgravia, SW1. 3D 47
Laid out in the early 19th cent. by Thomas Cubitt with George Baseui as his chief
architect. Imposing stucco classical style. A highly fashionable area. Fine examples of
Belgravian architecture include Belgrave Sq. and Eaton Sq.

Bloomsbury, WC1. 2D 19
Famous for its Georgian domestic architecture set around peaceful squares
including Bloomsbury, Bedford, Fitzroy, Tavistock and Russell Squares. A
highly fashionable 18th cent. residential area, especially so with intellectuals and
artists (including the Bloomsbury Group, early 1900). Now contains British
Museum, British Library and London University.

Bond Streets, W1. 2C 33
Comprising New and Old Bond Streets known as "The High Street of Mayfair".
Shops essentially concerned with quality include fashion, jewellery, antiques,
fine art and beauty specialists. New Bond Street has Sotheby's and Time and Life
Building (with Henry Moore stone relief).

Bow Street, WC2. 1D 35
Famous for the Royal Opera House, 1856–8 and the Bow St. Police Court and its
association with the Bow Street Runners. Famous residents have included
Henry Fielding, Grinling Gibbons, Charles Macklin and John Radcliffe.

Burlington Arcade, Piccadilly, W1. 3D 33
Regency shopping arcade built 1819, named after the Earls of Burlington. Original
curved windows. Beadle still employed to maintain the peace.

Carnaby Street, W1. 2D 33
Made a big noise in fashion during the late 1960's, now predominantly a Union
Jack tourist attraction, pedestrianized with coloured pavement.

Charing Cross, WC2. 1C 51
Originally a small village between the City and Westminster. Site of one of the
twelve Eleanor Crosses erected in 1291 by Edward I to commemorate the
journey of his Queen's funeral cortege from Notts to Westminster Abbey, now
occupied by the equestrian statue of Charles I (south side of Trafalgar Sq.) This marks
the official centre of London from which mileages are measured. A replica of the
cross stands in Charing Cross Station forecourt (Strand).

Downing Street, SW1. 2C 51
Row of 17th cent. houses named after their builder Sir George Downing. No. 10
is the official residence of the Prime Minister; No. 11 Chancellor of the Exchequer.

Ely Place, EC1. 3D 21
Previously the site of Ely Palace, London home of the Bishop of Ely; remains
include Ely Chapel (or St. Etheldreda) and the Old Mitre Tavern, now a private
cul-de-sac with beadle on duty at the gated entrance.

Fleet Street, EC4. 1C 37
Centre for the newspaper industry since the early 16th cent. when Caxton's
assistant Wynkyn de Worde set up a printing press here. Now most National

and London newspapers and related concerns have their offices in this area. Name derived from the River Fleet used now as part of the sewer system.

Grosvenor Square, W1. 2A 32
Laid out in 1695 by Sir Richard Grosvenor and associated with the United States since 1785. As H.Q. of U.S. Forces in Europe during World War II, was known as "Little America". Largely rebuilt in the last 40 years including the new American Embassy. Statue of Franklin D. Roosevelt.

Hammersmith Mall. AZ 5D 74
Divided into Upper and Lower Mall, is an attractive riverside promenade from Hammersmith to Chiswick. Amongst the many 18th cent. houses are Sussex House *c.* 1726 and Kelmscott House *c.* 1780 home of William Morris.

Hatton Garden, EC1. 2C 21
Centre of the diamond market. Name comes from Sir Christopher Hatton, Elizabethan statesman and Lord Chancellor, who lived at Ely Place nearby. Sir Thomas Coram who established the Foundling Hospital lived here.

King's Road, SW3. 3C 61
Chelsea's High Street, a centre of fashion where anything goes. Join the Saturday parade.

Lincoln's Inn Fields, WC2. 3A 20
Largest square in central London. Gardens noted for plane trees and once for duelling. Interesting buildings include Sir John Soane's House designed by himself 1812, contains his museum; Lindsey House built –c. 1640 possibly by Inigo Jones; and the Royal College of Surgeons 1835–7. Name of the square derives from the neighbouring Inn of Court.

Lombard Street, EC3. 2A 40
The centre of British Banking owes its name to the Lombard goldsmiths and money-lenders who established themselves here after the expulsion of the Jews in 1290. Numerous bank signs hang medieval fashion, over the pavement.

Mall The, SW1. 2D 49
Linking Buckingham Palace with Trafalgar Square this is used in all Royal Ceremonies such as Trooping of the Colour and State opening of Parliament. It formed the northern avenue to St. James's Park as remodelled by Le Nôtre for Charles II; built as a Royal "Pell Mell" alley, thus superseding Pall Mall – the original venue for this fashionable Italian croquet-like game. Relaid 1910 as part of the National Memorial to Queen Victoria.

Manchester Square, W1. 3A 16
Laid out 1776–88 and largely unspoilt. Hertford House built for the Duke of Manchester houses the Wallace Collection formed by the Fourth Marquess of Hertford and his son Sir Richard Wallace.

Oxford Street, W1. 1D 31 to 3B 18
Shopping centre famous for its stores. Follows the line of the Roman Road west from the City. In medieval times the route for the condemned to Tyburn Gallows. Now being partly pedestrianized with the addition of trees and seats.

Pall Mall, SW1. 1A 50
Derivation of "Pell Mell"; see The Mall. Famous for clubs, including the Athenaeum 1830 by Decimus Burton, Travellers' Club 1829–32 and Reform Club 1837–41 both by Sir Charles Barry.

Parliament Square, SW1. 3C 51
Originally laid out by Sir Charles Barry –c. 1868 when the Houses of Parliament were being built (the old Palace of Westminster having been destroyed by fire). Relaid for the 1951 Festival of Britain. Bounded by St. Margaret's Westminster with Westminster Abbey behind, New Palace Yard and the Houses of Parliament, Middlesex Guildhall the former County Hall. Statues of statesmen in the square include those of Churchill, Lincoln, Disraeli and Smuts.

Petticoat Lane, Middlesex St., E1. 3C 25
Sunday morning street market. Sells almost anything, although its name derives from the sale of cheap clothes.

Piccadilly Circus, W1. 3A 34
Laid out late 19th cent. as a junction to five main roads, Piccadilly, Regent Street, Shaftesbury Avenue, Coventry Street and Lower Regent Street, and famous for its array of neon advertisements. A pedestrian piazza surrounds the fountain memorial (including Eros) to the Earl of Shaftesbury. The Trocadero Centre houses besides traffic free shopping malls the "Guinness World of Records" and "London Experience" exhibitions both open to the public daily.

Portobello Road, W11. 2A 26
World famous Saturday antique and junk market.

Queen Anne's Gate, SW1. 3B 50
Built 1704, is noted as an example of Georgian domestic architecture, elaborately carved porches. Statue of Queen Anne near No. 13.

Regent Street, W1. 1C 33 to 3A 34
Part of a vast Regency Town Planning scheme by John Nash constructed 1811–26 to connect the Prince Regent's Carlton House on Pall Mall with Regent's Park. Famous for the Quadrant, Park Crescent and other terraces surrounding the Park.

Strand, WC2. 3D 35
Originally a riverside walk. Now famous for its hotels and theatres linking Trafalgar Square and Fleet Street. Other buildings include Somerset House, Law Courts, Bush House, Australia House, Charing Cross Station and two island churches, St. Clement Danes and St. Mary-le-Strand.

Threadneedle Street, EC2. 1A 40
Home of the Bank of England (nicknamed the Old Lady of Threadneedle Street), and the Royal Exchange. The Stock Exchange now has a new tower block in Old Broad Street

Trafalgar Square, WC2. 3C 35
Laid out as a memorial to Nelson's death and victory at Trafalgar 1829–41 by Barry. Dominated by Nelson's column completed 1843, bronze lions by Landseer, 1868 and fountains, 1948, designed by Lutyens. On the north side of the square are the correct British Standard Measurements. Important surrounding buildings include National Gallery, St. Martin-in-the-Fields, Canada and S. Africa Houses.

Victoria Embankment, SW1 and WC2. 2D 51 to 2D 37
Riverside promenade, lined with floodlit buildings at night from Westminster Bridge to Blackfriars Bridge. Constructed 1864–70 from land reclaimed from the Thames, by Sir Joseph Bazalgette; beneath runs the Circle and District tube line. Partly lined by Victoria Embankment Gardens and Temple Gardens.

Whitehall, SW1. 1C 51
Broad processional way between Trafalgar and Parliament Squares lined by Government Offices and Departments. Name derives from Whitehall Palace destroyed by fire 1698 (except for the Banqueting House). Other buildings include the Old Admiralty, Horse Guards, Dover House. The many statues and monuments include the Cenotaph.

STATUES AND MONUMENTS

Achilles, Hyde Park Corner, SW1. **2B 48**
Bronze statue made from cannon captured in the Peninsular War, commemorates Wellington. Westmacott, 1822.

Albert, Prince. 1819–61:
1. Albert Memorial, Kensington Gore, SW7. **2C 45** Monument by Scott. Statue of Prince Albert (with Catalogue of the Great Exhibition 1851 in his hand) by Foley. Unveiled 1876 by his widow, Queen Victoria.

2. Albert Ct., SW7. **3C 45**. Bronze statue of Queen Victoria's Prince Consort to commemorate the Great Exhibition of 1851. Durham, 1863.

3. Holborn Circus, EC1. **3D 21**. Equestrian. Bacon, 1874.

Aldrich-Blake, Dame Louisa, Tavistock Sq., WC1. **3B 10**
1866–1925 Woman Surgeon, Lutyens, Walker, 1927.

Alfred the Great, Trinity Church Sq., SE1. **3C 55**
849–99. First leader of all Englishmen. Legendary burner of cakes. A late 14th cent. work possibly the oldest statue in London. Removed from Palace of Westminster 1822.

Bacon, Francis, Gray's Inn, WC1. **2C 21**
1561–1626. Courtier, lawyer, writer. Considered by "Baconians" as author of Shakespeare's plays. Pomeroy, 1912.

Bazalgette, Sir J. W., Victoria Embankment, WC2. **1D 51**
Bronze mural monument to engineer responsible for Victoria Embankment, sewage system and Thames Bridges, d. 1891.

Beatty, Earl, Trafalgar Sq., WC2. **3C 35**
1871–1936. Admiral. Served in Sudan, China and World War I. Bronze bust. Wheeler, 1948.

Bedford, 5th Duke of, Russell Sq., WC1. **2C 19**
1765–1805. Landowner, agriculturalist. Westmacott, 1809.

Belgian Gratitude, Monument of, Victoria Embankment, WC2. **3A 36**
For British Aid given during World War I. Blomfield, Rousseau, 1920.

Boudicca/Boadicea, Westminster Bridge, SW1. **3D 31 51**
Queen (d. AD 62) with two daughters in War Chariot. Thorneycroft, 1902.

Browning, Robert, Warwick Gdns., W2. **2B 12**
1812–89. Poet. Commemorative mural at Little Venice.

Brunel, I. K., 1806–59. Visionary engineer, designer of great ships, bridges and the Great Western Railway. 1. Victoria Embankment, Temple Pl., WC2. **2B 36**
2 Paddington Station; Doubleday, erected 1982. **1C 29**

Bunyan, John, Southampton Row, WC1. **3A 20**
1628–88. Author of "The Pilgrim's Progress", 1903.

Burghers of Calais, Victoria Tower Gdns., SW1. **1D 65**
Bronze copy of group erected 1895 in Calais. Rodin, 1915.

Burns, Robert, Victoria Embankment Gdns., WC2. **3D 35**
1759–96. Scottish poet. Steeller, 1884.

Byron, Lord, Hyde Park Corner, SW1. **2A 48**
1788–1824. Poet. Died fighting for Greek Independence. Belt, 1880.

Cambridge, 2nd Duke of, Whitehall, SW1. **1C 51**
1814–1904. Soldier. Equestrian. Jones, 1907.

Canning, George, Parliament Sq., SW1. **3C 51**
1770–1827. Statesman. Chiefly in Foreign Office. Westmacott, 1832.

Carlyle, Cheyne Walk, SW3. **3A 68**
1795–1881. Author. Known chiefly for his "The French Revolution". Boehm, 1882.

Cavalry War Memorial, Serpentine Rd., Hyde Park, W1. **2D 47**
Commemorates dead of World War I. 1924.

Cavell, Nurse Edith, St. Martin's Pl., WC2. **3C 35**
1865–1915. Shot in Belgium for helping British prisoners escape in World War I.

Cenotaph, Whitehall, SW1. **2C 51**
Memorial to the dead of World Wars I and II. Designed by Lutyens, unveiled Armistice Day 1920. Remembrance Sunday service is attended here by the Sovereign, Members of Parliament, Leaders of the Armed Forces and representatives of the Commonwealth. Inscription reads "To the Glorious Dead".

Chaplin, Charlie, Leicester Sq., WC2. **2B 34**
1889–1977. Famed actor and producer of the silent film era. Doubleday, 1981.

Churchill, Sir Winston, Parliament Sq., SW1. **3C 51**
1874–1965. Prime Minister during World War II. Roberts-Jones. Unveiled Nov. 1st, 1973.

178 *STATUES & MONUMENTS*

Clive of Bengal, 1st Baron., King Charles St., SW1. **2C 51**
1725–74. Soldier and Statesman. Tweed. 1916.
Cook, Captain J., The Mall, SW1. **1C 51**
1728–79. Navigator and Maritime explorer. Brock, 1914.
Cromwell, Oliver, St. Margaret St., SW1. **3C 51**
1599–1658. Leader in Civil War against Charles I. Became "Protector of the Commonwealth of England, Scotland and Ireland". Thorneycroft, 1899.
Cunningham, Admiral Lord, Trafalgar Sq., WC2. **3C 35**
1883–1962. Sailor in World Wars I and II. Commander-in-Chief Mediterranean 1943.
Curzon of Kedleston, 1st Marquess, 1 Carlton House Terr., SW1. **1B 50**
1859–1925. Viceroy of India. Mackennal, 1931.
Devonshire, 8th Duke of, Whitehall, SW1. **1C 51**
1833–1908. War Secretary and Postmaster General. Hampton, 1911.
Disraeli, Benjamin, Parliament Sq., SW1. **3C 51**
1804–81. Prime Minister during Queen Victoria's reign. Raggi, 1883.
Elfin Oak, Kensington Gdns., W2. **3D 27**
Carved from old oak tree stumps. Innes, 1930.
Eros, Piccadilly Circus, W1. **3A 34**
Memorial to Earl of Shaftesbury. Gilbert, 1893.
Field Marshall Alexander of Tunis, Birdcage Wlk., SW1. **3A 50**
In Italian Campaign winter flying jacket. James Butler, 1985.
Foch, Marshal, Grosvenor Gdns., SW1. **1C 63**
1851–1929. French C.-in-C. World War. I. Given by France. Malissard, 1930.
Fox, C. J., Bloomsbury Sq., WC1. **2D 19**
1749–1806. Whig Politician. Westmacott, 1816.
Frere, Sir H. E. Bartle, Victoria Embankment Gdns., SW1. **1D 51**
1815–84. First High Commissioner for South Africa. Brock, 1888.
Gladstone, St. Clement-Danes, Strand, WC2. **2B 36**
1809–98. Four times Prime Minister under Queen Victoria. Thorneycroft, 1905.
Gordon, General, Victoria Embankment, SW1. **1D 51**
1833–85. Killed at Siege of Khartoum. Thorneycroft, 1888.
Guards Memorial, Horse Guards Parade, SW1. **2C 51**
Commemorates dead of World War I. Ledward and Bradshaw, 1926.
Guards Memorial, Waterloo Pl., SW1. **1B 50**
Commemorates dead of Crimean War. Bell, 1859.
Haig, 1st. Earl, Whitehall, SW1. **2C 51**
1861–1928. British Commander-in-Chief World War I. Equestrian. Hardiman, 1937.
Havelock, Sir Henry, Trafalgar Sq., WC2. **3C 35**
1795–1857. Soldier in India. Behnes, 1861.
Hill, Sir Rowland, G.P.O. King Edward St., EC1. **3B 22**
1795–1879. Originator of the Penny Post. Ford, 1882.
Hogarth, W., Leicester Sq., WC2. **3B 34**
1697–1764. Painter, Engraver, Satirist. Bust by Durham.
Hogg, Quintin, Portland Pl., W1. **3C 17**
1845–1903. Philanthropist. Frampton, 1906.
Hudson, W. H., Hyde Park, W2. **3A 30**
1841–1922. Memorial to Naturalist and Writer. "Rima" by Epstein, 1925.
Hunter, W., Leicester Sq., WC2. **3B 34**
1718–83. Anatomist and Obstetrician. Woolner.
Imperial Camel Corps Memorial, Victoria Embankment Gdns., WC2. **3A 36**
Commemorates dead of World War I.
Irving, Sir Henry, Charing Cross Rd., WC2. **3C 35**
1838–1905. Actor-Manager. Brock, 1910.
Jellicoe, Earl, Trafalgar Sq., WC2. **3C 35**
1859–1935. Admiral, First Sea Lord in World War I. Macmillan, 1948.
Jenner, E., Kensington Gdns., W2. **3C 29**
1749–1823. Famous for the Smallpox Vaccination. Calder Marshall, 1858.

Johnson, Dr. Samuel, St. Clement Danes, Strand, WC2. **1B 36**
1709–1784. Known for his Dictionary of the English Language. Fitzgerald, 1910.
Kennedy, John F., 1 Park Cres., W1. **1C 17**
1917–63. President of the United States of America. Assassinated 1963.
King Charles I. 1600–49 (executed 30th Jan.).
1. Banqueting Hall, Whitehall, SW1. **1C 51.** Lead bust –c. 1800.
2. Charing Cross, SW1. **1C 51.** Equestrian statue. Cast 1633. Hubert Le Sueur.
King Charles II. 1630–85. 1. Chelsea Hospital, SW3. **AZ 5E 76.** In Roman Dress.
Grinling Gibbons, 1692. 2. Soho Sq , W1. **1B 34.** Late 17th cent. Caius Cibber.
King Edward VII, Waterloo Pl., SW1. **1B 50**
1841–1910. Equestrian. Mackennal, 1921.
King George II, Golden Sq., SW1. **2A 34**
1683–1760. Supposed holding a lizard. J. Nost the Elder, 1720.
King George III, Junction of Pall Mall E. and Cockspur St., SW1. **3B 34**
1738–1820. Equestrian. Wyatt, 1836.
King George IV, Trafalgar Sq., WC2. **3C 35**
1762–1830. Regent 1810–20. Equestrian. Chantrey, 1843.
King George V, Old Palace Yard, SW1. **3C 51**
1865–1936. National Memorial to George V in association with the scheme for
provision of playing fields throughout the country.
King Henry VIII, St. Bart's Hospital Gateway, West Smithfield, EC1. **3A 22**
1491–1547. Bird, 1702.
King James II, Trafalgar Sq., WC2. **3C 35**
1633–1701. In Roman Dress. Grinling Gibbons, 1686.
King Richard I, Old Palace Yard, SW1. **3D 51**
1157–99. Equestrian statue in Crusading Armour. Marochetti, 1860.
King William III. 1650–1702. Joint ruler with Queen Mary.
1. Kensington Palace Gdns., W8. **2D 43.** Baucke, 1907.
2. St. James's Sq., SW1. **1A 50.** Equestrian, J. Bacon the Younger, 1808.
Kitchener of Khartoum and Brooke, 1st Earl, Horse Guards Pde., SW1. **2C 51**
1850–1916. Soldier, Sudan, Boer War. Sec. of State for War in World War I until
drowned at sea.
Lincoln, Abraham. 1809–65. Sixteenth President of U.S.A. Opposition to Slavery
precipitated Civil War between north and south. Parliament Sq., SW1. **3C 51**
Copy of that by A. Saint-Gaidens, presented by Americans, 1920.
Lister, Lord, Portland Pl., W1. **1B 16**
1827–1912. Surgeon Founder of antiseptic principle. Brock, 1924.
Livingstone, Dr., Royal Geographical Society, Kensington Gore, SW7. **3C 45**
1813–73. African Missionary and Explorer.
Machine Gun Corps Memorial, Hyde Park Corner, SW1. **2A 48**
Commemorates dead of World War I. Figure of David. Wood. 1925.
Markham, Sir Clements, Royal Geographical Society, Kensington Gore, SW7. **3C
45.** 1830–1916. Geographer. Bust erected by Peruvian Government.
Merchant Seamen's War Memorial, Trinity Sq., EC3. **2C 41**
Commemorates the dead in the two World Wars of the Merchant Navy, fishing
fleets, lighthouse and pilotage services.
"Monty". Field Marshall Viscount Montgomery of Alamein. Whitehall, SW1.
2C 51
Oscar Nemon, 1984.
Mill, John Stuart, Victoria Embankment, WC2. **2C 37**
1806–73. Philosopher and Political Economist. Woolner, 1878.
Monument, The, Fish Street Hill, EC3. **2A 40**
Commemorates the Great Fire 1666. Designed by Wren the stone column 202 ft.
high is 202 ft. from the origin of the fire in Pudding Lane, 311 steps to viewing platform.
Open Apr. to Sept., 09.00–17.40, Oct. to Nov. 09.00–15.45, Mon. to Sat. Sun.
14.00–17.40 May to Sept. only. Closed Christmas, Good Fri. Admission
charge.
Mountbatten. Earl Mountbatten of Burma, Horse Guards Parade, SW1. **2C 51**

In uniform of an admiral of the fleet. 1983.

Myddleton, Sir Hugh, Royal Exchange, EC2. **1A 40**
c. 1560–1631. Goldsmith and Businessman. Joseph, 1845.

Napier, Sir Charles, Trafalgar Sq., WC2. **3C 35**
1782–1853. Soldier in Peninsular War and India. Adams, 1856.

Nelson's Column, Trafalgar Sq., SW1. **3C 35**
Designer W. Railton, 184 ft. 10 in. high including the statue of Nelson. Statue is 17 ft. 4–4 in. tall by Baily. Erected 1840–3 at the same time as the laying-out of Trafalgar Square, a memorial to Nelson's death and victory at Trafalgar.

Newman, Cardinal, The Oratory, Brompton Rd., SW7. **1A 60**
1801–90. Convert from Church of England Orders to Roman Catholic Church in 1845. Chavalliaud, 1896.

Newton, Sir Isaac, Leicester Sq., WC2. **3B 34**
1642–1727. Mathematician and natural philosopher, famous for Law of Gravity. Bust by Calder Marshall.

Nightingale, Florence, Waterloo Pl., SW1. **1B 50**
1820–1910. Nurse and pioneer of hospital reform. Famed as "Lady of the Lamp" in Crimean War. Walker, 1913.

Pan, Knightsbridge, SW1. **2C 47.** Pan group, Epstein's last work, 1959.

Pankhurst, Mrs. Emmeline, Victoria Tower Gdns., SW1. **1D 65**
p1858–1928. Leader of Women's suffrage and mother of suffragettes Christobel and Sylvia. Walker, 1930.

Peabody, George, Royal Exchange, EC2. **1A 40**
1795–1869. American philanthropist and London merchant banker. Story, 1869.

Peel, Sir Robert, 1788–1850. Statesman. Creator of London Police, hence "Bobbie"
1. Parliament Sq., SW1. **3C 51.** Noble, 1876.
2. St. Botolph, Aldersgate Churchyard ("Postman's Park"), Aldersgate, EC1. **3B 22**

Peter Pan, Kensington Gdns., W2. **3C 29**
From James Barry's Children's Play. Frampton, 1911.

Physical Energy, Kensington Gdns., W2. **1C 45.** Equestrian bronze. Watts, 1907.

Pitt, William the Younger, Hanover Sq., W1. **1C 33**
1759–1806. Statesman, Prime Minister at 25. Chantrey, 1831.

Plimsoll, Samuel, Victoria Embankment Gdns., SW1. **1D 51**
1824–98. Fought against overloading of Freightershence Plimsoll line. Memorial erected by National Union of Seamen, 1929. Blundstone.

Queen Anne. 1665–1714. 1. Queen Anne's Gate, SW1. **3B 50** Originally intended for portico of St. Mary-le-Strand. 2. St. Paul's Cathedral, EC4. **1B 38** At west front, a replica of the original by Bird, 1712.

Queen Elizabeth I. 1533–1603. St. Dunstan-in-the-West, Fleet St., EC4. **1C 37** 1586. Originally on Lud Gate (moved 1766).

Queen Victoria, 1819–1900. 1. Kensington Palace Gdns., **W8. 1A 44** White marble, 1893. By her daughter Princess Louise. 2. The Mall, SW1. **2D 49** The Queen Victoria Memorial, unveiled 1911 as part of the National Memorial to her, designed by Sir Aston Webb, sculptured by Brock.

Raleigh, Sir Walter, Whitehall, SW1. **2C 51**
1552–1618. Elizabethan Courtier, Merchant Adventurer. Brought potatoes and tobacco to Britain. Macmillan, 1959.

Reynolds, Sir Joshua, 1723–92. Portrait painter. First President of Royal Academy. 1. Leicester Sq., WC2. **3B 34.** Bust by Weekes. 2. Royal Academy, Burlington Ho., Piccadilly, W1. **3D 33** Complete with brush and palette. Drury.

Roberts of Kandahar and Waterford, 1st Earl. Horse Guards Parade, SW1. **1C 51**
1832–1914. Soldier. Served in India, Boer War and for two days before his death in World War I. Bates, 1924. Copy of statue in Calcutta.

Roosevelt Memorial, Grosvenor Sq., W1. **2A 32**
1882–1945. President of U.S.A. 1932–45. Famous for Depression "New Deal" and as World War II leader. Reid Dick, 1948.

Rossetti, Dante Gabriel, Cheyne Walk, SW3. **AZ 7B 76**
1828–82. Pre-Raphaelite painter. Lived in Cheyne Row. Brown, 1887.
Royal Air Force Memorial, Victoria Embankment, SW1. **2D 51**
Blomfield and Reid Dick, 1923.
Royal Artillery Memorial, Hyde Park Corner, SW1. **2A 48**
Commemorates dead of World War I, has the inscription "Here was a royal
fellowship of death". Jagger and Pearson, 1925.
Royal Fusiliers Memorial, Holborn, WC1. **3C 21**
Commemorates the dead of the City of London Regiment.
Scott, Captain R. F., Waterloo Pl., SW1. **1B 50**
1868–1912. Polar explorer perished with his companions on return from the South
Pole. Lady Scott (his widow). 1915.
Shackleton, Sir Ernest, Royal Georgraphical Society, Kensington Gore, SW7. **3C
45.** 1874–1922. Polar explorer. 1932.
p**Shakespeare, William,** Leicester Sq., WC2. **2B 34**
1564–1616. World-famous Elizabethan dramatist, poet, actor. 1874.
Smuts, Field Marshal J. C., Parliament Sq., SW1. **3C 51**
1870–1950. South African soldier and statesman. Fought against Britain in Boer
War, for Britain in World War I. Epstein, 1956.
Speke Memorial, Kensington Gardens, W2. **3B 28**
African explorer, discovered source of the Nile. In form of Obelisk.
Stephenson, Robert, Euston Station Forecourt, NW1. **3A 10**
1803–59. Engineer. Son of George "Father of the Locomotive". Marrochetti, 1871.
Sullivan, Sir Arthur S., Victoria Embankment Gdns., WC2. **3A 36**
1842–1900. Composer, chiefly known for his collaboration with W. S. Gilbert in
Gilbert and Sullivan light operas. Bust by Goscombe John. 1903.
Temple, H. 3rd Viscount Palmerston, Parliament Sq., SW1. **3C 51**
1784–1865. Statesman. Prime Minister 1855 and again aged 75 in 1857. Woolner,
1876.
Tyndale, William, Victoria Embankment Gdns., SW1.**1D 51**
–c. 1484–1536. Religious reformer and translator of the Bible. Boehm, 1884.
Washington, George, Trafalgar Sq., WC2. **3C 35**
1732–99. First President of the United States. Commander of the Continental Army
in War of Independence. Presented by State of Virginia. 1921.
Wellington Arch (Quadriga Arch), Constitution Hill, SW1. **2A 48**
By Decimus Burton, built as an entrance gate to Hyde Park. The Quadriga group
1912, Jones, is in memory of Edward VII.
Wellington, Duke of, 1769–1852. British Commander-in-Chief in Napoleonic Wars
1. Hyde Park Corner, SW1. **2A 48**
    Figures cast from captured French cannon. Equestrian. Boehm, 1888.
2. Royal Exchange, EC2. **1A 40.** Equestrian, without stirrups. Chantrey, 1844.
Wesley, John, Wesley's Chapel, City Rd., EC2. **1A 24**
1703–91. Founder of the Methodist Church. Acton, 1891.
Whittington, Dick, Royal Exchange, EC2. **1A 40**
d. 1423. Thrice Lord Mayor of London. Carew.
Whittington Stone, Highgate Hill, N19. **AZ 1F 65**
Stone placed where Dick and his cat were supposed to have heard Bow Bells.
Wolseley, 1st Viscount, Horse Guards Parade, SW1. **1C 51**
1833–1913. Soldier. Served in Crimea, India, China, Boer War. Equestrian.
Goscombe John. 1917.
York, Duke of, Waterloo Place, SW1. **1B 50**
1763–1827. Column 124 ft. high with statue of the non-hero of the popular song
"led his ten thousand men up a hill and down again".

TELECOMMUNICATIONS SERVICES

TELEGRAPH SERVICES
British Telecom HQ, 81 Newgate St., EC1. 01-356 5000 **1B 38**
See below for British Telecom Services
Commercial Cable Co., Melbray Ho., Bastwick St., EC1. 24 hrs. 01-251 1577
AZ 1B 22. Reception of Cablegrams only 01-251 1500
Exchange Telegraph Co., 1 E. Harding St., EC4. (Head Office) 01-353 1080
AZ 1D 37. City office, 10 Throgmorton Av., EC2. 01-628 9361 **1A 40**
Gt. Northern Telegraph Co., 5 St. Helen's Pl., EC3. (Messengers & Enquiries)
01-588 4567 **1B 40**
R.C.A. Global Communications Inc., 47a Gt. Guildford St., SE1. 01-928 0227 **1B
54** Night Service 01-928 2758
Western Union Int., 34 Southwark Bri. Rd., SE1. 01-928 1232 **3C 39**

BRITISH TELECOM SERVICES
Alarm Calls. 191 Book through the operator.
Albumline. 01-246 8008, selected LP; weekly.
Bureaufax Office, Cardinal Ho., Farringdon Rd., EC1. 01-250 1117
BTI Bureau Services, Bureaufax, telex and translation bureau, Electra Ho., Temple
Pl., Victoria Embankment, WC2. 01-836 5432 **2B 36**
Challengeline. 01-246 8050. Daily Brainteasers.
Children's London, Events of Interest. 01-246 8007
Cricketline, Test Match Score Card, 154 (from London 01-numbers) during Test
Matches in England.
Discline, 160 18.00–08.00 and all Sat. & Sun. (from London 01- numbers).
FT Cityline, Financial Times Index & Business News. 01-246 8026
Golden Hitline, 01-246 8044. Hits from the 1960's & 70's.
International Telephone Bureaux. Direct lines to 160 countries; main foreign
currencies accepted; open daily.
Heathrow Airport, Open 08.00–20.30.
Westminster, 1 Broadway, SW1. **1A 64** Open 09.00–19.00.
IRN Newsline, 01-246 8080. News Bulletin updated hourly.
Leisureline. A selection of the main events of the day in and around London.
01-246 8041. For additional tourist information: 01-730 3488.
London Weather Centre. 01-836 4311
Overseas Calls: via the operator.
Afghanistan, Antarctica, Bhutan, Bourkina Fasso, China, Cocos Islands, Ghana,
Guinea, Iraq, Lebanon, Mauritania, Pitcairn Islands, Sudan, USSR, and Zaire: dial 158.
All other countries dial 155. International directory enquiries dial 153.
Puffin Storyline, Bedtime Stories. 01-246 8000 From 18.00.
Raceline, 168.
Recipeline. 01-246 8071
Ships Service (Telephone & Telegrams) 100.
Sportsline, 01-246 8020.
Starline, 01-246 8000. Daily horoscope.
Telegrams: International Telegrams and enquiries 193.
Telemessages. 190
Timeline. 123 The Speaking Clock (from London 01- numbers).
Traveline. 01-246 8021. Road conditions 50 miles radius of London.
Weatherline, London area 01-246 8091. N. Kent & Essex Coast 01-246 8096.
S. Kent & Sussex Coast 01-246 8097. Oxen, Berks & Bucks 01-246 8090.
Remote Communications: for details of radio telephones, radio paging.
Air Call, 01-834 9090

British Telecom, via local area telephone sales office.
Racal-Vodac Ltd., Vodafone: 0635-69000
Securicor Communications, 01-223 2101

THEATRES

For MUSIC HALL see page 40
Adelphi, Strand, WC2. 01-836 7611 **3D 35**
Albery, St. Martin's La., WC2. 01-836 3878 **2C 35**
Aldwych, Aldwych, WC2. 01-836 6404 **2A 36**
Ambassadors, West St., WC2. 01-836 1171 **1C 35**
Apollo, Shaftesbury Av., W1. 01-437 2663, 01-630 6262 **2B 34**
Apollo Victoria, Wilton Rd., SW1. 01-828 8665/01-630 6262 **2C 63**
Arts Theatre Club, 6 Gt. Newport St., WC2. 01-836 3334 **2C 35**
Ashcroft, Fairfield Halls, Park La., Croydon. 01-688 9291 **AZ 3D 134**
Astoria, 157 Charing Cross Rd., WC2. 01-734 4291 **1B 34**
Barbican Theatre, Silk St., EC2. 01-628 8795 C/Cards 638 8891 **2C 23**
Battersea Arts Centre, Lavender Hill, SW11. 01-223 8413 **AZ 3D 92**
BBC Paris Theatre Studios, Regent St., SW1. **3A 34**
Bear Gardens Arts Centre, Bankside, SE1. 01-928 6342 **3C 39**
Bloomsbury, 15 Gordon St., WC1. 01-387 9629 **1B 18**
Cambridge, Earlham St., WC2. 01-836 6056 **1C 35**
Chaucer Theatre, Sedgwick Centre, E1. 01-481 5204 **1D 41**
Churchill Theatre, High St., Bromley 01-460 6677 **AZ 2J 127**
Cockpit, Gateforth St., NW8. 01-402 5081 **1D 13.** Theatre and Arts Workshop.
Coliseum: See Concert Halls/Opera, p. 38.
Collegiate, 15 Gordon St., WC1. 01-387 9629 **1B 18**
Comedy, Panton St., SW1. 01-930 2578 **3B 34**
Cottesloe, see National Theatre.
Court Theatre (–Open Air), Holland Park W8. **3A 42.** No advanced booking.
Criterion, Piccadilly, W1. 01-930 3216 **3A 34**
Donmar Warehouse, 41 Earlham St., WC2. 01-836 1071 **1C 35**
Drury Lane (Theatre Royal), Catherine St., WC2. 01-836 8108 **2A 36**
Duchess, Catherine St., WC2. 01-836 8243 **2A 36**
Duke of Yorks, St. Martin's La., WC2. 01-836 5122 **3C 35**
Fortune, Russell St., WC2. 01-836 2238 **1A 36**
Garrick, Charing Cross Rd., WC2. 01-836 4601 **3C 35**
Globe, Shaftesbury Av., W1. 01-437 1592 **2B 34**
Greenwich, Crooms Hill, SE10. 01-838 7755 **AZ 7E 80**
Guildhall School of Music & Drama, Barbican, EC2. 01-628 2571 **2D 23**
Half Moon, 213 Mile End Rd., E1. 01-790 4000 **AZ 5J 63**
Hampstead Theatre Club, Swiss Cottage Centre, Avenue Rd., NW3. 01-722 9301
AZ 7B 44
Haymarket (Theatre Royal) Haymarket, SW1. 01-930 9832 **3B 34**
Her Majesty's, Haymarket, SW1. 01-930 6606 **3B 34**
ICA, The Mall, SW1. 01-930 3647 **1B 50**
Jeannetta Cochrane, Southampton Row, WC1. 01-242 7040 **3A 20**
L.A.M.D.A. London Academy of Music & Dramatic Art, Logan Pl., W8. 01-373
7017 **AZ 4J 75**
London Palladium, 8 Argyll St., W1. 01-437 7373 **1D 33**
Lyric, Shaftesbury Av., W1. 01-437 3686 **2A 34**
Lyric Hammersmith, Kings St., W6. 01-741 2311 **AZ 4A 58**
Lyttelton, see National Theatre.
Mayfair, Stratton St., W1. 01-629 3036 **3C 33**
Mermaid, Puddle Dock, Up. Thames St., EC4. 01-236 5568 **2A 38**
National Theatre, Upper Ground, SE1. 01-928 2252 **1B 52**
Gen. Information 633 0880. Three theatres Cottesloe, Lyttelton & Olivier.

New London Theatre, Parker St., Drury La., WC2. 01-405 0072 **1D 35**
Old Vic, Waterloo Rd., SE1. 01-928 7616 **2C 53**
Olivier, see National Theatre.
Palace, Shaftesbury Av., W1. 01-437 6834 **2B 34**
Phoenix, Charing Cross Rd., WC2. 01-836 2294 **1B 34**
Piccadilly, Denman St., W1. 01-437 4506 **2A 34**
Players, 173 Hungerford Arches, Villiers St., WC2. 01-839 1134 **3D 35**
Playhouse, Northumberland Av., WC2. **1D 51**
Prince Edward, Old Compton St., W1. 01-437 6877 **1B 34**
Prince of Wales, 31 Coventry St., W1. 01-930 8681 **3B 34**
Queen's, 51 Shaftesbury Av., W1. 01-734 1166 **2B 34**
Questors, 12 Mattock La., W5. 01-567 5184 **AZ 1B 72**
Regents Park (Open Air), Inner Circle, Regents Pk., NW1. 01-486 2431 **3D 7**
Richmond, The Green, Richmond, Surrey. 01-940 0088 **AZ 5D 88**
Riverside Studios, Crisp Rd., W6. 01-748 3354 **AZ 5E 74**
Round House, Chalk Farm Rd., NW1. 01-267 2564 **AZ 7E 44**
Royal Court, Sloane Sq., SW1. 01-730 1745 **3D 61**
Royalty, Portugal St., WC2. 01-405 8004 **1A 36**
Royal Opera House; see Concert Halls/Opera, page 38.
Royal Shakespeare Company; see Barbican Theatre.
Sadlers Wells, Rosebery Av., EC1. 01-837 1672 **AZ 4A 62**
St. George's, 49 Tufnell Pk. Rd., N7. 01-609 1198 **AZ 4G 45**
St. Martin's, West St., WC2. 01-836 1443 **2C 35**
Savoy, Strand, WC2. 01-836 8888 **2A 36**
Shaftesbury Theatre, Shaftesbury Av., WC2. 01-836 6596 **1C 35**
Shaw Theatre, 100 Euston Rd., NW1. 01-388 1394 **2C 11**
Strand, Aldwych, WC2. 01-836 2660 **2A 36**
Theatre Royal Stratford, Angel La., E15. 01-534 0310 **AZ 6F 49**
Tower Theatre, Cannonbury Tower, Cannonbury Pl., N1. 01-226 5111 **AZ 6B 46**
Vanbrugh Theatre Club, Royal Academy of Dramatic Art, Malet St., WC1. 01-580
    7982 **1B 18**
Vaudeville, Strand, WC2. 01-836 9987 **2D 35**
Victoria Palace, Victoria St., SW1. 01-834 1317 **1C 63**
Westminster, Palace St., SW1. 01-834 0283 **3C 49**
Whitehall, 14 Whitehall, SW1. 01-930 6692 **1C 51**
Wimbledon, The Broadway, SW19. 01-946 5211 **AZ 7J 107**
Wyndham's, Charing Cross Rd., WC2. 01-836 3028 **2C 35**
Young Vic, 66 The Cut, SE1. 01-928 6363 **2D 53**

Children's Theatre
**Children's Theatre and Puppet shows take place in many London Parks
between May and Sept. Details can be found in weekly entertainments guides.**

The following provide professional quality theatre for children.
Little Angel Marionette Theatre, 14 Dagmar Pas., Cross St., N1. 01-226 1787
AZ 1B 62
Polka Children's Theatre, 240 The Broadway, SW19. 01-543 4888 **AZ 7J 107**
Also run many children's "theatrical" activities; playground, toyshop.
Unicorn Theatre Club, Gt. Newport St., WC2. 01-836 3334 **2C 35**
Also run "Workshop" training for children 4 to 12 yrs.

Anna Scher Children's Theatre, 70/72 Barnsbury Rd., N1. 01-278 2101 **AZ 1A
62** Not a "theatre", but provide theatre classes for children out of school time;
occasional theatrical events by the children.

TICKET AGENCIES

Cinema, Concerts, Theatre, Sports and other events.
Abbey Box Office, 27 Victoria St., SW1. 01-222 2992 **1C 63**
Edwards & Edwards, Palace Theatre, Shaftesbury Av., W1. 01-734 9761 **2B 34**
Tickets for all London theatres, Stratford upon Avon & New York.
Group Sales Box Office, Norris Ho., Norris St., SW1. 01-930 6123 **3B 34**
Keith Prowse, Theatre, Sports and all Bookings. Head Office, Banda Ho.,
Cambridge Gro., W6. Theatre **01-741 9999**
Sport 01-741 8999. Concerts 01-741 8989, and at over 30 branches in London.
London Theatre Bookings, 96 Shaftesbury Av., W1. 01-439 4061 **2A 34**
London Visitor & Convention Bureau, Victoria Station, SW1. **2C 63**
Obtainable's, Panton Ho., 25 Haymarket, SW1. 01-839 5363 **3B 34**
Premier Box Office, 188 Shaftesbury Av., WC2. 01-240 2245 **2A 34**
Theatre & Concert Rail Club, PO Box 1. St. Albans, Herts.
Theatre Services, 19 Newport Ct., WC2. 01-439 1439 **2C 35**
Ticket Centre, 1b Bridge St., SW1. 01-839 6732 **3D 51**
Ticketmaster, 78 St. Martins La., WC2. 01-379 6433 **2C 35**

Half Price Tickets
Society of West End Theatre Kiosk, Leicester Sq., WC2. **2B 34**
Open from 14.00 (from 12.00 for matinee tickets); small service charge; no
telephone.

TOURIST INFORMATION CENTRES

For Hotel reservations see also Accommodation.

British Travel Centre, Rex Ho., 4/12 Lower Regent St., SW1. **3A 34**
What to see/Where to stay in England, Scotland, Wales and N. Ireland. Information
service linked to British Rail Ticket Office; American Express Travel Office for Bureau
do change, coach tours or theatre tickets, Books and gifts shop. Open daily.
TELEPHONE SERVICE 01-730 3400 (excluding information on London–see
below) Mon to Sat 09.00–18.00
London Visitor & Convention Bureau, Head Office, 26 Grosvenor Gdns., SW1.
Mail Only.
TELEPHONE SERVICE. 01-730 3488 (London information only) Mon to Fri 09.00–
17.30.
TOURIST INFORMATION CENTRES:
Information on all matters concerning visiting London and Britain. Multi-
   lingual.Victoria Station, forecourt. **2C 63.** Open 09.00–20.30 Daily (08.00–
   22.00 July & August). Tourist information, accommodation, tickets, bookshop
   with wide range of guide books and maps.
Harrods, Knightsbridge, SW3. 4th floor. **3B 46.** Open normal shop hours. Tourist
   information and bookings.
Selfridges, Oxford St., W1. Ground floor. **1A 32.** Open normal shop hours. Tourist
   information and bookings.
West Gate, Tower of London, EC3 **3C 41**. Tourist Information and bookings. Open
   10.00–18.00 Daily (10.15 Sun.) April to Oct. only.
Heathrow Central Underground Station, Tourist Information and bookings. Open
   09.00–18.00 Daily.
City of London Information Centre, St Paul's Churchyard, EC4. 01-606 3030 **1B 38**
Information on places and events within the "City". Open Mon. to Fri. 09.30–
17.00. Sats. Oct. to Mar. 10.00–12.30. April to Sept. 10.00–16.00.

Clerkenwell Heritage Centre, 33 St. John's Sq., EC1. 01-250 1039 **1A 22**. Open 09.00–18.00 Daily (except Oct. to March. Mon. to Fri. 09.00–16.00 only).
London Transport, 55 Broadway, SW1. **3B 50**
Information concerning Buses, Green Line Coaches, Underground Trains and special tickets. TELEPHONE SERVICES. 01-222 1234 24 hours.
TRAVEL INFORMATION CENTRES: Euston Tube Sta., Heathrow Central Tube Sta., King's Cross Tube Sta., Oxford Circus Tube Sta., Piccadilly Circus Tube Sta., St. James's Park Tube Sta., Victoria Tube Sta., Charing Cross Tube Sta.
Leisureline Information Service. For the main events of the day in and around London 01-246 8041. –In French 01-246 8043. In German 01-246 8045. For Children 01-346 8007

TOURS AND SIGHTSEEING EXCURSIONS

London Appreciation Society, 17 Manson Mews, SW7. 01-370 1100
An association of people interested in London. Members visit a great variety of interesting places both in and around London, many not normally open (not during June, July, Aug. or Sept.). Subscription.

BARBICAN Centre for Arts and Conferences. **2C 23**
For tours (excluding the theatre) apply with two to three weeks' notice; subject to staff availability. 01-638 4141 extension 303.

CANAL TRIPS for Canal Walks see page 86 and 189
Jason's Trip and Argonaut Gallery, Little Venice, W2. 01-286 3428 **2A 12**
Summer service from opposite 60 Blomfield Rd., W9. Evening trips (refreshments available) and Saturday extended tripsbook in advance.
Jenny Wren Canal Cruises, 250 Camden High St., NW1. 01-485 4433/6210 **AZ 1F 61** Summer service from Garden Jetty, 250 Camden High St. Seats can be booked by phone. Also restaurant boat available for lunch or dinner cruises. See "Fair Lady"Restaurant section.
London Waterbus Company, Camden Lock, NW1. 01-482 2550
From Little Venice **2A 12** or Camden Lock, Chalk Farm Rd. **AZ 7F 45** to London Zoo (joint Zoo tickets available) daily April to Oct. Also some extended trips. Weekends and holidays in Winter months. Evening trips and private hire available.

COACH TOURS
For London Transport special tickets see TRAVEL AND TRANSPORT Buses and Underground sub-section.
Cityrama Sightseeing Tour: London Cityrama 01-720 6663
Starts from Victoria (Grosvenor Gdns) **1C 63.**, Trafalgar Sq. **3C 35** and Broad Sanctuary **3C 51**.
Two hour circular tour with recorded commentary in eight languages.
London Crusader: National Express in association with London Transport; ½ day and full day tours to all tourist sights. Bookable at tourist and London Transport Information Centres, Victoria Coach Station and agents.
Culture Bus 01-629 4999. Operating at half hourly intervals around an 18 mile circuit to cover most of London's attractions, 20 stopping points and flat fare, re-boarding all day.
Round London Sightseeing Tour: London Transport.
Starts from Victoria (Grosvenor Gdns), **1C 63,** Marble Arch, **2C 31** and Piccadilly pCircus, **3A 34.** Two hour circular tour every day except Christmas Day. Not a conducted tour, an illustrated diagram is provided, no bookings accepted. April to Oct.: regular intervals between 09.00–20.00. Nov. to March: every hour 09.00–16.00.

Tour operators offering guided coach tours to famous places in and around London. COTTER TOURS, 1 Norris St., SW1. 01-930 5781.

EBDONS COACHES, 1/6 Powerscroft, Sidcup. 01-300 7606.
THOMAS COOK LTD., 45 Berkeley St., W1. 01-499 4000.
EVAN EVANS, 27 Cockspur St., SW1. 01-930 2377.
FRAMES, 7 Herbrand St., WC1. 01-837 6311.
GREY GREEN, 53 Stamford Hill, N16. 01-800 8010.
GUARDS OF LONDON, 111 Lots Rd., SW10. 01-351 0221.
LONDON CRUSADER, Western Ho., 237 Oxford St., W1. 01-437 0124.
LONDON TRANSPORT, 55 Broadway, SW1. 01-222 1234.
WEALDON OF LONDON, Falcon Estate, Central Way, Feltham. 01-844 0944

HELICOPTER TOUR, UK Air Taxis, Westland Heliport, Lombard Rd.,
SW11. 01-228 9114. 15 minute trip along the course of the River
Thames to Greenwich within sight of the Thames Barrier.

HOUSES OF PARLIAMENT
For a House of Commons debate queue at the St. Stephen's entrance or write to
M.P. in advance, sessions usually start Mon. to Thurs. 14.30 and Fri. 11.00.

LAW COURTS
Central Criminal Courts: (Old Bailey), Old Bailey, EC4.
Fifteen courts with access for the public, spectacular cases are tried in Court 1 and
can attract large numbers hoping to occupy one of the 28 Public Gallery seats.
–Royal Courts of Justice, Strand, WC2.
Twenty to thirty courts with access for the public. Courts generally sit between
10.30–16.30 weekdays only. The senior attendant at the main gate can arrange
tours, circumstances permitting, to interested visitors.

LONDON BRASS RUBBING CENTRES
St. James's Church, Piccadilly, W1. 01–437 6023 **3A 34.** Open Mon. to Sat. 10.00–
18.00, Sun. 12.00–18.00. All Hallows by the Tower, Byward St., EC3. **3C 41.**
Open Mon. to Sat. 11.00–17.45, Sun. 12.30–17.45. May to Oct. only. Materials
and instruction available. Brass Rubbing is also available at Westminster Abbey
3C 51 Mon. to Sat. 09.00–17.30.

LLOYDS, Lime St., EC3. 01-623 7100 **1B 40**
External observation lifts give views over the "City" and access for the public to
the Underwriting Room Viewing Gallery and exhibition of Lloyds history.

NATIONAL THEATRE
Tour the backstage and three auditoriums, duration 1–2 hours. Daily Mon. to Sat.,
bookings 01-633 0880

NEWSPAPERS
The following are among the National Daily's who will give conducted tours. Expect
a long waiting list.
Daily Express, Fleet St., EC4. 01-353 8000
Evening Tour 20.30 lasting 2 hrs. apply Group Technical Dept.
Daily Mail, Northcliffe Ho., Tudor St., EC4. 01-353 6000
Evening Tour 21.00 lasting 2 hrs., apply Production Manager, New Carmelite Ho.
New Carmelite St., EC4.
Daily Telegraph, 135 Fleet St., EC4. 01-353 4242
Evening Tour 20.45 lasting 2 hrs., apply General Manager.
Guardian, 119 Farringdon Rd., EC1. 01–278 2332
Evening Tour 20.30 lasting 3 hrs., apply Production Office.
The Times, 1 Pennington St., E1. 01-481 4100
Evening Tour 20.15 lasting 2–4 hrs., apply Visits Secretary.

PRIVATE GUIDES
The London Visitor & Convention Bureau publishes a list of Registered Guides
annually, special subject and languages are indicated. Bookings 01-730 3450
ext 244.

Guild of Guide Lecturers, Grandma Lees Restaurant. 2 Bridge St., SW1., 01-839 7438
The professional association of tourist guides in Gt. Britain. Book a guide direct or via Tour Guides Ltd. Free guide information and annual list.
British Tours/Undergraduate Tours, 6 South Molton St., W1. 01-629 5267 **1B 32**
Drive/Guide London Tours. One or half-day tours for sightseeing, shopping, pub crawls. Half, one, and multi-day tours from London of major historical places. Registered guides.
Driver Guides Association, Bookings 01-736 8882.
Spcially trained Driver Guides; both London and extended tours.
Prestige Tours, 13/16 Jacob's Well Mws., W1. 01-584 3118 **3A 16**
Personal sightseeing tours by registered guides who are also licensed London Taxi Drivers.
Take-a-Guide, 85 Lower Sloane St., SW1. 01-730 9144 **3D 61**
Personal sightseeing driver/guide service. Door to Door itineraries for half-day and full-day tours in London, day tours from London. Registered guides.
Specials, 243 Regent St., W1. 01-408 1611.
Large programme of tours and holidays for groups or individuals in London, UK or Europe. Specialist subjects and personal itineraries available.
Tour Guides Ltd, 164 N. Gower St., NW1. 01-388 8601 **3D 9**
Booking bureau for registered guides throughout UK; in association with Guild of Guide Lecturers.

RIVER TRIPS
London Visitor & Convention Bureau River Boat Information Service. 01-730 4812.
Piers: Charing Cross **1D 51.** Greenwich **AZ 5E 80.** Tower **3C 41.** Westminster **2D 51.** Festival Pier **1A 52**
There are hosts of passenger boats providing regular sightseeing river trips along the River Thames upstream as far as Hampton Court or downstream to the Thames Flood Barrier. Special services include luncheon cruises, floodlit cruises, disco cruises and audio-visual cruises. Boats are always available for private hire and group bookings.

From Westminster Pier 2D 51
Regular trips daily to Tower of London, Greenwich and Thames Barrier downstream (details 01-930 4097). Regular summer only services upstream to Kew Gardens, Richmond and Hampton Court Palace (details 01-930 2062).
From Tower Pier 3C 41
Regular trips daily downstream to Greenwich and Thames Barrier and upstream to Westminster (details 01-488 0344). Also ferry service to HMS Belfast.
From Charing Cross Pier 1D 51 and Festival Pier 1A 52
Regular summer services to Tower of London and Greenwich (details 01-930 0971).

Salter Bros. Steamers. Folly Bridge, Oxford 43421 and Windsor 65832.
Daily services between late May and early September.
From piers at Staines, Runnymede, Windsor, Maidenhead, Cookham, Marlow, Henley, Reading, Abingdon, Oxford and intermediate landing stages. Timetables, combined rail and river tours available. Light refreshments on most boats.

SEWAGE PUMPING STATIONS AND TREATMENT WORKS
Can include visit to any local works, the historic Abbey Mills Station (see PLACES OF INTEREST) or a modern automatic works. Weekdays only, apply to Divisional Manager, Metropolitan Public Health Division, Thames Water Authority, 50–64 Broadway, SW1.

STOCK EXCHANGE Old Broad St., EC2. 01-588 2355 **1A 40**
Visitors' Gallery open Mon. to Fri. 09.45–15.15. Last guided tour 14.30, advisable
to book.

VIEWING LONDON
By Coach or Helicopter see p. 186/187.
Lloyds, see page 187.
The Monument, see STATUES AND MONUMENTS.
St. Paul's Cathedral Galleries, see CATHEDRALS AND CHURCHES.
Tower Bridge Walkway, see BRIDGES & TUNNELS.
Westminster Cathedral, Campanile, see CATHEDRALS AND CHURCHES.

WALKING TOURS Interesting walks are organised by the following:
Citysights. 01-241 0323
City Walks. 01-908 4897
Discovering London. 0277 213704
London Walks. 01-882 2763
Royal London Walking Tours. 01-740 7100
Regents Canal: guided walks May–Dec. organised through the Inland Waterways
Association. 01-586 2510/2556. See also Canal Walks p. 86.
Streets of London. 01-882 3414

WEMBLEY STADIUM Empire Way. 01-902 8833 **AZ 4F 41**
Conducted tour behind the scenes. Dressing Rooms, Royal Box Steps, and audio-
visual history. Daily (except Thurs.) at 10.00, 11.00, 12.00 also 14.00, 15.00.
16.00 summer, 14.00, 15.00 winter; not during events or day before or after.

TRAVEL AND TRANSPORT

International Travellers Aid, Y.W.C.A, 2 Weymouth St., W1. **2C 17**
Help for travellers in difficulty. Will arrange escorts across London, especially
concerned with young people, au pairs. Reception office: Victoria Station. The
Kiosk, Platform 10. 01-834 3925, 01-834 3901 **2C 63**
Thomas Cook Airport Services. 01-897 7567/8.
Will meet, escort, assist with baggage, documentation, forward booking; including
children travelling alone and overseas visitors.
Universal Aunts Ltd., 250 Kings Rd., SW3. 01-351 5767
Will meet and escort children, students or adults to and from airports, stations
etc.; visa and passport advice; see also page 11.

AIRPORT LINKS
Heathrow to Central London/Central London to Heathrow
   Airbus: London Transport 01-222 1234
   A1 Heathrow–Victoria (Grosvenor Gdns.) **1C 63**
   A2 Heathrow–Paddington (Eastbourne Ter.) **1B 28**
   A3 Heathrow–Euston Station **2A 10**
   Flightline 767: National Bus Company 01-730 0202
   Heathrow–Victoria Coach Station **3B 62**
   Underground: London Transport 01-222 1234
   Piccadilly Line, from and to Heathrow Terminals 1 2 3 & 4.
Gatwick to Central London/Central London to Gatwick
   British Rail: Gatwick Airport Sta.–Victoria Sta. 01-928 5100 **2C 63**
   Flightline 777: National Bus Company 01-730 0202
   Gatwick–Victoria (Buckingham Pal. Rd.) **3B 62**
Heathrow to Gatwick/Gatwick to Heathrow
   Speedlink: direct express coach link.
   Jetlink 747: direct express coach link.

Luton to Central London/Central London to Luton.
   Flightline 757: National Bus Company 01-730 0202
   Luton–Victoria (Eccleston Bridge) **2C 63**
   British Rail: Luton Station—St. Pancras Station. 01-387 7070 (via bus or taxi to
   Luton Station).

AIRLINES—PASSENGER

AER Lingus, 223 Regent St., W1. **1C 33**
Pass. Res., Ireland and Europe 01-734 1212. Transatlantic 01-437 8000.
Aeroflot Soviet Airlines, 69 Piccadilly, W1. 01-493 7436 **1D 49**
Air Afrique, 177 Piccadilly, W1. 01-493 4881 **3D 33.** Pass. Res. 01-629 6114.
Air Canada, 140 Regent St., W1. **2D 33**
Ticket Office 439 7941. Flight Information 24 hrs. 897 1331. Enquiries, Booking,
Reconfirmations 759 2636.
Air France, 158 New Bond St., W1. 01-499 8611 **2C 33.** Pass. Res. 01-499 9511.
Air India, 17 New Bond St., W1. 01-493 4050 **2C 33.** Pass Res. 01-491 7979.
Air Jamaica, 36 Piccadilly, W1. Pass. Res. 01-734 1782
Air Malta, 23 Pall Mall, SW1. 01-839 5872 **AZ 1A 50**
Air New Zealand, 15 Charles II St., SW1. 01-930 1088 **3B 34**
Air UK, reservations 01-249 7033
Alitalia Italian Airlines, 27/28 Piccadilly, W1. **3A 34.** Pass. Res. 01-734 4040.
Admin. 01-759 2510
American Air Lines, 7 Albemarle St., W1. 01-629 0195 **3C 33** Pass. Res. 01-629
8817
Austrian Airlines, 50 Conduit St., W1. 01-439 1851 **2D 33.** Pass. Res. 01-439
0741
British Airways: Head Office, Speedbird Ho., Heathrow Airport 01-759 5511
Reservations, Fares, Advance Travel Information 01-897 4000
Passenger Flight Information Heathrow 01-759 2525, Gatwick, Crawley 518033
Sales Shops: 101 Cheapside, EC2 **1C 39,** 52 Grosvenor Gdns., SW1. **1C 63,** 421
Oxford St., W1. **1A 32,** 65 & 75 Regent St., W1. **3A 34,** 110 Strand, WC2.
3C 35, Victoria Station (Platform 13) SW1. **2C 63,** also Portman Hotel **1C 31** and
Hilton Hotel **1A 48**
British Caledonian Airways, Victoria Air Terminal, SW1. 01-834 9411 **2C 63**
Reservations Heathrow 01-668 4222, Gatwick, Crawley 518888
British West Indian Airways, 20 Regent St., SW1. 01-839 7155 **3A 34**
Canadian Pacific, 62 Trafalgar Sq., WC2. **3C 35**
Caribbean Airways, 6 Bruton St., W1. 01-491 3817 **3C 33**
Cathay Pacific Airways, 123 Pall Mall, SW1. 01-930 7878 **1A 50**
Continental Airlines, 50 Pall Mall, SW1. 01-839 1543 **1A 50**
Cyprus Airways, 29 Hampstead Rd., NW1. 01-388 5411 **3D 9**
Czechoslovak Airlines, 17 Old Bond St., W1. 01-499 6442 **3D 33**
Dan Air, Sales 36 New Broad St., EC2. 01-638 1747 **3A 24**
Eastern Airlines, 49 Old Bond St., W1. 01-409 3376 **3D 33**
Egyptair, 31 Piccadilly, W1. 01-734 2864. Res. 437 0812 **3A 34**
El Al Israel Airlines, 185 Regent Street, W1 01-437 9255 **2D 33**
Ethiopean Airlines, 85 Jermyn St., SW1. 01-930 9152 **3A 34**
Finnair, 56 Haymarket, SW1. 01-930 3941 **3B 34**
Ghana Airways Corp., 12 Old Bond St., W1. 01-499 0201 **3D 33**
Gulf Air, 73 Piccadilly, W1. 01-409 0191 **3A 34**
Iberia Airlines of Spain, 169 Regent St., W1. 01-437 9822 **2D 33**
Pass. Res. European 01-437 5622. Intercontinental. 01-439 7539
Icelandair, 73 Grosvenor St., W1. 01-499 9971 **2B 32**
Iran Air, 73 Piccadilly, W1. 01-409 0971 **1D 49**
Iraqi Airways, 4 Regent St., SW1. 01-930 1155 **3B 34**
Japan Airlines, 5 Hanover Sq., W1. 01-629 9244 **1C 33.** Pass. Res. 01-408 1000
Kenya Airways, 16 Conduit St., W1. 01-409 3121 **2C 33**

K.L.M. Royal Dutch Airlines, Time and Life Bldgs., New Bond St., W1. 01-492 0336 **2C 23.** Pass. Res. 01-568 9144.
Korean Air Lines, 66 Haymarket, SW1. 01-930 6513 **3B 34**
Kuwait Airways, 16 Baker St., W1. 01-486 6666 **1C 15**
Lufthansa German Airlines, 28 Piccadilly, W1. 01-408 0322 **3A 34**
Pass. Res. 01-408 0442
Malaysian Airlines, 25 St. George St., W.1. 01-499 6286 **2C 33**
Malev Hungarian Airlines, 10 Vigo St., W1. 01-439 0577 **3D 33**
Middle East Airlines S.A.L., 80 Piccadilly, W1. 01-493 6321 **1C 49**
Pass. Res. 01-493 5681
Nigeria Airways, 12 Conduit St., W1. 01-493 9726 **2C 33.** Pass. Res. 01-629 3717
Northwest Orient, 49 Albemarle St., W1. 01-629 5353 **3C 33**
Olympic Airways, 141 New Bond St., W1. 01-493 1233 **2C 33.** Pass. Res. 01-499 8712
Pakistan International Airlines, 45 Piccadilly, W1. **3D 33** Pass. Res. 734 5544.
Admin. 01-741 8066
Pan American World Airways, 193 Piccadilly, W1. 01-409 0688 **3D 33**
Peoplexpress, Gatwick Airport, Gatwick 502061
Polish Airlines (Lot), 313 Regent St., W1. 01-580 5037 **3C 17**
Portuguese Airways, 19 Regent St., SW1. 01-839 1031 **3A 34**
(Pass. Res. and Flight Enquiries) 01-828 0262
Qantas Airways, 169 Regent St., W1. 01-748 3131 **3D 33**
Pass. Res. and enquiries. 01-748 5050. Flight Information 897 1331
Royal Air Maroc, 174 Regent St., W1. 01-734 5943 **2D 33**
Royal Jordanian Airlines, 177 Regent St., W1. 01-734 2557 **2D 33**
Sabena Belgian World Airlines, 36 Piccadilly, W1. 01-437 6960 **3A 34**
Pass. Res. 01-437 6950
Saudi Arabian Airlines, 171 Regent St., W1. 01-995 7777 **2D 33**
Scandinavian Airlines, 52 Conduit St., W1. 01-734 4020 **2C 33**
South African Airways, 251 Regent St., W1. 01-437 9621 **1C 33**
Pass. Res. 01-734 9841
Sudan Airways, 12 Grosvenor St., W1. 01-629 3385 **2B 32.** Pass. Res. 01-499 8101.
Swissair, Travel Office, Swiss Centre, 3 New Coventry St., W1. 01-734 6737
2B 34 Pass. Res., 10 Wardour St., W1. 01-439 4144 **2B 34**
Syrian Arab Airlines, 5 Conduit St., W1. 01-493 2851 **2C 33**
TAP. See Portuguese Airways.
Thai Airways,41 Albemarle St., W1. 01-499 9113. Sales 491 7953 **3C 33**
Trans World Airlines Inc., 200 Piccadilly, W1. 01-636 4090 **3A 34**
Heathrow Terminal 3-flight enquiries etc. 01-759 5352
Trans-Australia Airlines, 49 Old Bond St., W1. 01-493 1934 **3C 33**
Turkish Airlines, 11 Hanover St. W1. 01-499 9240 **1C 33.** Pass. Res. 01-499 9247
UTA French Airlines, 177 Piccadilly, W1. 01-493 4881 **3D 33.**
Pass. Res. 01–629 6114
Varig Brazilian Airlines, 16 Hanover St., W1. 01-629 9408 **1C 33**
Pass. Res. 629 5824
Virgin Atlantic Airways, 7th Floor, Sussex Ho., High St., Crawley 549771. Pass
Res. Crawley 38222.
Yugoslav Airlines, 201 Regent St., W1. 01-734 6252 **2D 33**
Zambia Airways Corp., 163 Piccadilly, W1. 01-491 7521 **3D 33**

AIRPORT LINKS Heathrow/Gatwick/Luton to and from Central London, see page 189.

AIRPORTS
British Airports Authority, Gatwick Airport, Gatwick 517755.
Gatwick Airport, Horley, Surrey. Crawley 28822 and 01-668 4211 (flight enquiries Gatwick 31299).
For transport links with central London, see Airport Links page 189.

Heathrow Airport, Bath Road, Heathrow, Middx. 01-759 4321
For transport links with central London, see Airport Links page 189.
Luton Airport, Luton, Beds. Luton 36061. See Airport Links page 189.
Southend Airport, Southend-on-Sea. 40201
By train from Liverpool Street to Rochford then special bus.
Stansted Airport, Stansted, Essex. Bishop's Stortford 502380
By train from Liverpool Street to Bishop's Stortford.
Westland Heliport, Lombard Rd., SW11. 01-228 0181 **AZ 2B 92**

AIR CHARTER
Air London, from Gatwick Airport, Gatwick 31653
Biggin Hill Air Taxi, Biggin Hill 76137
British Air Ferries Ltd, Southend 354435.
British Airways, Charter flight enquiries Gatwick 36321
Cabair, from Elstree Aerodrome, Herts. 01-953 4411
Cal Air International, Gatwick 543661
Dan Air, Dancharter. 01-638 1747, from Gatwick Airport
Fairflight Charters, from Biggin Hill Aerodrome, Kent. Biggin Hill 74651
Helicopter Charter Enquiries, Westland Heliport, SW11. 01-731 5857
    Executive Aircraft Charter, 01-228 3232
London Airtaxi Centre, 36 New Broad St., EC2. 01-588 3578
McAlpine Aviation, from Luton Airport. Luton 24182
Tradewinds Airways, from Gatwick Airport. 01-668 9273
UK Air Taxis, Westland Heliport, SW11. 01-228 9114

BRITISH RAIL
British Railways Board H.Q., Euston Square, PO Box 100, NW1. **3A 10**
British Rail Travel Offices, Personal callers only. Cannon Street Station, EC4.
2D 39; Euston Station, NW1. **2A 10**; Kings Cross Sta., NW1, **1D 11**;
Paddington Sta., W2. **1C 29**; Waterloo Sta., SE1. **2C 53**; Victoria St., SW1. **2C 63**;
87 King William St., EC4. **2A 40**; 14 Kingsgate Pde. 66 Victoria St., SW1.
1D 63; 407 Oxford St., W1. **1A 32**; 170 Strand, WC2. **2B 36**; Regent St., SW1.
3B 34 also Heathrow Airport.

Main Line Termini and Principal Destinations
Charing Cross (and Waterloo East), Strand, WC2. 01-928 5100 **3D 35**
Southern Region. Principal Destinations include Ashford, Dover, Gillingham,
Hastings, Maidstone, Margate, Ramsgate, Sevenoaks, Tonbridge, Tunbridge Wells.
Euston, Euston Rd., NW1. 01-387 7070 **2A 10**
London Midland Region. Principal Destinations include Bangor, Barrow-in-Furness,
Birmingham, Carlisle, Chester, Coventry, Crewe, Glasgow, Holyhead,
Liverpool, Manchester, Northampton, Preston, Rugby, Shrewsbury, Stoke-on-
Trent, Wolverhampton, Isle of Man.
Kings Cross, Euston Rd., NW1. 01-278 2477 **1D 11**
Eastern Region. Principal Destinations include Aberdeen, Berwick-upon-Tweed,
Bradford, Darlington, Doncaster, Edinburgh, Grantham, Grimsby, Harrogate,
Hull, Leeds, Newark, Newcastle, Peterborough, Retford, Teeside, Wakefield, York.
Liverpool Street, EC3. 01-283 7171 **3B 24**
Eastern Region. Principal Destinations include Cambridge, Colchester, Ely,
Harwich, Ipswich, Kings Lynn, Lowestoft, Norwich, Southend, Stansted
Airport.
Marylebone, Marylebone Rd., NW1. 01-387 7070 **1B 14**
London Midland Region. Principal Destinations include Aylesbury, Banbury, High
Wycombe.
Paddington, Praed St., W2. 01-262 6767 **1C 29**
Western Region. Principal Destinations include Banbury, Bath, Birmingham,
Bristol, Cardiff, Cheltenham, Exeter, Fishguard, Gloucester, Hereford,
Newport, Oxford, Penzance, Plymouth, Reading, Swansea, Swindon, Worcester.
St. Pancras, Euston Rd., NW1. 01-387 7070 **2C 11**

London Midland Region. Principal Destinations include Bedford, Derby, Leicester,
Luton, Manchester, Nottingham, Sheffield, Luton Airport.
Victoria, Buckingham Palace Rd., SW1. 01-928 5100 **2C 63**
Southern Region. Principal Destinations include Ashford, Brighton, Canterbury,
Dover, Eastbourne, Folkestone, Gatwick Airport, Gillingham, Hastings,
Maidstone, Margate, Newhaven, Portsmouth, Ramsgate.
Waterloo, Waterloo Rd., SE1. 01-928 5100 **2C 53**
Southern Region. Principal Destinations include Ashford, Basingstoke,
Bournemouth, Dorchester, Exeter, Guildford, Hastings, Portsmouth, Reading,
Salisbury, Southampton, Weymouth, Winchester, Windsor, Woking, Heathrow
Airport via Staines or Woking, Isle of Wight.

Suburban Services
Charing Cross, Waterloo and Victoria serve the south, south-east and south-west
supplemented by the suburban termini at Blackfriars, **2A 38**; Cannon St.,
2D 39; Holborn Viaduct, **3A 22**; and London Bridge, **1A 56**, Tel.: 01-928 5100.
Euston and St. Pancras serve the Midlands, North and North West, 01-387 7070
Liverpool Street and Fenchurch Street serve Essex and East Anglia, 01-283 7171
Paddington the West, 01-262 6767 and King's Cross the North East, 01-278 2477

International Passenger Network, Inter-City Europe, General enquiries 01-
834 2345
The principal rail services link with shipping, hovercraft, coach and air services to
provide a through timetable to other European countries.
Charing Cross & Waterloo East, through services to Belgium, France, and West
Germany.
Euston, through services to Republic of Ireland, Northern Ireland, Isle of Man.
Kings Cross, through services to Norway.
Liverpool Street, through services to Austria, Belgium, Czechoslovakia, Denmark,
East Germany, Hungary, Italy, Netherlands, Norway, Poland, Romania,
Sweden, Switzerland, USSR, West Germany.
Paddington, through services to Eire.
Victoria, through services TO ALL EUROPEAN COUNTRIES.
Waterloo, through services to Channel Islands and Isle of Wight.

Car Ferry Services: Victoria Car Ferry Centre for Continental, Ireland and Channel
Islands, 01-834 2345. Isle of Wight services 01-928 5100 or Portsmouth 827744.

Motorail, London Reservations Office 01-387 8541
London to Carlisle, Edinburgh, Inverness, Newton Abbot, Penzance,
St. Austell, Stirling.

Passenger Train Information: see also **Main Line Termini.**
EASTERN REGION to W. Yorkshire, North-East, East Coast to Scotland. 01-278
2477 to East Anglia and South-East Essex. 01-283 7171
LONDON MIDLAND to Midlands, N. Wales, North-West to Scotland. 01-387 7070
SOUTHERN REGION to South-East and South. 01-928 5100
WESTERN REGION to West, South-West and S. Wales. 01-262 6767

Region Headquarters:
EASTERN. York Station Tel. York 53022
LONDON MIDLAND. Stanier Ho., Birmingham. 021-643 4444
SOUTHERN. Waterloo Station, SE1. 01-928 5151
WESTERN. 125 Ho., Swindon. 0793 26100

Sleepers Berths can be reserved at any **London Terminus.**
Kings Cross to Aberdeen, Billingham, Darlington, Durham, Dunbar, Dundee,
Edinburgh, Hartlepool, Leeds, Newcastle, Seaham, Stockton and Sunderland.
Euston to Aviemore, Barrow, Carlisle, Dumfries, Fort William, Glasgow, Grange-
over-Sands, Holyhead, Inverness, Kilmarnock, Liverpool, Manchester,
Motherwell, Perth, Preston, Stirling, Stranraer and Ulverston.

Paddington to Bridgend, Camborne, Cardiff, Carmarthen, Exeter, Haverfordwest, Hayle, Liskeard, Llanelli, Lostwithiel, Milford Haven, Neath, Newton Abbot, Par, Penzance, Plymouth, Port Talbot, Redruth, St. Austell, Swansea, Truro.

BUSES AND UNDERGROUND
Airport Bus Links, see page 189 AIR LINKS

London Regional Transport, Admin. H.Q., 55 Broadway, SW1. 01-222 5600 **3B 50 24 Hour Travel Enquiries.** 01-222 1234
Green Line Coaches, London Country Bus Services. Enquiry Office, Eccleston Bri., SW1. 01-834 6563 668 7261 **2B 62**. Green Line Coaches link outlying towns with central London. Limited stops and higher fares than other buses.

London Buses
DOUBLE-DECK RED BUSES, run an extensive network over Greater London during hours approx. 06.00–24.00 with 30 all-night routes to most parts of the greater London area.
SINGLE-DECK RED ARROW BUSES, run between rail terminals and the principal business and shopping areas.
London Explorer Pass. For overseas and UK visitors. Gives unlimited travel on London Transport Buses and the Underground in central and inner London for 1, 3, 4 or 7 day periods. Available from underground stations or Travel Information centres.
London Bus Passes. Unlimited travel on the Bus network without rush hour restrictions, but excluding sightseeing and coach tours. Available from Travel Centres, bus garages and certain underground stations.
Red Bus Rovers. Apply to all normal Red Bus Services, excluding sightseeing and coach tours; valid for one day only. Available from Travel Information Centres, bus garages and most underground stations.

London Transport Travel Information Centres
Heathrow Central, Charing Cross **3C 35**, St. James's Park **3B 50**, Euston **2A 10**, Kings Cross **1C 11**, Oxford Circus **1C 33**, Piccadilly Circus **3A 34** and Victoria **2C 63** Underground Stations. Victoria Station (BR), opposite platform 8 **2C 63**

London Underground: see back cover for tube map.
Cheap day returns available after 10.00.
First and Last Trains
Most tube trains run between 05.30–24.00 on weekdays last trains leaving from the centre of London approx. 24.00. They start later and finish earlier on Sundays.

COACHES It is necessary to book coach journeys in advance.

National Bus Company: express services to and from most principal destinations. Operates from Victoria coach station, see below. London Crusader, Western Ho., 237 Oxford St., W1. 01-437 0124 operate coach tours, see also pp. 186/187, and private coach hire.
Victoria Coach Station, 164 Buckingham Pal. Rd., SW1. 01-730 0202 Enquiries; 01-730 3499 Bookings. **3B 62**
For Green Line, Flightline and Jetlink services 01-668 7261.

CYCLE HIRE
Rent-a-Bike, 41 Floral St., WC2. 01-836 7830 **2C 35**
Wide range of bikes for hire, plus accessories. Bikes also for sale.

FOREIGN EXCHANGE–BUREAUX DE CHANGE
Heathrow Airport, 24 hour service provided by banks in rotation.
Victoria Station, 07.45–22.00 Daily, Thomas Cook Bureau de Change.

Central London facilities outside normal banking hours.
Post Office, Trafalgar Sq. **3C 35** Daily 08.00–20.00. Closed Sun. & Bank Hols.
American Express, 6 Haymarket SW1. 01-930 4411 **3B34** and branches.
Chequepoint, Head Office and exchange rate enquiries—01-439 7282

24 hour facilities at 37 Coventry St., W1. **3A 34,** 236 Earls Court Rd., SW5.
AZ 3J 75, 126 Bayswater Rd., W2. **3D 27,** 548 Oxford St., W1. **2C 31**
08.30–24.00 facilities at 89 Gloucester Rd., SW7. **1A 58,** 130 King's Rd., SW3.
3C 61, 58 Queensway, W2. **1D 27,** 24 Wardour St., W1. **1A 34,** 10–12
Exhibition Rd., SW7. **1D 59,** 41 Cranbourn St., W1. **2C 35,** 13/15 Davis St., W1.
1B 32, 1/7 Shaftesbury Av., W1. **2B 34.**

Thomas Cook Ltd, normally 09.00–17.30 Mon. to Sat. 71 Buckingham Palace Rd.,
SW1. **3B 62,** 1 Marble Arch, W1. (also Sun. am in summer) **2C 31,** C & A
Modes, 505 Oxford St., W1. **2D 31,** c/o Midland Banks at 1 Woburn Pl., WC1.
1C 19 and 39 Tottenham Court Rd., W1. **1A 18.**
Mon. to Fri. only at 54 Cornhill, EC3. **1A 40.**

LOST PROPERTY
Buses and Underground Trains. Visit Lost Property Office, 200 Baker St., NW1.
1C 15. Mon. to Fri. 09.30–17.30.
Railways. Visit Lost Property Office at Main Line Terminus.
Taxis. Visit Lost Property Office, 15 Penton St., N1. **AZ 2A 62**

MINI CABS
Central Companies with 24 hr. service.
A1 Mini Cab, 142 Churchfield Rd., W3. 01-992 8883 **AZ 1J 73**
Mini Cabs AABA, Kensington. 01-352 2284, Fulham 01-385 6673, Putney 01-736
1555.
Mini Cabs, 3 Acton Town Sta., W3. 01-994 2643.
Nova Radio Cars, 01-340 0909, 01-341 2121.

MOTORING
Automobile Association
HEAD OFFICE: Fanum Ho., Basing View, Basingstoke, Hants. Basingstoke 20123
RESCUE SERVICES: 24 HOUR SERVICE/MEMBERS ONLY. 01-954 7373
WEST END CENTRE: Fanum Ho., 5 New Coventry St., WC2. 01-954 7355 **3B 34**

National Breakdown Recovery Club
Cleckheaton Rd., Low Moor, Bradford. 0274 671299
RESCUE SERVICES: 24 HOUR SERVICE/MEMBERS ONLY. 0274 671234

Royal Automobile Club
HEAD OFFICE: P.O. Box 100, RAC Ho., Lansdowne Rd., Croydon. 01-686 2525.
RESCUE SERVICES: 24 HOUR SERVICE/MEMBERS ONLY. South of Thames 01-
681 3611. North of Thames Watford 33555.
WEST END ASSOCIATE OFFICE: 149 Pall Mall, SW1. 01-839 7050 **1A 50**

Car Hire
Avis Rent-a-Car. Trident Ho., Station Rd., Hayes, Middx. 01-848 8733.
SELF DRIVE in Central London: 35 Headfort Pl., SW1. 01-254 9862 **3A 48**; 92
Eversholt St., NW1. 01-387 5481 **1A 10**; Hilton Hotel, Park La., W1. 01-499
2919 **1A 48**; 141 Warwick Rd., W14. 01-373 3022 **AZ 7H 75**; Vintry Car Pk., Upper
Thames St., EC4. 01-236 5991 **2D 39**
CHAUFFEUR DRIVE SERVICE, Trident Ho., Station Rd., Hayes, Middx. 01-848
8765.
AIRPORT SERVICES: Gatwick, Crawley 29721, Heathrow 01-897 9321, Luton
36537.
Budget Rent-a-Car: Central reservations 01-441 5882 at locations throughout
London.
Car Hire Centre, Self Drive, 23 Swallow St., W1. 01-734 7661 **3D 33**
Central Chauffeur Services, 1 Hendre Rd., SE1. 01-237 4111 (24 hrs). **AZ 9D 148.**
Prestigious fleet of limousines, luxury saloons and vintage Rolls Royce. Also
luggage transportation.
Godfrey Davis, Self Drive, Wilton Rd., SW1. 01-834 8484 **2C 63**

RAIL DRIVE: Euston 01-387 9710; Kings Cross 01-278 5228; Liverpool St. 01-387 2276; Paddington 01-262 5655; Victoria 01-834 8484; Waterloo 01-834 8484. CHAUFFEUR DRIVEN 01-834 6701

AIRPORT SERVICES: Gatwick 0293 31062. Heathrow 01-897 0811.

Hertz, Self Drive and Chauffeur Driven. Head Office (Adm.), 1272 London Rd., SW16. 01-679 1777 at locations throughout London.

Kenning, Self Drive and Chauffeur. Selection with car telephone. 84 Holland Park Av., W11. 01-727 0123 **AZ 1G 75**

Rolls-Bentley Car Hire, 612 Streatham High Rd., SW16. 01-764 8583 **AZ 4J 109**

Swan National, Central Reservations, 305 Chiswick High Rd., W4. 01-995 4665 **AZ 5G 73**

Travelwise Self Drive, 77 Pavilion Rd., SW1. 01-235 0751 **1C 61**

Motorcycle and Scooter Hire
Scootabout, 59 Albert Embankment, SE1. 01-582 0055 **2A 66**

Central Car Parks: Open 24 hours
These, plus other car parks, parking meter areas and one way streets are marked on the A-Z Motorists Map of Inner London. *Parking meters are generally operative 08.30-18.30 Mon to Fri. 08.30-12.30 Sat.*

Europark Ltd., Burlington Garage, 3 Old Burlington St., W1. 01-437 2313 **2D 33**
National Car Parks Ltd. (N.C.P. Ltd) 21 Bryanston St., W1. 01-499 7050 **1C 31**

Abingdon St., SW1. 250. **1D 65**

Aldersgate St., EC1. 850.**2B 22**

Arlington House, Arlington St., SW1. 100. **1D 49**

Arthur Court Garage, Queensway, W2. 85. **2D 27**

Audley Square, South Audley St., W1. 310. **1A 48**

Barbican Centre, EC2. **2C 23**

Bedfordbury, WC2. **2C 35**

Bilton Towers, Gt. Cumberland Pl., W1. 160. **1C 31**

Bloomsbury Square, WC1. 450. **2D 19**

Brewer St., W1. 450. **2A 34**

Britannia Hotel, Adams Row, W1. 180. **3A 32**

Brunswick Square, WC1. 100. **1D 19**

Bury St., SW1. **1D 49**

Cadogan Place, SW1. 349. **1D 61**

Cale St., SW3. **3A 60**

Cambridge Circus, WC2. 350. **1B 34**

Carrington St., Shepherd Mkt., W1. 300. **1B 48**

Cavendish Square, W1. 545. **3C 17**

Caxton Ho., Cowcross St., EC1. **2A 22**

Charterhouse Sq., EC1. **2B 22**

Chelsea Cloisters, Sloane Av., SW3. 120. **3B 60**

Chiltern Garage, Chiltern St., W1. 394. **2D 15**

Churchill Hotel, Portman Sq., W1. 110. **1D 31**

Clipstone St., W1. 345 **2C 17**

Commercial St., E1. **1C 25**

Coptic St., WC1. **3C 19**

43a Crawford St., W1. **3B 14**

Cumberland Garage, Bryanston St. W1. 400. **1C 31**

Denman St., W1. 320. **2A 34**

Dolphin Sq., Chichester St., SW1. 300. **AZ 1E 77**

Dorset House, Marylebone Rd., NW1. 180.**2C 15**

Euston Station, NW1. 235. **2A 10**

Finsbury Sq., EC2. **2A 24**

Grand Metropole Hotel, Harbet Rd., W2. **3D 13**

Hamilton Place, W1. 60. **2A 48**

Hillgate House, Seacoal La., EC4. 180. **1A 38**

Hilton Hotel, Park La., W1.200. **1A 48**

Hyde Park Underground Car Park, W1. **3D 31**

Kendal Street, W2. 140, **1B 30**

Minories, EC2. 600. **1D 41**

Marriot Hotel, Grosvenor Sq., W1. **2A 32**

Museum Street, WC1. 350. **3C 19**

National Theatre, South Bank, SW1. **1B 52**

Paddington Station, W2. 50. **1C 29**

83 Park Lane, W1. 150. **3D 31**

Park Lane Hotel Garage, Brick St., W1. 190. **1B 48**

Paternoster Square, Ave Maria La., EC4. 277. **1A 38**

Pavilion Road, SW1. 311. **3C 47**

Park Tower Hotel, Knightsbridge, SW1. **3A 46**

Rochester Row, SW1. 299. **2A 64**

Rodwell House, Middlesex St., E1. 200. **3C 25**

Rossmore Court, 57 Park Rd., NW1. 80. **3B 6**

Royal Garden Hotel Car Park, Kensington, W8. 250. **2D 43**

Russell Court Garage, Coram St., WC1. 200. **1C 19**

Saffron Hill, EC1. 400. **2D 21**

Savoy Adelphi Garage, Savoy Pl., WC2. 450. **3D 35**

Semley Place, SW1. 422. **3A 62**

Smithfield Central Market, EC1. 370. **3A 22**

Warwick Way, SW1. 300. **3C 63**

Water Gardens Car Park, Burwood Pl., W2. 300. **1A 30**

Waterloo Station, 100. **2C 53**

Whitcomb Garage, Whitcomb St., WC2. 298. **3B 34**

Winter Garden Complex, Drury La., WC1. 450. **1D 35**

Young Street, W8. 270. **3D 43**

Car Pounds: To find which pound your car has been taken to contact nearest Police Station. If in doubt contact New Scotland Yard.

Broomfield St., E14. **AZ 5D 64**

Ditton Rd., Tolworth, Surbiton.

Donegal Street, N1. **AZ 2K 61**

Heathrow Airport

Horn's Rd., Barkingside. **AZ 5G 35**

Park Lane Garage, Park La., W1. **3C 31**

Talgarth Rd., W6. **AZ 5F 75**

Union Rd., West Croydon. **AZ 7C 124**

Willow Walk, SE1. **AZ 4E 78**

Motels: See also Accommodation section

Travel Lodge, M1 Scratchwood Service Area, Ellesmere Av., NW7. 01-906 0611 **AZ 2D 12**

Master Robert, 366 Gt. West Road, Hounslow Middx. 01-570 6261

Viking Motel, 162 Romford Rd., E15. 01-534 7861 **AZ 6G 49**

New Post House, Haverstock Hill, NW3. 01-794 8121 **AZ 5C 44**

Post House, London Airport (Heathrow), Sipson Rd., W. Drayton. 01-759 2323

Post House, Gatwick Airport, Povey Cross Rd., Horley. 0293 771621

Silvertown Transport Motel, Silvertown Way, E16. 01-476 3574 **AZ 6H 65**

24 Hour Breakdowns and Petrol: * indicates Petrol; † indicates Breakdown Service. *North of the Thames*

Acton
*STAR, 48 Horn La., W3. 01-992 0894 **AZ 7J 57**

Chalk Farm
*STAR, 81/85 Chalk Farm Rd., NW1. 01-267 3227 **AZ 1E 44**

Chiswick
*CHISWICK FLYOVER SERVICE STA., 1 Gt. West Rd., W4. 01-994 1119 **AZ 5B74**
*STAR—HOGARTH, Mawson La., W4. 01-994 8332 **AZ 6B 74**

College Park
*STAR, 875 Harrow Rd., NW10. 01-969 2389 **AZ 3D 58**

Ealing
†BRENT RECOVERY, 7 Culmington Parade, Uxbridge Rd., W13. 01-579 4275 **AZ 1B 72**

E. Finchley
†LYNTON GARAGE, Fortis Grn., N2. 01-883 4036 **AZ 4C 28**
*STAR, 178/192 High Road, N2. 01-883 3029 **AZ 1B 28**
*STAR, Cherry Tree Hill, Gt. North Rd., N2. 01-883 1741 **AZ 5C 28**

Enfield
*STAR—PONDERS END, 356/360 High St. 01-804 9736 **AZ 5D 8**

Hampstead
*STAR, 63 Fortune Green Rd., NW6. 01-435 2211 **AZ 4J 43**

Harlesdon
*STAR, 2/14 Hillside, NW10. 01-965 7199 **AZ 7J 41**

Harlington
*STAR—HARLINGTON, Sipsons Corner, Bath Road, Harlington, Middx. 01-897 3265

Heathrow Airport see Harlington.

Hornsey

*STAR, Crouch End, Tottenham La., N8. 01-348 1577 **AZ 5J 29**
Hounslow
*STAR, 1 Great West Road, Hounslow. 01-577 2270 **AZ 2B 86**
Islington
*STAR, 287/297 New North Rd., N1. 01-359 0099 **AZ 7C 46**
Kensington and Chelsea
†LION AUTO ENGINEERS, Netherwood Rd., W14. 01-602 5653 **AZ 3F 75**
Kilburn
†*CAVENDISH MOTORS, Cavendish Rd., NW6. 01-451 3211 **AZ 7G 43**
†MAYGROVE MOTORS, 59 Maygrove Rd., NW6. 01-624 0177, 01-328 1673 (24 hrs) **AZ 6H 43**
†RAYBURY MOTORS, 28 Malvern Mews, NW6. 01-286 8282 **AZ 3J 59**
Limehouse
*STEPNEY SERVICE STATION, 731 Commercial Rd., E14. 01-987 3750 **AZ 6G 63**
Maida Vale
*STAR—VALE, 383/393 Edgware Rd., W2. 01-723 9686 **1C 13**
Mill Hill
*†ARCADE MOTORS, Ellesmere Av., NW7. 01-959 1293. Scratchwood Service Area Workshops. For petrol approach via M1 only. 959 2150, 883 8030
North Kensington
*STAR, 235a Scrubs La., NW10. 01-743 9970 **AZ 5D 58**
Notting Hill
*STAR, 7 Pembridge Villas, W11. 01-229 6626 **2B 26**
Rayners Lane
*STAR, Alexandra Av., Harrow. 01-429 1303 **AZ 1D 38**
Ruislip Common
*STAR, Bury St., Ruislip. 71-37083
St. Marylebone
*STAR—HANOVER GATE, 129 Park Rd., NW8. 01-723 1901 **AZ 3C 60**
*STAR, 195 Old Marylebone Rd., NW1. 01-723 1630 **3A 14**
Stonebridge Park
*STAR—STONEBRIDGE PARK, North Circular Rd., NW10. 01-965 1229 **AZ 3F 57**
Wembley
*STAR—WEMBLEY, Watford Rd., Wembley. 01-904 7740 **AZ 7A 24**
Wood Green
*STAR, 573 Lordship La., N22. 01-888 2741 **AZ 2A 30**

South of the Thames
Addiscombe
*STAR, 155 Addiscombe Rd., E. Croydon. 01-645 4435 **AZ 1F 135**
Battersea
*PARKGATE SERVICE STATION, 15 Parkgate Rd., SW11. 01-223 1926 **AZ 7C 76**
Bermondsey
*STAR—BERMONDSEY, 171 Grange Rd., SE1. 01-237 4171 **AZ 3E 78**
Clapham
*STAR, 474/488 Wandsworth Rd., SW18. 01-622 4213 **AZ 3F 93**
Croydon
*STAR, 40 Croham Rd. 01-680 8181 **AZ 5D 134**
*STAR—PURLEY WAY, 514 Purley Way, W. Croydon. 01-688 5019 **AZ 7K 123**
Colliers Wood
*STAR—COLLIERS WOOD, 1/7 High St., SW19. 01-542 7628 **AZ 7B 108**
New Malden
*STAR, 59 Kingston Rd. 01-942 1539 **AZ 3H 119**
Penge
†QUEENS MOTORS, 89 Maple Rd., SE20. 01-659 5900 **AZ 1H 125**
*STAR, 204/212 High St., SE20. 01-778 8504 **AZ 6J 111**
South Norwood

*STAR, South Norwood Hill, SE25. 01-653 1906. **AZ 2E 124**
Wimbledon
†LYON HOUSE FILLING STATION, Harfield Rd., SW19. 01-946 9365 **AZ 7H 107**

PASSPORTS, VISAS AND VACCINATIONS

British Passports can be obtained only through the Passport Office.
Visitors passports valid for one year to most European Countries and Canada are obtained by application to any Post Office.

British Airways Immunisation Centre, 75 Regent St., W1. 01-439 9584 **3A 34**
Thomas Cook Passport Dept., can obtain necessary visas for foreign countries; their Vaccination Centre on the spot vaccinations and certificates; 45 Berkeley St., W1. 01-499 4000 **3C 33**
Passport Office, Clive Ho., Petty France, SW1. 01-213 3434 **3A 50**
Open Mon. to Fri. 09.00–16.30. Emergencies (excluding Holiday Travel) Mon. to Fri. 16.30–18.30. Sat., Sun. and Public Hols. 10.00–12.00 (Closed Christmas Day).

RIVER TRANSPORT see Tours and Sightseeing Excursions.

SAFE DEPOSIT BOXES Berkeley Safe Deposit Co., 13/15 Davis St., W1. 01-409 1122 **1B 32** and at Victoria Station forecourt 01-828 0053/0014 **2C 63**

SHIPPING LINES—PASSENGER

London Cruise Terminal, Port of London Authority, Tilbury Docks. 03752 3444

Bl Lines, 155 Regent St., W1. 01-734 4681 **2D 33**
Blue Star Line, Albion Ho., Leadenhall St., EC3. 01-488 4567 **1B 40**
Brittany Ferries, Albert Johnson Quay, Portsmouth 819416
Chandris Lines, 5 St. Helen's Pl., EC3. 01-588 6991 **1B 40**
Channel Island Ferries, Wharf Rd., Portsmouth. 0705 819416
Cunard Line, 1 & 8 Berkeley St., W1. 01-499 9020 **1C 49**
Danish Seaways, DFDS, 199 Regent St., W1. 01–434 1523 **2D 33**
Fred Olsen Bergen Lines, 11 Conduit St., W1. 01-491 3760 **2C 33**
Hoverspeed, International Hoverport, Dover 01-554 7061. Dover (0304) 214514 and 208013
Isle of Man Steam Packet Co., P.O. Box 5, Imperial Bldgs, Douglas, I.O.M. Douglas 3824
Isle of Scilly Steamship Co., 16 Quay St., Penzance, Cornwall. Penzance 2009
North Sea Ferries, King George Dock, Hedon Rd., Hull 795141
P & O Ferries, Head Office, 79 Pall Mall, SW1. 01-930 4343. Ferries 01-240 9071. Cruises 01-283 8080
Prins Ferries, Latham Ho., Minories, EC3. Pass. Res. 01-481 3211
Sally Line, 81 Piccadilly W. 01-409 2240 **3A 34**
Sealink UK, HQ and Admin., Eversholt Ho., Eversholt St., NW1. 01-387 1234
   Sealink Travel Centre, Victoria Station. Reservations and enquiries 01-834 8122.
   Ferry/Train connected services UK to Europe 01-834 2345.
Tor Line, Admin: Anzani Ho., Trinity Av., Felixstowe. Pass. Res. 0394 273131
Townsend-Thoreson Car Ferries, 127 Regent St., W1. 01-437 5644 **2D 33**

TAXIS Look for yellow "FOR HIRE" sign and hail.

Taxi Ranks: at most Main Line Stations and large hotels; other central ranks include
   Harrington Rd., SW7. 01-589 5242 **2C 59**
   Holbein Pl., SW1. 01-730 2664 **3D 61** Moorgate, EC2. 01-606 4526 **3D 23**
   St. Georges Sq., Sw1. 01-834 1014 **AZ 1E 77** Warwick Av., W9. 01-286 2566 **1A 12**
Radio Taxicabs. 01-272 3030. **Computer Cab Co. Ltd.** 01-286 0286. **Dial a Cab.** 01-253 5000

TRAVEL AGENTS AND TOUR OPERATORS

AA Travel, 5 New Coventry St., W1. 01-930 2462 **3B 34** and branches.
American Express, 6 Haymarket, SW1. 01-930 4411 **3B 34** and branches
Christian Travel International, 76 Church Rd., SE19. 01-771 5142 **AZ 1E 24**

And at other addresses throughout central London and UK.
Cosmos Air Holidays, 1 Bromley Com., Bromley. 01-464 3444 **AZ 4A 128**
Evan Evans Tours, 27 Cockspur St., SW1. Reservations 01-930 2377 **3B 34**
Frames Tours, 46 Albermarle St., W1. 01-493 3181 **3C 33**
Galleon World Travel, 45 Cathedral Pl., EC4. 01-248 1011 **1B 38**
Global of London, 200 Tottenham Ct. Rd., W1. 01-637 3333 **2A 18**
Hickie Borman Grant, 24 Charles II St., SW1. 01-839 7611 **3B 34**
Keith Prowse Travel, Banda Ho., Cambridge Gro., W6. 01–741 7441 **AZ 4D 74**
and at branches throughout London.
Lunn-Poly Holidays & Travel, Upstream Buildings, Shell Centre, SE1. 01-928 7631 **1B 52** and branches.
National Travel, 191 Rushey Green, SE6. 01-697 2156 **AZ 7D 96**
Olympic Holidays, 17 Old Court Pl., W8. 01-727 8050 **2C 43**
Pickfords, 400 Gt. Cambridge Rd., Enfield. 01-366 1211 **AZ 7A 8** and branches.
P & O, Cruises 01-283 8080; Air Holidays 01-247 1611
Sovereign Holidays, London Airport Heathrow. Reservations, 01-897 4545
Student Travel Centre, 18 Rupert St., W1. 01-434 1306 **2A 34**
Thomson Holidays, Greater London Ho., Hampstead Rd., NW1. 01-387 9321 **1D 9**
Thomas Cook Ltd., 45 Berkeley St., W1. 01-499 4000 **3C 33** and branches throughout London and UK.
Wallace Arnold Tours, 8 Park La., Croydon (Admin.). 01 688 7255 **AZ 3D 134**
British Holidays 01-462 7733. Continental Holidays 462 7711
W. H. Smith Travel, 124 Holborn, EC1. 01-242 9826 **3C 21** and branches.
Youth Hostels Ass., 14 Southampton St., WC2. 01-836 8541 **2D 35**

TOURIST OFFICES
Austrian Nat. Tourist Office, 30 St. George St., W1. 01-629 0461 **2C 33**
Bahama Islands Tourist Off., 23 Old Bond St., W1. 01-629 5238 **3D 33**
Belgian National Tourist Off., 38 Dover St., W1. 01-499 5379 **3C 33**
British Tourist Authority, Nat. Tourist Information Centre, and British Travel Centre see p. 185. Head Office, Admin. only, Thames Tower, Blacks Rd., W6. 01-846 9000
Bulgarian National Tourist Off., 18 Princes St., W1. 01-499 6988 **1C 33**
Canadian Office of Tourism, Canada House, Trafalgar Sq., SW1. 01-629 9492 **3C 35**
Cyprus Tourist Centre, 213 Regent St., W1. 01-734 2593 **2D 33**
Danish Tourist Board, 169 Regent St., W1. 01-734 2637 **2D 33**
Egyptian Tourist Information Centre, 168 Piccadilly, W1. 01-493 5282 **3D 33**
English Tourist Board, Admin. only. 4 Grosvenor Gdns., SW1. 01-730 0791 **1B 62**
Finnish Tourist Board, Finland Ho., 66 Haymarket, SW1. 01-839 4048 **3B 34**
French Government Tourist Off., 178 Piccadilly, W1. 01-491 7622 **3D 33**
German Travel Bureau (DER), 15 Orchard St., W1. 01-486 4593 **1D 31**
Greek Tourist Agency, 320 Regent St., W1. 01-580 3152 **3C 17**
India Government Tourist Off., 7 Cork St., W1. 01-437 3677 **3C 33**
Intourist Moscow Ltd. Information Bureau, 292 Regent St., W1. 01-580 4974. **1C 33**
Irish Tourist Off., Ireland Ho., 150 New Bond St., W1. 01-493 3201 **2C 33**
Israel Government Tourist Off., 18 Gt. Marlborough St., W1. 01-434 3651 **1D 33**
Italian State Tourist Dept., 1 Princes St., W1. 01-408 1254 **1C 33**
Jamaica Tourist Board, 50 St. James's St., SW1. 01-493 3647 **1D 49**
Japan National Tourist Organisation, 167 Regent St., W1. 01-734 9638 **2D 33**
Kenya Tourist Off., 13 New Burlington St., W1. 01-734 6296 **2D 33**
London Visitors and Convention Bureau, National Tourist Information Centre, Victoria Station, SW1. 01-730 3488. See p. 185. Head Office Admin. and Mail only, 26 Grosvenor Gdns, SW1. 01-730 3450.
Luxembourg National Tourist Off., 36 Piccadilly W1. 01-434 2800 **3A 34**

Malta National Tourist Organization, 207 College Ho., Wrights La, W8. 01-938 2668 **3C 43**
Mexican National Tourist Council, 7 Cork St., W1. 01-734 1058 **3C 33**
Netherlands National Tourist Off., 143 New Bond St., W1. 01-499 9367 **2C 33**
New Zealand Government Tourist Bureau, New Zealand Ho., 80 Haymarket, SW1. 01-930 8422. **3B 34**
Norwegian National Tourist Off., 20 Pall Mall, SW1. 01-839 6255 **1A 50**
Polish Travel Agency Tazab, 273 Old Brompton Rd., SW5. 01-373 1186 **3A 58**
Portuguese National Tourist Off., 1 New Bond St., W1. 01-493 3873 **2D 33**
Scottish Tourist Office, 19 Cockspur St., SW1. 01-930 8661 **3B 34**
South African Tourist Corp., 1 Warwick St., W1. 01-439 9661 **2D 33**
Spanish National Tourist Off., 57 St. James's St., SW1. 01-499 0901 **1D 49**
Swiss National Tourist Off., Swiss Centre, 1 New Coventry St., W1. 01-734 1921 **2B 34**
Turkish Tourist Office, Egyptian Ho., 170 Piccadilly, W1. 01-734 8681 **3A 34**
Welsh Tourist Board, 34 Piccadilly., W1. 01-409 0969 **3A 34**
Yugoslav National Tourist Off., 143 Regent St., W1. 01-734 5243 **2D 33**

WORSHIP

For Church of England and Roman Catholic Church Services see under CATHEDRALS AND CHURCHES.

ARMENIAN

Armenian Church of St. Sarkis, Iverna Gdns., W8. 01-937 0152 **AZ 3J 75**
Sundays 10.00, 11.00.

AUSTRIAN

Austrian Catholic Centre, 29 Brook Grn., W6. 01-603 2697 **AZ 3F 75**
Sundays 20.00.

BAPTIST

Bloomsbury Central Baptist Church, Shaftesbury Av., WC2. 01-836 6843 **3C 19**
Sundays 11.00, 18.30
Metropolitan Tabernacle/Spurgeons, Elephant & Castle, SE1. 01-735 7076 **AZ 4B 78**
Sundays 11.00, 18.30.

BELGIAN

Our Lady of Hal., 165 Arlington Rd., NW1. 01-485 2727 **AZ 1F 61**
Sundays 08.30, 10.00, 11.00, 12.00, 17.00, 18.30, 19.30.

BUDDHIST

London Buddhist Centre, 51 Roman Rd., E2. 01-981 1225 **AZ 3J 63**
Open throughout the week, regular meditation and worship sessions.

CHINESE

Chinese Church in London-Centre and Office, 4 Earlsfied Rd., SW18. 01-870 2251 **AZ 1A 108**
Services at the Welsh Methodist Church, 82a Chiltern St., W1. Sundays 14.00 Mandarin Service, 15.30 English Service.

CHRISTIAN SCIENCE

First Church of Christ Scientist, Sloane Ter., SW1. 01-730 8584 **2D 61**
Sundays 11.00, 19.00. Wednesdays Testimony Meetings 19.00.
Second Church of Christ Scientist, 104 Palace Gdns. Ter., W8. 01-229 2682 **1C 43**
Sundays 11.00, 19.00. Wednesday Testimony Meetings 19.30.
Third Church of Christ Scientist, Curzon St., W1. 01-499 1271 **1B 48**
Sundays 11.00 plus 19.00 in summer. Wed. Testimony Meetings 12.15, 19.00.

CHURCH OF SCOTLAND
Crown Court Church, Russell St., WC1. 01-836 5643, 584 2321 **1A 36**
Sundays 11.15, 18.30.
St. Columba's, Pont St., SW1. 01-584 2321 **1B 60**
Sundays 11.00, 18.30.
DANISH CHURCH
Danish Church, St. Katherine's Precinct, Regent's Park, NW1. 01-935 7584 **1B 8**
First Sunday in Month 11.00, otherwise at 16.00.
DUTCH CHURCH
Dutch Church, Austin Friars, EC2. 01-588 1684 **1A 40** Sundays 11.00.
FINNISH
Finnish Church and Social Centre, 33 Albion St., SE16. 01-237 1261 **AZ 2J 79**
Sundays at 19.30 (except 1st Sun. in monthat 11.00).
FRENCH
Eglise Catholique de Notre Dame de France, 5 Leicester Pl., WC2. 01-437 9363
2B 34
Sundays (day before 18.00) then 10.00, 11.15, 12.15, 18.30. Weekdays 08.00,
12.15, 18.00. Saturdays 08.00.
Eglise Protestants Francaise de Londres, 9 Soho Sq., W1. 01-437 5311 **1A 34**
Sundays 11.00.
GERMAN
Deutsche Evangelische Christus Kirche, 19 Montpelier Pl., SW7. 01-589 5305
3A 46
Sundays 11.00. First Sunday in month 18.30.
Deutsche Lutherische St. Marien Kirche, Sandwich St., WC1. 01-794 4207
3C 11
Sundays first and third in month 11.00, otherwise 16.00.
GREEK ORTHODOX
St. Sophia's, Moscow Rd., W2. 01-723 4787 **2C 27**
Sundays 10.00.
HINDU
Hindu Centre, 39 Grafton Terr., NW5. 01-485 8200 **AZ 5D 44**
First Sunday in the month at 16.00.
HUNGARIAN
Hungarian Reformed Church, 17 St. Dunstan's Rd., W6. 01-748 8858 **AZ 5F 75**
Sundays 17.00.
INDEPENDENT EVANGELICAL
Westminster Chapel, Buckingham Gate, SW1. 01-834 1731 **3D 49**
Sundays 11.00, 18.30.
INTER-DENOMINATIONAL
Chapel of St. George, Heathrow Airport. Always open and shared by all
denominations.
ITALIAN
St. Peter's. Back Hill EC1. 01-837 1528 **1C 21**
Sundays 09.00, 10.00, 11.00, 12.15, Weekdays 10.00. 19.00.
JEHOVAH'S WITNESSES
Watch Tower Ho., The Ridgway, NW7. 01-959 6773 **AZ 4J 13**
Kingdom Hall, 7 Pratt Mews, NW1. **AZ 1G 61**
Sundays 15.00. Fridays 19.30.
JEWISH
Central Synagogue (Orthodox), Great Portland St., W1. 01-580 1355 **2C 17**
Daily 08.00 and at other variable times.
Liberal Jewish Synagogue, 28 St. John's Wood Rd., NW8. 01-286 5181 **3D 5**
Saturdays 11.00. Fridays 20.15.
West End Great Synagogue, 21 Dean St., W1. 01-437 1873 **1B 34**
Saturdays 09.30. Dusk1 hour before sunset. Fridays at sunset. Daily 07.45, 17.30.
Sundays 08.30.

LIBERAL CATHOLIC CHURCH
St. Peter's Chapel, 52 Victoria Rd., W8. 01-351 1765 **1A 58**
Sundays 11.00 (entrance in Eldon Rd.).

LITHUANIAN
Lithuanian Church, 21 The Oval, E2. 01-739 8735 **AZ 2H 63**
Sundays 09.00, 11.00. Weekdays 20.00. Holidays of Obligation 11.00, 20.00.

LUTHERAN
St. John's Lutheran Church, St. Anne and St. Agnes, Gresham St., EC2. 01-904 2849 **3C 23**
Sundays, in English at 11.00, in Estonian at 16.15 on 1st and 3rd Sundays. In Latvian at 17.00 on 2nd and 4th Sundays.

METHODIST
Central Hall, Storey's Ga., SW1. 01-222 8553 **3B 50**
Sundays 11.00, 18.30. Tuesdays 18.30.

Hinde St. Church, Hinde St., W1. 01-935 6179 **3A 16**
Sundays 10.00, 11.00, 18.30.

Wesley's Chapel, City Rd., EC1. 01-353 2262 **1A 24**
Sundays 11.00. Wednesdays Holy Communion 08.30. Wednesday Lunch Hour Service 12.45. Daily prayer meetings at 08.00 and 17.30.

MOSLEM
The London Central Mosque, 146 Park Rd., NW8. 01-723 7613 **2A 6**
Friday 13.30 March–October. 13.00 Nov.–Feb.

NORWEGIAN
St. Olav's (Lutheran), 1 Albion St., SE16. 01-237 5587 **AZ 2J 79**
Sundays 11.00, 19.30. See also St. Olave, Hart St., EC3. p. 23.

PENTECOSTAL
Assemblies of God, 141 Harrow Rd., W2. 01-286 9261 **3D 13**
Sundays 11.00, 18.30. Wed. 19.30.

POLISH
St. Andrew Bubola's Roman Catholic Church, 1 Leysfied Rd., W12. 01-743 8848 **AZ 3C 74**
Sundays 09.00, 10.00, 11.00, 12.00, 17.00. Weekdays 09.00, 09.30.

ROMANIAN
Guild Church of St. Dunstan in the West, Floot St., EC4. 01-242 6027 **1C 37**
Sundays 10.00. Tues. 17.30. Wed. and Fri. 14.00. Sat. 16.05. Saints Days 11.00, 12.00.

RUSSIAN
Orthodox Church in Exile, Cathedral of the Dormition, Emperors' Ga., SW7. **2A 58**
Sun. 10.00. Sat. 17.00. Information 01-748 4232.

SALVATION ARMY
Regent Hall, 275 Oxford St., W1. 01-629 5424 **1C 33**
Sundays 11.00, 15.00, 18.30.

SERBIAN
Serbian Orthodox Church, Lancaster Rd., W11. 01-727 8367 **AZ 6G 59**
Sundays 11.00 and Orthodox Feast Days at 11.00.

SEVENTH DAY ADVENTISTS
New Gallery Centre, 123 Regent St., W1. 01-734 8888 **2D 33**
Sundays 18.30. Saturdays Seminars 10.30.

SPANISH
Spanish Catholic Chaplaincy, 47 Palace Ct., W2. 01-229 8815 **3C 27**
Sundays 12.00, 18.00. Ring for times of Mass at other Spanish churches.

SPANISH AND PORTUGUESE
Spanish and Portuguese Synagogue, 9 Lauderdale Rd., W9. 01-286 4189 **3A 4**
Daily 07.30. Sat. and Sun. 08.00. See also Bevis Marks Synagogue p. 101.

SOCIETY OF FRIENDS (QUAKERS)
Friends House, 173 Euston Rd., NW1. 01-387 3601 **3A 10**
Sundays 11.00.
Westminster Meeting House, 52 St. Martin's La., WC2. 01-836 7204 **2C 35**
Sundays 11.00. Tuesday 13.00. Wednesday 18.15. Thursday 13.00.
SWEDISH
Swedish Protestant Lutheran Church, 6 Harcourt St., W1. 01-723 5681 **2B 14**
Sundays 11.00.
SWISS CHURCH
Swiss Church in London, 79 Endell St., WC2. 01-340 9740 **1C 35**
Sundays at 11.00 in French and (except 4th Sunday) at 10.00 in Dutch and German.
UKRAINIAN
Ukrainian Catholic Cathedral, 21 Binney St., W1. 01-629 1534 **1A 32**
Sundays 10.30.
UNITARIAN
Essex Church, Palace Gardens Terrace, Notting Hill Ga., W8. 01-727 8920 **3C 27**
Sundays 11.00.
UNITED REFORMED
City Temple, Holborn Viaduct, EC1. 01-583 5532 **3D 21**
Sundays 11.00, 18.30, Thursday 13.15.
Regent Square Church, Regent Sq., WC1. 01-837 6523 **3D 11**
Sundays 11.00, 18.30.
WELSH
St. Benet Guild Church, Queen Victoria St., EC4. 01-723 3104 **2B 38**
Sundays 11.00, 17.00.
Welsh Presbyterian Church, 265 Willesden La., NW2. 01-459 2690 **AZ 6E 42**
Sundays 10.45, 17.45.

24 HOURS/EMERGENCIES

AMBULANCE FIRE OR POLICE—Tel. 999. No coins needed.

BREAKDOWNS see Travel and Transport: Motoring.

CASUALTIES Emergency Casualty Depts. for accidents in Central London.
New Charing Cross, Fulham Palace Rd., W6. 01-748 2040 **AZ 5E 74**
Moorfields Eye Hospital, High Holborn. WC1. 01-836 6611 **1D 35**
University College Hospital, Gower St., WC1. 01-387 9300 **1A 18**
Medent Emergency Clinic, Chapel Place, Oxford St., W1. 01-499 1991 **1B 32**
Private clinic open to anyone in need of swift, effective treatment for minor
accidents and ailments; X-ray; medicine; and surgery. Open 08.00–20.00 weekdays,
09.00–18.00 Sat. Closed Sun. No appointment required.

CHEMISTS
Bliss Chemists, 24 hrs. 50 Willesden La., NW6. 01-624 8000 **AZ 6E 62**

EATING
Heathrow Airport, Buffet Bars Terminals 1, 2 & 3 24 hrs.
Up all Night, 325 Fulham Rd., SW10. **AZ 2G 91**
Open 12.00 till 06.00.
The American, 335 Fulham Rd., SW10. **AZ 1A 76**
Open to 24.00 daily; to 24.30 Fri. and Sat.
American Hamburger, 455 Oxford St., W1. **2D 31**
Open to 24.00 daily.
Wimpys open late
Piccadilly Circus till 02.00 Fri. and Sat., otherwise 24.00.

Victoria, 333 Vauxhall Bri. Rd., till 01.00 daily.
South Kensington, 85 Gloucester Rd., till 02.00 daily.
113 Baker St., till 24.00 daily.

GAY SWITCHBOARD
01-837 7324. 24-hour general advice, information and support telephone service for homosexual men and women.

MONEY
Heathrow Airport, 24-hour banking service provided by the principal banks in rotation.
24-hr. Bureau de Change: at 37 Coventry St., W1. **3A 34.** 236 Earls Court Rd., SW5. **AZ 3J 75.** 126 Bayswater Rd., W2. **3D 27.** 548 Oxford St., W1. **2C 31**

NURSE AND MIDWIFE (State registered).
B.U.P.A. Nursing Services, 36 Dover St., W1. 01-629 4233 **3C 33**
British Nursing Ass., Private Nurses/Midwives, 470 Oxford St., W1. 01-629 9030 24 hrs. **2C 31**

PETROL See Travel and Transport: Motoring.

PETS
Blue Cross Animal Hospital, 1 Hugh St., SW1. 01-834 4224, 24 hrs. **2C 63**
Elizabeth Street Veterinary Clinic, 55 Elizabeth St., SW1. 01-730 9102 **2A 62**
Vet on call 24 hours.
P.D.S.A. People's Dispensary for Sick Animals.
Night Service—East London 01-550 6644, South London 686 3972. Head Office, P.D.S.A. House, South St., Dorking, Surrey. Dorking 888291.
Dispensaries throughout London for those unable to afford normal veterinary treatment.
Royal Society for the Prevention of Cruelty to Animals, Manor Ho., The Causeway, Horsham, Sussex. 0403 64181. Emergency Services—North of Thames 01-272 6214, South 01-789 8252.

POST OFFICE 08.00-20.00 Mon. to Sat. 10.00–17.00 Sun. & Bank Hols. Closed Christmas Day.
Trafalgar Square, 24 William IV St., WC2. **3C 35**
General Enquiries 01-930 9580. Bureau de Change closed Sun.

RAPE CRISIS CENTRE 01-837 1600

RELEASE 01-289 1123 (603 8654 24 hrs.).

SAMARITANS: 01 283 3400.
Local Branches: Enfield 889 6888. Bexley, Dartford 01-301 1010. Brent. 459 8585. Croydon 681 6666. Ealing 560 2345. Harrow 427 7777. Hillingdon Uxbridge 53355. Kingston 399 6676. Lewisham, Greenwich, Southwark 692 5228. Orpington 33000. Putney 789 9121. Redbridge 478 7273. Waltham Forest 01-520 1181.

STUDENTS NIGHTLINE 01-581 2468
Help and information telephone service for students in London. Operational 18.00–08.00 nightly during term times. Otherwise answerphone.

TRANSPORT INFORMATION
London Transport. 01-222 1234

REFERENCE TO MAPS

Key to Maps ··	Pages 2-3
Airline Offices ··	✛
Churches ··	✚
Cinemas ··	◖◗
Clubs ··	▨
Commonwealth Representatives ······························	✦
Consulates, Embassies & Legations ·······················	✳
Hotels ··	◇
National Tourist Offices ··	⊗
Police Stations ··	▲
Post Offices ··	★
Pubs ··	➡
Restaurants ··	▩
Statues & Monuments ···	✳
Theatres ··	▭
Toilets ··	T

Dual Carriageway ··	☰
Class A Roads ···	═
Class B Roads ···	─
British Rail Lines & Stations ·································	─□─
Underground Stations ··	○
Map Continuation ··	▷28

Scale: 10½″ to 1 Mile 1:6034

0	110yds.	220yds.		¼ Mile
100 Metres	0		200	400

These Maps are based upon the Ordnance Survey Map with the Sanction
of the Controller of Her Majesty's Stationery Office.
Crown Copyright Reserved.

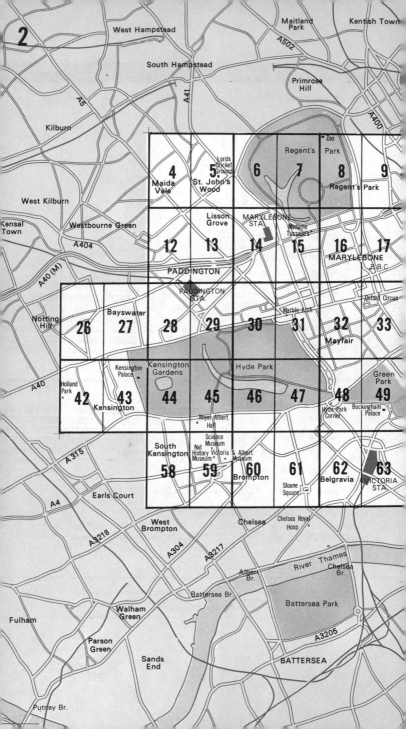

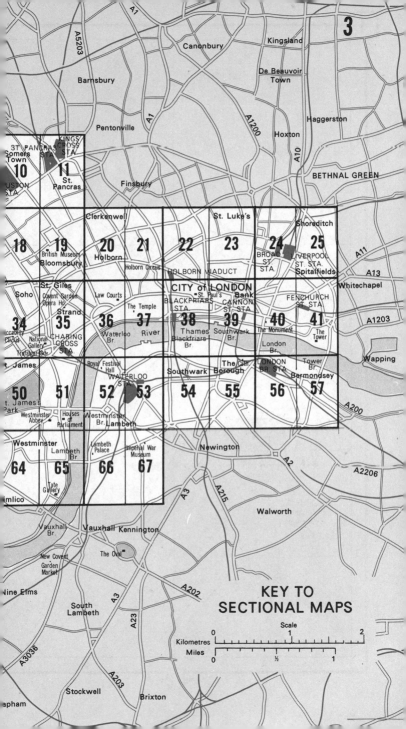

KEY TO
SECTIONAL MAPS

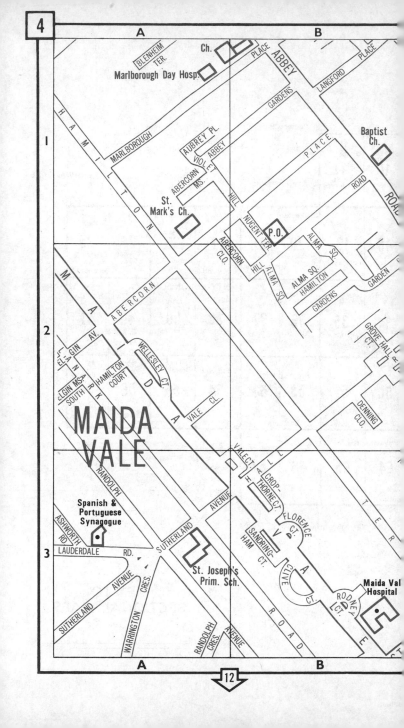

A

B

Ch.

BLENHEIM TER.

PLACE

ABBEY

LANGFORD

PLACE

Marlborough Day Hosp.

HAMILTON

MARLBOROUGH

GARDENS

Baptist Ch.

1

AUBREY PL.

VIOL

ABBEY

PLACE

ABERCORN

MS.

HILL

NUGENT TER.

ROAD

ROAD

St. Mark's Ch.

P.O.

ABERCORN

CLO.

HILL

ALMA SQ.

ALMA SQ.

ALMA SQ.

HAMILTON

GARDEN

M

A

I

D

ABERCORN

GARDENS

GROVE HALL

CT.

2

ELGIN

AV.

ELGIN MS.

SOUTH

PARK

HAMILTON

COURT

WELLESLEY CT.

VALE

VALE CL.

D

A

DENNING

CLO.

MAIDA
VALE

VALE

VALE

CT.

CROP-

THORNE CT.

H

A

RANDOLPH

AVENUE

FLORENCE

CT.

ER

Spanish & Portuguese Synagogue

SANDRING-

HAM CT.

V

D

ASHWORTH RD.

3

LAUDERDALE

RD.

SUTHERLAND

CLIVE

A

CT.

Maida Val Hospital

AVENUE

CRES.

St. Joseph's Prim. Sch.

RODNEY

CT.

E

SUTHERLAND

WARRINGTON

CRES.

RANDOLPH

CRES.

AVENUE

ROAD

A

B

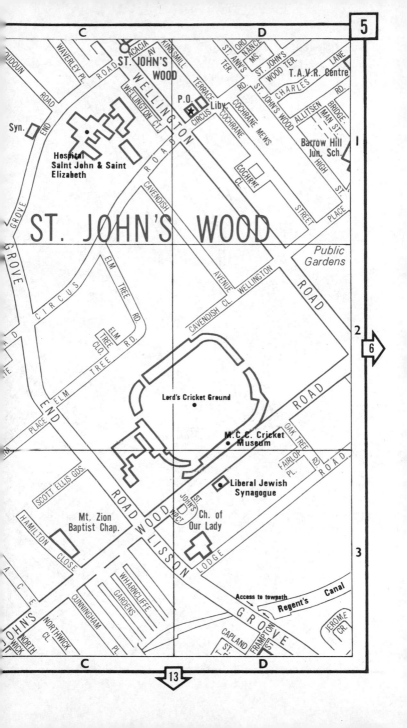

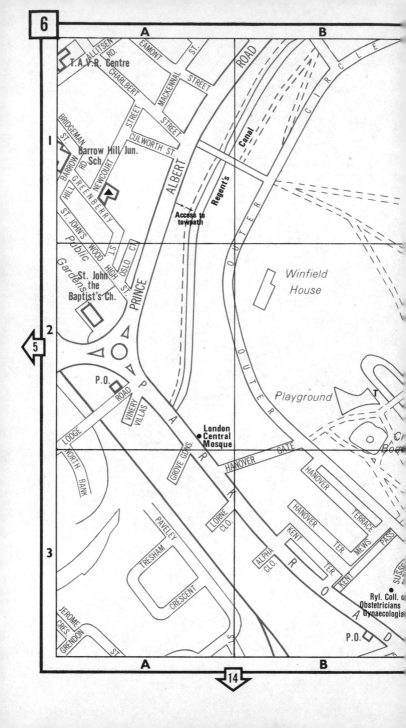

A

B

ALLITSEN RD.

EAMONT

ST.

T.A.V.R. Centre

MACKENNAL

STREET

CHARLBERT

STREET

STREET

ROAD

CIRCLE

BRIDGEMAN ST.

CULWORTH ST.

Canal

I

Barrow Hill Jun. Sch.

NEWCOURT

ALBERT

Regent's

BARROW HILL RD.

GREENBERRY

OSLO CT.

Access to towpath

ST. JOHN'S WOOD

ST.

HIGH

OUTER

Public Gardens

PRINCE

ST.

Winfield House

St. John the Baptist's Ch.

2

5

⬦ ○ ◁

P.O.

ROAD

A

OUTER

Playground

T

LODGE

VINERY VILLAS

P

London Central Mosque

NORTH BANK

GROVE GDNS.

R

HANOVER

GATE

Ci Boa

HANOVER

HANOVER

TERRACE

PAVELEY

LORNE CLO.

KENT

TER.

MEWS

3

TRESHAM

ALPHA CLO.

R

KENT

PASS

SUSSE

JEROME CRES.

CRESCENT

O

Ryl. Coll. o Obstetricians Gynaecologis

GRENDON

ST.

S

P.O.

D

A

B

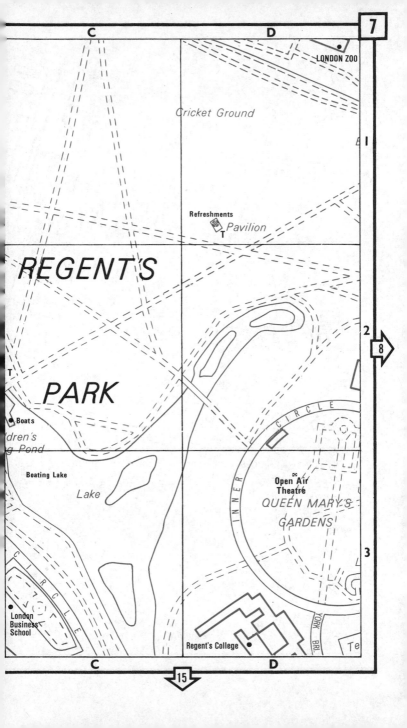

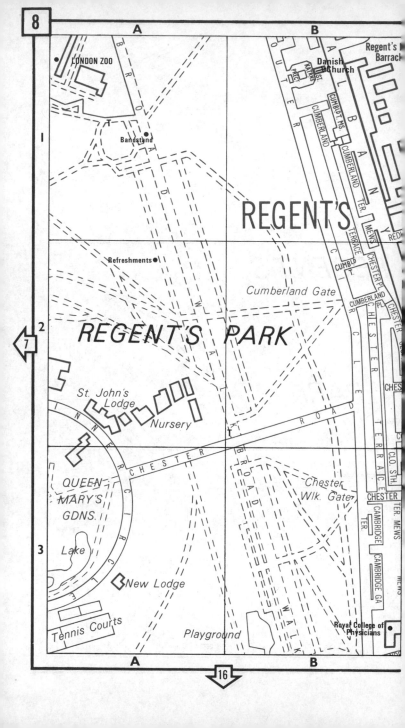

A

B

● LONDON ZOO

Danish
Church

Regent's
Barracks

B
R
O
A
D

KATENS ST.
REC.

KENT PAS.

CUMBERLAND

CUMBERLAND TER.

CUMBERLAND

B
A
N
Y

TERRACE

MEWS

REDI

● Bandstand

1

REGENT'S

W
A
L
K

● Refreshments

CUMBLD
T.

CHESTERPL

Cumberland Gate

CUMBERLAND
PL.

CHESTER

C
I
R
C
L
E

2

REGENT'S PARK

CHES

CLO. STH.

7

I
N
N
E
R

C
I
R
C
L
E

St. John's
Lodge

Nursery

ROAD

CHES

CHESTER

TER MEWS

CHESTER

C
I
R
C
L
E

CHESTER

B
R
O
A
D

ROAD

Chester
Wlk. Gate

CHESTER

TERRACE

QUEEN
MARY'S
GDNS.

Lake

W
A
L
K

CAMBRIDGE
TER.

CAMBRIDGE GA

3

◇ New Lodge

Tennis Courts

Playground

W
A
L
K

Royal College of
Physicians ■

HILTNS

A

B

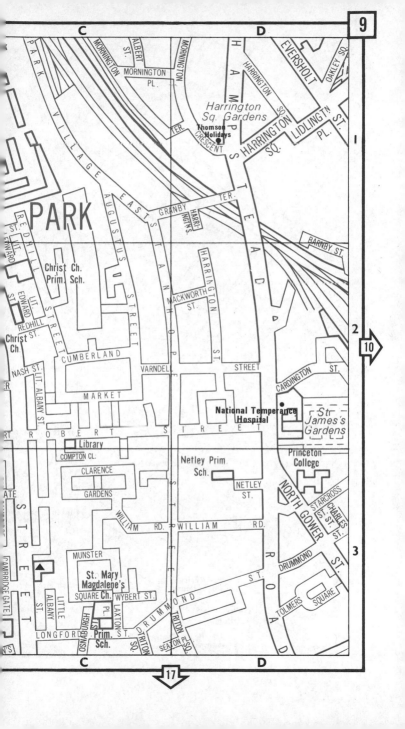

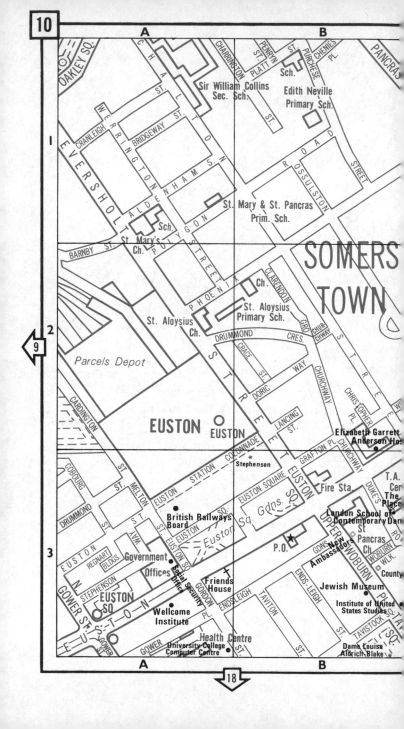

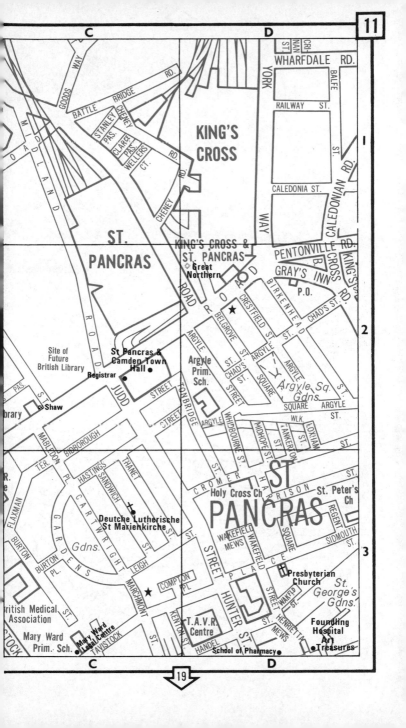

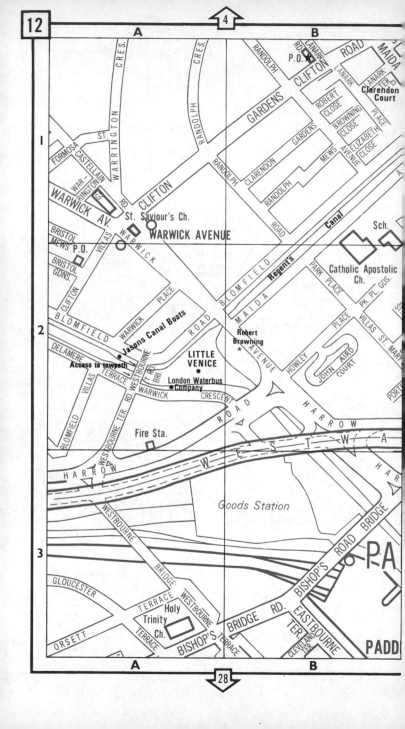

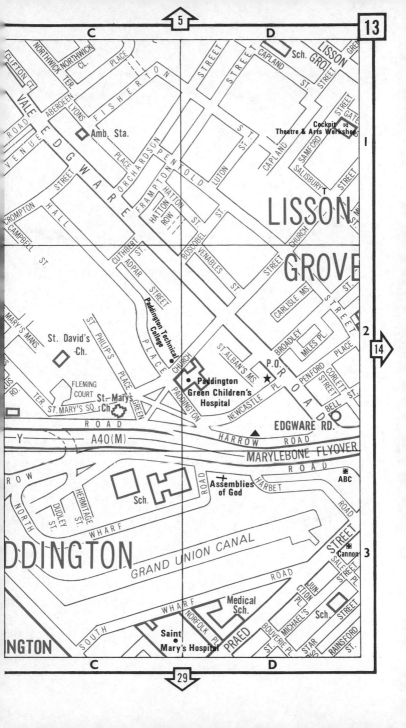

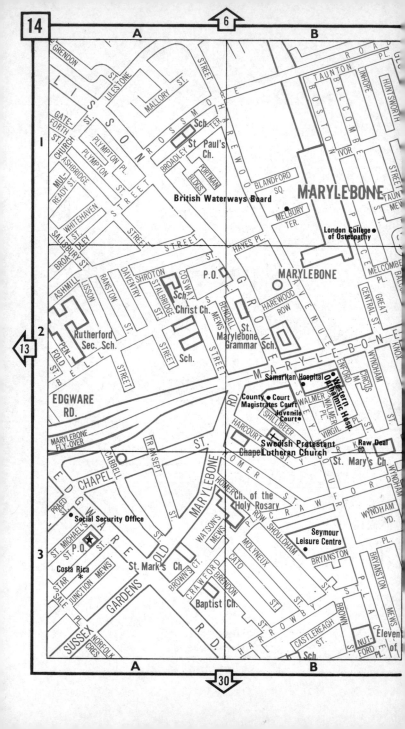

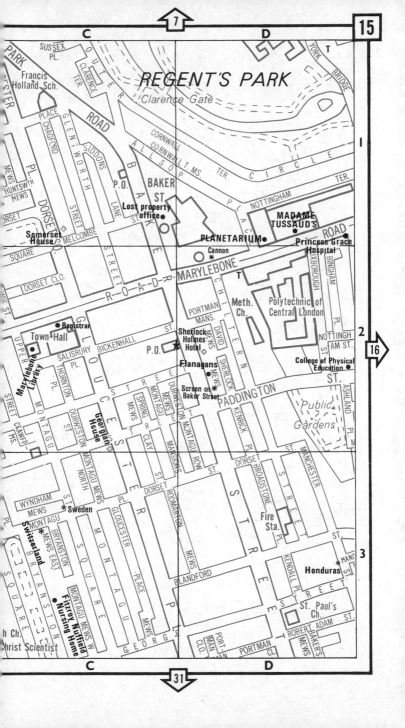

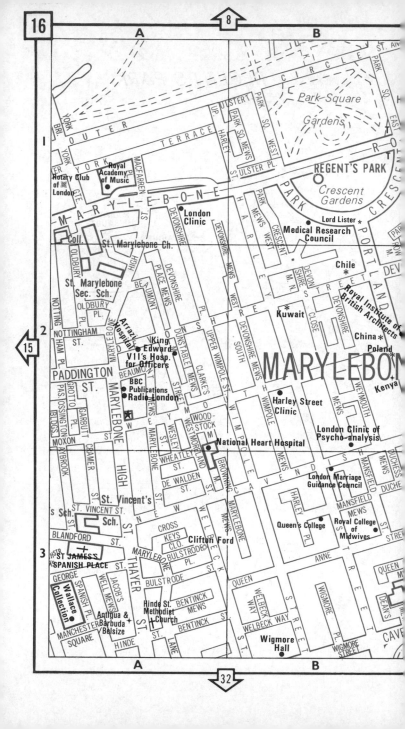

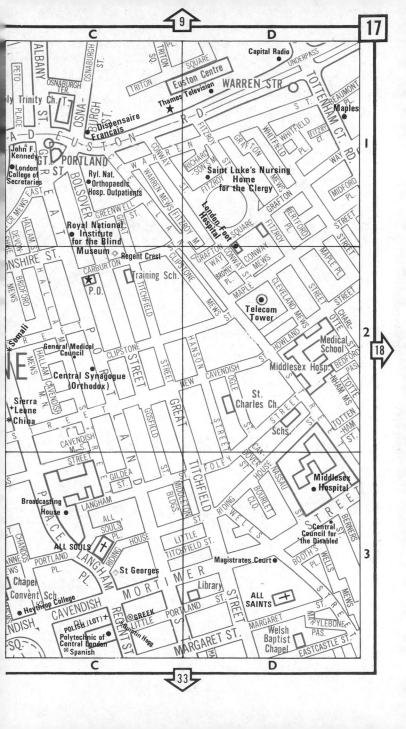

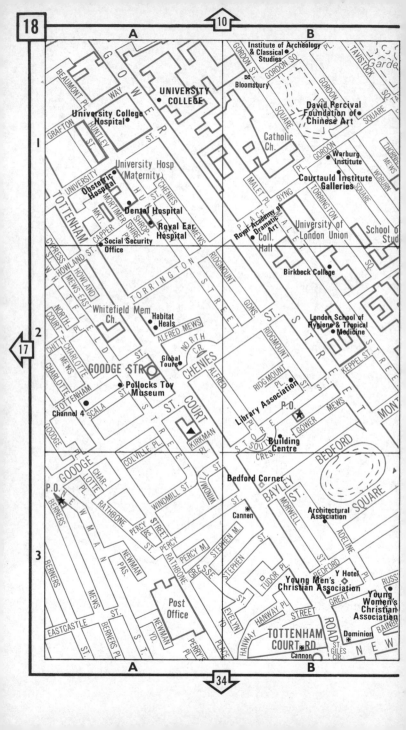

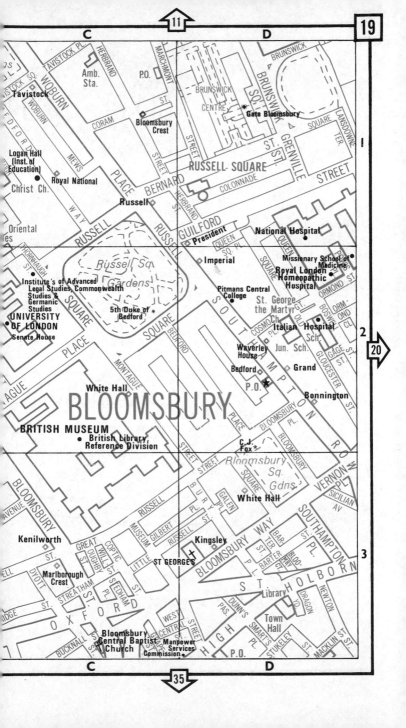

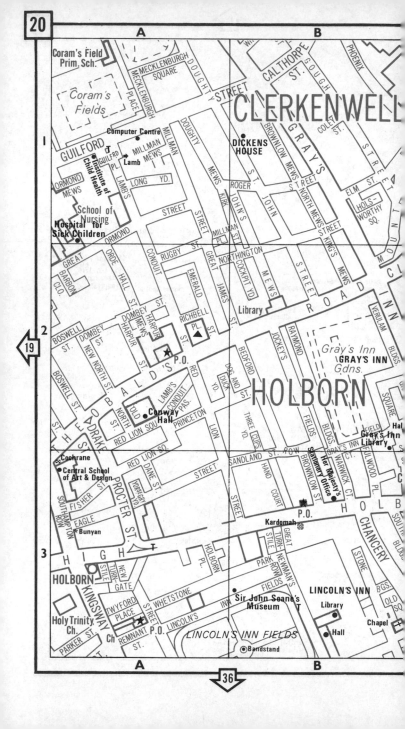

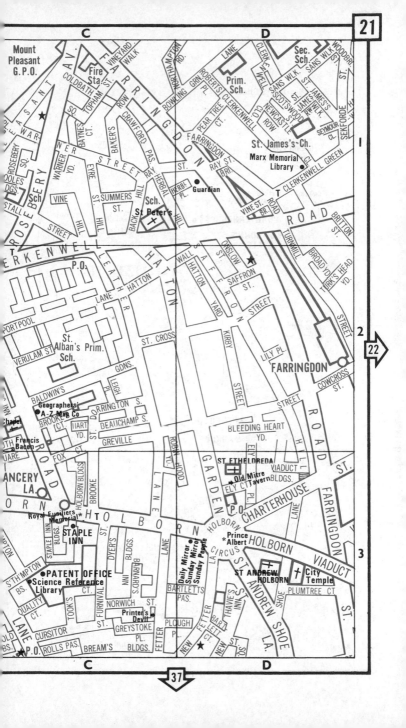

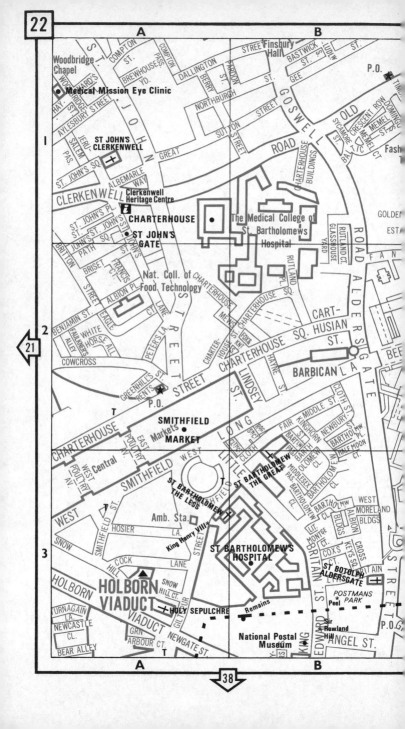

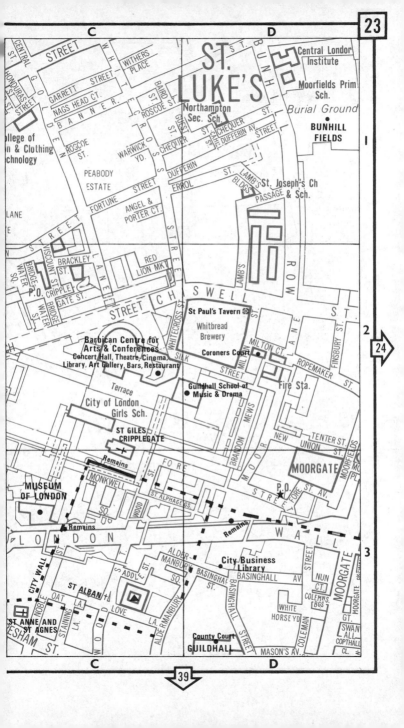

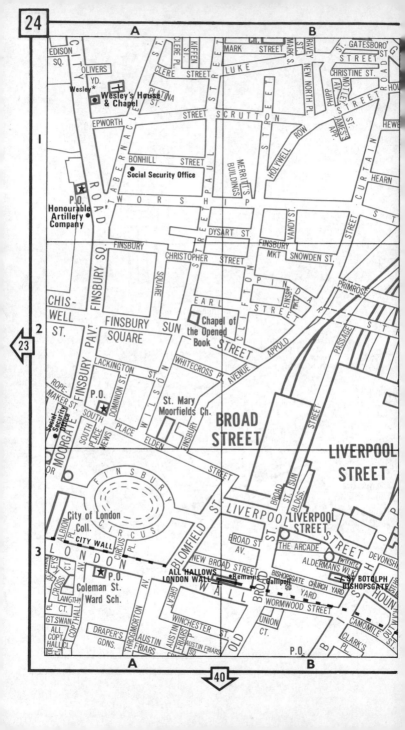

EDISON SQ.

CITY ROAD

OLIVERS YD.

Wesley* ✠ Wesley's House & Chapel

EPWORTH STREET

CLERE ST. CLERE PL. KIFFEN ST. CLERE STREET PLATINA ST.

MARK STREET MARK S. RAVEY ST. NEW NORTH PL. GATESBORO' STREET CHRISTINE ST.

LUKE STREET

SCRUTTON STREET

PHILIP STREET

AYLEY ST. OTLEY STREET

JAMES'S ST. APP.

HEWE

1

TABERNACLE ST.

BONHILL STREET

• Social Security Office

WORSHIP STREET

PAUL STREET

MERRITT'S BUILDINGS

HOLYWELL ROW

CURTAIN ROAD

HEARN

ST.

P.O. ★
Honourable •
Artillery
Company

FINSBURY SQ.

FINSBURY

FINSBURY SQUARE

FINSBURY PAVT.

SQUARE

CHRISTOPHER STREET

DYSART ST.

EARL

STREET

FINSBURY MKT. VANDY ST. SNOWDEN ST.

FINSBY. MKT.

PRIMROSE STR

PASSAGE

CHIS-
WELL
ST.

Chapel of
the Opened
Book

SUN STREET

WILSON ST.

CLIFTON STREET

APPOLD

ST.

2 ◀ 23

LACKINGTON ST.

DOMINION ST.

WHITECROSS PL.

FINSBURY AVENUE

ROPE-
MAKER ST.
•Social
Security
Office

P.O. ★

SOUTH PLACE

SOUTH PLACE MEWS

St. Mary
Moorfields Ch.

FINSBURY ST.

ELDEN ST.

BROAD
STREET

LIVERPOOL
STREET

MOORGATE

OR

FINSBURY CIRCUS

BLOMFIELD STREET

LIVERPOOL STREET

BROAD ST. SUN BLDGS.

STREET

LIVERPOOL STREET

HO

City of London
Coll.

CITY WALL

BROAD ST. AV.

THE ARCADE

ALDERMANS WLK.

DEVONSHIRE

3

LONDON

ALBION

CROSS CT. KEYS CT. LANGTHN CT.

WALL

CIRCUS PL.

New Broad St.

ALL HALLOWS
LONDON WALL

GREAT

WINCHESTER ST.

•Remans

BISHOPSGATE CHURCH YARD
Gallipol•

WENTW

ST. BOTOLPH
BISHOPSGATE

BROAD ST. OLD

P.O. ★
Coleman St.
Ward Sch.

GT.SWAN ALL. COPT. HALL CT.

THROGMORTON AV.

COPTHALL AV.

DRAPER'S GDNS.

AUSTIN FRIARS

AUSTIN FRIARS

AUSTIN FRIARS SQ.

WORMWOOD STREET

UNION CT.

HOUNDSDITCH

CAMOMILE ST

CLARK'S PL

P.O.

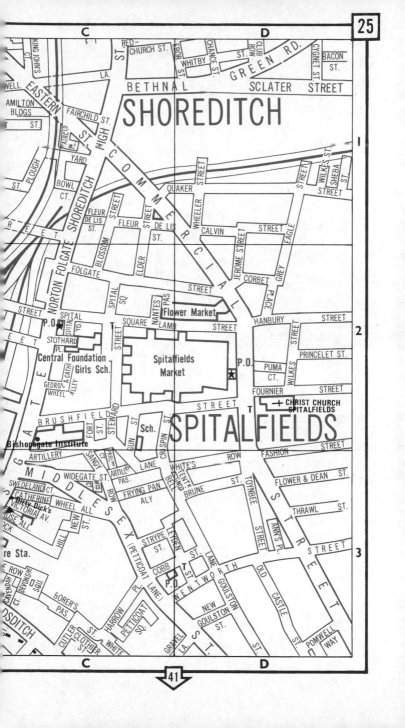

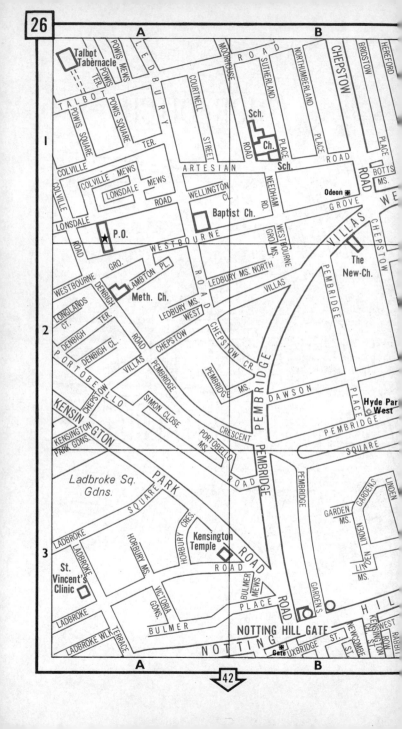

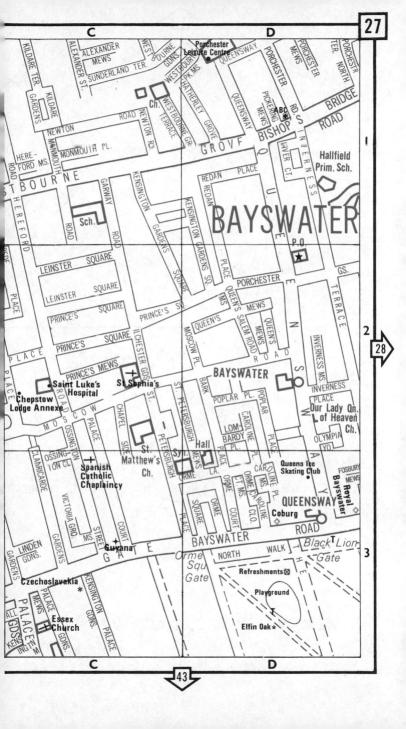

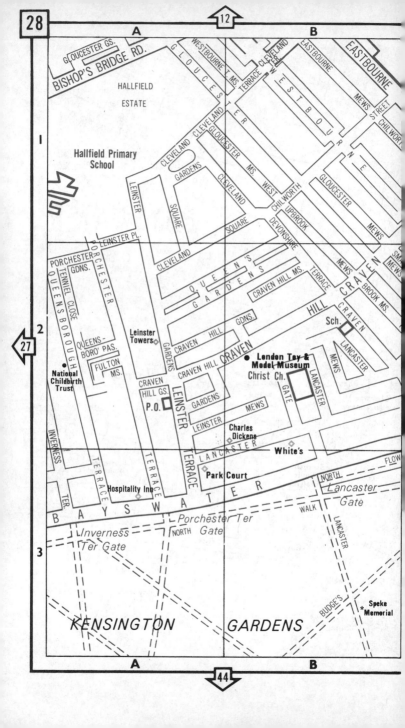

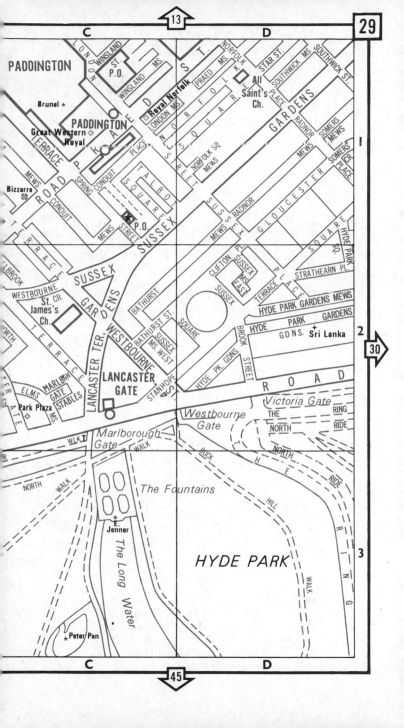

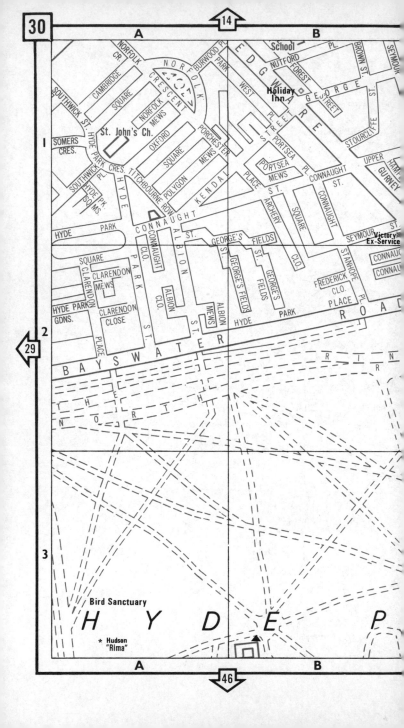

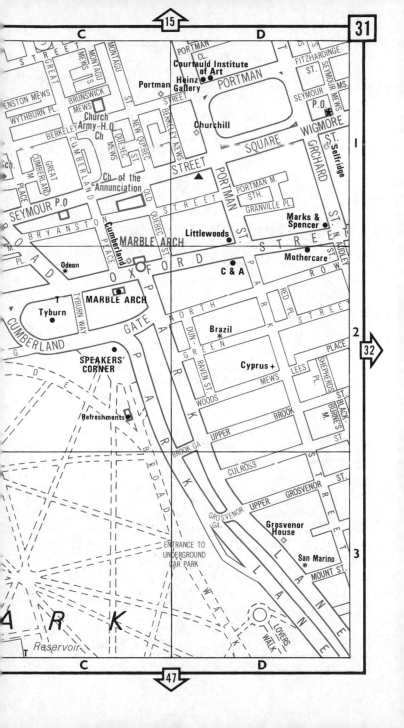

STREET
PORTMAN
CL.
FITZHARDINGE
ST.
SEYMOUR MS.

Courtauld Institute of Art
Portman
Heinz
Gallery

PORTMAN

SEYMOUR MEWS

P.O.

ENSTON MEWS
WYTHBURN PL.
BRUNSWICK
MEWS
Church
Army-H.Q
Ch

MONTAGU
STREET
MONTAGU S²

Churchill

WIGMORE
ST.

Selfridge

ch.

GREAT
CUMBERLAND
PLACE
IM

BERKELEY
MEWS
QUE-BEC
MEWS
NEW QUEBEC
ST.

BERKELEY MEWS

SQUARE

ORCHARD

Ch of the Annunciation

STREET

PORTMAN

PORTMAN M.
STH.

ST. N.

ST. N. AUDLEY

I

SEYMOUR P.O

STREET

GRANVILLE PL.

Marks & Spencer

BRYANSTON

Cumberland

QUEBEC

MARBLE ARCH

Littlewoods

PORTMAN ST.

STREE

M.
PL.

Odeon

Cumberland
PLACE

O X F O R D

C & A

PARK

Mothercare

ROW

RED
PL.

STREE

T
MARBLE ARCH

TYBURN WAY

Tyburn

GATE

NORTH

DUN-
GREEN

Brazil
*

STREE

PLACE

SHEPHERDS
PL.

2
32

CUMBERLAND

PARK

RAVEN ST.

Cyprus +

LEES

MEWS

ST. BLACK-
BURNE'S
M.

G

D
E
SPEAKERS' CORNER

WOODS

BROOK

ST.
BLACK-
BURNE'S
ST.

Refreshments

UPPER

BROOK GA.

P
A
R
K

CULROS3

ST.

B
R
O
A
D

GROSVENOR
GA.

UPPER GROSVENOR

STREE

W
A
T

Grosvenor House

T

ENTRANCE TO
UNDERGROUND
CAR PARK

L
A
N
E

San Marino
*

3

MOUNT ST.

A R K

LOVERS
WALK

T Reservoir

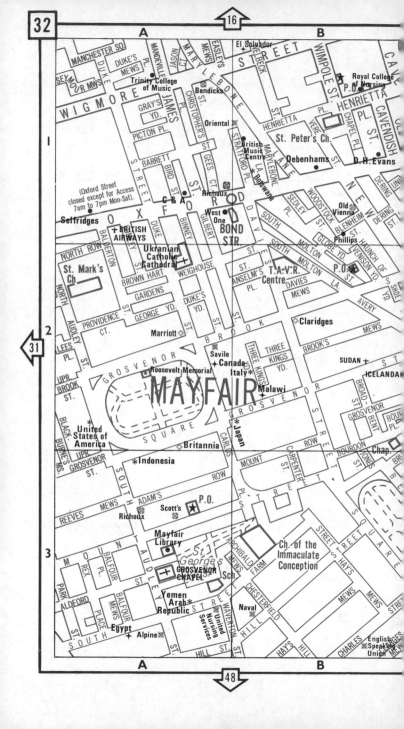

A   B

MANCHESTER SQ.

SEYMOUR MWS

DUKE ST

DUKE'S MEWS

MANDEVILLE PL.

EASLEY'S MEWS

El Salvador

BEEBECK STREET

WIMPOLE ST.

CANAL

P.O.

★ Royal College of Nursing

Trinity College of Music

Bendicks

HENRIETTA

WIGMORE

JAMES

GRAY'S YD.

ST. CHRISTOPHER'S PL.

Oriental

HENRIETTA ST.

VERE ST.

CHAPEL PL.

CAVENDISH

PICTON PL.

St. Peter's Ch.

1

BARRETT

STREET

BIRD ST.

GEES CT.

STRATFORD PL.

MARYLEBONE LA.

British Music Centre

Debenhams

D.H. Evans

(Oxford Street closed except for Access 7am to 7pm Mon-Sat.)

C & A

Richoux

OXFORD

Selfridges

DUKE STREET

BINNEY ST.

GILBERT ST.

West One

BOND STR

DAVIES

SOUTH MOLTON

SEDLEY PL.

WOODSTOCK ST.

Old Vienna

BLENHEIM ST.

DERING ST.

NEW

Phillips

Haunch of

P.O.

★ BRITISH AIRWAYS

Ukranian Catholic Cathedral ✚

WEIGHOUSE ST.

SOUTH MOLTON LA.

MOLTON ST.

★ T.A.V.R. Centre

DAVIES MEWS

P.O. ★

VENISON YD.

S. MOLTON

SHEL

St. Mark's Ch.

NORTH ROW

BROWN HART

GARDENS

DUKE'S YD.

ST. ANSELM'S PL.

BROOK ST.

AVERY ROW

NORTH AUDLEY ST.

PROVIDENCE CT.

GEORGE YD.

◇ Claridges

2

LEES PL.

Marriott

BROOK

THREE KINGS YD.

THREE KINGS

BROOK'S MEWS

SUDAN ✚

ICELAND

31

UPR BROOK ST.

GROSVENOR

Savile

✚ Canada Italy ✦

MAYFAIR

GROSVENOR STREET

BROAD-BENT

GROSVENOR

BOURDON PL.

BLACKBURNE MS.

UPR GROSVENOR ST.

Roosevelt Memorial ★

SQUARE

Malawi ●

CARLOS

ROW

BOURDON ST.

Chap.

BR.

United States of America ★

Britannia ◇

★ Japan

✱ Indonesia

SOUTH

ADAM'S ROW

MOUNT ROW

CARPENTER ST.

JONES ST.

SQUARE

REEVES MEWS

Richoux

MEWS

Scott's ★ P.O.

AUDLEY

STREET

STREET

HAY'S

3

MOUNT

REX PL.

BALFOUR

Mayfair Library

St. George's

✚ GROSVENOR CHAPEL

FARM ST.

ARCHIBALD MEWS

Ch. of the Immaculate Conception

HAY'S MEWS

MEWS

STREET

PARK

ALDFORD

BALFOUR MEWS

Yemen Arab Republic ✱

Sch

CHESTERFIELD

ST.

Egypt ✱

Alpine

SOUTH

✱ United Nursing Services

Naval ✚

WATERTON ST.

English Speaking Union

HILL

HAY'S

CHARLES

STR

A   B

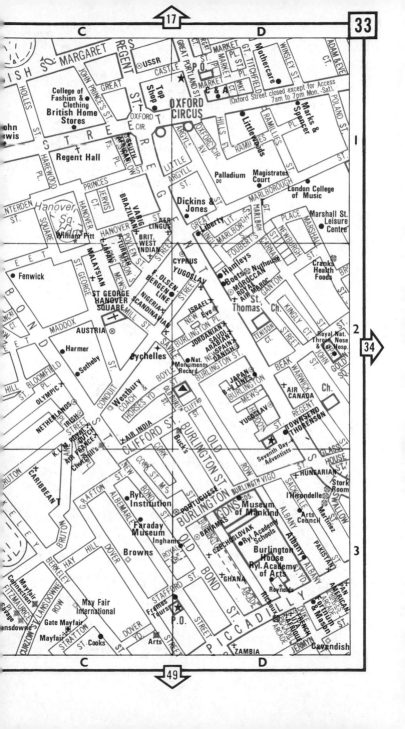

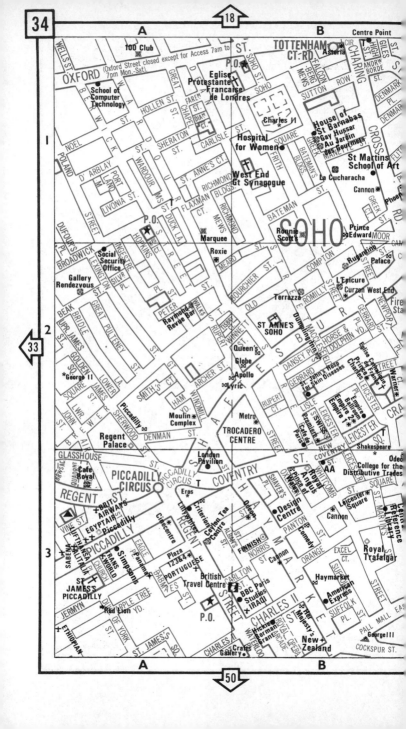

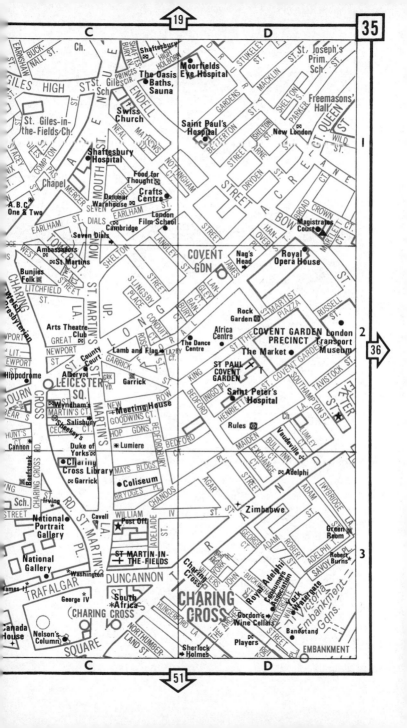

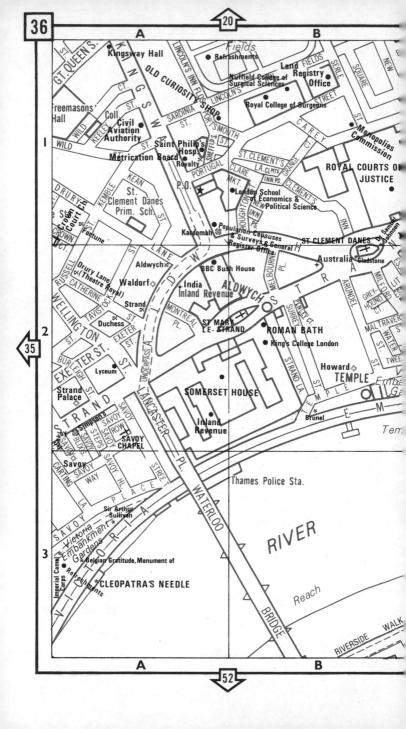

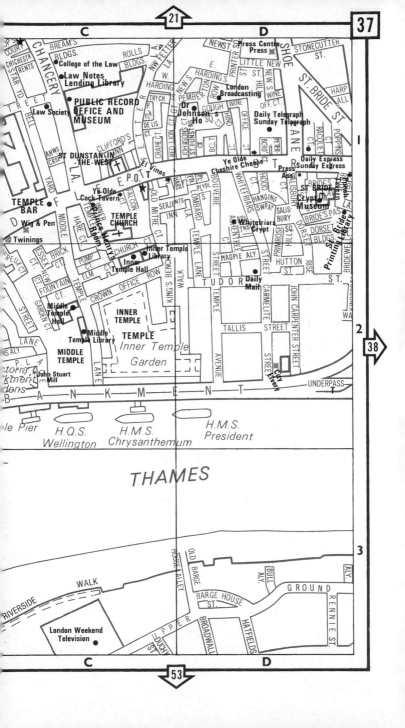

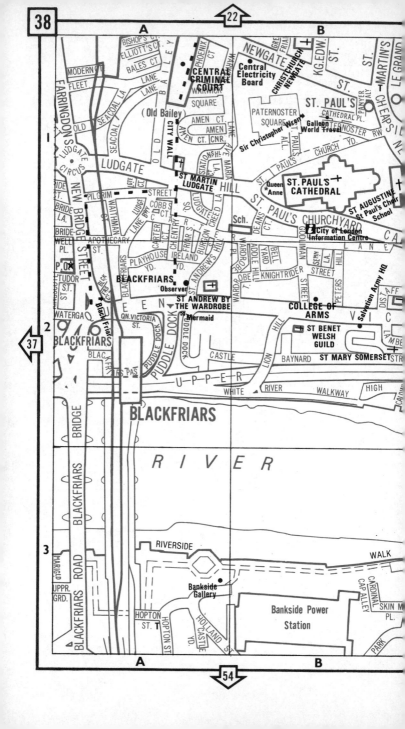

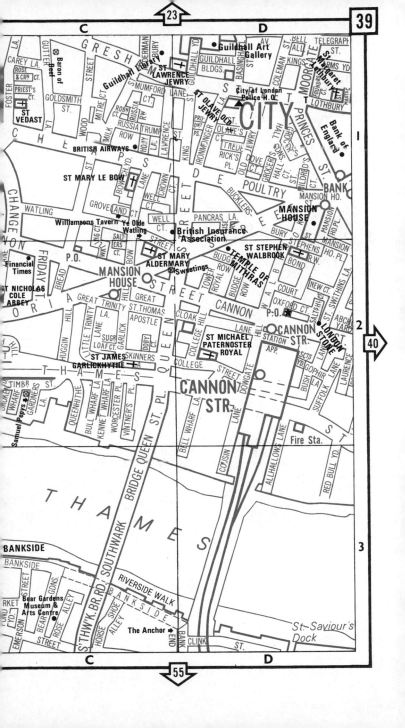

A · B

COPTHALL BGS.

P.O.

BISHOPSGATE

✝ ST ETHELBURGA

TOKENHOUSE YARD

ANGEL CT.

THROGMORTON AV.

AUSTIN FRIARS

✝ Dutch Church

BROAD ST.

ST. HELEN'S PL.

GREAT ST. HELEN'S

🏛 City of London

☒ Overseas Bankers

LOTHBURY

THROGMORTON ST.

ST.

P.O.

ADAMS CT.

CROSBY SQ.

✝ ST HELEN BISHOPSGATE

BROWN BLDGS.

BARTHOLOMEW CT.

STOCK EXCHANGE

OLD

CAPEL CT.

STREET

WHITE

SHAFTS CT.

UNDERSHAFT

✝ ST ANDREW UNDERSHAFT

1 BANK OF ENGLAND

THREADNEEDLE

ROYAL EXCHANGE

RY. EXCHANGE BLDGS.

RY. EXCHANGE AV.

UPPER

ST. MICHAEL'S

City Unity

LS

PETER CORNHILL

LEADENHALL STREET

★

P.O. LLOYDS

C O R N H

CASTLE CT.

ST. MICHAEL'S

BENGL

BLS

LEADENHALL

KINGTON

LEADENHALL MARKET

★

CORN H

POPES HEAD AL.

ABCHURCH

CHANGE AL.

George and Vulture

CENTRAL

LIME

LEADENHALL PL.

ST.

FENCHURCH

AV.

LOMBARD

✝ ST MARY WOOLNOTH

Institute of Bankers

NICH. LAS LANE

BIRCHIN LA.

BELL INN YD.

P.O.

BULLS HED PAS.

BEEHIVE PL.

FEN CT.

CLEMENT'S LANE

✝ ST EDMUND THE KING

STREET

SHIP TAVERN PAS.

CULLUM ST.

HOGARTH AL.

DUNSTER

2
39

CANNON

✝ ST MARY ABCHURCH

☒ Gresham

WILLIAM

NICHOLAS LANE

PLOUGH CT.

GRAC. ECH. CT.

LOMBARD CT.

GRACECHURCH

F E N C H U R C H

BRABNT LA.

ST. BENET'S

ST. BENET'S CTPL.

PHILPOT LA.

TURNER'S AL.

ROOD LA.

✝ ST MARGARET PATTENS

MINCING

LANE

Customs & Excise Department

POULTNEY HILL

LA. Old Wine Shades

ST CLEMENT EASTCHEAP

ST. MARTIN'S

TALBOT CT.

★

EASTCHEAP

GREAT

TOWER

ST.

LAURENCE POUNTNEY

ARTHUR ST.

MONUMENT

Square Rigger

MONUMENT

THE MONUMENT

HILL

MILES LA.

MONU MENT

KING'S HEAD CT.

PUDDING LA.

ST. GEOS LA.

BOTOLPH LA.

LOVAT LA.

BOTOLPH ALY.

ST. MARY

✝ ST MARY AT HILL

ST. DUNT'S

ST. DUNT'S HI.

ST DUNSTAN'S HILL

HARP LA.

BAKERS HALL CT.

BYWARD ST.

UPR. THAMES

FISH ST. HILL

FISHMONGERS HALL ST.

SWAN LA.

OLD SWAN

LOWER

STREET

ST. BOTOLPH

ST. MARY

✝ ST DUNSTAN-IN-THE-EAST

CROSS LA.

CUSTOMS HOUSE

Social Security Office

✝ ST MAGNUS THE MARTYR

Old Billingsgate Market

THAMES

WHARF

London Bridge Sports Centre

3

LONDON BRIDGE

RIVER THAMES

Upper Pool

A · B

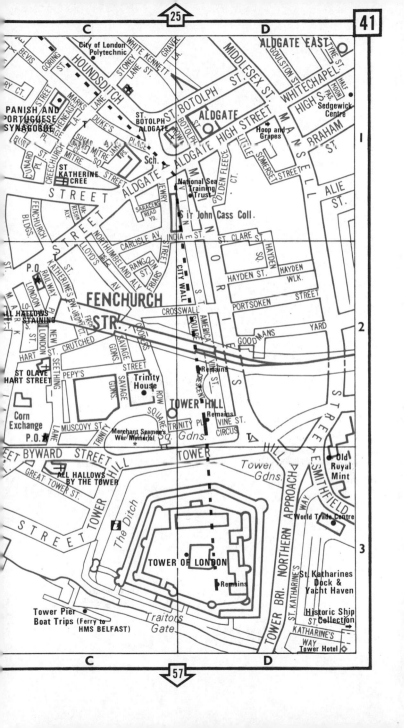

C **D**

ALDGATE EAST

City of London
Polytechnic

WHITE KENNETT ST.
GRAVEL
TYNE ST.
HALF MOON

HOUNDSDITCH
STONEY LA.
LANE ST.
MIDDLESEX ST.
GOULSTON ST.
WHITECHAPEL HIGH S.

MARKS LANE
HENEAGE LA.
DUKE'S
ST. BOTOLPH
ALDGATE
BRAHAM ST.
Sedgewick
Centre

PANISH AND
PORTUGUESE
SYNAGOGUE
GORING ST.
BEVIS
MARKS
CREECHURCH LA.
MITRE ST.
MITRE SQ.
SUGAR
PLACE
DUKE'S
JAMES
ST. BOTOLPH
ALDGATE
Hoop and
Grapes
MANSELL ST.

1

ST.
KATHERINE
CREE
ALDGATE HIGH STREET
LITTLE
SOMERSET STREET

STREET
FENCHURCH
BLDGS.
Sch.
JEWRY
National Sea
Training
Trust
GOLDEN FLEECE CT.
ALIE ST.

STREET
RISMA
NORTHUMBERLAND ALL.
CARLISLE AV.
SARACENS
HEAD YD.
INDIA ST.
Sir John Cass Coll.
ST. CLARE ST.
HAYDEN
SQ.
HAYDEN ST.
HAYDEN
WLK.

P.O.
Railway
KATHERINE'S RW.
LONDON
LLOYD'S AV.
RANGOON ST.
FRIARS
CITY
WALL
MINORIES
PORTSOKEN
STREET
HAYDEN ST.

ALL HALLOWS
STAINING
LO-
NDON ST.
MARK
LANE
ST.
NEW
CRUTCHED
HART
ORMOND CT.
ST.
CROSSWALL
CRESCENT
AMERICA SQUARE
GOODMANS
YARD

FENCHURCH
STR.
ST. OLAVE
HART STREET
SEETHING
LANE
PEPY'S
SAVAGE
GDNS.
Trinity
House
VAULTS ST.
Remains

Corn
Exchange
MUSCOVY ST.
TRINITY LANE
SQUARE
ROW
SAVAGE GDNS.
TOWER HILL
Remains
TRINITY PL.
VINE ST.
CIRCUS

P.O.
BYWARD STREET
TOWER HILL
Merchant Seamen's
War Memorial
Sq. Gdns.
TOWER HILL
Tower
Gdns.
E. SMITHFIELD
Old
Royal
Mint

ALL HALLOWS
BY THE TOWER
GREAT TOWER ST.
TOWER HILL
The Ditch
Tower Gdns.
NORTHERN APPROACH
WAY
World Trade Centre

3

STREET
The Ditch
TOWER OF LONDON
Remains
ST. KATHARINE'S
TOWER BRI.
St. Katharines
Dock &
Yacht Haven

Tower Pier
Boat Trips (Ferry to
HMS BELFAST)
Traitors
Gate
KATHARINE'S
WAY
Historic Ship
Collection
Tower Hotel

C **D**

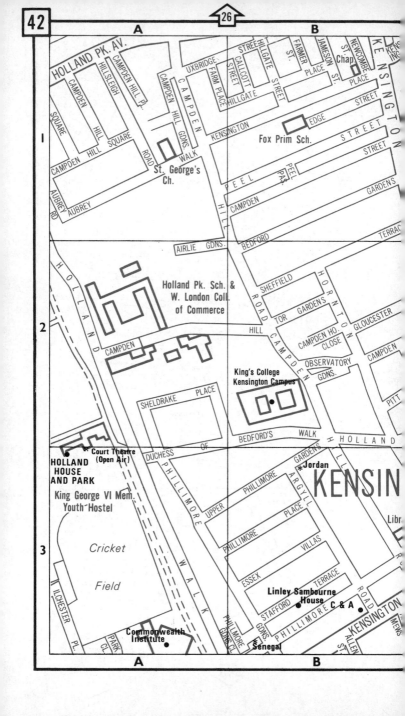

A

B

HOLLAND PK. AV.

KENSINGTON

STREET
HILLGATE ST.
FARMER
JAMESON ST.
NEWCOMBE
Chap
PLACE

UXBRIDGE
CALLCOTT STREET
HILLGATE STREET
PLACE
STREET

CAMPDEN
HILLSLEIGH
CAMPDEN HILL PL.
CAMPDEN HILL GDNS.
FARM PLACE
HILLGATE

CAMPDEN
HILL
SQUARE
HILL SQUARE
EDGE
Fox Prim Sch.
STREET

1

CAMPDEN
HILL
ROAD
WALK
KENSINGTON
STREET

St. George's Ch.
PEEL
PEEL PAS.
GARDENS

AUBREY RD.
AUBREY
HILL
CAMPDEN
STREET

AIRLIE GDNS.
BEDFORD
TERRAC

HOLLAND

SHEFFIELD
HORNTON

Holland Pk. Sch. &
W. London Coll.
of Commerce
TOR GARDENS
GLOUCESTER

2

CAMPDEN
ROAD
Campden Ho.
CLOSE
CAMPDEN

HILL
CAMPDEN
OBSERVATORY
GDNS.
PITT

King's College
Kensington Campus

SHELDRAKE
PLACE

BEDFORD'S
WALK
HOLLAND

OF
DUCHESS
Court Theatre
(Open Air)
GARDENS
Jordan
KENSIN

HOLLAND
HOUSE
AND PARK

PHILLIMORE

ARGYLL
HILL

King George VI Mem.
Youth Hostel

UPPER
PHILLIMORE
PLACE
KENSIN

Libr

3

Cricket

PHILLIMORE
VILLAS

Field

WALK
ESSEX
TERRACE

ILCHESTER

Linley Sambourne House
C & A

STAFFORD
PHILLIMORE
KENSINGTON

PARK CL.

Commonwealth
Institute
PHILLIMORE GDNS.
GDNS.
ALLEN ST.
MEWS

Senegal

A

B

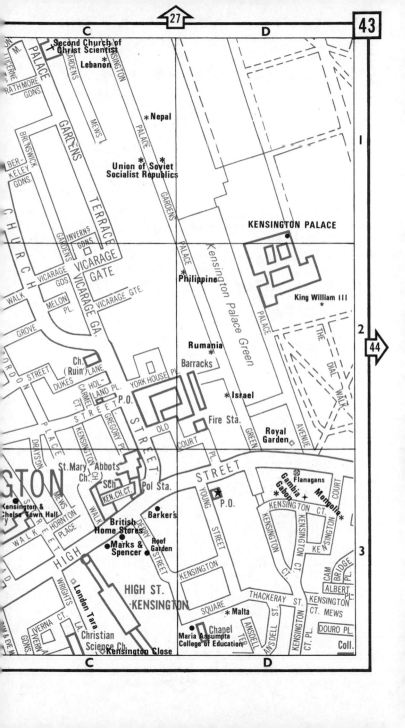

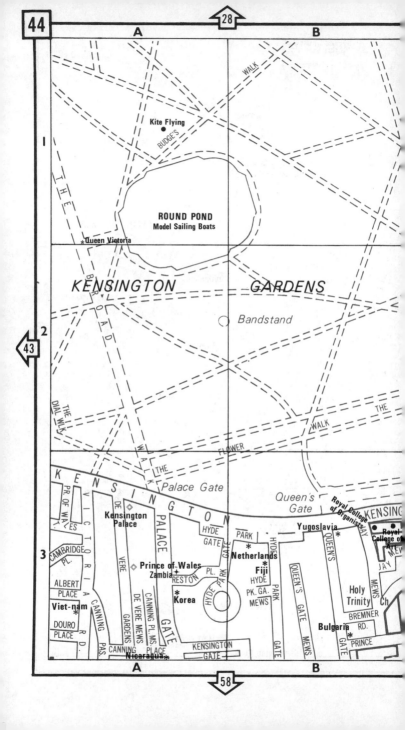

A B

1

Kite Flying
BUDGE'S
WALK

THE BROAD WALK

ROUND POND
Model Sailing Boats

* Queen Victoria

KENSINGTON GARDENS

2

◯ *Bandstand*

THE DIAL WALK

THE WALK

THE WALK

FLOWER WALK

3

KENSINGTON

Palace Gate

Queen's Gate

Royal College of Organists

KENSINGTON

PR. OF WALES T.
VICTORIA RD.

Kensington Palace ◇

DE VERE GARDENS

PALACE GATE

HYDE GATE

Yugoslavia *

Royal College of *

JAY

CAMBRIDGE PL.

Prince of Wales ◇
Zambia +
RESTON PL.

PARK *
Netherlands *

HYDE PARK GATE

Fiji *
HYDE PK. GA. MEWS

QUEEN'S GATE

QUEEN'S

MEWS

Holy Trinity Ch.

ALBERT PLACE

DE VERE MEWS

CANNING PL. MS.

Korea *

HYDE PARK MEWS

BREMNER RD.

Viet-nam *

CANNING PAS.

DOURO PLACE

CANNING RD.

GARDENS

KENSINGTON GATE

KENSINGTON GATE

Bulgaria *

QUEEN'S GATE MEWS

PRINCE

Nicaragua *

A B

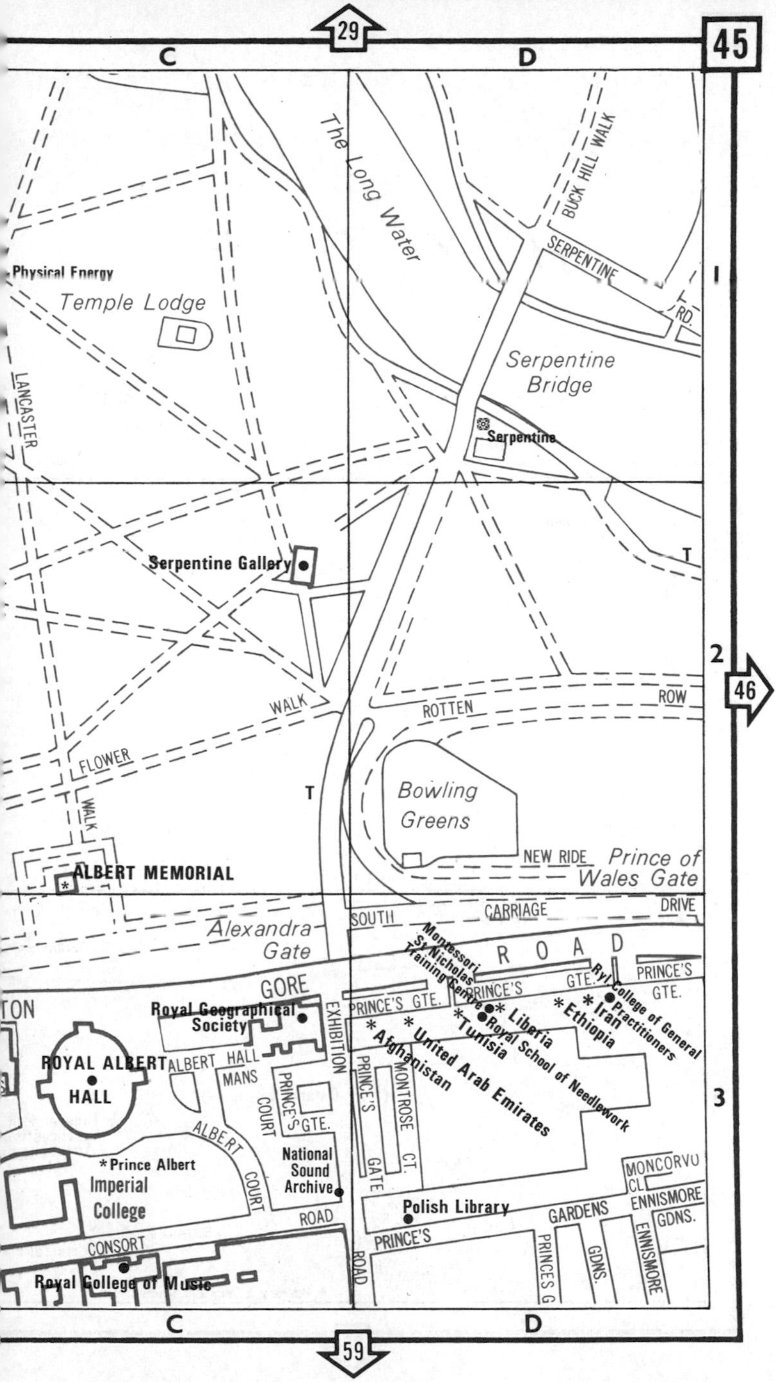

C D

Physical Energy

Temple Lodge

The Long Water

BUCK HILL WALK

SERPENTINE

RD

1

Serpentine
Bridge

LANCASTER

Serpentine

Serpentine Gallery

T

WALK

ROTTEN ROW

FLOWER

WALK

T

Bowling
Greens

NEW RIDE Prince of
Wales Gate

ALBERT MEMORIAL

Alexandra
Gate

SOUTH CARRIAGE DRIVE

ROAD

Montessori
St Nicholas
Training Centre

PRINCE'S

GTE.

R¹
College of General
Practitioners

PRINCE'S
GTE.

GORE

Royal Geographical
Society

EXHIBITION

PRINCE'S GTE.

Liberia

Royal School of Needlework

Iran

Ethiopia

TON

ROYAL ALBERT
HALL

ALBERT HALL
MANS

PRINCE'S GTE.

Tunisia

United Arab Emirates

Afghanistan

MONTROSE CT.

3

PRINCE'S GATE

ALBERT COURT

ROAD

Prince Albert

Imperial
College

National
Sound Archive

Polish Library

PRINCE'S

MONCORVO
CL.

ENNISMORE

GDNS.

GARDENS

PRINCES G

GDNS.

ENNISMORE

CONSORT

Royal College of Music

ROAD

C D

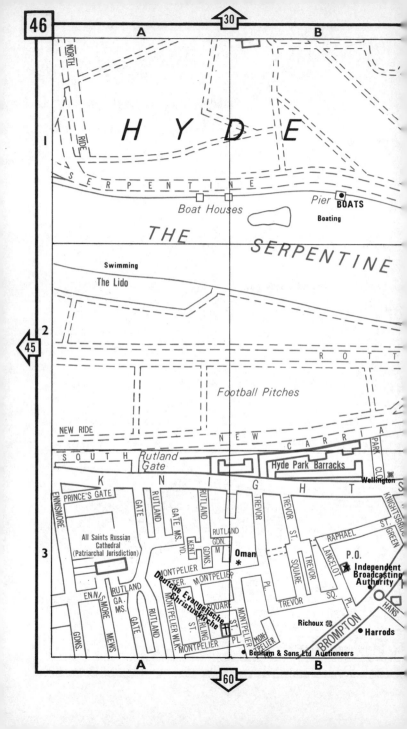

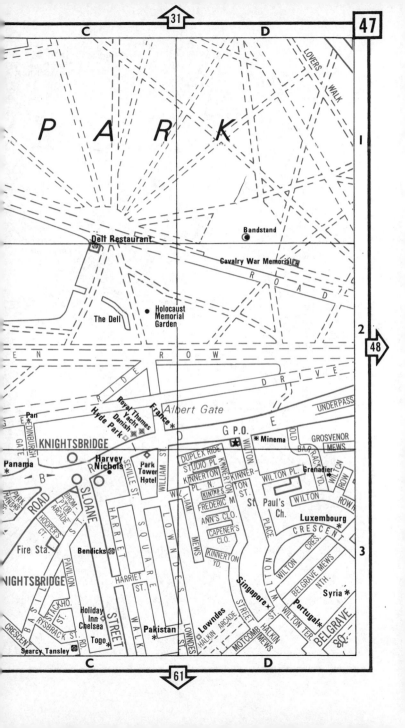

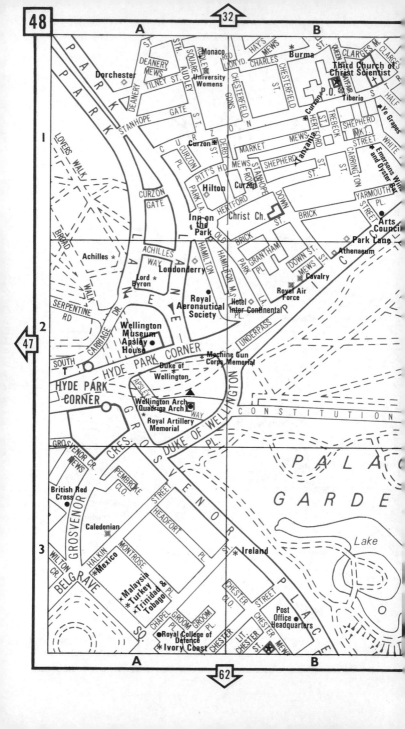

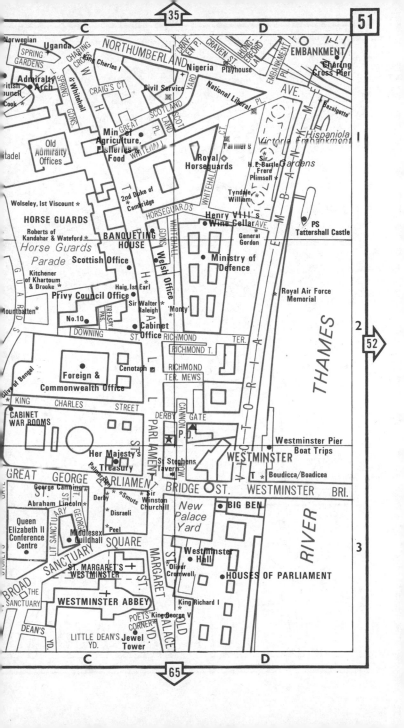

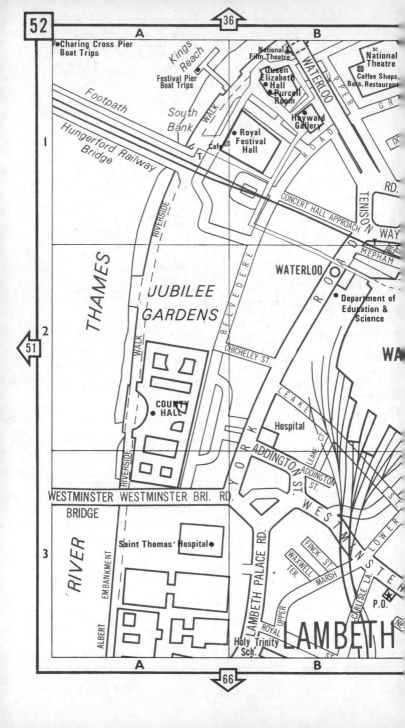

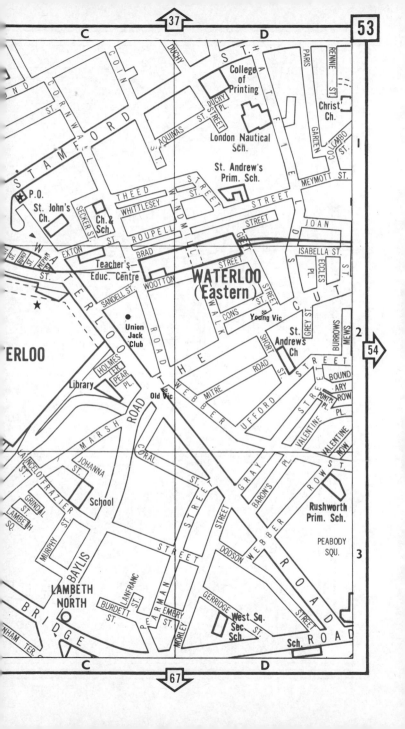

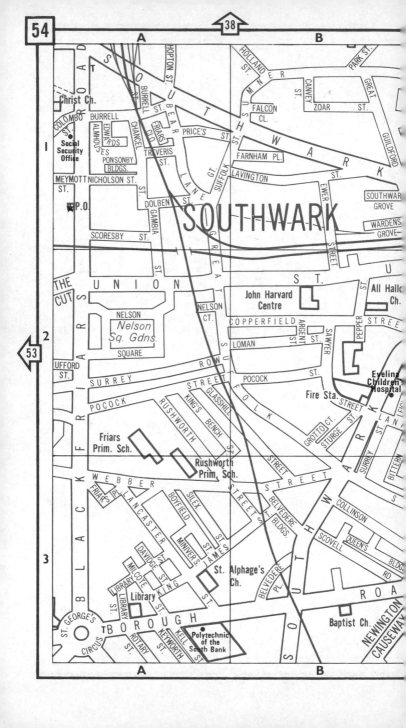

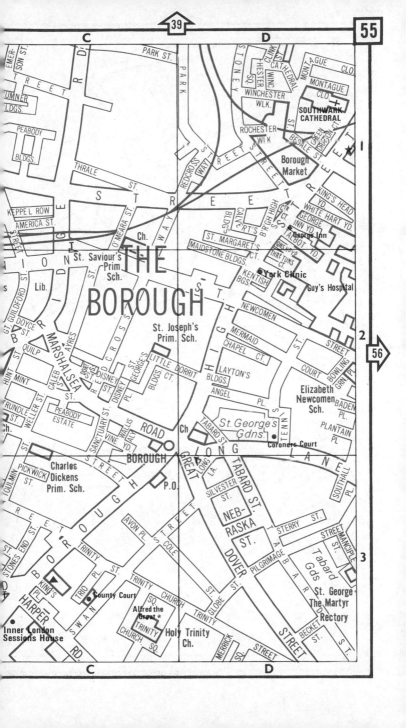

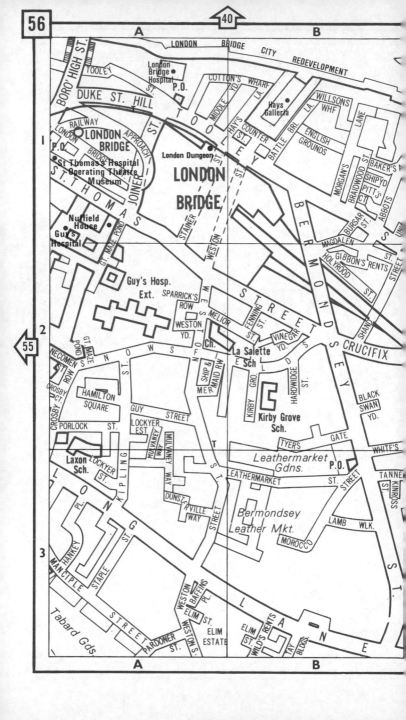

55

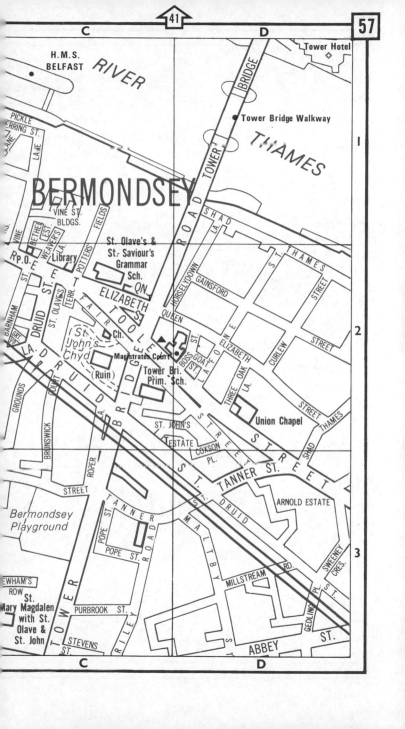

C D

Tower Hotel

H.M.S.
BELFAST

RIVER

PICKLE
ERRING ST.
LANE
HERRING LANE

Tower Bridge Walkway

THAMES

1

BERMONDSEY

VINE ST.
BLDGS.

BETHEL
WEST
WEAVER'S

VINE

Rp.O.E.

FIELDS

SHAD
LA.

ROAD
TOWER
BRIDGE

St. Olave's &
St. Saviour's
Grammar
Sch.

Library

POTTERS

Lib.

QN.

ST. THAMES

STREET

ELIZABETH

ST.

TOOLEY

HORSELYDOWN

GAINSFORD

ST.

DRUID ST.
BARNHAM ST.

ST. OLAVES

TERR.

FAIRDELL

QUEEN

Ch.

St.
John's
Chyd

BRIDGE STREET

LA.

Magistrates Court

(Ruin)

BOSS ST.
GOAT ST.
LAFFONE

ELIZABETH

CURLEW

STREET

STREET

GROUNDS

COURT
LA.

DRUID

Tower Bri.
Prim. Sch.

THREE OAK LA.

STREET

THAMES

BRUNSWICK

ROPER

ST. JOHN'S

ESTATE

COXSON
PL.

STREET

SHAD

ST.

2

STREET

Union Chapel

STREET

ROPER

TANNER ST.

ARNOLD ESTATE

Bermondsey
Playground

TANNER
POPE ST.
POPE ST.

MALTBY

ST. DRUID

ROAD

MILLSTREAM

RD.

SWEENEY
CRES.

GEDLING PL.
ST.

3

EWHAM'S
ROW
St.
Mary Magdalen
with St.
Olave &
St. John

TOWER

PURBROOK ST.

RILEY

STEVENS
ST.

ABBEY

ST.

C D

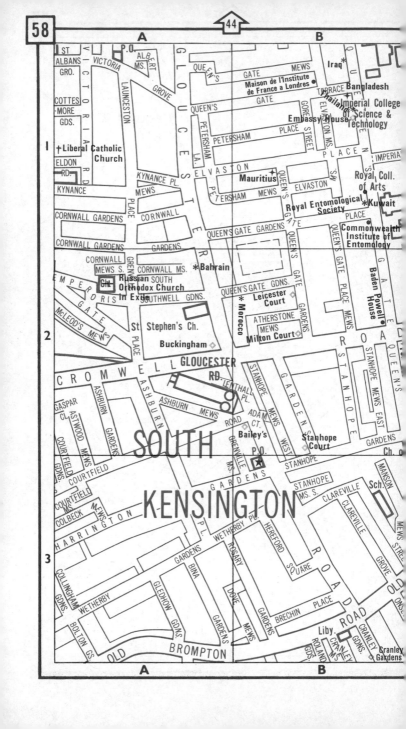

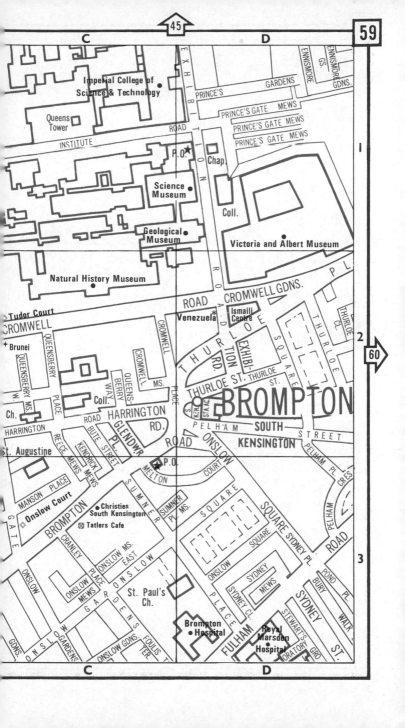

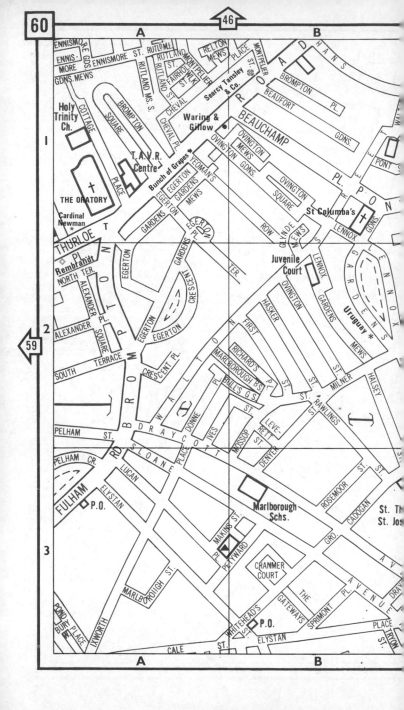

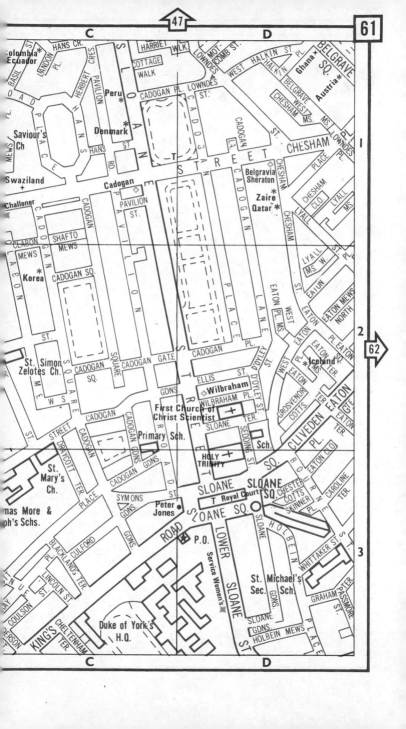

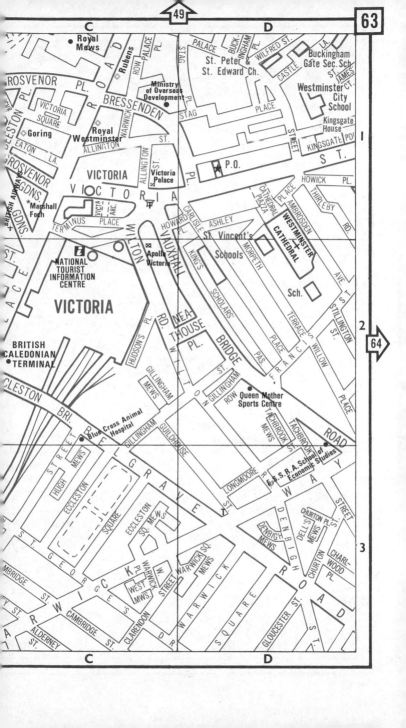

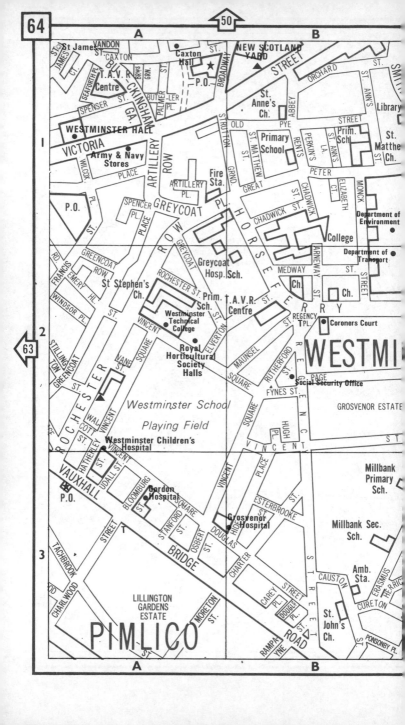

A B

St James's VANDON ST.
CAXTON ST.
St. JAMES'S CT.
Caxton Hall
NEW SCOTLAND YARD
STREET
ORCHARD ST.
SMITH
T.A.V.R. Centre
BREWS. GRN.
BUTLER PL.
PALMER PL.
P.O.
BROADWAY
STRUTTON
ABBEY
PYE
St. Anne's Ch.
ORCHARD
ST. ANN'S
Library
BUCKINGHAM GA.
SEAFORTH PL.
SPENSER ST.
WESTMINSTER HALL
VICTORIA
WILCOX PLACE
Army & Navy Stores
ARTILLERY ROW
Fire Sta.
ARTILLERY PL.
OLD
ST. MATTHEW ST.
Primary School
PERKIN'S RENTS
STREET
ST. ANN'S LA.
Prim. Sch.
St. Matthe Ch.

1

P.O.
SPENCER PLACE
GREYCOAT
PLACE
GREYCOAT ROW
GREYCOAT ST.
HORSEFERRY
GREAT
CHADWICK ST.
CHADWICK
PETER
ST.
ELIZABETH CT.
MONCK ST.
Department of Environment
College
Department of Transport

GREENCOAT
FRANCIS
RD.
EMERY HL.
GREENCOAT ROW
St Stephen's Ch.
ROCHESTER ST.
Greycoat Hosp. Sch.
Prim. Sch.
MEDWAY ST.
Ch.
ARNEWAY ST.
Ch.
MONCK STREET

WINDSOR PL.
STILLINGTON GREENCOAT ST.
VINCENT ST.
VANE ST.
Westminster Technical College
ELVERTON ST.
T.A.V.R. Centre
FERRY
REGENCY TPL.
Coroners Court

2

WESTMI

ROCHESTER
WALL COTT ST.
HATHERLEY ST.
Royal Horticultural Society Halls
VINCENT SQUARE
MAUNSEL
SQUARE
RUTHERFORD ST.
FYNES ST.
PAGE ST.
Social Security Office
GROSVENOR ESTATE

Westminster School Playing Field
HUGH ST.
REGENCY ST.
VINCENT ST.

Westminster Children's Hospital

VAUXHALL
P.O.
UDALL ST.
VINCENT ST.
Gordon Hospital
BLOOMBURG ST.
STANFORD ST.
SQUARE
OSBERT ST.
DOUGLAS ST.
ESTERBROOKE ST.
HIDE PL.
Grosvenor Hospital
PLACE
Millbank Primary Sch.

Millbank Sec. Sch.

STREET
BRIDGE
CHARTER ST.
STREET
CAUSTON ST.
Amb. Sta.

3

TACHBROOK ST.
CHARLWOOD
LILLINGTON GARDENS ESTATE
MORETON ST.
CAREY PL.
DOUGLAS PL.
RAMPAYNE ST.
ROAD
St. John's Ch.
ERASMUS ST.
CURETON ST.
PONSONBY PL.
FRE. RIC.

PIMLICO

A B

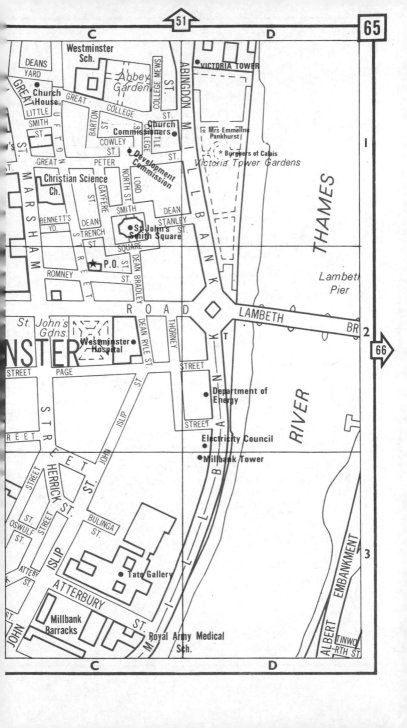

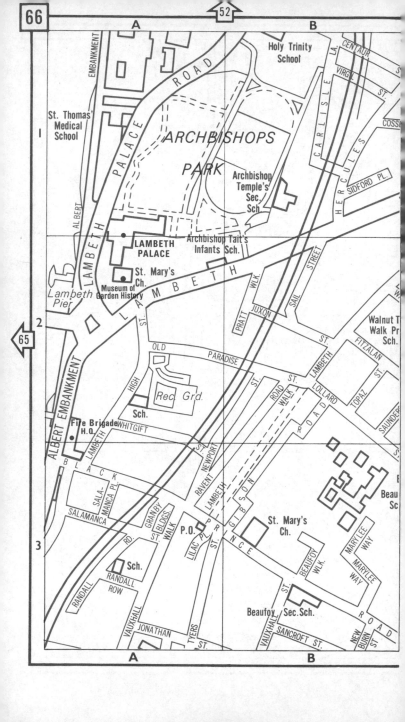

52

A   B

Holy Trinity
School

EMBANKMENT

St. Thomas'
Medical
School

PALACE

ROAD

CARLISLE LA.

CENTAUR

VIRGIL

ST.

HERCULES

COSSE

ARCHBISHOPS

PARK

Archbishop
Temple's
Sec.
Sch

SIDFORD PL.

1

ALBERT

LAMBETH

LAMBETH
PALACE

Archbishop Tait's
Infants Sch.

St. Mary's
Ch.

Museum of
Garden History

Lambeth
Pier

LAMBETH

ST.

PRATT WLK.

JUXON ST.

SAIL STREET

Walnut T
Walk Pr
Sch.

65

2

ROAD

WALK

FITZALAN

LOLLARD

TOPAZ ST.

SAUNDER

ST.

OLD

PARADISE

LAMBETH

ALBERT EMBANKMENT

HIGH ST.

Rec Grd.

Sch.

Fire Brigade
H.Q.

WHITGIFT

BLACK

LAMBETH

WALK

ST.

NEWPORT ST.

RAVENT

LAMBETH

GIBSON

ROAD

St. Mary's
Ch.

B
Beau
Sc

SALA-
MANCA PL.

SALAMANCA

RD.

GRANBY ST.

BLDGS.

WALK

P.O.

LILAC PL.

PRINCE

ST.

BEAUFOY WLK.

MARYLEE
WAY

MARYLEE
WAY

3

Sch.

RANDALL

RANDALL
ROW

VAUXHALL

JONATHAN

TYERS ST.

ST.

Beaufoy Sec.Sch.

VAUXHALL

SANCROFT ST.

NEW
BURN ST.

ROAD

A   B

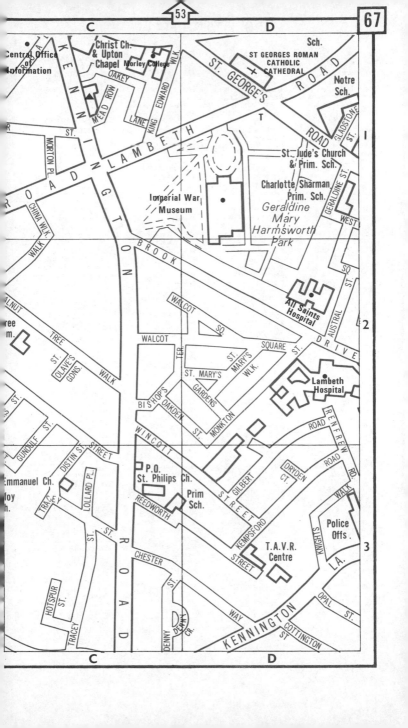

INDEX TO STREETS

Printed and bound in England by Hazell Watson & Viney Ltd., Aylesbury, Bucks.